E.J. SYMONS

MICROECONOMICS:

*the theory of
economic allocation*

microeconomics

the theory of economic allocation

C. A. Tisdell
Department of Economics
Australian National University

John Wiley & Sons Australasia Pty Ltd
Sydney   New York   London   Toronto

Copyright © 1972 by John Wiley & Sons Australasia Pty Ltd

All rights reserved

No part of this book may be reproduced by any means, nor transmitted, nor translated into a machine language without the written permission of the publisher

ISBN and National Library of Australia card numbers:
Cloth: 0 471 87440-X
WIE: 0 471 87441-8
Library of Congress catalog card number: 70-180250

Printed by Wing Tai Cheung Printing Co., Hong Kong

Contents

Preface	vii
1 Scarcity and Economising	7
2 Optimisation, Economic Behaviour and Choice	17
3 Economic Efficiency and Markets	41
4 Equilibrium, Statics and Dynamics	56
5 Prices and Pure Competition	63
Appendix: Elasticities of Demand and Supply	83
6 The Theory of Consumption	92
Appendix: Convex Sets and the Theory of Consumption	127
7 Production, Costs and Supply	134
Appendix: Sets and the Theory of Production	163
8 The Pricing and Supply of Products under Perfect Competition	175
9 Imperfect Competition	194
Appendix: Game Theory and Oligopolistic Behaviour	221
10 The Pricing and Employment of Factors	227
11 General Equilibrium	241
12 Input-Output Analysis	253
13 Welfare Economics	264
14 More on Markets, Efficiency and Growth	287
15 Linear Programming, Activity Analysis and Economic Choice	304
16 Resource Allocation over Time	322
17 Objectives of the Firm: Profit Maximisation Reconsidered	335
18 Measurement and Estimation in Microeconomics	347
19 Returns to Scale and Barriers to Entry	359
20 Markets and Knowledge, Research and Innovation	368
21 The Government and Resource Allocation	377
22 The Operation of Socialist Economies: Some Theories	400
Index	418

To Mariel and Ann-Marie

Preface

This book is designed primarily as a university text to meet the needs of a one-year intermediate course in microeconomics. Nevertheless, the material has been presented in a way which offers considerable flexibility. Thus it can be used for shorter and less advanced courses depending upon one's selection of its material and the way in which it is supplemented. Portions of it have also been specifically marked for distinction groups or those interested in a more extensive and deeper treatment of the subject. Some chapters may also provide useful background reading for parts of specialised undergraduate courses, such as business economics, public finance, mathematical economics, comparative economic systems, industry economics and welfare economics.

The text is based upon my lectures in microeconomics for second-year undergraduate students of the Australian National University. These students have a wide range of abilities, needs and interests and some, but not all, do additional specialised or distinction work in microeconomics. All have some knowledge of the differential calculus, although this is slight in a few cases. I suspect that their background knowledge is much the same as at universities elsewhere. Hence, I have used *elementary* differential calculus whenever this seemed appropriate as an aid to understanding but diagrammatic and verbal explanations are also given. Consequently, an elementary knowledge of the differential calculus is an advantage in following the subject-matter, but by no means a prerequisite.

Sections which treat more specialised topics or which require a more substantial mathematical background have been printed on a screen, like this paragraph. These should interest students who wish to delve more deeply into the subject and should be of value for distinction or more advanced work.

Concepts from the "new maths" are introduced and applied but only in sections which can be avoided if one wishes to do this. Aspects of sets, point sets, convex sets, etc., which are touched on in the screened sections are invaluable for a better understanding of economising and help us to realise the nature and limitations of traditional microeconomics. They give us powerful tools and extraordinary insights into optimising and (linear) programming procedures.

However, the discussion is not made subservient to a study of mathematical techniques. Constructs can both aid and hamper the flow of ideas and since space and time are limited one must strike a balance in presentation. In this book, techniques and tools are introduced only if they are to be subsequently used to communicate either contemporary or traditional ideas about microeconomics.

The first four chapters deserve special mention. These set microeconomics in a wider social and economic framework than is frequently done and examine generally our notions of optimisation, equilibrium, statics and dynamics. These notions are basic to microeconomic thought and are repeatedly used in the discussion. Most texts on microeconomics deal very superficially with these topics (some even neglect them altogether) and soon become involved in the details of market analysis. Consequently, general patterns and issues, and the relevance of the analysis to the alleviation of scarcity are lost with the result that the reader is often confused or becomes disinterested.

This book does not hide the controversial nature of microeconomic theory. It emphasises that new ideas, methods and debates constantly arise in the field of microeconomics and old debates continue, for example, those about the organisational efficiency and the advantages of free markets as compared to the alternative of central control of resource allocation. Consideration is given to "second-best" solutions, workable competition and countervailing power so as not to judge the performance of the economy solely by the unrealistic norm of perfect competition. The significance for market operations of the inescapable realities of decreasing costs, externalities and knowledge limitations are explored. Technical progress, invention, innovation and research are given special attention and the possible conflict between static allocative efficiency and economic growth is examined. In demand theory, unlike most other texts which overlook this problem, the book stresses the prime significance of social influences. The text also examines the allocation of resources by the public sector. This topic is often neglected in microeconomic texts but is important in its own right, especially when one considers that a substantial proportion (20-30 per cent) of the gross national product of advanced western countries is directly allocated by governments. The economics of socialism is also discussed, for it illustrates well the universal nature of economic problems.

Throughout I have been influenced by the point of view which has been so well expressed by Wesley C. Mitchell,

> No science is likely to prosper unless it is being subjected to ever new criticisms, unless its devotees are not only willing but eager to find all limitations which inhere in the science as it has been passed on to them and regard the work of their greatest predecessors with unrelenting criticism.*

When this sceptical view is combined with positive suggestions for reformulating the science, the vitality of the subject is assured.

I wish to thank Burgess Cameron, Gavin Ford, Fred Gruen, Owen Stanley and Cliff Walsh for their comments on part or all of the material of this manuscript. I am also grateful to individual students who, in my Economics II classes of 1964 and 1966-71 inclusive, challenged some of my ideas and either caused these to be reformulated or abandoned. My thanks to Miss Felicity Adams who, assisted by Mrs I. Everitt and Mrs B. Palmer, typed the whole manuscript both efficiently and cheerfully. I wish also to thank the Department of Economics, S.G.S., in the Australian National University, for making typing assistance available for the production of the manuscript.

Throughout the whole period of writing my dear wife Mariel has been a continual source of encouragement. This was so even though Ann-Marie was born in June.

Canberra, A.C.T. CLEM TISDELL
July, 1971

---

* WESLEY C. MITCHELL, *Types of Economic Theory from Merchantilism to Institutionalism*. Edited with an Introduction by JOSEPH DORFMAN, 2 vols, Augustus M. Kelley, Publishers, New York, vol. I, p. 536, 1967-69.

CHAPTER 1

Scarcity and Economising

Economics is the science of administration of scarce resources in human society. (Lange.)[1]

Civilisation should look forward to a day when the material product of industrial activity shall become rather its by-product, and its primary significance shall be that of a sphere for creative self-expression and the development of a higher type of individual and of human fellowship. (Knight.)[2]

Scarcity is a Basic Problem

While a few societies are comparatively rich, a majority of people are constantly struggling in order to obtain the necessities of life. Today, possibly two-thirds of the world's population is undernourished and engaged in the struggle for a precarious existence. For centuries this has been the lot of most of mankind.[3]

Whether a society is rich or poor, scarcity is a basic problem. This is so even in affluent countries like the United States and Sweden. Yet clearly, scarcity is not as great a problem for these countries as, say, for India. Nevertheless, it is a problem because the desires of individuals for goods and services exceed the available quantities of goods and services. Because desires are excessive in *relation* to the available quantity of commodities relative scarcity exists and the art of economising is socially significant in all existing countries. Thus relative scarcity gives economics importance. As we shall see, by adopting superior forms of economic organisation and by using more reliable economic principles, a society can reduce relative scarcity and poverty. Indeed, many societies could virtually eradicate poverty but none are able to eliminate relative scarcity by mere changes in their economic organisation. Even if the world's known resources were to be efficiently employed using existing technical knowledge, everyone's desire for commodities could not be simultaneously satisfied and relative scarcity would still be a basic problem. From now on scarcity should be understood as relative scarcity in the sense of its being impossible to satisfy simultaneously everyone's desire for commodities.

Consequences of Scarcity

Conflict is an inevitable consequence of scarcity. Since everyone's desire for commodities cannot be simultaneously satisfied, all individuals are to some extent in conflict or competition with one another for the commodities which can be made available. Such conflict or competition is unavoidable and may be overtly expressed or be repressed. The exact manner in which competition expresses itself depends upon the rules and customs of any society.

We may consider some of these rules for sharing in the wealth and opportunities of society to be fair and others to be unjust. Most of these rules not only affect the distribution of commodities between individuals but also the overall level of production. The most primitive factor which decides between competitors is physical force, but happily it is of limited importance in more civilised countries, all of which have very complex rules and mechanisms for discriminating between individuals.[4]

In a pure capitalist society, one's share in total output depends on the net value of the commodities which flow from the land, labour and capital which one owns or hires. Subject to prevailing prices, one is free to hire factors and to accumulate capital and land. Values in this society are determined by the free interplay of the forces of supply and demand through a price mechanism which will be discussed later. In a communist society, one is not free to accumulate capital and land nor to hire factors for one's personal profit. These avenues for increasing one's share in national income are absent. The rules of the game differ. Nevertheless, there is still conflict and competition between individuals for the available commodities. The demands of all cannot be met and in the U.S.S.R., for example, rewards and shares are determined by a complex system of social priorities. In practice, in the U.S.S.R., a scientist receives a much bigger share in output than an unskilled worker in a low priority industry. Output is not shared equally.

As long as wants exceed available means, competition and conflict between individuals for the available commodities and economic opportunities cannot be eliminated. In these circumstances, one must live with competition and organise so that it takes a desirable form. This rather than the elimination of competition is a reasonable social goal.

Different Approaches to the Problem

Mankind as a whole wishes to see scarcity reduced and many scientists, reformers and social philosophers have addressed themselves to this task. Many too have not been motivated by this task and yet their discoveries have certainly helped to reduce scarcity. There are various general methods of approach to this problem and we can best distinguish between them by imagining two ways in which scarcity (that is relative scarcity) can be reduced. Scarcity can be eased by reducing desires while holding the available quantities of goods and services constant, or it can be diminished by increasing the availability of commodities while keeping the intensity of desires unchanged. Both methods result in a more even balance between wants and means. Some religious leaders, for example, Buddhist and Christian, and philosophers maintain that excessive desire for material goods is the cause of much avoidable unhappiness and that individuals can and should reduce their desire for material possessions.

The researches and findings of scientists and economists have a different bearing on the problem. By using their findings it is possible to expand the quantity and quality of commodities. Nevertheless, the scientist and the economist do work in unlike spheres. The scientist reveals new laws of nature which, for example, may involve biological, chemical and physical matters. These laws can be harnessed to provide a greater and more diverse output from the same resources. Knowledge about inheritance leads to more productive species in agriculture, knowledge about nuclear material opens up new methods of generating electricity, and we could go on adding to the list. The method in which the scientist adds to a society's potential for reducing scarcity is clear. The way in which an economist proceeds may be less clear.

The economist investigates the organisation of society itself and the ways in which this organisation affects scarcity.[5] Given the preferences of individuals and the state of the arts and technology, a society's organisation may be such as to make goods and services scarcer than they need be. Thus the study of economics may be no less important for human progress and happiness than the study of natural science. Rousseau may still be correct in believing that: "The most useful and least advanced of all sciences is that of man."

In this book some of the laws and theories of economics are outlined. It examines the influence of alternative forms of social organisation on resource allocation, and debates the merits and drawbacks of various economic structures particularly markets as means for reducing scarcity.

Universality of the Problem

Is scarcity really a universal phenomenon? Some may doubt it. For example, they may point to surpluses in the production of crops, such as wheat in 1970, as evidence of this.

But wheat surpluses only exist because the prices which are paid to producers of wheat are artificially maintained by governments. True, such surpluses indicate an ability to produce more wheat than is consumed at current prices. Furthermore, it may be possible to produce more wheat than would be consumed even if wheat were free, but such increased production is at the expense of other commodities. For example, as more land is allocated to wheat production the output of other cereals, meat, timber etc., is certain to fall. Given our present technology and resources and assuming economic efficiency, an expansion in wheat production increases the scarcity of other commodities. Thus scarcity remains a problem. It is a problem in the sense that, given our present technology, resources and tastes, it is impossible to satisfy fully and simultaneously everyone's desire for every commodity. There are possibly no commodities which are plentiful everywhere. Even space commands a price in some places. On the face of it, the problem of scarcity is universal.

Four Economic Ways of Dealing with Scarcity

As a first approximation, it is useful to imagine that there are four ways of fighting scarcity in a country. These are:
  (i) by ensuring that scarce resources are in fact fully employed;
  (ii) by seeing that employed resources are efficiently used in the sense that it ought to be impossible to employ them in any alternative way, so as to satisfy wants more fully;
  (iii) by stimulating economic growth, for example by developing new technologies which expand the potential of resources; and
  (iv) by altering the distribution of income and thus mitigating the impact of scarcity on some individuals without reducing overall scarcity.

In short, scarcity can be alleviated by ensuring full employment, economic efficiency and growth and by redistributing income. *All* of these factors are influenced by the types of markets which prevail. While many books on microeconomics concentrate on the efficiency aspect alone, or principally, this book does not lose sight of the other influences. Of course, the above scheme is only a convenient simplification but it provides a starting point for further enquiry.

Full Employment

What is really meant by saying that resources should be fully employed? Paradoxically, it is not implied that resources such as labour should be employed to their physical capacity. Nor is it even implied that extra labour should be employed so long as it can make any additional positive contribution to output. In our own society, this would mean that we would all have to forgo much of our present leisure and this, few of us would do willingly for the value of the additional output. Thus our problem cannot be approached in these terms because leisure too is valued. The problem must be approached differently.

We may fruitfully approach the problem by considering the relevance of Pareto's criterion. V. Pareto suggested that economic welfare is not at a maximum if it is possible to make someone better off without making anyone else worse off.[6] Thus a social optimum requires that it be impossible by any economic re-organisation to do this. Adopting Pareto's view, resources are not optimally employed if it is possible to make someone better off without making anyone worse off.

Singling out labour, labour is not optimally employed in Pareto's sense if any individual is willing to work for the net value of his marginal product and is unable to do so. If any individual is willing to work for his net addition to output given the employment of other factors and individuals, his employment increases his own satisfaction without making anyone else worse off. Desired output is lower than it need be if anyone who is willing to work for his marginal product is unable to obtain employment. His involuntary unemployment results in economic waste and avoidable distress, and is prima facie evidence of deficiencies in the organisation of his society.

Few if any societies have been or are completely free of involuntary unemployment. In times of economic depression, capitalist societies have experienced much involuntary unemployment amongst labour, as in the 1930s for example. But with the adoption of the types of policies which were advocated by J. M. Keynes,[7] depressions have become less violent and cause less economic waste. But depressions are not the sole causes of involuntary unemployment. Minimum wage legislation and trade union pressure to maintain wages can also add to involuntary unemployment. Handicapped and others who have a far smaller marginal product than average and who are willing to work for a correspondingly lower wage may remain unemployed as a result of these policies. Also, the conditions placed on government grants to the needy may add to scarcity in an undesired way. In extreme cases, a government transfer payment, for example, invalid pension, old-age pension and so on, may be reduced by one dollar per week for each dollar earned. Thus, it can happen that it is no longer in the individual's self-interest to work for the value of his marginal product even if he would otherwise wish to. Thus desired output is lower than it could be.

Unemployment, too, occurs for frictional reasons, since it takes time to transfer resources from one place to another or from one use to another. The loss involved on this account can be reduced by improving knowledge about opportunities, by facilitating the retraining of labour where this is appropriate, and, in general, by improving communications.

Economic Efficiency

The question of maintaining economic efficiency would not be very complex if it merely involved the requirement that a society's output from its resources should be maximised. But output consists of a diverse bundle of commodities and the problem of valuing this bundle arises. Furthermore, the supply of resources which will be willingly supplied for production is a variable quantity. This, for example, is true of labour. Thus the question is not so simple in practice and it is normally necessary to approach the efficiency question in Pareto's manner. To do so at this stage would be to introduce too much complexity.

Nevertheless, a few simple points can be seen from a physical model. Imagine a society which is producing only one product by means of labour and land. Further assume that labour is in fixed supply. Society's problem is to maximise its output given the supply of labour and the availability of land. A requirement for this maximum may be that some of the land remain unused.

Consider the following case. A country is divided into two regions and the marginal physical productivity of labour is always higher in Region 1 than in Region 2 for any possible allocation of labour. Take the example shown in Fig. 1.1 and assume that the aggregate supply of labour is N. Then all of this labour should be used in Region 1 and Region 2 should not be used assuming that labour is essential to its use. To use Region 2 is only to add to scarcity not reduce it.

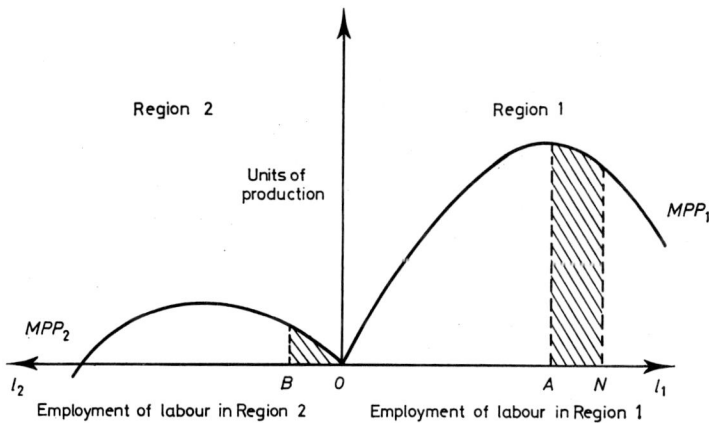

Fig. 1.1

The marginal physical productivity of labour in Region 1 is shown by the curve MPP_1 and that in Region 2 by the curve MPP_2. Each curve represents the *addition* to output of each *additional* unit of labour in the appropriate region. If any labour is allocated to Region 2 scarcity is increased. For example, if AN of labour is transferred from Region 1 to Region 2, output in Region 1 *falls* by the equivalent of the hatched area in the neighbourhood of A and output in Region 2 *increases* by the equivalent of the hatched area in the neighbourhood of B. Clearly, the gain in production in Region 2 does not compensate for the loss in production in Region 1 and aggregate output falls. The real cost of employing labour in Region 2 is the output forgone in Region 1.

In practice problems akin to this one arise. No doubt it is physically possible to grow agricultural products in some of the most niggardly regions of the world. But to do so would only be to add to scarcity. The Russians by using parts of Siberia for wheat production, Australians by using the Gibson Desert for agricultural production or Americans by developing the less promising parts of Alaska for this purpose, might well add to scarcity. It is more economic to leave these regions unused for the co-operating resources which are required to bring them into agricultural production are more productive elsewhere. For example, it would be more productive to use the capital and labour which would be required to produce crops in the Gibson Desert in the higher rainfall areas of Australia. This is so given existing technical knowledge.

Again, it may not be economic to employ a factor fully because beyond a certain rate of application its use decreases output. The factor's marginal product is negative after a point. For example, if the application of water to a growing crop exceeds a certain margin, the yield of the crop falls. The excess application creates biological problems for the plants and encourages fungal attacks etc. Even if water were freely available in a region, it can be uneconomic to employ it completely. To do so would subtract from production.

It is useful to distinguish between technical efficiency and economic efficiency as defined by Pareto. Technical efficiency does not ensure economic efficiency even though it is a prerequisite for economic efficiency. Technical efficiency requires that each productive unit adopts the technique which, in the existing state of knowledge, maximises its output from its employed resources. For economic efficiency to occur, it is additionally required that resources be optimally allocated between productive units, commodities, etc. The distinction can be made by using a simple example.

Modify the example given in Fig. 1.1. Suppose now that we consider two productive units, such as firms, instead of two regions and, as before, imagine that only one factor is variable and that only one product is produced. The problem is to maximise the firms' aggregate output given a fixed aggregate employment of the variable factor which we shall call labour.

First, technical efficiency must prevail if the maximum is to be reached. Whatever level of labour each firm employs it must use the method which ensures the maximum output from its employed resources. If there are two known methods of producing the output and the relationships are as indicated in Fig. 1.2 for Firm 1, then Firm 1 ought to adopt method A if it employs less than $\hat{l}_1$ of labour and method B if it

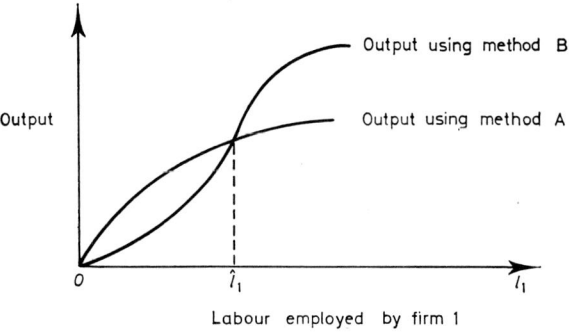

Fig. 1.2

Scarcity and Economising

employs more labour than this. If however, the curve of output using method A is higher everywhere than for B, method A should be used exclusively.

Assuming that optimal methods or techniques are employed let us imagine that the marginal physical productivity curves for the two firms are as indicated in Fig. 1.3. The two firms are assumed to be technically efficient.

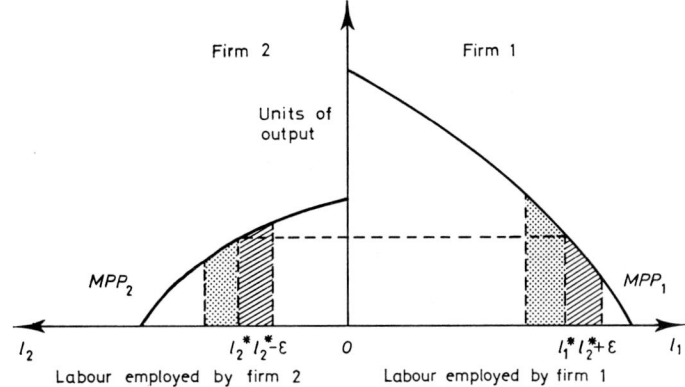

Fig. 1.3

Suppose that the aggregate employment of labour by these two firms is $L = l_1^* + l_2^*$. Then output is not maximised for this employment unless l_1^* of L is allocated to Firm 1 and l_2^* of L is allocated to Firm 2. Unless the marginal physical products of these firms are equal output is not at a maximum despite the presence of technical efficiency. As can be perceived from the diagram any other allocation reduces the aggregate output from the employed labour. An increase in Firm 1's employment of labour by ε, increases its output by the hatched area but reduces that of Firm 2 by the larger area which is hatched. Aggregate output goes down. Similarly, if Firm 2's usage of labour is increased by ε, its output rises by the dotted area but that of Firm 1 falls by an even bigger dotted area. In cases such as this, any impediment which prevents equalisation of the marginal productivities of firms is a cause of economic inefficiency. In these circumstances, it is possible to produce a larger output without changing the quantity of employed resources. This is so even if each firm is technically efficient.

Naturally, if we take into account the greater complexity of production and its diversity, the conditions required for economic efficiency are more complex and greater attention must be given to tastes. But even then technical efficiency can exist and economic efficiency can be absent. Even if technical efficiency exists, it may be possible to make someone better off without making anyone else worse off. It may, for example, be possible to increase the output of one desired product without decreasing the output of any other and without changing the employment of factors. Attention will be given to these more complicated cases later in the book. The influence of different market forms on economic efficiency will be particularly examined.

Economic Growth

Growth of the economic potential and of the resources of a country also may help it to reduce scarcity. The actual and potential output of an economy can grow for many reasons. Population may grow and provide more labour; capital may accumulate by saving and investment; additional resources, such as minerals, may be discovered; and improvements of economic knowledge may make a greater output possible from the same resources.

But the mere growth of national output does not ensure economic plenty, for

$$\text{Average Income per head} = \frac{\text{National Output}}{\text{Population}}.$$

Hence, if population expands at a faster rate than national output, average income per head falls. Both the growth of population and of output are important.

In discussing optimal growth, value judgements cannot be avoided. Should a nation maximise income per head if to achieve this it needs to limit its population? Should it be prepared if necessary to accept some reduction in income per head for the sake of a greater population? Using various assumptions about utility and assuming that maximisation of the overall level of utility in a community is desired, it is possible to show that overall utility can be increased in some circumstances by increasing population at the expense of income per head if necessary. Under other circumstances, overall utility is decreased by this.

A model, which is due to Ricardo,[8] emphasises the relationship between the growth of output and of population. Assume that if income per head is above the subsistence level, population increases and if the opposite is the case it decreases. Imagine too that as the population and hence available labour varies the country's output varies, so that there is a functional relationship between the country's output and population. For a given state of technology and quantities of resources other than labour, such a function is shown by $f_1(N)$ in Fig. 1.4. In the case which is illustrated, output increases but at a decreasing rate. In other words, diminishing marginal productivity prevails. If the line OA represents the national output required to support any level of population at subsistence level, the economy is in equilibrium if population and output correspond to the co-ordinates of E_1. If there is an improvement of scientific knowledge which shifts the production function suddenly to $f_2(N)$, the system is then in disequilibrium at E_1 and will only reach a new equilibrium at E_2. Initially, income per head rises above subsistence, but as population increases it moves back to subsistence level. In these circumstances, improvements in productivity per head are eventually eroded by population growth.

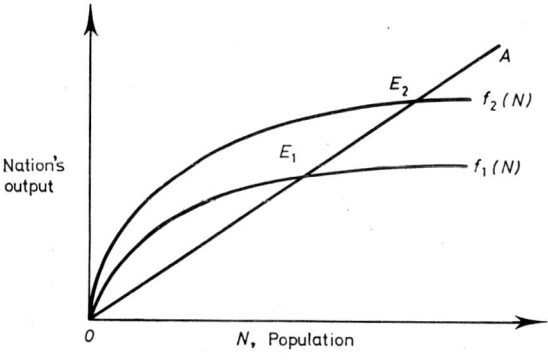

Fig. 1.4

Empirically, incomes per head will only continue to rise if improvements in productivity due to technical progress or additions to other resources besides labour outstrip the deterioration in productivity per head caused by a rising population.

Is Ricardo's model reasonable? If you cannot accept his views about population growth and the nature of the production function, then you will not be convinced that it is a reasonable representation of reality. Nevertheless, his model points to fundamental issues. To understand these issues and alternative growth models one requires, amongst other things, a thorough knowledge of the *tools* of microanalysis. Some of these tools are presented later.

Markets too affect economic growth. The degree of competition in a market can influence the rate of invention and adoption of new techniques. As will be seen, the organisation of society is important in this respect.

Income Redistribution

The burden of scarcity between individuals can be altered by redistributing income. However, measures designed to accomplish this very often reduce total output. For example, income taxes which are collected for this purpose may well reduce effort. But a society may be prepared to forgo some total output for the sake of a more equitable distribution of income. One economic problem is how to achieve a desired income distribution while at the same time keeping national output at the maximum possible level.

The distribution of income in any society is affected by its organisation. In our own society, it is materially affected by the resources which one commands and the net market value of commodities which flow from them. This will be thoroughly investigated.

A distinction ought to be made between the distribution of personal income and the distribution of income in the form of wages, rent and profit to factors. If a capitalist society were in fact divided into exclusive classes of labourers, landlords and capitalists, much might be learnt about the distribution of personal income by studying factor rewards. But our society is not divided exclusively in this manner and it is necessary to be cautious in drawing inferences about personal incomes from such results.

Can a society in fact really alter its distribution of income? Certainly, a society can alleviate the hardships of its most needy, but some economists have doubted if income distribution can really be fundamentally changed in its overall pattern. For example, Vilfredo Pareto claimed that inequality in the distribution of personal income has a constant nature and put forward an expression, now known as Pareto's distribution, to describe it.[9] Economists such as Cobb and Douglas have maintained that there is a constancy in labour's share in national income.[10] In many western economies, there has been a remarkable long-term tendency for wages to remain at around two-thirds of overall income.

On the question of income redistribution, value judgements cannot be avoided. Not only must one decide on a fair way to divide income between the living but also one needs to consider the extent to which present generations should forgo consumption and vary their behaviour in order to reduce scarcity for future generations. The problem is inescapable, while ever scarcity exists.

Because scarcity exists every nation is concerned about the employment of its resources, the efficiency with which they are used, economic growth and the distribution of income. All of these are influenced by economic organisation and there are many different types of economic and social organisation. Let us look at the binding force behind some of them.

Organisational Mechanisms

In every society, there are accepted rules or patterns of social behaviour. As biologists point out, even various species of animals have established social patterns. But man, because of his intellectual abilities, has in the long run considerable control over his established social patterns and norms. He is also capable of establishing a wider range of social rules and mechanisms. The prevailing rules of the game decide

(i) what is produced,
(ii) how it is produced, for example, by what methods and resources and by whom, and
(iii) to whom the fruits of production are distributed.

Social rules change over time—sometimes drastically and quickly. The rules prevailing now clearly differ from those of the Middle Ages. In some cases, these have been modified in an evolutionary way as in the United Kingdom but in others such as the U.S.S.R. they have been modified by revolution.

The governing mechanisms of economic conduct are sometimes classified into

(i) those which rely on custom and tradition,
(ii) those which involve central control or dictatorship, and
(iii) those which use market forces.

But this classification is artificial for most organisation inextricably involves more than one of these factors. Custom may reinforce dictatorship and market forces may be bolstered by tradition e.g., profit maximisation is approved of in some societies. In no country today is any one of these methods relied on exclusively. The countries which are more capitalistic rely on market forces to a considerable extent for their organisation, but central command and tradition also play a role, for example, individuals are sometimes drafted or conscripted into the armed forces, some posts may be filled by tradition and certainly many posts are filled in a traditional *manner*. Posts on legislative bodies are, for example, filled in a traditional manner. While central command is important in communist countries, prices too are used to help with administration.

Custom

It is difficult to know whether our Society is less custom and tradition-bound than in the Middle Ages. Certainly individuals have more social mobility and work mobility now than in that age, and prescriptions of the Church are less heeded but, on the other hand, we now have firmly entrenched traditions about such matters as democracy, liberty, the rights of the individual and free competition. Work and social mobility seems to have increased. No longer are there strong social pressures to ensure that sons carry on the occupation of their fathers. Yet social prejudice still hinders work mobility to some extent, for example, prejudices against women and various races may adversely affect their promotion opportunities. Not only does custom have some influence on factor employment, but it may also affect income distribution. In most societies, kinship influences sharing patterns. In most Asian countries, children have a social responsibility to support their ageing parents. However, in many western countries, with advent of the Welfare State, children have become less responsible in this respect and this sometimes has disgraceful consequences. Parents are sometimes neglected materially and deserted. It is interesting to note that even prehistoric man had fixed sharing patterns supported by tradition and custom. For example, the emus, kangaroos and so on which Australian Aboriginal tribes managed to hunt down were shared according to strict rules. Under these rules the softer portions of the animals were allocated to the old members of the tribe.

Command

Command also plays a role in resource allocation, and in many cases an acceptable role. Most of us are subject in some respect to the authority of others. In the internal operations of business enterprises and most economic bodies directives from above have an important place. In our society, rates and taxes are collected by order of the appropriate bodies. True they are not collected at the whim of any one individual or dictator but they are levied by representative bodies. As Thoreau found,[11] the individual has no freedom to opt out of these arrangements. The Soviet Union relies to a greater extent on directives from above to organise its overall economy. But even there command is not all-pervading. The Communist Party uses material incentives to coax *its* desired level and composition of production from the economy. Manpower is not allocated by fiat, but wage differentials are paid in order to allocate labour in accordance with the Communist Party's preferences. Prices play an important part in the organisation of the economy even though a *freely* operating price mechanism is absent. Most countries do not extensively issue commands from above to allocate their resources, except in times of national emergency. For example, under emergency wartime conditions governments sometimes allocate labour by command.

Market Forces and Prices

Systems of organisation which use prices are amongst the most efficient known to man. Pricing systems can be constructed so as to allocate resources in accordance with the wishes of a central authority, or prices may be determined as a result of the strivings of individuals, subject to the natural restrictions of markets, to optimise their own personal economic position.

In modern economies, specialisation in production, knowledge, resources and so on, is a fundamental fact of existence. As a result of this specialisation production is much greater than it otherwise would be. But in order for a society to gain the full benefits of specialisation, it needs efficient methods of exchanging goods and services. As markets improve, the spur to specialise and the gain from specialisation increase. In the earliest times, goods were exchanged by barter and markets were geographically restricted and imperfect. But since the process of individual calculation is difficult a barter system is cumbersome when no item is accepted as a *numéraire*; that is one in terms of which all exchange rates are stated. The customary use of a particular commodity as a *numéraire*, such as gold, speeds up individual economic calculation and has other advantages. In our society, the monetary unit, not gold, provides the *numéraire*. Exchange, free or otherwise, is a dominant feature of all modern economies. In the more developed economies, some individuals consume none of the goods and services which they produce, and most people only consume a small fraction of their own production.

The effect of prices on economic activity depends upon the aims of individuals as well as on the manner in which individual reward varies with the individual's adjustment to price changes. Traditionally, consumers are assumed to use their incomes so as to maximise their satisfaction and producers are assumed to act so as to maximise their profit. But even if this were not so, prices could still be used to manipulate an economy to some extent if there happened to be any regular relationship between these and economic activity. Nevertheless, under some conditions, it is *necessary* for firms to maximise their individual profits if Pareto's necessary condition for a maximum of social welfare is to be satisfied.

Prices provide an economical way of transmitting signals about the economic value of commodities. If coupled with suitable inducements to those controlling resources, they provide a powerful and efficient means for organising economies. Prices may be determined or altered by central authorities or they may be left to be determined by the interplay of the forces of individual self-interest. Let us consider the latter possibility.

Under free competition the allocation of resources and prices are determined by the interplay of economic units, acting in their own self-interest. The role which each individual plays in production, the methods employed, the commodities produced and the general allocation of resources are not the outcomes of customary stipulations or central command, but result from the striving of each individual, subject to the impersonal constraints of the market, to achieve the most that he can from his resources. Such a system works. As Frank Knight puts it:

> Each person in [a free exchange] system seeks his own satisfaction without thought of the structure of society or its interests; and the mere mechanical interaction of such self-seeking units organises them into an elaborate system and controls and co-ordinates their activities so that each is continuously supplied with the fruits of the labour of one vast and unknown multitude in return for performing some service for some multitude also large and unknown to him.[12]

The system operates through prices and material incentives. If demand for a particular commodity rises then initially its price tends to be forced up. It becomes profitable to produce extra amounts of the commodity and resources flow into its production as firms try to increase their individual profits.

Does the system work well? The question is not an easy one to answer. Externalities apart, it has been shown that if the conditions required for perfect competition prevail, Pareto's necessary condition for a social optimum is satisfied. In practice these conditions are not satisfied though they are sometimes approximated. Yet even in the absence of perfect competition, competition may be sufficient to give some results which are like those under perfect competition. Competition is then said to be workable.

Economists have isolated conditions under which there is an identity of economic self-interest and of social interest. Their discovery is a fundamental one, even though the required conditions are not exactly fulfilled in the real world and discovery is of an abstract Euclidean character. If the required economic conditions are satisfied, all an economic unit need know, in order to promote a Paretian social optimum by acting in its own self-interest, is the prices of things which it buys and sells. These prices are determined so as to equilibrate supplies and demands in markets by mere mechanical forces. The prices are determined by the market and no economic unit is able individually to influence these. Decisions are completely decentralised and no great deal of information is needed for decision-making. For example, no producer need know for whom or what his produce is finally destined, nor need he know of the more remote origins of his inputs.

Adam Smith, indeed, made a major advance in economic thought when he asserted in 1766 that competition promoted the public good.[13] He stated, for example, that:

> Every individual is continually exerting himself to find out the most advantageous employment for whatever capital he can command. It is his own advantage, indeed and not that of society which he has in view. But the study of his own advantage naturally, or rather necessarily, leads him to prefer the employment which is most advantageous to society.[14]

In his time, Adam Smith's views were radical. Philosophers such as James Steuart Denham[15] agreed with Smith that individuals looked to their own self-interest but they drew a different conclusion. They believed that individual behaviour would be contrary to the social interest unless the government regulated it carefully.

The idea that competition is in the public interest is still accepted with qualifications in many countries today. For example, John F. Kennedy has stated:

> It is well to remind ourselves from time to time of the benefits we derive from a free-market system. The system rests on the freedom of consumer choice, the profit motive and vigorous competition for the buyer's dollar. By relying on these spontaneous economic forces, we secure these benefits: (a) Our system tends automatically to produce the kinds of goods that people want in the relative quantities in which people want them. (b) The system tends automatically to minimise waste. If one producer is making a product inefficiently, another will see an opportunity for profit by making the product at a lower cost. (c) The system encourages innovation and technological change. . . .[16]

However, perfect competition does not arise automatically in all markets. In a *laissez-faire* system, a system in which the government does not intervene, serious deviations from competition may occur. Unfortunately, we are not always fully assured of the above benefits in a freely competitive economy, even though substantial benefits are likely to be obtained. It is worthwhile to mention some of the difficulties.

Consumers' sovereignty is an important ingredient of the competitive system. Increased demand by consumers for any product raises its price and raises the profitability of producing it. Businessmen normally increase production in response to this increased demand in order to increase their individual profit. The allocation of resources changes in response to variations in the demands of consumers. Are consumers in fact sovereign? It is sometimes suggested that consumers are manipulated by the suggestive advertising of big business and that where competition is weak they are only supplied goods with inferior characteristics to the ones which would be supplied in a more competitive market. The goods may also be supplied in smaller volume.

Should consumers be sovereign? In other words, should individuals be free, subject to market constraints, to consume whatever they wish? The legislature of all countries seems to have answered this in the negative. Prohibition may, for example, be placed on the sale of drugs or literature of certain types or, as in one country, on certain "pop-song" recordings. Liberals have generally opposed encroachments on individual freedom in this manner.

If the government does not interfere in the economic system, the correct mix of commodities may not eventuate. Even if the government intervenes the correct mix need not eventuate, as we shall see later. Under free competition, the correct mix may not occur because (a) monopolies may exist in some sectors. The forces of competition are then absent and the monopolist may restrict his production below the socially desirable level in order to maximise his profit. Too little of the monopolised product is then produced. (b) Externalities may also arise in production and consumption. In such a case the private cost and benefits from an activity do not reflect the social costs and benefits. For example, where a factory disposes of pollutants free of charge, and these adversely affect other people, the costs of production borne by it are less than the costs to the community as a whole. In this case, a diseconomy exists, and too much of the commodity may be produced or socially optimal techniques may not be employed. (c) Imperfections of knowledge may cause one good to be produced in excess while others are in short supply. For example, in agriculture shortages in some commodities tend to be followed by gluts at a later time, as farmers adjust to the earlier high prices. The glut in turn is followed by a shortage and a so-called cobweb relationship exists. (d) It is in the very nature of some goods that they cannot be provided by the market mechanism. These are called public goods or social goods. The enjoyment of such goods cannot be made subject to price payments. The exclusion principle does not operate. Individuals who do not pay for a service may nevertheless enjoy the benefits stemming from it. Even though the service involves a net gain to all, it might not be provided at all unless contributions are compulsory. Services such as the judicial system, defence and campaigns affecting the general state of public health are of this type.

Markets for all the benefits which they may provide do have their limitations. The whole matter is carefully examined in this book. The influence of markets on innovation and technological progress will not be neglected.

Different systems of economic organisation have their advantages and drawbacks some of which have already been noted. A system in which occupations are hereditary may give little scope for change and be the cause of inefficiency in the allocation of manpower. Persons are not allowed by this customary system to move into the economic roles, in which the economic value of their marginal product is greatest. In a central command economy in which manpower is directed by fiat, lack of knowledge on the part of central planners or their personal whims may be such as to reduce output from this resource. The deficiencies of these systems can be far greater than those of free competition.

Social Welfare

But how do we measure economic deficiencies? It is too imprecise, as has already been noted, to say that the effectiveness of the system should be measured by its ability to reduce scarcity. Some method of reducing diverse commodities to a simple index of social welfare is needed. A number of different views have been put forward.

One view, due principally to Jeremy Bentham,[17] originated in the nineteenth century and was held by later economists such as John Stuart Mill[18] and Pigou.[19] It was

Scarcity and Economising

stated that society should maximise the overall sum of human happiness or utility. Furthermore, it was maintained that commodities are capable of yielding utility to the consumers of them, and that utility is capable of measurement and is comparable between individuals. The optimal allocation of income then depends upon the way in which the utility functions of individuals are related to their income. If the functions are identical and increase with income at a decreasing rate, perfect income equality maximises overall utility. If the functions differ as, for example, Edgeworth[20] believed them to do, inequality of income may be necessary to maximise overall utility. But given any distribution of income, overall utility is not at a maximum unless economic efficiency in Pareto's sense exists.

The Utilitarian Doctrine has been attacked violently. Doubts have been expressed about the measurability of utility and the possibility of making meaningful interpersonal comparisons of utility. Nevertheless, men are forced to make interpersonal comparisons. While the Utilitarian Doctrine seems to be without scientific basis, it has enabled us to spell out the consequences of various interpersonal comparisons, comparisons which some are forced to make.

Because of the disrepute into which the Utilitarian view fell, a weaker view due to Vilfredo Pareto has prevailed.[21] Pareto merely noted a necessary condition for a social optimum given that all are to count. A necessary condition for a social optimum is, as he maintained, that it should be impossible to make anyone better off without making someone else worse off. His position has been attacked on the grounds that it tends to preserve the *status quo* and is of little value in practice, because most economic reforms affect income distribution. If income redistribution is involved, his criterion is silent for then some gain and some lose. But Pareto's criterion has definite consequences for the optimal employment of labour and the efficient allocation of resources some of which have previously been noted.

It is impossible to proceed any distance in economics without coming up against problems of optimisation, be these at the social or individual level. The next chapter looks more closely at the problem of optimisation. This one has given us an account of the basic economic problem and the general methods by which economies are organised.

NOTES AND REFERENCES

[1] OSKAR LANGE, "The Scope and Method of Economics", *The Review of Economic Studies*, 1945-46, 13, p. 19.

[2] FRANK H. KNIGHT, "Social Economic Organization", an extract from *The Economic Organization*, reprinted in W. BREIT and H. M. HOCHMAN (Eds), *Readings in Microeconomics*, Holt, Rinehart and Winston, New York, 1968, p. 4.

[3] For some further information on world poverty see, for example, H. KOHLER, *Economics: The Science of Scarcity*, Dryden Press, Hinsdale, 1970, Ch. 26.

[4] Seniority, racial origin, sex, educational performance may all be used to discriminate against individuals, sometimes when these have no bearing at all on the value of the individual's product, his productivity. Even ballot or chance systems are sometimes used, for example, for drafting into the Australian army.

[5] Economics, the science of administration of scarce resources, has both positive and normative aspects as well as purely logical aspects. Positive economics is concerned with describing actual economic relationships, normative economics with the ways in which economies *ought* to be operated. The distinction is discussed in Chapter 13, "Welfare Economics".

⁶ V. Pareto (1848-1923), *Cours d'économie politique*, 2 volumes, F. Rouge, Lausanne, 1896-97 and *Manuel d'économie politique*, 2nd ed., Giard, Paris, 1927.
⁷ J. M. Keynes, *The General Theory of Employment, Interest and Money*, Macmillan, London, 1936.
⁸ D. Ricardo, *Principles of Political Economy and Taxation* (1817), in P. Sraffa (Ed.), *Works of David Ricardo*, Vol. 1, Cambridge University Press, London, 1951.
⁹ See, for example, G. Tintner, *Mathematics and Statistics for Economists*, Rinehart & Company, New York, 1953, Ch. 5.
¹⁰ C. W. Cobb and Paul H. Douglas, "A Theory of Production", *American Economic Review*, 1938, **18**, pp. 139-65.
¹¹ H. D. Thoreau, *Walden and On the Duty of Civil Disobedience*, Holt, Rinehart and Winston, New York, 1964. Also see O. Thomas (Ed.), *Walden and Civil Disobedience*, W. W. Norton, New York, 1966.
¹² Frank H. Knight, "Social Economic Organization", op. cit. in Breit and Hochman, op. cit., pp. 17-18. Reprinted by kind permission of Frank H. Knight.
¹³ Adam Smith, *The Wealth of Nations*, 1st ed. 1776, Everyman's ed., J..M. Dent & Sons, London, 1910.
¹⁴ Ibid., Everyman's ed., Vol. 1, p. 398.
¹⁵ Sir James Steuart Denham (1712-1780), *An Enquiry into the Principles of Political Economy*, A. Miller and T. Cadell, London, 1717.
¹⁶ From a speech of J. F. Kennedy to business magazine and newspaper publishers, September 1962. Quoted by A. A. Alchian and W. R. Allen, *Exchange and Production Theory in Use*, Wadsworth, Belmont, 1969, p. 60. Reprinted by permission of Wadsworth Publishing Company, Inc.
¹⁷ Jeremy Bentham (1748-1832). For an assessment of his contribution, see Wesley C. Mitchell, *Types of Economic Theory*, Vol. 1, Augustus M. Kelley, New York, 1967, pp. 193 et seq.
¹⁸ John Stuart Mill (1806-1873). See W. Levi (Ed.), *The Six Great Humanistic Essays of John Stuart Mill*, Washington Square Press, 1963 (especially "Utilitarianism", pp. 243-85) and *Collected Works*, University of Toronto Press, Toronto, 1963.
¹⁹ A. C. Pigou (1877-1959), *Economics of Welfare*, 4th ed., Macmillan, London, 1938.
²⁰ F. Y. Edgeworth, *Mathematical Psychics*, Kegan Paul, London, 1881.
²¹ V. Pareto, references given in Reference 6.

FURTHER READING

Alchian, A. and W. Allen, *Exchange and Production Theory in Use*, Wadsworth, Belmont, 1969, Ch. 1.
Heilbroner, R., "The Three Solutions of the Economic Problem", Ch. 3 and "The Wonderful World of Adam Smith", Ch. 27 in M. L. Joseph, N. C. Seeber and G. L. Bach (Eds), *Economic Analysis and Policy*, Prentice-Hall, Englewood Cliffs, 1964.
Knight, F. H., "Social Economic Organization", Reading 1 in W. Breit and H. Hochman (Eds), *Readings in Microeconomics*, Holt, Rinehart and Winston, New York, 1968.
Kohler, H., *Scarcity Challenged*, Holt, Rinehart and Winston, New York, 1968, Ch. 1.

CHAPTER 2

Optimisation, Economic Behaviour and Choice*

I. Why are Economists interested in the Mathematics of Optimisation?

Economists have increasingly turned to mathematics in order to portray the economic world. Sometimes their enthusiasm has led to the building of elegant mathematical models of little relevance to the economic world but mostly the use of mathematics marks a step forward. Axioms and assertions become more precise and, therefore, more easily sorted out. The possibilities for measuring and testing have also grown.

Economists are, of course, interested in many branches of mathematics but as the science now stands the theory of mathematical *extrema* is of central importance. This is so for the following reasons:

(i) frequently, we are concerned with finding the *best* economic strategy or course of action; that is, best in relation to some set of aims. This is generally equivalent to finding a strategy which maximises or minimises a relevant objective function: a function which has the power of value ordering the alternative strategies. The aim may be to maximise economic welfare, find an optimal course of action for the government or to find a strategy which maximises the profit of the firm. In general, these can be reduced to problems in the mathematics of extrema. The purpose of such an exercise is to indicate the policy which *should* be pursued if one has a specific set of objectives. The problem is of the prescriptive type;

(ii) interest in the mathematics of extrema comes also from another source. Economic theorists frequently assume that economic agents act so as to maximise or minimise particular types of objective functions. Optimisation then *describes* and *predicts* actual behaviour. For example, orthodox economic theory is based on the assumption that firms maximise their profit and consumers their utility. Given the constraints in the system this can be used to describe and predict the behaviour of firms and consumers if the basic assumptions of the theory are correct.

The central role of optimisation in economic theory has not gone unchallenged. H. Simon,[1] for example, has expressed doubts as to whether optimisation theories are very satisfactory descriptions of actual behaviour. His attention has turned to adaptive theories. But many adaptive approaches can be explained in terms of

---

* Readers may wish to omit Sections III, IV, and V, until they have read Chapter 6.

attempts to move towards an optimum. I shall not enter into the controversy here, but it is a fundamental one.

The optimisation approach gained great support from the nineteenth century belief in the rationality of man. Thinkers of that century were agog with man's success in discovering scientific laws. Surely, optimisation in his social behaviour was not beyond the ken of man. Economists of the nineteenth and early twentieth century made sweeping assumptions about the rationality and optimising behaviour of man. In the last quarter of this century, important modifications have been made in the economic view of behaviour. In particular, imperfections of knowledge have been shown to have important consequences for optimising behaviour.

Because economic units are frequently assumed to act rationally, optimisation is central to economic theory. In economic theory, optimisation and rationality are inextricably linked. For example, Lange states that, "An economic unit is said to act rationally when its objective is the maximisation of a magnitude."[2] Hence, in the study of economics it is vital to know some simple points about the mathematical theory of extrema.

II. Simple Points about the Mathematical Theory of Extrema

Until recently there has been a considerable lag between the development of mathematical techniques and their application in economic theory. Although Leibniz and Newton, for example, developed the differential calculus before the turn of the seventeenth century, its implications for economics were not generally comprehended until just before the turn of the twentieth century. True, Cournot[3] had applied it in 1838 but his work was generally neglected and it was not until the advent of Jevons,[4] Marshall[5] and the Austrian School[6] that the relevance of the differential calculus to economic problems was appreciated. It has now been firmly embedded as a useful tool for economists.

Why is it a useful tool? It is valuable, amongst other reasons, because it gives a method of finding an extremum by knowing *limited* characteristics of the function to be maximised. Thus problem solving is made easier. In general, this is an important property to be sought in any mathematical method for finding extrema. Furthermore, it is an analytical technique as opposed to a computational one. This provides the theorist with considerable flexibility. While the maximum and minimum of many functions might be found by sheer enumeration, the effort which is involved is often tremendous and except in the case of refined computational methods, which rely on mathematical properties, is devoid of generalisation. Many efficient search methods are in fact, based on the properties of the derivatives of functions.

Marginal analysis is concerned with small changes at the margin and is integrally related to the differential calculus. In order to find the maximum or minimum of many functions all we need to know are some properties of the way in which the total value of the function *changes* as the independent variables change. If one wishes to maximise the value of a function which is dependent upon one variable, for example, production per week, then one increases the value of the dependent variable until the additional gross benefit from doing so equals the additional cost of doing so. At a point where the net benefit is zero, an extremum usually (but not invariably) exists and it will be a maximum if some conditions to be mentioned later are satisfied.

Take a simple case. Imagine that a firm wishes to maximise its profit which depends

Optimisation and Choice

on the difference between its total revenue and total cost both of which depend upon the firm's level of output in any week. Its profit is therefore a function of its weekly output. Its assumed marginal profit as a function of its weekly output is shown in Fig. 2.1. If production is at all profitable, profit is clearly maximised by producing $\bar{x}$ units per week. If output is at any level less than $\bar{x}$, say at $\bar{x} - \varepsilon$,

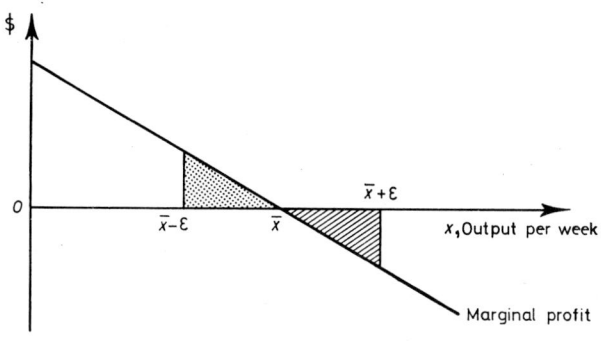

Fig. 2.1

profit can be increased by adding to output until $\bar{x}$ is reached. For example, expanding output from $\bar{x} - \varepsilon$ to $\bar{x}$ increases profit by the equivalent of the dotted triangle. To go beyond $\bar{x}$ is to reduce profit. To increase output from $\bar{x}$ to $\bar{x} + \varepsilon$ is to reduce profit below the maximum level by the equivalent of the hatched triangle. In this case in order to find the true maximum one need only consider the *additions* to profit by varying output in the *neighbourhood* of the point where marginal profit is zero. *The maximum occurs for the output at which marginal profit is zero.* A small decision area is involved and only a limited knowledge of the properties of the profit function is required to find the maximum.

This example has been chosen so as to avoid difficulties. As will be seen below the questions involved can be more complex. Indeed, there are some problems to which the differential calculus and marginal analysis cannot be applied. But assuming application of the differential calculus, let us examine more closely the question of finding an extremum.

III. Marginalism, the Differential Calculus and Extrema

Broadly, a function is only differentiable everywhere if it is continuous and smooth, that is without kinks. The functions shown in Figs 2.2 and 2.3 are discontinuous and

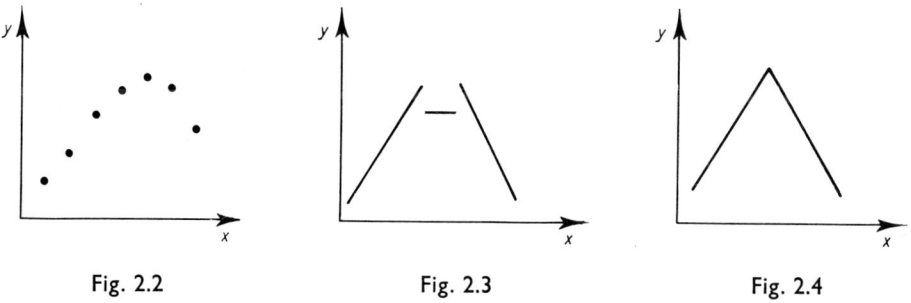

Fig. 2.2   Fig. 2.3   Fig. 2.4

not differentiable everywhere and that shown in Fig. 2.4 involves a kink. In cases like this the differential calculus cannot be used in order to find the maxima of the functions. Functions of this kind can occur for economic problems. If a factor input cannot be varied in small quantities but only in large discrete quantities, the relationship between output and quantity of the input may not be unlike the function in Fig. 2.2. But a great number of economic situations can be characterised by differentiable functions so let us first examine these in more detail.

Take the function which is illustrated in Fig. 2.5. The function is supposed to be differentiable everywhere and is useful for illustrating the relationship between derivatives and extrema. It is clear that a relative extremum of y only occurs at points where $f(x)$ is stationary, i.e., at points where the rate of change of $f(x)$ is zero. Relative extrema occur at the values x_0, x_1 and x_3. While the condition that the rate of change of $f(x)$ be zero is necessary for a relative extremum of the function it is not sufficient because the rate of change of a function is also zero at an inflection point. In this case, an inflection point occurs at x_2.

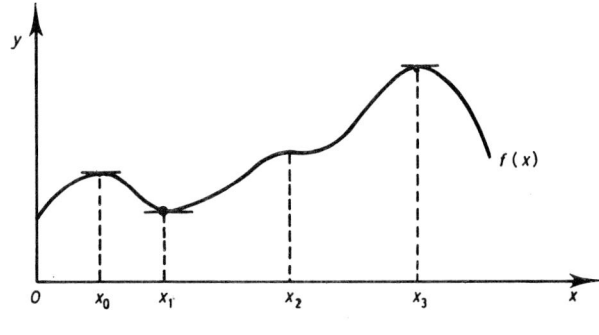

Fig. 2.5

The first derivative of $f(x)$, that is, its rate of change, is shown roughly in Fig. 2.6. It is the marginal curve corresponding to $f(x)$. As indicated the derivative of $f(x)$ is zero for extrema as well as for the inflection point. If the first derivative is zero, we may have a maximum, a minimum or an inflection point of the function. Further information is needed in order to distinguish between these possibilities. Fig. 2.6

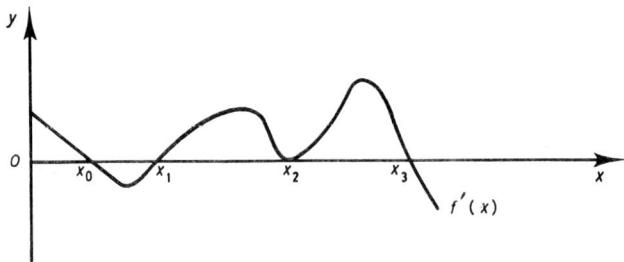

Fig. 2.6

gives a clue to the required information. Given that $f'(k) = 0$ where k is any value of x, $f(k)$

(i) is a relative maximum of $f(x)$ if $f'(x)$ changes from positive to negative in the neighbourhood of k,
(ii) is a relative minimum of $f(x)$ if $f'(x)$ changes from negative to positive in the neighbourhood of k,
(iii) and *may* be an inflection point of $f(k)$ if $f'(x)$ does not change its sign in the neighbourhood of k but need not be.

Given that $f(k)$ possesses a second derivative, the satisfaction of the previous conditions depends upon the sign of the second derivative. If $f'(k) = 0$, $f(k)$ is

(i) a relative maximum of $f(x)$ if $f''(k)$ is negative, i.e., if the slope of the tangent to $f'(k)$ is negative,
(ii) a relative minimum of $f(x)$ if $f''(k)$ is positive, i.e., if the slope of the tangent to $f'(k)$ is positive, and
(iii) may be an inflection point if $f''(k) = 0$, but need not be.

It is quite possible for $f(k)$ to be either a maximum or a minimum value of $f(x)$ even if $f''(k) = 0$. In such a case, $f(k)$ may be in respectively a "flat upland" or a "flat valley". A flat upland case is shown in Fig. 2.7. In that case $f(k)$ is clearly a maximum value of $f(x)$ even though $f''(k) = 0$.

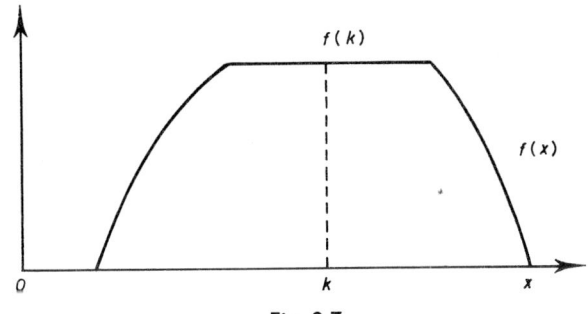

Fig. 2.7

In cases where $f''(k) = 0$ it is sometimes possible to resolve whether the function has a maximum, minimum or stationary value by considering derivatives of higher order. Any standard calculus text will outline the method which uses Taylor's series.

It has been assumed above that $f(x)$ is defined for an unlimited range. If $y = f(x)$ is defined for a limited range of values $a \leqslant x \leqslant b$, the end-points, $x = a$ and $x = b$, must be examined as possible extreme points.

Furthermore, $y = f(x)$ has been assumed to be differentiable everywhere. If it is not, one must examine every point at which it fails to have a derivative for a maximum or minimum value might occur there.

To summarise: given that a function $y = f(x)$ is differentiable everywhere, the critical points of it, that is, those for which its first derivative or its rate of change or its marginal value is zero, are either maximum, minimum or inflection values of it. The condition $f'(x) = 0$ is sometimes referred to as the first order or necessary condition for an extreme. A critical point is a local maximum if $f''(x) < 0$ and a minimum if $f''(x) > 0$. $f(x)$ is a local maximum if $f(x)$ changes at a decreasing rate or if the marginal values of $f(x)$ are diminishing in the neighbourhood of the critical point. Conditions such as these are referred to as second-order conditions. On checking these one *may* be able to decide that the critical point is a maximum or a minimum value. The evaluation of the second derivative is an essential step towards resolving the nature of the critical points.

The conditions which are mentioned indicate *local* extrema—points which are maxima or minima within a small neighbourhood. The greatest of the local maxima is naturally the global maximum and the smallest of the local minima is the global minimum. Generally, our main problem is to find either the global maximum or the global minimum of a function. Classical differential methods do not always ensure that the global extremum required in a problem will be discovered. For example, the direct method of observing the variation of $f(x)$ in the range $0 \leqslant x < x_1$ could lead to the mistaken conclusion that the global maximum of $f(x)$ occurs for $x = x_0$ when in fact it occurs for $x = x_3$. Myopic marginalist procedures can easily lead one astray in cases like this.

But if the relevant function has suitable properties one can be sure that any local maximum is also a global maximum or any local minimum is also a global one. If for example, $f''(x) < 0$ everywhere, that is if $f(x)$ changes at a diminishing rate or in other words is a strictly concave function, then any stationary value of $f(x)$ is a global maximum. Assumptions of this nature have been widely employed in economics and will be discussed below in further detail.

Most problems of economic optimisation involve maximising subject to constraints. Normally, they involve maximisation of an objective function, subject to limitations such as those imposed by the available resources and technology, but so far only unconstrained functions have been discussed. However, problems which have been raised in that context also occur for constrained optimisation problems and frequently simple constrained problems can be converted into equivalent unconstrained ones. However, let us specifically consider marginalism and constrained maximisation problems.

The method devised by Lagrange for solving constrained optimisation problems has been widely used either explicitly or implicitly in economics.[7] The most common textbook statements of the optimal allocation of a consumer's income and of the optimal employment of resources are based in an assumed applicability of this method. This method requires that the objective and constraint functions be continuous and differentiable. Furthermore, all the functional constraints must be equalities and no non-negativity constraints must be present.

The essence and the limitation of Lagrange's method might best be illustrated by an example. Imagine that an economic agent wishes to maximise an objective function

$$U = f(x_1, x_2) \qquad (2.1)$$

subject to

$$Y \geqslant p_1 x_1 + p_2 x_2 \qquad (2.2)$$

and

$$\left. \begin{array}{l} x_1 \geqslant 0 \\ x_2 \geqslant 0 \end{array} \right\} \qquad \begin{array}{l} (2.3) \\ (2.4) \end{array}$$

where x_1 and x_2 are controlled variables and Y, p_1 and p_2 are constants. U is a continuous and differentiable ordering or objective function, Equation (2.2) is a functional constraint and Equations (2.3) and (2.4) are non-negativity conditions.

The model may reasonably describe a consumer's choice problem under perfect

Optimisation and Choice

competition if U is interpreted as his utility, Y as his income, p_1 and p_2 as the prices of commodities, x_1 and x_2 where these symbols represent their quantities. Given that the consumer can purchase only two commodities, the problem is to maximise utility subject to the constraint that expenditure *must not exceed* available income and subject to the proviso that negative quantities of the commodities are not available. The consumer is under no obligation to spend his total income.

In this case, the feasible set of (x_1, x_2) values forms a triangle in an (x_1, x_2) plane. In fact, the triangle represents the intersection of, or if you like, the points in common of the half-planes described by the restrictions of (Equations (2.2), (2.3) and (2.4)). Only points contained in the triangle simultaneously satisfy all the inequality restrictions. The nature of the feasible set is illustrated in Fig. 2.8 where the feasible set is $\triangle OBC$. Only points in the positive quadrant satisfy the non-negativity conditions and only points below BC satisfy the budget restraint. The equation of the line BC is found by rearranging

$$Y = p_1 x_1 + p_2 x_2 \tag{2.5}$$

to give

$$x_2 = \frac{Y}{p_2} - \frac{p_1}{p_2} x_1 \tag{2.6}$$

and thus its slope is equal to the relative prices of the commodities. The objective function U can be projected onto the (x_1, x_2) plane as a series of contours or indifference curves. Depending on the nature of these contours a global maximum of U may either occur at a boundary point of the feasible set, or at an interior point.

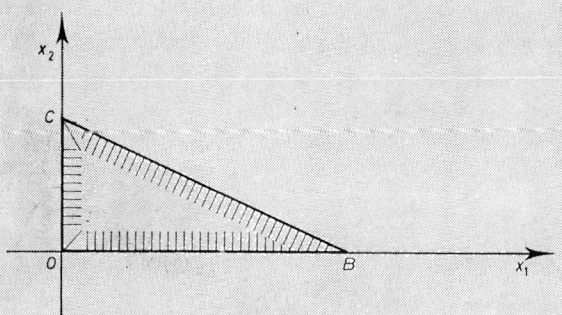

Fig. 2.8

The traditional approach to this problem has been to solve it by using Lagrange's method. This assumes that a global maximum of U occurs on the boundary of the feasible set in the interior of the positive quadrant, or that if this maximum occurs at the boundary of the feasible set and the positive quadrant an equality of particular derivatives is satisfied there. In terms of Fig. 2.8, the Lagrange and traditional economics approach assumes that a global maximum occurs between points B and C on the line BC. In rare cases a global maximum at points B and C is also allowable. In all cases, the maximum is assumed to occur for a set of *marginal equalities*.

Using Lagrange's method the problem which is solved *rather than* the original one, is as follows:

Maximise $\qquad\qquad U = f(x_1, x_2)$ (2.7)
subject to $\qquad\qquad Y = p_1 x_1 + p_2 x_2.$ (2.8)

Note that no inequalities are mentioned in this problem at all. The consumer is assumed to spend the whole of his income and negative values for quantities are not specifically excluded. The method of finding the necessary conditions for a maximum involves maximising a new equation which is formed from the previous two with the addition of an undetermined multiplier, the Lagrange multiplier, λ. In the case above, we form

$$z = f(x_1, x_2) + \lambda(p_1 x_1 + p_2 x_2 - Y)$$

and examine this function for critical points. On differentiation one can show that these occur for x_1, x_2 values for which the following equations are simultaneously satisfied:

$$\frac{\frac{\partial f}{\partial x_1}}{p_1} = \lambda \qquad (2.9)$$

$$\frac{\frac{\partial f}{\partial x_2}}{p_2} = \lambda \qquad (2.10)$$

$$Y = p_1 x_1 + p_2 x_2. \qquad (2.11)$$

An economic interpretation of these conditions, as will be learnt later, is that the marginal utility of the last dollar spent on one commodity should *equal* that from the other *and* total income must be exactly spent. It can also be shown that these conditions are satisfied whenever the slope of the budget line (*BC* in Fig. 2.8) is equal to the slope of a contour or indifference curve of $U = f(x_1, x_2)$. A critical point occurs at point *A* in Fig. 2.9 and classical restrictions on the nature of the objective function are such as to ensure that it is at a global maximum for the values of x_1 and x_2 at *A*.

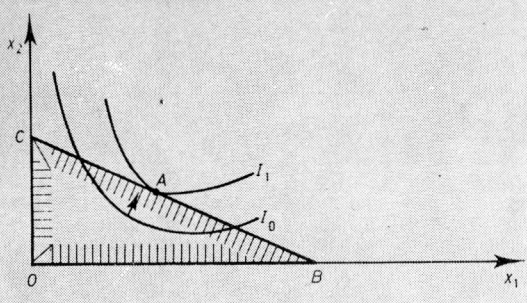

Fig. 2.9

For example, it is normally assumed that any individual prefers a greater quantity of commodities to less. Clearly, in the case of nuisance goods this is not so and corner point solutions at *O*, *B* and *C* are liable to occur in practice, and these may render the classical conditions of marginal equalities and expenditure of total income inappropriate. This is easily illustrated assuming that the original problem is the one which really requires to be solved.[8]

DIFFICULTY 1

The global maximum of U may occur at a corner-point such as C, and there the slope of the budget line and the indifference curve may differ. In that circumstance solving the Lagrange problem will lead to a solution which involves a negative value for x_1 if the objective function is conceptually defined for negative values of x_1. Thus the suggested solution is not really one at all. This is illustrated in Fig. 2.10. The Lagrange approach suggests that A corresponds to a global maximum, but in view of the inequality restrictions, C in fact corresponds to the global maximum. At C the slope of the budget line BC differs from that for the highest attainable indifference curve I_2. The rate of decline of the budget line is greater than that of the indifference curve.[9]

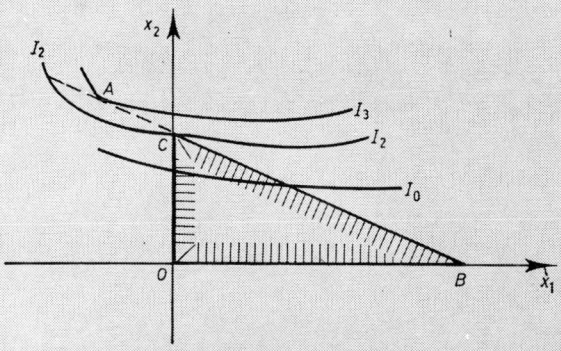

Fig. 2.10

DIFFICULTY 2

The maximum of U may not occur in a boundary point of the feasible set but at an interior point. An interior solution is indicated in Fig. 2.11. In the application to consumption, point A, the point corresponding to a global maximum, is a satiety point. If the search for a maximum is confined to points on the budget line BC, the

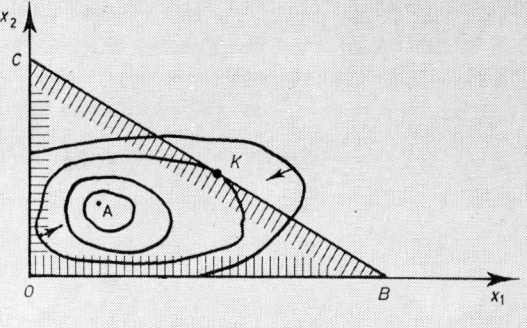

Fig. 2.11

global maximum will not be found. Lagrange's method does confine the search to points on BC and is not capable of resolving the general problem. Note also that a point such as K corresponds to a relative maximum, given that one is constrained to BC. In other circumstances, we shall find that points like K correspond to constrained minima. The second-order conditions must be checked.

Kuhn and Tucker[10] have developed methods which are designed to cope with both of the above difficulties and which allow the type of problem which was first posed to be solved in principle. Kuhn and Tucker have extended classical optimisation techniques so as to allow for corner-point solutions and for non-negativity conditions and for either interior or boundary solutions. An exposition of their method may, for example, be found in Lancaster's *Mathematical Economics*. If the objective function is not continuous, their method is inadequate and for some problems, since it can involve an evaluation of all corner-points, may not be practical.

Even if restraints are present, the difficulty of distinguishing between local and global optima may occur. In Figs 2.12 and 2.13 the feasible set consists of the points on and in $\triangle OBC$. In Fig. 2.12, two local boundary maxima occur, one at D and the other at A. A corresponds to a global maximum. In Fig. 2.13 two interior local maxima occur. One corresponds to point D and the other to A. By placing restrictions on the concavity, convexity etc. of the objective functions, economists frequently rule out multiple local optima. This will be discussed further.

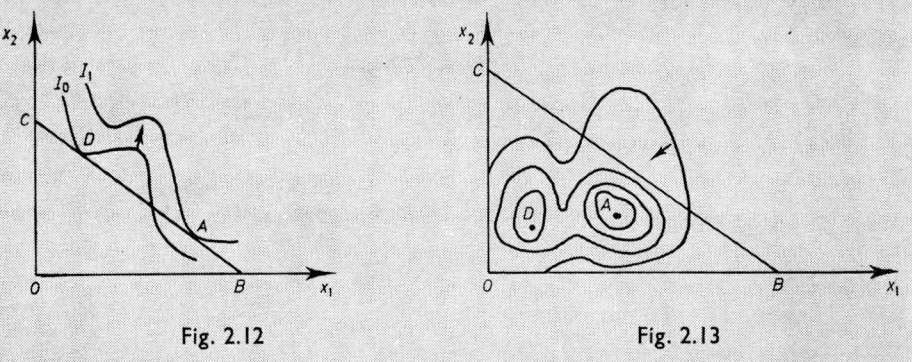

Fig. 2.12 Fig. 2.13

In the examples considered above, the feasible set is of a particularly simple form. By varying the nature of the feasible set one can manufacture corner-point solutions where none existed before and one can create multiple local optima. To illustrate, let us vary the nature of the feasible set given in Fig. 2.9. With the feasible set as indicated in Fig. 2.14 two local maxima occur, namely at D and A, and in Fig. 2.15 a maximum occurs at A which is now a corner point so that marginal equivalences are irrelevant.

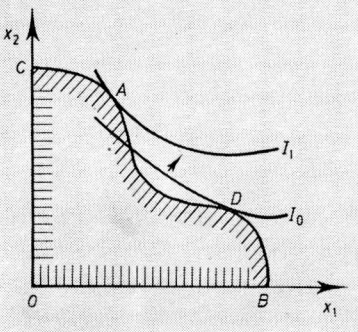 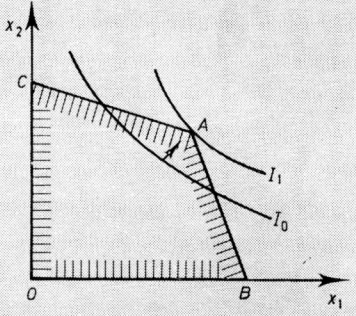

Fig. 2.14 Fig. 2.15

By placing restrictions on the general nature of the objective function and the feasible set, the possibility of multiple maxima or minima can be ruled out and the conditions required for an extremum can be narrowed down. The convexity and quasi-concavity properties of objective functions and the convexity, or otherwise, of feasible sets are very important in this regard. These are discussed below.

Before discussing these matters, let us note at this stage that present economic theory differs say from theoretical physics in one important respect. There seem to be few if any universally accepted constants in economic theory and the theory mostly relies on the general properties of functions and sets. The specific form of the functions and sets involved in an economy is rarely known or are so variable as to be of little value in economic generalisation. Hence, it is most important that the general properties be fruitfully classified. Classification in terms of convexity properties has proven to be very helpful. Also, the modern approach by way of set theory has not only resulted in new generalities, but in increased simplicity. In terms of this new approach, it is very easy to see why the theories of Hicks in *Value and Capital*[11] and that of Samuelson in the *Foundations of Economic Analysis*[12] are particular ones.

IV. Convex Functions

Let X represent the set of possible x values for $f(x)$ i.e., the range of possible x values. x can represent a point in any finite number of dimensions. It is an n-tuple. Then $f(x)$ is a *convex* function if

$$f[tx_0+(1-t)x_1] \leqslant tf(x_0)+(1-t)f(x_1) \qquad (2.12)^*$$

$$[x_1, x_0 \in X; \quad 0 \leqslant t \leqslant 1],$$

and $f(x)$ is a *strictly convex* function, if $x_1 \neq x_0$ and $0 < t < 1$, and (2.12) is a strict inequality. If the inequality of (2.12) is reversed, $f(x)$ is a *concave* function and if the reversed strict inequality holds, $f(x)$ is a *strictly concave* function.

The propositions are easily illustrated. Take the two-dimensional function shown in Fig. 2.16. It is a strictly convex function since the chord joining any different two points of it lies above the function, except at the end-points of the chord. As indicated for $t = 0.5$, inequality (2.12) is a strict one. In this figure

$$A = f[tx_0+(1-t)x_1] = f[0.5x_0+0.5x_1]$$

and

$$B = tf(x_0)+(1-t)f(x_1) = 0.5f(x_0)+0.5f(x_1).$$

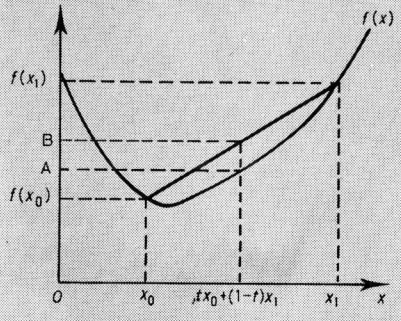
Fig. 2.16

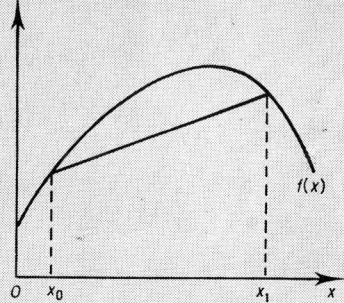
Fig. 2.17

The function shown in Fig. 2.17 is strictly concave because the chord joining any two points of it is, except for the end-points, below the function. Both types of functions occur in economic theory. For example, production functions are sometimes assumed to be strictly concave everywhere, that is, subject to diminishing marginal productivity and diminishing returns everywhere.

Next, visualise this classification in three dimensions. The functions, for example of suitable parts of a sphere and on ellipsoid can either be globally concave or globally convex. Take a half or less of a ball by cutting it straight through once. Then if the base of this piece is placed on, say, the base plane (that is the floor of a usual three-dimensional diagram) the function representing its surface is *strictly concave*. The chord joining any two points of the surface is below it, except at the end-points. If this piece of ball is then, for example, rotated through 180°, the function representing its surface becomes *strictly convex*. In Fig. 2.18 a strictly concave function in three dimensions is indicated and a strictly convex one is represented in Fig. 2.19. Production and utility functions of the general form represented in Fig. 2.18 are commonly assumed in economics.

Fig. 2.18 Fig. 2.19

It might be noted that a linear function is *both* convex and concave, but is never strictly convex or concave. For a linear function, (2.12) always reduces to an equality.

If a function is strictly convex or strictly concave it need not be differentiable everywhere as the convex example shown in Fig. 2.20 indicates. An infinite number of tangents can be drawn at $f(\bar{x})$.

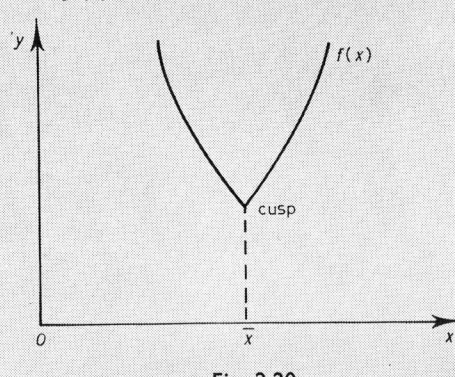

Fig. 2.20

However, if $f(x)$ is a twice differentiable function and if its second derivatives have suitable properties $f(x)$ is convex, concave or strictly so.

Optimisation and Choice

In the two-dimensional case, if for all values of $y = f(x)$,

$$\frac{d^2 f}{dx^2} > 0, \text{ then } f(x) \text{ is strictly convex;}$$

if $\quad \dfrac{d^2 f}{dx^2} = 0, f(x)$ is convex and concave; and

if $\quad \dfrac{d^2 f}{dx^2} < 0, f(x)$ is strictly concave.

In the general multidimensional case, if $f(x)$ is a twice differentiable function, its convexity properties, or lack of these, can be inferred from the nature of the matrix of the second derivatives of $f(x)$. This matrix is called a Hessian.[13] For the record only, if this Hessian is positive (negative) semidefinite for all possible values of x, $f(x)$ is convex (concave). If the Hessian is positive (negative) definite for all possible values of x, $f(x)$ is strictly convex (concave).[14]

The following is an important theorem for much of existing economic theory. If $f(x)$ is a strictly concave (convex) function, it has at most one local maximum (minimum). This local maximum (minimum) is a global maximum (minimum). If $f(x)$ is a strictly concave (convex) function, it is also the case that any critical value of the function corresponds to a global maximum (minimum). Thus in many cases it is sufficient merely to search for points at which the marginal (first order) conditions are zero. On finding such a point, one can be sure that it corresponds to a global maximum if the function is (globally) concave and a minimum if the function is (globally) convex. Where a function is strictly concave (convex) usual myopic search procedures are certain to lead towards the global maximum (minimum) if it exists. In the former case, no multiple maxima exist and in the latter no multiple minima occur.

Other properties of convex and concave functions also have application in economics. For example, it follows from (2.12) that

$$f(E[x]) \leq E[f(x)] \tag{2.13}$$

if $f(x)$ is convex. Here E may represent the mathematical expectation or average of the value in parentheses. If $f(x)$ is strictly convex and not all the x values of (2.13) are the same, (2.13) is a strict inequality.

The reverse respective positions hold if $f(x)$ is concave and strictly concave. A strictly concave case is illustrated in Fig. 2.21. If $f(x)$ is taken to represent utility

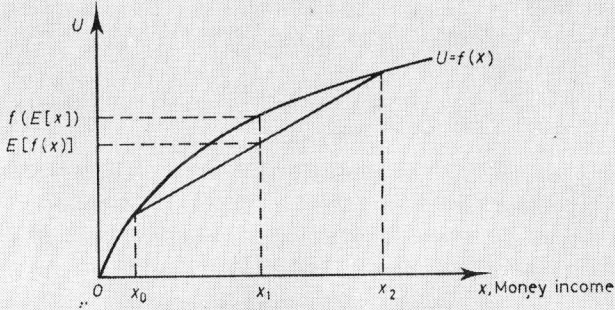

Fig. 2.21

from money income, x, the sure prospect of an income of $x_1 = 0.5x_0 + 0.5x_2$ yields a higher level of expected utility than a prospect of x_0 or x_2 with a probability of 0.5 each. The reverse position would hold if marginal utility were increasing with income rather than diminishing.

This by no means exhausts the number of valuable theorems which can be derived from the convexity properties of functions or can be shown to hold in view of these. But at this stage, the problem of optimisation is our principal concern. The quasi-concavity of functions is important in this regard. However, it is not possible to grasp the concept adequately without discussing sets and convex sets. Indeed, a discussion of these is essential, especially to bring out constrained optimisation problems fully.

V. Sets and Convex Sets

A set is a collection of objects of any kind. The set may be described by complete enumeration or by some property possessed by the objects. The whole numbers, for example, from 1 to 10 inclusive form a set. We could name all these numbers 1, 2, ... 9, 10, and describe the set in this way or by reference to the property mentioned in the last sentence. The objects of a set are called its elements or members and notation $x \in S$ indicates that x is a member or element of S whereas $x \notin S$ indicates that it is not.

If the set consists of a finite number of elements, we can describe it by using the following notation

$$S = \{x_i\} \quad i = 1, \ldots, n \tag{2.14}$$

which indicates a set of n elements. The set mentioned above is

$$S = \{1, 2, \ldots, 9, 10\} \tag{2.15}$$

or we might describe it by some property. The following also describes the above case:

$$S = \{x \mid 1 \leq x \leq 10 \text{ and } x \text{ is a whole number}\} \tag{2.16}$$

that is, the collection of values such that [this is indicated by the stroke] x is a whole number from 1 to 10 inclusive. A set need not be a collection of points but such a collection forms a set. Possibly the properties of point sets are of most interest in economics so in order to illustrate some set-notation, I have selected examples from this area.

Two sets A and B are said to be *equal* if they contain the same elements. This is indicated by $A = B$. The sets

$$A = \{x, y \mid y = a + bx, x \geq 0\} \tag{2.17}$$

and

$$B = \{x, y \mid \lambda y = \lambda(a + bx), x \geq 0\} \tag{2.18}$$

are equal. They make up the same line segment.

A *subset* B of a set A is a set all of whose elements are in A. This is written as $B \subset A$ to be read as "B is contained in A" or "B is a subset of A". If both $B \subset A$ and $A \subset B$ then $A = B$ for the sets consist of the same elements. However, if $B \subset A$ but $A \not\subset B$ then B is a *proper subset* of A. Some elements of A are not elements of B. If

$$B = \{x, y \mid y = a + bx, x \geq 10\} \tag{2.19}$$

then B is a proper subset of A, if A is described by Equation (2.17). To give another example. Let A consist of all (x, y) values on the circumference of or in the interior of a circle with a radius r centred at the origin, that is

$$A = \{x, y \mid x^2 + y^2 \leq r^2\}. \tag{2.20}$$

Imagine that

$$B = \{x, y \mid x^2 + y^2 \leq k^2\}. \tag{2.21}$$

Then $A = B$ if $k = r$ and B is a proper subset of A if $k < r$. In Fig. 2.22, B is shown as a proper subset of A.

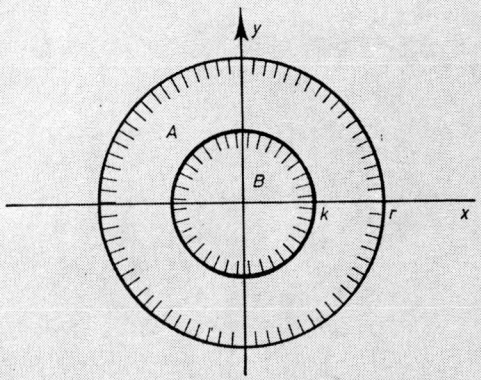

Fig. 2.22

The *intersection* or product of two sets A and B written $A \cap B$ and read as "A cap B" is a set, C, containing all elements which are *common* to A and B. There may be no elements common to A and B in which case $A \cap B$ is an *empty set*; it has no members. This is written as $A \cap B = \phi$, and the sets A and B are said to be *disjoint*.

Consider the following examples. Let

$$A = \{x, y \mid y = a + bx\} \tag{2.22}$$

and

$$B = \{x, y \mid y = c + dx\} \tag{2.23}$$

Then if $a \neq c$ and $b \neq d$, $A \cap B$ consists of the single value at which these lines cross. It is their unique solution. If $a \neq c$ and $b = d$, $A \cap B = \phi$. The lines have no point in common. The sets are disjoint. If $a = c$ and $b = d$ the lines are identical and they have all points in common. The three respective cases are indicated by the examples in Figs 2.23, 2.24 and 2.25. Note that in the first case $A \cap B$ consists of the non-empty set $\{x = 0, y = 0\}$.

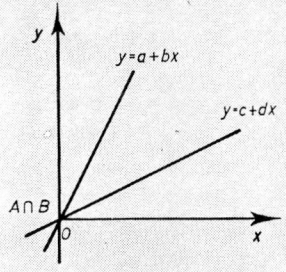
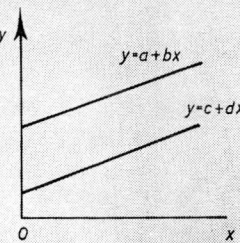
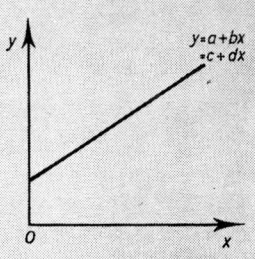

Fig. 2.23   Fig. 2.24   Fig. 2.25

To take a further example. Let
$$A = \{x, y \mid x^2 + y^2 \leqslant r^2\} \tag{2.24}$$
and
$$B = \{x, y \mid (x-h)^2 + y^2 \leqslant k^2 \text{ where } k \geqslant 0\}. \tag{2.25}$$
Then if $h = r+k$, $A \cap B$ consists of one point, namely the point of tangency of the circles, if $h > r+k$ the sets A and B are disjoint and if $h < r+k$ the sets have several points in common. Examples of these three possibilities are shown respectively in Figs 2.26, 2.27 and 2.28. In Fig. 2.26, $A \cap B = C = (r, o)$; in Fig. 2.27, $A \cap B = \phi$; and in Fig. 2.28 $A \cap B = C$ consists of the eye-shaped segment indicated by the dots.

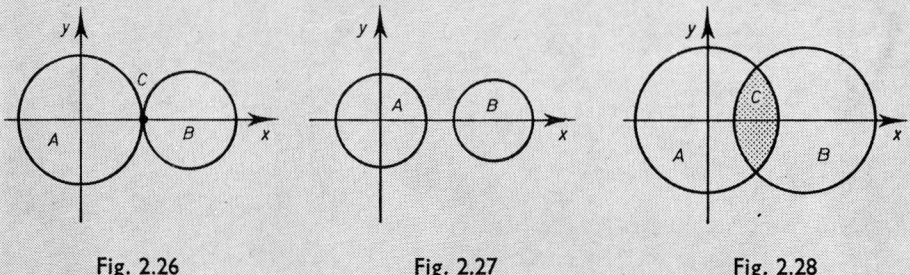

Fig. 2.26   Fig. 2.27   Fig. 2.28

Not only is the intersection of sets important to the concept of a solution but feasible sets are often defined in economics by the intersection of various relations. For example, the feasible set in linear programming problems is defined by the intersection of a number of linear inequalities. The idea of intersection can be extended to m sets. The set C of all the elements common to m sets is indicated by

$$C = \bigcap_{j=1}^{m} A_j.$$

The *union* of two sets, $A \cup B$ read "A cup B" is the set which contains all elements in either A or B or both. If in Figs 2.26, 2.27 and 2.28, all the points of the closed discs A and B are shaded, then all shaded points together form $A \cup B$. The notation extends to m sets. The union of m sets, $A_1, A_2, \ldots A_m$ is indicated by

$$\bigcup_{j=1}^{m} A_j.$$

The complement of the set B consists of all elements not in B. The complement of B with respect to a particular set, say A, consists of all those elements of A which are not in B. It is indicated by $A \sim B$. In the case illustrated in diagram 2.22, $A \sim B$ consists of all points on the outer circle, plus all points between the inner and the outer circle.

I shall not consider the ordering and quasi-ordering of sets here but will defer that until the revealed preference theory of demand is discussed. Rather let us consider the concept of a convex set. The concept is of great importance for almost all of economic analysis. In economic theory we are principally concerned with point sets, that is, sets whose elements are points or vectors in Euclidean space. A point or vector set S is *convex* if the line segment joining any (and every) pair of points in the set is comprised entirely of points of the set. More formally, a point set S is said to be *convex* if $\lambda x_1 + (1-\lambda)x_2 \in S$ whenever $x_1, x_2 \in S$ and $0 \leq \lambda \leq 1$. Hence, in geometrical terms, a convex set is connected, that is, "solid" and is not re-entrant.

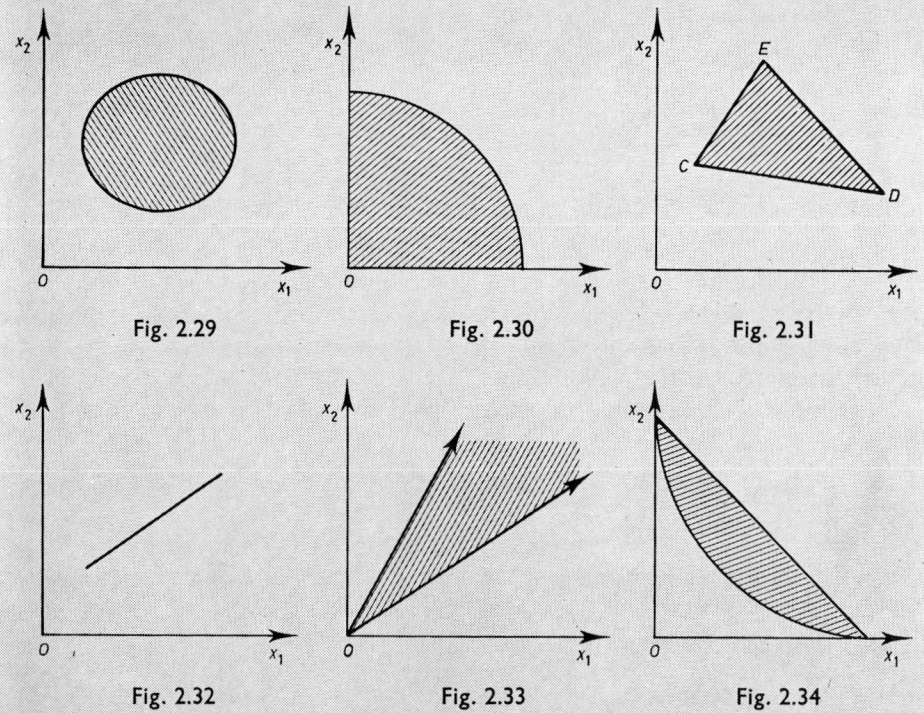

Fig. 2.29   Fig. 2.30   Fig. 2.31

Fig. 2.32   Fig. 2.33   Fig. 2.34

The shaded figures shown in Figs 2.29 to 2.34 are convex. Note that the set shown in Fig. 2.33 has no upper bound but is nevertheless convex. It is also easy to imagine convex sets in three dimensions. The set consisting of the points on an inside of a solid ball is a convex set. Any hyperplane is a convex set. A Euclidean space, any linear subspace, a halfspace are convex sets.

Examples of non-convex sets are shown in Figs 2.35 to 2.40. The line segment for two points of each set is shown and includes points not in the set. The first three sets are re-entrant, the next two have "holes" in them and the last is not connected.

A set is *compact* if it is both strictly bounded and closed. A set is strictly *bounded* if we can specify a hypersphere, however large, which contains all the points of the set. All the sets shown in the last 12 figures except those in 2.33 and 2.39 are bounded.

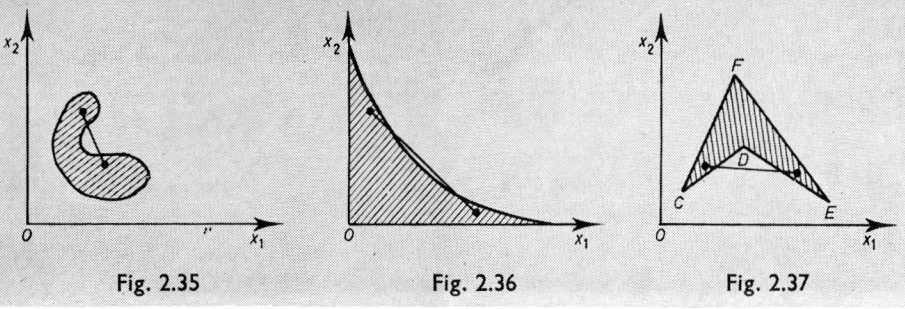

Fig. 2.35   Fig. 2.36   Fig. 2.37

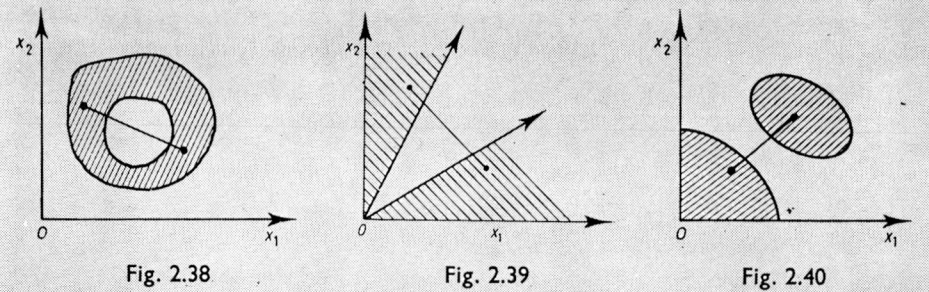

Fig. 2.38   Fig. 2.39   Fig. 2.40

A set is *closed* if it contains all of its boundary points. A point x is a *boundary point* of a set S if the neighbourhood of x, no matter how small, contains points some of which are in S and some of which are not in S. A set which does not contain any of its boundary points is said to be open. Nearly all sets of economic interest are closed and most seem to be strictly bounded.

The concept of openness and closedness might be made clearer by two examples. The set

$$A = \{x, y \mid y = x, 0 \leqslant x \leqslant 1\} \quad (2.26)$$

is closed and

$$B = \{x, y \mid y = x, 0 < x < 1\} \quad (2.27)$$

is open. One is a closed line segment, the other is an open line segment. The set

$$A = \{x, y \mid x^2 + y^2 \leqslant r^2\} \quad (2.28)$$

is closed whereas

$$B = \{x, y \mid x^2 + y^2 < r^2\} \quad (2.29)$$

is open. The boundary points of both sets are the points on a circle with radius r but the second set does not contain the points on the circumference.

An *extreme point* of a set is a point of the set which cannot be expressed as a linear combination of any two different points of the set.[15] In Fig. 2.31, the points C, D and E are extreme. In Fig. 2.37, the points C, E and F are extreme but the point D, for example, is not. All the points on the circumference of the figure in Fig. 2.29 are extreme points. The set of all the extreme points of a set is called the *extremal* of the set. A compact convex set is spanned by the linear combinations of its extreme points. A set is *strictly convex* if all of its boundary points are extreme points, for example, a closed disc forms a strictly convex set. The only boundary points of the set which are contained on the line segment joining any two boundary points of a *strictly convex set* are the end-points of the segment.

The *convex hull* of S is the smallest convex set which contains S. We may write it as $Co(S)$. If S is a closed convex set then this set and its convex hull coincide. Thus the convex hulls of the sets of Figs 2.29 to 2.34 are the original sets. But the convex hull of a non-convex set differs from the non-convex set, for example, the convex hull of the set in Fig. 2.37 consists of the points on and in $\triangle CFE$. Nevertheless, the extremal of a set is always contained in the convex hull of a set.

We are now in a position to return meaningfully to the constrained optimisation problem and to note the following propositions:

(a) *Weierstrass's Theorem:* A continuous function defined over a non-empty compact set attains a maximum and a minimum value at least once over the set.

(b) *The Solution Principle:* If $f(x)$ is continuous function defined for x over some closed feasible set X, its maximum (and minimum) value occurs either in an interior point of X or in a boundary point. By taking (i) the critical points of $f(x)$, that is those for which the first derivative of f is zero for all possible variations of the variables, (ii) the boundary points of X and (iii) all the points where $f(x)$ is not differentiable, we are certain to find in the set the values of x which maximise and minimise $f(x)$. If $f(x)$ is differentiable everywhere then steps (i) and (ii) suffice. However, to enumerate all the values of $f(x)$ for these sets is frequently impractical. Thus it is useful to have rules which, in certain general cases, inform us that we can disregard some of these possibilities and so narrow down the feasible solution set.

(c) *Global Optima:* If $f(x)$ is a continuous function defined over a *closed convex* set, every local optimum of $f(x)$ is a global maximum if $f(x)$ is a concave function and a global minimum if $f(x)$ is a convex function.* Both in production and consumption theory concavity of the objective function and the existence of a closed feasible set are often assumed.

If $f(x)$ is a *strictly concave* (convex) continuous function defined over a compact convex set, the global maximum (minimum) of this function occurs for a *unique* value of x. Once again conditions of this type are often assumed in production and consumption theory.

QUASI-CONCAVITY

The following is an important property of convex and concave functions:

(i) if $f(x)$ is convex, the set $V = \{x \mid f(x) \leqslant f(x^*)\}$ is convex where x^* is any point $\in X$;

(ii) if $f(x)$ is strictly convex, V is a strictly convex set;

(iii) if $f(x)$ is concave the set $V = \{x \mid f(x) \geqslant f(x^*)\}$ is convex; and

(iv) if $f(x)$ is strictly concave this set is strictly convex.

The contours shown in Fig. 2.11 correspond to an assumed strictly concave objective function. Take any contour, that is $\{x \mid f(x) = f(c)\}$ where c is any point. This contour forms the boundary of the set $\{x \mid f(x) \geqslant f(c)\}$. In words, this contour, in the consumption case, is the boundary of all the commodity bundles which give the consumer as much or more utility than the bundle $x = c$. The set consists of all bundles which are ranked superior or equal to c. A set V for a strictly concave function is indicated in Fig. 2.41 by a hatched area. The set shows all values of (x_1, x_2) which yield values of $f(x_1, x_2)$ in excess of or equal to that for $c = (\bar{x}_1, \bar{x}_2)$. The set is strictly convex. The usual smooth indifference curves which are encountered in consumption theory also have this property. Two of these are indicated in Fig. 2.42. In the top set, the contour I_1 is, for example, strictly convex.

While functions which are [strictly] concave (convex) have the properties referred to above, some functions which are not [strictly] concave (convex) also have these properties. Any function which satisfies the property of (i) is quasi-convex and if it satisfies the property of (ii) it is *strictly* quasi-convex. Functions which satisfy the properties mentioned in (iii) and (iv) are respectively quasi-concave and *strictly*

---

* *By the way, the concept of a convex set and convex function should not be confused. The collection of points on a convex function need not form a convex set.*

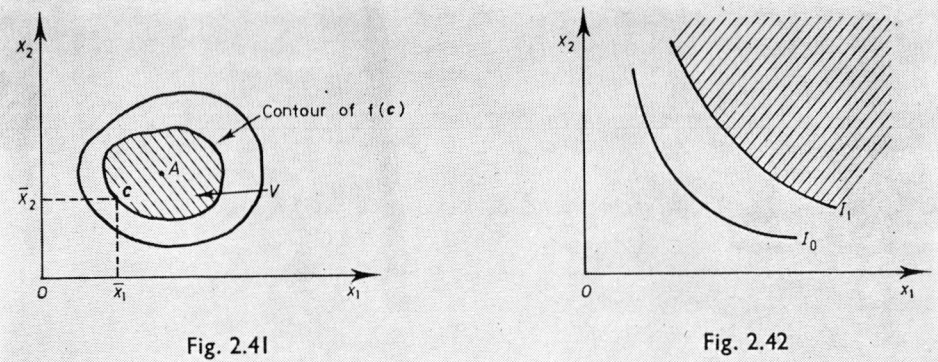

Fig. 2.41   Fig. 2.42

quasi-concave. To take an example, the surface of a trumpet cut in half longitudinally is represented by neither a convex nor a concave function. But its contours are like those shown in Fig. 2.42. The surface is represented by a strictly quasi-concave function. A function of this type can easily arise in economic problems, for example, if increasing returns to scale prevail in production but the rate of technical substitution of factors diminishes. A quasi-concave function is sometimes referred to as a concave-contoured function.

If $f(x)$ is a quasi-concave function defined over a closed convex set any local maximum of it is a global maximum. If $f(x)$ is a *strictly* quasi-concave function defined on a compact convex set, X, $f(x)$ has a global maximum for a *unique* value of x. In such cases nearsighted computational techniques can be used to search for a maximum. However, it is sometimes useful to know in advance whether the optimum will occur at an interior point of the feasible set or on the boundary.

(d) *Interior and Boundary Optima:* It follows from the solution principle mentioned in (b) that if $f(x)$ is a differentiable function which is defined on a compact set and which has no critical points in the interior of the set that its maximum and minimum values occur for values of x in the boundary of the feasible set. Given that $f(x)$ is differentiable and defined on a compact set, X, and has no interior critical points, its maximum occurs for a *unique* value of x in the *boundary* of the feasible set if

(i) $f(x)$ is strictly quasi-concave [this includes strict concavity as a special case] and the feasible set, X, is convex; or

(ii) $f(x)$ is quasi-concave and the feasible set is strictly convex; or

(iii) $f(x)$ is strictly quasi-concave and X is strictly convex.[16]

Analogous results hold for the minima of quasi-convex functions.

If, for example, $f(x)$ increases or decreases monotonically with x, we can rule out the possibility of interior critical points. In economics assumptions such as these are often employed, for example, the non-satiety assumption of consumer demand theory.

(e) *A Linear Objective Function:* A linear objective function is an important special case. It is both a *convex* function *and* a concave function, but is not strict of course. In economic theory linear functions frequently arise especially in the theory of perfectly competitive markets. In these markets, for example, the firms' profit can

Optimisation and Choice

be expressed as a linear function of its output of products and its employment of factors.

A linear function has no critical points. Hence, from proposition (c),

(i) a linear function, $f(x)$ which is defined on a compact set, X, reaches its global maximum and minimum values in the *boundary* of the set.

(ii) Furthermore, it reaches a global maximum and a global minimum value in *extreme* points of the set. Thus the set of extreme points, the extremal of the set, contain values of x which yield the global maximum of $f(x)$ and the global minimum of $f(x)$. One need only check the x values in the extremal to be sure of finding an x value which globally maximises $f(x)$. This principle is used in linear programming.

To test all of the extreme points by enumeration may be impossible; for example if the feasible set is a closed disc, the boundary points consist of the infinite number on the circumference of the disc. But in many cases the extreme points are finite and techniques are available to help in the rapid location of an optimum.

Mention might be made here of a convex polyhedral set or polytope, since we shall come across it in linear programming discussions later. It is a convex set with a finite number of extreme points. The intersection of a finite number of closed half-spaces form a closed convex polyhedral set. A closed half-space consists for example of the points on and to one side of a line in two-dimensional space, and the points on and to one side of a plane in three dimensions. The linear inequality restrictions used in linear programming yield closed half-planes.

Some illustrations for the linear case follow. The contours of $f(x)$ are linear and parallel and in the cases shown $f(x)$ is assumed to increase with x. In Fig. 2.43, local maxima occur at A and B and the minimum at D. A is the global maximum. Given that $f(x)$ is convex (concave), and it is in the linear case, the possibility of non-global local maxima (non-global local minima) can be ruled out if the feasible set is convex. In Fig. 2.43, the set is not convex and thus multiple maxima are not ruled out. In Fig. 2.44, the set is compact convex polyhedral with extreme points at A, B, C and D. The minimum of the indicated linear function occurs at D, its maximum occurs for any value of x in the closed interval from A to B. The value of x which maximises the function is not unique. If the feasible set were, however, *strictly* convex and compact, the x value which maximises $f(x)$ would be unique. So would be the x value which minimises $f(x)$.

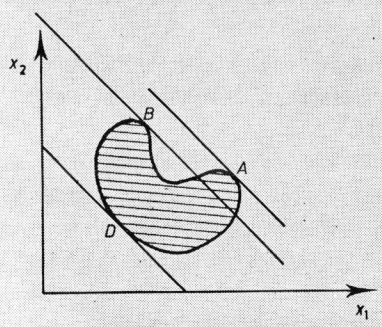

Fig. 2.43

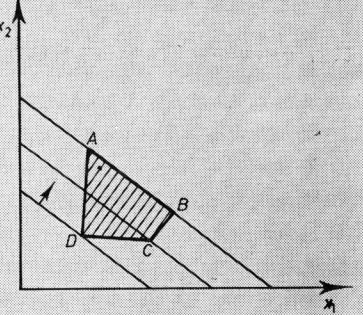

Fig. 2.44

In Fig. 2.45 the intersection of three closed half-lines are indicated. These are the intersections of the sets $\{x_1 \mid x_1 \geq 0\}$, $\{x_2 \mid x_2 \geq 0\}$, and $\{x_1, x_2 \mid x_2 \leq b - ax_1\}$. They form the simple closed compact polyhedral set with extreme points at O, B and C.

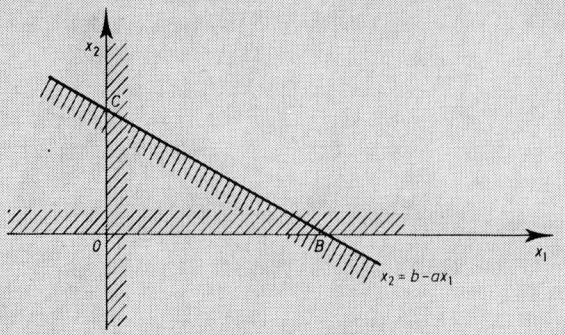

Fig. 2.45

At this stage let us take stock. We observed that the classical method of Lagrange for optimising has definite limitations, for example, it does not cope with interior solutions or inequality restrictions. The problem of multiple local maxima (minima) was also raised. We next enquired whether there might be any *general* properties of functions and feasible sets which might, if they are satisfied, allow us to avoid some of these difficulties. It was discovered that the quasi-concavity (convexity) properties of the objective function and the convex nature or otherwise of the feasible set are of fundamental importance in this regard. Our discussion of the "new maths" could go much further. Already it has yielded some valuable insights and it is applied to economic problems later. (See especially the appendices to Chapters 6 and 7 and applications in Chapters 15 and 22.) Those who are interested beyond this are referred to the references at the end of this chapter.

VI. Modifications to the Optimisation Approach

Recently economists have begun to stress limitations on the possible optimising behaviour of man yet even within these new restrictions man is normally assumed to be trying to *maximise* some objective function. For example, it is now stressed that
(a) lack of knowledge does exist and does influence rational behaviour;
(b) in many circumstances individuals are not a law unto themselves but have a few rational competitive opponents which, as von Neumann and Morgenstern[17] suggest, creates problems for a simple maximisation approach;
(c) it may be impossible, as Arrow[18] has pointed out, to define a social welfare ordering for society, which also meets certain "reasonable requirements"; and
(d) there are problems in co-ordinating a group and informing its members even when the members have a common goal or objective function to be maximised.[19]
Modifications to the traditional approach are being made. In most modifications, maximising behaviour in one form or another is still important even if Simon sees defects in this approach. No doubt the debate will continue.

NOTES AND REFERENCES

[1] H. SIMON, (i) "A Behavioral Model of Rational Choice", *Quarterly Journal of Economics*, 1955, **79**, pp. 99-118: (ii) *Models of Man*, John Wiley, New York, 1957.

[2] O. LANGE, "The Scope and Method of Economics", *Review of Economic Studies*, 1945-46, **13**, p. 30.

[3] AUGUSTIN COURNOT, *Researches into the Mathematical Principles of the Theory of Wealth*, first published 1838. English translation by N. BACON, The Macmillan Company, New York, 1897.

[4] WILLIAM S. JEVONS (1835-1882), *Theory of Political Economy*, 1st ed., 1871; 4th ed., Macmillan, London, 1911.

[5] ALFRED MARSHALL (1842-1924), *Principles of Economics*, 1st ed., 1890; 8th ed., Macmillan, London, 1920.

[6] Includes MENGER (1840-1921), VON WIESER and BÖHM-BAWERK. Carl Menger's *Grundsätze der Volkswirtschaftslehre* was published in 1871. Translation by J. DINGWALL and B. HOSELITZ, *Principles of Economics*, Free Press, Glencoe, 1950.

[7] For an outline of Lagrange's method and some economic applications see, for example, R. G. D. ALLEN, *Mathematical Analysis for Economists*, Macmillan, London, 1960, pp. 366 et seq. and G. C. ARCHIBALD and R. G. LIPSEY, *An Introduction to a Mathematical Treatment of Economics*, Weidenfeld and Nicolson, London, 1967, Ch. 11.

[8] However, note that neo-classical consumption theory can be recast to allow for non-expenditure of all income by treating savings as a desired commodity and then applying Lagrange's method. While difficulty 2 below them seems unimportant, difficulty 1 remains.

[9] The analytical importance of this difficulty should not be underestimated. As a result of it, neo-classical demand theory predicts responses of consumption to relative price changes when, in fact, no response occurs. If optimal consumption is at C as in Fig. 2.10, relative prices of the products may change and yet the optimal level of consumption does not alter. But if non-negativity conditions are ignored, and if A is treated as the optimum, this non-response will not be apparent.

[10] H. W. KUHN and A. W. TUCKER, "Nonlinear Programming", in J. NEYMAN (Ed.), *Proceedings of the Second Berkeley Symposium on Mathematical Statistics and Probability*, University of California Press, Berkeley, 1951.

[11] J. R. HICKS, *Value and Capital*, Clarendon Press, Oxford, 1939; 2nd ed., 1946.

[12] P. A. SAMUELSON, *Foundations of Economic Analysis*, Harvard University Press, Cambridge, 1947.

[13] See, for example, A. C. CHIANG, *Fundamental Methods of Mathematical Economics*, McGraw-Hill, New York, 1967, p. 321.

[14] Cf. S. KARLIN, *Mathematical Methods and Theory of Games, Programming and Economics*, Vol. I, Addison-Wesley Publishing, Reading, 1959, p. 406.

[15] That is, it cannot be obtained by multiplying the two different points by the constants λ and $1-\lambda$ where $0<\lambda<1$.

[16] In neo-classical economic theory, the consumer's choice problem corresponds to (i); the production model for the perfectly competitive firm to (ii); and under imperfect competition the firm's decision problem may correspond to (iii). The consumer's objective is utility maximisation and the firm's objective is profit maximisation and the feasible sets are determined by income, market and technological restraints.

[17] J. VON NEUMANN and O. MORGENSTERN, *Theory of Games and Economic Behavior*, 1st ed., Princeton University Press, Princeton, 1944; Wiley Science Edition, New York, 1964.

[18] K. J. ARROW, *Social Choice and Individual Values*, John Wiley, New York, 1951.

[19] A considerable amount of research on these problems has been done by J. Marschak and R. Radner. See, for example, J. MARSCHAK, "Towards an Economic Theory of Organization and Information", Ch. 14 in R. M. THRALL, C. H. COOMBS and R. L. DAVIS (Eds), *Decision Processes*, John Wiley, New York, 1954 and R. RADNER, (i) "The Evaluation of Information in Organizations", *Proceedings of the Fourth Berkeley Symposium on Probability and Statistics*, Vol. I, University of California Press, Berkeley, 1961, pp. 491-530; (ii) "Team Decision Problems", *The Annals of Mathematical Statistics*, 1962, **33**, pp. 857-81.

FURTHER READING

General

ARCHIBALD, G. C. and R. G. LIPSEY, *An Introduction to a Mathematical Treatment of Economics*, Weidenfeld and Nicolson, London, 1967, Ch. 7.

BAUMOL, W. J., *Economic Theory and Operations Analysis*, 2nd ed., Prentice-Hall, Englewood Cliffs, 1965, Chs. 1-4.

MITCHELL, WESLEY C., *Types of Economic Theory*, Kelley, New York, 1967, Vol. I, Ch. 2, pp. 35-76.

SAMUELSON, P., *The Foundations of Economic Analysis*, Harvard University Press, Cambridge, 1963, pp. 7-10, 21-3.

More Advanced (mostly involve outlines of properties of convex sets and functions).

ALLEN, R. G. D., *Mathematical Economics*, 2nd ed., Macmillan, London, 1959, pp. 383-7.

ARCHIBALD and LIPSEY, op. cit., Ch. 11.

BAUMOL, op. cit., Ch. 7.

HADLEY, G., *Linear Algebra*, Ch. 6, Addison-Wesley, Reading, 1961.

KARLIN, S., *Mathematical Methods and Theory of Games, Programming and Economics*, Addison-Wesley, Reading, 1959, Vol. I, Appendix B.

KOOPMANS, T. C., *Three Essays on the State of the Economic Science*, McGraw-Hill, New York, 1957, Essay I, Sec. I.

LANCASTER, K., *Mathematical Economics*, The Macmillan Company, New York, 1968, Chs. 2, 4 and 5, and R4, R8.4, R8.6.

CHAPTER 3

Economic Efficiency and Markets

I. Exchange and Markets

It is contended in Chapter 1 that markets can be very effectively used in order to organise economies. Prices in markets effectively transmit information and prompt individuals to take economic action in their own self-interest. Such action can be socially optimal and stems from motives which seem to be very strong. But not all markets are equally likely to be economically efficient, and different types of markets have different side-effects. Throughout this book, this proposition is going to be continually investigated.

The exchange of goods and services is commonplace and fundamental to our present economy. Few, if any of us, are economically self-sufficient. Most of us specialise to some extent in our productive activity exchanging part of our product, or the income derived from it, for the products of others; and many do not consume any of their own product and live solely by exchange.

Free exchange normally involves a gain to both parties to the exchange otherwise there could be no incentive on the part of at least one party to participate. At least, it involves an *expected* gain on the part of both parties. If the parties are adequately informed about the qualities of the articles which are available for exchange, then the expected gain will also be *realised*. If parties are misinformed exchange may not be beneficial for both parties. If a buyer overestimates the quality of an article, then *ex post facto* he may be disappointed with his purchase and be worse off than before the exchange. It will be assumed that all traders have adequate knowledge of the quality of the commodities which are available for exchange.

In that case, any institutional mechanism which facilitates exchange increases the scope for mutually agreeable trades. Markets provide mechanisms which make it easier and less costly to negotiate exchanges. In organised markets, information about offers of exchange is provided at low cost and very often simplified, and low cost methods of making actual transfers are available. Consider, for example, markets in securities and real estate.

While markets can be organised on a barter basis such markets are cumbersome, especially when no commodity is used as a common *numéraire*, that is, one in terms of which all exchange rates are expressed. Considerable advantages stem from having money (paper and bank money) as a *numéraire* and a general medium of exchange. Paper money is a portable commodity of little value in itself whereas this cannot be said of most alternative commodities.

By facilitating exchange, markets encourage specialisation in production if this is profitable. In many circumstances, as a result of improvements of skills and simple physical relationships, specialisation in production enables a greater output to be produced from the same resources. The existence and the size of the market is important in this respect. Thus markets not only extend the scope for mutually agreeable trading but as a result of specialisation may add to total output, so increasing the volume of goods which are available for trading. In essence, an efficient exchange system gives a double bounty.

II. Classification of Markets

Markets can be classified in a variety of ways: by the type of commodity traded; the degree of knowledge in the market; the number of participants; the ease with which new suppliers can enter the market, and so on. There is no unique classification and one must be guided by the purpose of the exercise.

In the main, economists have found that classification of markets according to the ability of participants to influence the terms of exchange is useful. From a Paretian point of view it makes a great deal of difference whether sellers or buyers can individually influence the terms of exchange. If no individual buyer or seller can influence the terms of exchange (price of commodity) in a market then pure competition exists.[1] If, in addition, all traders in the market are completely informed about exchange opportunities in the market, perfect competition exists. It is assumed in both cases that traders seek to maximise their individual gain from economic activity. If any buyer or seller, or any group of traders who are in actual coalition, are able to influence the terms of exchange in a market, competition is imperfect.[2] Thus there are four possible combinations which are set out in Table 3.1:

Table 3.1

Influence on Price or Terms of Trade in a Market

Individual seller	Individual buyer	Classification	
		Supply side	Demand side
None	None	PC	PC
Some	None	IC	PC
None	Some	PC	IC
Some	Some	IC	IC

where PC represents perfect or pure competition and IC represents imperfect competition.

Most markets involve imperfect competition and this is frequently on the supply side. In the absence of governmental intervention, the markets for agricultural products, such as wheat, tobacco leaf and oats, are likely to be purely competitive. No buyer and no seller is in a position to influence the general price of wheat by his own individual decisions in the market. But the markets for most manufacturing goods are, for example, imperfect. Products are differentiated and many suppliers are in a position to influence the price of their product and the general conditions of trade in a market. In other words, product loyalty permits the manufacturer of some goods to raise his price above the general level in a market and yet retain some of his

Efficiency and Markets

custom. If a wheat grower were to do this he could expect no sales. In some cases' the ability to influence price is insignificant, in other cases important.

There is normally, but not inevitably, a relationship between the numbers in a market and their ability to exert an individual influence on price. As the numbers involved on both the selling and buying side increase in a market the probability that any trader can individually influence price diminishes. However, one must be careful. It is quite possible to have only one supplier in a market and for perfect competition to exist. If new suppliers can enter easily and if the commodity can be supplied at the same *constant* cost per unit by potential entrants, the actual supplier can exert no influence over the selling price of the good. Nevertheless, there does seem to be a rough empirical connection between numbers in a market and the ability to influence price. Economists have, therefore, *tended* to associate these factors.

Imperfectly competitive markets have been divided into a number of categories. The following classification (Table 3.2) is a common one.

Table 3.2

Imperfect Market Situation	Classified Structure
One seller	Monopoly
One buyer	Monopsony
A *few sellers* who recognise that their market behaviour influences that of other sellers	Oligopoly
A *few buyers* who recognise that their market behaviour influences that of other buyers	Oligopsony
A *large number of sellers* with no recognised interdependence in market behaviour	Monopolistic competition

To give some examples of these market structures consider the following. In most regions the supply of public utilities is provided by a monopoly. Generally, there is one seller of electricity, one of telephone services, one of postal services in any region. In countries with small markets, it is not uncommon to have monopolies in the supply of manufactured goods (for example, there are at present a steel monopoly and a glass monopoly in Australia.) Monopsony is not quite so common. In some countries all gold has to be sold to the central bank, and occasionally (as for tin in the case of Australia) there may be only one smelter for a mineral. This may give a monopsony position to the owners of the smelter.

Oligopoly is fairly common, especially in larger markets. Oligopolies exist in the supply of steel and aluminium in the United States and in automobile and petroleum industries. Markets for these products, except for steel, are also oligopolistic in Australia.

Oligopsony is not so rare either. Suppliers of raw materials and primary products, which require processing, frequently must sell in oligopsonistic markets. There may be few processors of a primary product, especially within an area in which it can be economically transported. Many small retail businesses seem to be monopolistically competitive. They can ignore their individual effect on the overall market situation but, nevertheless, have some ability to increase the price of their product or service and yet retain some custom. Later, each of these market-types, as well as purely and perfectly competitive markets, are examined in detail.

As market structures change so too do the transactions characteristics of markets. For example, transaction costs may be higher in a market in which a single buyer faces a single seller (a *bilateral monopoly* situation) than under perfect competition. No negotiations are involved in a perfectly competitive exchange situation, but negotiations may be long and uncertain in a bilateral monopoly situation. Under perfect competition the conditions of exchange are not subject to negotiation for the terms are impersonally settled by the market as a whole.

III. Reputed Advantage of Perfectly Competitive Markets

Some market structures, it is claimed, are more conducive to minimising scarcity or maximising social welfare than others. Traditionally, economists have held that perfectly competitive markets are superior in this respect. Certainly, this doctrine has been qualified. Yet it is hard to escape the view that the main theme of the classical and neo-classical economists has been that perfectly competitive markets lead, apart from a few minor deviations, to a social optimum. To be more precise, the traditional view is that *an economy reaches a Paretian optimum if externalities are absent and if all markets are perfectly competitive.* An externality arises from the provision of a service (or disservice) by one economic agent for others at a price which does not reflect its marginal social value. Externalities may be favourable to others or unfavourable. To give some examples, if farmers in the headwaters of a river system apply greater quantities of fertilisers, those in the lower reaches may gain by the deposition of silt of higher quality. Farmers in the lower reaches will pay nothing for this gain. Pollutants from factories are sometimes disposed of free or at little cost to their owners. Such pollutants may damage the production of others or injure the consumption of others of clean air and surroundings and the price of disposal ought to reflect this. Classical and neo-classical economists are well aware of the type of allowance which must be made for externalities. But with increases in the wealth of societies externalities have become increasingly important.

However, the classical position is subject to further qualifications, qualifications which have become very important also with the economic growth of many countries. We shall merely touch on them here. The technological conditions of production in many industries is such that if the most efficient technique is used, perfect competition cannot exist. Perfect competition is incompatible with the existence for firms of internally decreasing average costs of production. Decreasing costs of this type occur in automobile manufacture and in many manufacturing industries. To have large numbers of plants producing such goods is to add to scarcity. Economic efficiency may require production by one plant only.

True perfect competition might be created in some of these industries by *prohibiting* the use of all techniques which lead to continually falling average cost. However, this will reduce output from any employed quantity of resources and, as compared with the alternative, may involve a considerable Paretian reduction in economic welfare. The artificially induced situation of perfect competition may be

Efficiency and Markets

Pareto optimal in relation to the restricted use of techniques yet be inferior to the alternative which, because of the existence of oligopolies or monopoly, may not be Pareto optimal. Even assuming given techniques, perfect competition need not be optimal from an economic efficiency point of view.

Professor Schumpeter has stressed another problem.[3] If we take economic growth into account perfectly competitive markets may not be optimal. Market imperfections by enabling higher returns to be reaped from innovation and invention may stimulate these activities. Thus even though an economic system is not Pareto optimal at any point of time because of the existence of market imperfections, nevertheless if invention, technical knowledge and innovation is greater, the economy may be in a situation which is Paretian superior to that which would prevail under continuous perfect competition.

This brief survey indicates that no particular market form is always superior for overcoming scarcity. It is necessary in each case to be pragmatic and to examine the exact nature of the technological relationships and the economic growth aspect. In the remainder of this chapter conditions will be considered under which perfect competition is Pareto optimal. The models to be discussed are extremely simple in order to give a first flavour of this type of theoretical problem.

IV. Efficiency of Perfect Competition: Illustrated in a Simple Case

Taking a simple case, the aim is to show that perfectly competitive market conditions imply Pareto optimality if suitable conditions are satisfied. A market is perfectly competitive if the following conditions hold:

(i) no buyer or seller is able to influence prices by his individual trading behaviour;
(ii) every economic agent is completely informed about his relevant production or consumption possibilities;
(iii) economic agents always predict prices correctly, and
(iv) act to maximise their gain which is interpreted to mean that firms maximise their profit and that consumers maximise their level of satisfaction;
(v) factors of production are perfectly mobile.

The implications of these conditions will be examined now for a simple case. Imagine that one product, which is in universal demand, is produced by one specific but variable factor which I shall call labour, or l. The product will be designated as X. It could be wine for example. Furthermore, suppose that the marginal product of labour is positive for any feasible employment of l and that it declines with increases in the employment of l. Then a Pareto optimum can only exist if the output of X (wine) is at a maximum for any employed quantity of l (labour). This requires that the marginal product of labour in producing X be the same for all firms (productive units) which employ l.

To see this mathematically, let X indicate the aggregate output of the commodity, x_i represent its output by the ith firm, and l_i indicate the ith firm's employment of l, and L represent any given employment of l in the industry. The production function of the ith firm may then be represented as

$$x_i = f_i(l_i) \qquad (3.1)$$

where $f_i' > 0$ and $f_i'' < 0$. If $i = 1, \ldots n$ productive units exist, the problem is to maximise

$$\left. \begin{array}{c} X = \sum_{i=1}^{n} f_i(l_i) \\ \text{subject to} \\ \sum_{i=1}^{n} l_i = L. \end{array} \right\} \quad (3.2)$$

Using Lagrange's method, the following conditions are necessary for maximising output from the available labour:

$$\frac{df_i}{dl_i} = \lambda \quad i = 1, \ldots n, \quad (3.3)$$

and

$$L - \sum_{i=1}^{n} l_i = 0. \quad (3.4)$$

λ is a Lagrange multiplier.

Conditions (3.3) indicate that the marginal product of the factor must be equal for all firms. If conditions (3.3 and 3.4) are satisfied, a maximum exists because $f_i'' < 0$ by assumption.

This necessary condition for a Paretian optimum can be indicated by means of the figures shown in Fig. 3.1. The marginal product functions of two firms are indicated. Given that these firms employ between them a particular quantity of labour, the output of that labour cannot be at a maximum unless the labour is allocated so that its marginal product is the same for both firms. For example, assume that the firms employ sixty units of labour between them. Given the employment of labour and the example below, the output of X can only be at a maximum if twenty units go to Firm 1 and forty units go to Firm 2 for then the appropriate marginal products are equal. If a different allocation is arrived at, output is lower. For example, if thirty units go to each firm, the output of Firm 1 is increased by the dotted area and the output of Firm 2 is decreased by the hatched area so aggregate output clearly declines. The same type of thing happens if employment of labour of Firm 2 is pushed above forty units at the expense of that of Firm 1.

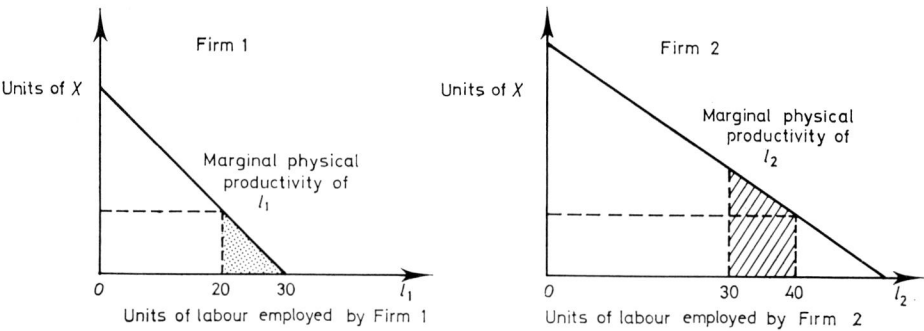

Fig. 3.1

Efficiency and Markets

One particular allocation of labour is optimal and no other is. Theoretically, this optimal allocation of labour could be achieved by fiat or order. In the above particular instance, twenty men could be ordered to Firm 1 and forty to Firm 2. Alternatively, the allocation might be left to a perfectly competitive market. Under these conditions, we wish to show that the optimal allocation will prevail. We wish to show that the set of conditions for maximum output as expressed in Equations (3.3) and (3.4) will be satisfied under perfect competition.

Under perfect competition the price of X must be the same for all firms and the price of l must be the same everywhere. Let p and w represent these prices respectively. Each firm maximises its profit, π. The ith firm maximises

$$\pi_i = px_i - wl_i$$
$$= pf_i(l_i) - wl_i. \tag{3.5}$$

The necessary condition for a maximum is that marginal profit be zero, that is

$$\frac{d\pi_i}{dl_i} = pf_i'(l_i) - w = 0. \tag{3.6}$$

This is satisfied when

$$f_i'(l_i) = \frac{w}{p} \tag{3.7}$$

that is when the marginal product of l is equal to the real wage rate in terms of X. Since $\frac{w}{p}$ is necessarily the same for all firms, so is $f_i'(l_i)$. Firms by maximising their profit on the basis of the same product and factor prices equalise their marginal products and thus under these circumstances optimally allocate l.

That the maximum output of X for any aggregate employment of l will be achieved under perfect competition can be seen from the following: under perfect competition, the price per unit of X must be the *same* for each firm and so must be the wage rate, w. Any firm which charged more than the others for X would make no sale and any which failed to pay the going wage rate would be unable to attract labour or would lose labour to those firms which are prepared to pay more. The equality of prices for all economic agents in conjunction with the profit maximisation assumption implies that the output of X is at a maximum for any given employment of l. Take any firm, for example, Firm 1. In order to maximise its surplus (profit) the firm should employ the quantity of labour which equates the marginal product of its labour and the (real) wage rate. Because the real wage rate is the same for all firms under perfect competition, they must be led by their attempts to maximise their own individual profits to equate their marginal products. Consequently, since their marginal products are rendered equal, the aggregate output of X must be automatically maximised for any given employment of labour. Thus the spur to individual gain leads to the satisfaction of an economic efficiency condition for the industry as a whole. It matters little whether firms are cognisant of this social purpose or not.

If one is unclear about the type of economic behaviour which maximises the firm's profit, the following illustration may help. Figure 3.2 is meant to indicate the type of situation which is faced by any firm in the industry, say Firm 1. The marginal physical product curve which is marked *MPP* traces out the additions to the firm's output which can be expected from changes in its employment of labour. The real cost of a unit of labour is represented by R_0 and equals the number of units of X which must be exchanged for one unit of labour. In a monetary economy, it equals the money wage rate of labour divided by the price of X. Given the existence of perfect competition, the firm's real cost of an extra unit of labour is constant and, hence, its marginal real cost curve of labour is a straight line marked MFC. At any stage, the firm's surplus consists of the difference between the sum of the contributions to output of each unit of labour employed less the total real cost of employing those units. In Fig. 3.2, the firm's surplus for an employment of l_1 is represented by the area under MPP from O to l_1 *less* the area under MFC from O to l_1. Given this, one can see that in Fig. 3.2 the quantity of labour which equates the marginal product of labour with its real marginal cost, namely $\bar{l}_1$ in this case, maximises the firm's surplus. If any other quantity of l_1 is employed, it can be shown that the firm's surplus is lower.

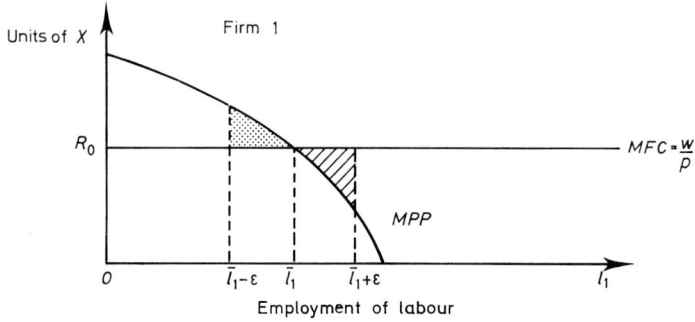

Fig. 3.2

For example, if the firm employs $\bar{l}_1 - \varepsilon$ of labour its surplus can be increased by the equivalent of the dotted area if it employs an additional ε of labour. Similarly, if $\bar{l}_1 + \varepsilon$ of labour is employed the firm can increase its surplus by the equivalent of the hatched area if it reduces its employment of labour by ε. Since R_0 is the same for all firms under perfect competition, profit maximisation leads them to equate their marginal products from employing labour. In consequence, aggregate output from the overall labour which is employed is maximised.

But will the *aggregate* employment of labour be optimal under perfect competition? Nothing has been said about that so far. Let us take this up. If any labourer (unit of labour) wishes to work for a real wage rate which is not more than his net addition to the physical product, total welfare can conceivably be increased by employing him. At the stated wage rate the labourer gains by being employed and the total product remaining to the rest of society is unchanged or greater. Now it has been argued that perfect competition will lead to the full employment of labour in the sense that all who wish to work for a wage not greater than their marginal product will be employed.

In the above example, the argument runs as follows: if the real wage rate is less than the marginal physical product of labour, firms will find it profitable to employ more labour, and to do so will bid up the real wage rate. They will continue to bid for more labour until the real wage rate equals its marginal product. If, on the other hand, the real wage rate is in excess of the marginal product of labour, firms will

Efficiency and Markets

reduce their bids and their employment of labour because it is unprofitable to employ all labour which is willing to work at such a real wage rate. Fig. 3.3 helps to illustrate the position. The aggregate quantity of labour, L, is shown on the X axis. The marginal physical productivity of labour overall is indicated by MPP_L which also indicates the aggregate demand for labour as the real wage rate varies. The curve SS indicates the aggregate quantity of labour which individuals as a whole are willing to supply at different real wage rates. In the case shown in Fig. 3.3, competition must result in a

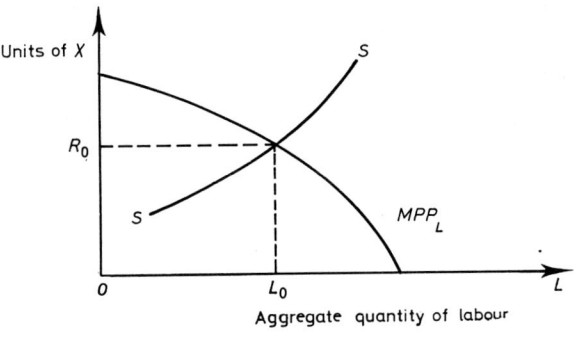

Fig. 3.3

real wage rate of R_0 and an aggregate level of employment of L_0. If the real wage rate is less than R_0, it exceeds the marginal physical productivity of labour. It is then profitable to employ extra labour if necessary by raising real wage bids. This will be true until the real wage is bid up to R_0 where it equals the marginal physical productivity of labour. At that wage rate, L_0 of labour will be employed. No labour will be involuntarily unemployed. All who wish to work at the going real wage will find work.

But it could be that the model leads us astray at this point. Certainly in a real complex economy pure competition may *not* lead quickly to full employment. This is a problem of central importance in macroeconomics and will not be discussed here.

V. The Efficiency of Perfect Competition: Another Example

In the previous example there is only one product and the only exchange considered is that of labour for a part of the product. But today almost an infinity of different products seems to exist and individuals and regions *specialise* in the production of these, exchanging one product against the other principally by using money as a medium. Specialisation in production with subsequent exchange is characteristic of modern economies and makes possible a greater output than otherwise would be the case. Hence, any scheme to increase self-sufficiency needs to be scrutinised very closely. As Samuelson has put it:

> The economies of mass production upon which modern standards of living are based would not be possible if production took place in self-sufficient farm households or regions. Specialisation of function permits each person and region to use to best advantage any differences in skill and resources. . . .[4]

But specialisation may even pay if there are no differences in skill and resources, and indeed, if there are no differences in tastes. Exchange itself may be mutually profitable to the parties concerned because technological advantages stem from changes in their specialisation or because there are differences in their tastes. A great deal of the discussion in international trade theory centres on the advantages of exchange and specialisation. Let us look at the matter more closely.

Once again a criterion for economic efficiency is needed and I shall continue to use that of Pareto.[5] The aggregate output of employed resources must be maximised if a Paretian optimum is to occur. This, of course, assumes that all the goods which are produced are wanted. Because aggregate output consists of a diverse bundle of goods, the necessary condition for a Paretian optimum needs to be stated in terms of a vector inequality. Relative to the overall levels of employed resources, it should be impossible to increase the output of any product without decreasing that of any other, otherwise a Paretian optimum does not exist. Clearly, output cannot be at a maximum if the output of any good can be increased without decreasing that of any other.

Taking a simple model and allowing for multiple products, let us find the conditions or degree of specialisation in production which maximises the output from a group's employed resources. After doing this, we next turn to consider whether perfect competition ensures the optimal degree of specialisation.

Imagine that only two products can be produced. We may call them wheat and rice and designate their quantities by y and x respectively. Take any economic unit. It may be an individual, a firm, even an economic region or country in which many firms produce. For its given employment of factors, there are combinations of Y and X such that it is impossible to increase the output of one without decreasing that of another. These combinations as a whole form the unit's *production possibility frontier* or its product transformation function. For an economic unit, say number one, its production possibility frontier might be of the form indicated in Fig. 3.4. The frontier

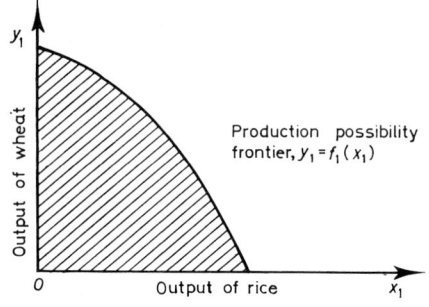

Fig. 3.4

indicates the maximum possible levels of output of wheat which are consistent both with the quantities of rice indicated on the X axis and a given employment of resources. In the case shown, the production possibility frontier is strictly concave, and the production possibility set (hatched) is a convex set. Strict concavity of the frontier implies that as the output of rice is increased larger amounts of wheat have to be forgone in order to produce an extra unit of rice. In other words, the *marginal rate of substitution* of wheat for rice increases as the quantity of resources which is devoted to rice increases. The marginal rate of substitution of wheat for rice is equal to the (absolute) slope of the product transformation function and indicates the amount of

Efficiency and Markets

wheat which must be forgone in order to obtain a small increase in the output of rice.[6]

Assuming that all economic units of the group have strictly concave production possibility frontiers, optimal specialisation requires (if corner solutions are ruled out) that the marginal rate of product substitution be the same for all units. If this condition is met it is impossible to increase the group's output of one product without decreasing that of another. That the units' marginal rates of product transformation should (normally) be equal can be seen from the following. (This may be skipped by anyone with very limited mathematical knowledge.)

If the group's aggregate output is to be at a maximum, the overall output of Y must be maximised for any overall output of X. Where y_i and x_i represent the outputs of Y and X respectively of the ith unit and

$$y_i = f(x_i) \tag{3.8}$$

is its transformation frontier, and assuming n members of the group, we need to find the condition under which

$$Y = \sum_{i=1}^{n} y_i = \sum_{i=1}^{n} f_i(x_i) \tag{3.9}$$

is at a maximum subject to

$$\sum_{i=1}^{n} x_i = \bar{X}. \tag{3.10}$$

$\bar{X}$ represents any overall output of X. Using the Lagrange method, the necessary condition for the maximum is that

$$\frac{dy_1}{dx_2} = \frac{dy_2}{dx_2} = \ldots = \frac{dy_n}{dx_n} = \lambda \tag{3.11}$$

for

$$\sum_{i=1}^{n} x_i = \bar{X} \tag{3.12}$$

where λ is a Lagrange multiplier. Equation 3.11 implies that each unit should allocate its production of X and Y in a manner which makes the marginal rates of product transformation equal for all units. Otherwise the units have not optimally specialised.

Note that this rule implies that optimal specialisation depends on *comparative marginal* advantage and not on absolute advantage. Though one unit may be at an absolute disadvantage in producing all products nevertheless, with the resource distribution given, it ought to specialise more in that area in which it has a marginal comparative advantage. Take the case illustrated in Figs 3.5 and 3.6. Imagine that both units have the same given quantity of variable resources. Unit 1 has a comparative marginal advantage in wheat and an absolute advantage in both lines when compared with Unit 2. The above rule implies that if aggregate output is to be maximised, Unit 1 should specialise comparatively in wheat and Unit 2 in rice.

We now turn to the next problem. Will perfect competition lead to optimal specialisation in the production of the products? It can be shown that in the absence of externalities it does. A general proof cannot be given at this early stage in the book because it requires too much prior knowledge, but a satisfactory simple demonstration can be. Imagine that all the economic units are firms and that they have contracted

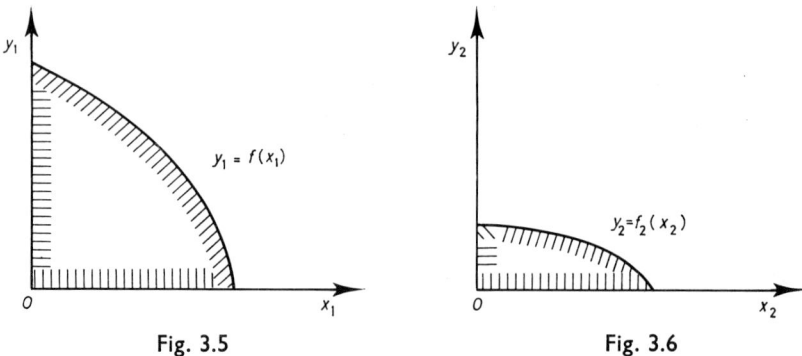

Fig. 3.5   Fig. 3.6

for given quantities of factors in advance at a stipulated cost. Having done this the cost of their factors is determined and their remaining problem is one of directing these to produce more or less of the two products. The firm under perfect competition chooses its composition of production to maximise profit. Let p_x and p_y represent respectively the prices of product X and Y and A_i the ith firm's contracted cost. It maximises

$$\pi_i = p_x x_i + p_y y_i - A_i \tag{3.13}$$

subject to

$$y_i = f_i(x_i), \tag{3.14}$$

that is, it maximises its profit subject to its product transformation function. Substituting Equation (3.14) into (3.13),

$$\pi_i = p_x x_i + p_y f_i(x_i) - A_i. \tag{3.15}$$

Since x_i is a controlled variable, the necessary condition for a maximum is that

$$\frac{d\pi_i}{dx_i} = p_x + p_y f_i'(x_i) = 0, \tag{3.16}$$

or, rearranging

$$f_i'(x_i) = -\frac{p_x}{p_y} \tag{3.17}$$

which is the same as

$$\frac{dy_i}{dx_i} = -\frac{p_x}{p_y}. \tag{3.18}$$

In other words, the marginal rate of substitution of Y for X equals the price of X divided by the price of Y if the firm is maximising profit. At this point, the value of the units of Y, which are forgone to get the last unit of X, are just equal to the market value of one unit of X. Under perfect competition product prices are the *same* for all firms and each maximises profit. Hence, it must be true that

$$\frac{dy_1}{dx_1} = \frac{dy_2}{dx_2} = \ldots = \frac{dy_n}{dx_n} = -\frac{p_x}{p_y}. \tag{3.19}$$

In other words, perfect competition brings the marginal rates of product transformation of all units into equality. The necessary condition for maximising aggregate output is thus satisfied. Given the concavity of the product transformation functions

Efficiency and Markets

(and the absence of corner solutions), the duality is established. Perfect competition maximises output in this case.

The ith firm's profit maximising behaviour can be represented pictorially by superimposing its isoprofit lines on a figure showing its production possibility frontier. An isoprofit line indicates all combinations of (x_i, y_i) which yield a given level of profit. To find, for example, those which yield the profit π_i^0 we rearrange

$$\pi_i^0 = p_x x_i + p_y y_i - A_i \tag{3.20}$$

to give

$$y_i = \frac{\pi^0 + A_i}{p_y} - \frac{p_x}{p_y} x_i. \tag{3.21}$$

Since p_x and p_y are constants under perfect competition, this gives a straight line in the (x_i, y_i) plane which, given that other things are constant and p_y is positive, is higher the greater is π^0. Given p_x and p_y, the firm's profit can be represented in the (x_i, y_i) plane by a series of parallel lines which are in fact contours of its profit function. The firm maximises its profit for the combination of X and Y which puts it on its highest attainable isoprofit line. In Fig. 3.7 the series of parallel lines are isoprofit lines. The highest attainable one is marked AC and the optimal product combination of the firm is indicated by point B. There the slope of the isoprofit line, that is $-p_x/p_y$, equals the slope of the product transformation function, namely dy_i/dx_i.

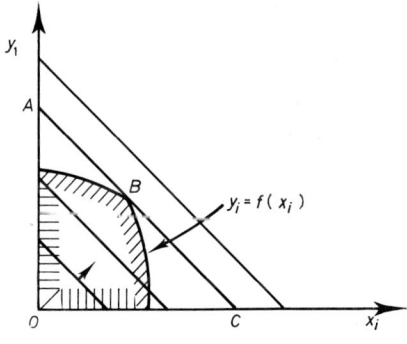

Fig. 3.7

In the cases considered above, the production possibility frontier is assumed to be strictly concave. One consequence of this is that *if* a positive quantity of both goods is to be produced, aggregate output will not usually be at a maximum if any unit specialises completely. Furthermore, if the unit's product transformation functions are identical, aggregate output cannot be at a maximum unless the product-mix of all is the same. Neither of these propositions is true if the product transformation curves of the units are convex. If the curves are convex it may pay the units to specialise completely even if positive quantities of both products are to be produced. To illustrate this, assume two units with identical product transformation functions as shown by ABC in Fig. 3.8. If the units are producing at point B, their marginal rates of product transformation are ëqual. However, aggregate output is not at a maximum, it is at a minimum. We can easily indicate that if one unit specialises completely in Y (for example, cars) and the other in X (for example, chemicals), aggregate output is increased. If both units are at B, their aggregate output is $(2x_i^0, 2y_i^0)$. If one specialises completely in X its output will be $OC > 2x_i^0$ and if the other switches entirely to Y its output will be $OA > 2y_i^0$. Hence, aggregate output is increased by complete specialisation.

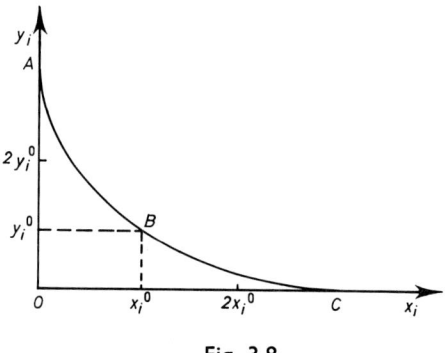

Fig. 3.8

In circumstances where transformation functions are strictly concave, perfect competition may not be able to exist. If there are few individual producers and they specialise, there will be even fewer producers of each commodity. Thus the likelihood increases that a producer has some control over the market price or terms of exchange.

VI. Difficulties

The models above which have explored the possible optimality of perfect competition have had regard to production only and have completely neglected consideration of the optimal exchange of production. But at a more advanced level this problem is amenable to analysis too, and it can be shown that under *suitable* conditions perfect competition leads to a Paretian optimum. However, this does not imply that, in the absence of governmental interference, an economy will achieve a Paretian optimum. Under such circumstances, some firms may engage in restrictive trade practices, for example. Also, important externalities may occur. Action might be needed to deal with these matters.

Yet there are more fundamental difficulties. In some industries, the individual units experience falling (long run) average costs if they use the most efficient technology. Under these circumstances, the cost of producing any aggregate volume of output in the industry is not minimised unless just *one* unit produces. Under normal circumstances, a single firm is bound to be able to influence the price of its product. Economic efficiency is incompatible with perfect competition in this case.

In practice, the assumptions about knowledge are rarely, if ever, completely satisfied. Firms and economic units may, indeed, make their decisions on the basis of different price expectations and consequently a Paretian optimum will not be reached.

Again there are some goods, public goods, which cannot be supplied through a market because their enjoyment cannot be made subject to a price payment. Non-contributors to a service of this type may gain just as much from it as contributors. For example, farmers in a river valley who do not contribute to flood control work may nevertheless gain along with contributors. The project, even though it is desired by all, may not come into existence unless the government intervenes.

Finally, mention of Schumpeter's point ought to be made once again. Although perfect competition may lead to economic efficiency at any point of time it may be inferior to alternative market forms from a growth point of view. Alternative forms may lead to greater growth of technology.

Clearly, one should not be deceived by the elegant mathematical proofs that under suitable conditions perfect competition leads to a Paretian optimum. The suitable conditions are most unlikely to be satisfied and there is Schumpeter's point to remember. Yet even a utopian model gives us a benchmark and a starting point for modifications.

NOTES AND REFERENCES

[1] This is a crude definition. See Chapter 5 for a more complete definition.
[2] Our definitions would be more symmetrical if the term "imperfect competition" applied to cases in which traders have perfect knowledge and are able to influence the terms of trade, and the term "impure competition" to cases in which knowledge is not perfect but traders influence the terms of exchange.
[3] J. SCHUMPETER, *Capitalism, Socialism and Democracy*, 4th ed., George Allen and Unwin, London, 1954, Chapters 7 and 8.
[4] P. SAMUELSON, K. HANCOCK and R. WALLACE, *Economics*, Australian edition, McGraw-Hill, Sydney, 1970, p. 52.
[5] Economic welfare, according to Pareto, can only be at a maximum if it is impossible to make someone better off without making others worse off.
[6] Expansion of rice output is at the increasing marginal cost of wheat output, and vice versa.

FURTHER READING·

ALCHIAN, A. and W. ALLEN, *Exchange and Production Theory in Use*, Wadsworth, Belmont, 1969, Ch. 3.
DORFMAN, R., *Prices and Markets*, Prentice-Hall, Englewood Cliffs, 1967, Chs 1, 7 and 8.
HANSEN, B., *Lectures in Economic Theory*, Studentlitteratur, Lund, 1967, Part II, Lecture 9.
KOHLER, H., *Scarcity Challenged*, Holt, Rinehart and Winston, New York, 1968, Chs 15 and 17.
TISDELL, C., "Uncertainty and Pareto Optimality", *The Economic Record*, December 1963, pp. 405-12.
TISDELL, C., "On the Theory of Externalities", *The Economic Record*, March 1970, pp. 14-25.

CHAPTER 4

Equilibrium, Statics and Dynamics

I. Definitions of Concepts

The notions of equilibrium, stability, statics and dynamics are of fundamental importance in economic thought. We may, therefore, with advantage discuss them early in our studies.

Economic models may involve time explicitly and integrally in which case they are *dynamic models*, or they may take no explicit account of time and merely concentrate on equilibrium situations in which case they are *static models*. In a dynamic model, the variables are functions of time which itself is an important variable. The time-variable may be introduced either as a continuous variable or as a discrete one. While it may be more natural to think of time as a continuous stream, it is sometimes more useful to treat it as being composed of a series of discrete points. In such cases, a period such as a week, month or year is treated as a point; a point at which important changes can take place. The Swedish School,[1] for example, found this method to be very useful for analysing changes in economic activity and it has been valuable for examining "cobweb" relationships in markets which will be discussed later.

In static models the passage of time does not enter explicitly into the model. Static models have been the most widely used models in economics and comparative statics has been used as a vehicle for policy recommendations. Different equilibria are compared in *comparative statics*. The equilibrium of a model may change as economic conditions alter and this will be reflected by changes in the structure of parameters of the model. Most of the fundamental works in economics, including J. R. Hicks' *Value and Capital*[2] and J. M. Keynes' *The General Theory of Employment, Interest and Money*,[3] have relied almost exclusively on the method of comparative statics.

But no definition has yet been given of equilibrium. An *equilibrium state* is one which in the absence of any changes outside the system or model is self-perpetuating. Such an equilibrium may be *stable* or *unstable*. Roughly an equilibrium state is stable for any disturbance if after that disturbance the system eventually returns to original equilibrium state. But the analysis of stability requires a consideration of dynamic factors. Not everyone is agreed on this,[4] but writers such as R. G. D. Allen,[5] B. Hansen,[6] R. Kuenne[7] and P. Samuelson[8] have taken this point of view and I accept this position.

It is worthwhile to quote two of these economists. For example, Kuenne says:

> ... let us note that whether we use the term *stability* to describe the quality of an equilibrium or a system, it can only be relevant to dynamic systems, that is to systems that have explicit time assumptions in their interrelationships: Stability characterises a path or set of paths in the time dimension, and if these paths do

Equilibrium, Statics and Dynamics

not exist in the solution, or exist only in the implicit sense that we move the solution through time in a constant manner, stability analysis does not apply. Thus to analyse the stability of a static model or of that model's equilibrium is impossible, and when we seem to do this we are in fact implicitly building a dynamic model and analysing its properties.[9]

Again, Samuelson states:

But the problem of stability of equilibrium cannot be discussed except with reference to dynamical considerations, however implicit and rudimentary.[10]

Let us, therefore, look a little more closely at dynamic models and the nature of their solutions.

II. Dynamic Models and the Nature of Their Solutions

The variables of a dynamic model and its solutions involve time in an integral way. Its interrelationships are vitally dependent on time and thus its solution is a path through time. Frequently, the model is specified in terms of differential or difference equations and the problem is by integration or other means to find the time-path which is consistent with these.

Imagine that we have a model in which a variable x is a function of time. This function may be of many forms but let us suppose that the time-path of x depends solely on its initial value. Given that x_0 is the initial value of x (its value at time zero) some of the possible paths which $x(t)$ might trace out are shown in Fig. 4.1. These are all possible types of solutions to dynamic models. The indicated time-paths can be described as follows:

(1) monotonically increasing and unbounded;
(2) monotonically increasing but converging to a limit;
(3) constant or stationary;
(4) explosive oscillatory;
(5) damped oscillatory;
(6) undamped oscillatory;
(7) monotonically decreasing but converging to a limit; and
(8) monotonically increasing and unbounded.

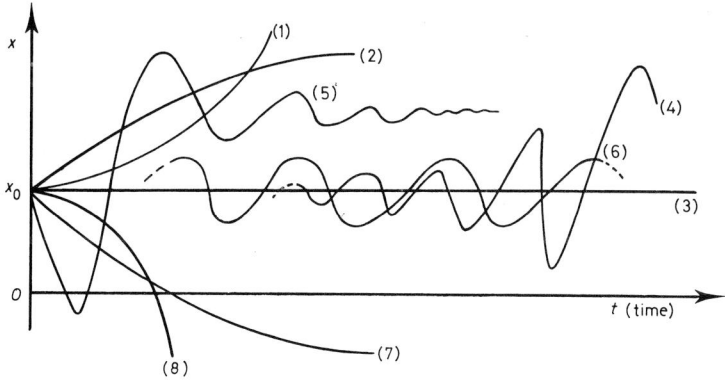

Fig. 4.1

This is an extremely small sample of the possible time-paths of dynamic systems. Note that time-paths (2), (3), (5) and (7) have an important property in common. As t becomes very large these solutions get arbitrarily close to limiting or *stationary* values or, indeed, do attain them. The rate of change of the functions becomes zero or very close to it, as time elapses. These stationary values are frequently equilibrium values of the model, that is values which once attained remain unchanged. For the time being, a value $\bar{x}$ of x will be regarded as an equilibrium value in a model if once that value is attained, x remains unchanged in the absence of a disturbance external to the model. Such an equilibrium may be stable or unstable.

III. More on Stability and Equilibrium

It is useful to distinguish between:
(a) the stability of a process, system or model, and
(b) the stability of an equilibrium value of the model.

A model is globally stable for a particular variable if that variable always tends to a stationary value (not necessarily the same one) no matter what is its initial value. It is locally stable if for limited initial values of the variable the system tends to stationary values in the variable. In Fig. 4.2, $\bar{x}_0$ and $\bar{x}_1$ are assumed to be equilibrium values. The system for initial values of $x > \hat{x}$ is assumed to tend to $\bar{x}_1$ and for $x \leqslant \hat{x}$ the system tends to $\bar{x}_0$. It is *globally* stable. Some possible paths towards the stationary values are indicated.

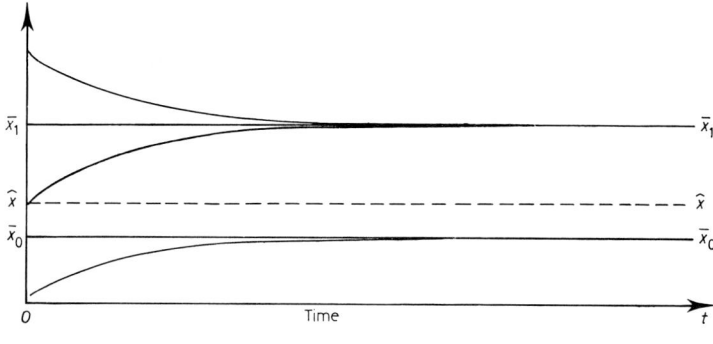

Fig. 4.2

On the other hand, the equilibrium values $\bar{x}_1$ and $\bar{x}_0$ are stable only for certain displacements of the initial value of x away from these values. $\bar{x}_1$ is stable for any initial displacement of x_1 in the interval $\hat{x} < x \leqslant \infty$. The value of x returns to $\bar{x}_1$ if displacements are in this area. The equilibrium $\bar{x}_1$ is *locally* stable. It is not globally stable because for some displacements of x the value of x does not return to $\bar{x}_1$. If an equilibrium *value* re-establishes itself after any initial disturbance, it is stable in the large. If it does this for small displacements in the neighbourhood of the equilibrium, it is stable in the small.

The identification of equilibrium with a stationary value of a system is a useful one which has been commonly adopted in economics. Note that it does not rule out the possibility of change in the values of variables of the system. The value x may be an absolute value, a percentage rate of change of another variable, a rate of change, and

Equilibrium, Statics and Dynamics

so on. If it is a percentage rate of change of a variable X, then equilibrium is consistent with X's rising, say, at constant percentage rate through time.

Stationary values of a model need not be its only interesting long-term regular characteristics. A process may for any initial value eventually settle into characteristic paths or solutions, which even if they do not tend to a limit may have simple properties. For example, depending upon a model's initial values, its relevant variable might eventually trace out one of a set of sine waves. If initially the relevant variable is on one of these waves and is disturbed, it may nevertheless (for small disturbances) return to this wave again.

Again, we might have a process in which the value of x always tends to return to certain bounds. It may wander between the bounds endlessly unless exogenously disturbed. A particular case is indicated in Fig. 4.3. The value of x may return to $x_1 \leqslant x \leqslant x_2$ for any disturbance beyond those limits, for example, if it is disturbed to x_0 or x_3. Clearly, the useful generalities which can be made along these lines are

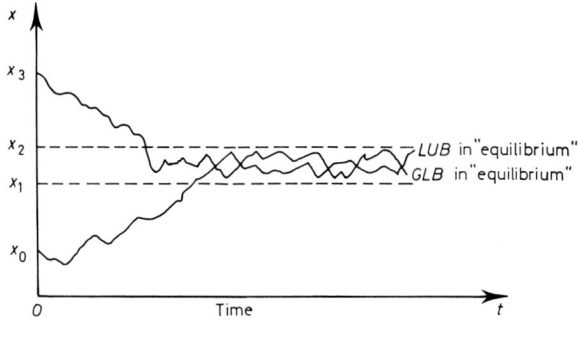

Fig. 4.3

large and though stationary values are important we should not forget that they are a particular case of more general regularities. In view of this it is worthwhile to keep Kelvin Lancaster's advice in mind, namely " 'Stability' is like 'equilibrium', a term with strong intuitive connotations that must be defined suitably in each particular case."[11] Provided the definition is clear it ought to be possible to avoid confusion.

IV. The Relationship between Static and Dynamic Models

A static model involves a "snapshot" of a dynamic process. It is a representation of it at an instant of time, but time relationships do not enter explicitly into the static model's relationships.

A static model may be compatible with more than one dynamic process or model. However, if one requires a process to be stable, it can be shown that this often limits the type of static models which are compatible with the dynamic process. For example, by placing a stability requirement on various dynamic market models one often limits the compatible slopes of demand and supply functions.

The stationary solutions of dynamic models correspond to the equilibrium points of static models. The easiest way to illustrate this is to take a particular case for a purely competitive market.

In Fig. 4.4 a comparative static model of a market is shown. The curve marked D_a indicates the amount of commodity X which consumers are willing to buy, at all possible prices of it as at March, 1970 and the curve S indicates the quantities of X which producers are willing to supply, at various prices during the same period. For 1970 and for any month in which the supply and demand curves are S and D_a the equilibrium price and quantity respectively are P_0 and X_0. In the absence of any general changes, consumers are just willing to purchase X_0 at price P_0 and producers are just willing to supply this quantity and are willing to do so period after period. However, suppose that in March, 1971 the demand curve suddenly shifts to D_b. It might do so, for example, if population increases or if tastes change in favour of X. With the supply curve unchanged the equilibrium price rises to P_1 and the equilibrium quantity to X_1. But there is no guarantee that *actual* price and quantity will instantaneously adjust to equality with these new equilibrium levels. The actual nature and time-path of adjustment need to be considered.

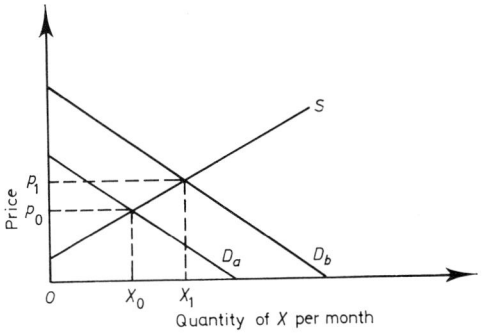

Fig. 4.4

Imagine that the market is in its original equilibrium from March, 1970 to March, 1971 and that, after the disturbance created by the shift of the demand curve, no further shifts take place. A *possible* time-path for price is shown in Fig. 4.5. Taking March, 1970 as the initial period and indicating the time-path of price by a semi-continuous line for simplicity, the price of X remains stationary at P_0 for one year,

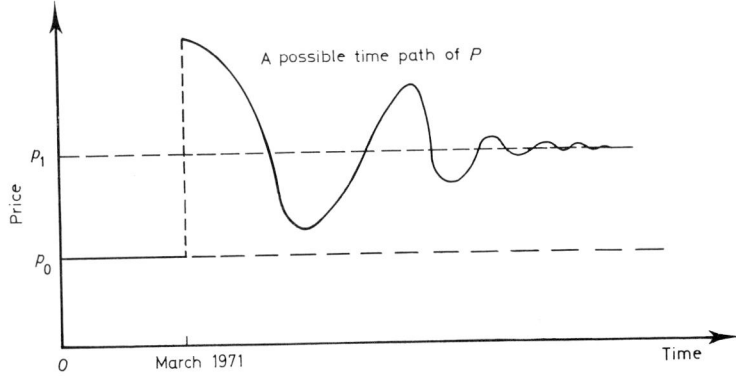

Fig. 4.5

Equilibrium, Statics and Dynamics

suddenly increases and then with damped oscillations tends to P_1. Even though it tends to P_1, it is considerably divergent from P_1 in the initial months.

The above example is a simplified one. In practice, the system may be shooting towards ever changing equilibrium values and may never reach any. This raises important issues about the value of comparative static analysis.

V. The Relative Merits of Static and Dynamic Models

Static models contain less detail than dynamic models do. From this point of view they are easier to construct. They are also compatible with a large number of dynamic models but they achieve this generality at the expense of details about time. This can be a very great cost to pay for simplicity. Comparative static models can give rise to very misleading policy conclusions.

Comparative statics is likely to be a misleading method of analysis if movements from one equilibrium to another are slow. If these are fast, the method may give a useful approximation. This can be illustrated by Fig. 4.6. Comparative statics may indicate a change in a variable x from its initial value of x_0 to an equilibrium value of $\bar{x}_1$. If policy is based in the assumption that $\bar{x}_1$ will prevail, it may be misguided if the path to $\bar{x}_1$ is as indicated by curve 3 but is likely to be less misguided the closer the path comes to being a vertical line from x_0.

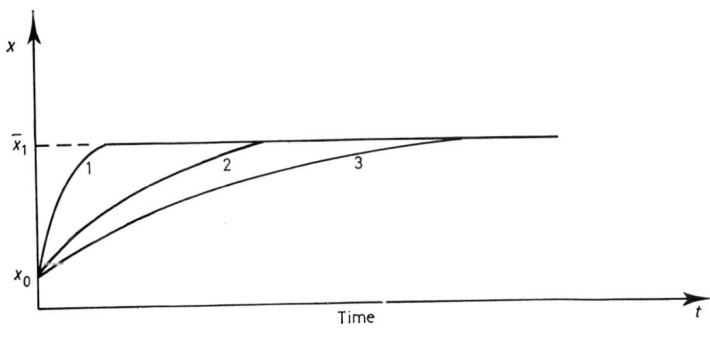

Fig. 4.6

It might also be noted that while it is of some value to know that an equilibrium value such as $\bar{x}_1$ is stable in the large, this by itself is not of much practical value. If it takes aeons to reach the equilibrium value (and this cannot be ruled out) the knowledge alone that the equilibrium is stable will not be of much relevance here and now. In many cases, one must trace out the actual time-paths themselves and consider other qualities of these in order to make a rational policy decision. One cannot concentrate on the equilibrium values alone.

NOTES AND REFERENCES

[1] For further details see B. SELIGMAN, *Main Currents in Modern Economics*, The Free Press of Glencoe, New York, 1962, Ch. 7, "The Swedish Contribution".
[2] J. R. HICKS, *Value and Capital*, 2nd ed., Clarendon Press, Oxford, 1946.
[3] J. M. KEYNES, *The General Theory of Employment, Interest and Money*, Macmillan, London, 1936.

⁴ Henderson and Quandt do not seem to agree. See J. M. HENDERSON and R. E. QUANDT, *Microeconomic Theory*, McGraw-Hill, New York, 1958, pp. 110 et seq.
⁵ R. G. D. ALLEN, *Mathematical Economics*, 2nd ed., Macmillan, London, 1959, p. 11.
⁶ B. HANSEN, *Lectures in Economic Theory*, 3rd ed., Studentlitteratur, Lund, 1968, Part I, p. 2.
⁷ R. KUENNE, *Microeconomic Theory of the Market Mechanism*, The Macmillan Company, New York, 1968, p. 29.
⁸ P. A. SAMUELSON, *Foundations of Economic Analysis*, Harvard University Press, Cambridge, 1947, p. 262.
⁹ KUENNE, op. cit., p. 29. Reprinted by kind permission of The Macmillan Company.
¹⁰ SAMUELSON, op. cit., p. 262.
¹¹ K. LANCASTER, *Mathematical Economics*, The Macmillan Company, New York, 1968, p. 195.

FURTHER READING

ALLEN, R. G. D., *Mathematical Economics*, Macmillan, London, 1959, Chs 1 and 2.
FRISCH, RAGNAR, "On the Notion of Equilibrium and Disequilibrium", *Review of Economic Studies*, 1935-36.
HANSEN, B., *Lectures in Economic Theory*, Studentlitteratur, Lund, 1969, Part I, Ch. 1.
KUENNE, R. E., *The Microeconomic Theory of the Market Mechanism*, Macmillan, New York, 1968, Ch. 1.
*SAMUELSON, P. A., *Foundations of Economic Analysis*, Harvard University Press, Cambridge, 1963, Chs 9 and 10.

* Advanced.

CHAPTER 5

Prices and Pure Competition

I. The Static Framework of Pure Competition

A. PURE COMPETITION AND ITS ROLE IN ECONOMIC ANALYSIS

Already we have noted that the ability of participants to determine the terms of exchange differ in different markets and that economists have used this to classify markets. In purely and perfectly competitive markets, no individual participant, by acting alone, is able to influence the price of the commodity traded in the market or the terms of its exchange. The operation of a purely competitive market is analysed in this chapter.

Purely competitive markets are extremely important types of markets. They are of particular interest since

(i) they roughly typify some actual markets, for example, the markets in some agricultural products;

(ii) several markets, for example, most markets for agricultural goods, would almost be purely competitive in the absence of governmental intervention;

(iii) the basic model gives a point of reference. It can be used as a starting point and allowance can be made for such things as labour immobility and other frictions if necessary. The procedure is akin to that of a physicist who takes the law of gravitation (in a vacuum) as basic and then makes allowance for air resistance etc. The actual conception of a purely competitive market involves an abstraction from reality, but a very useful abstraction. Even if no market exactly satisfies the conditions required for pure competition, the ideal or pure type is a valuable reference point;

(iv) if appropriate assumptions are made about the knowledge of participants, a purely competitive market becomes perfectly competitive. Under certain circumstances, if all markets in a market economy are perfectly competitive economic efficiency prevails.

A purely competitive market has the following characteristics:

(a) no buyer and no seller is individually able to influence the price of the commodity which is traded on the market. The price of the commodity is set by the market as a whole. This normally involves a large number of buyers and sellers with none transacting a significant fraction of the total trade in the markets;

(b) the commodities which are traded (whether they be products or resources) are homogeneous in the opinion of buyers. At identical prices, buyers have no reason to favour one source of supply to another. Combined with the self-interest assumption (see (c) below) this implies that the price of the commodity must be the same throughout the market *if* knowledge is perfect;

(c) buyers and sellers act in their own anticipated self-interest and are able to do so without artificial restriction imposed, for example, by a government. Buyers and sellers are free to enter and leave a market if they so desire. In general, firms or productive units are assumed to act in a way which maximises their anticipated profits, while consumers maximise their anticipated utility or satisfaction through their purchases;

(d) commodities are perfectly mobile. Factors and products can be transported anywhere in the market at no cost whatsoever and will be if it is in the self-interest of any economic agent to do so.

Perfect competition exists if a suitable *additional* assumption about knowledge is satisfied. It certainly exists if all economic units (decision-makers) possess perfect knowledge about prices in all markets and know all about the qualities and technological characteristics and possibilities of all commodities. But this knowledge-assumption is really stronger than is required. Each unit's knowledge of a *limited* set of prices and technological characteristics may be sufficient to give the results which are ensured by the more global knowledge condition. A local or limited knowledge sometimes results in the perfectly competitive outcome and economists have examined some of the circumstances under which this is so.

As previously mentioned, under pure and perfect competition no individual is able alone to determine or influence the price of a commodity in a market, but the price is determined by the market as a whole, that is by the combined actions of all participants in the market. We shall now investigate the elements which affect the price of a commodity in an isolated market: the workings of a single market will be examined using partial analysis. Except for changes associated with the workings of the particular market, everything else in the economy including prices in other markets is assumed to be constant. This might be defended on the grounds that the market is small in relation to the whole market economy so that changes in it have negligible effect outside the market. If interdependencies are important, we must use general not partial analysis.

In order to examine a market using partial analysis, the concepts of the market demand curve and market supply curve are needed. These two curves together determine the equilibrium price of the commodity and have considerable influence on actual market prices. The analysis of the market given here is for a product, but an analogous treatment is possible for resource markets and will be discussed later. Static and comparative static models are considered first and then some dynamic ones.

B. THE MARKET-DEMAND FUNCTION

The overall demand for any product depends upon many factors. The quantity of any product which will be purchased by consumers depends, amongst other things, on their tastes, incomes and the distribution of incomes, the size of the population, expectations, wealth and, most importantly, on the prices of other products as well as the price of the product itself.

The partial market-demand curve for a product indicates the various quantities of products which consumers are willing to purchase at each possible price of the product other things being held constant. The other things which are held constant include

(i) consumers' tastes and preferences,
(ii) the number of consumers,
(iii) consumers' incomes,
(iv) the prices of other goods,
(v) the range of available goods,
(vi) the price expectations of consumers, and
(vii) their wealth.

In the next chapter the determinants of demand are discussed in detail. But for now let us accept the proposition that *other things being equal* consumers' demand for a product can be expressed as a function of the price of that product alone. Take a particular product, X. The prices of other products being given and incomes being given as well as other things, the aggregate demand for X in a particular period might be expressed as

$$X^d = X^d(p) \tag{5.1}$$

where X^d is the aggregate quantity of X demanded, and p is its price. In this demand function the quantity demanded is the dependent variable and price is the independent variable. The normal mathematical convention would therefore be to show p on the x axis of a graph and X^d on the y axis. But since Marshall, economists have broken with this convention when drawing supply and demand curves. They draw the inverse function of (5.1). For example, imagine that in a particular instance function (5.1) is the linear one

$$X^d = a - bp. \tag{5.2}$$

Its inverse is

$$p = \frac{a}{b} - \frac{1}{b}X. \tag{5.3}$$

These two functions are indicated in Figs 5.1 and 5.2 respectively. Usually economists represent the demand function with the axes marked as in Fig. 5.2.

In the particular instance shown, the demand function slopes downward which indicates that, when other things are constant, consumers wish to consume a greater quantity of the product as its price decreases. Is it usual for the demand curve to

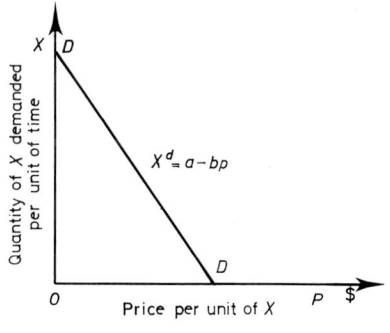

Fig. 5.1

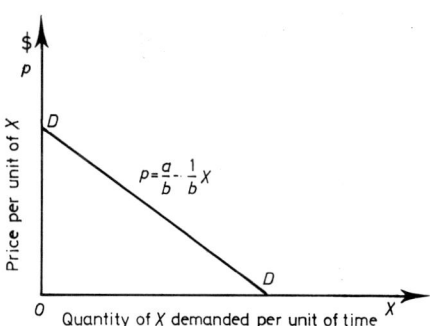

Fig. 5.2

slope downwards? Empirical and theoretical evidence suggests that downward sloping demand curves are common. But it is not impossible for a demand curve to be upward sloping over some of its range. This can happen if the product is an inferior one. A reduction in its price raises *real* income and enables consumers to substitute preferred goods for the inferior one. It can also happen if consumers tend to judge the quality of a product by its price or if the Veblen effect[1] is present. The Veblen effect occurs if there is a class of consumers who wish to impress others by the high prices which they pay for commodities. We shall discuss these effects in the next chapter.

Shifts or changes in the demand curve should be clearly distinguished from movements along a demand curve. A movement along the demand curve for a product occurs if its price changes and all other factors remain constant. On the other hand, a change or shift in the demand curve may occur if other things change. It may, for example, eventuate if

(i) consumers' tastes alter, or

(ii) if the number of consumers vary, or

(iii) if their income alters, or

(iv) if the price of other goods changes.

In Fig. 5.3, the result of a fall in the price of X from p_1 to p_0 is illustrated assuming other things constant. The quantity of X which is demanded rises from X_1 to X_2. This case involves a movement along the curve. In Fig. 5.4, the demand function is shown to shift up from DD to $D_1 D_1$. More of X is demanded at any given price. For example, consumers after the shift in the demand function are willing to buy X_3 of X at a price of p_1, whereas originally they were only willing to buy X_1 of it. A shift upward of the demand curve *might* be caused by an increase in population, an increase of income, by a fall in the price of a complementary product or by a rise in the price of a substitute, by a change of taste in favour of the product, and so on. However, increases of income or a reduction in the price of a complementary product are not certain to have this result if the product in question is an inferior one.

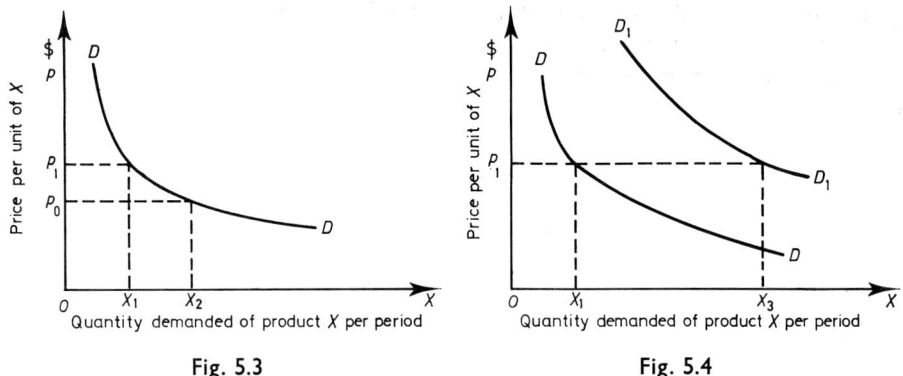

Fig. 5.3   Fig. 5.4

C. THE MARKET-SUPPLY FUNCTION

The market-supply schedule of a product indicates the quantity which sellers are willing to sell at each possible price of the product other things being assumed constant.

Prices and Pure Competition

It shows the quantity of a product which suppliers are willing to supply to a market as a function of the product's price alone. The quantity which suppliers are willing to supply of a product X depends amongst other things on

(i) the price offered for the product,

(ii) on the prices offered for the supply of other products,

(iii) on the state of technology, and

(iv) on the prices of resources which need to be used in order to produce the product.

A market-supply curve is usually drawn on the assumption that the state of technology is constant and all prices except the price of the product are constant. Sometimes the number of suppliers is assumed to be constant but this is not always done. The whole question of underlying assumptions will be clarified in Chapter 8.

For the time being let us accept the proposition that, if certain other things are held constant, the quantity of the product which suppliers are willing to supply and exchange can be expressed solely as a function of the product's price. In other words, (other things being constant) there is a market-supply function which can be expressed by

$$X^s = X^s(p) \tag{5.4}$$

where X^s represents the quantity supplied to the market. In a particular instance, it might be of the form

$$\left. \begin{array}{ll} X^s = 0 & \text{for } p < \hat{p} \\ X^s = -\alpha + \beta p & \text{for } p \geqslant \hat{p} \end{array} \right\} \tag{5.5}$$

In this case nothing is supplied to the market if price is $\hat{p}$. If price exceeds this, positive quantities are supplied as indicated by the linear expression. A particular instance of this supply function is shown in Fig. 5.5. It indicates that the quantity supplied tends to increase with the price which is offered. The inverse of the supply function of Fig. 5.5. is shown in Fig. 5.6. It is usual for economists to give the supply function in the inverse form. Normally (there may be exceptions) the supply function has a positive slope because increasing supplies can only be obtained at increasing additional cost. A discussion of the slope of the function will, however, be delayed until Chapter 8.

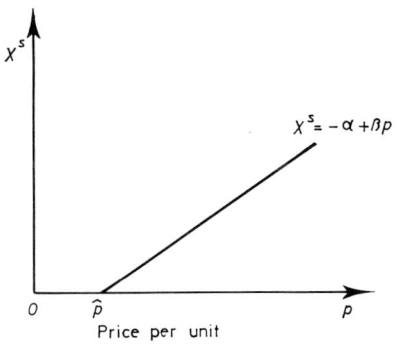

Fig. 5.5

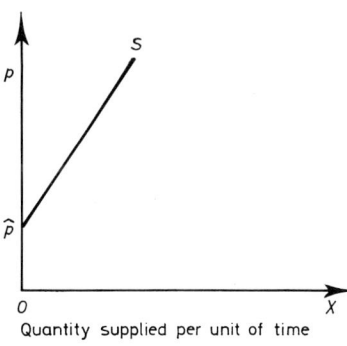

Fig. 5.6

Also, in this case, shifts in the supply function ought not to be confused with movements along the function. A movement along the supply function for a commodity results from a change in the commodity's price other things being held constant. A movement along the supply curve is shown in Fig. 5.7. A reduction in the price of the product from p_1 to p_0 results in a fall in the quantity supplied from X_1 to X_0. Figure 5.8 illustrates a shift of the supply curve. If the supply curve moves from SS to $S_1 S_1$ more is supplied at any given price. For example, X_0 is originally supplied at p_0 but after the shift in the supply curve X_2 is supplied. A movement such as the one indicated might come about as a result of improvements in technology.

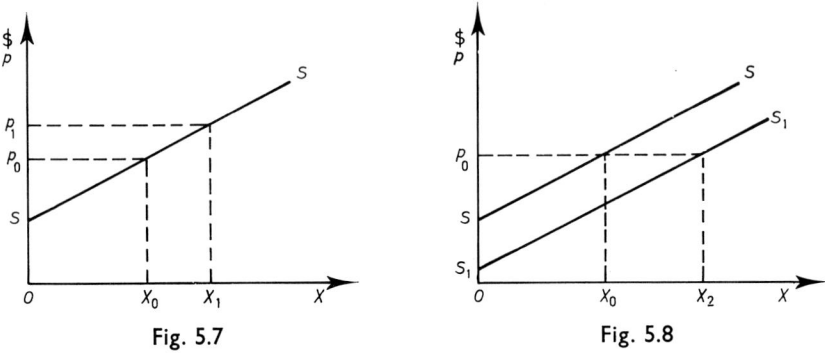

Fig. 5.7   Fig. 5.8

D. EQUILIBRIUM PRICE AND OUTPUT

The demand and the supply functions together determine the *market-equilibrium* price for a product. If the market-equilibrium price prevails, then the quantity of the product which consumers are willing to buy is just equal to the quantity which producers are willing to supply. In the absence of any exogenous changes, the market-equilibrium price is self-sustaining. Neither the buyers nor the sellers have any incentive to change their behaviour if the equilibrium price and transactions position is reached.

The equilibrium price and quantity correspond to the values at which the demand and the supply curves intersect. Algebraically they are found by solving the equations which represent the supply and demand curves. For example, $\bar{p}$ and $\bar{X}$ are respectively the equilibrium price and equilibrium quantity of transactions for the case shown in Fig. 5.9 where the industry supply curve is SS and the demand curve DD. At a price

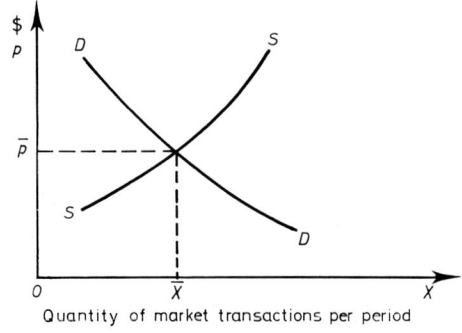

Fig. 5.9

Prices and Pure Competition

$\bar{p}$ for X, buyers are willing to buy $\bar{X}$ of the product and sellers are willing to sell $\bar{X}$ of it. If traders in the market are at the equilibrium point, they will be satisfied to remain there from period to period unless the market demand or supply curve shifts.

The equilibrium price and transaction quantity can be held to be important from several points of view. First, it represents a point of permanence and actual market prices and quantities may tend to it. This raises the matter of stability, essentially a dynamic factor, and this will be discussed below. Second, the equilibrium price and quantity is the only one which can simultaneously satisfy the expectations of buyers and sellers. If the equilibrium price and quantity of transactions does not prevail, either the expectations of buyers or sellers or both must be less than fully realised.

Two "oddities" might be mentioned at this stage. It is possible for multiple equilibria to occur in markets and for some goods to be free goods, and to be less than fully employed or used. Figures 5.10 and 5.11 represent the respective cases. In Fig. 5.10, the demand curve is backward-bending. It slopes upward for some of its length and this may occur because of a Veblen effect or because individuals judge quality by price. Equilibria occur at (X_0, p_0) and (X_1, p_1). To determine which, if any, will actually prevail in the long run, one needs to consider the dynamics of the market process. In Fig. 5.11, the supply curve is SAS and in equilibrium the product is free with $\bar{X}$ of it being consumed. The remainder $A - \bar{X}$ is unused.

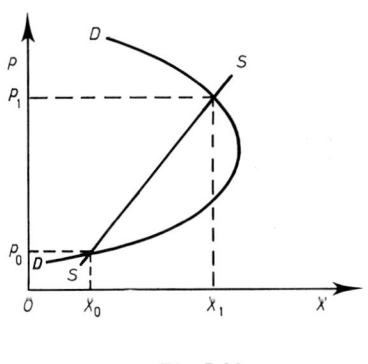
Fig. 5.10

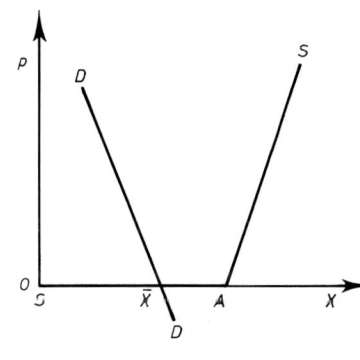
Fig. 5.11

E. COMPARATIVE STATICS: SHIFTS OF THE DEMAND AND SUPPLY CURVES

If the study of markets were to be merely confined to the discussion of whether or not an equilibrium exists and to the manner in which it is determined, the study would be of very limited value. As Samuelson has said:

> Simply to know that there are efficacious "laws" determining equilibrium tells us nothing of the character of these laws. In order for the analysis to be useful it must provide information concerning the way in which our equilibrium quantities will change as a result of changes in the parameters taken as independent data.[2]

As a result of shifts in the demand and supply curve for a product, its equilibrium price and quantity of transactions alters. If the market tends to the equilibrium values, then changes in these indicate the new values to which price and quantities tend. The study of changing equilibria is called *comparative statics*. The practical relevance of this method was discussed in the last chapter.

If the supply curve is upward-sloping and the demand curve is downward-sloping (and neither is perpendicular), an increase in demand, that is a shift upward in the demand curve, other things being constant, causes the equilibrium price and quantity of a product to increase. This is illustrated in Fig. 5.12. A shift upwards in the demand schedule from $D_0 D_0$ to $D_1 D_1$, other things constant, causes the equilibrium price to rise from p_0 to p_1 and the equilibrium quantity to increase from X_0 to X_1. If the supply curve is horizontal, the equilibrium quantity will increase while equilibrium price remains constant. If the supply curve is vertical, equilibrium price rises while equilibrium quantity remains unchanged.

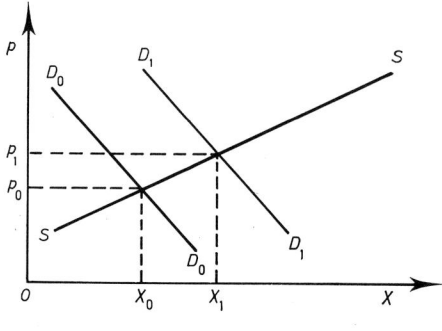

Fig. 5.12

Let us now consider shifts in the supply curve assuming that the supply function is upward-sloping and the demand curve is downward-sloping and neither is perpendicular. In these circumstances, a shift upward in the supply curve [if X is shown on the X axis, otherwise a shift downward if p is shown on the X axis] causes the equilibrium price to rise and the equilibrium quantity to decrease. This is illustrated in Fig. 5.13. A shift upward in the market supply curve from $S_0 S_0$ to $S_1 S_1$ increases the equilibrium price from P_0 to P_1 and decreases the equilibrium quantity from X_1 to X_0.

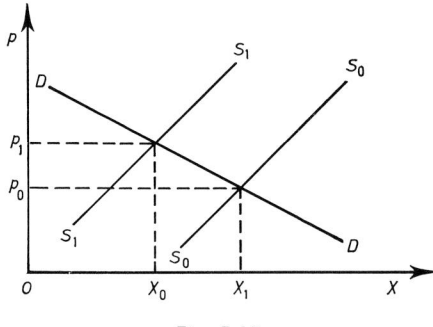

Fig. 5.13

Mention has already been made of factors which may cause the supply and demand curves to shift. Shifts of the demand curve may arise because of changed tastes, for example, or increased population. The supply curve may shift, for example, because of alterations in the price of resources or because of technological change.

Prices and Pure Competition

In the examples discussed above, the supply and demand curves are of normal slope. The demand curve has a negative slope while the supply curve is positively sloped. Under these circumstances a shift in the curve gives the "normal" effects on equilibrium. For example, an upward movement in the demand curve, other things constant, causes the equilibrium price and quantity to increase. If the curves are not normal, other results may occur. For example, if the supply curve is downward-sloping, an increase of demand may actually reduce the equilibrium price.

It is interesting to examine algebraically the equilibrium properties of a linear market model, in order to illustrate the effect on equilibrium of shifts in the supply and demand curves. Later some of the crucial influences on the direction of the change in equilibrium will be shown to be important in determining whether a market equilibrium is stable or not. Though a linear model is used here the effect of a parameter shift in the supply or demand curve can be generalised.[3]

Let the demand curve for the product be represented by

$$X^d = a + bp \tag{5.6}$$

and the supply curve be represented by

$$X^s = \alpha + \beta p \tag{5.7}$$

where X is the quantity of the product, p its price, and a, b, α, and β are coefficients which may be of any sign. In equilibrium, the quantity of the product which sellers are willing to supply should be just equal to the amount which buyers are willing to buy. In equilibrium (assuming its existence)

$$X^s = X^d. \tag{5.8}$$

Therefore,

$$a + bp = \alpha + \beta p \tag{5.9}$$

and the equilibrium price is

$$\bar{p} = \frac{a - \alpha}{\beta - b}. \tag{5.10}$$

Substituting this value into the supply function, the equilibrium quantity is

$$\bar{X} = \alpha + \frac{\beta(a - \alpha)}{\beta - b}. \tag{5.11}$$

These equilibrium expressions can be used to study the effect of changes in the coefficients (parameters) of the supply and the demand functions. Changes in these describe shifts of the curves. For example, let us imagine that the demand curve shifts up in a parallel fashion, other things being constant. This implies that parameter a increases. How do the equilibrium price and quantity levels change? To decide on the direction of the change, we can differentiate Equations (5.10) and (5.11) partially with respect to a. The results are:

$$\frac{\partial \bar{p}}{\partial a} = \frac{1}{\beta - b} \tag{5.12}$$

and

$$\frac{\partial \bar{X}}{\partial a} = \frac{\beta}{\beta - b}. \tag{5.13}$$

We note several things. The sign of the changes depends only on the slopes of the supply and demand functions. β is the slope of the supply function and b is the slope of the demand function. If $\beta - b$ is positive, equilibrium price increases as a result of the shift upward in demand, but equilibrium output need not increase. In the normal case, $\beta > 0$ and $b < 0$, and hence, both of the above expressions are positive. The shift upward in demand increases both the equilibrium quantity and the equilibrium price. Similarly, the results of other parameter changes can be deduced.

II. The Dynamics of Market-Adjustment

A. THE ASSUMPTIONS OF WALRAS AND MARSHALL

In statics and comparative statics, equilibria and shifts of equilibria are studied. But statics by itself gives no indication of whether an equilibrium is stable or unstable, or the speed with which a system tends to an equilibrium or away from it once disturbed. Only dynamics is capable of resolving these fundamental issues.

The issues are of fundamental theoretical and practical importance. Frequently, comparative static models are used for policy purposes. This may be a justifiable simplification if "the" equilibrium of the model is a stable one and the system moves to it speedily. However, if the equilibrium is not stable or if the system only moves to it slowly, then serious, even disastrous, errors can be made by relying on comparative statics. In some policy problems, one must explicitly consider the time-path of the process. But even in market adjustments a large number of equilibrating processes are conceivable.

Two different processes have, for example, been suggested by Walras[4] and Marshall.[5] Walras' view is that the variation of price depends upon whether at the current price the quantity demanded exceeds the quantity supplied. If the quantity demanded exceeds that which is supplied, price rises; if these quantities are equal, price is steady; otherwise it falls. The mathematical relationship is

$$\frac{dp}{dt} = f(X^d - X^s)$$

where $f(0) = 0$ and $f > 0$ for $X^d - X^s > 0$. If we assume that the rate of change in price is greater the greater is the divergence between the quantities demanded and supplied, $f' > 0$.

In a more particular case, where k is a constant

$$\frac{dp}{dt} = k(X^d - X^s) \text{ where } k > 0. \tag{5.14}$$

In Fig. 5.14, if $p = p_3$ there is an excess of supply and price falls. This is so also if $p = p_2$ but it falls at a slower rate as p approaches $\bar{p}$ for the difference between demand and supply is smaller. Similarly, if $p = p_0$, price is forced up by the competition of buyers. In the case shown in (5.14), as in any case in which the supply and demand curves are of normal slope, the equilibrium $(\bar{p}, \bar{X})$ is *stable* given Walrasian reaction assumptions. The equilibrium is also stable given Marshallian assumptions.

Marshall assumes that sellers react to an excess of the demand price (the price which buyers are willing to pay) above the supply price (the price at which suppliers are just willing to sell) for a given quantity of supplies by increasing their *supplies*.

Prices and Pure Competition

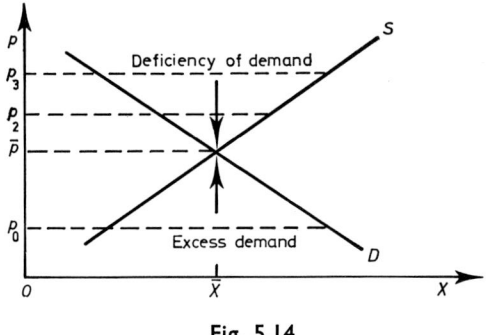

Fig. 5.14

This is illustrated in Fig. 5.15. If supplies are below the equilibrium level, $\bar{X}$, the demand price exceeds the supply price and supplies increase. For example, if $X = X_1$, the demand price is p_2 and exceeds the supply price, p_0, and supplies expand. If on the other hand, $X > \bar{X}$ the supply price exceeds the demand and supplies contract. This continues until $X = \bar{X}$ for then the demand and the supply price are equal.

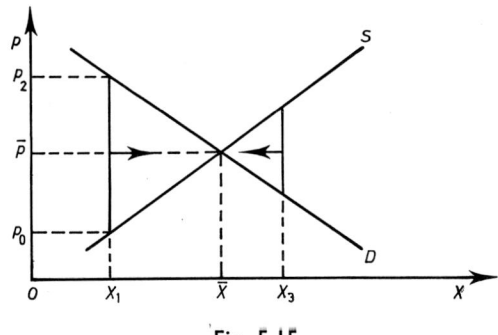

Fig. 5.15

Supplies contract, for example, if $X = X_3$ because consumers are not willing to pay the price which producers require to supply this much. The equilibrium $(\bar{p}, \bar{X})$ is stable given Marshallian reaction assumptions. Indeed, if the supply and demand curves have normal slopes both Walrasian and Marshallian assumptions ensure that the market-equilibrium price and quantity are stable.

But an equilibrium can be stable under one set of adjustment assumptions and unstable for the other. For example, if the supply curve cuts the demand curve from above, the market-equilibrium is stable for Walrasian assumptions and unstable for Marshallian ones. This is indicated in Fig. 5.16. If X happens to exceed $\bar{X}$, output continually expands under Marshallian conditions or if X is less than $\bar{X}$ it continually contracts. In the former Marshallian case, the demand price exceeds the supply price, and further expansion of supplies only increases the difference. Under Walrasian assumptions, if $p < \bar{p}$ then the quantity demanded exceeds the quantity supplied and price is forced up. If $p > \bar{p}$, the opposite is the case and price is forced down. Stability is achieved at $\bar{p}$. Hence, the equilibrium $(\bar{p}, \bar{X})$ is stable under Walrasian adjustments but unstable under Marshallian ones.

D

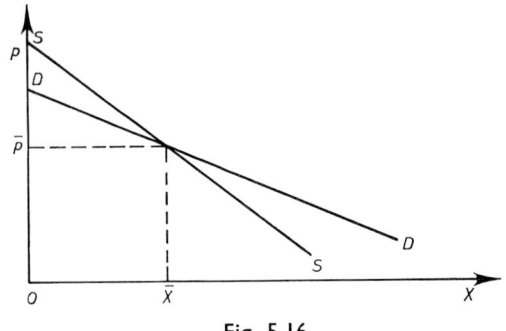

Fig. 5.16

Samuelson[6] and others have noted important *correspondences* between the stability of various dynamic market models and the equilibria of comparative statics. *If Walrasian adjustment assumptions are made, then an increase in demand does involve a higher equilibrium price if (and only if) the market is stable.* A higher equilibrium price is associated with stability and vice versa. Equilibrium quantity may change in any direction. Nothing is implied about the sign of its change. It can also be shown that *if Marshallian adjustment patterns occur, then an increase in demand does involve a higher equilibrium quantity if (and only if) the market is stable.* The equilibrium quantity and stability (but not price) are associated.

It is interesting to follow the argument at least for the Walrasian case. Assume that the demand and supply functions are as set out in Equations (5.6) and (5.7) respectively, and the reaction function is as indicated by Equation (5.14). We may substitute (5.6) and (5.7) into (5.14) to get

$$\frac{dp}{dt} + k(\beta - b)p = k(a - \alpha) \tag{5.15}$$

which is a linear differential equation of the first order in p. Its solution is

$$p(t) = \frac{a - \alpha}{\beta - b} + Ce^{-k(\beta - b)t} \tag{5.16}$$

where C is the constant of integration. If $t = 0$,

$$p(0) = \frac{a - \alpha}{\beta - b} + C \tag{5.17}$$

so rearranging and noting (5.10),

$$C = p(0) - \bar{p}. \tag{5.18}$$

Substituting into Equation (5.16) and replacing $\frac{a - \alpha}{\beta - b}$ by $\bar{p}$,

$$p(t) = \bar{p} + (p(0) - \bar{p})e^{-k(\beta - b)t}. \tag{5.19}$$

The expression $(p(0) - \bar{p})$ indicates the deviation of the initial condition (price) from the equilibrium price level. Clearly, the system is stable and tends towards the equilibrium price level $\bar{p}$ if

$$\beta - b > 0. \tag{5.20}$$

If Equation (5.20) is the case, then as $t \to \infty$ the last term of Equation (5.19) tends to zero so that $p(t)$ tends to the limit $\bar{p}$. This is the stationary solution of Equation (5.16).

Prices and Pure Competition

If the condition of Equation (5.20) is fulfilled this dynamic system tends to the equilibrium price of the static system, which is described by Equations (5.6), (5.7) and (5.8). Indeed, the dynamic system above degenerates to this static system if

$$\frac{dp}{dt} = 0 \qquad (5.21)$$

since Equation (5.14) then becomes

$$0 = k(X^d - X^s) \qquad (5.22)$$

which, when rearranged, is equivalent to Equation 5.8. This static system corresponds to the above dynamic one.

Note that the condition for stability of the dynamic system (5.20) is exactly the condition required in the static model for equilibrium price to increase with a shift up in demand (see Equation 5.12). In both cases $\beta - b$ must be positive. Thus under Walrasian reaction assumptions, a market can only be stable if increased demand leads to an equilibrium price increase, and an equilibrium price increase will occur in a market as a result of a shift up in demand if (and only if) the market is stable. The change in equilibrium quantity is not only dependent on the sign of the stability condition $(\beta - b)$ but also on the sign of β. (See Equation 5.13). Hence, Walrasian stability does not require output to increase as a result of an upward shift in demand.

We may illustrate the connection. In the normal case shown in Fig. 5.12, equilibrium price increases as a result of an upward shift in demand. The market is stable under Walrasian assumptions. Four cases are shown in Figs 5.17 to 5.20. The first two situations are stable and the second two involve an unstable equilibrium.

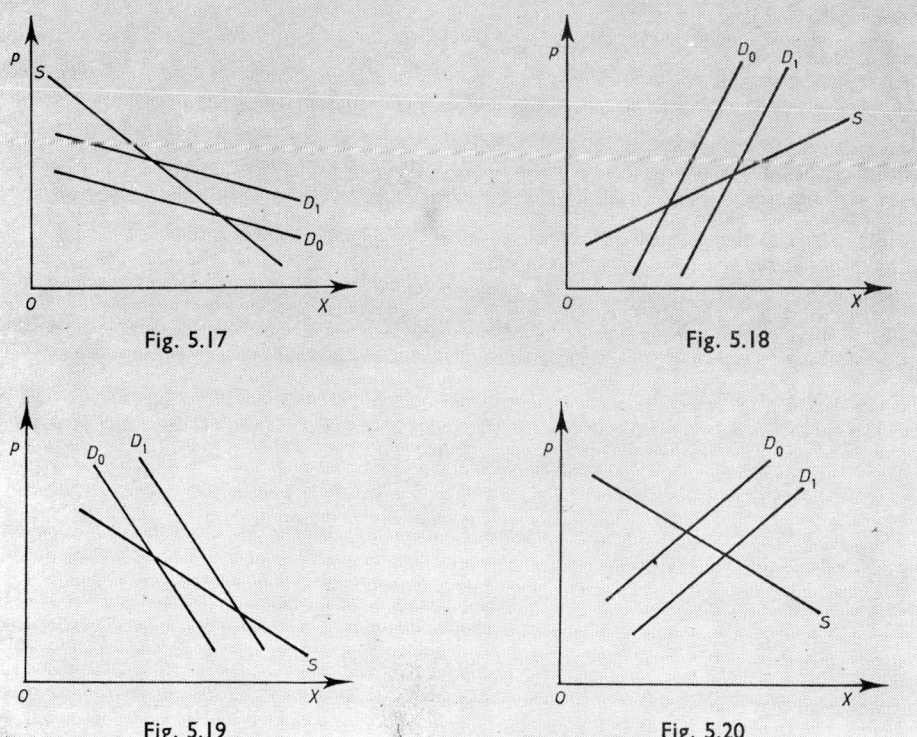

Fig. 5.17

Fig. 5.18

Fig. 5.19

Fig. 5.20

In the stable cases, equilibrium price increases and in the unstable cases it decreases. Equilibrium quantity decreases in one of the stable cases and increases in the other one. For the unstable cases, too, equilibrium quantity increases in one instance and decreases in the other. This indicates that equilibrium quantity is not related to stability under Walrasian assumptions.

Under Marshall's excess price hypothesis, the position is different. If Marshall's assumption applies, the main burden of adjustment comes from variations in supply. The supplied quantity rather than price is regarded as the independent variable. Marshallian stability requires that the equilibrium *quantity* increases when demand increases. However, it does not require the equilibrium price to increase. Once again, there is a connection between comparative statics and dynamics. If equilibrium quantity increases in the static market model, as a result of an increase in demand, the market is stable for *Marshallian assumptions*. If the market is stable under Marshallian assumptions, an upward shift in demand increases the equilibrium quantity. Thus there is a simple correspondence. This is easily shown mathematically.[7]

B. A COBWEB MODEL

In the dynamic models which have been considered so far, time has been treated as a continuous variable. Other models of market-adjustment are available which treat time as a discrete variable. One of them is the simple cobweb model which can be used to generate fluctuations not unlike those observed in some agricultural markets. The supply of pigs, cattle, onions and other commodities can be approximated in their fluctuation by using modified cobweb models. Only the simplest one is discussed here.

Time is supposed to be divided into a number of equal intervals, for example, years; and for each period one price and supply level is recorded. The level of output or supply in any one period is decided in the previous period. This may be technically necessary since some products take time to come to maturity, for example, crops and animals. Suppliers are assumed to determine their supplies for period $t+1$ in period t by supposing that the price of t will prevail in period $t+1$. In any period, price is adjusted so as to clear all the available supplies of that period so no inventories or stocks are held.

Under these circumstances, the market exhibits the following stability characteristics if the supply and demand curves are linear and of the normal slopes (that is if the demand curve is sloping downward and the supply curve is sloping upward):

(i) if the absolute slope of the demand curve exceeds that of the supply curve, disturbances lead to increased oscillation of price and quantity and explosive movement away from equilibrium;

(ii) if the absolute slope of the demand curve equals that of the supply curve, any disturbance leads to fluctuations in price and quantity of constant amplitude about the equilibrium;

(iii) if the absolute slope of the demand curve is less than that of the supply curve, the oscillations are damped and price and quantity converge to the equilibrium.

The following six figures illustrate these cases. Situations, shown in Figs 5.21, 5.23 and 5.25, correspond to the above respective cases and 5.22, 5.24, 5.26 are their corresponding time-profiles for prices, given that price is initially p_0.

Prices and Pure Competition

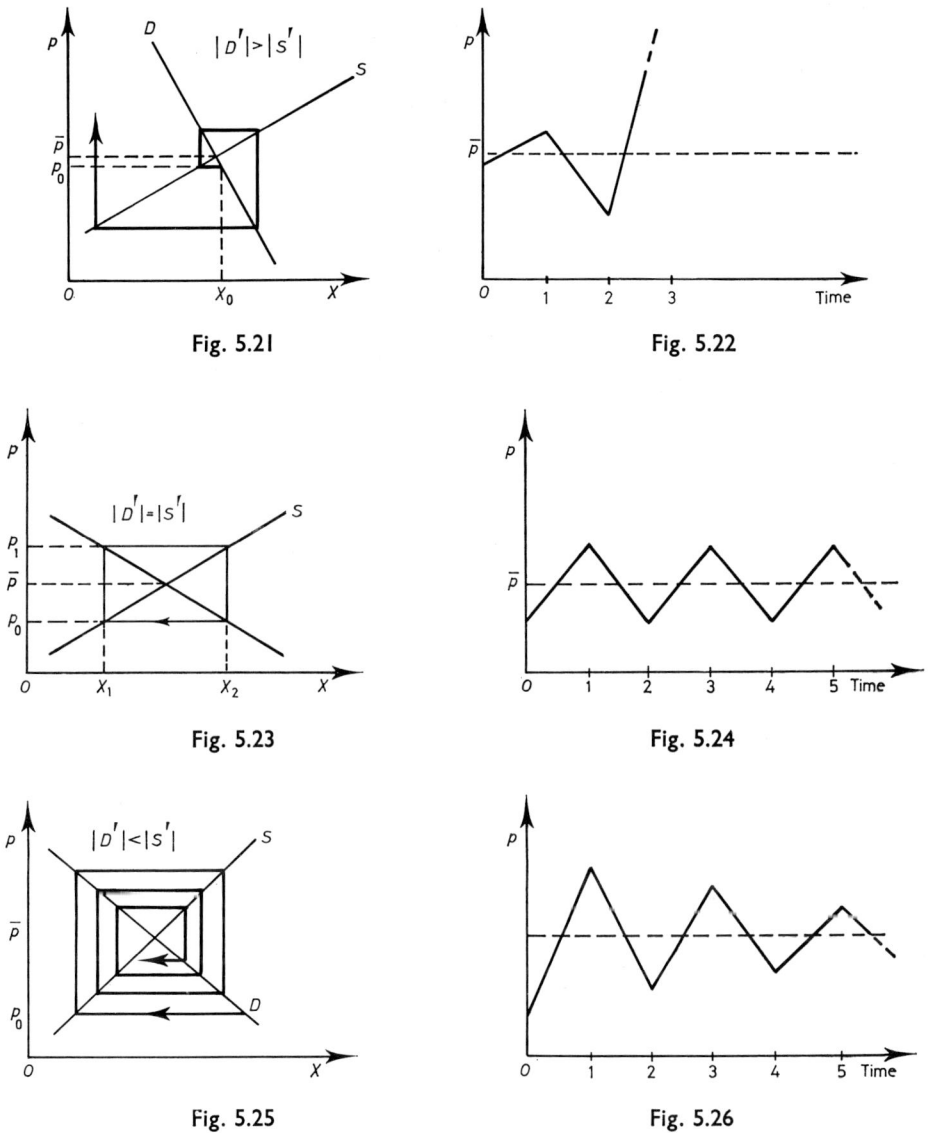

Fig. 5.21   Fig. 5.22   Fig. 5.23   Fig. 5.24   Fig. 5.25   Fig. 5.26

The oscillatory properties for the supply or output quantities are similar to those for prices, but above-equilibrium price levels correspond to below-equilibrium output levels.

The type of process can be described by considering the case shown in Fig. 5.23. Initially price is p_0. In the initial period, demand might have been lower than now shown or supplies might have been greater, for example, due to a good season. *In the absence of any shifts in the supply and demand curves*, the following pattern emerges. In period 1 suppliers supply X_1 to the market, assuming that p_0 will prevail. This quantity is below equilibrium and is cleared at a price of p_1 which is above equilibrium. In period 2 suppliers supply X_2 since they believe that the price of the product will be p_1. In fact, their expectations are not realised and a price of p_0 occurs in order to clear the excess supplies. In period 3 supplies are based upon the assumption that p_0 will prevail, but price turns out to be p_1. Producers are proven to be always wrong in their expectations and the market oscillates steadily about its equilibrium values.

Now, it might be held that if regularities of this kind occur that sellers will soon learn about them. The shrewd seller would predict p_0 when the others are predicting p_1 and vice versa. Thus the cycle may be eliminated in the end. While this is possible there are difficulties. If all or most suppliers switch their predictions, movement to equilibrium is not assured. Indeed, if this happens in one period (for the case just discussed) then the results of that period are just like the last one and all producers are wrong in their expectations. The other problem, in practice, is that supply and demand curves are shifting so that a cycle is unlikely to work itself out in a pure form. Decision-makers may find it extremely difficult to distinguish between a cyclic change and one which is due to a shift in demand and supply functions. On the whole, it seems very naïve to rule out the possibility of cycles such as those described above on the grounds that economic agents are rational.

In reality, cycles are likely to be generated in a more complex pattern than those discussed above, but before discussing this, mention ought to be made of an important point. Under Marshallian and Walrasian adjustment assumptions, markets were shown to be *stable* for normal slopes of the demand and supply curves. In the cobwebs discussed previously, the market curves are of normal slope. However, the equilibrium is stable in some circumstances and unstable in others. This underlines the point that stability cannot be analysed independently of dynamic considerations.

The above cobweb models are fairly special ones. They assume a fixed time lag and allow no variation within a period. The forecast assumptions are also fairly particular ones. The price predicted by producers for supplies of t is equal to the price of $t-1$, that is

$$p_t^* = p_{t-1} \qquad (5.23)$$

when p_t^* is the price predicted for t. Many other theories are possible, for example, predicted price may be a linear function of the actual price of τ preceding periods, that is

$$p_t^* = \lambda_1 p_{t-1} + \lambda_2 p_{t-2} + \ldots + \lambda_\tau p_{t-\tau}. \qquad (5.24)$$

Another limitation is the assumption that the expectations of producers (suppliers) are identical. Nevertheless, the simple model gives us an important starting point for speculation and application.

III. Some Applications of the Analysis

The very simple market models which have been discussed so far have many applications. Clearly, if the market accords with these models, they can be used for predictive purposes. One can, for example, trace through the effect on price of a shift of demand. A decision to expand production of the good concerned or to commence production of it might, for example, hinge on the result.

The effect of quotas and of price control is also apparent. Consider the examples given in Figs 5.27 and 5.28. If supplies are limited by quota to $X_0 < \bar{X}$, X_0 is supplied which is exactly cleared by the market at a price of p_1 which exceeds the equilibrium price. Individual suppliers will wish to expand their supplies since on an individual basis this is profitable. However, such an expansion may reduce the suppliers' profit as a group. Normally, legal restraints will be necessary to restrict supplies to the quota.

In Fig. 5.28 the effect of price control is illustrated. If transactions are only permitted at a price of $p_0 < \bar{p}$, the quantity which is demanded exceeds that which is supplied. Price does not serve its rationing function. In the absence of other means of rationing, queues may form and arbitrary methods of allocation may be used. If price is fixed by regulation at p_1 which is above the equilibrium level, suppliers wish to supply a greater quantity than that which is demanded. Secret attempts to undercut price are likely and some sellers may by chance obtain none or very little of the market sales. The interference in the market may take another form rather than the prohibition of sales at less than a price of p_1. A government authority may buy all supplies at p_1 (this is not unlike the situation which exists for many agricultural products) and sell to consumers at the same price. However, in that case its revenues will fail to cover its outlays and its losses will need to be met from general governmental revenues (for example, from taxation receipts). Furthermore, stocks of the product will build up and create a disposal problem.

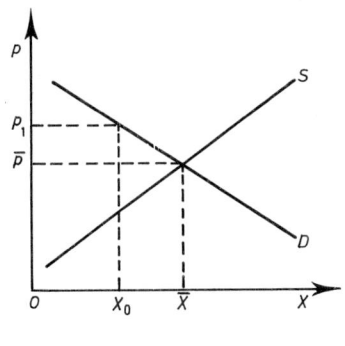

Fig. 5.27

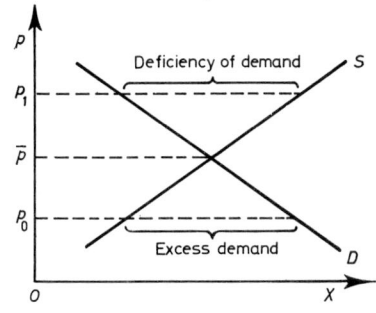

Fig. 5.28

The analysis can also be used to study the effect on government revenue, price and production of products which are subjected to a tax. Let us briefly consider the situation for a specific tax on supplies, that is, one which is of constant value per unit of supplies. If output (supplies) are shown on the X axis, the tax shifts the supply curve upward everywhere by the per unit value of the tax. If the tax per unit is $\$T$ the curve moves up by the equivalent of this amount. Supplies at a price of $p+T$ are now equivalent to those previously at a price of p. The situation is illustrated in Fig. 5.29 for a normal case.

In Fig. 5.29 the supply curve is shown to shift up from S_0 to S_1 as a result of the imposition of a tax per unit of T on the sales of X. Equilibrium price rises by $\bar{p}_1 - \bar{p}_0$ which is less than the tax per unit. This is regarded as the *incidence* of the tax on consumers. $T - (\bar{p}_1 - \bar{p}_0)$ is its incidence on producers. The equilibrium quantity falls from $\bar{X}_0$ to $\bar{X}_1$ so that the equilibrium revenue raised by the tax per unit of time is $T\bar{X}_1$. A comparative static model has been applied to the problem.

An appropriate dynamic model would be more informative. From it, we could learn about the path from one equilibrium to the other. The adjustment process may

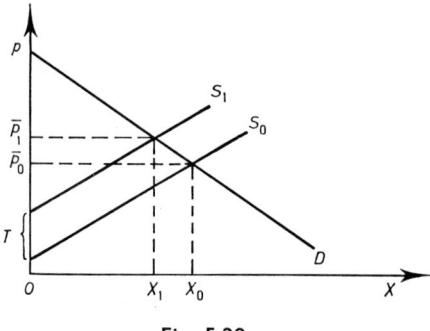

Fig. 5.29

be such that tax receipts are substantially above $T\bar{X}_1$ for a number of periods after introduction of the tax and this could be of practical importance.

The shift in the equilibrium price and quantities (in the linear case) depends on the slopes of the supply and the demand curves. The less pronounced the absolute slope of the demand or the slope of the supply curve, the less the variation in price; and the greater is the reduction in quantity as a result of the tax. The incidence of the tax also depends on slopes of the supply and demand curves. The greater is the absolute slope of the demand curve and the smaller is the slope of the supply curve, the greater is the incidence of the tax on consumers. If the demand curve is vertical or if the supply curve is horizontal the full incidence of the tax is on consumers. You might wish to illustrate this for yourself and show the position algebraically.

Subsidies can be regarded as negative taxes on transactions and can be analysed in a similar manner. The effect of a subsidy (quantity being shown on the X axis) is to shift the supply curve downwards. While comparative statics may give a lead to the effects of the subsidy, once again it may be misleading to ignore dynamics. In the short run, the costs to the government of the subsidy may be much less than in the equilibrium position.

IV. Problems Connected with Equilibrium

The common shortcomings of comparative statics have already been mentioned. Comparative statics by itself gives no guide to the stability or otherwise of equilibria and does not describe the time-paths of the variables which are being considered. In some circumstances, it is perilous to ignore these factors. This has been discussed in this and the preceding chapter.

There is, however, another point of interest. The impression is sometimes given in economics textbooks[8] that increases in mobility of factors and of general responsiveness of supplies to price variations make it more likely that markets will speedily converge towards their equilibrium values. But this is not so.

To convince oneself of this, you need only recall the simple cobweb model, which was presented earlier in the discussion of normal market curves. In that case, if stability is present, the more responsive supply is to price, the slower the convergence to equilibrium. If instability is present, the more responsive supply is to price changes, the faster the movement is away from equilibrium. Also, other things being equal, the more responsive is supply to price changes, the more likely is it that the market equilibrium is unstable.

Cobweb models for interrelated markets can also be constructed which imply a similar result. Such a model might be constructed to explain labour movements between regions or occupations depending upon wage differentials. If labour mobility or responsiveness in relation to a wage differential is excessive, the system can be unstable or may converge more slowly than otherwise to its equilibrium.

Sometimes it is contended that the knowledge of market participants can be an important determinant of the existence of, and stability of, equilibrium. Under some circumstances, knowledge of the behaviour of others leads towards an equilibrium but in still other cases it renders the outcome indeterminate. In certain purely competitive market situations, if participants are fully informed about the plans of others only the equilibrium price and quantities can prevail. But this is not true in all situations. If the supply curve cuts the demand curve from above and if planned output initially happens to be greater than its equilibrium level under Marshallian assumptions, the outcome is indeterminate in the long run. Knowledge does not suffice to make it determinate.

Von Neumann and Morgenstern have been particularly interested in the influence of knowledge on the existence of equilibrium.[9] They have shown that equilibrium is in some cases incompatible with certain knowledge about the behaviour of others. They claim that situations of this type can arise in imperfectly competitive markets especially in duopoly and oligopoly situations.

These markets will not be discussed now, but a simple example will serve to bring out their interest. Consider a situation in which two competitors are involved and imagine that the gains of one are the losses of the other. Designate these competitors as 1 and 2 and imagine that 1 has only the alternative strategies a_1 and a_2 and the only alternative strategies of 2 are β_1 or β_2. The gain and loss of the competitors depends on their joint strategy and each is assumed to aim either to maximise his gain or minimise his loss. The table below indicates a hypothetical situation which they may face. The numbers in its body represent the gain to individual 1 and the loss to 2 as a result of the joint strategy listed in the corresponding column and row. For example, 4 is the gain to 1 (the loss to 2) when 1 adopts strategy a_1 and 2 adopts strategy β_1. In the case shown (a_1, β_2) is clearly the equilibrium strategy set. Knowing

$$\begin{array}{c} & \beta_1 & \beta_2 \\ a_1 & \begin{bmatrix} 4 & & 3 \\ 1 & & 2 \end{bmatrix} & \begin{array}{c} ③ \\ 1 \end{array} \\ & 4 & ③ \end{array}$$

that his opponent has selected a strategy from the equilibrium set, a competitor can only maximise his gain (minimise his loss) by also choosing a strategy from the equilibrium set. But in the circumstances indicated in the next table no equilibrium exists in terms of the simple (unmixed) strategies which are available. For example, (a_1, β_1) cannot be stable. If competitor 2 believes that competitor 1 will adopt a_1,

$$\begin{array}{c} & \beta_1 & \beta_2 \\ a_1 & \begin{bmatrix} 4 & & 3 \\ 2 & & 5 \end{bmatrix} & \begin{array}{c} ③ \\ 2 \end{array} \\ & ④ & 5 \end{array}$$

then β_2 is optimal for competitor 2. But if 1 believes that 2 believes this, 1 should choose α_2. In turn, competitor 2 should adopt β_1 and so on. No equilibrium exists if each competitor "knows" the behaviour of the other. In situations like this von Neumann and Morgenstern have shown that equilibrium can be achieved by the individuals selecting their strategies *at random* using suitable probabilities.[10] Neither party then has advance knowledge of the actual strategy which is adopted by the other. Hence, in cases like this, some imperfection of knowledge must be created in order to achieve equilibrium or determinancy at all. How mightily different is that thought.

NOTES AND REFERENCES

[1] The effect is discussed in Ch. 6, Sec. VI.
[2] P. A. SAMUELSON, *Foundations of Economic Analysis*, Harvard University Press, Cambridge, 1963, p. 257. Reprinted by permission of Harvard University Press.
[3] See, for example, K. COHEN and R. M. CYERT, *Theory of the Firm*, Prentice-Hall, 1965, p. 54.
[4] L. WALRAS, *Elements d'économie politique pure* (1874). Translation by W. JAFFE, *Elements of Pure Economics*, Irwin, Homewood, 1954.
[5] A. MARSHALL, *Principles of Economics*, 1st ed., 1890; 8th ed., Macmillan, London, 1920.
[6] SAMUELSON, op. cit., Ch. 9 and p. 284.
[7] See, for example, SAMUELSON, op. cit., p. 264.
[8] Cf. R. HAVEMAN, *The Economics of the Public Sector*, Wiley, New York, 1970, pp. 26-7.
[9] O. MORGENSTERN, "Perfect Foresight and Economic Equilibrium", *Zeitschrift für Nationalökonomie*, 1935, **5**.
J. VON NEUMANN and O. MORGENSTERN, *Theory of Games and Economic Behavior*, 1st ed., 1943; 2nd ed., 1946, Princeton University Press, Princeton; John Wiley Science Edition, 1964. See especially Ch. 1.
[10] Op. cit., Wiley Science Edition, Ch. 3, Sec. 17.

FURTHER READING

ALLEN, R. G. D., *Mathematical Economics*, 2nd ed., Macmillan, London, 1959, Ch. 1.
ARCHIBALD, G. C. and R. G. LIPSEY, *An Introduction to A Mathematical Treatment of Economics*, Weidenfeld and Nicolson, London, 1967, Ch. 13.
COHEN, K., and R. M. CYERT, *Theory of the Firm*, Prentice-Hall, Englewood Cliffs, 1965, Ch. 4.
HANSEN, B., *Lectures in Economic Theory*, 3rd ed., Studentlitteratur, Lund, 1969, Part I, Lecture 2.
MORGENSTERN, O., "Perfect Foresight and Economic Equilibrium", *Zeitschrift für Nationalökonomie*, 1935, **5**.
RICHARDSON, G. B., "Equilibrium, Expectations and Information", *Economic Journal*, 1959, **69**, pp. 223-37.
SAMUELSON, P. A., *Foundations of Economic Analysis*, Harvard University Press, Cambridge, 1947, Chs 9 and 10.

APPENDIX TO CHAPTER 5

Elasticities of Demand and Supply

A. THE CONCEPT OF AN ELASTICITY

The concept of an elasticity was first widely employed in the physical sciences. In the 1890s, Alfred Marshall noted that the concept could be of value in economics and applied it to a number of economic problems.[1] Subsequently, the value of the concept seems to have become overrated and this has culminated in a reaction. For example, a leading economist (P. Samuelson) was to say in the 1940s,

> Not only are elasticity expressions more or less useless, but in more complicated systems they become an actual nuisance. . . .[2]

Nevertheless, the concept is of some value in generalisation since it is independent of the units of measurement. It is still widely used in economic analysis.

In general, an elasticity measures the responsiveness of one variable to changes in another variable. But most significantly it concentrates on *proportional* changes. The elasticity of one variable with respect to another is the proportional change in the former as a result of a proportional change in the latter divided by the latter's proportional change. If

$$x = f(p), \quad (A5.1)$$

the elasticity of x with respect to p, where ϵ represents this elasticity, is

$$\epsilon = \frac{\frac{dx}{x}}{\frac{dp}{p}} = \frac{p}{x}\frac{dx}{dp} \quad (A5.2)$$

$$= \frac{d(\log x)}{d(\log p)}. \quad (A5.3)$$

It is not the absolute change, $\frac{dx}{dp}$, but the *proportional* change. In consequence, the elasticity of a function is independent of the units in which the variables are measured. Therefore, theorems based upon elasticities can be given very diverse applications.

B. THE OWN PRICE ELASTICITY OF DEMAND FOR A COMMODITY

The own price elasticity of demand for a commodity measures the response in proportionate terms of the quantity demanded of the commodity for a proportionate change of its price, all other things being constant. As we shall show later, a firm's or an industry's total revenue or income is related to this elasticity. Knowing this elasticity, one can predict whether an increase in price or a decrease in quantity supplied to a market will increase or decrease revenue.

But let us return to the measurement of this elasticity. If we take any particular commodity, X, its own price elasticity is

$$\epsilon = \frac{\text{proportional change in the amount of } X \text{ demanded}}{\text{proportional change in the commodity's price}}$$

where all other things, bar the change of the commodity's price, are constant. Clearly, the demand curve can be tied in with this definition.

Let

$$p = f(X) \qquad (A5.4)$$

represent the demand curve for the commodity where p is its price and X is the quantity demanded of it. The elasticity of demand for X with respect to the commodity's price is

$$\epsilon = \frac{\frac{dX}{X}}{\frac{dp}{p}} = \frac{dX}{dp} \cdot \frac{p}{X} \qquad (A5.5)$$

$$= \frac{dX}{dp} \cdot \frac{p}{g(p)} \qquad (A5.6)$$

where $g(p)$ is the inverse of Equation (A5.4). This formula gives the elasticity for any particular value of p. In any specific instance, the elasticity can be evaluated by algebraic or geometrical means.

Take an algebraic example first. Imagine that $g(p)$ is a linear expression,

$$X = a - bp. \qquad (A5.7)$$

The quantity demanded is a linear and declining function of price. Applying the formula of Equation (A5.6), we see that

$$\epsilon = -b \cdot \frac{p}{X}$$

$$= -b \cdot \frac{p}{a - bp} \qquad (A5.8)$$

and the elasticity depends on p. Take a special case of Equation (A5.7), namely

$$X = 10 - 0.5p. \qquad (A5.9)$$

Then,

$$\epsilon = -0.5 \frac{p}{10 - 0.5p}. \qquad (A5.10)$$

The elasticity varies with p as the following table indicates. The table shows the elasticities which correspond to selected values of p.

p	ϵ
20	$-\infty$
15	-3
10	-1
5	-0.33
0	0

Elasticities of Demand and Supply

The demand curve which corresponds to Equation (A5.9) is graphed in Fig. A5.1 and the selected point elasticities are indicated. Note that the elasticity of demand varies along this curve. The elasticity is greatest absolutely when prices are highest. If the absolute elasticity is greater than 1, demand is said to be elastic; if equal to 1, it is said to be of unitary elasticity; and if less than 1, it is described as inelastic.

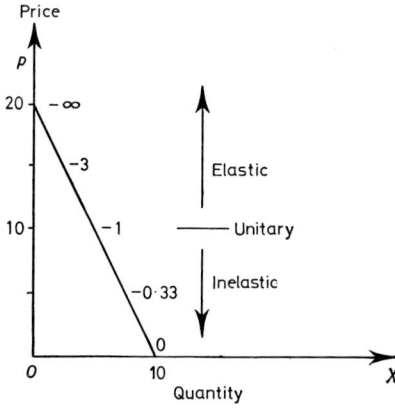

Fig. A5.1

Although the slope or rate of change of this demand curve is constant, its elasticity is not. While we might normally expect the elasticity to vary along a demand curve, there are some curves for which this is not so.

If the demand curve is of the form

$$X = ap^\beta \tag{A5.11}$$

where a and β are parameters, the price elasticity of X is a constant equal to β. Usually we expect β to be negative for a demand curve. The easiest way to see that the elasticity must be a constant equal to β is to rewrite Equation (A5.11) in terms of logarithms. We obtain

$$\log X = \log a + \beta \log p. \tag{A5.12}$$

Hence,

$$\epsilon = \frac{d(\log X)}{d(\log p)} = \beta \tag{A5.13}$$

which is independent of p. If $\beta = -1$, we have the interesting special case where the demand curve is a rectangular hyperbole. Total revenue is constant no matter what price is asked. This must be so, since by substituting $\beta = -1$ into Equation (A5.11) and rearranging it,

$$pX = a. \tag{A5.14}$$

Besides the algebraic approach to evaluation of a demand elasticity there is also a geometric approach which deserves brief mention. Take the linear demand curve EC shown in Fig. A5.2 and suppose that we wish to find its elasticity at any point, K. Drop a perpendicular from K to meet the X axis in B. The own price elasticity of the function at point K can then be shown to be equal to $-\frac{BC}{OB}$.

Proof:

$$\epsilon = \frac{dX}{dp} \cdot \frac{p}{X} = 1 / \frac{dp}{dX} \cdot \frac{p}{X} \qquad (A5.15)$$

$$= 1 / -\frac{BK}{BC} \times \frac{BK}{OB}$$

$$= -\frac{BC}{BK} \times \frac{BK}{OB}$$

$$= -\frac{BC}{OB}.$$

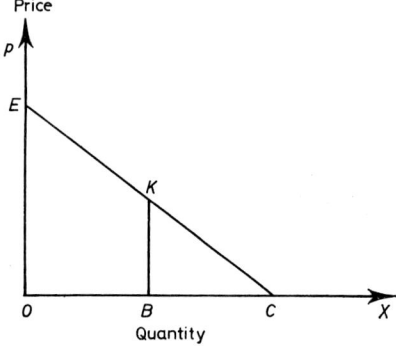

Fig. A5.2

If the demand function is not linear and we wish to find its elasticity at a point K on the curve geometrically, we draw a tangent to the curve at K. Let the tangent cut the X and Y axes at C and E respectively. Drop a perpendicular from K to meet the X axis in B. The elasticity of the demand function at the point K is equal to $-\frac{BC}{OB}$. This is illustrated for the demand curve shown in Fig. A5.3. The proof is straightforward. Indeed, the previous proof also applies here.

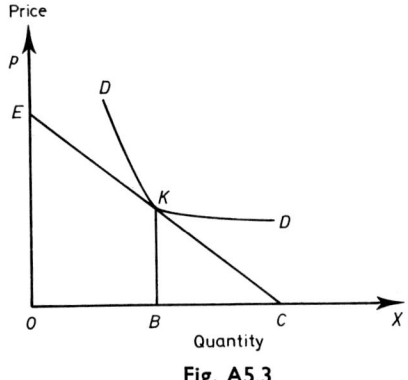

Fig. A5.3

There is a very important *relationship between the effect of a price change on total revenue and the elasticity of demand.* Total revenue (to a firm or an industry) equals

Elasticities of Demand and Supply

the total quantity of a commodity which is sold times the price per unit of the sales. If R represents total revenue, X the quantity of sales and p the price per unit of these,

$$R = pX. \tag{A5.16}$$

If the demand function is

$$X = g(p), \tag{A5.17}$$

this can be more fully expressed as

$$R = pg(p). \tag{A5.18}$$

The firm or industry may wish to know if its total revenue will increase when the price of its commodity is increased. A knowledge of the elasticity of demand at the current price can help in answering this query. Briefly, a (small) price increase raises total revenue if demand is inelastic, lowers it if demand is elastic and leaves it unchanged if demand is of unitary elasticity.

Proof:

The product differentiation rule may be used to differentiate

$$R = pX = pg(p)$$

with respect to price. The change of total revenue for a change of price is

$$\frac{dR}{dp} = p\frac{dX}{dp} + X. \tag{A5.19}$$

Equation (A5.19) can be re-expressed as

$$\frac{dR}{dp} = X\left(\frac{p}{X}\frac{dX}{dp} + 1\right) \tag{A5.20}$$

$$= X(\epsilon + 1). \tag{A5.21}$$

If the demand curve is of normal slope, ϵ is non-positive. Given that $\epsilon \leq 0$,

$$\frac{dR}{dp} \gtreqless 0$$

can be expressed accordingly as

$$|\epsilon| \lesseqgtr 1.$$

If the absolute elasticity of demand is less than unity (if demand is inelastic), an increase in price increases total revenue. If it is of unitary elasticity, an increase of price leaves total revenue unchanged. If the demand is elastic, an increase of price reduces total revenue. Letting η represent the absolute elasticity, $|\epsilon|$, our findings can be set out in the following table.

Table A5.1

η value	Nature of demand	$\frac{dR}{dp}$	Change of total revenue as a result of a price increase
$\eta < 1$	Inelastic	> 0	Increases
$\eta = 1$	Unitary	$= 0$	Unchanged
$\eta > 1$	Elastic	< 0	Decreases

Going back to Fig. A5.1, we note that, if price is less than 10, a small price increase raises total revenue, but, if price is above 10, a price increase reduces total revenue. Normally, if the demand curve is linear, demand is elastic at "high" prices and inelastic at low ones. One may be tempted to think that this is a general rule for all demand curves.

It clearly is not. Take the case quoted in Equation (A5.11). The elasticity of demand is in no way affected by the price. If $\beta = -1$, variations of price cannot be effective as means to increase revenue. This is the rectangular hyperbole case.

The formula which is given above measures elasticity at a point, and makes use of the differential calculus. There are also elasticity measures which take discrete changes into account.[3]

Textbooks traditionally list a number of *factors which are likely to influence the own price elasticity of demand for a product*. One standard text[4] suggests that the demand for a product tends to be more elastic

(i) the closer are the available substitutes, that is the more easily other products can be substituted for it or contain more closely its properties. Thus aluminium can be substituted for copper in some uses and for steel in others. Both the demand for copper and steel are more elastic as a result.

Demand is also said to be more elastic

(ii) the greater is the range of uses for the product,
(iii) the higher is the proportion of income spent on it, and
(iv) the higher is its price.

Yet the result which is supposed to follow from factors (ii) to (iv) is by no means assured. If the increased range of uses does not duplicate that of any other product, demand need not become more elastic. Certainly, as we have noted previously, demand need not be elastic at high prices. [Consider, for example, Equation (A5.11).]

C. CROSS-ELASTICITY OF DEMAND

It is known that the demand for most products depends not only on their own price but also, at least, on the price of related goods. Thus the demand for butter clearly depends not only on the price of butter but also on the price of margarine and similar products. It would be useful to have some indicator of the responsiveness of the demand for butter to variations in margarine prices. This type of interdependence and its measure is also of vital interest for many other products.

The concept of the cross-elasticity of demand is considered to be of value in this respect. It measures the *relative* change in the demanded quantity of one product for a relative change in the price of another. The cross-elasticity of demand for a product, say 1, with respect to changes in the price of another, say 2, is the percentage change in the quantity demanded of 1 divided by the percentage change in the price of 2.

To be more precise, imagine that the demand for commodity 1, X_1, is a function only of its price and that of the other commodity, all other factors being kept constant. Further, imagine this to be so also for commodity 2, X_2. The demand functions might be respectively expressed as

$$X_1 = f_1(p_1, p_2) \quad \text{(A5.22)}$$

and

$$X_2 = f_2(p_1, p_2). \quad \text{(A5.23)}$$

Elasticities of Demand and Supply

The cross-elasticity of demand for commodity 1 with respect to the price of commodity 2 can be expressed as

$$\theta_{12} = \frac{\text{Relative change in the demanded quantity of 1}}{\text{Relative change in the price of 2}}$$

$$= \frac{\partial X_1/X_1}{\partial p_2/p_2} = \frac{\partial X_1}{\partial p_2} \cdot \frac{p_2}{X_1} \qquad (A5.24)$$

Similarly, the cross-elasticity of demand for commodity 2, with respect to the price of 1, is

$$\theta_{21} = \frac{\partial X_2}{\partial p_1} \cdot \frac{p_1}{X_2} \qquad (A5.25)$$

Incidentally, we could build up a table (matrix) of elasticities for this case, as shown below. The term θ_{11} represents the own price elasticity for commodity 1, and θ_{22}

$$\begin{bmatrix} \theta_{11} & \theta_{21} \\ \theta_{12} & \theta_{22} \end{bmatrix}$$

represents that for commodity 2.

Cross-elasticities have been used to indicate the substitutability and complementarity of goods. It is commonly accepted that products are substitutes if their cross-elasticities are positive, and complements if these are negative. Thus we might expect lamb and beef as substitutes to have positive cross-elasticities. A rise in beef prices, other things being equal, might be expected to raise the consumption of mutton. On the other hand, if we take pipe-tobacco and pipes (complements), a rise in pipe-tobacco prices, other things being equal, might be expected to lead to a fall in the demand for pipes.

Yet we can run into difficulties with this approach because of the income effect.[5] Manufacturing beef (burger-mince) is to some extent a substitute for better cuts of steak. On the definition given above, we might expect a fall in the price of manufacturing beef (other prices and things being constant) to lead to an increased consumption of this type of beef. But, if manufacturing beef is an inferior product, the consumer may take advantage of his increase in real income (which results from the price fall) to reduce somewhat his expenditure on this type of beef and increase his consumption of the better cuts.

The cross-elasticity notion has been rather half-heartedly suggested as a means for defining the limits or boundaries of an industry.[6] The naïve view is that, if goods have high cross-elasticities, then they belong to the same industry; if not, they belong to different industries. The concept is of little value in this respect. We might note the following problems:

(i) how high must the cross-elasticities be before goods belong to the same industry?

(ii) cross-elasticity chains may be formed by products with no natural gaps; and

(iii) the emphasis is solely on the demand side but, if goods are closely related in production, we may sometimes wish to treat them as being in the same industry.

D. SUPPLY ELASTICITIES

On the supply side, there are elasticities which correspond to all those which have been mentioned on the demand side. The own elasticity of supply of a product indicates the relative increase of its supply for a relative increase in its price, other things being constant. It might be represented by

$$\eta_s = \frac{\text{relative change in quantity supplied}}{\text{relative change in the product's price}}.$$

Algebraically, where X is the quantity supplied,

$$\eta_s = \frac{p}{X} \cdot \frac{dX}{dp} \tag{A5.26}$$

where $\frac{dX}{dp}$ is the slope of the supply curve and, if the supply function is known, the elasticity is easily found by algebraic means. It can also be found by geometric means.

Take the linear supply curve CS which is shown in Fig. A5.4. To find its elasticity at any point, B, drop a perpendicular from that point to meet the X axis in a point A. From the point at which the supply curve cuts the Y axis (C) draw a horizontal line which cuts AB in K. The supply elasticity at the point B is then equal to AB/BK.

Proof:

Substituting in Equation (A5.26),

$$\eta_s = \frac{AB}{OA} \times \frac{CK}{BK}$$

$$= \frac{OA}{BK} \times \frac{AB}{OA}$$

$$= \frac{AB}{BK}.$$

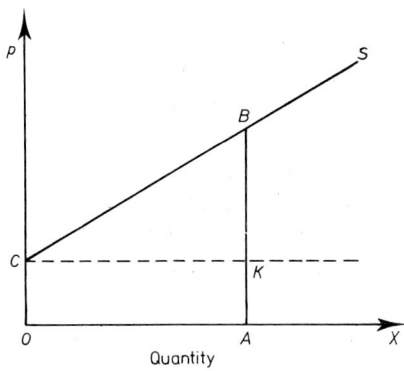

Fig. A5.4

In the case shown, $\frac{AB}{BK} > 1$, so the supply situation is elastic. Indeed, this is true for all points on a linear supply curve, if it intersects the positive part of the Y axis.

If such a curve passes through the origin, the points exhibit unitary elasticity and, if its intercept with the Y axis is negative, its points exhibit inelasticity.

If the supply curve is not linear and one wishes to find the elasticity of a point, B, on it, construct a tangent through B to cut the Y axis in C. Drop a perpendicular from B to cut the X axis in A and draw a line from C at right-angles to AB to cut AB in K. The elasticity of the supply curve at point B is equal to $\dfrac{AB}{BK}$.

Cross-elasticities of supply are analogous to those for demand. The reader should have no difficulty in deriving the corresponding formulas.

NOTES AND REFERENCES

[1] ALFRED MARSHALL, *Principles of Economics*, 1st ed., 1890; 8th ed., Macmillan, London, 1920.
[2] P. A. SAMUELSON, *Foundations of Economic Analysis*, Harvard University Press, Cambridge, 1947, p. 126.
[3] The interested reader is referred to G. J. STIGLER, *The Theory of Price*, Revised ed., The Macmillan Company, New York, 1952, pp. 35-6.
[4] R. H. LEFTWICH, *The Price System and Resource Allocation*, 3rd ed., Holt, Rinehart and Winston, New York, 1966, p. 41.
[5] See J. M. KUHLMAN and R. G. THOMPSON, "Substitution and Value of Elasticities", *American Economic Review*, 1965, **55**, pp. 506-10. Reprinted in D. KAMERSCHEN, *Readings in Microeconomics*, John Wiley, New York, 1969.
[6] R. TRIFFIN, *Monopolistic Competition and General Equilibrium Theory*, Harvard University Press, 1941, Ch. 3.

FURTHER READING

ALLEN, R. G. D., *Mathematical Analysis for Economists*, Macmillan, London, 1938, pp. 254-60.
MARSHALL, A., *Principles of Economics*, 8th ed., Macmillan, London, 1920, Book III, Ch. 4, and Book V, Chs 1-3.
ROBINSON, JOAN, *Economics of Imperfect Competition*, 1st ed., 1933; 2nd ed., 1969, Macmillan, London, Ch. 2.
SAMUELSON, P., *Foundations of Economic Analysis*, Harvard University Press, Cambridge, 1947, pp. 125-9.
STIGLER, G. J., *The Theory of Price*, Revised ed., The Macmillan Company, New York, 1952, Ch. 3, Sec. III; and Ch. 4.
STONIER, A. W. and D. C. HAGUE, *A Textbook of Economic Theory*, 2nd ed., Longmans, London, 1957, Ch. 1.
TRIFFIN, R., *Monopolistic Competition and General Equilibrium Theory*, Harvard University Press, 1941, Ch. 3.

CHAPTER 6

The Theory of Consumption

I. Introduction

Market demand and supply curves result from individual choices by numerous consumers and producers and so the choices of individuals have important implications for the nature of market demand and supply curves. By studying the behaviour of individual economic units, while at the same time abstracting from any idiosyncrasies of isolated units, it is possible to draw valuable inferences about the characteristics of market demand and supply curves; and to have the satisfaction of isolating the components which together make up the market curves. In this chapter, the relationship between the demand curves of individuals and those for the market are explored, and the corresponding exercise for supply curves is worked through in the next chapter.

In the last century, several economic theories of consumption have been advanced. By the end of the nineteenth century, Jevons,[1] Walras[2] and Marshall[3] and economists of the Austrian School[4] developed a rigorous theory which supposes that consumers obtain utility (satisfaction) from the consumption of different quantities of goods and that this utility can be measured cardinally. The demand of any consumer for a commodity results from his maximisation of his utility, subject to the restraints imposed by his limited income and by market prices. This theory, however, was soon attacked. Pareto,[5] Slutsky,[6] Allen[7] and Hicks[8] rejected the earlier assumption about measurable utility. In their view, the earlier postulate was empirically unwarranted and also unnecessary. Not only is it impossible to measure by how much an individual prefers one combination of commodities to another, but it is also unnecessary for the construction of a fruitful theory of demand. As these economists have shown, an adequate theory of demand can be based upon the mere preference rankings by individuals of their alternative consumption possibilities. It is merely necessary to know whether any combination is preferred to, is indifferent to, or is less preferred than, any other combination of commodities. On the basis of this consideration a preference field can be constructed for the consumer and his choice of commodities, given the constraints posed by his income and by market prices, can be predicted. But how does one obtain knowledge about an individual's preference ordering of his alternative consumption bundles? Does one infer the preference ordering from introspection? Or, does one seek a statement from the individual about his preferences or ought one try to infer the individual's preferences from his observed behaviour? All approaches have been tried and all have their shortcomings. The last approach has been explored comparatively recently by Samuelson[9] and Hicks[10] in their revealed preference theory of demand.

Theory of Consumption

Other significant developments have also occurred. Von Neumann and Morgenstern have introduced a measurable utility concept which is applicable to the choice of risky alternatives.[11] Lancaster[12] and others have analysed demand not in terms of the desire for products as such but in terms of desire for their inherent characteristics or qualities. These theories ought to make it easier to predict the demand for new or potential products. Finally, earlier presentations of the theory of demand were limited by the available, and generally accepted, mathematical techniques. With the extension of knowledge about mathematical techniques, the theory of demand has been widened to take account of a greater range of possibilities, for example, by Debreu.[13] This chapter and its appendix outlines these developments and the earlier theories. In the discussion, it is contended that one of the serious shortcomings of accepted theory is its failure to take adequate account of social influences on demand.

II. Neo-Classical Marginal Utility Theory

Neo-classical demand theory is based on the premise that different quantities of goods yield varying quantities of utility (satisfaction) to any consumer. It is imagined that for any period of time in which the consumer's tastes are constant, the preference of the consumer can be represented by a cardinal utility measure which is a continuous and differentiable function of the quantities consumed. This requires the goods to be variable in extremely small quantities. Wheat and water would satisfy the assumption well but houses, for example, involve some "lumpiness" and may not satisfy it. Again, the utility function is supposed to be defined for all alternative combinations of products.

The consumer's objective is to maximise his utility from consumption. In pursuing this objective, however, he is constrained by his available resources and the market prices of commodities. For simplicity, it will be assumed that an individual's sole resource, during the period under consideration, is his (given) income. The neo-classical theory can then be stated as follows:

Assume that n products are available for consumption and let x_i represent an individual's consumption of the ith commodity where $i = 1, \ldots, n$. The individual aims to maximise his utility, U, which can be represented by the cardinal utility function

$$U = U(x_1, x_2, \ldots, x_n). \tag{6.1}$$

But the individual is not free to vary his consumption of products just as he pleases. He is limited in his possibilities by his available income and by the terms on which he can exchange it for products (that is by market prices). If perfect competition prevails, as neo-classicists assumed, the prices of the products are independent of the individual's consumption. Represent these market prices by $p_i(i = 1, \ldots, n)$ where p_i is the price of the ith good, and let M represent the consumer's money income for the period being considered. In the absence of borrowing, the individual's total expenditure during the period cannot exceed his total money income. Neo-classicists also reasoned that his optimal expenditure would not be less than total income since they ruled out the likelihood that an individual might, within the bounds of his limited income, be satiated by all goods. (For qualifications, see Chapter 16.) Thus the effective restraint is

$$\sum_{i=1}^{n} p_i x_i = M. \tag{6.2}$$

The problem then becomes one of maximising utility (function 6.1) subject to the expenditure of total income (function 6.2).

The nature of the solution depends upon the general properties of consumers' utility functions. Neo-classical economists considered these functions to be continuous, to be at least twice differentiable and, for practical purposes, to be strictly concave and monotonically increasing. Consequently, any critical value of the above constrained problem (any combination of products which satisfy the first order conditions for a maximum of utility subject to the constraint) yields a global maximum of utility. The second order conditions for a maximum are automatically satisfied whenever the first order conditions (conditions for a stationary point) are satisfied. Furthermore, the linearity of the constraint in conjunction with the strict concavity of the utility function ensures that the constrained critical value of the utility function occurs for only one combination of products. For any individual, with given tastes and a given income, his consumption choice can be predicted uniquely once market prices are given.

Before giving the principles which can be used to determine an individual's consumption-choice, it may be appropriate to mention the law of diminishing marginal utility. This law, which has been widely regarded as an important one for neo-classical demand theory, is implied by the strict concavity of the utility function. However, diminishing marginal utility does not imply that the consumer's utility function is strictly concave. In consequence, the significance of the law of diminishing marginal utility has been exaggerated and the assumption is certainly not required to ensure (nor does it ensure) that demand curves slope downwards. Unfortunately, a few texts suggest otherwise. The law of diminishing marginal utility states that if an individual's consumption of all other goods remains constant, his utility increases with his increased consumption of any good but at a diminishing rate. Mathematically, this amounts to

$$\frac{\partial U}{\partial x_i} > 0 \qquad (i = 1, \ldots, n)$$

for $0 < x_i$ and

$$\frac{\partial^2 U}{\partial x^2_i} < 0 \qquad (i = 1, \ldots, n).$$

The total utility function for any product, the consumption of others given, is a monotonically increasing and concave function. The marginal utility curve which indicates an individual's additional utility from an additional unit of the product (consumption of other goods being constant) is downward-sloping and non-negative in value. Total utility and marginal utility curves which meet this description are shown in Figs 6.1 and 6.2 respectively for product 1. Where the consumption of all goods, 2, ..., n, is fixed at levels $\bar{x}_i$, the utility function of Fig. 6.1 is $U(x_1, \bar{x}_2, \ldots, \bar{x}_n)$ which can be expressed just as a function of x_1.

Neo-classical economists were, of course, aware that functions such as $U(x_1, \bar{x}_2, \ldots, \bar{x}_n)$ might be monotonically decreasing for large values of x_1. Consumption of any product, beyond a point, might yield negative marginal utility. However, this

Theory of Consumption

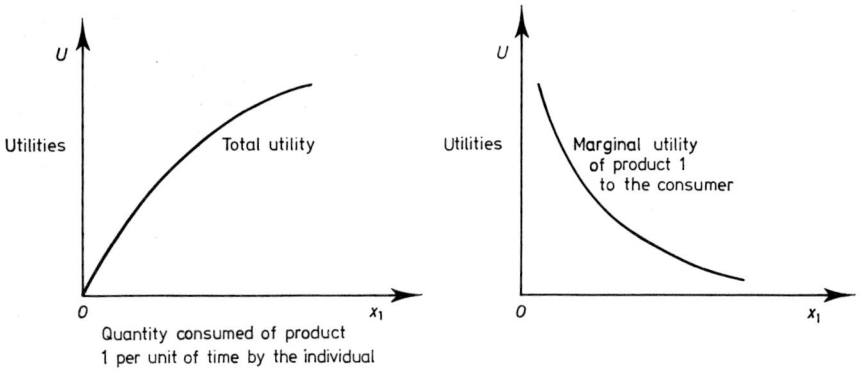

Fig. 6.1 Fig. 6.2

was felt to be inconsequential for theory since no individual, given his income limitations, was likely to become satiated by any product. Furthermore, convexity in part of the utility function was envisaged as a possibility, for example, by Marshall. At very low levels of consumption of a product, increasing marginal utility may occur. Marshall assumed that this would rapidly give way to diminishing marginal utility and be of no consequence. Thus the assumptions mentioned above were the effective ones. Ruling out the possibility of corner-point solutions (the possibility that it may be optimal to consume none of one or more commodities), neo-classical economists had only to find the necessary conditions (first-order conditions) for a maximum of an individual's utility function subject to his constraints to predict his demand for products. Let us derive their necessary conditions.

The necessary condition for a maximum of the utility function of Equation (6.1) subject to the income restriction of (6.2) can be found by using Lagrange's mathematical method. If perfect competition exists in the goods market, prices are independent of purchases by individual consumers and so the prices of Equation (6.2) are constants. Consequently, since the appropriate second-order conditions are ensured by the neo-classical assumptions about strict concavity of the utility function and non-satiety is supposed, the maximum feasible value of utility occurs for purchases of the various goods which ensure that

$$\frac{\frac{\partial U}{\partial x_1}}{p_1} = \frac{\frac{\partial U}{\partial x_2}}{p_2} = \ldots = \frac{\frac{\partial U}{\partial x_n}}{p_n} = \lambda \tag{6.3}$$

and that Equation (6.2) is satisfied. λ is an undetermined multiplier which in this case equals the common marginal utility of the last cent of expenditure on each good. Less formally, the consumer is in equilibrium and has allocated his income optimality if he just disposes of his total income and allocates it to ensure that

$$\frac{MU \text{ of product 1}}{p_1} = \frac{MU \text{ of product 2}}{p_2} = \ldots = \frac{MU \text{ of product } n}{p_n}. \tag{6.4}$$

This condition implies that the utility derived from the expenditure of the *last* cent on any one product must be the same as the utility derived from the expenditure of the *last* cent on any other. The marginal utilities of expenditures on the various goods (not the marginal utilities from consumption of the goods) must be equal if the consumer is to be in equilibrium.

This is easily illustrated for a case where only two products are available and the utility derived from any one product depends only on the individual's consumption of that product. In this separable utility case and assuming given prices, the marginal utility of expenditure on product 1 and 2 might be as shown in Figs 6.3 and 6.4, respectively. With an income of $O_1A + O_2B$, it is optimal to allocate O_1A to product 1 and O_2B to product 2, for then the marginal utility of expenditure on the two products is equal. If, for example, AA' less of income is allocated to 1 and $BB' = AA'$ extra is allocated to 2, total utility clearly falls. It falls by the difference between the dotted figure and the hatched one.

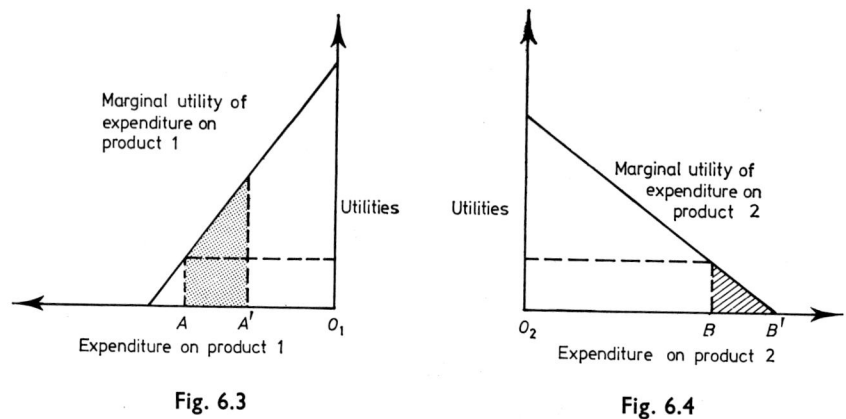

Fig. 6.3   Fig. 6.4

Given the consumer's optimising behaviour, we can enquire into the effect upon consumption of variations in different parameters. Assuming given tastes which, of course, imply that there is no variation of the consumer's utility function, we may consider the effect upon the quantity demanded of a commodity if its price rises while all other prices and income are constant, or the effect if the consumer's income rises and prices remain constant. These effects are least confusingly analysed by means of indifference curves. The use of such curves does not require one to abandon the assumption of cardinal utility. These curves can be regarded, if one retains the cardinality assumption, as contours of the utility function. Since indifference curves are introduced in the next section and the above relationships are explored later, let us consider the next approach.

III. The Indifference Curve (Ordinal) Approach of Hicks and Allen

The assumption of cardinal utility has been rejected by Pareto,[14] Slutsky,[15] Allen and Hicks[16] as a suitable basis for demand theory. In their opinion, the assumption lacks any empirical foundation and is not needed to construct a satisfactory theory of demand. As they have shown, an adequate theory of demand can be constructed by merely considering the preference orderings which individuals have for their alternative consumption possibilities.

The ordinal approach to demand theory of Hicks and Allen is broadly outlined in this section. While their theory is more general than the cardinal neo-classical utility

Theory of Consumption

theory, it is nevertheless a particular theory for, amongst other things, it assumes that the preference orderings of consumers possess special properties. Whether or not these limitations are justifiable will be examined later. But we might note now that economists, such as Debreu, have relaxed the assumptions of Hicks and Allen.

A. ORDERINGS AND INDIFFERENCE CURVES

In the theory of consumer's choice, as in many theories of rational choice, two main components are involved. These are a preference ordering of alternative possible choices and an attainable region of alternative choices. Together these determine the optimal feasible choice. In order to predict the behaviour of consumers one needs to specify their preference rankings of alternative commodity bundles and their set of attainable bundles. The consumer is assumed to purchase the consumption bundle which is his preferred one of the attainable set.

Hicks[17] assumes that the consumer's preference ordering of the possible consumption bundles is a *weak* ordering which is transitive and complete (universal). As opposed to a strong ordering a weak ordering allows the individual to be indifferent about alternatives. Given any two alternative consumption possibilities, the consumer either prefers one to the other or is indifferent about them. Completeness or universality implies that there are no possible consumption alternatives for which the consumer cannot decide whether he prefers one to the other or is indifferent about them. Transitivity introduces a consistency requirement. Let A, B, C, represent alternative bundles of goods and let ">" indicate "preferred to" and "=" indicate "indifference". Then, if

$$A > B > C$$
or if
$$A = B > C$$
or if
$$A > B = C$$

transitivity requires that $A > C$. If any consumer indicates that he prefers A to B and prefers B to C, the theory assumes that he will be consistent and express a preference for A rather than C, if A and C are presented to him as alternatives.

Other assumptions are also employed by Hicks:

(i) No individual is indifferent between any two alternative consumption bundles, A and B, if A consists of more of some goods than B and no less of any.

(ii) Indeed, Hicks goes further. He supposes that combination A will always be preferred. A combination of commodities which consists of more of some goods than another and no less of any is preferred. This implies that the individual cannot be satiated by any product. (This hypothesis can be made more acceptable by treating savings as a product.)

(iii) The preference ordering of the consumer of his alternative combinations of commodities can be represented by one of a number of possible functions, which is continuous and differentiable. The order of preference is indicated by the value of the function. It is merely necessary that any combination which is preferred to another be indicated by a higher value of the function and those of indifference be shown by equal values of it. In the simple case when only one product is variable and greater quantities of it are preferred, any function which increases with increased quantities of the product indicates the correct order of preference.

(iv) The consumer's preference ordering is dependent only on his own consumption of commodities. It is not influenced by the consumption of others.

(v) Product-combinations about which the consumer is indifferent, that is any indifference curve of his, form a convex function (usually a *strictly* convex function) of the quantities of the products. Normally, these indifference curves are continuous and differentiable.

The meaning and implications of these axioms can best be appreciated by limiting choice to two products. However, the analysis has analogous implications no matter how many products are involved.

Imagine that a hypothetical consumer's choice is limited to two products, 1 and 2. Represent his possible quantities of consumption of these in a given period of time by x_1 and x_2 respectively and suppose that his tastes are unchanged over the period. Those combinations of product 1 and 2 which are as equally desired by the consumer as some particular combination can be shown by an indifference curve. For example, the indifference curve, I_0I_0, shown in Fig. 6.5, links the combinations of product 1 and 2 which in the hypothetical consumer's estimation are just as desirable as a combination of three units of product 1 and two units of product 2, and no more desirable. In the case shown, the consumer is indifferent between (three units of product 1 and two units of product 2) and (five units of product 1 and one unit of product 2).

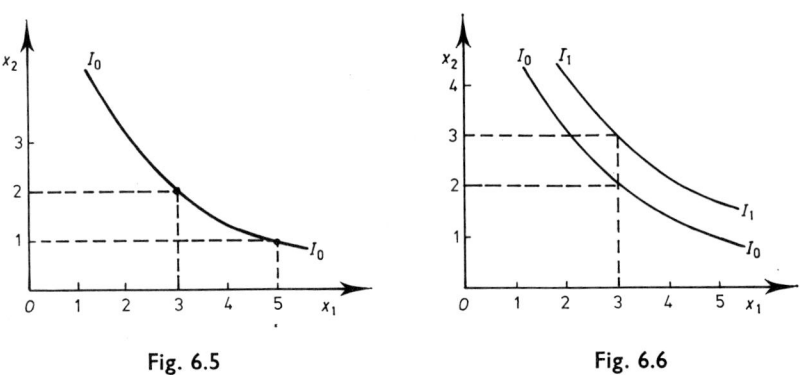

Fig. 6.5　　　　　　　　　　Fig. 6.6

An infinite number of different indifference curves exist. Every combination which involves more of one product and no less of the other is preferred and is on a higher indifference curve than its alternative. The combination (3, 3) indicated in Fig. 6.6 is preferred to (2, 3) and is on a higher indifference curve I_1I_1. All combinations along I_1I_1 are preferred to those on I_0I_0. In general, the above assumptions imply that the further is movement in Fig. 6.6 in a north-easterly direction the more preferable is the combination encountered.

Having introduced the concept of the indifference curve, it is possible to be more explicit about the *properties of indifference* curves which are implied by the above suppositions.

(a) Supposition (i) above implies that indifference curves are *without thickness* and

Theory of Consumption

do not intersect. It is easy to see that this is so. If indifference sets have thickness or cross the supposition is not satisfied. In Fig. 6.7 an indifference region is indicated by the thick cross-hatched area. But such an area indicates that the consumer is indifferent between combinations such as A and B. Since B involves more of both products than A, supposition (i) is contradicted. In Fig. 6.8, two indifference curves are shown as crossing. But if this is so the consumer must be indifferent about combinations such as A and B, even though B involves more of both goods, and indifferent about combinations C and D even though C involves less of both goods. This would contradict assumption (i).

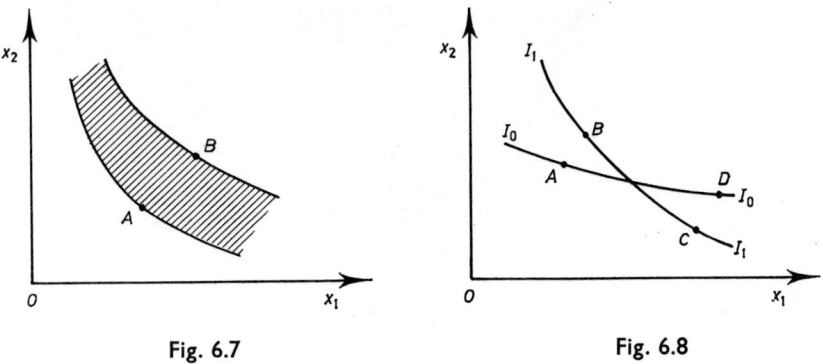

Fig. 6.7　　　　　　　　　　　Fig. 6.8

(b) Supposition (ii) implies that a consumer cannot be satiated by any product. Hence, it is inferred that higher indifference curves correspond to preferred combinations *and* indifference curves slope downwards. Take any ray (vector) of zero to 90° slope. Combinations further out along it (moving NE. rather than SW.) are preferred and are on higher indifference curves. In Fig. 6.9 this is true of combinations along OC, AB and AD for example. Movements outward along these vectors involve more of at least one product and no less of another. In Fig. 6.10, three indifference curves which do not slope downwards are shown. All imply that the individual is indifferent about more of at least one product and no less of the other and thus contradict supposition (ii). For example, taking I_0I_0, the individual is indifferent about (x_1^*, x_2^*) and $(\bar{x}_1, x_2^*)$ even though a greater quantity of product 1 is available in the latter case.

(c) Supposition (iii) ensures that an indifference curve corresponds to every possible combination of goods.

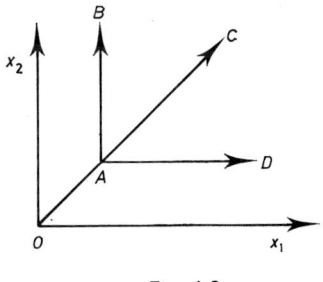 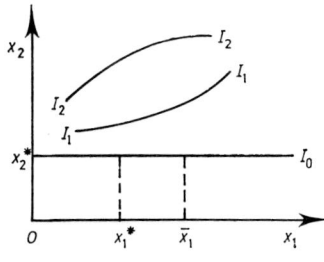

Fig. 6.9　　　　　　　　　　　Fig. 6.10

(d) The *strict* convexity and differentiability assumption about indifference curves (v) is equivalent to supposing that the *marginal rate of substitution* of one product for another is decreasing. The marginal rate of substitution of product 2 for product 1 (MRS_{21}) is the amount of 2 which the consumer is just willing to forgo for an additional unit of product 1. In the limit, the marginal rate of substitution is the (absolute) rate of change of the indifference curve or its (absolute) slope. The concept is illustrated in Fig. 6.11. At combination C the MRS_{21} is 2 and at combination D it is 0.25. In

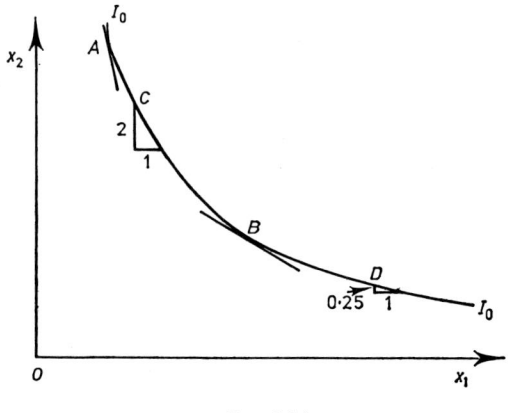

Fig. 6.11

the limit it is equivalent to the absolute slopes of the tangents at the relevant combination. As can be seen, when the indifference curve is strictly convex the absolute slope of the tangents to it decrease. The consumer is only prepared to sacrifice smaller quantities of 2 for additional units of 1, as his quantity of product 1 increases and that of 2 decreases. This empirical proposition, like the law of diminishing marginal utility, is supposedly supported by observation. Note, by the way, that the convexity of indifference curves is not implied by the mere presence of diminishing marginal utility.

It may be of value to give some examples of the type of indifference curves and indifference maps which are ruled out by Hicks' assumptions. Indifference curves of the shape which are shown in Fig. 6.12 are excluded. However, Hicks does consider

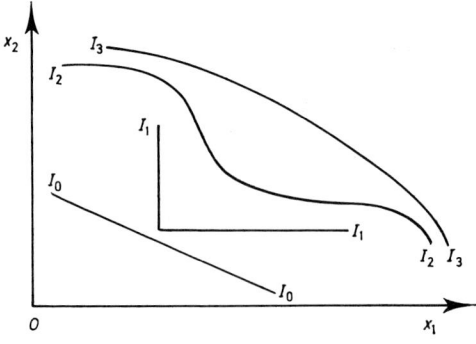

Fig. 6.12

Theory of Consumption

the straight-line and right-angled types, I_0I_0 and I_1I_1, as limiting cases. If the two products are *perfect substitutes* their indifference map consists of parallel straight lines, and if they are *perfect complements* the map consists of a series of right-angled indifference curves like I_1I_1. The indifference curve I_2I_2 is *strictly* concave over a range and I_3I_3 is *strictly* concave. Curves of this type are ruled out. In the case of I_3I_3, the marginal rate of substitution of product 2 for 1 is increasing, *not* decreasing. The possibility that this may, indeed, happen for *some* goods should not be lightly discounted. But at this stage, let us retain Hicks' assumptions.

The Hicksian assumptions either rule out the sort of indifference map indicated in Fig. 6.13 or focus attention merely on region **I** as the relevant region. The map has been divided into four regions. In region **I**, the individual is satiated by no goods, and in region **III** he is satiated by both and increased quantities of either are a nuisance. In region **II**, product 2 only is a nuisance product and in region **IV** product 1 alone is unwelcome in increased quantities. The only relevant region for consumers is considered by Hicks to be region **I**. He reasons, no doubt, that with his limited resources the consumer will never be able to attain region **III**, and sectors **II** and **IV** are irrelevant since with the types of attainable sets which consumers have, the optimum occurs in **I** and never in **II** or **IV**. A final point, before considering attainable consumption sets, is that one should not be deluded into supposing that all sets of indifference curves are segments taken from a field like the one shown in Fig. 6.13. If this were so, it would, for example, be impossible to have concave indifference curves with higher ones corresponding to preferred combinations.

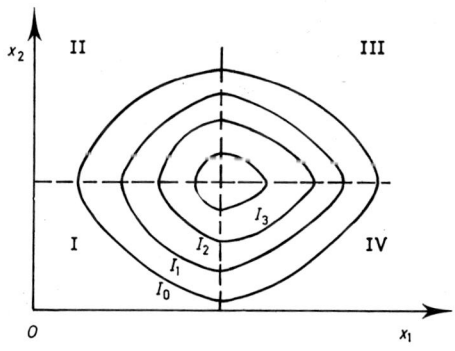

Fig. 6.13

Taking the Hicksian preference map as given, let us now consider the consumer's set of attainable consumption possibilities, for it is a fundamental assumption of the demand theory that the consumer selects the combination from his attainable set which is highest on his preference scale.

B. THE ATTAINABLE SET OF CONSUMPTION POSSIBILITIES

The *attainable set* is determined by two factors: the prices of the goods, and the individual's money income. The attainable set is enlarged by an increase in income or by a reduction in prices. The influence, if any, which the individual has on the prices of the products determines the shape of the attainable region. Examples of two types of attainable consumption sets are shown by the hatched areas in Figs

6.14 and 6.15. A given income is assumed. The first case corresponds to a situation in which the individual has no influence on the price of product 1 or 2. The second corresponds to a situation in which an individual drives up the price of at least one of the goods as he increases his purchases of it. Since most consumers are not in this position, the Hicksian theory of demand is based on the assumption of perfect competition in buying. In other words, it is supposed that the consumer has no influence on prices. Given the Hicksian preference map and a convex attainable set (like those of Figs 6.14 and 6.15), the consumer's optimal choice must be along its north-east boundary. The consumer allocates his total income. The line of this boundary is called the budget line or in a perfectly competitive market may also be called the price-line. *Assuming a perfectly competitive market*, let us derive this budget line from basic data.

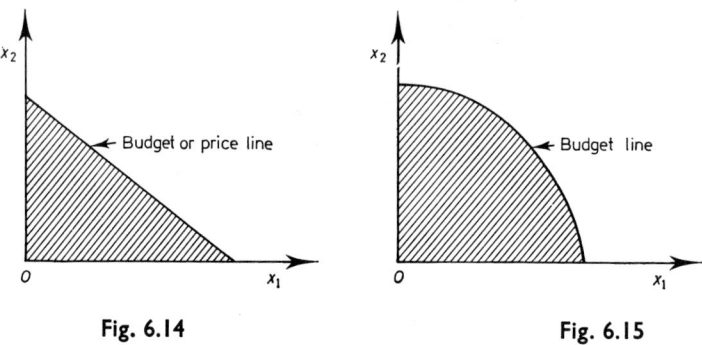

Fig. 6.14 Fig. 6.15

The quantities of the two available goods are x_1 and x_2. Let their prices be represented by p_1 and p_2 and indicate the individual's money income by M. If all of his income is spent on these two commodities (the only ones available), it must be true that

$$M = p_1 x_1 + p_2 x_2. \tag{6.5}$$

The combinations of (x_1, x_2) which satisfy this equation clearly depend on the values of M, p_1 and p_2. The budget line can be found by rearranging Equation (6.5). This gives a budget line

$$x_2 = \frac{M}{p_2} - \frac{p_1}{p_2} x_1 \tag{6.6}$$

and, of course, is found by first subtracting $p_1 x_1$ from both sides of Equation (6.5) and then dividing through by p_2. In particular one should note that the slope of the budget line is $-p_1/p_2$ and thus depends on the *relative* prices of the products. It is steeper the higher is the price of product 1 relative to product 2. Fig. 6.16 illustrates this. The budget line **1** in Fig. 6.16 involves a higher relative price for product 1 than does budget line **2**. Budget line **3** which is parallel to **2** involves the same relative prices as for **2**. Line **3** may, for example, result from increased money income (absolute prices constant). It can also result if relative prices and money income are unchanged but absolute prices are lowered in comparison to **2**. Note also that the intercept on the x_1 axis is M/p_1 and on the x_2 axis M/p_2, that is the number of units of the commodity which can be purchased if all income is devoted to it.

Theory of Consumption

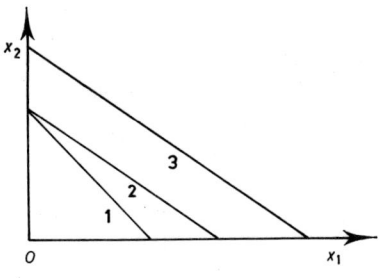

Fig. 6.16

C. CONSUMER'S EQUILIBRIUM

Given the attainable set (given income and prices) and the consumer's tastes as indicated by his preference map, what combination of goods does the consumer choose? In Fig. 6.17 a typical Hicksian budget line and preference map is shown for a consumer. It is clear that with this budget line and sets of preferences the individual's (optimal) choice is the combination at C. All other combinations along the budget line KL or below it are inferior to the one at C. They are on lower indifference curves.

Notice that at point C the slope of the indifference curve is equal to the slope of the budget line. Since the absolute slope of an indifference curve indicates the marginal rate of substitution of product 2 for product 1 and since the slope of the budget line is $-p_1/p_2$, in equilibrium at C,

$$MRS_{21} = p_1/p_2. \tag{6.7}$$

The allocation of income which equates the marginal rate of substitution with the price ratios of the products is optimal. Given the total expenditure of income, there is only one point along KL where this condition is satisfied.

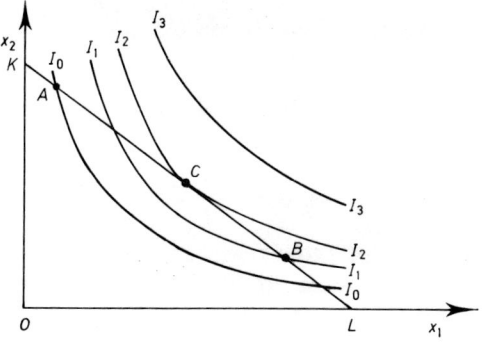

Fig. 6.17

That C is the equilibrium point can be alternatively explained. The slope of an indifference curve represents the quantity of product 2 which an individual is *willing* to give up for an additional unit of product 1. The slope of the budget line indicates the amount of product 2 which the consumer *would have to* give up in the market to obtain an additional unit of 1. A point such as A cannot be an equilibrium point, for the absolute slope of the indifference curve exceeds that of the budget line and the individual is willing to give up more of product 2 for a unit of product 1 than is demanded by the market. At points beyond C, the individual is not prepared to forgo product 2 at the rate of exchange dictated by the market. Only at point C is the individual's preference rate of exchange equal to the market rate.

The conditions for consumer equilibrium are entirely consistent with those suggested by neo-classical demand theory. Indifference curve $I_2 I_2$ is the contour of a utility function, $U(x_1, x_2)$. Where c is the appropriate constant value of the function, $I_2 I_2$ consists of all values of x_1 and x_1 which satisfy

$$U(x_1, x_2) - c = 0. \tag{6.8}$$

Differentiating this expression with respect to x_1 and x_2,

$$\frac{\partial U}{\partial x_1} dx_1 + \frac{\partial U}{\partial x_2} dx_2 = 0 \tag{6.9}$$

or representing the appropriate marginal utilities of the goods by MU,

$$MU_1 dx_1 + MU_2 dx_2 = 0. \tag{6.10}$$

Rearranging, the slope of the indifference curve is

$$\frac{dx_2}{dx_1} = -\frac{MU_1}{MU_2}. \tag{6.11}$$

As indicated near Equation (6.7), in Hicks' theory the consumer is not in equilibrium unless

$$\frac{dx_2}{dx_1} = -\frac{p_1}{p_2} \tag{6.12}$$

or, put differently,

$$\left|\frac{dx_2}{dx_1}\right| = MRS_{21} = \frac{p_1}{p_2}. \tag{6.13}$$

Consequently from Equation (6.7), equilibrium requires that

$$\frac{MU_1}{MU_2} = \frac{p_1}{p_2} \tag{6.14}$$

or rearranging that

$$\frac{MU_1}{p_1} = \frac{MU_2}{p_2}. \tag{6.15}$$

This is the same condition as the neo-classical condition stated in Equation (6.4).

However, neither the neo-classical nor the Hicksian equilibrium condition is a really general one. Even given the ambit of Hicks' assumptions, condition (6.7) need not be satisfied and yet a consumer may be in equilibrium. If negative quantities of products are impossible, then even with a Hicksian indifference map it may be optimal for the consumer to consume nothing of some products. In equilibrium the equalities of Equation (6.7) need not hold. Typically individual consumers do not consume anything of some products and we would expect an adequate theory of demand to predict this. Hicks' theory can explain this but so, too, can some different theories. Let us explore corner-point solutions, using the Hicksian assumptions about the budget line and preferences.

Theory of Consumption

The Hicksian condition for an optimum can easily be extended. Given Hicks' assumptions, the individual's optimal consumption level occurs for a combination which is either in the interior of the budget line or at one of its extreme points. If the optimum is at an interior point, the equilibrium condition of (6.7) must be satisfied. If the optimum occurs at an extreme point, condition (6.7) may, but need not be satisfied. Represent the consumer's budget line by KL where K corresponds to its value for $x_1 = 0$ and L corresponds to its value for $x_2 = 0$. Given a Hicksian preference map, the optimum occurs at K (for $x_1 = 0$), if at that point

$$MRS_{21} \leqslant \frac{p_1}{p_2} \tag{6.16}$$

or at L (for $x_2 = 0$), if at that point

$$MRS_{21} \geqslant \frac{p_1}{p_2}. \tag{6.17}$$

If Equation (6.16) holds, the absolute slope of the indifference curve at K is less than or equal to that of the budget line. If Equation (6.17) is satisfied, the absolute slope of the indifference curve at L exceeds or equals that of the price line. In Figs 6.18 and 6.19, extreme-point equilibria are indicated at K and L respectively. In the second case, and given the market exchange rate, an individual would be willing to forgo additional units of product 2 for additional units of product 1 at L. However, his supply of product 2 is exhausted and no further improvement is possible.

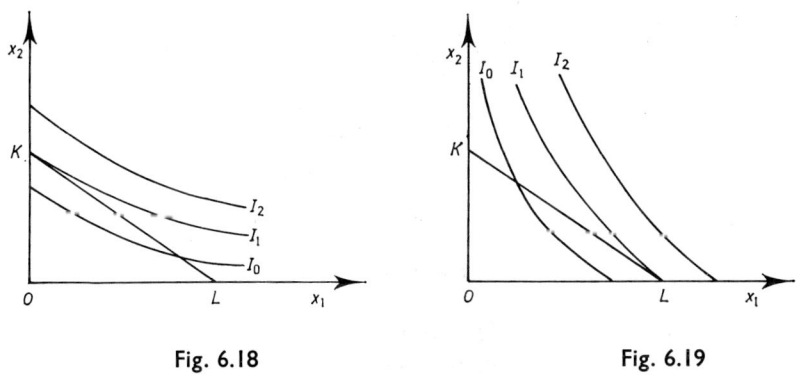

Fig. 6.18   Fig. 6.19

Having derived the conditions which specify an individual's choice of commodities, if he has given tastes, a given income, and encounters specified prices, we can now enquire into the effect of changes in these factors upon his choice. In consequence, propositions are derived about the influence of variations in prices and income upon the demand for commodities. In the analysis, it is supposed (as Hicks does) that the consumer's optimum allocation of income occurs for an *interior* combination along his budget line. Corner-point equilibria are ruled out.

D. THE PRICE-CONSUMPTION CURVE AND THE DEMAND CURVE

An individual's price-consumption curve can be used to derive his partial demand curve for a commodity. This latter curve expresses the quantity demanded of the commodity as a function of its price, the prices of other goods, income and taste being assumed to be constant. A consumer's price-consumption curve (or, as it is sometimes called, his *offer curve*) is the collection of all of his equilibrium consumption bundles for all possible prices of the product, his income, tastes and other prices being constant. An individual's price-consumption curve for any product consists of all of his equilibrium *bundles* of commodities if the price of the product alone is varied. The concept can be easily understood by considering a two-product world.

Suppose that the consumer's tastes and the price of product 2 are constant and that his income stands at a fixed level, M. Consequently, as the price of product 1 rises his budget line will rotate about a fixed point on the x_2-axis and become steeper. As the price of product 1 varies, new equilibria of consumption of x_1 and x_2 are established. Together these equilibrium combinations form the price-consumption curve for product 1. This is illustrated in Fig. 6.20. The budget line is AB when the price of product 1 is p_1^* and rises to AC when the price of product 1 falls to p_1'. In the first case, the consumer is in equilibrium at E_1 and in the second case at E_2. Thus E_1 and E_2 are on his price-consumption curve. As the price of product 1 changes, while the level of income and the price of 2 are constant, other equilibrium bundles besides E_1 and E_2 arise. The curve of all such bundles is a price-consumption curve. In the case shown, it might be a curve like FE_1E_2G.

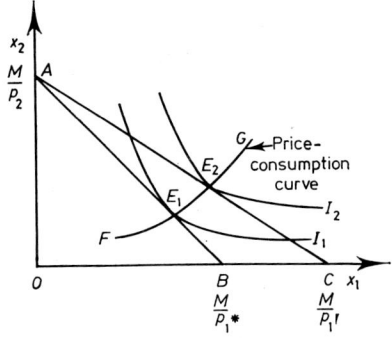

Fig. 6.20

The individual's demand curve for product 1 (tastes, income and other prices constant) can be derived by using his price-consumption curve. Let $E_1 = (x_1^*, x_2^*)$ and $E_2 = (x_1', x_2')$. The individual consumes x_1^* of product 1 if its price is p_1^* and, a greater quantity, x_1' if its price is lowered to p_1'. Thus two points can be plotted on this individual's demand function. These are indicated in Fig. 6.21. By moving along

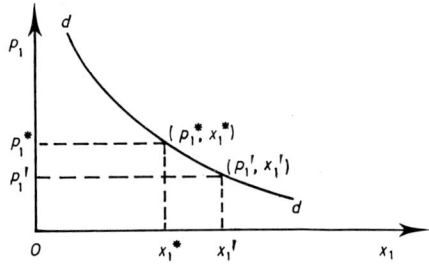

Fig. 6.21

the price-consumption curve and taking account of the price of product 1, the individual's complete demand curve for product 1 as a function of its price can be traced out. Because the price-consumption curve of Fig. 6.20 is positively sloping, the demand curve for product 1 is downward-sloping. However, it is possible for the price-consumption curve to slope negatively. In that case, the demand curve may not have its usual downward slope and could slope upward. This will be carefully considered once the income effect has been introduced.

E. THE INCOME-CONSUMPTION CURVE AND ENGEL FUNCTIONS

The influence of the level of an individual's income upon his demand for products has not been considered. Let us consider this influence now by introducing income-consumption curves and Engel functions. These are analogous to the price-consumption and demand curves which were discussed in the previous section.

An individual's income-consumption curve consists of all of his equilibrium bundles of commodities for all alternative income levels, prices and his tastes being assumed constant. Such a curve is indicated in Fig. 6.22 by $RSTV$, where the price of both commodities is assumed to be constant. Consequently, increases of income cause the budget line to move up in a parallel fashion. Two budget lines are indicated in Fig. 6.22. AB corresponds to an income of M' and CD corresponds to a higher income of M^*. In the former case, the consumer is in equilibrium when he purchases combination S. In the latter case the equilibrium is at T. At the given prices, both S and T are on the individual's income-consumption curve. Similarly, other points on the income-consumption curve may be found. Together they form a curve like $RSTV$.

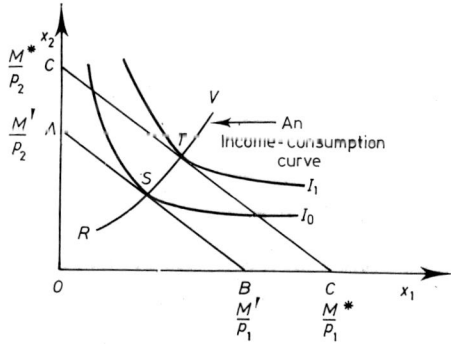

Fig. 6.22

The income-consumption curve which is shown in Fig. 6.22 is positively sloped. As income rises, so does the quantity which is consumed of both commodities. Both goods are normal goods. However, it is possible for an income-consumption curve to be negatively sloped. In that case the consumption of one of the goods decreases with increases of income. It is an inferior good. For example, in Fig. 6.23 product 1 is inferior and in Fig. 6.24 product 2 is inferior.

An individual's Engel[18] curve for any product can be derived from his income-consumption curve. The Engel curve of a product relates the quantity consumed of the product to income, prices and tastes being assumed constant. For a normal

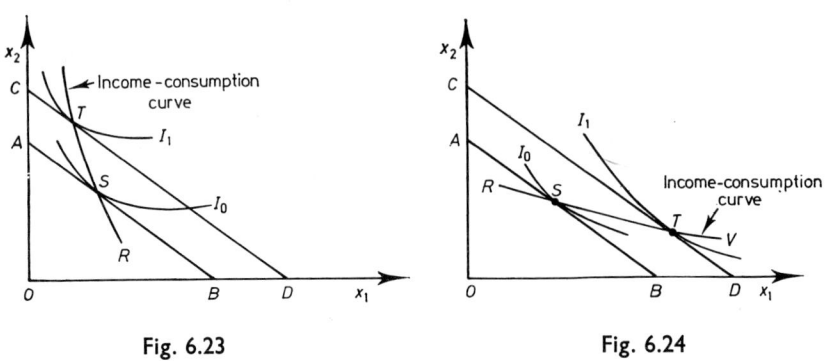

Fig. 6.23

Fig. 6.24

good, the Engel curve slopes upwards and for an inferior good it slopes downward. If the situation of Fig. 6.22 applies, the Engel curve of product 1 (and for product 2) is positively sloping. Points along the Engel curve may be found by plotting equilibrium quantities of x_1 from the income-consumption curve against the corresponding income. For example, if in Fig. 6.22 $S = (x_1', x_2')$ and $T = (x_1^*, x_2^*)$, (M', x_1') and (M^*, x_1^*) are points on the Engel curve for product 1. Similarly, other points of the Engel curve can be found by considering the other equilibria along the income-consumption curve. In this case, the Engel function is the normal one shown by the rising continuous line in Fig. 6.25. However, if the income-consumption curve is declining as in Fig. 6.23, the Engel curve for product 1 is declining like the dotted curve shown in Fig. 6.25. However, a declining income-consumption does not imply

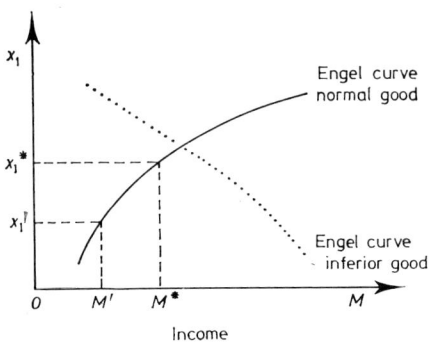

Fig. 6.25

that both goods are inferior. One must be normal. In the case shown in Fig. 6.24, product 1 is a normal good.

F. THE INCOME AND SUBSTITUTION EFFECTS OF A PRICE CHANGE

A fall in the price of a commodity influences the quantity demanded both by a substitution and an income effect. The income effect occurs since a fall in the price of a commodity, all other prices constant, increases an individual's real income or purchasing power. The substitution effect is a result of the fall in the relative price of the commodity. The substitution effect favours increased consumption of the com-

Theory of Consumption

modity whose price has declined, whereas the income effect may operate either towards its increased or decreased consumption or may be neutral. To measure the substitution effect one eliminates the influence of real income changes, and to gauge the income effect one eliminates the impact of the substitution effect. However, two different views of real income exist. For Hicks,[19] money incomes which yield the same psychic level of satisfaction (enable one to reach the same indifference curve) correspond to the same level of real income. For Slutsky,[20] money incomes which barely enable one to purchase the same initial bundle of commodities give the same level of real income. The qualitative predictions of demand theorems are the same for both approaches. Conceptually Hicks' measure is the more satisfactory, but Slutsky's measure has the considerable advantage that it lends itself readily to measurement and econometric study. Both methods of measuring the income and substitution effects of a price change will now be illustrated. The slope of the demand curve for any product depends on these two effects.

HICKS' SEPARATION OF INCOME AND SUBSTITUTION EFFECTS

Consider the two-product case. In Fig. 6.26, the consumer is shown to be in equilibrium at A when the price of product 1 is p_1^*, and the price of product 2 and his income stands at some specific level. If the price of product 1 falls to p_1' while his money income and the price of the other product remain unchanged, his budget line rotates outwards and a new equilibrium is established at B. In consequence, his consumption of product 1 increases from x_1^* to x_1'. The increase of $x_1' - x_1^*$ consists of a component which can be ascribed to the income effect and another which can be ascribed to substitution effect. In equilibrium B the individual's real income is higher than in equilibrium A. To eliminate the difference in real income, reduce the individual's money income (given the lower price, p_1', of product 1) until he is just able to attain the same level of satisfaction as at A. The budget line through B is reduced in a parallel fashion until it is tangential to the indifference curve $I_2 I_2$. At this reduced level of income, equilibrium is achieved at point C and $\bar{x}_1$ of product 1 is consumed. The influence on the consumption of product 1 which stems from the rise of real income (due to the price fall) is $x_1' - \bar{x}_1$. The substitution effect which is purely the result of the change in relative prices, real income being constant, is $\bar{x}_1 - x_1^*$. Substitution results from the variation of the price or budget line around the indifference curves

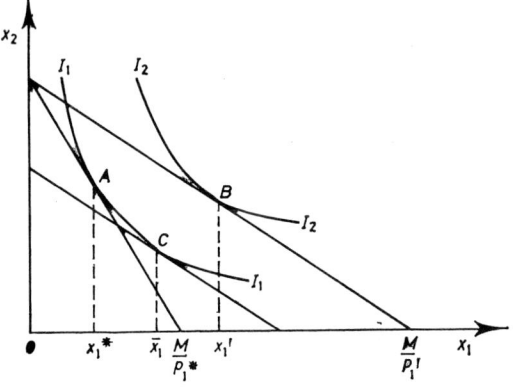

Fig. 6.26

I_1I_1. Adding these two components together, one obtains the total effect on the demand for product 1 of its price rise, namely the increase in demand $x_1' - x_1^*$.

If the individual's indifference curves are *strictly* convex, twice differentiable, and negatively sloping (as is usually assumed), the substitution effect always favours a greater consumption of the product whose price has fallen, all other things being assumed constant. In such a case, as the tangent to any indifference curve rotates, a new consumption-bundle eventuates each time and the substitution effect holds.

Ignoring the income effect and given the usual assumption about indifference curves, the substitution effect indicates that the demand curve for a commodity slopes downward: it suggests that the quantity demanded of a product varies inversely with its price. But the income effect cannot be ignored. While it normally reinforces the substitution effect, more of any product being consumed at higher levels of income, it does not always do so. If the product is an inferior one, the increase in real income due to its fall of price will counteract the substitution effect. However, only rarely will it offset, or more than offset, the substitution effect and thus cause the demand curve for a product to slope upwards rather than downwards.

A case in which the income effect causes the demand curve for product 1 to slope upwards is shown in Fig. 6.27. With a fall in the price of product 1 from p_1^* to p_1', other prices and the consumer's income and tastes constant, the individual's equilibrium level of consumption shifts from point A to point B, and his consumption of product 1 falls. The slope of the demand curve for product 1 is perverse. The real income influence of the price reduction upon the consumption of product 1 is equal to $x_1' - \bar{x}_1$ and is negative; and the substitution effect is the positive value $\bar{x}_1 - x_1^*$. On addition, the income effect outweighs the substitution effect and the total effect is the negative value $x_1' - x_1^*$. The demand for product 1 falls as its price declines. Of course, a negative income effect does not in itself imply that the demand curve has a

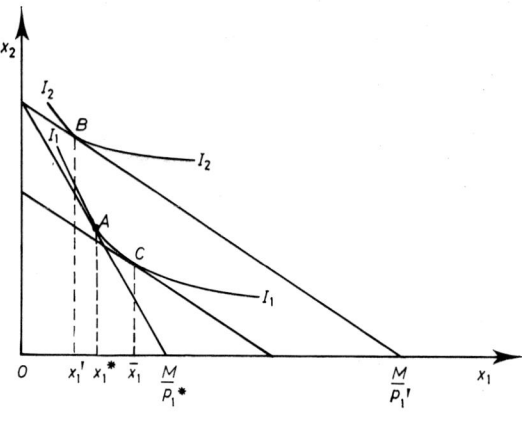

Fig. 6.27

positive slope. Not only must the income effect be negative, but it must also outweigh the substitution effect if the demand curve for a product is to have a positive slope. The mere fact that a product is an inferior one does not imply that its demand curve is necessarily upward-sloping. However, if the product is a normal good, the theory

Theory of Consumption

implies that the individual's demand curve for the product is definitely downward-sloping.

SLUTSKY'S SEPARATION OF INCOME AND SUBSTITUTION EFFECTS

If the real income of a consumer varies as the result of a price variation, Slutsky eliminates this effect by altering the consumer's income so that the consumer can just purchase his previous equilibrium bundle of products at the new prices. If, as in the previous example, the price of product 1 falls, Slutsky isolates the income effect of this by reducing the consumer's income until combination A is just attainable at the new set of prices. Income is not reduced, as in Hicks' case, until the indifference curve $I_1 I_1$ is just reached. After income is reduced at the new set of prices so that the individual's budget line passes through A, equilibrium is established at point D in Fig. 6.28. In this case, the substitution effect is the change in x_1, which occurs as a result of moving from equilibrium A to D and the income effect is the variation of x_1, which is involved in the movement from equilibrium D to B. As with the previous method, the substitution effect is always in favour of a product which has a price decrease and the income effect may operate in either direction. Proof of the sign of the substitution effect will be given in the section on revealed preference.

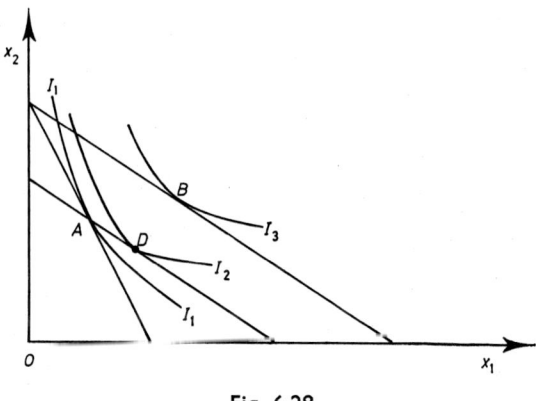

Fig. 6.28

G. THE NATURE OF THE DEMAND CURVE

The previous theory gives us useful guidelines about the nature of the demand curve. If the theory holds, the demand curve for any particular product must slope downwards unless it is an inferior good. But even if it is an inferior good, the income effect may not completely counteract the substitution effect and the demand curve might still slope downward.

Downward-sloping demand curves are the rule for normal goods, that is for goods which have positively sloping Engel curves. Few goods, if any, are so inferior that the income effect counteracts completely the substitution effect. In cases where this happens, the demand curve has a positive slope and the product is called a "Giffen good" in honour of Mr Giffen who, in the nineteenth century, reputedly suggested potatoes as such a product. But the prevalence of inferior goods can only be detected by empirically specifying the Engel curves of products. Our presumption is that Giffen goods are rare. However, pure theory goes no further than to indicate that not all goods can be inferior, and all goods must be normal beyond some price level. The former proposition must be so since if total expenditure is increased, expenditure on all products cannot be decreased. The latter holds since income places an upper bound on the possible expenditure on any commodity.

However, the above theory neglects some possible influences on consumption. If the individual judges the quality of a product by its relative price, this may give rise to a perverse demand curve over a range. Social influences may also give rise to perverse *market* demand curves. But before considering these, let us indicate the (traditional) relationship between the demand curves of individuals and those of the whole market. The traditional view is that market demand curves can be obtained by aggregating individual demand curves like the one obtained in Fig. 6.21. Simple aggregation is possible since with given tastes, incomes and other prices, the demand of any individual for a particular commodity depends only on the price of the commodity. In Fig. 6.29, the simple aggregation procedure is illustrated for the demand curves of two individuals. Typically, of course, more than two individuals are involved and the example is only illustrative. The demand curve of individual 1 for product 1 is

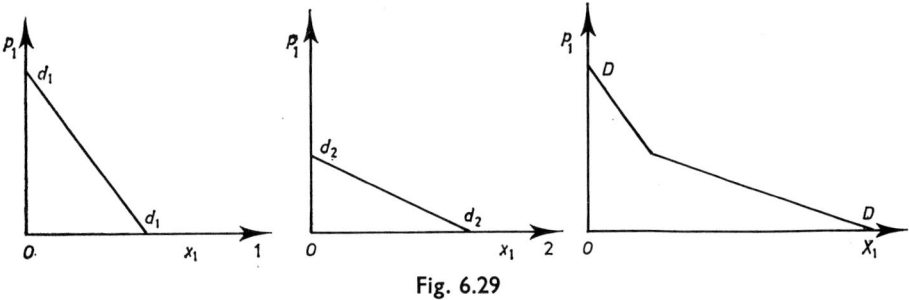

Fig. 6.29

illustrated by $d_1 d_1$ and for individual 2 by $d_2 d_2$. Adding these two demand curves together, total demand is DD.

But does such an additive procedure always yield the market demand curve? Definitely not. Under certain conditions, social influences may make it impossible to find the market demand curve by adding the demand curves of all individual consumers. The Hicksian theory can be misleading because it ignores these influences. It takes no account of phenomena like the "bandwagon" and Veblen effects nor of the possibility that some individuals gauge the quality of a product by its volume of sales and obtain real advantages or disadvantages from buying a (durable) product which has large sales, for example, in terms of more (or less) reliable after-sales service. Apart from possible income influences, Veblenesque factors may cause a market demand curve to slope upwards over a range. Other social effects also influence the market demand curve in characteristic ways and make the above addition of individual demand curves inappropriate. These social influences will be discussed in Section VI.

IV. Consumer's Surplus and the Excess Burden of Indirect Taxes

Let us digress for a moment to indicate the application of indifference curve analysis to two important matters. The first is the concept of consumer's surplus. The second is the excess burden of indirect taxes as compared to direct ones.

A. CONSUMER'S SURPLUS

The concept of consumer's surplus has had a troubled history and, indeed, a number of concepts exist.[21] All stem from the realisation that most consumers pay less for their purchases of a product than they could be forced to pay. I shall use the following definition.

> *The consumer's surplus from his purchase of any quantity of a product is the difference in dollars between the amount which the consumer pays for this purchase and the maximum amount which he would be prepared to pay rather than do entirely without the product.*

The concept can be clarified by considering the individual's indifference map. As before, imagine that two products, 1 and 2, are available for purchase. But to increase the generality let us imagine that product 2 is Hicks' composite product. It is money expenditure on all products bar product 1, assuming that the prices of these other products are constant and that expenditure on them is optimally allocated. The individual's indifference map can then be shown in the usual way if money expenditure (on all goods, except product 1) is shown on the Y-axis and quantity of product 1 is indicated on the X-axis. Such an indifference map is illustrated in Fig. 6.30.

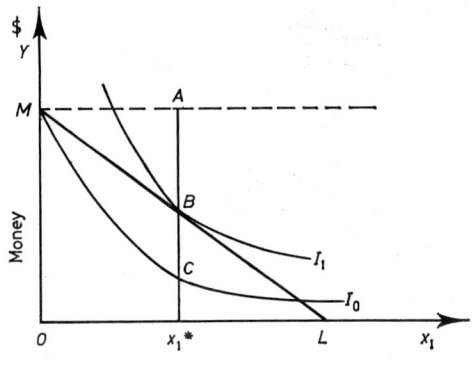

Fig. 6.30

Figure 6.30 shows that the individual is willing to forgo AC of income (money) to purchase x_1^* of product 1 rather than go without it entirely, that is, rather than be at M. If the individual pays less than this amount, he obtains a surplus, and the surplus is the difference between AC and the amount which he actually pays. If product 1 is so priced that budget line ML applies, the consumer's surplus is BC since he only forgoes AB of income for x_1^* units of product 1.

The concept, despite its difficulties, is of value. It gives a guideline as to whether or not any economic undertaking should be commenced. Clearly, if consumers are not willing, at any level of the operations of the undertaking, to forgo [as calculated by the above method] sufficient to cover the costs of operations, the undertaking involves a social loss and should not be commenced. However, some enterprises (for example, public enterprises which make their services freely available) may run at an accounting (private) loss and yet give a social gain.

Both Dupuit[22] and Marshall[23] stressed the possible application of the concept of consumer's surplus to the evaluation of public undertakings. However, they proposed to measure the consumer's surplus for any product by an area under the consumer's partial demand curve for the product. If a consumer pays a price of p_1^* for x_1^* units of product 1, they proposed as the measure of his consumer's surplus

$$\int_0^{x_1^*} f(x_1)dx_1 - p_1^* x_1^*$$

where $f(x_1)$ is his demand curve for the product. Marshall reasoned that, *if* the marginal utility of money is constant, this area indicates the amount which the individual might have been forced to pay over and above what he paid for his purchases of the product. His surplus is indicated in Fig. 6.31 by the hatched area.

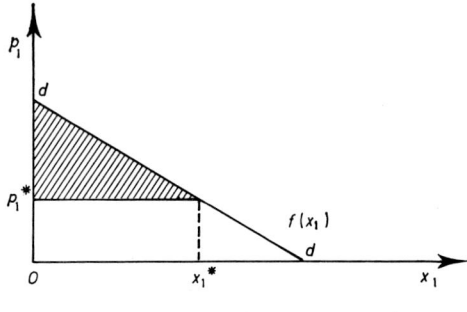

Fig. 6.31

Only in very special circumstances is this area equal to BC, the surplus, obtained directly from the indifference curves.[24]

B. EXCESS BURDEN OF AN EXCISE (INDIRECT OR SALES) TAX COMPARED TO AN INCOME (DIRECT) TAX

If the government wishes to collect a specific amount of revenue by taxation, it is preferable to collect it by an income (direct) tax rather than by a partial sales tax. It is argued that the former method puts the taxpayer in a preferable position. In order to illustrate the argument consider Fig. 6.32. In this diagram, Hicks' composite good, "money", is shown on the Y-axis and the quantity of product 1 is indicated on the

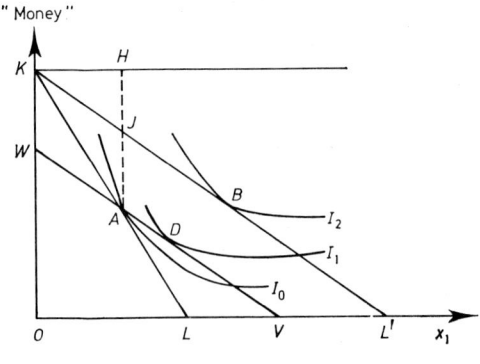

Fig. 6.32

X-axis. The indifference map of an individual is also indicated. Imagine the individual's income to be OK and the price of product 1 to be such that his budget line before tax is KL'. If an excise tax is imposed on product 1, the after-tax budget line rotates downward (with a fixed point at K) because the tax raises the price of product 1. Imagine that after the imposition of the excise tax the individual's budget line becomes KL. This new equilibrium is established at A. Of the AH of income exchanged for product 1, AJ is received by the government as taxation revenue. The same quantity of taxation revenue could be raised by imposing an income tax (direct tax) of KW. But if this is done, the individual will reach a new equilibrium at point D since WV is now his after-tax budget line. Point D is on a higher indifference curve than point A. Hence, the consumer prefers the direct tax. For the usual preference map and given the implicit assumptions employed above, the individual is better off with the direct rather than the indirect tax. (A formal proof of this can be given by the consistency method discussed in Section V.)

The same type of argument also suggests that *per capita* subsidies or grants rather than specific purpose grants or subsidies are preferable. An individual can always reach a higher indifference curve by a general subsidy of the same amount than by subsidies tied to a limited range of products. However, specific purpose subsidies may be justified on the grounds of externalities, or possibly merit grounds. This is not to say that governments justify their subsidies on these grounds. In the main, actual government subsidies are for particular purposes and may very well be the outcome of political compromise rather than economic wisdom. The mechanics of politics sometimes prevents social improvements.

The above argument is limited. It does not take account of the possible variation in the per-unit costs of production, as demand is altered by taxation (it assumes constant per-unit costs), nor does it study the variation in the supply of effort which may be occasioned by taxation. Musgrave[25] discusses these factors in some detail and the interested reader might consult his work.

V. Revealed Preference Approach

In 1947, Samuelson[26] suggested the revealed preference approach to the theory of demand. By adopting very simple axioms about consistency and by using observations of consumer behaviour, it was shown to be possible to obtain a theory of demand. Hicks[27] and others also contributed to this new line of approach. They demonstrated that, if an individual's tastes do not change and some simple assumptions are satisfied, an individual's indifference system can be pieced together by observing his purchases as prices and his income are varied. Furthermore, theorems, such as the substitution theorem, can be shown to hold. In this section, the method for obtaining indifference curves from observation by letting the attainable set vary[28] will not be discussed but consistency tests and the substitution effect will be. Many of the simple axioms which are used in revealed preference theory are already implicity assumed in the earlier theories of Pareto, Slutsky and Hicks.

A. CONSISTENCY TESTS

Given some simple axioms, certain choices by a consumer indicate that he has changed his tastes or that he is inconsistent. Assume that

(i) the consumer has a *weak* preference ordering[29] over his consumption possibilities, and

(ii) prefers any combination of commodities which involves more of one product and no less of any other.

Imagine that on two different occasions, the consumer is faced by different sets of consumption possibilities which involve the possible consumption of the same two products, 1 and 2. (Product 2 may be Hicks' composite commodity.) For instance, in Fig. 6.33 the consumer's attainable set on the first occasion is shown as ONQ and as OML on the second occasion. The figure $ONPL$, which is hatched, is the product or intersection of these two sets and consists of the commodity bundles which are available on both occasions. If tastes have not changed, it can be shown that the choice of two different bundles in the set $ONPL$ is inconsistent with the above assumptions. Thus, for example, the choice of bundle 1 on the first occasion and of bundle 2 on the second occasion involves an inconsistency.

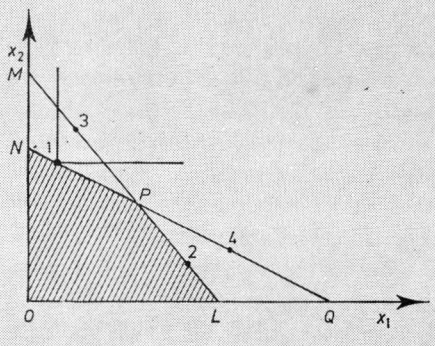

Fig. 6.33

Let us show this. Combinations 1 and 2 are available on both occasions; thus the choice of one and then the other implies that one is not preferred to the other. It implies $1 = 2$. But 3 is available on the second occasion and, by assumption (ii), 3 is preferred to 1 since it involves more of both products. But if $3 > 1$ and $1 = 2$, it follows that $3 > 2$. Hence the consumer is revealed to be inconsistent by choosing 2 in preference to 3 when 3 is available.

Given the above axioms, the chosen bundle must be upon the consumer's budget line. Furthermore, it can be shown by the type of argument just given, that the choice of any two different combinations, one of which is in NP and one of which is in PL, involves an inconsistency, or a change of tastes. But no inconsistency is implied by a choice first of a combination along PQ and then of one anywhere along ML.

B. THE SUBSTITUTION EFFECT OF A PRICE CHANGE

The consistency argument of the last section enables us to show for Samuelson's cost-difference method or Slutsky's method of allowing for real income variation, that the substitution effect cannot lead to a reduction in the consumption of a product as its price falls, other things being constant. Axioms (i) and (ii) of the last section are assumed to hold.

The following simple proof applies: assume other prices, the individual's income and tastes to be constant, and let the price of product 1 decrease so that the consumer's budget line as shown in Fig. 6.34 shifts from ML to ML'. Suppose that the consumer purchases combination A when ML is the case and combination B when ML' is the case. To isolate the real income effect of the price decline by using Slutsky's method, it is necessary to reduce the individual's money income until his budget line, given the new prices, just passes through point A, thus indicating that the consumer could just purchase his original combination if he wished to. After this reduction of income the individual's new budget line is NQ.

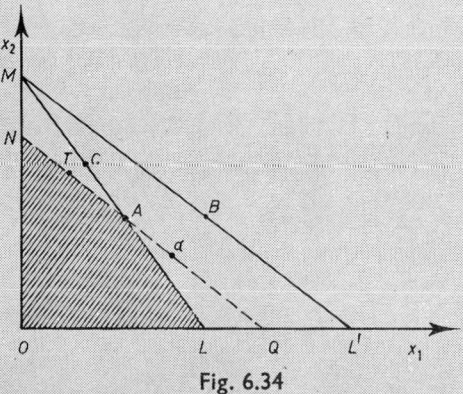

Fig. 6.34

With his new budget line at NQ, it can be shown that the consumer's new equilibrium cannot be to the left of A. It must either be at A or to its right and, hence, the consumption of product 1 cannot be decreased by the substitution effect. To prove this we imagine that the equilibrium occurs to the left of A and show that a contradiction is involved.

Let T be chosen when NQ is the budget line. A was chosen when ML was the budget line. Hence, if a weak-ordering exists, the implication is that A is indifferent to T, $A = T$. But, by axiom (ii) above, C is preferred to T, $C > T$. Hence, $C > A = T$, C is preferred to A. However, on the first occasion both C and A were available and the consumer chose A. He revealed an inconsistency. Only if his choice, given budget line NQ, is at A or to its left along NQ is an inconsistency avoided.[30] No inconsistency arises if the choice after elimination of the income effect is at a for example. In such case, the consumption of x_1 is increased. Hence, the substitution influence never leads to a decline in the consumption of a product if its price falls and the above axioms are satisfied.

Thus if a product is a normal good, the individual's demand curve for it slopes downward. If no social influences are present, and if the good is normal for all individuals, its market demand curve will also slope downwards. But social influences cannot always be ignored and there is the awkward possibility that individuals may judge the quality of a product by its price. Both these factors, but especially the former, require modifications of traditional demand theory.

VI. Social Influences on Demand

Our tastes are to a great extent conditioned by the society to which we belong. This alone, however, does not render traditional demand theory inadequate, because it is still *possible* (at least over a short period of time) that our preference for any bundle of commodities is independent of the demand for or consumption of these commodities by others. But even casual observation indicates that the demand of individuals for several commodities depends upon the consumption of these commodities by others. This view is reinforced by the nature of advertisements, which are designed to increase the sales of products. An inspection will reveal that many of these stress the consumption of the product by *others*. Consumption by a special group may be selected for mention or inferred or the total volume of sales may be indicated. One can reasonably conclude that these factors do influence demand, and empirical study might reveal that the major part of consumer's expenditure is influenced by these factors. For the sale of durable goods, for example, automobiles and houses, social influences seem to be very important.

The study of social influences upon demand has lagged behind other research and the theory is incomplete. However, some work has been done by Leibenstein[31] which provides useful analysis.

Take any product, X, and let x_j represent the quantity of it which is demanded by the jth individual. Traditional demand theory asserts, if the jth individual's income, his tastes and other prices are constant, that his demand for product X depends solely upon p, the price of product X. The dependence might be represented by

$$x_j = g_j(p). \tag{6.18}$$

Consequently, if income, tastes and all other prices are constant and if there are m consumers, the market demand for the product is

$$X = \sum_{j=1}^{m} g_j(p) \tag{6.19}$$

where X represents the aggregate quantity demanded of X. But if the individual's demand also depends upon the consumption of others, demand curve of Equation 6.18 must be modified.

Social interdependence can be quite complex. The individual's consumption might not only depend upon the total consumption by others but it might depend upon the distribution of the consumption amongst categories of consumers. However, there is only room here to consider dependence on aggregate consumption. In this case, if the jth individual's tastes and income and other prices are constant, his demand for commodity X might be represented by

$$x_j = g_j(p, \hat{X}) \tag{6.20}$$

where $\hat{X}$ is his estimate of the quantity of good X consumed in the market as a whole.

Two possibilities concern us. Possibly $\frac{\partial x_j}{\partial \hat{X}} > 0$ or this inequality may be reversed.

If the former inequality holds, the individual consumes greater quantities at any price, the greater is the quantity which he expects others to consume. According to Leibenstein's terminology,[32] the individual is subject to a "bandwagon" effect. If the opposite situation exists, the individual is a "snob". Clearly, in either case his consumption of X can be varied by influencing his estimate of group consumption.

In any market, the demand of some individuals may be of the snob-type, the demand of others may be of the bandwagon-type and the demand of still others may be unaffected by the aggregate level of demand. The proportions of these types in any market may show considerable variation. At one extreme all participants may be snobs or all may be anxious to increase their purchases in common with everyone else.

Consider the case in which individual demands are all of the bandwagon-type. At each level of p, price of product X, there is only one value of $\hat{X}$ which *ex post facto* can be justified by the actual quantity purchased. Given p, there is only one value of $\hat{X}$ which coincides with actual purchases. At this value of $\hat{X}$, expectations are exactly realised and all consumers are in equilibrium. An industry demand curve, based upon the assumption that all expectations are realised, is represented in Fig. 6.35 by D_G. Other demand curves can be drawn, which do not suppose that consumers are in overall equilibrium. For example, a market-demand curve may be drawn on the assumption that all consumers predict that the quantity demanded in the whole market will be of some level, A. Such a curve is indicated in Fig. 6.35 by D_A. The curve is steeper than D_G. If all consumers assume that X will equal A, an upward bias is caused by their overestimation of X for prices in excess of p_A and a downward bias is introduced by their underestimation of X at prices less than p_A. If all consumers suppose that X will equal B, and $B > A$, an aggregate demand curve such as D_B can be drawn. Their expectations in the former case will only be justified if $p = p_A$ and in the latter case if $p = p_B$. Similarly, other curves can be drawn for different expected levels. We observe that the bandwagon effect causes the market demand curve (D_G) to be more elastic than if social influences are held constant. Also, the diagram enables one to separate the social impact and purely individualistic variation of demand which result from a price change. A reduction of price from p_A to p_B increases demand from A to B. Of this increase AX^* may be attributed to individualistic factors and X^*B to the bandwagon effect. Individualistic movements are reinforced by the bandwagon effect.

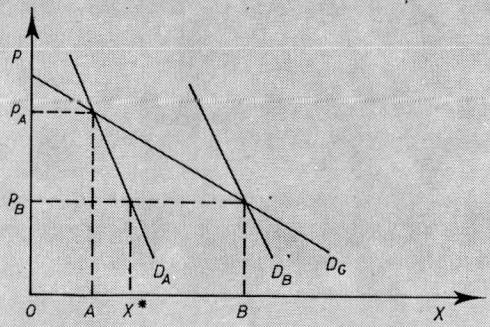

Fig. 6.35

If all consumers in the market are snobs, similar sets of curves to those shown in Fig. 6.35 can be drawn. However, they are related in a different way. The curve D_G is now more inelastic than the demand curves based upon constant expectations about X. The relationship between these curves and D_G is indicated in Fig. 6.36. The effect of a fall in price from p_A to p_B (after the new equilibrium is established) upon the increase of the quantity demanded can be divided into an individualistic and a snob component. The individualistic component is equal to AX^* but the snob influence subtracts BX^* from that to give a net effect of AB.

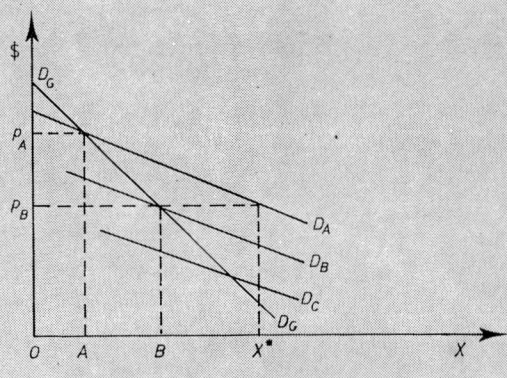

Fig. 6.36

Motives other than the bandwagon and snob motives may give rise to demand situations which are similar to those described. For example, if individuals judge the quality of a product by its aggregate volume of sales, a bandwagon-type demand curve results when their estimate of quality rises with volume, and a snob-type curve results when their estimate of quality is reduced with increased sales volume. Again, if the quality of after-sales service is expected to rise (fall) with sales volume, a bandwagon-type (snob type) demand curve occurs.

Many other social factors also exert controls on demand. In certain circumstances, individuals may enhance their social standing by purchasing higher priced goods, provided that their purchase is conspicuous to the group whom it is hoped to impress. This has been called the Veblen effect, in honour of Thorstein Veblen[33] who, in the nineteenth century, stressed the importance of social influences upon demand. The Veblen effect can cause the market demand curve to slope upwards, at least over a range. This can also happen if individuals judge the inherent qualities of a product by its price, and rate these more highly the higher is its price.

Social influences may also be important on a different plane. They can cause the indifference curves of consumers to be other than convex. Certain combinations of *commodities* can be socially taboo. Some implications of this will be discussed in the appendix.

So far the discussion has been based upon the supposition that consumers have adequate knowledge and are not uncertain of the qualities or amounts of their purchases. In practice, this condition need not be satisfied. However, von Neumann and Morgenstern have advanced a theory to predict the consumer's (or individual's) choice under conditions of risk. Let us consider their view.

VII. Von Neumann and Morgenstern's Theory of Choice

If certain behavioural assumptions are satisfied, von Neumann and Morgenstern have shown[34] that an index can be constructed which enables one to predict behaviour in risky situations. By using the index, behaviour can be forecast for situations which have not been previously observed. Their theory is not empty for it could conceivably be contradicted by observations. However, it is not a hedonistic theory, despite the fact that their index is unfortunately called a utility index, but a purely behavioural one. This is true even though their index possesses cardinal properties.

The behavioural axioms which underlie von Neumann and Morgenstern's theory are as follows (in the following ">" indicates "preferred to" and "=" designates "indifferent to"):

(i) if A and B are any two possible alternatives (either of which may involve gains influenced by chance), then either $A > B$ or $A < B$ or $A = B$. The preference ordering is a complete weak ordering. The individual is not permitted to be undecided about his preference;

(ii) if A, B and C are three alternatives and if $A \geqslant B$ and $B \geqslant C$, then $A \geqslant C$. Preference relations are assumed to be transitive;

(iii) if $A > B$ and D is an alternative, a lottery which involves A as a prize with a *positive* probability of p and D as a prize with a probability of $(1-p)$ is preferred to one in which B has a probability of p and D has a probability of $(1-p)$; and

(iv) if $A > B$ and $B > C$, there is a probability, p, between zero and unity, such that if A has this probability and C has the probability $(1-p)$, the individual will be indifferent about taking a chance on A or C or having B with certainty. In other words, the individual can always be induced to take a risk (the chance of a loss) if the probability of gain is made high enough (without being made certain).

The axioms do appear to be reasonable ones.[35] If they hold, consistency requires that an individual act to maximise the expected value of his "utility" function.

An individual's "utility" function can be constructed by first assigning an arbitrary number to his least preferred alternative and a higher arbitrary number to his most preferred alternative. Numbers are then assigned to all other alternatives by observing the probability of the best and worst alternatives required in a lottery, in order to make the individual indifferent about the lottery and the alternative under consideration. For example, consider four alternatives, A, B, C and D where the preference relation is $A > B > C > D$. Assign a number, r, to D and a number, s, to A where s exceeds r. The utility number to be assigned to B depends upon the chances required in a lottery in which A and D are the prizes to make the individual indifferent about the lottery and the certainty of B. Imagine that the individual is indifferent if A has a probability of p and, therefore, D has a probability of $(1-p)$. The utility (number) assigned to B is then $ps+(1-p)r$. In a similar fashion a number can be assigned to C and the individual "utility" function can be constructed. Once numbers are assigned in this manner, they can be used to predict behaviour. Faced with any set of alternatives, the consistent individual (one acting in accordance with von Neumann and Morgenstern's axioms) must choose the alternative which maximises the expected value of his utility index. The expected utility of any alternative is equal to the sum of its possible utility values, times their probability of occurrence. Thus, *having set the arbitrary constants* and, for example, having assigned utilities as follows: $U(A) = 10$; $U(B) = 6$; $U(C) = 5$; and $U(D) = 1$, we could conclude that the individual would prefer (an 0.5 chance of B or C) to (an 0.2 chance of A and an 0.8 chance of D). At least we are predicting this to be so,

$$0.5U(B)+0.5U(C) > 0.2U(A)+0.8U(D)$$

because $3+2.5 > 2+0.8$.

But, to reiterate, the index is not unique because two constants are arbitrarily determined. Given one index, any other index which is a linear transform of it also gives the same predictive results.

A more concrete example may be of value. Imagine that the individual is faced with alternative money payoffs, returns or income levels and prefers those of higher value. Suppose that payoffs between $0 and $1000 are possible and assign a utility of 0 units to $0 and 10 units to $1000. This last assignment is arbitrary; we might have used 1 and 5, or 3 and 19, etc. Having assigned these values, the utility values for other payoffs can be calculated. Suppose that the individual is indifferent between $500 with certainty and the chance of $1000 with a probability of 0.7 or $0 with a probability of 0.3. The appropriate utility assignment for $500 is then

$$0.3 \times 0 + 0.7 \times 10 = 7.$$

In a similar fashion, utilities can be assigned to all payoffs between zero and $1000. On completion, the utility function might be like the one shown in Fig. 6.37 by $U(\pi)$ which is a strictly concave function.

The utility function can be used to make forecasts. For example, the individual prefers the certainty of $500 to an 0.5 probability of $250 or $750. The expected utility in the former case is β and α in the latter and as the diagram indicates, $\beta > \alpha$. He would always be prepared to trade the lottery alternative for the certain one. Indeed, he would be prepared to trade the lottery alternative for the certainty of π^* dollars or

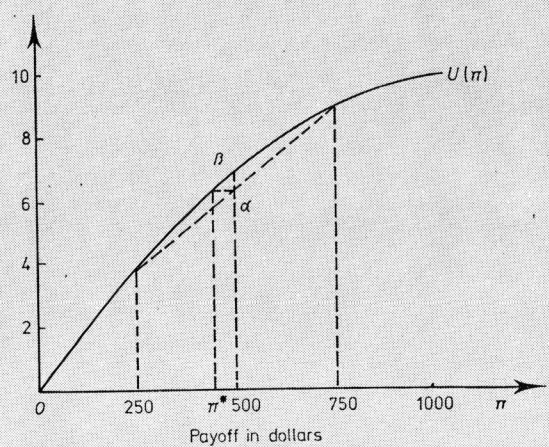

Fig. 6.37

more. The utility associated with π^* just equals α, the utility for the risky alternative. Note that the individual is willing to exchange his risky alternative for less than its actuarial value ($500). This occurs because his utility function is *strictly* concave. He is a risk-averter.

The form of the utility function indicates the individual's attitude towards risk. If the function is *strictly* concave, he is a risk-averter and is prepared to pay a premium to avoid risk. If it is *strictly* convex he has a preference for risk and, if it is linear, his attitude towards risk is neutral.

The possible applications of this theory are great. It has been applied to the demand for insurance[36] and can be applied to all trading in income rights and in this respect it sheds new light on the notion of liquidity preferences.[37] However, there is not room to consider these fascinating applications here. No doubt, it could be also adapted to help explain a consumer's decision to try a new product when he is uncertain of its characteristics.

Before considering demand theory which emphasises the demand for characteristics, we might note that certain criteria for choice under uncertainty are inconsistent with von Neumann and Morgenstern's axioms. Furthermore, the form of a utility function may imply that certain, apparently unrelated, rules for choice under uncertainty maximise expected utility. For example, if the individual's utility function is linearly dependent upon his money gain, then the maximisation of expected gain *also* maximises expected utility. If the utility function is quadratic, then preferences based on expected gain and the variance of gain (provided that these preferences take a particular form) maximise expected utility. But, at this stage, it is impossible to explore these matters.[38]

VIII. The Characteristics Approach and Other Developments

A limitation of traditional demand theory is its inability to predict the demand for new or differentiated products. This stems principally from its specification of preferences in terms of products rather than the intrinsic properties of products. Recently, economists such as Lancaster[39] have been exploring the alternative of basing demand theory upon the demand for the properties inherent in products. The difficulties involved in this approach need no emphasis. For example, how do we define and measure a relevant characteristic? But it is not always easy to define a product either.

A commodity is regarded as a bundle of characteristics, and can be defined in terms of these. To give a very simple example, various types of garden fertilisers differ in so far as they contain different elements for plants and elements combined in different proportions. Let us imagine that the home-gardener is interested in only two characteristics of fertilisers, namely the amount of available nitrogen and phosphorus which they contain. Let N and P represent the quantity of these characteristics as measured in some suitable unit. Then different fertilisers are likely to contain these ingredients in dissimilar proportions. Some may be relatively richer in nitrogen than others. It is also reasonable to suppose that any fertiliser will contain a fixed amount *per-unit* weight of these ingredients irrespective of the total quantity used.

Taking two fertilisers, products 1 and 2, their nitrogen to phosphorus ratios per unit are indicated in Fig. 6.38 by the slopes of OF_1 and OF_2 respectively. Given that the individual's budget for fertiliser is M, OF_1 represents the maximum amount of the characteristics which the individual can purchase by spending his budget only on product 1. At F_1, N_1 of nitrogen is available. This is found by the following formula:

$$\frac{M}{p_1} \times a_{IN},$$

where p_1 is the price of product 1 and a_{1N} is its content of nitrogen per unit. F_1 is clearly further from the origin, other things being equal, the lower is the price of the product or the greater is its per-unit content of characteristics. Similarly, the maximum available quantity of the characteristics if all the individual's fertiliser budget is spent on product 2 is shown as F_2. By combining the products in different proportions, any combination along the frontier F_1F_2 is attainable if there are given prices, a given budget, and only two products.

The individual is assumed to have a preference ordering of the different quantities of the characteristics. Imagine the preference ordering to have Hicksian properties. Then an equilibrium in terms of characteristics is defined by the tangency of F_1F_2 and the highest attainable indifference curve. Such an equilibrium is shown at E_1 in Fig. 6.38. This solution can in turn be used to determine the optimal quantities of each product. In the case shown, quantities of both fertilisers are purchased.

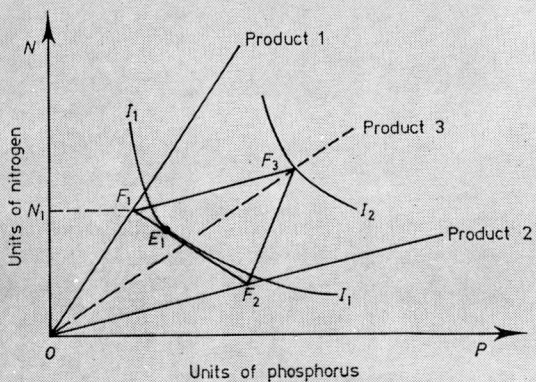

Fig. 6.38

Suppose that a new product presents itself as a possibility and that except for its existence the previous situation remains unaltered. The characteristic line for the new product 3 is indicated by OF_3 in Fig. 6.38. Its mix of characteristics is an intermediate one. Depending upon the product's price and its "density" of characteristics, the maximum amount of characteristics which can be obtained by spending \$$M$ upon it may be below F_1F_2 or above it. If it is below F_1F_2 we would not expect product 3 to be purchased. If it is above F_1F_2, we would expect product 3 to be purchased, but not necessarily to be exclusively purchased. In the case illustrated, it is possible to purchase a maximum of OF_3 of the characteristics by spending \$$M$ on product 3. The consumption possibility frontier is $F_1F_3F_2$ and product 3 is exclusively purchased *in this case*. A number of other propositions can be derived but this is sufficient to indicate the flavour of the approach.

If one is not slightly uneasy about the knowledge assumptions which underlie demand theory, the characteristics approach is likely to make one aware of possible problems. Many individuals are very ignorant of the characteristics of products and there is the further complication that some ignorance may be optimal since it involves time and effort to obtain knowledge. One may wish to dismiss these factors as microcomplications but random variations, *en masse*, may have important global implications. They are an interesting aspect to which Baumol[40] and others have given some attention.

Other generalisations and extensions of the theory of demand either have taken place or are proceeding. Demand theorems for a wider class of preference orderings than those of Hicks have been explored by economists such as Debreu,[41] corner-solutions have been examined and generally the restrictions upon the attainable set of consumption possibilities have been relaxed. Some of these aspects are explored in the appendix to this chapter.

NOTES AND REFERENCES

[1] W. S. JEVONS, *Theory of Political Economy*, 1st ed., 1871; 4th ed., Macmillan, London, 1911.
[2] L. WALRAS, *Elements d'économie politique pure*, 1874. Translation by W. JAFFE, *Elements of Pure Economics*, Irwin, Homewood, 1954.
[3] A. MARSHALL, *Principles of Economics*, 1st ed., 1890; 8th ed., Macmillan, London, 1920.
[4] This school includes Menger, von Wieser and Böhm-Bawerk. CARL MENGER'S work, *Grundsätze der Volkswirtschaftslehre*, outlining marginal utility theory, was published in 1871. Translation by J. DINGWALL and B. HOSELITZ, *Principles of Economics*, Free Press, Glencoe, 1950.
[5] V. PARETO, *Cours d'économie politique*, 2 vols, F. Rouge, Lausanne, 1896-1897. *Manuel d'économie politique*, 2nd ed., Giard, Paris, 1927.
[6] E. SLUTSKY, "Sulla Teoria del Bilancio del Consumatore", *Giornale del Economisti*, 1915, **51**, pp. 1-26. Reprinted, in translation, pp. 27-56 of A.E.A., *Readings in Price Theory*, Allen and Unwin, London, 1953.
[7] R. G. D. ALLEN. See Reference 8.
[8] J. R. HICKS and R. G. D. ALLEN, "A Reconsideration of the Economic Theory of Value", *Economica*, 1934, **1**, pp. 52-76 and pp. 196-219. J. R. HICKS, *Value and Capital*, 1st ed., 1939; 2nd ed., Clarendon Press, Oxford, 1946.
[9] P. A. SAMUELSON, "Consumption Theory in Terms of Revealed Preference", *Economica*, 1948, **15**, pp. 243-53.
[10] J. R. HICKS, *A Revision of Demand Theory*, Clarendon Press, Oxford, 1956.
[11] J. VON NEUMANN and O. MORGENSTERN, *Theory of Games and Economic Behavior*, Science Edition, John Wiley, New York, 1964, appendix.
[12] K. LANCASTER, (i) "Change and Innovation in the Technology of Consumption", *American Economic Review Supplement*, May 1966, pp. 14-23; (ii) "A New Approach to Consumer Theory", *Journal of Political Economy*, 1966, **74**, pp. 132-57.
[13] G. DEBREU, *Theory of Value*, John Wiley, New York, 1959.
[14] PARETO, op. cit.
[15] SLUTSKY, op. cit.
[16] ALLEN and HICKS, op. cit.
[17] J. HICKS, *Value and Capital*, 2nd ed., Clarendon Press, Oxford, 1946. All references to Hicks throughout this section are relevant to *Value and Capital*. My terminology is, however, not always the same as his.
[18] For more details of Engel curves, see J. TINBERGEN, *Econometrics*, Blakiston, New York, 1951, Sec. 26.
[19] HICKS, *Value and Capital*, op. cit.
[20] SLUTSKY, op. cit.
[21] See, for example, P. A. SAMUELSON, *Foundations of Economic Analysis*, Harvard University Press, Cambridge, 1963, pp. 197 et seq.
[22] JULES DUPUIT, "On the Measurement of the Utility of Public Works", *International Economic Papers*, 1952, **2**, pp. 83-110. Reprinted in A.E.A., *Readings in Welfare Economics*, George Allen and Unwin, London, 1969. Translated by R. H. BARBACK from "De la Mesure de l'Utilité des Travaux Publics", *Annals des Ponts et Chaussées*, 2nd series, 1844, **8**.

[23] A. Marshall, op. cit.
[24] See Hicks, *Value and Capital*, op. cit., pp. 38-41.
[25] A. Musgrave, *The Theory of Public Finance*, McGraw-Hill, New York, 1959.
[26] See Reference 9.
[27] See Reference 10.
[28] For a simple exposition of this, see W. J. Baumol, *Economic Theory and Operations Analysis*, 2nd ed., Prentice-Hall, Englewood Cliffs, 1965, pp. 200-2.
[29] A weak preference ordering allows indifference.
[30] This is so, provided that the individual's tastes are unchanged.
[31] H. Leibenstein, "Bandwagon, Snob, and Veblen Effects in the Theory of Consumer's Demand", *Quarterly Journal of Economics*, 1950, **64**, pp. 183-207, reprinted in D. Kamerschen, *Readings in Microeconomics*, John Wiley, New York, 1969.
[32] Ibid.
[33] Thorstein Veblen (1857-1929), *The Theory of the Leisure Class*, Allen and Unwin, London, 1924.
[34] J. von Neumann and O. Morgenstern, *Theory of Games and Economic Behavior*, Science Edition, John Wiley, New York, 1964, appendix.
[35] This is not to imply that they are necessarily applicable. For a discussion of their limitations, see Robert M. Strotz, "Cardinal Utility", *American Economic Review*, 1953, **42**, pp. 384-97.
[36] K. J. Arrow, "Uncertainty and the Welfare Economics of Medical Care", *American Economic Review*, 1963, **53**, pp. 941-73 and 1965, **55**, pp. 154-8. See also D. S. Lees and R. G. Rice, "Uncertainty and the Welfare Economics of Medical Care", *American Economic Review*, 1965, **55**, pp. 140-53.
[37] See J. Tobin, "Liquidity Preference as Behaviour towards Risk", *The Review of Economic Studies*, 1958, **25**, pp. 65-86.
[38] For further discussion see, for example, C. Tisdell, *The Theory of Price Uncertainty, Production and Profit*, Princeton University Press, Princeton, 1968, Ch. 2.
[39] See Reference 12.
[40] W. J. Baumol and R. Quandt, "Rules of Thumb and Optimally Imperfect Decisions", *American Economic Review*, 1964, **54**, pp. 23-46.
[41] See Reference 13.

FURTHER READING

Baumol, W. J., *Economic Theory and Operations Analysis*, 2nd ed., Prentice-Hall, Englewood Cliffs, 1965, Ch. 9.
Henderson, J. and R. Quandt, *Microeconomic Theory*, McGraw-Hill, New York, 1958, Ch. 2.
Hicks, J. R., *Value and Capital*, 2nd ed., Clarendon Press, Oxford, 1946, Preface, Chs 1 and 2.
Leibenstein, H., "Bandwagon, Snob and Veblen Effects in the Theory of Consumers' Demand", *Quarterly Journal of Economics*, 1950, **64**, pp. 183-207.
Marshall, A., *Principles of Economics*, 8th ed., Macmillan, London, 1920, Book III.
*Samuelson, P., *Foundations of Economic Analysis*, Harvard University Press, Cambridge, 1947, Ch. V.

---

* Advanced.

APPENDIX TO CHAPTER 6

Convex Sets and the Theory of Consumption

In Section V of Chapter 2, the relevance of the mathematics of convex sets to the theory of consumption was noted and it is supposed that the reader is reasonably familiar with that section. The discussion can now be carried further. The special nature of Hicks' demand theory[1] can be further clarified and demand theory can be extended to allow for more diversity in the nature of the preference orderings. In this appendix, Hicksian restrictions on the individual's preference function are successively relaxed and the implications for demand functions of doing this are explored. However, before proceeding with this task, some background knowledge about hyperplanes may be necessary.

A. SEPARATING AND SUPPORTING HYPERPLANES[2]

Our interest in hyperplanes stems from the fact that under perfect competition, a consumer's budget line can be regarded as a hyperplane. The relationship of hyperplanes to sets also concerns us, since a consumer's preferences can be arranged in sets and his equilibrium can be viewed as the point of intersection of a hyperplane and one of these sets. But more of this later. Let us specify some properties of hyperplanes in relation to sets.

A *hyperplane*, H, divides a space into two half-spaces. In two-dimensional space a straight-line is a hyperplane and in three dimensional space a plane is a hyperplane and in N-dimensional space an $N-1$ linear relationship is a hyperplane. A *separating* hyperplane for any two sets is one which ensures that one set is contained in one of the half-spaces defined by H and the second is contained in the other half-space defined by H. A *bounding* hyperplane to a set is one which ensures that all elements of the set are contained in one of the closed half-spaces which the hyperplane defines. A *supporting* hyperplane to a set is one which intersects *only* boundary points of the set. Figures A6.1 and A6.2 illustrate these concepts in two-dimensional space. In Fig. A6.1, H is a separating hyperplane for the two hatched sets. It also bounds both. In Fig. A6.2, H' is a supporting hyperplane to the hatched set (and is also a bounding

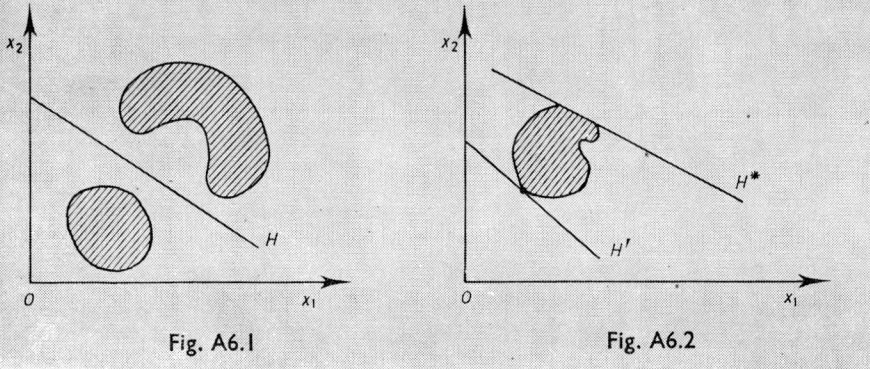

Fig. A6.1   Fig. A6.2

one). So also is H^*. H' intersects the set at one point only whereas H^* coincides with a linear segment of the set.

The following theorems can be shown to hold:
(a) if x^* is any boundary point of a closed convex set, S, it has a supporting hyperplane through x^*. While every boundary point of a closed convex set has a supporting hyperplane, those of non-convex sets do not. Boundary points of the convex set indicated by the hatched area in Fig. A6.3 have supporting hyperplanes and one, H^*, is shown for the point x^*. The non-convex set shown in Fig. A6.4 obviously has no supporting hyperplane at its boundary point, x^*;

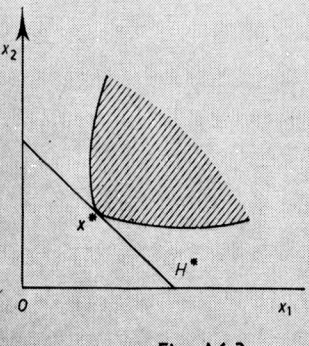
Fig. A6.3

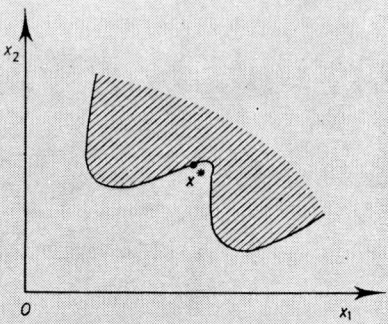
Fig. A6.4

(b) but every boundary point of a closed convex set does not have a unique supporting hyperplane. Boundary points may share the same hyperplane. Furthermore, several supporting hyperplanes may exist at one boundary point. In Fig. A6.5, the supporting plane at x^*, H^*, is, for example, the same as that at x'. In Fig. A6.6 the supporting plane to the set at x^* is not unique. The hyperplanes H^* and H' (and others not shown) are also supporting hyperplanes;

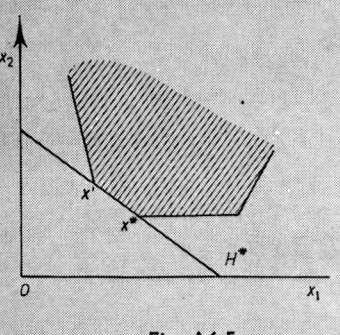
Fig. A6.5

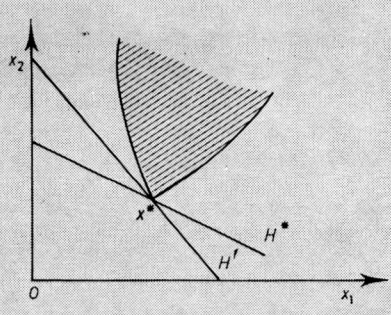
Fig. A6.6

(c) if a set is closed and *strictly* convex, no two different boundary points of it share a common supporting hyperplane. But strict convexity does not rule out the possibility that a boundary point of a set may possess multiple supporting planes. The set shown in Fig. A6.6, for example, is strictly convex but it has a number of supporting hyperplanes at the boundary point, x^*;

(d) however, if a set is closed and strictly convex and if its boundary is differentiable everywhere, each boundary point is on a unique supporting hyperplane to the set.

B. RELEVANCE TO DEMAND THEORY

Let x represent the vector of the quantities of products which a consumer may consume and let $U(x)$ be a function which represents his ordinal preference for the alternative bundles. If x^* represents any value of x (any bundle of products), the set of bundles which the individual finds to be indifferent to or preferred to x^* are defined by

$$S(x^*) = \{x \mid U(x) \geq U(x^*)\}. \tag{A6.1}$$

The set, $S(x^*)$ may vary if x^* varies. For any given value of x^*, $S(x^*)$ consists of bundles on or above the indifference curve corresponding to $U(x^*)$. It consists of all product-bundles which are *no less* preferred by the individual than x^*. In Hicksian demand theory, the sets $S(x^*)$ are strictly convex, and consist of bundles on and above indifference curves.

If $U(x)$ is assumed to be a continuous function, if perfect competition prevails, and if, in view of his limited income, the consumer cannot be satiated by all goods, his equilibrium consumption-bundle occurs at the point where his budget line is a supporting hyperplane to a set $S(x^*)$ whose boundary points are his highest attainable indifference curve. The traditional case is shown in Fig. A6.7 for two products. As indicated, if the consumer's budget-line is ML, his optimal consumption-bundle is B, since this places him upon his highest attainable indifference curve. Now, B is a boundary point of $S(B) = \{x \mid U(x) \geq U(B)\}$. It is a boundary point of the set indicated by the hatched area. $S(B)$ consists of points on or above $I_1 I_1$. ML is clearly a supporting hyperplane to set $S(B)$ and supports it at B. Equilibrium occurs for the intersection of a budget supporting hyperplane and a preferred set of this type.

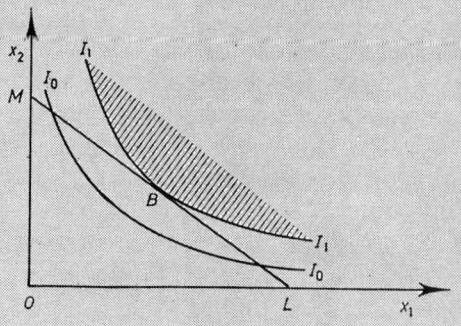

Fig. A6.7

In Hicks' theory (if pure substitutes and complements are ruled out as possibilities) an individual's budget-line in conjunction with his preference map determines a *unique* optimal consumption-bundle for the individual. Furthermore, the individual's budget-line can be so varied that *any* consumption-bundle is optimal. For example, any bundle may be made optimal by altering product prices while holding the individual's income constant. Again, if boundary solutions are ruled out and an individual's money income is given, any variation of product prices leads to a change in the individual's consumption. Any new budget hyperplane involves a change of consumption. These results follow from the assumption that $U(x)$ is a continuous, strictly concave function, which is at least twice differentiable (and which possesses indifference curves which are strictly convex and twice differentiable) and the further supposition that an individual cannot be satiated by *any* product. It will be shown below that if the assumption about the strict concavity and differentiability of $U(x)$ is relaxed (or the assumption about the convexity and differentiability of indifference curves is relaxed) that each of the above propositions no longer holds. In other words, the following Hicksian propositions do not hold:

(i) given an individual's tastes, ruling out boundary solutions, and given his money income, any change of money price changes his consumption;
(ii) given money income and tastes, the choice of a bundle of commodities results from a unique set of prices;
(iii) the optimal consumption-bundle is unique if money income, prices and tastes are given;
(iv) if money income is constant, the consumer can be induced to purchase any combination of products by altering product prices suitably.

Let us relax Hicks' assumptions and consider the consequences.

(a) If the consumer's indifference curves are strictly convex but are not everywhere differentiable, propositions (i) and (ii) do not hold. This can be seen from Fig. A6.6, if the boundary of its hatched set is regarded as an indifference curve. (Strictly, if non-satiation by any product is supposed, this curve should be negatively sloping.) At x^*, a cusp-point, the set is supported by a number of different hyperplanes. This indicates that different sets of prices, income being constant, result in the choice x^*. The set of prices corresponding to this choice is not unique and a change of prices does not necessarily lead to a change of choice.

(b) If the indifference curves are convex (but not necessarily *strictly* so), proposition (iii) does not hold. Consider the case shown in Fig. A6.5. If the consumer's budget-line is H^* and if his highest attainable indifference curve is indicated by the boundary of the hatched set, consumption-bundles anywhere along the linear segment common to this indifference curve and the budget-line are optimal. The choice involves a chance element. Consequently, the partial demand curves for both products may not be *functions* of their price, but relations.

(c) If indifference curves are not convex, proposition (iv) does not hold. As indicated in Fig. A6.4, the set $S(x^*)$ has no supporting hyperplane at x^*. If the boundary of this hatched set is an indifference curve, it is impossible to devise a budget-line which will result in the choice x^*, using constant prices.

Further examples of non-convex indifference curves are shown in Figs A6.8 and A6.9. The indifference curve $I_1 I_1$ in Fig. A6.8 is concave between points B and C and the indifference curves of Fig. A6.9 are *strictly* concave throughout. Under perfect competition the consumer cannot be induced to purchase any combination in the dotted area of Fig. A6.8. For any budget-line which passes through this area, a superior alternative bundle is to be found outside the area. In consequence of the strict concavity of the indifference curves in Fig. A6.9 the individual either purchases one product or the other exclusively. He cannot be persuaded by price variations to purchase both products simultaneously. A combination such as D will never be purchased.[3]

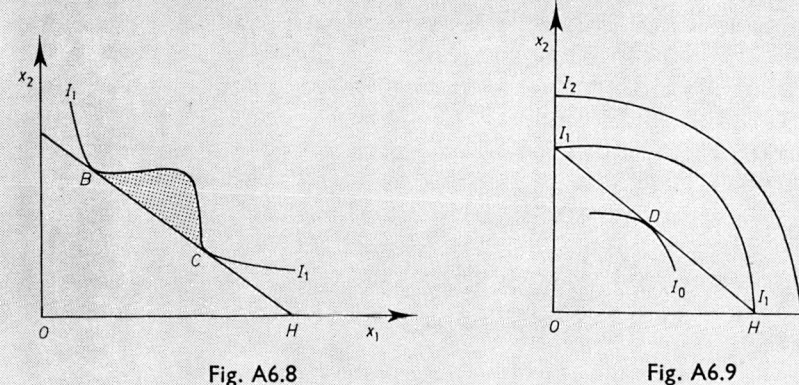

Fig. A6.8   Fig. A6.9

Concavity of indifference curves may arise for many reasons. There may be social taboos on the mixing of some products or of consuming these in particular proportions, and indeed increasing marginal rates of substitution for some goods (like those in Fig. A6.9) may not be uncommon. Expenditure on hobbies might be influenced by marginal rates of substitution like this. Many prefer to specialise in one or a few hobbies and purchase the goods which are appropriate rather than to dabble in many. Again, a consumer may prefer to concentrate his spending on a limited range of products because in that way he becomes known to the sellers of the products, and may "rate" with them whereas if he spreads his expenditure he may remain anonymous. If goods are durable and complex a consumer may also concentrate his outlay on a few products for this may ensure that his knowledge about the products is better. All of these factors may give rise to strictly concave indifference curves. Non-convex indifference curves are associated with *some* goods and there is no reason to suppose that this is very rare. Consequently, traditional demand theory has an important shortcoming.[4]

C. SOME EXTENSIONS OF TRADITIONAL DEMAND THEORY

Debreu[5] has indicated circumstances in which Hicksian demand theory can be readily extended. If a consumer, given his wealth constraint, cannot be satiated by *all* goods and if his (ordinal) utility function is continuous and (*strictly*) *quasi-concave*, the condition for consumer's equilibrium is similar to the Hicksian one. The condition is identical if we add the provision that all indifference curves are differentiable. Debreu's assumptions are much more general than those of Hicks. Hicks assumes a strictly concave utility function and no satiation by any product.

It will be recalled that the concept of a quasi-concave function was discussed in section V of Chapter 2. Taking the example of this appendix, $U(x)$ is a strictly quasi-concave function if

$$S(x^*) = \{x \mid x \geqslant U(x^*)\}$$

is strictly convex where x^* is any value of x. In other words, the utility function is strictly quasi-concave if all bundles which are equally or more preferred to every particular bundle, x^*, form a strictly convex set. The set of bundles on and surrounded by an indifference curve must be strictly convex if $U(x)$ is *strictly* quasi-concave. A strictly concave utility function possesses this property but so to do other functions. (See Chapter 2, Section V.)

In the two-product case, Debreu's assumptions permit indifference curves like those illustrated in Fig. A6.10 (but do not permit the ends of these to join up). Two ridge-lines are shown in Fig. A6.10 by dotted lines. The top ridge-line is the income-consumption path if product 2 is free but not product 1, and the bottom ridge-line is the consumer's income-consumption path if product 1 is free but product 2 is not. Debreu's assumptions imply that the two-ridge lines do not meet in the interior of the figure. The consumer's equilibrium consumption-bundle occurs on a ridge-line or at one of the points contained within the ridge-lines. It only occurs on a ridge-line if one of the products is free. This is, of course, on the assumption that the individual is unable to influence market prices. We *note* that, given differentiability, the indifference curves between the ridge-lines are of the *Hicksian* type, and the consumer is in equilibrium when the Hicksian equilibrium conditions are satisfied, that is, if he allocates all of his income and if the marginal rate of substitution of product 1 for product 2 equals the price of product 1 divided by the price of product 2. Assuming a budget-line of KL, a consumer's equilibrium is indicated at point A in Fig. A6.10. Given this type of map; Hicks' procedures for obtaining price-consumption curves, demand curves and Engel curves can be repeated. But this theory differs from that of Hicks. For example, given Debreu's theory, it is not always possible by a suitable variation of prices to induce the consumer to purchase every commodity-bundle, for example, the consumer cannot be induced to purchase bundle D in Fig. A6.10.

Corner-point equilibria may also arise under Debreu's assumptions. A corner-point optimum is indicated in Fig. A6.11. With a budget-line of KL, the optimum occurs at L and a marginal inequality holds there. Thus the conditions for the consumer's equilibrium are the same as those suggested in Section III, Chapter 6.

In three-dimensions, Debreu's assumptions allow each indifference curve to look like an egg-shell with one end removed. In this three-product world, the individual may be satiated by up to two products. For n products, Debreu's assumptions allow the individual to be satiated by up to $n-1$.

If the assumed differentiability of the indifference curves is dropped then, given the other assumptions, it is still true that the consumer's equilibrium occurs at a

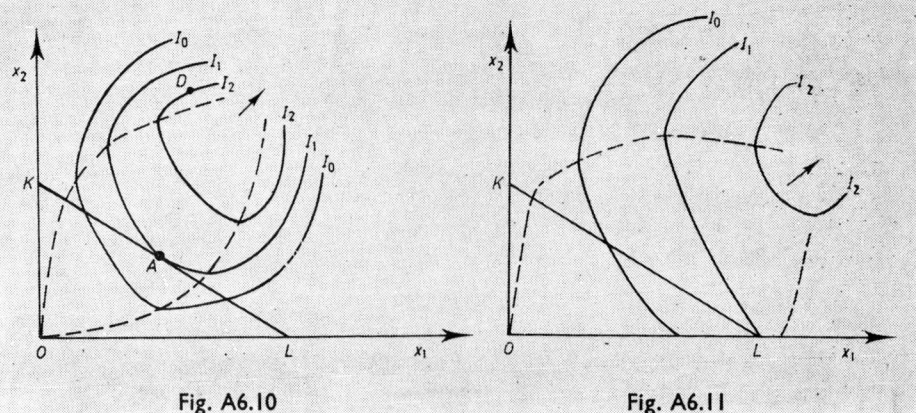

Fig. A6.10   Fig. A6.11

point where the budget-line is a supporting hyperplane to the highest attainable indifference set. This follows from Debreu's non-satiation assumption which is more reasonable than that of Hicks.

Other extensions of the theory of consumer choice are possible. Quasi-concavity of the utility function, for example, does not allow the type of indifference map shown in Figs A6.8 and A6.9. In some circumstances, it is desirable, too, to suppose that $U(x)$ is a discrete function, for example, if the products are only available in large units. Advances in integer programming enable a number of theorems to be derived in this case. But it is not the purpose of this appendix to give a compendium of all extensions of demand theory. It does, however, indicate that important extensions have been made and that intellectual inquiry in this field is far from moribund.

NOTES AND REFERENCES

[1] As outlined in *Value and Capital*, 2nd ed., Clarendon Press, Oxford, 1946.
[2] For further mathematical details on this subject see G. HADLEY, *Linear Algebra*. Addison-Wesley, Reading, Mass., 1961, Sec. 6.6; and K. LANCASTER, *Mathematical Economics*, The Macmillan Company, New York, 1968, R.4.3.
[3] This is relevant to the possibility of controlling an economic unit or an economy by a price system. In this particular instance, a consumer cannot be induced to select D, by setting any set of (fixed) prices for the commodities. As is pointed out in Chapter 22, this limits the possibilities for control under socialism.
[4] Demand curves for cases (a), (b), (c) and (d) have not been specifically given. But the reader, after considering the appendix to Chapter 7, should be easily able to decide on the nature of these curves. The reader might also refer to J. QUIRK and R. SAPOSNIK, *Introduction to General Equilibrium Theory and Welfare Economics*, McGraw-Hill, New York, 1968, Sec. 2-3.
[5] G. DEBREU, *Theory of Value*, John Wiley, New York, 1959.

FURTHER READING

*DEBREU, G., *Theory of Value*, John Wiley, New York, 1959.
KUENNE, R. E., *Microeconomic Theory of the Market Mechanism*, The Macmillan Company, New York, 1968, Ch. 2.
QUIRK, J. and R. SAPOSNIK, *Introduction to General Equilibrium and Welfare Economics*, McGraw-Hill, New York, 1968, Chs 1 and 2.
WALSH, V., *Introduction to Contemporary Microeconomics*, McGraw-Hill, 1970, pp. 206-11.

---

* Advanced.

CHAPTER 7

Production, Costs and Supply

Introduction

As we have just seen, knowledge about the choices of individual consumers places the theory of demand on a firm foundation and enables forecasts to be made about the nature of the market demand for products. So too, on the supply side, the study of the decisions of individual idealised producers enables us to isolate the components of aggregate supply and to predict its properties.

The basic unit of decision-making, on the supply side of the market for a product, is the firm. The firm is an idealised microadministrative unit which determines within the span of its control the output of a particular product or of a number of products. The firm controls its employment of resources and their use in the production of goods. In any market, the aggregate supply of a product and use of resources to produce this product are the combined result of decisions by individual firms. The economic theory of production abstracts from the structure and organisation of firms to concentrate solely on their decisions to produce products and to employ factors of production.

The traditional theory assumes that firms aim to maximise their profit. But this assumption has been subject to considerable challenge in recent years; for example, Berle and Means[1] have suggested that the separation of ownership and management, which is typical of the modern corporation, makes the assumption inappropriate. Nevertheless, the appropriateness of the supposition is as yet undecided and it does provide valuable limiting cases from which welfare propositions can be derived. Hence, much of this analysis is developed on the basis that the profit maximisation hypothesis holds. The hypothesis and competing hypotheses are scrutinised in Chapter 17.

The firm is not free to raise its profit to any level. It is constrained by the technical possibilities which exist for producing goods and by the market both for its product and for the resources which it employs. The known technology sets restraints upon the firm's production possibilities. For example, it is impossible to produce a product from nothing and given a particular quantity of resources there is, with the known technology, a maximum output of any product which can be obtained by its use. The relationship between the input of factors and the maximum output of a product is expressed by a production function. In addition to the technical restrictions, market restrictions must be taken into account. Does the firm influence the price of the product or the price of factors as it varies its output? How high is the price of the product and what are the comparative prices of factors? All these elements modify a firm's strategy for profit maximisation.

Production, Costs and Supply

Let us analyse the fundamentals of that strategy, first limiting ourselves to the simple case where the firm produces one product by means of one variable resource, and then considering the one product and two variable factor example which permits factor substitution. Later some further extensions and refinements of production analysis are discussed.

I. The Firm's Production: A Single Product and Single Factor Case

The case in which the firm produces a single product using a single factor has already been encountered in Chapters 1 and 3 in introducing the notion of economic efficiency. The opportunity now arises to consider the case in detail.

A. THE PRODUCTION FUNCTION

A firm's production function, given the known technology, indicates its maximum output from its employment of each combination of factors. The function presumes technical efficiency, a presumption which may not always be justified. Firms may lack knowledge of generally-known techniques or because of general inefficiency and lack of desire for change or maximum profit may not always switch to the technically most efficient method of production. But even in these circumstances a function which relates their realised output to their inputs has relevance. On the basis of this sub-production relationship predictions can be made and profit can also be maximised subject to it. However, I shall adopt the assumption of technical efficiency because the logic of the argument is much the same and, under perfect competition, there are pressures to ensure technical efficiency. However, these pressures may be less strong in other markets, for example, monopoly markets.

If the firm is producing one product, X, by means of one variable input, L, its production function for a particular period might be represented by

$$x = f(l) \tag{7.1}$$

where x is its output of product X and l is its employment of L. On the assumption of technical efficiency and two available techniques with production relationships $f_1(l)$ and $f_2(l)$ as shown in Fig. 7.1, the firm's production function is the upper boundary of the two curves as shown by the heavy line. Technique 1 is most efficient for an output of $\hat{x}$ or less and technique 2 is superior for higher levels of output.

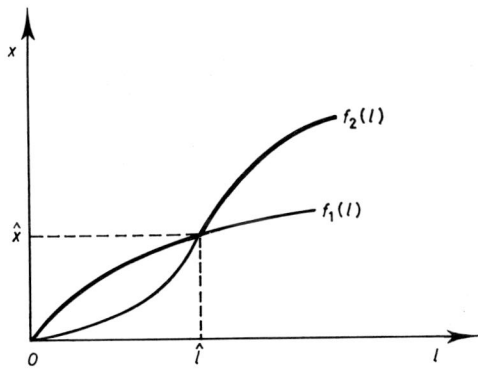

Fig. 7.1

What are the properties of the production function? It is usually assumed to be a continuous and differentiable function. While this assumption is a reasonable abstraction in many circumstances, there are others in which factors are "lumpy" and available only in large discrete quantities. This, for example, might be true of various types of chemical plants.

The production function is also normally assumed (definitely in perfectly competitive markets) to be strictly concave within the firm's decision region. This relationship is usually postulated, where one input is variable, in terms of the *law of eventually diminishing marginal productivity*. The law states that if, in the absence of technical change, the input of one resource is increased while the input of all other resources is held constant, total product increases but, after a certain point, it rises at a decreasing rate and may eventually decline after a sufficiently large amount of the variable input is employed. In other words, the marginal product of a factor, all other factors being constant, falls after a certain point. The production functions shown in Figs 7.2 and 7.3 accord with the law. The marginal product of L, the additional output of X from the employment of an additional unit of L, declines continually in

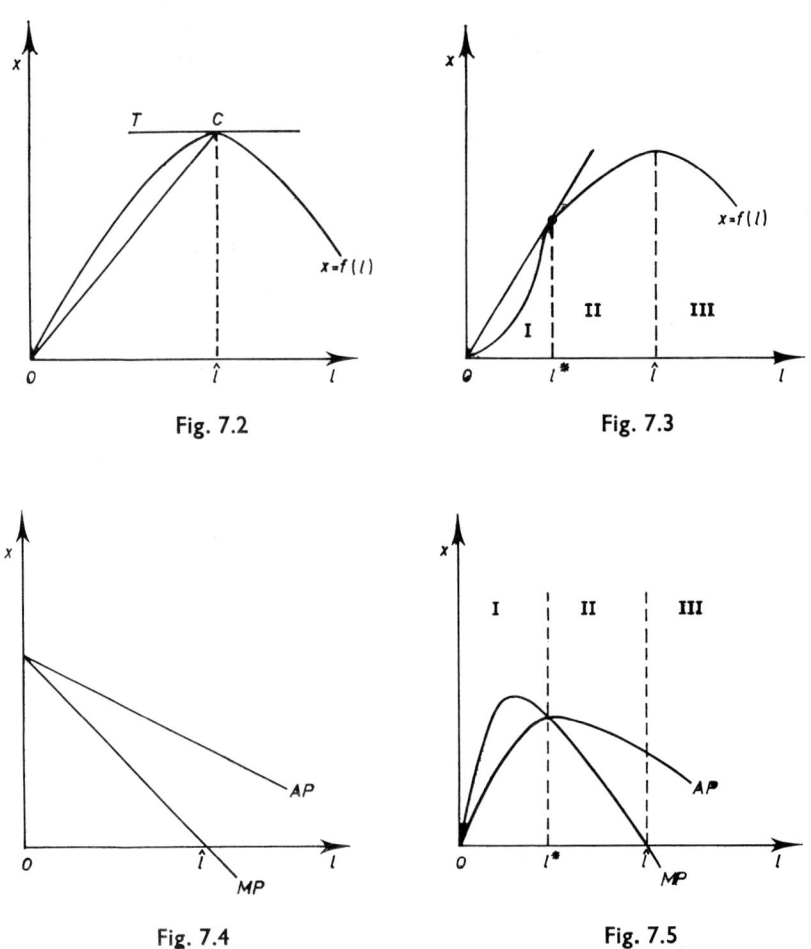

Fig. 7.2

Fig. 7.3

Fig. 7.4

Fig. 7.5

the case shown in Fig. 7.2, but it at first rises in the case illustrated in Fig. 7.3. The corresponding type of marginal product functions for these curves are shown in Figs 7.4 and 7.5, by *MP*. The average product functions $f(l)/l$, are also indicated by *AP*. Note that if the average product function is increasing, the marginal product function is above it, and if the average product function is decreasing, the marginal product function is below it. The marginal product of any employment of L is given by the slope of the tangent to the production function for that employment, and the average product is given by the slope of a ray from the origin to the relevant point on the production function. Thus in Fig. 7.2, the marginal product of $\hat{l}$ is zero since the tangent TC has zero slope, whereas the average product of $\hat{l}$ of the factor is positive since OC has a positive slope.

In Figs 7.3 and 7.4, three regions are marked. If firms maximise profit, production in region **III** does not occur. If perfect competition prevails, production in sector **I** does not maximise profit. This should be clear from the discussion of the next part of this section and the appendix to this chapter. However, if perfect competition does not prevail (for example, if monopoly exists) production in region **I** may be optimal. (See Fig. A7.11 and surrounding discussion. The appendix to this chapter clarifies the issues raised here.) *Under perfect competition*, the only relevant production region is that in which both average and marginal products are decreasing without marginal product being negative. Or, put differently, it is the region in which the production function is increasing and is *strictly* concave.

B. THE SUPPLY DECISIONS OF THE FIRM BRIEFLY EXAMINED

The decisions of firms to supply products and employ factors will be discussed in several later chapters. But at this stage, brief sketches of the theory may be helpful in setting our bearings. Basically, two components influence the production and employment decisions of profit maximising firms. One is the nature of their production function. The other is the type of markets which exist for their products and the nature of the markets in which they purchase their factors of production. This is easily perceived if the firm's profit maximising problem is stated formally. In the one product and one variable factor case, the problem is to maximise

$$\pi = px - wl \qquad (7.2)$$

subject to
$$x = f(l) \qquad (7.3)$$

where π represents the firm's profit, p the price of its product and w the price of L; and the other symbols are as previously used. The firm aims to maximise the difference between its total revenue and total cost given the technical restrictions posed by the production function. But p and w may not be independent of the firm's production decisions. It is always possible that p depends upon the firm's supplies of the product to the market, for example, if it has a monopoly it may depress the price of the product as it supplies greater quantities to the market, and its usage of L may influence w, for example, if it is the sole buyer of the resource. It is possible for

$$p = \phi(x), \text{ where } \phi'(x) \neq 0 \qquad (7.4)$$

and/or for
$$w = \psi(l), \text{ where } \psi'(l) \neq 0. \qquad (7.5)$$

Relationships of this type must be taken into account by profit maximising firms. Markets in which these influences are important are discussed in later chapters.

Let us concentrate here on the case in which $\phi'(x) = 0$ and $\psi'(l) = 0$, the case in which the firm has no influence on market prices, the case of perfect competition in both the product and the factor market. Market prices still affect the perfectly competitive firm's production decisions but for it p and w are constants.

To solve for the perfectly competitive firm's profit maximising output and employment of the factor, substitute Equation (7.3) in Equation (7.2) to give

$$\pi = pf(l) - lw. \tag{7.6}$$

Differentiating this expression with respect to l,

$$\frac{d\pi}{dl} = p\frac{df}{dl} - w. \tag{7.7}$$

If π is to be at a maximum (boundary maxima excluded), it is necessary for $\frac{d\pi}{dl}$ to equal zero. This is so if

$$p\frac{df}{dl} = w \tag{7.8}$$

or

$$\frac{df}{dl} = \frac{w}{p}. \tag{7.9}$$

Now, $\frac{df}{dl}$ is the marginal physical product of L and p is the price per unit for which X is sold so $p\frac{df}{dl}$ is the value of the marginal product of L. Hence, L must be employed at a level which ensures that the value of its marginal product equals its price per unit if the necessary condition for a maximum profit is to be satisfied. Alternatively, the factor L should be employed in a quantity which equates its marginal physical product with its real cost in terms of product X.

This is only a first order condition for a maximum of π. The second order condition that $\frac{d^2\pi}{dl^2}$ is negative must also be satisfied. This is satisfied if

$$\frac{d^2f}{dl^2} < 0, \tag{7.10}$$

that is if the marginal physical productivity of L is declining at its employed level.

The optimal employment of L is indicated for a simple case in Figs 7.6 and 7.8. There the marginal physical product of L is assumed to decline continually and the

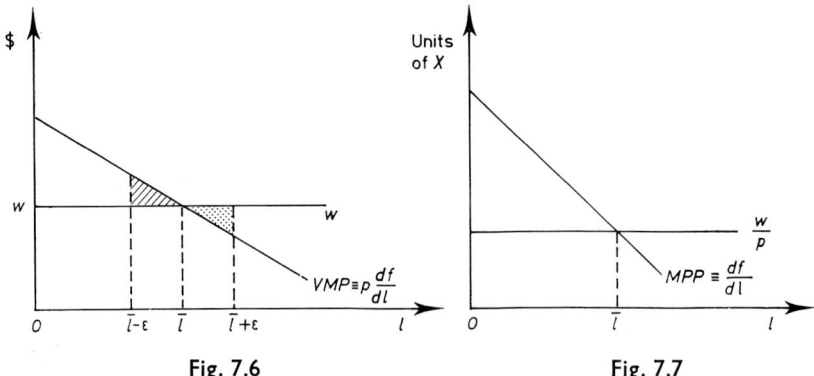

Fig. 7.6 Fig. 7.7

Production, Costs and Supply

profit maximising employment of l is shown by $\bar{l}$. Both versions of the problem give an identical solution. The first figure corresponds to Equation (7.8) and the second to Equation (7.9). That $\bar{l}$ maximises profits may be supported with the following illustration. If $\bar{l}-\varepsilon$ of factor L is employed by the firm, the employment of an additional ε units increases its revenue by more than its cost. Consequently profit rises by the amount shown by the hatched area in Fig. 7.6. To increase employment beyond $\bar{l}$ say to $\bar{l}+\varepsilon$ is to reduce profit. The reduction of profit is indicated by the dotted area of Fig. 7.6. Only for the employment $\bar{l}$ is profit maximised.

Once the optimum value of L is found, the profit maximising output and the maximum level of profit are easily determined. In the case above, the profit maximising level of output is

$$\bar{x} = f(\bar{l}). \qquad (7.11)$$

The maximum level of profit is found by substituting $\bar{l}$ into Equation (7.6).

The profit maximising solution can be illustrated in another way. In an (l, x) plane a series of isoprofit lines can be superimposed on the production function. The optimum occurs at the point of tangency between the highest attainable isoprofit line and the production function.

An isoprofit line indicates levels of L and X which yield the same profit. It is constructed independently of whether the combinations are feasible or not. For example, all the combinations corresponding to a profit of π' can be found by rearranging the equation

$$\pi' = px - wl$$

to give

$$x = \frac{\pi'}{p} + \frac{w}{p}l. \qquad (7.12)$$

The combinations of (l, x) which yield a profit of π' are on this line. Similarly, other isoprofit lines can be found for all the other possible levels of profit. Given w and p, these are all parallel lines and higher ones correspond to greater levels of profit. A series of such isoprofit lines is depicted in Fig. 7.8: π_1 corresponds to combinations giving a profit of π_1, π_2 corresponds to those giving a profit of π_2, etc. A production function $x = f(l)$ for the firm is also shown in the figure. The highest attainable profit occurs at the point where π_2, the highest attainable isoprofit line, is just tangential to the production function. This happens for an employment of L of $\bar{l}$ and an output of X of $\bar{x}$.

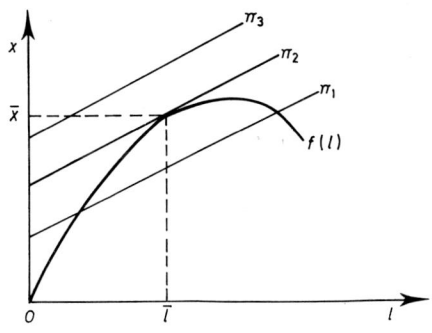

Fig. 7.8

From Equation (7.12), the slope of any isoprofit function is $\frac{w}{p}$. Thus, ruling out boundary solutions, the optimum occurs for a value at which the slope of an isoprofit line equals the slope of the production function. In other words, the optimum corresponds to a value of l which ensures that

$$\frac{w}{p} = \frac{df}{dl}.$$

This condition for profit maximisation agrees with our previous result in Equations (7.9) and (7.8).

A number of relationships hold. It is clear, for example from Fig. 7.7, that the employment of l rises as $\frac{w}{p}$ (the factor to product price ratio) falls if the marginal physical product of the factor is declining. The slower is the decline in the marginal physical productivity of L the greater is the variation in L for a reduction in $\frac{w}{p}$. In turn, the output of X rises as the employment of L increases and by a greater amount the greater is the marginal physical product of L. Consequently, the supply of the product is increased by a decrease in the price of the factor, other things unchanged, or by a rise in the price of the product, if other things are constant. But note that if w and p rise in equal proportions the ratio $\frac{w}{p}$ is unchanged and so too is the firm's supply of the product and its usage of the factor.

Still another method of determining the firm's profit maximising output and employment of the factor exists. This approach expresses costs as a function of output rather than as a function of the employment of the factor used. It is particularly useful if several factors are employed since it readily enables the problem to be separated into different components. Let us briefly consider this approach.

The inverse of the production function $x = f(l)$ indicates the amount of L required to produce various quantities of X *assuming maximum technical efficiency*. Let the inverse of this function be represented by

$$l = g(x). \tag{7.13}$$

(Note that only the monotonically increasing portion of the production function is relevant and *this* has an inverse.)

Total cost can be expressed as

$$wl = wg(x)$$
$$= C(x). \tag{7.14}$$

Consequently, the firm's aim can now be stated as follows: it aims to maximise

$$\pi = px - C(x). \tag{7.15}$$

Ruling out boundary maxima, the output of X must be such that

$$\frac{d\pi}{dx} = p - \frac{dC}{dx} = 0, \tag{7.16}$$

if profit is to be at a maximum and if perfect competition prevails. If profit is to be at a maximum, it is necessary for output to be such that

$$p = \frac{dC}{dx}, \tag{7.17}$$

Production, Costs and Supply

that is for output to be such that p, the additional revenue from the last unit produced, equals the additional cost of the unit. The firm should expand its output until the marginal cost of production just equals the price which it receives for each unit of the product (which also equals its marginal revenue from sales). Not only must the first-order condition be satisfied, but so, too, must the second-order condition. Otherwise profit may well be at a relative minimum or an inflection level. The second-order condition for a maximum requires that $\frac{d^2\pi}{dx^2} < 0$. This is satisfied if $\frac{d^2C}{dx^2}$ is positive, that is if marginal cost is increasing. Thus the optimum level of the firm's output occurs for a level at which marginal cost equals price *and* marginal cost is increasing. In Fig. 7.9, the optimal level of output is $\bar{x}$. If the optimal level of output is known, the maximum level of profit can be found by substituting $\bar{x}$ in Equation (7.15) and

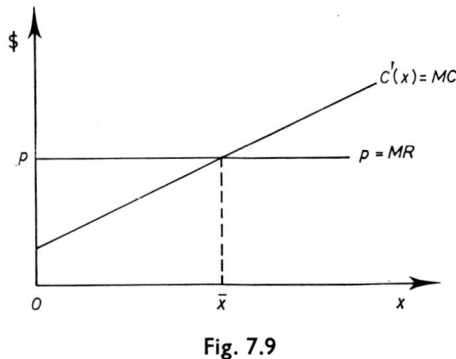

Fig. 7.9

the optimal employment of the factor can be discovered by substituting $\bar{x}$ into Equation (7.13). Thus the whole of the firm's problem of using resources to maximise profit is solved.

If the price of the factor is given, the marginal cost curve of the firm throughout its positively sloping region may be regarded as the product supply curve of the firm. (This is a first approximation since the possibility that average revenue may not cover average variable costs is disregarded.) Thus in Fig. 7.9, as the price of X is raised, other things being constant, the firm's supply of X increases if it acts to maximise its profits Clearly, its supply response is greater the less steep is the marginal cost curve. This curve is less inclined the slower is the rate at which the marginal productivity of factor L falls.

The formal relationship between the slope of the marginal cost function and the production function is as follows:
from Equation (7.14),

$$\frac{dC}{dx} = wg'(x)$$
$$= w\frac{1}{f'(l)} \qquad (7.18)$$

by the inverse differentiation rule. Hence,

$$\frac{d^2C}{dx^2} = -\frac{wf''(l)}{[f'(l)]^2} \qquad (7.19)$$

by the quotient differentiation rule. $\dfrac{d^2C}{dx^2}$ is the slope of the marginal cost curve and, given that $f''(l)$ is negative, this slope is smaller the lower is $f''(l)$, the slower is the rate of diminishing marginal productivity. The relationship between the production function and the cost function is comparatively simple in this case. It is less so in the multiple factor case.

It can be concluded in the single product and single factor case that the supply curve of a perfectly competitive firm's product is upward-sloping and its steepness depends upon the rate with which the marginal productivity of the variable factor diminishes.

II. The Firm's Production: A Single Product and Two Factor Case

This case differs from the former in one important respect. It permits the substitution of factors for one another in the production of goods, and consequently increases the realism of the model. Furthermore, it brings out certain formal similarities between the firm's decision problem and those of the consumer.

A. THE FIRM'S PRODUCTION FUNCTION AND ISOQUANTS

As before, the firm's production function indicates its maximum possible output from its employment of each combination of factors. If the firm produces one product by using two variable inputs, 1 and 2, its production function might be represented by

$$x = F(l_1, l_2)$$

where x indicates its output of product X and l_1 and l_2 are its level of employment of inputs 1 and 2 respectively.

What properties are possessed by a typical production function of this kind? Normally, it is assumed to possess the following properties:

(i) it is *strictly* concave (at least in the relevant decision area) and continuous and at least twice differentiable; and

(ii) if the application of any factor (or factors) is increased and that of the others is held constant, the output of the product is altered.

Assumption (i) implies that the set of factor quantities required to produce an output of any particular value or greater is *strictly* convex, that is it implies the quasi-concavity of the production function. Assumption (ii) implies that *isoquants*, which are the counterparts to indifference curves in production theory, have no thickness and do not intersect. (The argument need not be repeated here, since it is identical to that given previously for indifference curves.) An isoquant links those input combinations which yield the same specific level of output. For example, the circular line indicated in Fig. 7.10 by Q_2 represents an isoquant, a contour line, of the firm's production function. It links the combinations of l_1 and l_2 which yield a specific level of output, for example, an output of 50 units of X. It shows, for example, that the following combinations of (l_1, l_2) produce the same level of output: (3, 1), (1, 2) and (5, 2).

The isoquant shown in Fig. 7.10 might be selected from a field of isoquants such as the one represented in Fig. 7.11. In that field the isoquants marked by a higher subscript of Q correspond to higher levels of output. For any movement along a

Production, Costs and Supply

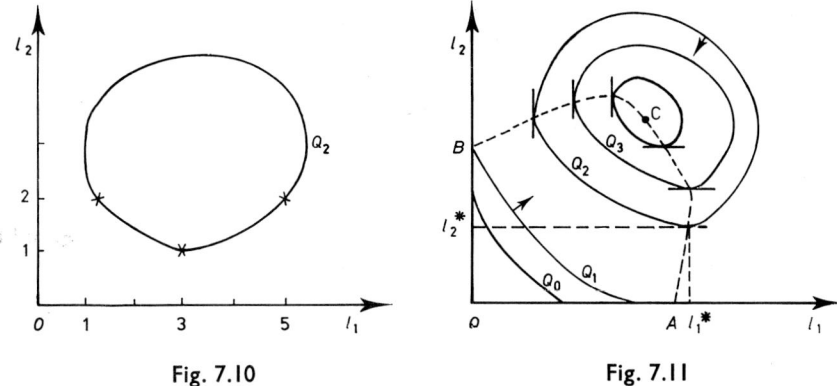

Fig. 7.10   Fig. 7.11

north-easterly ray in this diagram (with increases of both factors 1 and 2 in fixed proportions) output at first increases but then reaches a maximum and declines.

Concave production functions do not always possess an isoquant map like that illustrated in Fig. 7.11. Indeed, Hicks[2] assumes that typically all isoquants are negatively sloped throughout, and are *strictly* convex. In that case, given concavity of the production function, the further an isoquant is to the north-east, the greater is its associated output. The isoquant map is like that indicated in Fig. 7.12. The supposition of such a map might be defended on two grounds, namely that production functions are normally of a type which yields this kind of map or, even though production functions are not of this type, production functions are of this kind, *within the relevant decision area* for the firm. For example, in Fig. 7.11, isoquants have these properties in the relevant decision area which lies between the two dotted *ridge lines AC* and *BC*. Along the ridge line *BC*, which joins vertical points on the isoquants, each employment of l_2 is such that for the corresponding employment of l_1 any additional employment of l_2 causes total output to fall. The marginal product of factor 2 is negative and, even if factor 2 were free, there would be no incentive to use greater quantities of it with the employed quantity of input 1 indicated on the ridge line. Analogously, the ridge line *AC* gives the limits to the possible profitable employment of factor 1 for given quantities of employment of factor 2, for example, l_1^* is the limit of *possible* profitable employment of input 1 if l_2^* of factor 2 is employed because the total product falls for a greater employment of l_1.

An isoquant map of the Hicksian type is indicated in Fig. 7.12. The isoquants are

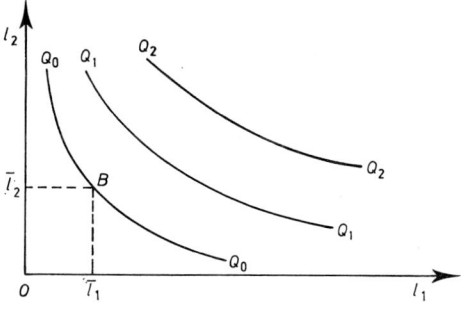

Fig. 7.12

strictly convex and negatively sloped and the higher ones correspond to greater levels of output. The *strict* convexity of the isoquants reflects the diminishing rate of substitution of one factor for the other as the employment of the other is increased. Thus, as the employment of input 1 increases, the rate of technical substitution of input 2 for input 1 decreases. The rate of technical substitution of input 2 for input 1 is the minimum amount by which input 2 can be decreased, if the quantity of input 1 is increased by one unit and output is to remain unaltered. More precisely, the marginal rate of substitution of the two factors at a given level of employment is equal to the absolute rate of change of (slope of the tangent to) the corresponding isoquant at their relevant employment values, for example, the rate of technical substitution of factor 2 for factor 1 at an employment of $(\bar{l}_1, \bar{l}_2)$ in Fig. 7.12 is the absolute slope of the tangent to Q_0Q_0 at point B. The rate of technical substitution of input 2 for input 1 can be represented by

$$RTS_{21} = \left| \frac{dl_2}{dl_1} \right| \qquad (7.20)$$

where $\frac{dl_2}{dl_1}$ is the slope of the isoquant at the relevant point.

Incidentally, the slope of an isoquant can be computed from first principles. The input combinations which yield any specific output, x^*, must satisfy

$$F(l_1, l_2) = x^*, \qquad (7.21)$$

and form the isoquant corresponding to an output of x^*. Differentiating Equation (7.21) the variations of l_1 and l_2 which satisfy the equation must satisfy

$$\frac{\partial F}{\partial l_1} dl_1 + \frac{\partial F}{\partial l_2} dl_2 = 0. \qquad (7.22)$$

Hence, the slope of the isoquant is

$$\frac{dl_2}{dl_1} = -\frac{\partial F}{\partial l_1} \bigg/ \frac{\partial F}{\partial l_2} \qquad (7.23)$$

$$= -MPP_1/MPP_2, \qquad (7.24)$$

where the marginal physical productivity of the appropriate factor is indicated by *MPP*. (The marginal physical product of any factor is the variation of output which results from a small increase in the use of that factor, if technology and the utilisation of all other factors are constant.) The RTS_{21} equals the ratio of MPP_1 to MPP_2. RTS_{21} is equal to the ratio of the marginal physical productivities of the factors. This result will be utilised later in discussing the firm's profit maximising decisions.

The rate at which factors can be substituted in production is important because the responsiveness of the economic system to factor price changes is influenced by it. Two limiting cases of substitutability are worthy of special note. One is the case in which the factors of production are perfect substitutes and the isoquants are straight lines so that the rate of technical substitution of the factors is constant. The other is the case in which the factors are required in fixed proportions so that each isoquant consists of two linear segments which meet at right angles. Isoquant maps of these respective types are shown in Figs 7.13 and 7.14. The latter one allows no factor substitution.

Production, Costs and Supply

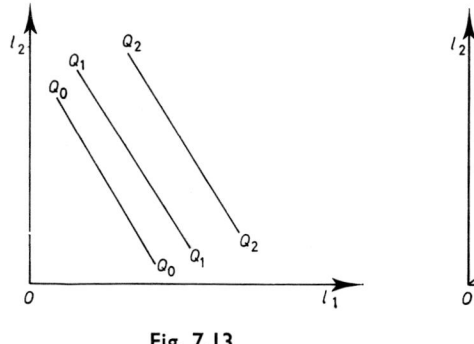

Fig. 7.13

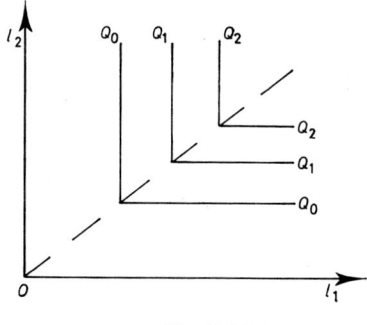

Fig. 7.14

B. THE FIRM'S PROFIT MAXIMISING BEHAVIOUR

In the one product, two variable factor example, as in the previous case, the determination of the firm's optimal employment of factors can be approached in two different ways. The optimal employment of the factors may be determined first and can then be used to find the optimal output. Alternatively, optimal output may be found by means of a cost function and then be used to locate the optimal employment of factors. The latter approach will be emphasised, since it enables a traditional type of supply curve for the firm's product to be drawn without difficulty. However, it has the disadvantage that it conceals the significance of factor prices to some extent. (Compare the discussion in the appendix of this chapter.) Let me briefly indicate the first approach and then spend more time on the second approach.

The firm's aim is to maximise its profit function

$$\pi = px - (w_1 l_1 + w_2 l_2) \tag{7.25}$$

subject to its production restrictions as indicated by the production function,

$$x = F(l_1, l_2). \tag{7.26}$$

(Note that no fixed cost is shown in Equation (7.25). The conditions for maximum profit are unaffected by its inclusion, that is by the inclusion of a cost term which does not vary with the employment of the factors.) As previously, assume that perfect competition exists in both the product and the factor markets so that p, w_1 and w_2 are constants from the firm's point of view.

The maximum of this constrained problem may be found by Lagrange's method or more directly by substituting Equation (7.26) into (7.25) and maximising with respect to l_1 and l_2. This substitution gives

$$\pi = pF(l_1, l_2) - w_1 l_1 - w_2 l_2. \tag{7.27}$$

Hence,
$$d\pi = \left(p\frac{\partial F}{\partial l_1} - w_1\right)dl_1 + \left(p\frac{\partial F}{\partial l_2} - w_2\right)dl_2 \tag{7.28}$$

and no change in profit occurs for very small variations of l_1 and l_2 if the following equations are both satisfied:

$$p\frac{\partial F}{\partial l_1} - w_1 = 0 \tag{7.29}$$

$$p\frac{\partial F}{\partial l_2} - w_2 = 0. \tag{7.30}$$

It is necessary for these conditions to be satisfied if profit is to be at a maximum (boundary maxima being ruled out).

The partial derivatives $\frac{\partial F}{\partial l_1}$ and $\frac{\partial F}{\partial l_2}$ represent the marginal physical products of factors 1 and 2 respectively and these, when multiplied by the price of the product, give the respective values of the marginal products of the factors. Thus the above equations may be restated as the requirements:

$$pMPP_1 = w_1 \tag{7.31}$$

$$pMPP_2 = w_2 \tag{7.32}$$

or

$$VMP_1 = MRP_1 = w_1 \tag{7.33}$$

$$VMP_2 = MRP_2 = w_2 \tag{7.34}$$

since under perfect competition the value of the marginal product equals the marginal revenue product (MRP, the additional revenue from the sale of the extra units of the product due to the employment of an extra unit of the factor). Each factor should be hired up to the level at which the addition to the firm's revenue of the product of the last unit hired just equals the cost of that unit.

The above conditions are only first-order conditions for a maximum. However, the strict concavity of the production function ensures that the second-order conditions are satisfied and that the solutions to Equations (7.29) and (7.30) are unique. Let $(\bar{l}_1, \bar{l}_2)$ satisfy these equations. Then, the profit maximising output level can be found by substituting in the production function, $x = F(\bar{l}_1, \bar{l}_2)$. It is clear from Equations (7.31) and (7.32) that the solutions are unchanged if all prices (factor and product prices) alter in the same proportion. It is also evident from this set of equations that, if profit is maximised, the factors are combined so that

$$\frac{MPP_1}{w_1} = \frac{MPP_2}{w_2}. \tag{7.35}$$

In other words, the contribution to output of the last cent's worth of factor 1 equals the contribution of the last cent's worth of factor 2. This condition alone does not, however, ensure profit maximisation. This, if it is not already evident, can clearly be seen from the next approach which will be discussed now.

If the firm wishes to maximise profit, it must minimise its cost of producing any output which it does produce. Let us, therefore, consider the combinations of factors or inputs which minimise its cost of producing each alternative level of output. To do so, the concept of an isocost function is needed. An isocost function indicates those factor employments which result in the same level (equal level) of cost or require the same expenditure by the firm. It is the counterpart of the budget line of consumer theory.

The perfectly competitive firm's isocost line for any given level of expenditure can be found by rearranging its cost function

$$C = w_1 l_1 + w_2 l_2 \tag{7.36}$$

to give

$$l_2 = \frac{C}{w_2} - \frac{w_1}{w_2} l_1 \tag{7.37}$$

Production, Costs and Supply

and then substituting the appropriate specific level of expenditure for C. Thus the isocost line for an expenditure of C^* is

$$l_2 = \frac{C^*}{w_2} - \frac{w_1}{w_2}l_1 \qquad (7.38)$$

and is indicated in Fig. 7.15 by the line AB. This is a straight line with negative slope and its slope depends on the relative prices of the factors. It cuts the l_2 axis at $\frac{C^*}{w_2}$ and the l_1 axis at $\frac{C^*}{w_1}$. These intercepts represent respectively the quantity purchased of factor 2 if total expenditure is allocated to input 2 and the quantity purchased of factor 1 if all expenditure is on factor 1.

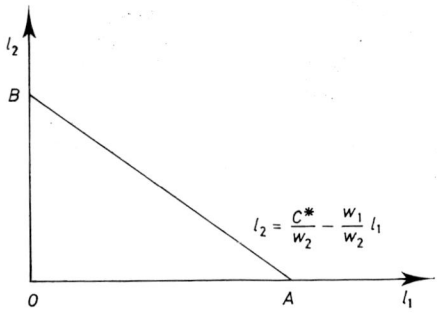

Fig. 7.15

The isocost line AB in Fig. 7.15 indicates those input combinations of (l_1, l_2) which, *given* the prices of the factors, the firm is able to purchase by an expenditure of C^*. If factor prices are unchanged, then for a greater expenditure the firm is able to reach a higher cost curve, for example, CD in Fig. 7.16. Indeed, given the factor prices, there are an infinite number of parallel isocost lines to AB, and the higher ones correspond to greater levels of expenditure. The effect of a rise in the price of one factor, if the price of the other is unaltered, is to change the slope of the isocost lines. In Fig. 7.16, the isocost line $A'B$ occurs for the expenditure C^* if the price of factor 1 rises while the price of factor 2 remains unchanged. These variations are analogous to those for the consumer's budget line.

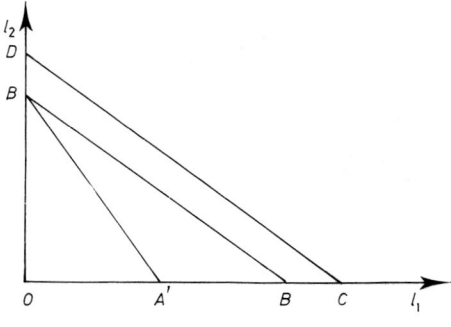

Fig. 7.16

If isoquants are *strictly* convex, and if the production function is continuous, any isocost line is tangential to one isoquant at *one point only*. The combination of inputs at that point minimises the cost of producing the output appropriate to the isoquant or it maximises the possible output from the expenditure corresponding to the isocost line. In the Hicksian case illustrated in Fig. 7.17, the input combination at point H both minimises the cost of producing an output of Q_1 and maximises the output from an expenditure of C^* if this is the expenditure corresponding to isocost AB. Thus we note a duality. The input combination at H minimises the cost of producing

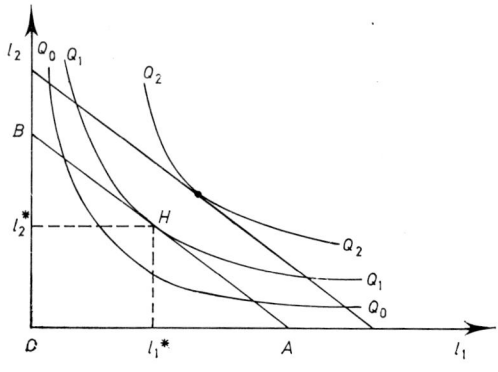

Fig. 7.17

Q_1 since the isoquant $Q_1 Q_1$ intercepts higher isocosts than AB at all points other than H. The combination maximises the output for an expenditure of C^* since the isocost line AB intercepts lower isoquants than $Q_1 Q_1$ at all other points.

At the cost minimisation point H, the slope of the isocost line is equal to the slope of the isoquant, $Q_1 Q_1$. At a point such as this,

$$\frac{dl_2}{dl_1} = -\frac{w_1}{w_2} \qquad (7.39)$$

where $\dfrac{dl_2}{dl_1}$ is the slope of the isoquant. Consequently, since

$$RTS_{21} = \left| \frac{dl_2}{dl_1} \right|, \qquad (7.40)$$

the condition which must be satisfied if the cost of producing a particular level of output is to be at a minimum is

$$RTS_{21} = w_1/w_2. \qquad (7.41)$$

For the cost to be at a minimum for producing a specific output, the factors must be hired up to the point where the rate of technical substitution of input 2 for input 1 equals the price ratio of input 1 to input 2.

From Equation (7.24),

$$RTS_{21} = MPP_1/MPP_2. \qquad (7.42)$$

Hence, the condition which is expressed by Equation (7.41) amounts to the requirement that

$$MPP_1/MPP_2 = w_1/w_2$$

Production, Costs and Supply

or that

$$\frac{MPP_1}{w_1} = \frac{MPP_2}{w_2} \qquad (7.43)$$

which is the same condition as was obtained in Equation (7.35) for the optimal combination of factors. Equation (7.43) implies that inputs are not optimally combined unless the marginal contribution to output of the last cent spent on each is the same. If this condition is unsatisfied, the firm's output can be produced at lower cost or a greater output can be produced by its existing expenditure. Because of the nature of the Hicksian production map, whenever the above necessary condition is satisfied, so too are the sufficient conditions for minimising the costs of producing a particular level of output.

The condition of Equation (7.43) can be used to deduce the consequences for employment of changes in the prices of inputs. If the price of one input rises relative to the other, it is clear that its use in producing the same level of output declines if isoquants are declining and *strictly* convex and twice differentiable, that is of the type indicated in Fig. 7.17. However, no substitution takes place if the inputs are required in fixed proportions (for example, the case indicated in Fig. 7.14), for then the rotation of an isocost line around the isoquant does not alter the point of tangency of the line and the isoquant.

The condition for minimising cost of any output has further application. It can be used to trace out the firm's *expansion path* and this in turn can be used to express the firm's costs as a function of its output. The firm's expansion path is analogous to the income-consumption path of a consumer and indicates, at given factor prices, the factor combinations which minimise the firm's costs for each of its possible levels of output. The path reveals the way in which the firm's cost minimising combination of inputs changes as its output varies. Such a curve, which links the points of tangency of the isocost curves and isoquants, is shown by $OHJE$ in Fig. 7.18. H is the minimum cost combination for $x = x_1$ and J is the minimum cost combination for the output

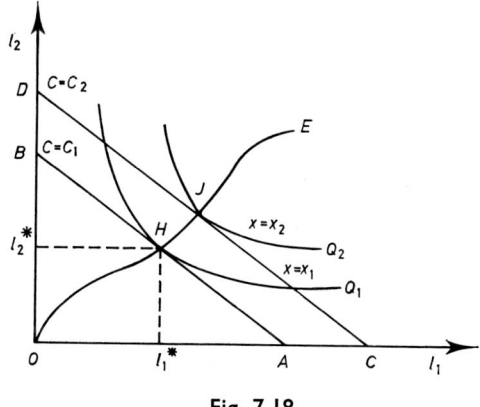

Fig. 7.18

$x = x_2$, where AB and CD are the respective relevant isocost lines corresponding to costs of C_1 and C_2. Linking all such points, the expansion path $OHJE$ is obtained at the given factor prices. (A different expansion path may be relevant at different factor prices.) All of the input combinations along OE minimise the cost of different levels of output. A profit maximising firm must produce at some point along its expansion path. Our task now is to determine its profit maximising point on this path, given that it is free to vary its output. To do this it is necessary to consider the firm's costs as a function of its output.

The firm's costs as a function of output is usually computed on the assumption that factors are so combined as to minimise the cost of any specific level of output. Thus a part of the profit-optimising problem is already supposed to be solved and the firm's cost as a function of output is, in fact, its lower limit of cost. This should be borne in mind since, if organisational slack is present, costs may be in excess of this limit.

To illustrate: from Fig. 7.18, if output x_1 is produced at minimum cost, it costs the firm C_1. Thus (x_1, C_1) is a point on the firm's cost curve (as defined above). So, too, is (x_2, C_2) since C_2 is the minimum cost of producing x_2. The two points are shown in Fig. 7.19. Similarly, other cost and output combinations can be obtained and a total-cost function, such as that shown by $C(x)$ in Fig. 7.19, can be constructed. The total-cost function shown increases at an accelerating rate thus indicating rising

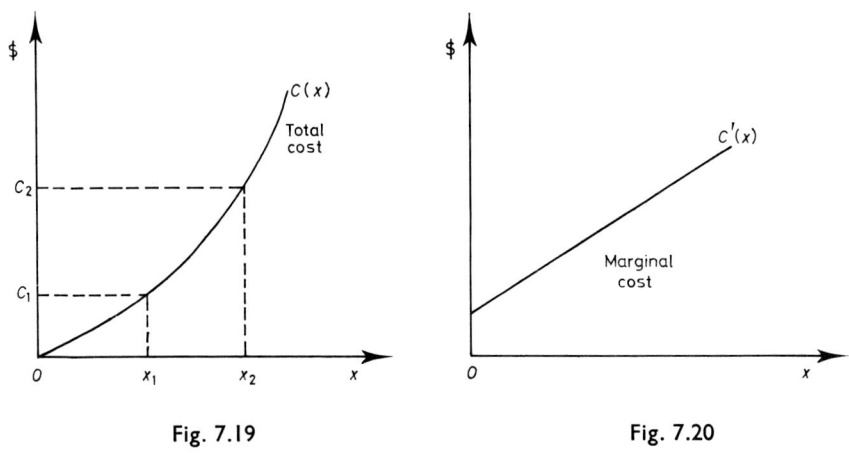

Fig. 7.19   Fig. 7.20

additional costs as a result of the firm's expansion. The corresponding marginal cost curve is indicated in Fig. 7.20. It expresses the additional cost which results from the production of an additional unit of the product. More precisely, marginal cost is the rate of change or first derivative of the total-cost function.

Given the cost function $C(x)$, the level of output which maximises the perfectly competitive firm's profit can now be determined. It is the output which maximises the difference between the firm's revenue and its costs, that is the output which maximises

$$\pi = px - C(x). \tag{7.44}$$

A necessary condition for this to be at a maximum is that

$$\frac{d\pi}{dx} = p - C'(x) = 0. \tag{7.45}$$

This condition is satisfied if

$$p = C'(x), \tag{7.46}$$

that is if the level of output is such that the additional revenue from an extra unit of output just equals its additional cost. Output must be such that price (= marginal revenue under perfect competition) equals marginal cost. In Fig. 7.21, this equality is satisfied for an output of $x = x_1$. Clearly, an expansion of output beyond x_1 adds

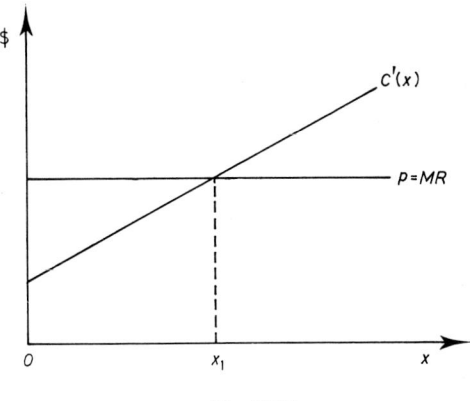

Fig. 7.21

more to cost than to revenue, since its addition to the area under the marginal cost curve exceeds its addition under the marginal revenue curve. If output is below x_1, the opposite situation holds.

Thus the whole of the firm's profit maximising strategy can be determined. To maximise profit it should produce an output of $x = x_1$. This output should be produced at minimum cost (in this case C_1) and consequently, as is indicated in Fig. 7.18, it ought to employ l_1^* of input 1 and l_2^* of input 2. In order to maximise its profit, a perfectly competitive firm

(i) must produce an output which equates the marginal revenue (equals, under perfect competition, the price per unit) of the product to its marginal cost of producing the product; and

(ii) must combine factors of production in a proportion which equates the marginal productivity per dollar of each input employed. The last condition is equivalent to the rule that the rate of technical substitution of factors be equated to the price ratios of the factors.

Given the assumptions used above (the cost function is *strictly* convex, the production function is *strictly* concave and both increase monotonically), these conditions suffice to determine the firm's profit maximising level of output and its optimal usage of factors.

Assuming that firms maximise profits, these conditions imply various supply relationships. If factor prices are constant, the firm's supply function of its product (the function which relates its supply of the product to the product's price) is the positively sloping portion of its marginal cost curve (above its minimum average variable cost point). This will be explained at length in the next chapter. In the case illustrated in Fig. 7.21, the supply curve coincides with the firm's marginal cost curve since the marginal cost curve increases throughout its length. The rise of marginal cost occurs because the total cost function is *strictly* convex due to *decreasing returns to outlay*. In consequence, the perfectly competitive firm's supply curve of the product as a function of the product's price alone is positively sloped. A more detailed discussion of this is given in the next chapter.

The term *returns to outlay* has not been defined nor has the concept of *returns to scale* been introduced. "Returns to outlay" indicates the relationship between a firm's output and its expenditure on inputs, if inputs are combined to minimise the cost of each output. It relates output to costs on the assumption that the firm adjusts along its expansion path. If output rises at an increasing rate as expenditure increases, increasing returns to outlay prevail; if it advances at a constant rate, constant returns to outlay occur; and if it climbs at a decreasing rate, decreasing returns to outlay prevail. Returns to outlay are indicated by the *inverse* of the cost function $C(x)$. If decreasing returns to outlay occur, $C''(x) > 0$, the marginal cost curve is positively sloped. For constant returns to outlay $C''(x) = 0$ and for increasing returns $C''(x) < 0$, the marginal cost curve is negatively sloped.

Consider the example given in Fig. 7.22, where the price of the factors is assumed to be constant. The lower isocost line corresponds to the cost of C_0 and the others to multiples of C_0 as indicated. The three isoquants, Q_0, Q_1 and Q_2, correspond to outputs of 10, 15 and 20 units of X. Constant returns to outlay prevail since output increases in the same proportion as the increase of costs. Had the isoquants been marked 10, 15 and 17.5 respectively, then decreasing returns to outlay would have been indicated. Note that the expansion path may, but need not, be linear and if it is linear, decreasing or increasing returns to outlay may be associated with it.

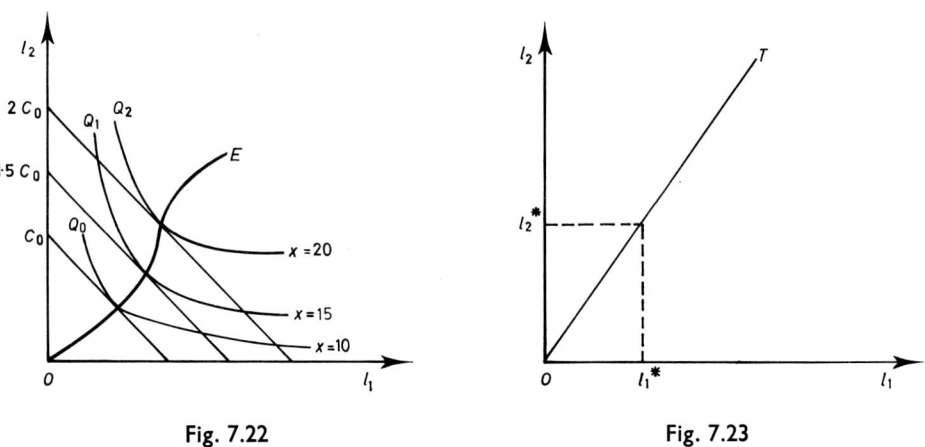

Fig. 7.22   Fig. 7.23

"Returns to scale" refers to the relationship between the firm's output and the quantity of resources employed by it, if the inputs are *combined in some fixed proportions*. Hence, a firm's scale line is always a straight line like that indicated by OT in Fig. 7.23. The scale line OT is drawn on the assumption that factors are combined in the proportion l_2^*/l_1^*. Constant, decreasing, or increasing returns to scale arise depending upon whether output increases by the same proportion, a lesser or a greater fraction than a fractional increase in the use of factors. Thus, if resource use is increased from (l_1^*, l_2^*) to $2(l_1^*, l_2^*)$ and if the output $F(2l_1^*, 2l_2^*)$ is less than

$2F(l_1^*, l_2^*)$, decreasing returns to scale occur. A doubling of the inputs (l_1^*, l_2^*) less than doubles output.

So far production theory has been outlined for (i) a single product and single factor case, and (ii) for a single product and two factor case. Production theory for the two product and single factor case can also be easily outlined by diagrams and simple mathematics, and the interested reader is referred to Henderson and Quandt, *Microeconomic Theory*.[3] The two product and two input case lends itself to some diagrammatic exposition and cannot be neglected even in this brief survey.

III. The Two Product and Two Factor Case

The two product and two factor case is of particular interest since it permits substitution of both factors and products. It is also a model which is frequently used in expositions of international trade theory and welfare economics. A knowledge of at least its bare essentials is necessary.

Take two products X_1 and X_2 and two factors L_1 and L_2. Indicate the firm's output of X_1 by x_1 and of X_2 by x_2. Let l_{11} and l_{12} represent the quantity of factor 1 allocated to products 1 and 2 respectively, and l_{21} and l_{22} represent the corresponding allocation of factor 2. Then if the firm's production function can be separated into the components

$$x_1 = F_1(l_{11}, l_{21}) \tag{7.47}$$

and
$$x_2 = F_2(l_{12}, l_{22}), \tag{7.48}$$

the profit maximising solutions of the last section apply, *mutatis mutandis*. The decisions about the production of each product can be made independently. Each factor should be employed in producing each product up to the point where the value of the marginal product of the factor equals the factor's price. This, of course, assumes perfect competition in both the factor and product markets. Alternatively, each product should be produced at a level which equates its price per unit to its marginal cost and, for each product, the marginal product per dollar of each factor should be the same (or the rate of technical substitution of the factors should equal their price ratios). The separation of the production functions which is indicated in Equations (7.47) and (7.48) is not always realistic since the output of product 1 may be influenced by activity in producing 2 and vice versa. Such interdependence can be allowed for. But let us keep to the simple model since it illustrates concepts which are applicable in more complicated cases.

The first such concept is the firm's *efficiency-locus*. For a *given* quantity of factors employed by the firm, the locus indicates all input combinations, such that it is impossible to increase the firm's output of one product without decreasing the output of another. If factors are not combined in proportions indicated by this locus it is possible by merely reallocating the employed factors to increase the output of one product without decreasing that of another. Clearly, economic inefficiency arises if factors are not combined in proportions dictated by the efficiency-locus. In Fig. 7.24, the firm's efficiency-locus is indicated by O_1ABO_2 in an Edgeworth-Bowley Box. The length of the base of this box is equal to the specific amount of L_1 employed by the firm and its height indicates the specific amount of L_2 employed. From the origin O_1, the isoquants corresponding to $x_1 = F_1(l_{11}, l_{22})$ are depicted. $Q_0{}^1 Q_0{}^1$ is one of these and $Q_1{}^1 Q_1{}^1$ is another and corresponds to a higher output of X_1. From the origin O_2, the isoquants corresponding to the production function $x_2 = F_2(l_{12}, l_{22})$ are indicated. Two associated isoquants are shown by $Q_0{}^2Q_0{}^2$ and $Q_1{}^2Q_1{}^2$. The latter one corresponds to the higher output.

The efficiency-locus consists of the points of tangency of all of these isoquants. A is one point of tangency and consequently is on the efficiency-locus but C is not. The combination of factors at point C is inefficient. Combination A is superior to that at C since in comparison to C it ensures that the output of X_1 is the same but that of X_2 is greater. Indeed, any factor combination on the segment AB of the efficiency-locus is superior to combination C. However, once the firm reaches its efficiency-locus it cannot increase the output of one product without decreasing that of the other, if its employment of resources is constant.

Along the efficiency-locus, the rates of change of the isoquants for the different products (the rates of technical substitution of the factors) in producing the products are equal. Only if these rates are equal will output be at a maximum, given the factors which are employed. Under perfect competition, this efficiency condition is automatically satisfied since the rate of technical substitution of factors is equated to the same factor-price ratio for each product. This last condition, as has been shown, is necessary for the firm's profit maximisation. (See Equation 7.42 and the discussion.)

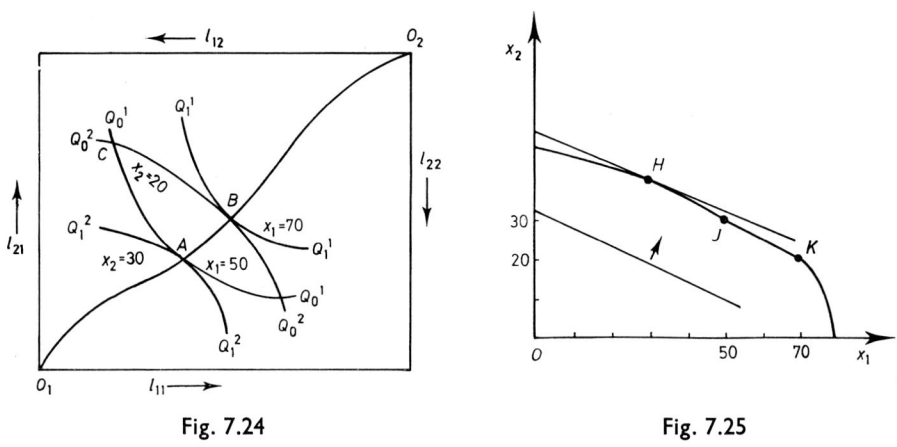

Fig. 7.24   Fig. 7.25

The firm's *product transformation function* can be found from its efficiency-locus. For the efficiency-locus shown in Fig. 7.24, a corresponding product transformation function is indicated by the curve HJK in Fig. 7.25. This curve shows the maximum amount of X_2 which is consistent with the production of various quantities of X_1, given the quantity of factors employed. The absolute slope of the product transformation function is the rate of product transformation (RPT), the rate at which one product can be substituted for another given maximum technical efficiency. Under perfect competition, profit maximisation requires that

$$RPT = \frac{p_1}{p_2}. \tag{7.49}$$

This is easily seen. *Given* the employed factors and factor prices, all costs are fixed, so profit is at a maximum if revenue is maximised. Revenue is equal to

$$R = p_1x_1 + p_2x_2, \tag{7.50}$$

and a series of isorevenue curves may be drawn in Fig. 7.25.[4] Each isorevenue curve is specified by

$$x_2 = R/p_2 - (p_1/p_2)x_1 \qquad (7.51)$$

where the appropriate value of R is substituted. Isorevenue lines have a slope of $-p_1/p_2$ and higher lines correspond to greater revenue. Consequently, revenue and profit reach a maximum at a point like H in Fig. 7.25, if the product transformation function is *strictly* convex. At such a point, the slope of the product transformation curve and the isorevenue line is equal and thus the above proposition relating to condition Equation (7.49) holds. At the profit maximising point, the comparative value which consumers place on the products (as indicated by the price ratios) just equals the comparative marginal costs of the products in terms of one another. This is an important result for welfare economics.

IV. Costs: Some Details

In previous sections, it has been pointed out that a firm's cost can be expressed as a function of its output of products. It was also stressed that *the* cost curve is constructed on the assumption that inputs are combined so as to minimise the cost of each level of output. However, details about the nature of cost curves were avoided. Some details are required in order to derive a firm's supply function adequately and different cost relationships also have operational significance for the firm.

Economists usually include additional items in costs to those included by accountants. The inclusion of these additional cost allowances is justified on the basis of the *opportunity cost* doctrine. The doctrine implies that the relevant cost of any activity is the reward forgone by not undertaking the most rewarding alternative activity. To give an example, suppose that capital can be invested in one stock to give a yield of 12 per cent per year and the alternative highest yield is 10 per cent. Then the opportunity cost of investing in the first stock is 10 per cent and its net yield (after allowing for the best alternative forgone) is 2 per cent. On the basis of this doctrine, economists include an allowance for the normal or average rate of profit in the cost component of an undertaking. Under perfect competition, this allowance indicates the maximum rate of return which would be available to the firm by using its resources in alternative productive activities.

Also, on the basis of the opportunity cost doctrine, other implicit costs are added to the firm's explicit costs. The cost of each factor in any activity is the highest alternative reward which is forgone. Thus, in the case of a farm owner-manager who is paid no explicit salary, the cost of his services is to be reckoned at the best price which they will fetch elsewhere in the economy.

Time has not entered explicitly or integrally into our discussion of costs so far. Some allowances must be made for it since its passage clearly influences the possibilities for varying the employment of factors and for altering costs. However, time will not yet be allowed for explicitly, but will be taken into account by a device of comparative statics.

Alfred Marshall[5] popularised this approach by dividing the possibility for the variation of factors into three categories. He abstracted three possibilities: (i) no factors variable, (ii) some particular set of factors variable but others in fixed supply, and (iii) all factors variable. Although mathematically these categories are not specifically related to clock-time, Marshall implicitly related clock-time and these categories in a rough way. Hence, he indicated that the possibility (i) occurs in the very short period, the possibility (ii) occurs in the *short period*, and the possibility (iii) arises in the *long period*.

However, as Knight has observed,[6] Marshall's division of the possibilities for variation into three neat categories is artificial. Take the production function

$$x = F(l_1, l_2, l_3) \quad (7.52)$$

in which three factors are involved. The number of possible combinations in which factors may or may not vary is large. *One* possibility is that (i) no factors are variable, (ii) L_1 is variable but no others, (iii) both L_1 and L_2 are variable but no others, and (iv) all factors are variable. This would give, using Marshall's analogy, a four "period" model. Other patterns of variation are also possible. Clearly, Marshall's categories do involve an abstraction. But all theory involves abstraction and Marshall's has proved to be a useful one. Thus it will be adopted in developing the static theory of production.

In the very short run no factor is variable. In the short run only a particular set of factors is variable, such as labour and raw materials; and others, such as buildings, land, machinery, and top management, are in fixed supply. The quantities of fixed resources employed by the firm determine the firm's *scale of plant* and this sets a limit to its production possibilities in the short run. In the long run, the firm is free to vary its scale of plant since all factors are variable. The different possibilities for variation influence the cost curves of the firm. Let us consider its short-run and long-run cost curves.

SHORT-RUN COST CURVES

In the short run the firm incurs costs for variable factors and fixed factors. Thus its total cost (*TC*) is equal to its total variable cost (*TVC*), plus its fixed cost (*TFC*)

$$TC = TVC + TFC.$$

To give a particular example, which ought not be taken to limit the generality of the analysis, suppose that the firm's production function is

$$x = F(l_1, l_2) \quad (7.53)$$

and imagine that in the short run L_1 is variable but L_2 is fixed at some level l_2^*. Then, the firm's short-run production function is

$$x = F(l_1, l_2^*)$$
$$= \phi(l_1) \quad (7.54)$$

and its short-run cost as a function of output can be derived from this by the method suggested in Section I. Its short-run cost function includes a variable component to allow for the possible variation of L_1 and a fixed component to allow for the costs of the fixed factor L_2. The cost function may be expressed as

$$C(x) = V(x) + A \quad (7.55)$$

where $V(x)$ represents total variable cost and A represents fixed costs. An example of such a function is given in Fig. 7.26. Variations of scale alter the relevant short-run cost function. Given the employment of the fixed factors, what is the typical slope of the total-cost curve $C(x)$? Marshall and others are of the opinion that typically the cost function is first concave and then convex.[7] Increasing returns to outlay are likely

Production, Costs and Supply

at first, but these are followed by decreasing returns to outlay. Thus the *strictly* convex cost function assumed earlier is usually only applicable for higher levels of outputs. A total-cost curve which accords with the Marshallian assumptions is shown in Fig. 7.26.

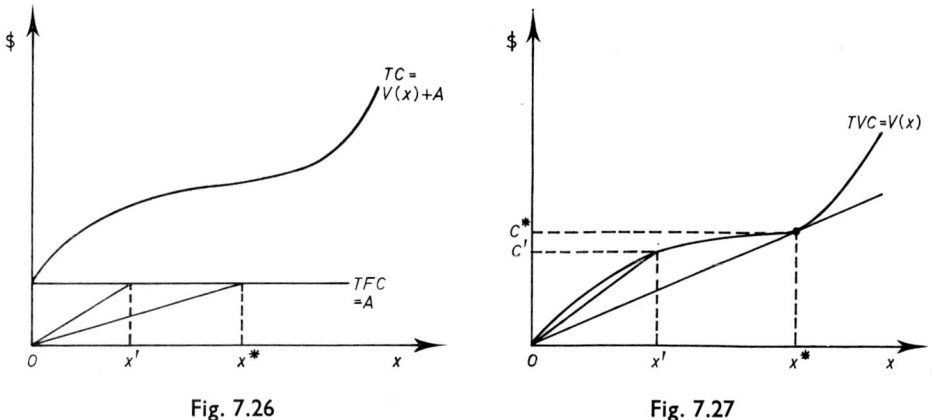

Fig. 7.26   Fig. 7.27

From the short-run total cost curves, a number of important per-unit short-run cost curves can be derived and related. These are: the average fixed-cost curve, the average variable-cost curve, the average total-cost curve (usually called average cost), and the marginal-cost curve.

Average fixed cost equals total fixed cost per unit of output, that is TFC/x. In this particular case, it equals $A/x = Ax^{-1}$. Total fixed cost as a function of output is always a rectangular hyperbole. The average fixed cost of any level of output in Fig. 7.26 can be computed by taking the slope of the ray to the fixed cost associated with that output. For example, the AFC of x' is A/x'.

Average variable cost is equal to the total variable cost divided by output, that is to TVC/x or $V(x)/x$. For any value of x, it is equal to the slope of the ray to $V(x)$ at that value. The total variable-cost function, $V(x)$, is graphed in Fig. 7.27. The average variable cost for an output of x' equals C'/x' or the slope of the ray to (x', C'). Note that the slope of such a ray decreases as x increases to x^*. Then it rises again. Consequently, the firm's average variable-cost function is U-shaped like $SAVC$ in Fig. 7.29.

Average cost is equal to total cost divided by output, that is to TC/x or $C(x)/x$. It is indicated, for example, by the slope of a ray from the origin to the corresponding point on the ATC curve. Thus in Fig. 7.28, the average cost of the output $\hat{x}$ is $\hat{C}/\hat{x}$ and this is equivalent to the slope of the ray from O to $(\hat{x}, \hat{C})$. Clearly, as x increases towards $\hat{x}$ the slope of such a ray declines and for outputs greater than $\hat{x}$ it rises. Consequently, for a total-cost curve of this type, the average cost curve is U-shaped with a minimum at $\hat{x}$. Such a curve is indicated in Fig. 7.29 by SAC.

Finally, the marginal-cost curve indicates the addition to cost of an additional unit of output. It is the first derivative of the total-cost function with respect to output. It is

$$\frac{dC}{dx} = \frac{dV}{dx} \qquad (7.56)$$

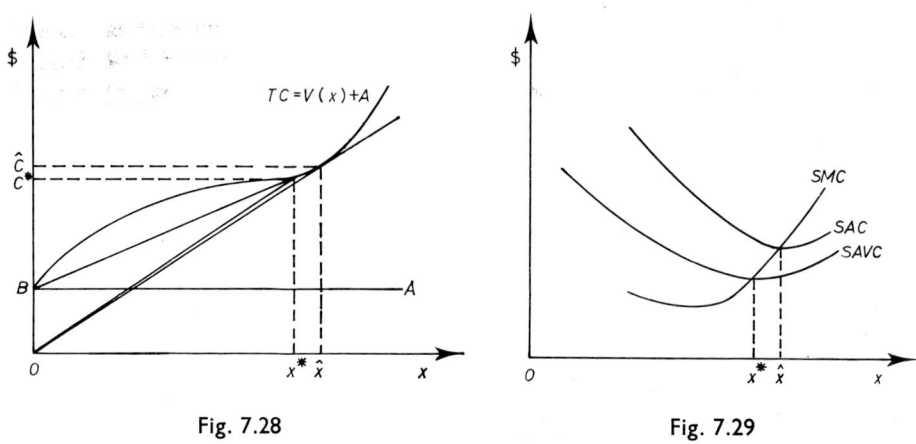

Fig. 7.28   Fig. 7.29

since fixed costs have no influence on the extra cost of an extra unit of output. The marginal cost of any output is equal to the tangent to the total-cost curve at that output. In the case shown in Fig. 7.29, marginal cost is positive for all levels of output but declines at first for low levels of output and then increases. (The slope of the tangent to $C(x)$ declines and then rises.) Consequently, the marginal-cost curve is U-shaped. Note, too, that the tangent at (x^*, C^*) coincides with the ray from B and so marginal cost and average variable cost are equal for that output. Also, at $(\hat{x}, \hat{C})$ the tangent and the ray from O coincide and consequently average total cost and marginal cost are equal for an output of $\hat{x}$. The relationship between the short-run cost curves is illustrated in Fig. 7.29. The marginal-cost curve is below the average cost and the average variable-cost curves when these are decreasing, and above these curves when they are increasing. Hence, the marginal-cost curve passes through the minimum of the average variable-cost curve and the minimum of the average cost curve. As a general rule, if the average value of a function is decreasing, its marginal value is below it and if it is increasing, its marginal value is above it.

LONG-RUN COST CURVES

In the long run, the firm is free to vary all of its inputs. Its operations can be of any scale, its scale of plant can be varied. Consequently, no costs are fixed in the long run.

The firm's long-run total-cost curve indicates its minimum total cost of each level of output if it is free to vary all of its factors. The long-run total-cost curve is the envelope of the short-run total-cost curves. It consists of segments of different short-run total-cost curves.

To take an example, assume that production function of Equation 7.53 is applicable. In the long run both factors are variable and the long-run cost curve could be obtained by the procedure suggested in Section II for obtaining a cost curve. Alternatively, the short-run cost curves for various given employments of L_2 might be derived first. Imagine for simplicity that only three different levels of employment or scale, namely $l_2^1 > l_2^2 > l_2^3$, are possible. For each of these alternative levels of employment of L_2, a short-run total-cost curve can be computed. Let the corresponding short-run total-cost curves be $C_1(x)$, $C_2(x)$ and $C_3(x)$. Examples of these cost curves are shown in Fig. 7.30 by STC_1, STC_2 and STC_3 respectively. If only these three alternative

Production, Costs and Supply

long-run employments of L_2 are available, the firm's long-run total-cost curve is the scallop-like heavy lower boundary of the short-run total-cost curves of Fig. 7.30. Clearly, this boundary indicates the minimum long-run cost of producing each output, for example, the cost of producing an output of x' is minimised in the long run only if the firm employs l_2^2 of L_2, that is adopts scale 2. The short-run average-cost curves corresponding to the respective short-run total-cost curves are represented in Fig. 7.31 by SAC_1, SAC_2 and SAC_3. The envelope of these curves, shown by the heavy lower boundary line, is the long-run average-cost curve of the firm and indicates the minimum average cost of producing each output if all factors are variable.

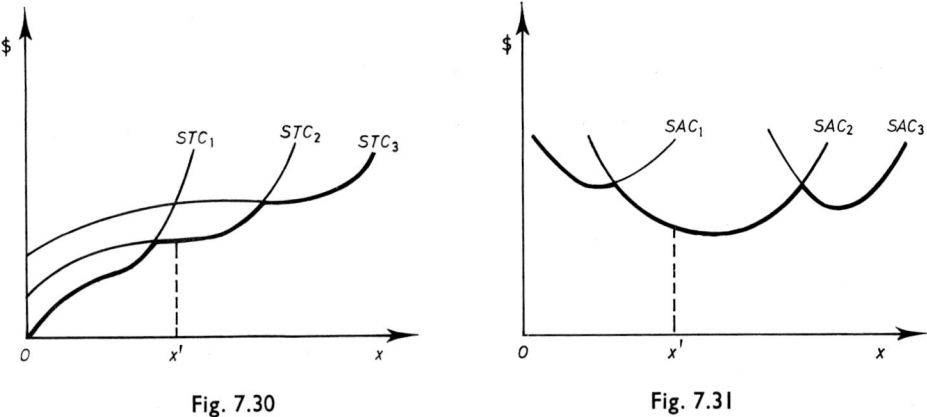

Fig. 7.30   Fig. 7.31

The long-run cost curves of Figs 7.30 and 7.31 are both kinked since the variability of L_2 has been restricted to a discrete number of possibilities. If L_2 is allowed to vary in a continuous fashion, then with the usual type of production function the long-run cost curves should become smooth. If increasing returns to outlay prevail for low outputs and decreasing returns arise for higher outputs, the long-run average-cost curve is U-shaped. Marshall assumed this to be the case. A long-run average-cost curve which meets this description is shown in Fig. 7.32, and a short-run average-cost curve corresponds to each segment of it. Three of these short-run cost curves are indicated by SAC_1, SAC_2 and SAC_3. On the downward portion of the $LRAC$ curve,

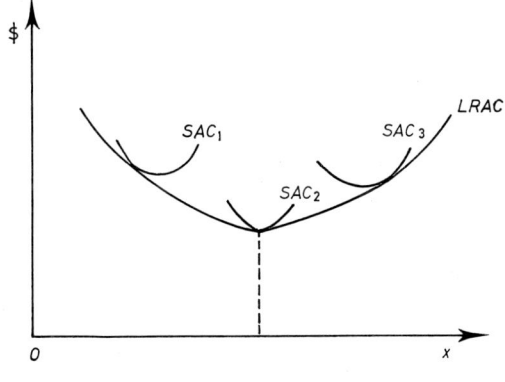

Fig. 7.32

the minimum of the SAC curves occur to the right of their "point of tangency" with the $LRAC$ curve, and to the left if $LRAC$ is increasing. At the point of minimum $LRAC$, there is a corresponding minimum for a short-run average-cost curve.

Long-run marginal cost ($LRMC$) indicates the change in the firm's cost if its output is increased by one unit and its scale of plant is freely variable. Long-run marginal cost is the rate of change or first derivative of the firm's long-run total-cost function. The firm's long-run marginal-cost curve passes through the minimum of its $LRAC$ curve. It is below the $LRAC$ curve if $LRAC$ is decreasing and above the $LRAC$ curve if $LRAC$ is increasing (this relationship is shown in Fig. 7.33). The interrelationship between short- and long-run per-unit cost curves is illustrated in Fig. 7.33. Note that when short-run average cost *equals* long-run average cost, short-run marginal cost and long-run marginal cost are equal, for example, this is so for the output x' in Fig. 7.33. This equality holds because the short-run total-cost and long-run total-cost curves are identical for the range of the equality of their average costs. Hence, the short- and long-run total-cost curves must have the same rate of change because they are identical for this range.

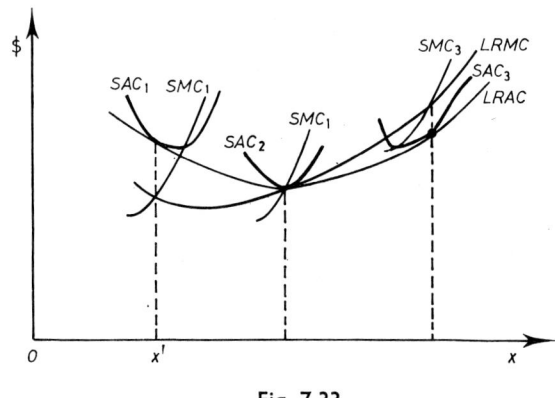

Fig. 7.33

Both the short-run and long-run cost curves are used in the next chapter to discuss the supply curve of the perfectly competitive firm in more detail and to derive the supply curve for the industry.

V. Some Special Production Functions

Some special production functions ought to be mentioned, since they commonly occur in economic theories. Homogeneous production functions are an important type. Homogeneous functions have the property that if their independent variables are increased by some proportion, the dependent variable is always increased by a given power of this proportion. If the production function is homogeneous then an increase of inputs by some proportion always increases the output by this proportion raised to particular power. Clearly, returns to scale are easily defined for such a function. If the power mentioned is greater than one, increasing returns to scale occur; if it is equal to 1, constant returns are the rule; and if it is less than one, decreasing returns are the case. Thus a production function

is homogeneous of degree k if
$$x = F(l_1, l_2)$$

$$F(\lambda l_1, \lambda l_2) = \lambda^k F(l_1, l_2) = \lambda^k q. \quad (7.57)$$

Here λ is a positive real number and a constant. The equation indicates that if both inputs are increased by a multiple λ, output is increased by the multiple λ^k.

The firm's expansion path for *any* homogeneous production function is a straight line. This can be shown from the fact that the partial derivatives of a homogeneous function of degree λ are homogeneous of degree $\lambda - 1$. For example, if

$$\frac{\partial F}{\partial l_1} = F_1(l_1, l_2) \quad (7.58)$$

then for F, homogeneous of degree k,

$$F_1(\lambda l_1, \lambda l_2) = \lambda^{k-1} F_1(l_1, l_2). \quad (7.59)$$

If constant returns to scale occur, the production function is homogeneous of degree one. Consequently,

$$F_1(l_1, l_2) = \lambda^0 F_1(l_1, l_2)$$
$$= F_1(l_1, l_2), \quad (7.60)$$

and marginal products are unchanged by an increase of factors in the same proportion. However, marginal products may change if the proportion in which the factors are combined alters. Hence, if constant returns to scale exist, the marginal productivity of the factors can be expressed solely as a function of the proportion in which the factors are combined.[8]

The function

$$x = a_1 l_1 + a_2 l_2 \quad (7.61)$$

is homogeneous of degree one. But here marginal products are also independent of factor proportions, for example, $\dfrac{\partial F_1}{\partial l_1} = a_1$. The function

$$x = A l_1^a l_2^{1-a} \quad (7.62)$$

is also homogeneous of degree one (or linearly homogeneous). In Equation (7.62), A and a are parameters. Function (7.61) has an important history in economics. Interpreting one of the independent variables as labour and the other as capital, Douglas[9] found that this equation fitted his observations on output, capital and labour for several economies as a whole. On the basis of his findings, he argued that the constancy of the share of labour in national income could be explained by the marginal productivity theory of distribution. This theory and his result is discussed in Chapter 10.

It should be noted that the Cobb-Douglas function, Equation (7.62), is a special case of the power function

$$x = A l_1^a l_2^\beta \quad (7.63)$$

where β is a parameter. Functions of this kind are homogeneous and their degree of homogeneity is $k = a + \beta$. Since Equation 7.63 is log linear, this can be an advantage if a curve has to be fitted to raw data. Equation 7.63 may be re-expressed as

$$\log x = \log A + a \log l_1 + \beta \log l_2. \quad (7.64)$$

The cost functions, of course, reflect the homogeneity of production functions. Total cost is a straight line and marginal cost is constant if the production function is homogeneous of degree zero. The total cost function is *strictly* concave if the production function is homogeneous of greater degree than one, and *strictly* convex if it is homogeneous of a degree less than one.

The properties of production functions which ensure a constant elasticity of substitution between factors (in response to factor price changes) have also been explored in the literature and have been fitted to data. The Cobb-Douglas function is a special case of a *CES* function.[10]

NOTES AND REFERENCES

[1] A. BERLE and G. MEANS, *The Modern Corporation and Private Property*, The Macmillan Company, New York, 1932.

[2] J. R. HICKS, *Value and Capital*, 2nd ed., Clarendon Press, Oxford, 1946, Ch. VII.

[3] J. HENDERSON and R. QUANDT, *Microeconomic Theory*, McGraw-Hill, New York, 1958.

[4] In this figure, the two parallel straight lines (which are unmarked) are isorevenue curves.

[5] A. MARSHALL, *Principles of Economics*, 8th ed., Macmillan, London, 1920.

[6] FRANK H. KNIGHT, "Cost of Production and Price over Long and Short Periods", *Journal of Political Economy*, 1921, **29**, pp. 304-35. Reprinted in FRANK KNIGHT, *The Ethics of Competition and Other Essays*, Harper, New York, 1936.

[7] Not all economists are of the opinion that total cost curves are of this nature. Dissenting views are given in Chapters 18 and 19.

[8] For further details see, for example, R. G. D. ALLEN, *Mathematical Analysis for Economists*, Macmillan, London, 1938, pp. 320-1, 343, 371-4; and HENDERSON and QUANDT, op. cit. pp. 62-7.

[9] PAUL H. DOUGLAS, "Are There Laws of Production?", *American Economic Review*, 1948, **37**, pp. 1-41.

[10] For further details on these and related types of production functions, the reader might consult A. A. WALTERS, *An Introduction to Econometrics*, W. W. Norton, New York, 1970, Ch. 10.

FURTHER READING

BAIN, J., *Price Theory*, Holt, Rinehart and Winston, New York, 1952, Ch. 3.

BAUMOL, W. J., *Economic Theory and Operations Analysis*, 2nd ed., Prentice-Hall, Englewood Cliffs, 1965, Ch. 11.

COHEN, K. J. and R. M. CYERT, *Theory of the Firm*, Prentice-Hall, Englewood Cliffs, 1965, Chs. 6 and 7.

HENDERSON, J. and R. QUANDT, *Microeconomic Theory*, McGraw-Hill, New York, 1958, Ch. 3.

HICKS, J. R., *Value and Capital*, Clarendon Press, Oxford, 2nd ed., 1946, Chs. 6 and 7.

KNIGHT, FRANK H., "Cost of Production and Price over Long and Short Periods", *Journal of Political Economy*, 1921, **29**, pp. 304-35. Reprinted in F. H. KNIGHT, *The Ethics of Competition and Other Essays*, Harper, New York, 1936.

MARSHALL, A., *Principles of Economics*, 8th ed., Macmillan, London, 1920.

VINER, J., "Cost Curves and Supply Curves", *Zeitschrift für Nationalökonomie*, 1931, **3**, pp. 23-36. Reprinted in A.E.A., *Readings in Price Theory*, Allen and Unwin, London, 1953.

APPENDIX TO CHAPTER 7

Sets and the Theory of Production

A. RELEVANT THEOREMS

The properties of point sets find valuable applications to the theory of production for, as a rule (but not always), a firm's set of production possibilities can be represented by a compact point set. A number of theorems exist concerning the maximisation or minimisation of a function subject to a compact set and we have already noted some in Chapter 2. In particular, we noted a number of theorems about the maximisation of a linear function subject to a compact set. These theorems are of particular relevance for under perfect competition the firm's profit function is linear and its aim is to maximise this function subject to its set of production possibilities.

This appendix concentrates on the production and supply curves of perfectly competitive firms so we are chiefly concerned with the properties of linear functions defined on compact sets. The following theorems will be used:

(i) a linear function which is defined on a compact set, S, reaches its maximum (and minimum value) in a boundary point of the set;

(ii) indeed, it reaches its maximum (and its minimum) value in an extreme point of the set. Yet this theorem does not exclude the possibility of the linear function reaching its maximum (and minimum) value at other boundary points, for example, all of those points on a facet of a compact set (if it has a facet) may maximise or minimise the linear function. Hence, we shall find the next theorem particularly relevant;

(iii) the maximum and minimum value of a linear function subject to a compact set, S, may occur *and* can only occur for boundary points of the set S which are also boundary points of the convex hull of the set. To be more precise, let B be the set of boundary points of a convex set S and C be set of boundary points of the convex hull, $Co(S)$, of S. The maximum and minimum value of a linear function subject to S can only occur for values in the set $D = B \cap C$. Also, every element of D has the possibility, depending on the exact nature of the linear function, of maximising or minimising this function.

Theorem (iii) enables us to rule out a certain set of boundary points as possibilities for maximising or minimising a linear function subject to a compact set, S. The set of boundary points $F = B - B \cap C$ can never maximise or minimise a linear function subject to a compact set S. F is an empty set if S is convex but otherwise it is not empty.

The above theorem accords with our observations in the appendix to Chapter 6 about supporting hyperplanes to a set. We observed in the Appendix to Chapter 6 that no supporting hyperplane to a set S could exist at a point of a set such as F. Supporting hyperplanes did exist for all points in a set such as D but an element of this set did not necessarily have a unique supporting hyperplane.

Theorems (i) and (ii) were illustrated in the last section of Chapter 2 and Theorem (iii) is best illustrated by direct reference to production theory.

B. PRODUCTION OF A SINGLE PRODUCT USING A SINGLE VARIABLE FACTOR

Production of a single product by using a single variable factor is discussed in Section I of Chapter 7 and the same notation will be used here. It will be recalled that assuming *perfect competition*, the problem for the firm was stated to be one of maximising its linear profit function

$$\pi = px - wl \qquad (A7.1)$$

subject to its production function

$$x = f(l). \qquad (A7.2)$$

This is the traditional formulation of the problem.

But the production function does not fully represent the production possibilities of the firm. It only isolates the most efficient possibilities. These are the only relevant possibilities (for profit maximisation) but it is sometimes analytically more useful to describe the whole set of production possibilities. In the above case, the set of production possibilities is

$$P = \{l, x \mid l \geqslant 0, 0 \leqslant x \leqslant f(l)\} \qquad (A7.3)$$

and can be represented by the set of points on and below the production function such that x is non-negative. An example of P for a strictly concave production function is shown in Fig. A7.1. The set P consists of all feasible input-output combinations including interior combinations, such as the one at D, which may result because the firm uses inferior techniques or fails to employ all of hired factor, L.

The set which is shown is compact and convex, indeed it is *strictly* convex in its boundary values $\{(l, x) \mid x > 0 \text{ and } x = f(l)\}$. A production set does not always possess these convexity properties nor is it always compact. It is possible that, no matter how large l is, production is positive so that the production possibility set is unbounded. This might be overcome by limiting the production set to values which occur for l lower than or equal to the value of l corresponding to the maximum level of output *if* a finite maximum exists. It is never optimal to operate beyond the maximum output level if profit maximisation is the firm's goal.

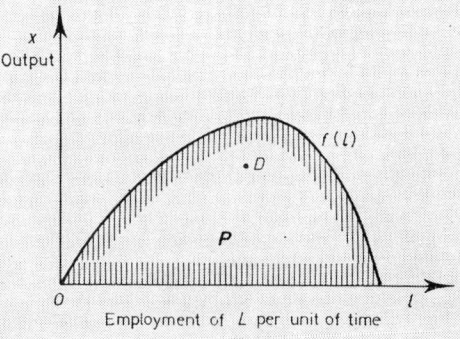

Fig. A7.1

Sets and Production

The profit function of a perfectly competitive firm can be represented by a series of parallel isoprofit lines in the (l, x) plane. Rearranging Equation (A7.1), the isoprofit line which corresponds to any specific value of π is given by

$$x = \frac{\pi}{p} + \frac{w}{p}l. \tag{A7.4}$$

Consequently, the slope of any isoprofit line is $\frac{w}{p}$ (equals the factor's price divided by the product's price) and, assuming positive prices, is positively sloped. If the price of the product is positive, higher isoprofit lines (those for a higher value of x, given l) correspond to higher profit levels and, hence, the highest attainable isoprofit line is reached for a value of (l, x) on the production function.

If the production function, $f(l)$, is *strictly* concave and twice differentiable (a production function of the type indicated in Fig. A7.1), the employment of L which maximises the firm's profit occurs for

$$\frac{w}{p} \geqslant f'(l). \tag{A7.5}$$

The variable factor is only employed in an optimal quantity if its marginal product is less than or equal to its real price per unit. If $\frac{w}{p} > f'(l)$ for all possible levels of L, the optimal level of employment of L is $l = 0$ and a corner-point solution occurs. Such a solution is indicated in Fig. A7.2. Note that the highest attainable isoprofit line, π_3, is a supporting hyperplane to the set P at point O. A conventional solution is shown in Fig. A7.3. The highest attainable isoprofit line is π_2 and is a supporting hyperplane to the set P. It supports the set at $(\bar{l}, \bar{x})$ and there $\frac{w}{p} = f'(l)$. The profit maximising input-output combination is $(\bar{l}, \bar{x})$.

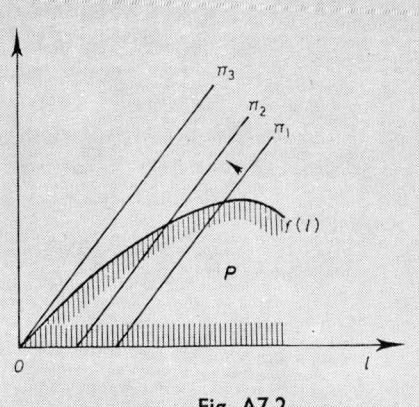

Fig. A7.2

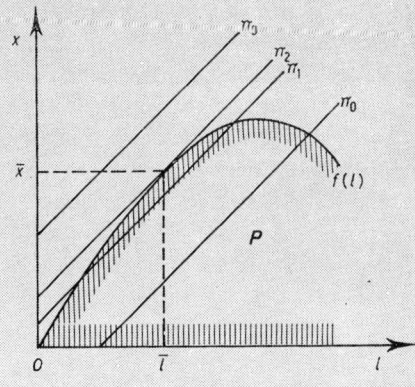

Fig. A7.3

If the firm's production function, $f(l)$ is strictly concave and twice differentiable, its supply function of product X (for positive values of x) is a continuous smooth function[1] which rises with $\frac{p}{w}$, the product's price to the factor's price. The supply function OAS shown in Fig. A7.4 satisfies this property. It has a vertical stretch at OA

since for low enough values of $\frac{p}{w}$, zero output is optimal. Supply functions of this type have the property that a single level of ouput corresponds to each price-ratio, $\frac{p}{w}$. Note that the supply function considered here differs from the Marshallian function introduced in Chapter 7 (and further discussed in Chapter 8). The Marshallian function relates output to variations of the product's price alone, the price of the factor being held constant. The supply function which is examined here stresses the importance of *relative* prices which are only implicitly taken into account in Marshall's formulation.

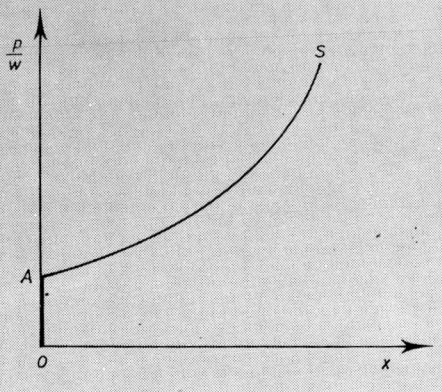

Fig. A7.4

If the production function is *strictly* concave, a single level of optimal output corresponds to each value of $\frac{w}{p}$. But *strict* concavity of the firm's production function does not ensure that the firm's supply curve for the product rises smoothly. A *strictly* concave production function which is not differentiable everywhere may have kinks in it. These kinks are associated with vertical stretches in the supply curve $x = S(p/w)$. The relationship is illustrated in Figs A7.5 and A7.6. A kink occurs in the *strictly* concave production function at the point (l^*, x^*). The production set has a number of different supporting hyperplanes at this point. Hence, there is a corresponding vertical stretch in the supply curve OAS of Fig. A7.6 which indicates a

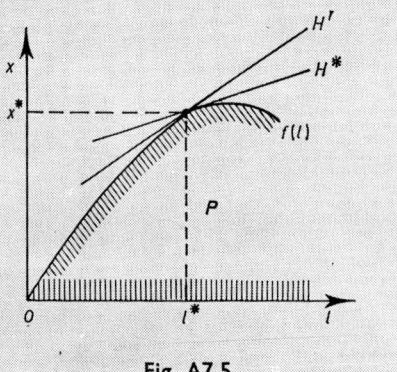

Fig. A7.5

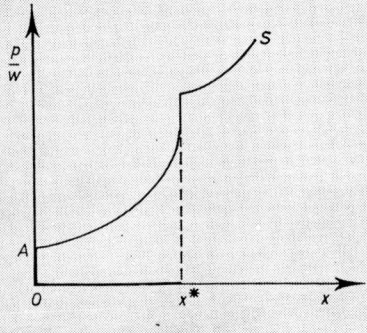

Fig. A7.6

Sets and Production

range of variation of the product-factor price ratio, p/w, which does not influence supply. A kink in a production function may arise if there is a sharp change of technique.

If the firm's production function is concave without being *strictly* so, a single level of output (supply) does not correspond to each value of $\frac{p}{w}$. For some values of $\frac{p}{w}$ the associated level of supply is indeterminate within a range. The production function which is represented in Fig. A7.7 consists of linear segments and is concave, but not *strictly* so. The associated type of supply curve is shown in Fig. A7.8. The dashed segments of the supply curve indicate indeterminacy and correspond to cases in which a supporting hyperplane is along one facet of the production function. For $\frac{p}{w} = A$ any output between zero and x^* is possible. For $\frac{p}{w} = B$ any output between x^* and x' is possible. *But* for any value of $\frac{p}{w}$ between A and B only an output of x^* is possible. This is, of course, assuming profit maximisation. A production function of this type which is shown in Fig. A7.7 is empirically possible if, for example, the production relationship which is associated with each technique is linear. Cases such as this frequently arise in linear programming problems.

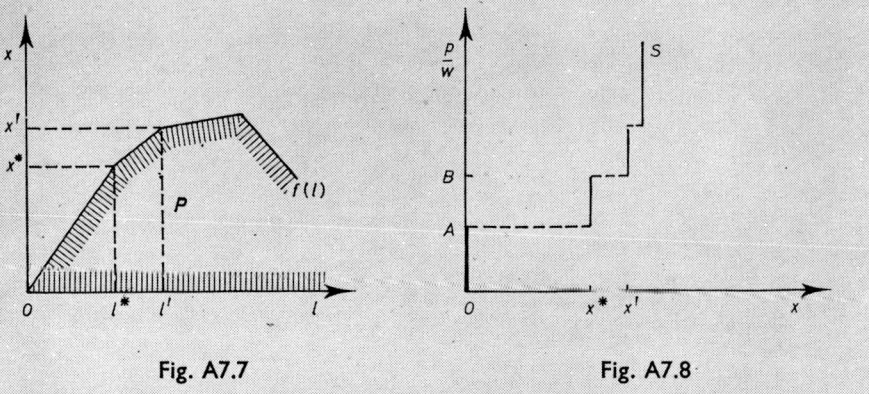

Fig. A7.7   Fig. A7.8

If the production function is *not concave* (in consequence, the production *set* is not convex in the boundary formed by the production function), some attainable values of x may never be supplied.[2] The firm cannot be induced to supply certain quantities of output by any manipulation of $\frac{p}{w}$. To illustrate, take the case which many economists regard as typical. Imagine that increasing returns prevail at first but that these give way to decreasing returns so that the production function is like the one shown in Fig. A7.9. Quantities of the product of between O and x^* will *never* be supplied by the firm.

This follows from theorem (iii) above. The set of boundary points of the production set $\{l, x | 0 \leqslant l \leqslant l^*, x = f(l)\}$ are equivalent to the set F which is mentioned in the exposition of theorem (iii). They are boundary points of the set P which are *not* boundary points of its convex hull, $Co(P)$. The set P has no supporting hyperplanes at boundary points in this set. It does, however, have supporting hyperplanes in all other boundary points.

If the input and the product are not free, boundary points of the set $\{(l, x) | l > 0$ and $x = 0\}$ can be ruled out on the principle that these cannot maximise profit. Also boundary points on the production function beyond its maximum value can be ruled out. Consequently, the relevant production set is the combination at O and the points on $f(l)$ between l^* and the maximum of $f(l)$ including the end-points. Supporting hyperplanes to P may occur at any of these points. Hence, the supply function of the firm is like that shown in Fig. A7.10. It is a discontinuous function consisting of two parts, OA and CS. At a price less than OA none of product X is supplied. At a price of OA the firm may *either* produce none of the product or produce x^* of it for in either case its profit is the same. The same hyperplane (isoprofit line) supports the set P at point O and at (l^*, x^*). Thus there is some indeterminancy in supply. After price rises above this Vinerian level of indeterminancy, supply rises smoothly with increases in $\frac{p}{w}$.

The firm never supplies an output between zero and x^*.[3] No manipulation of $\frac{p}{w}$ can result in supplies in this range. While for every value of $\frac{p}{w}$ except OA there is a corresponding uniquely optimal level of supply, for every value of output there is not a corresponding value of $\frac{p}{w}$ which results in that output. There may be no value of $\frac{p}{w}$ which results in a particular output or (for $\frac{p}{w} < OA$) there may be several values of $\frac{p}{w}$ which lead to the same output. Thus we are really concerned with problems of the mapping of one set into another.[4]

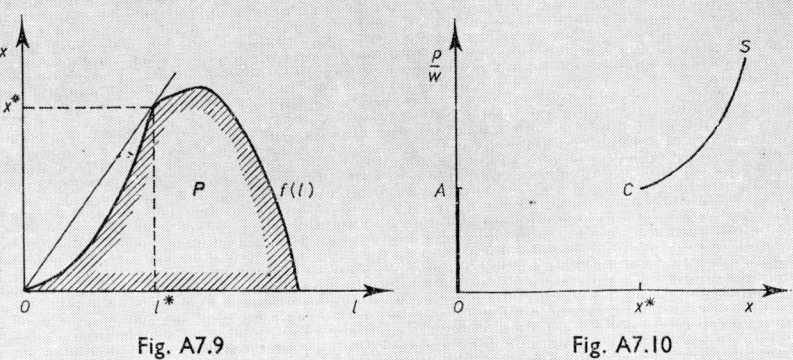

Fig. A7.9   Fig. A7.10

Given that a firm's production function is typically of the nature shown in Fig. A7.9, its supply function is of the form indicated in Fig. A7.10. Theorem (iii) stated above proved to be very helpful in determining this supply function. But it is well to remind ourselves that we have been assuming perfect competition which ensures linearity of the relevant objective function. If the objective function is not linear, all of the three theorems above can be violated. The firm's objective function will not be linear if it operates in imperfect markets, for example, if it has a monopoly in the supply of its product.

Figure A7.11 gives an example which could apply to a monopolist. His production set is indicated by P and his isoprofit lines by π_0, π_1, etc., and reflect the non-linearity of his profit function. He maximises profit for the input-output combination (l', x'). While this is a boundary point of the set P it is not a boundary point common to P and the set of boundary points of $Co(P)$. It is a member of the set F.

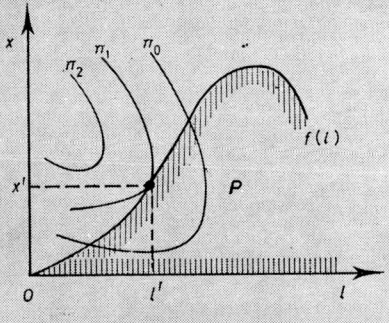

Fig. A7.11

Production of a single product using two variable factors will not be specifically discussed. The results of the Appendix to Chapter 6 can be applied to it *mutatis mutandis* by interpreting the individual's budget line as the firm's isocost limitation, his indifference curves as isoquants and the product prices as factor prices.

C. PRODUCTION OF TWO PRODUCTS

The theory of the production of two products was discussed in Chapter 7. Since the model obtains much application particularly in trade theory, it is worthwhile to analyse some of its supply characteristics.

A firm's product transformation frontier indicates for the firm's given employment of factors the maximum output of any product which is compatible with specified levels of output of the other products. The method of obtaining this frontier was outlined in the discussion of Figs 7.24 and 7.25. Using the notation of Chapter 7, the firm's production possibility frontier for a specific employment of resources can be represented by a function

$$x_2 = G(x_1). \tag{A7.6}$$

But this function does not represent the whole set of product combinations which the firm could produce; it indicates only the most efficient set. For analytical purposes, it is sometimes useful to specify the whole set of attainable product combinations which we shall also specify by P. The attainable production possibility set is

$$P = \{(x_1, x_2) | x_1 \geq 0 \leq x_2 \leq G(x_1)\}. \tag{A7.7}$$

Such a set is shown in Fig. A7.12 for a product transformation curve which is *strictly* convex and twice differentiable. It is a compact set.

If perfect competition prevails, the firm's profit can be shown by the linear expression

$$\pi = p_1 x_1 + p_2 x_2 - A, \tag{A7.8}$$

where A is the cost to the firm of its specific level of resources. Theorem (iii) clearly applies here because the firm's objective function is linear and is to be maximised subject to its compact product possibility set, P. The firm's isoprofit lines are all hyperplanes.

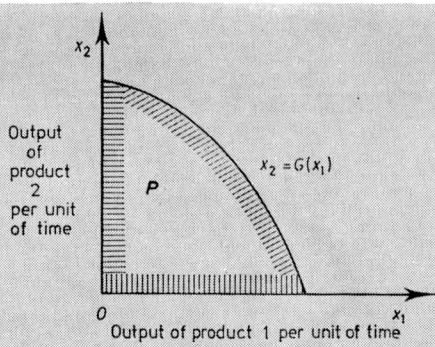

Fig. A7.12

If no price can be negative and at least one product price is positive, the maximum level of the firm's profit must occur for points along its production possibility frontier. Given that the production set P is *strictly* convex in this frontier (except at its end-points) and is twice differentiable (except at the end-points), every point on the frontier (except the end-points) possesses a unique supporting hyperplane for the set. The supply of any product depends on its relative price. The supply curve for product 1, for example, is like that shown in Fig. A7.13 if the product transformation frontier is downward-sloping as in Fig. A7.12. If the relative price of product 1 is sufficiently low (less than or equal to AO) none of product 1 is supplied. A supply curve of this nature may be the usual one.

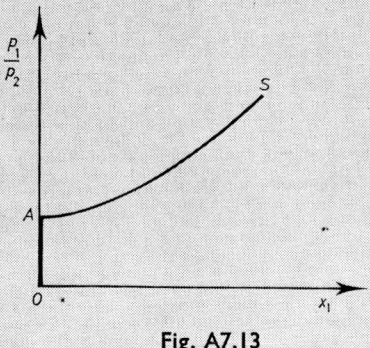

Fig. A7.13

Nevertheless, it is possible for P to be compact and *strictly* convex in its production frontier *and* for a non-zero end-point to arise in the supply function of one or more of the products. For this result, we assume that product prices cannot be negative, and that one is always positive. The production set P which is shown in Fig. A7.14 accords with the properties just mentioned. It implies a supply curve for product 1 like that shown in Fig. A7.15. Some of X_1 is supplied, no matter how low its relative price. This arises because at low levels of output of product 1 the production of products 1 and 2 are complementary. (Professor K. Campbell of Sydney University has observed such a relationship between beef and wool. Cattle in small numbers improve pastures for sheep.) In consequence, an output of product 1 of x_1^* or greater is always supplied. Supplies of product 1 cannot be reduced below x_1^* by reducing the relative price $\frac{p_1}{p_2}$. Even if p_1 is zero, x_1^* of product 1 is produced by the firm. Nevertheless, there is *only one* corresponding quantity of supply for each value of $\frac{p_1}{p_2}$. This is not so if the production possibility frontier is other than *strictly* concave.

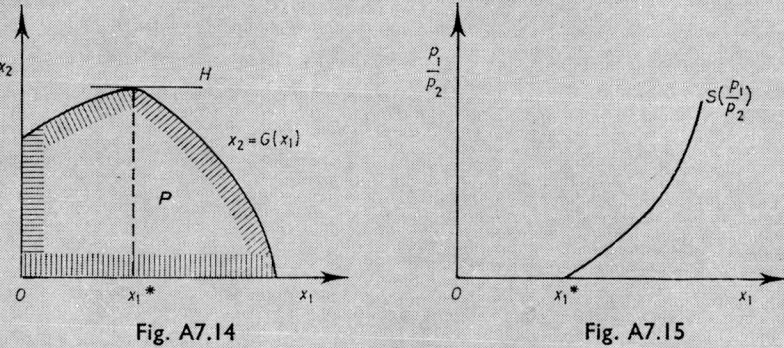

Fig. A7.14 Fig. A7.15

Consider some cases in which the firm's product transformation frontier is negatively sloped throughout but is not *strictly* concave. If this function is concave but not *strictly* so, the firm's supply curve for any product will have vertical stretches and horizontal areas of indeterminancy. The supply curve of product 1 in Fig. A7.17 which corresponds to the product transformation of Fig. A7.16 illustrates this. The vertical stretches of the supply relation indicate a range of price ratios for which a definite quantity of product 1 is supplied. The dashed horizontal stretches indicate quantities which may be supplied at particular prices, for example, at a price of OA any quantity in the range $O \leqslant x_1 \leqslant x_1'$ is liable to be supplied. The vertical stretches correspond to cases in which supporting hyperplanes (isoprofit lines) to the set P occur at corner-points and the horizontal stretches correspond to cases in which the supporting hyperplane is along a facet (a flat-face) of $x_2 = G(x_1)$. Production possibility sets of the form shown in Fig. A7.16 arise in linear programming problems.

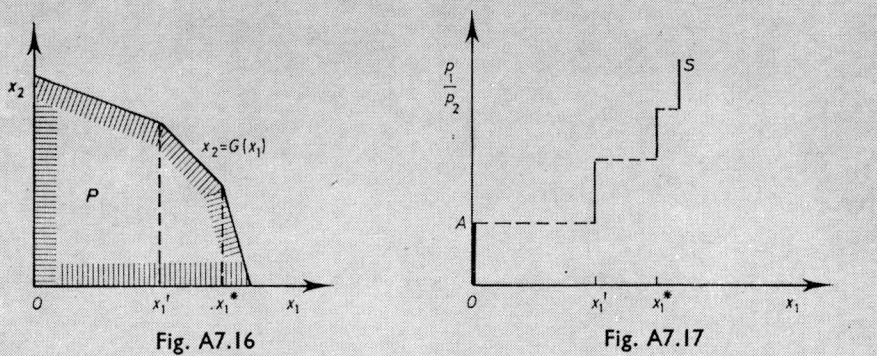

Fig. A7.16 Fig. A7.17

Allow the product transformation function to have strictly convex stretches so that the set P is non-convex. The firm's supply curve for each product can then be shown to be discontinuous. Certain quantities of each product (quantities which can be produced) will not be supplied at any ratio of product prices. This is illustrated for two cases. In Fig. A7.18, the firm's product transformation curve is *strictly* convex for a part of its range and in Fig. A7.20 it is *strictly* convex throughout. The corresponding respective supply functions are indicated in Figs A7.19 and A7.21. The first consists of the segments OAB and CS and the second consists of the segments OA and CS. Both supply curves have a gap because boundary points of P below the hyperplane marked H are in set F (theorem (iii)). A linear function cannot reach a maximum at a point of this set (F) because its points are not boundary points both of P and of the convex hull of P. A profit maximising, perfectly competitive firm will never produce a combination which corresponds to one of these points.

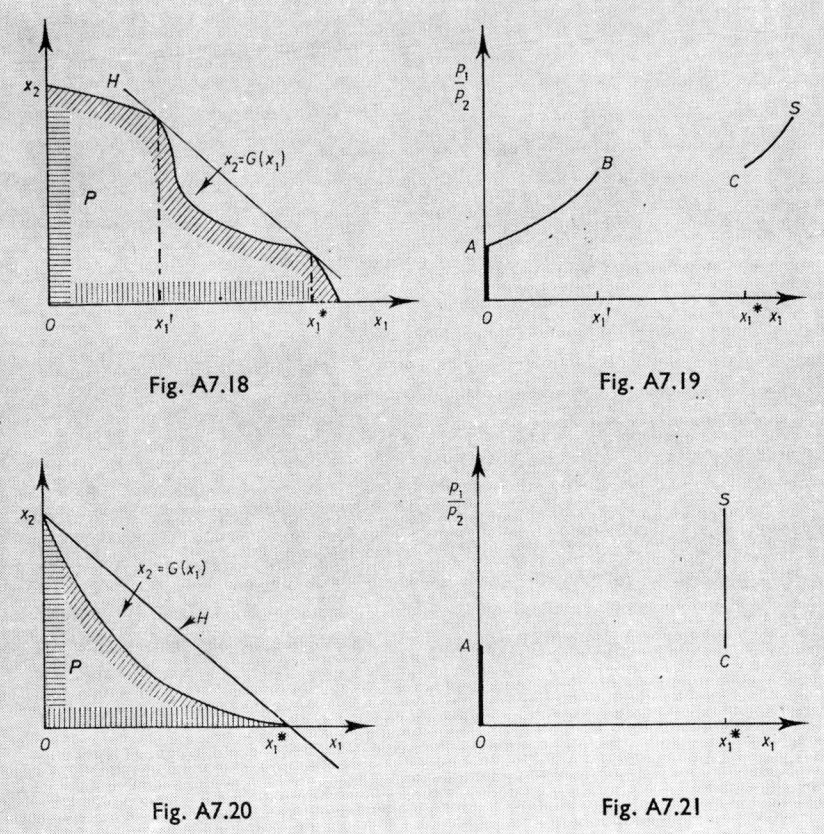

Fig. A7.18   Fig. A7.19

Fig. A7.20   Fig. A7.21

Let us interpret one of the supply curves. Take the one in Fig. A7.21, for example. It implies that the firm does not supply any of product 1 if the product's relative price, $\frac{p_1}{p_2}$, is less than OA. If the price ratio $\frac{p_1}{p_2}$ is equal to OA the firm is indifferent about supplying zero of product 1 or x_1^* of it. Supply is to some extent indeterminate at this price ratio. As can be seen in Fig. A7.20, at this price ratio the set P has the same supporting hyperplane at point $(0, G(0))$ as at $(x_1^*, 0)$. Each of these commodity bundles yields the same profit to the firm and chance determines which bundle it supplies. However, for $\frac{p_1}{p_2}$ in excess of OA no chance element is involved. The firm

Sets and Production

supplies $x_1{}^*$ of the product. In this case, the firm, depending upon relative prices, specialises completely in the production of either one product or the other.

Each type of production set which is being considered above has its empirical counterpart, even though some sets may seem to be unusual. Furthermore, each helps us to understand better the exact nature of traditional economic assumptions about production sets. In addition, the examples amply demonstrate that theorems based upon the properties of sets can widen our understanding of the economic universe in a simple manner.

It ought to be remembered, however, that the theorems which were used above relied on the linearity of the firm's profit function. If a firm's profit function is non-linear, the implications of theorems (i), (ii) and (iii) do not hold. The firm's profit function: (a) need not reach a maximum in a boundary point of P; (b) nor in one of its extreme points; and (c) it may reach its maximum in the set F. This is illustrated in Figs A7.22 and A7.23. In Fig. A7.22 the firm's profit function reaches a maximum at the interior point $(\hat{x}_1, \hat{x}_2)$ of the set P, the set of product possibilities. The firm may be a monopolist and influence the price of both products and depress these as it increases its sales. In Fig. A7.23 the firm's profit function reaches a maximum in a boundary point of set P at $(\hat{x}_1, \hat{x}_2)$. However, this point is in the set F. In neither case does the firm's profit function assume its maximum value at one of the extreme points of P. Consequently, the linearity assumption is important. But useful theorems can be deduced for other objective functions which possess general properties and are defined on sets (see Chapter 2).

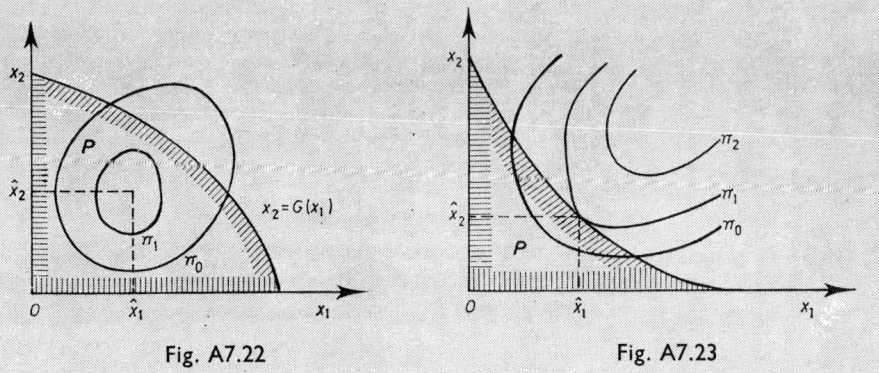

Fig. A7.22 Fig. A7.23

This chapter indicates that important advances are being made in economics by the use of topological and set concepts. The concepts enable the theory of production to be extended and simplified. One can go much further than has been done here. But I hope that I have at least given a flavour of the possibilities.[5]

This Appendix has not considered the supply relationships for an industry as a whole. This is not difficult to do. After reading Chapter 8, the interested reader may wish to extend the models outlined here to the whole industry. In the manner of Marshall, both short-run and long-run supply curves can be established. It might be borne in mind that some of the discontinuities of supply which arise in individual supply curves may disappear at the industry level (compare Figs 8.7 and 8.8 and the relevant discussion), and interesting supply *relationships* rather than functions may arise (compare Fig. 8.9 and the relevant discussion).

NOTES AND REFERENCES

[1] Smooth except at its end-point.
[2] The whole discussion of this Appendix is relevant to the possibility of controlling or managing economic units by a price system (see Chapter 22).
[3] This assumes that perfect or pure competition prevails.
[4] See K. LANCASTER, *Mathematical Economics*, The Macmillan Company, New York, 1968, pp. 342 and 343, and also J. QUIRK and R. SAPOSNIK, *Introduction to General Equilibrium Theory and Welfare Economics*, McGraw-Hill, New York, 1968, Ch. 2.
[5] The matters touched on here are crucial to the possibility of control by a price system. This should be apparent already, but it is followed up in Chapter 22.

FURTHER READING

GLICKSMAN, A. M., *An Introduction to Linear Programming and the Theory of Games*, John Wiley, New York, 1963, Ch. 2.

HADLEY, G., *Linear Algebra*, Addison-Wesley, Reading, Mass., 1961, Ch. 6.

KOOPMANS, T. C., *Three Essays on the State of Economic Science*, McGraw-Hill, New York, 1957, Essay I, Sec. I.

QUIRK, J. and R. SAPOSNIK, *Introduction to General Equilibrium Theory and Welfare Economics*, McGraw-Hill, New York, 1968, Ch. 2.

CHAPTER 8

The Pricing and Supply of Products Under Perfect Competition

I. Introduction and Definitions

Perfect competition is a limiting form of competition, sometimes approached by actual forms of competition but rarely if ever attained. As defined by economists, perfect competition is an abstraction, an ideal type. But this imaginary form of competition is not of little value because it is unrealistic, just as many mathematical concepts which have no *exact* counterpart in practice, for example, the line and the point, nevertheless find considerable application. Some markets do approach a state of perfect competition and perfectly competitive markets provide benchmarks by which to judge the efficiency or economic inefficiency of markets which are less than perfect.

In a perfectly competitive market,

(i) no single buyer or seller is able to influence the price at which he buys or sells products and resources;

(ii) no group of traders bands together to influence the terms of exchange of products and factors;

(iii) all traders are informed about revelant market prices and all are familiar with technological production possibilities and characteristics of goods;

(iv) every trader acts within his resource rights to foster his own self-interest (consumers maximise "utility" and firms maximise profit);

(v) except for the general restrictions placed upon mobility of resources by time (only some factors are variable in the short run), resources which are at all variable are geographically perfectly mobile without transport cost. Goods also are geographically mobile without transport costs;

(vi) Resources which are mobile can be freely employed by their owners in any industry. Resources are free to enter or leave any industry. No buyer is artificially restrained from bidding for or buying any commodity.

Condition (i) is likely to be fulfilled if there are a large number of buyers and sellers in the market and each trades in a negligible fraction of the quantity of any commodities traded. Thus no single citrus-fruit grower is likely to be able to influence the price of citrus fruit, and neither is a single consumer likely to exert an influence on the price. The trade of each is a negligible fraction of the trade in the whole market for citrus fruit. It is also said that if perfect competition is to prevail, products and factors must be homogeneous in the eyes of buyers. But a factor or product can be defined, and usually is, by the homogeneity requirement: if two cars are different in the eyes of consumers they can be regarded as different products.

If the above assumptions are fulfilled any product has the *same price everywhere* as do all variable factors of production. If any firm asks more than the market price for its product, this is immediately known by households and the firm makes no sales. Any firm that attempts to pay a variable factor of production less than its next best alternative reward, immediately loses the factor. Any trader who charges less than the going price for a product is swamped by demand and can raise his profit by increasing his price to the going level. If any firm pays a factor more than its market price (the factor's next best alternative reward), the firm is forgoing profit since it could lower its payment to the factor and retain the factor. If the firm does not act to maximise its profit, it is contravening condition (iv). In a perfectly competitive market, no trader has the *power* to sell commodities at a price above the market price and none has the *incentive* to purchase commodities at a price in excess of the market rate. Hence, all traders, both households and firms, trade and adjust their activities to common market rates. Each is a *price-taker* and a quantity-adjuster. If no individual influences market prices, then how are prices determined? As has been already indicated in Chapter 3, prices are determined collectively.

The purpose of this chapter is to explain in more detail the collective determination of prices under perfect competition. It concentrates on product prices and explores supply relationship in detail and indicates the connection between the supply curve for the individual firm and that for a market. The determination of the prices of factors of production is dealt with in a separate chapter.

The exposition is essentially Marshallian.[1] All prices, bar those of the market under consideration, are assumed to be constant. Thus partial analysis is used. Furthermore, the Marshallian division of resource variability for the very short, short, and long periods is adopted and firms are supposed to hold no stocks or inventories. Under these conditions, we reach the Marshallian conclusion that demand exerts a greater influence than cost on the determination of price in the short run whereas the position is reversed in the long run. Let us examine the short- and long-run positions.

II. Price and Supply in the Short Run

Taking a product, X, assume that it is exchanged in a perfectly competitive market. Following the example of Marshall,[2] the product might be fish.

In the very short run, the supply of the product is limited to the amount on hand since no factors are variable and there is, by assumption, no storage. Hence, during the interval of time considered, all the available quantity of the product is supplied to the market and the price rations this fixed supply to consumers. In the very short run, the number of firms is, of course, also fixed. Let there be $i = 1, \ldots, n$ firms in the industry and represent the supply of the ith firm by x_i and that of the whole industry by X. In the very short run the supply of the ith firm will stand at some specific level, $\hat{x}_i$ and, hence, the total supply available to the market is the fixed quantity

$$X = \sum_{i=1}^{n} \hat{x}_i = \hat{X}. \tag{8.1}$$

The total supply available to the market is shown by the vertical supply curve in Fig.

Pricing and Supply

8.2 and is the addition of the supplies of the individual firms. The supply curves of the individual firms are also vertical and the supply curve for the ith firm is for example indicated in Fig. 8.1 by s. An industry demand curve is indicated by D in Fig. 8.2 and may be obtained by the methods discussed in Chapter 6. The curves S and D intersect for a price of $\bar{p}$ and this is the only price which can prevail in the market if perfect knowledge exists and traders pursue their own interests. It is the equilibrium price in the very short run. The demand curve for the output of the ith firm is shown by the horizontal line marked d in Fig. 8.1. It is horizontal because the firm is so small in relation to the market that it is unable to influence demand by any feasible variation of its supplies. All of the firm's supplies are purchased at a price of $\bar{p}$. The firm makes no sales if it attempts to charge a price in excess of $\bar{p}$ and it is forgoing profit if it sells its supplies at a price of less than $\bar{p}$.

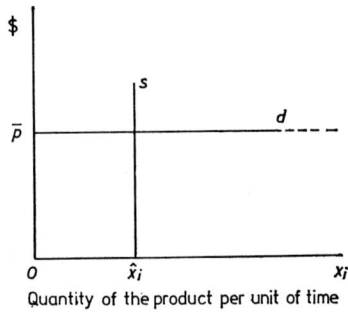

Fig. 8.1

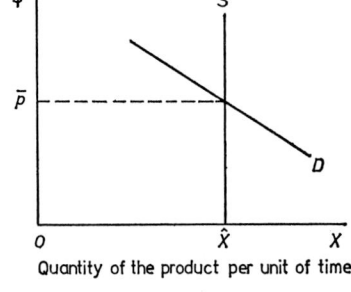

Fig. 8.2

In the *short run*, firms are able to vary their supplies by changing their employment of variable factors but other factors or their scale of plant remain fixed. Thus in Marshall's example, if the equilibrium price is determined each day, in the *very* short run (the market period) supply is limited to the catch of fish on hand. But in the short period, fishermen can, for example, stay at sea longer and extra hands can be hired so some variation of daily supply is possible. However, the number of luggers and firms that are operating cannot be varied in the short run so the variation is less than that in the long run. In the short run, some factors are variable and others are fixed and there is no entry nor exit of firms.

Taking any firm, the ith, let us derive its short-run supply curve for product X assuming that it aims to maximise profit and that factor prices are constant. Furthermore, imagine that its production function depends only on its own economic activity, so that consequently its costs depend only on its own output. (This was implicitly assumed in the last chapter and is relaxed later in this chapter.) Suppose, too, that in the typical case the firm at first experiences increasing returns to outlay as it increases output but that this is followed by decreasing returns. Its short-run total-cost curve for its particular scale of plant is of the type shown by STC in Fig. 8.3. A short-run total-cost curve of this nature was discussed at the end of Chapter 7. The total revenue received by the firm as a result of its output (equals quantity sold) is equal to the going market price for the product times the quantity of its output and thus can be shown by the straight line, TR, in Fig. 8.3. The slope of this straight line is equal to the market price which is unaffected by the supplies of any individual firm. The firm's profit is the difference between its total revenue and costs and varies with its output. The ith firm's profit function is indicated by π in Fig. 8.3 and reaches a maximum for an output of $\bar{x}_i$. At that output the slope of TR curve equals the slope of the STC curve which is increasing in slope. Marginal revenue (equals price under perfect competition) equals (increasing) marginal cost at this profit maximising output. Note that the slopes of the TR curve and the STC curve are also equal for an output of x_i^0 but this gives a relative minimum of profit since the slope of the total profit function is increasing at this point, and consequently, the slope of the total-cost curve is decreasing. Note further that

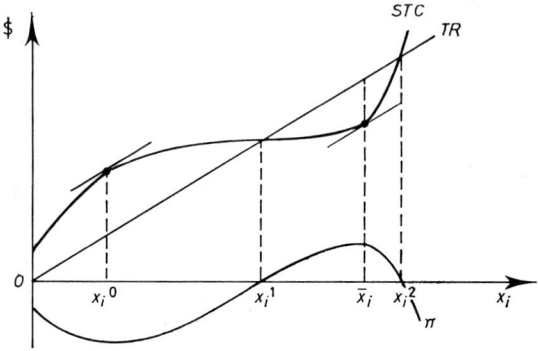

Fig. 8.3

break-even outputs are x_i^1 and x_i^2. At these levels of output total revenue just covers total cost. Also, the positive intercept of STC on the Y axis is fixed cost and the negative intercept of π is a loss equal to fixed cost.

The corresponding per-unit cost curves for the case shown in Fig. 8.3 are illustrated in Fig. 8.4. At a market price of $\bar{p}$, the ith firm's marginal revenue curve is a horizontal line equal to $\bar{p}$. Its short-run marginal and average cost functions are U-shaped. The short-run marginal-cost curve equals marginal revenue for two levels of output but the profit maximising output, $\bar{x}_i$, corresponds to that at which marginal cost is increasing. The firm's maximum profit is indicated by the hatched area in Fig. 8.4. Note that

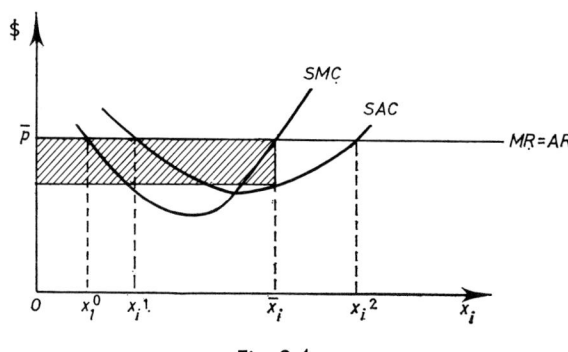

Fig. 8.4

the output which minimises the cost of production per unit (that corresponding to the minimum of the short-run average cost curve) does *not* maximise profit in this case.

Pricing and Supply

This output only maximises profit if the market price equals the firm's minimum average cost in which case the MR curve is tangential to the average-cost curve. If market price exceeds or equals minimum short-run average cost, the firm supplies an output which equates the price of the product and its increasing marginal cost. Consequently, at least for prices greater than or equal to minimum average cost, the firm's supply curve is equal to the positive portion of its short-run marginal-cost curve.

What, however, happens if the market price of the product is less than the firm's minimum average cost of production? Clearly the firm is unable to make a profit at any level of output. Should it cease production? Only if this minimises its loss. It does not pay the firm to shut down if it can more than cover its variable costs of operation. Any excess of revenue over and above its variable costs provides a contribution to meeting its fixed cost and reduces its loss. However, if the firm is unable to meet its variable costs at any level of output, then it pays the firm to shut down its operations. Otherwise, the firm adds to its inevitable loss of fixed costs.

In Figs 8.5 and 8.6 a case is illustrated in which the firm is indifferent about whether it produces an output of $\bar{x}_i$ or shuts down. The total curves are shown in Fig. 8.5 and the corresponding per-unit curves in Fig. 8.6. Market price (the slope of the TR curve) is assumed to be equal to the minimum of the firm's average variable cost, and equals the slope of MT in Fig. 8.5. At this price, the maximum interior value of π (at $\bar{x}_i$) is just equal to its end-point value, ON. OM equals total fixed cost and equals $|ON|$. If price is less than the minimum value of average variable cost, the interior maximum of π is lower (the loss is greater) than at the end-point value, $x=0$. It pays to cease production. Hence, the firm's short-run supply curve consists of its marginal-cost curve above the minimum of its average variable-cost curve. (The possibility of the MC curve having several minima is assumed away but in the light of the discussion of Chapter 2, is not difficult to deal with.)

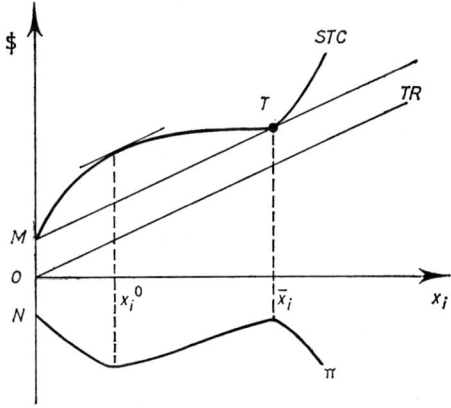

Fig. 8.5

Given a U-shaped average-cost curve, the supply curve of the firm really consists of two parts. It is a discontinuous curve of the type shown in Fig. 8.7. There a supply curve for the ith firm is shown by the lines OA and BC. OA equals the minimum value of the firm's average variable cost and BC is the segment of the firm's short-run

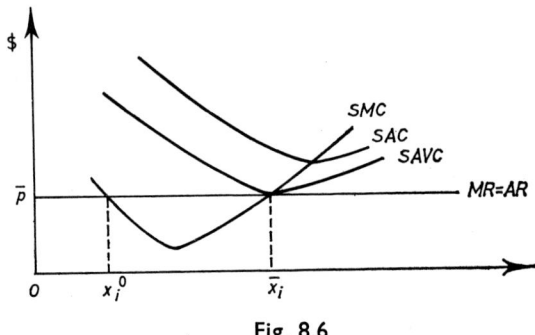

Fig. 8.6

marginal-cost curve equal to or above its average variable-cost curve. The firm's supply curve indicates that at a price of less than OA, it produces no output. For a price of OA, the firm is indifferent about producing an output of zero or $\bar{x}_i$ since both levels of output yield the same profit, namely a loss which is just equal to the firm's fixed cost. For this price, there is some indeterminancy in the firm's supply function. This also gives rise to a corresponding indeterminancy in the supply function for the industry. Most texts ignore this problem. To eliminate the indeterminancy, we might suppose that the greater output is preferred if profits from two alternative levels of output are equal. But by using such methods of analysis we avoid significant issues. We should also note that an output greater than zero but less than $\bar{x}_i$ is never produced by the firm, no matter what the price is.

Imagine that all firms in the industry have the same supply curve as the ith. Then, ruling out external economies and diseconomies, the supply curve for the industry is equal to the summation of the supply curves of the individual firms. The industry supply curve is indicated in Fig. 8.8 by $OADS$. At a price of less than OA, zero output is supplied by the industry. At OA, a dashed stretch is shown and indicates that at this price an output between zero and $\bar{X}$ may be produced by the industry because some firms may produce nothing and others might produce $\bar{x}_i$. Hence, there is an indeterminancy in the industry supply function but not a *certain* gap in supply as in the case of the individual firm.[3]

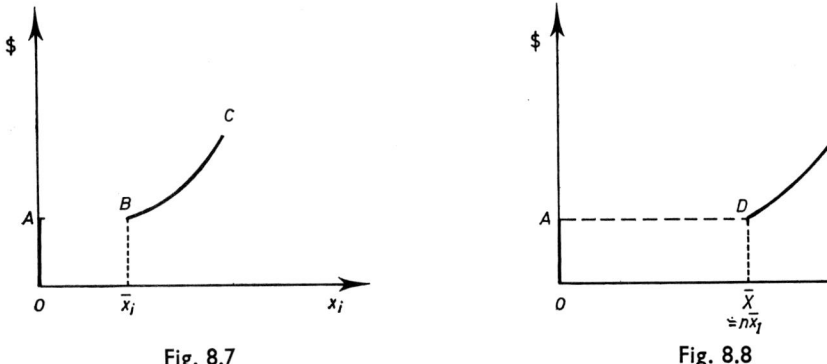

Fig. 8.7   Fig. 8.8

Cost curves may differ between firms in an industry in the short run and this changes the character of the industry supply curve. Imagine that the minimum average variable costs of the firms can be placed in an ascending order and that the highest such cost has some finite value. Allowing for indeterminancy, the typical short-run supply relationship for the industry might then be like that depicted in Fig. 8.9. The supply relationship consists of the dotted set in the neighbourhood of K (which indicates the area of indeterminancy of supply at various prices) and the segment KS as well as the line OK. No firm supplies any output at a price of OK or less. At prices between OK and p_1 there is some indeterminancy of supply. For example, if $p = p_0$, supply falls in the range $X_0 \leq X \leq X_1$. The range of firms definitely supplying the market, and the band of those who might or might not supply the market, change. If price is at or above p_1, all firms within the industry supply the market and the supply is a (fully determinant) function of price. The upper limit of the dotted set in the neighbourhood of K results if all those firms who are on the margin of doubt about whether to produce the commodity or not, do not produce. The lower limit of the set corresponds to the case where this group of firms decides to produce at the level where price equals minimum average variable cost. Hence, the supply *relationship* itself is determinate. The supply relationship which is depicted in Fig. 8.9 differs from the conventional representation. Conventionally, the industry supply curve for a product is shown as function of the product's price. No indeterminancy is involved in the traditional relationship. This representation is not accurate and in some circumstances involves a serious abstraction. A traditional industry supply curve is shown in Fig. 8.10 by OKS. It is reasonable to suppose that such a curve is the lower boundary of the relationship shown in Fig. 8.9 which implies that if firms are *indifferent* (on the basis of profit) about producing or not producing, they choose to produce. The consequences of the traditional supply relationship will be explored in this chapter. However, the traditional theory ought to be recognised as a special case. *Observe* that, if the supply relationship of Fig. 8.9 is accepted, the equilibrium *price* and output is to some extent indeterminate if the industry demand curve intersects the dotted supply set.

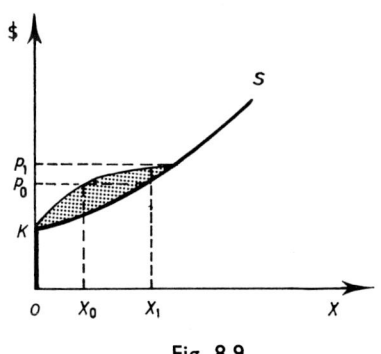

Fig. 8.9

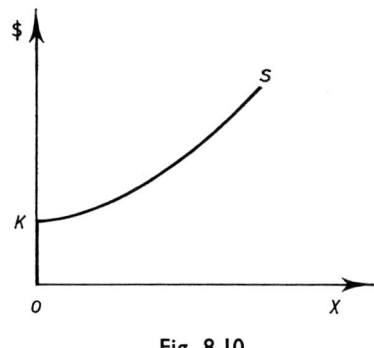

Fig. 8.10

It has been shown how a short-run industry supply function can be obtained from the supply functions of the firms within an industry. Unless the marginal-cost curve of each firm when above its minimum average cost point is vertical, the industry short-run supply curve is not vertical but is positively sloped. Typically, the industry supply curve is like OKS in Fig. 8.10. Variations of demand which result in short-run equilibria for a price of K or less do not affect supply but variations of equilibria in excess of K do influence supply. While supply does not respond to price changes in the *very* short run, it usually responds to price variations in the short run as firms alter their employment of variable factors. Thus initially market price is solely subject to the influence of demand but costs exert some impact in the short run. Equilibrium market price responds markedly to demand fluctuations in the very short run but, in the short period, variations of supply dampen the price movement. This is illustrated in Figs 8.11 and 8.12. Figure 8.12 indicates the position for the industry and 8.11 mirrors the industry changes for a firm within the industry.

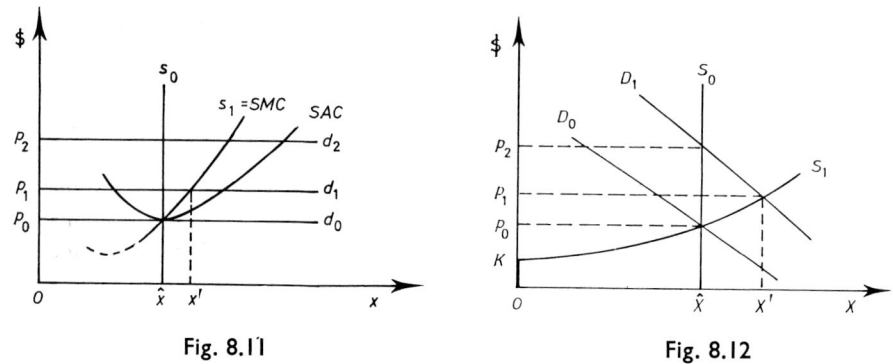

Fig. 8.11   Fig. 8.12

Imagine that the industry is initially in a short-run situation in which supply is S_1 and demand D_0, and that it is producing the equilibrium output $\hat{X}$ and selling this at p_0. The firm shown just manages to earn normal profit in this situation. Suppose that the demand for the output of the industry suddenly expands to D_1. In the very short run, industry supplies remain unaltered at $\hat{X}$ and the equilibrating market prices rises to p_2. The firm shown in Fig. 8.11 earns above-normal profits, which equal $p_2\hat{x} - p_0\hat{x}$ or $(p_2-p_0)\hat{x}$, a rectangle which can be easily identified in the diagram. At a price of p_2, the firm finds it profitable to expand output in the short run. But as several firms expand output in the short run, the market equilibrating price is forced down to p_1. At this price, the firm (shown) still makes above-normal profit but less than in the very short run. The firm's supply expands from $\hat{x}$ to x' and the industry supply increases from $\hat{X}$ to X'. The short-run equilibrium price is lower than that in the very short run but, because of increasing marginal costs, is higher than it was initially.

In the long run, even more variation of supply is possible than in the short run. In the long run, firms can alter their scale of plant, as well as their use of factors which are variable in the short run, and firms can enter and leave the industry. Consequently, price is even less subject to influence by fluctuations of demand in the long run. Let us examine the long-run supply relationships.

III. Price and Supply in the Long Run

Consider first the long-run supply curve of a firm. In the long run, the firm is free to vary its scale of plant and will take advantage of this if it increases profit. To maximise its profit in the long run, the firm should supply an output which equates its (increasing) long-run marginal cost to its marginal revenue (equals price) unless it is unable to cover its long-run average cost at any positive output. In the latter case, it should

Pricing and Supply

cease production of the product. However, this does not mean that the firm should cease producing altogether. It may transfer its resources to the production of another product, for it will be recalled that costs are based on opportunities forgone. It follows that the supply curve of the firm is equal to its long-run marginal-cost curve (above) and equal to its minimum of long-run average cost and consists of a vertical segment for prices less than minimum long-run average cost. Figure 8.13 indicates a supply curve for a firm and is comprised of the lines OA and BC. BC is equal to the long-run marginal-cost curve at and above the firm's minimum of long-run average cost.

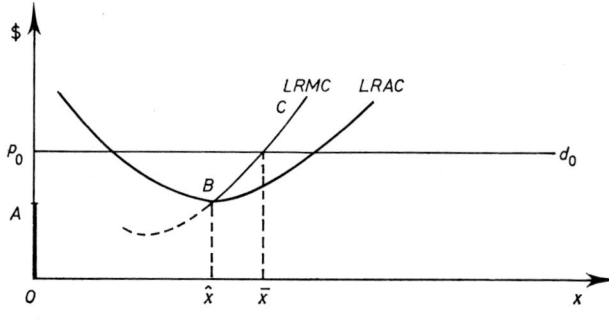

Fig. 8.13

At a price of less than OA the firm (shown) supplies none of product X. If the price of the product is OA, the firm is indifferent about producing $\hat{x}$ of the product or none of it. There is an area of indeterminacy. For prices in excess of OA, positive quantities of X are supplied as indicated by the rising $LRMC$ curve. At a price of p_0, for example, the firm supplies $\bar{x}$ of the product.

If we were to suppose that entry is not possible in the long run (this could happen because of artificial restrictions or entry may require an even longer period than variations of existing plant) but exit is possible, the industry supply curve would be found by the addition of supply curves of the type shown in Fig. 8.13. The supply relationships are akin to those for the short term, and excess profit may persist in the long run if blockaded entry is supposed. The supply curve for the industry is, however, flatter than the short-term one. The same sort of indeterminacy problem arises in this case as in the short-run case and I shall not discuss this again.

However, it is of value to compare the industry supply curves for the very short run, short run, and long run in this case, using the traditional assumptions. Given an initial equilibrium at E, these supply curves are related in the manner illustrated in Fig. 8.14: S_0 is the supply curve for the very short period, S_1 for the short period, and S_2 for the long period, assuming that entry of new firms is impossible.

It can easily be seen that shifts of the demand function (up or down) which change the equilibrium have a greater impact on price in the very short run than in the short run, and less effect in the long run than in the short, so I shall not clutter up the figure with examples.

In the long run, it may be more reasonable to suppose that the industry is open rather than closed and this is, indeed, the traditional assumption. Entry and exit are assumed, as a rule, to be free in the long run. Under these circumstances, and if factor prices are unaffected by the industry's variation of supply, the long-run supply curve

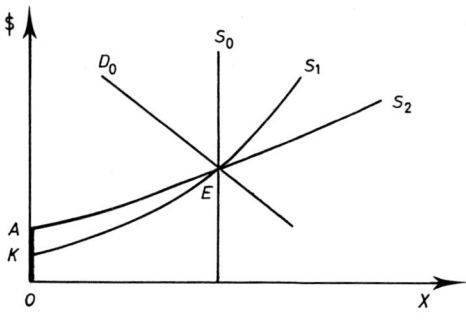

Fig. 8.14

of the product becomes a horizontal straight line, and no firm within the industry is able to earn other than normal profits. In the long run, every firm operating in the industry is marginal as far as that industry is concerned, for in the long run all factors are mobile and consequently long-run differences of efficiency between firms (for example, arising from superior management or other superior resources) are compensated for by differential rates of reward to the factors which are responsible for such differences. Thus a firm with superior management may be able to appropriate in the short run some of the extra returns due to the superior management, but in the long run the salary of this management will be forced up by the competition of other firms for it and thus the initial advantage of the firm will be lost. The long-run cost curve of each firm is computed on the basis that each factor obtains a reward equal to the best alternative forgone and where appropriate includes implicit costs (for example, an allowance for the salary of an owner-manager).

In the long run, the long-run average-cost curve of each firm which is operating in the industry is just tangential to its marginal revenue (equals demand curve) for its product. The typical long-run equilibrium position of a firm in an open industry is shown in Fig. 8.15. In this case, the firm's long-run optimal output is either $\bar{x}$ or zero. Its profits operating in the industry are just equal to those which it could alternatively earn by not producing X and producing another product optimally. It is, indeed, a marginal firm and is indifferent about producing the particular product or not. This was noted by Jacob Viner in his 1931 article and, as he pointed out, it is liable to result in some indeterminancy of supply.[4]

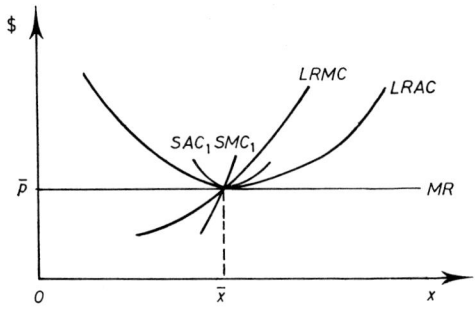

Fig. 8.15

Pricing and Supply

If the price of factors remain constant as the industry's output varies (that is if no *pecuniary* economies or diseconomies are present and if technological externalities which are unpriced are ruled out), the long-run supply curve of the industry is a horizontal straight line equal to the minimum long-run average cost of production of the product. Such a long-run supply curve is indicated in Fig. 8.17 by LRS and for comparison the per-unit cost curves for an equilibrium firm are shown in Fig. 8.16.

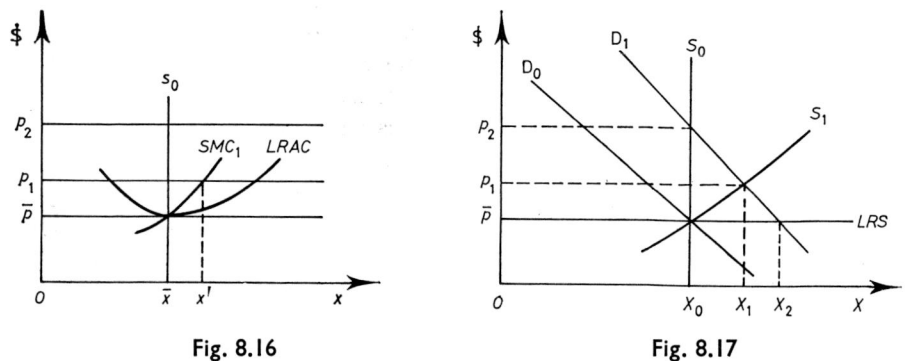

Fig. 8.16   Fig. 8.17

Let us now trace through the full repercussions of a sudden rise in the overall demand for the product from D_0 to D_1, assuming that the industry is initially in long-run equilibrium and that the firm shown is, in fact, a producer of product X. Initially, the industry is in long-term equilibrium when it is producing an output of X_0 and trading at a price $\bar{p}$ and the firm is maximising its profit at an output of $\bar{x}$. Now imagine that industry demand suddenly rises to D_1. In the very short period, the equilibrium price rises from $\bar{p}$ to p_2 and supply is unaltered. Firms within the industry make above-normal profit. In the short run, some factors can be varied but the scale of plant cannot be altered and firms are unable to enter or leave the industry. The equilibrium price of the product drops from p_2 to p_1 and output expands from X_0 to X_1. This expansion of output is made possible solely by existing firms operating their existing plants at increased capacities. Above-normal profits persist in the industry but are lower than in the very short run. The firm which is taken as an example has also expanded its output from $\bar{x}$ to x'.

At a price of p_1 and *in the absence of entry*, existing firms in the industry would find it profitable to expand their scale of plant in the long run (to move along their $LRMC$ curves). A *new equilibrium* would be established for the industry at the point of intersection of D_1 and a supply curve, such as that shown by S_2 in Fig. 8.14. Established firms would earn above-normal profit in this closed industry. But this new equilibrium could not persist in an open industry since new firms will enter to take advantage of the favourable profit opportunities in the industry. In an open industry, in which prices of the factors are constant, price is forced down to the minimum of long-run average cost, and the long-run supply curve is LRS.

In Fig. 8.17, the new long-run equilibrium is established for an industry output of X_2 and a product price of $\bar{p}$. As a result of the increased demand, the quantity supplied to the market has increased by $X_2 - X_0$. The whole of this increase results from supplies by new firms. All firms produce an output which minimises their $LRAC$. After an initially profitable period, the firm shown in Fig. 8.16 returns to its old level of activity and just makes a normal profit. As a result of the profit motive and competition, supplies have responded to the demands of consumers and consumers have been supplied with the product at minimum attainable cost. The system is efficient in the economic sense and this point will be taken up later.

Is it reasonable to suppose that the expansion or contraction of industry will always have no influence on factor prices? Pecuniary diseconomies or economies are only likely to be absent if the industry is a relatively small user of available factors, or if factors are in perfectly elastic supply. Otherwise, as the industry expands, factor prices are likely to rise (the increasing cost industry possibility) or factor prices may fall (the decreasing cost possibility). In the former case, the long-run supply curve for the industry is upward-sloping and in the latter case it is downward-sloping.

Consider the possibility of increasing costs due to the industry's expansion. Both the short-run and the long-run total cost of each firm is then not only a function of its own output but is also dependent upon the industry's total output. However, some texts only consider this diseconomy to be present in the long run and neglect any short-run impact of industry expansion on factor prices. In practice, I doubt whether this is justifiable since factor supplies are likely to be even more inelastic in the short run than in the long run.

If factor prices are dependent upon industry output, it is impossible to obtain the short-run supply of the industry by simply adding together the portion of the marginal-cost curves of firms above their average variable cost. In an increasing cost industry the nature of the error is indicated in Fig. 8.18. For simplicity, assume that all firms have identical costs and that each is producing an output $\bar{X}/n$, there being n firms in the industry. At the output of $\bar{X}$, the sum of their marginal costs gives a fake supply curve indicated by OA and BC. The true supply curve which allows for the impact of industry output on factor prices is like the curve $OLMS$. In the short run, less output is supplied at prices above $\bar{p}$ than is indicated by the fake supply curve and greater quantities of output are supplied at prices less than $\bar{p}$ than the fake supply curve indicates. The results here apply, *mutatis mutandis*, to the long-run supply curve for a *closed* industry.

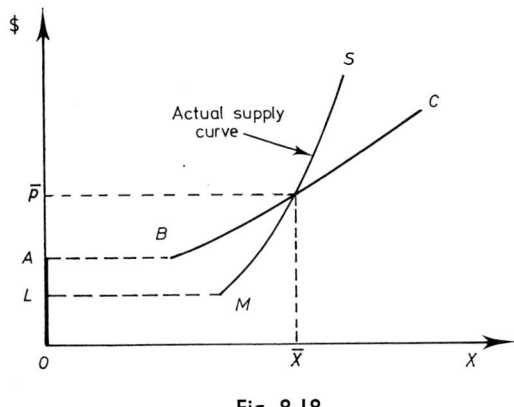

Fig. 8.18

Figures 8.19 and 8.20 trace through the repercussions of an increase of demand on the supply and price of a product in an increasing cost industry. Figure 8.19 indicates

Pricing and Supply

the long-run equilibria of the typical firm and the situation for the industry is depicted in Fig. 8.20. Imagine that the industry is initially in long-run equilibrium at the original

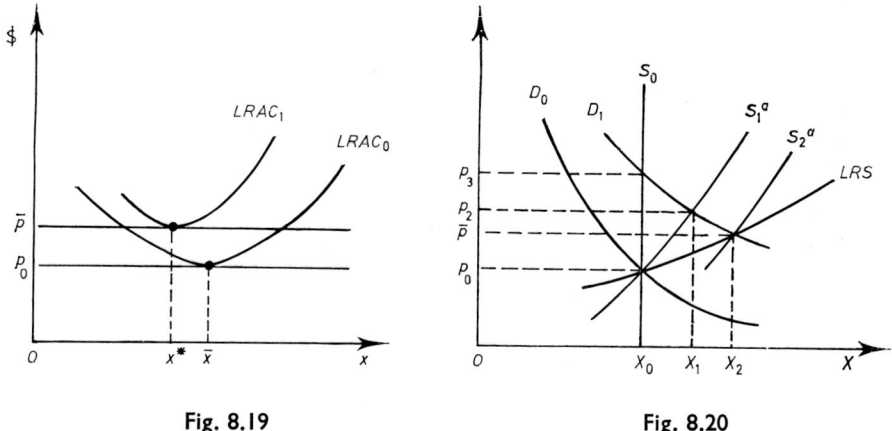

Fig. 8.19　　　　　　　　　　　Fig. 8.20

level of demand indicated by D_0, X_0 is supplied to the market, the price of the product is p_0, and all firms producing the product are only making normal profit. The firm whose cost curve is depicted in Fig. 8.19 produces an output of $\bar{x}$. With a sudden rise in demand to D_1, price rises in the very short period (sometimes called the market period) to p_3 and existing firms earn above-normal profits. In the short run, existing firms increase their supply of the product, equilibrium price settles down to p_2 and the industry supply increases to X_1. The new equilibrium is at the intersection of the demand curve D_1 and the short-run supply curve, $S_1{}^a$. However, $S_1{}^a$ is not obtained by simply summing the individual marginal cost curves, given X_0. As pointed out in Fig. 8.18, account must be taken of the influence on the price of factors of the industry's expansion of output. In the short run, existing firms continue to earn above-normal profit and in the long run this induces the entry of additional firms. Long-run equilibrium is established, given the demand curve D_1, at an output X_2 and a price $\bar{p}$. Due to increasing costs, however, the long-term price is higher than in the first long-term equilibrium. The long-term supply curve, LRS, indicates the supplies of the industry on the assumption that the industry is completely open and assumes that adjustments have been made for changes in the price of factors, which result from variations of industry output.

In the new long-run equilibrium, all firms in the industry once again just manage to make a normal profit. The firm depicted in Fig. 8.19 is in equilibrium producing an output of x^* and its long-run average cost has shifted up from $LRAC_0$ to $LRAC_1$ as a result of the rise of factor prices. In this case, its long-run output is lower than initially. *A priori*, there is no way of telling whether its output will be higher or lower than previously. This depends upon the manner in which the prices of the different factors change. However, we can be sure that industry supply will respond to increased demand by rising. The extra output may be completely or partly supplied by new firms.

Both the possibility of constant or increasing costs for an industry in the long run seem more plausible than the possibility of decreasing costs. The expansion of the output of an industry, however, may result in a decline in the price of inputs if the suppliers of the inputs experience decreasing costs, due to an increase of their total output. Suppliers may experience decreasing cost due to technological economies. Expansion of their total sales may allow increased specialisation of factors of production with resultant economies.

It is, of course, also possible that the industry supplying the product will experience technological economies. But these must be external to individual firms if an equilibrium is to exist for any individual firm. If economies can be achieved by the expansion of individual firm's output and if this results in a declining marginal cost function, the firm has no equilibrium level of output if price is independent of its output. As Joan Robinson has indicated,[5] under these conditions perfect competition must break down and give way to imperfect competition. The assumption cannot be retained that an individual firm is unable to influence the market price of the product. The difficulty is demonstrated in Fig. 8.21. A declining marginal-cost curve for a firm is shown and market price is assumed to be constant at $\bar{p}$. Profit is at a relative minimum for an output of x^* and, for output beyond x^*, increases without limit as x (the firm's output) is increased, since for all greater levels of output marginal revenue exceeds marginal cost. There is no upper limit to the size of the firm. But perfect competition is compatible with decreasing costs if the decrease in a firm's cost is independent of its own variation of output and results from an expansion of the output of an industry as a whole.

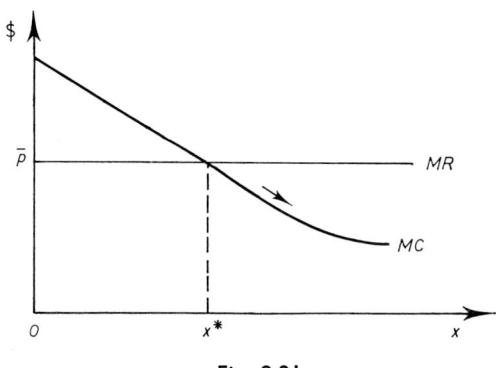

Fig. 8.21

In Fig. 8.22, the long-run equilibrium price of a decreasing cost industry is shown to decline from p_0 to $\bar{p}$ as a result of a rise in the demand curve from D_0 to D_1. The short-run supply curves are positively sloping indicating net diseconomies to the industry's expansion in the short run. The long-run economies are assumed to be external to firms. In both long-run equilibria, firms producing in the industry just manage to make normal profit. The corresponding equilibria of one firm is shown in Fig. 8.23. In the first long-run position, its optimal output is x^*, and its long-run average costs are $LRAC_0$. As a result of the industry's expansion, the firm's long-run average costs fall to $LRAC_1$ and it produces an output of x' and just makes a normal profit. Note that the equilibrium industry output expands as the result of the increased demand. Given Marshallian (dynamic) reaction assumptions, the long-run equilibrium is stable (see the discussion in Chapter 5) since the (absolute) slope of the demand curve exceeds that of the long-run supply curve. The long-run equilibrium is unstable

Pricing and Supply

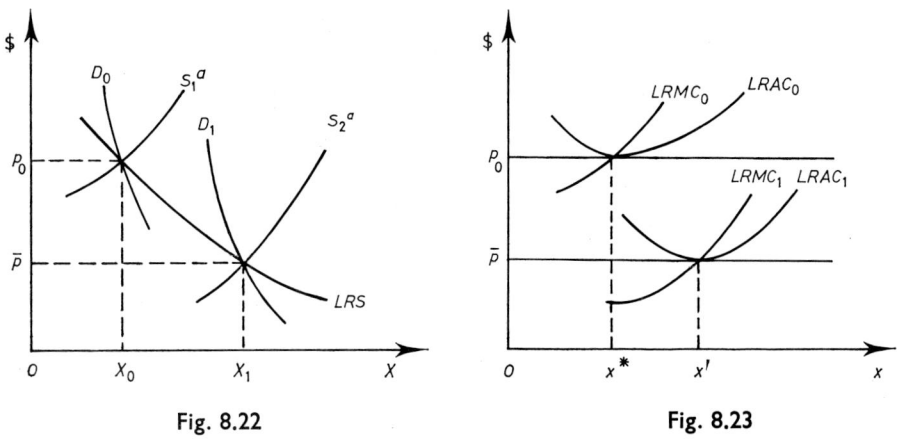

Fig. 8.22 Fig. 8.23

given Marshallian assumptions if the demand curve cuts the long-run supply curve from below. Yet, an equilibrium does exist. However, and this accords with our results of Chapter 5, an increase of demand reduces the equilibrium output and given Marshallian reaction assumptions the equilibrium is *unstable*. This reduction of equilibrium output is illustrated in Fig. 8.24 where, as a result of an increase in demand from D_0 to D_1, the long-run equilibrium output of the industry drops from X^0 to X^*. (Note that, although short-run supply curves for the industry were not shown in the above exposition to decline, they can be allowed to do so. If external economies are

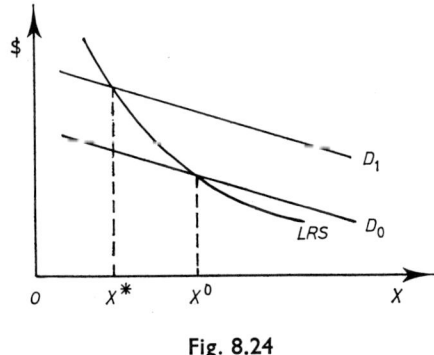

Fig. 8.24

present in the short run and *no* internal economies which give decreasing marginal cost for the expansion of individual firms exist, this situation is compatible with the existence of perfect competition. The explanation is analogous for that of the long run.)

Now, we should remind ourselves that the model of the market, which has been outlined, is a static model and that we have exclusively used the method of comparative statics. This was so cleverly done by Marshall that we are always liable to forget that his method is not dynamic. His "periods" of time do have some implicit relationship to clock-time and may give a rough approximation to the actual state of affairs. Nevertheless, from a theoretical and policy point of view the static nature of the model may give misleading results. All actual happenings are dynamic. The problem was

IV. Efficiency and Perfect Competition

The economic efficiency of perfect competition was discussed in a preliminary manner in Chapter 3 and there is very little which can profitably be added to the argument at this stage. The discussion of Section III of Chapter 7 helps to explain optimal specialisation of production, which was first considered in Section V of Chapter 3. If externalities are absent, perfect competition not only results in optimal specialisation in production but it also ensures that the composition of production is Pareto optimal from the consumers' point of view. It can be shown that a Pareto optimum requires (given that preferences and technological relationships satisfy the properties traditionally assumed by economists) the marginal rates of indifferent substitution of goods by consumers to be equal and these in turn must be equal to the marginal rates of product transformation of firms which must be equal to one another. (The latter, in turn, implies the fulfilment of equalities in the rates of factor substitution. See Fig. 7.24.) Because prices are the same for all under perfect competition and each supplier aims to maximise his profit and each consumer his utility, their individual self-interest ensures that they act unwittingly to fulfil the conditions for a Pareto optimum. The conditions will be discussed more adequately in Chapter 13 on "Welfare Economics".

However, a number of points can be made along Marshallian lines. First, perfect competition ensures that the cost of producing any level of *industry* output is at a minimum. (Pareto relevant externalities are ruled out.) It ensures that costs are at a minimum relative to the possibilities of variation in the employment of factors or the allocation of resources. Thus imagine that there are n firms in an industry and let the total cost of the ith firm be indicated by $C_i(x_i)$ where x_i is its own output. We need to find the conditions required for a minimum of industry cost

$$C = \sum_{i=1}^{n} C_i(x_i) \qquad (8.2)$$

subject to or given that industry output is to be at any level

$$X^* = \sum_{i=1}^{n} x_i. \qquad (8.3)$$

Solving by Lagrange's method, the first-order conditions are that

$$C_1'(x_1) = C_2'(x_2) = \ldots = C_n'(x_n) \qquad (8.4)$$

or

$$MC_1 = MC_2 = \ldots = MC_n, \qquad (8.5)$$

and that

$$\sum_{i=1}^{n} x_i = X^*. \qquad (8.6)$$

The total industry output must be distributed so that the marginal cost of each producing firm is equal. Furthermore, it can be demonstrated that the allocation of the output must ensure that the marginal-cost of all producing firms is increasing.

Pricing and Supply

For simplicity, suppose that the marginal-cost curves of firms increase throughout their range; diminishing returns is the rule, then the requirement that the marginal costs of firms be equal can be illustrated by the example given in Fig. 8.25. There the production conditions for only two firms are shown because of limitations of space, but we must imagine that there are in practice a large number. Suppose that the industry wishes to produce an output of $X^* = x_1^* + x_2^*$ at minimum cost and that there are only two firms in the industry. The allocation of x_1^* of X to firm 1 and x_2^* to firm 2 equalises their marginal costs and minimises the cost of producing X^*. Imagine a different allocation of output, say, $x_1^* - \varepsilon$ to firm 1 and $x_2^* + \varepsilon$ to firm 2. Obviously the cost of producing X^* increases. The cost of firm 1 falls by the dotted area but that of firm 2 rises by the hatched area which clearly is greater than the dotted area. The marginal cost of the firms must be equal if the cost of an industry's output is to be minimised.

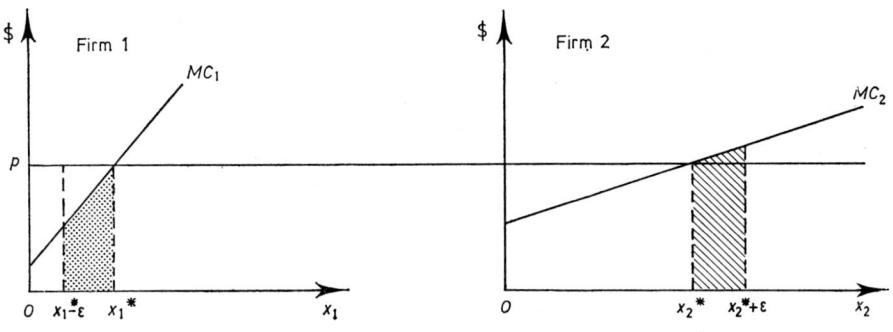

Fig. 8.25

Perfect competition ensures this equality. The price of the product is the same for both firms. For example, it might be p as indicated in Fig. 8.25. In order to maximise its profit, firm 1 equates p and its marginal cost. Likewise, firm 2 equates p and MC_2. Thus the marginal costs of the firm are equalised. These costs are equalised because each firm acts to maximise profit, and the product's price is the same for each.

However, should we be impressed about the fulfilment of this efficiency condition? Not really. A profit maximising monopolist with several plants would also equate the marginal cost of all plants which he operates (but not to the price of his product). He will also minimise the cost of any level of output. Yet, under perfect competition, this condition is automatically satisfied. Furthermore, the monopolist has the option of deviating from this allocation if he does not wish to maximise profit. He still may make above-normal profit and survive. But in the long run, with free entry, firms in a perfectly competitive industry have little option but to maximise profit and thus indirectly meet this condition.

Yet one wonders whether the social value of perfect competition resides so much in its cost minimising attributes. Surely, its most important attribute is that given the costs of production and the income distribution, it results in a composition of output which Pareto optimally meets the desires of consumers.[6] The outcome can be roughly indicated by Fig. 8.26. The supply curve shown there is the marginal cost to society of the industry's output given a certain degree of possible variability of resources. The demand curve, D, indicates the value to consumers of an additional unit of product. If industry output is less than $\bar{X}$ (say at X_0) the extra value to consumers of an additional unit of output (p_1) exceeds its additional cost to society in terms of alternatives forgone (OA). Thus, consumers can gain by increased production. At outputs beyond $\bar{X}$, the cost of additional output (which reflects the value of alternatives forgone) exceeds the value to consumers of extra quantities of X. Thus, production beyond $\bar{X}$ involves a loss to consumers. Only at $\bar{X}$ is the value of the product and its cost in terms of alternatives forgone just balanced. This is the output which, in the absence of externalities, eventuates under perfect competition. Under imperfect competition, a lower output is likely.

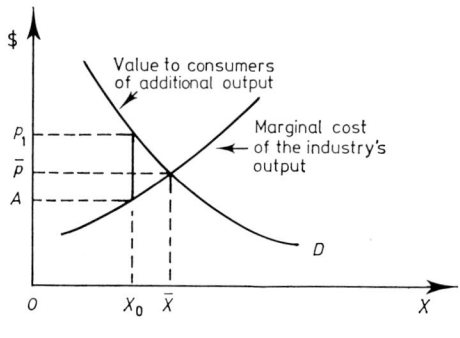

Fig. 8.26

Under perfect competition, there are long-run pressures to ensure cost minimisation which may not be present under imperfect competition.[7] Firms which fail to adopt the most efficient methods and which fail to maximise profit may not survive. We cannot say that they will definitely not survive because even normal profit may leave some leeway for sub-normal profit. But we might expect this to be a small margin indeed if capital accumulation proceeds far enough. In the short run, even perfectly competitive firms may have some discretion about whether or not to maximise profit and indeed, may have limited discretion in the long run. We have merely assumed that firms will choose to maximise profit. This might not be justified. It is a crucial assumption.

NOTES AND REFERENCES

[1] A. MARSHALL, *Principles of Economics*, 8th ed., Macmillan, London, 1920.
[2] Ibid.
[3] If x_i is sizable for each firm, the possibilities along AD may be discrete.
[4] JACOB VINER, "Cost Curves and Supply Curves", *Zeitschrift für Nationalökonomie*, 1931, 3, pp. 23-46. Reprinted in A.E.A., *Readings in Price Theory*, Allen and Unwin, London, 1953, especially pp. 210-12.
[5] JOAN ROBINSON, *The Economics of Imperfect Competition*, Macmillan, London, 1st ed., 1938; 2nd ed., 1969, p. 4. See also, P. SRAFFA, "The Laws of Return under Competitive Conditions", *Economic Journal*, 1926, 36, pp. 535-50.
[6] But it cannot be overstressed that this assumes the absence of externalities.
[7] This statement must be weighed and interpreted in the light of factors which are mentioned in Chapter 9. In particular, static efficiency may not be very attractive if it is achieved at the expense of technical progress.

FURTHER READING

BAIRN, J. S., *Price Theory*, Holt, Rinehart and Winston, New York, 1952, Ch. 4.

COHEN, K. J. and R. M. CYERT, *Theory of the Firm*, Prentice-Hall, Englewood Cliffs, 1965, Ch. 8.

MARSHALL, A., *Principles of Economics*, 8th ed., Macmillan, London, 1920, Book V, Chs. 1-5.

ROBINSON, JOAN, *The Economics of Imperfect Competition*, 2nd ed., Macmillan, London, 1969, Book III.

STONIER, A. W., and D. C. HAGUE, *A Textbook of Economic Theory*, 2nd ed., Longmans, London, 1957, Ch. 6.

CHAPTER 9

Imperfect Competition

I. Introduction

Logically, all markets which are not perfect can be regarded as imperfect. But in practice economists single out one factor to differentiate between perfect and imperfect markets. In imperfectly competitive markets some of the participants are able to influence the terms of exchange, whereas in perfectly competitive markets none are able to affect the terms of trade. This method of differentiation is satisfactory if knowledge is perfect in all markets but otherwise may be misleading.[1]

If some traders do influence the terms of trade this has implications for economic behaviour and economic efficiency which are explored in this chapter. We shall continue to concentrate on the market for products which, within the traditional circular flow of an economy, involves the exchange of the incomes of households for goods. The other principal market is that in which households supply factors for incomes and is discussed in the next chapter. All these markets will be linked together in the discussion of general equilibrium in Chapter 11.

In the market for goods, it is reasonable to suppose that households (consumers) are unable to alter individually the price of a product (or other conditions of sale), but that firms (sellers) may be able to do so. Thus the demand curve of a firm operating in an imperfectly competitive market is not a horizontal straight line as under perfect competition but is downward-sloping. By withholding or reducing its supplies to a market, an imperfectly competitive firm can raise the price which buyers are willing to pay for its product. Figures 9.1 and 9.2 represent possible demand curves for a firm's product in an imperfectly competitive and a perfectly competitive market respectively.

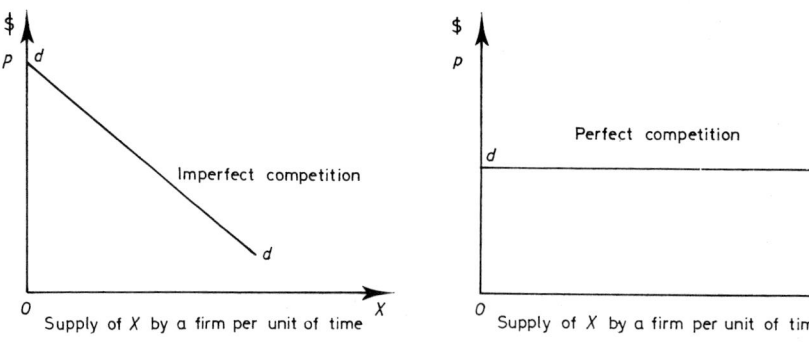

Fig. 9.1   Fig. 9.2

Imperfect Competition

In both markets consumers are price-takers, but firms are price-makers under imperfect competition[2] and price-takers under perfect competition.

The motivation of firms in supplying goods is important. Traditionally firms, no matter whether their market is perfect or imperfect, have been assumed to strive for maximum profits. However, as far as imperfectly competitive markets are concerned, the profit maximisation hypothesis has not gone unchallenged. Berle and Means,[3] Baumol[4] and others have suggested alternative hypotheses which not only give rise to differences in observed behaviour but also have different welfare implications. For example, under Baumol's hypothesis that firms maximise their value of sales subject to a satisfactory level of profit,[5] the welfare loss due to monopoly is smaller than in the traditional case. The alternatives to profit maximisation will be explored in a special chapter (17) and the arguments given here will rely on the profit maximisation hypothesis which is still staunchly defended, for example, by Edith Penrose.[6]

If profit maximisation is assumed, then prices and supplies can be readily determined for markets in which monopoly or monopolistic competition prevails. But this is not true for oligopolistic markets (markets in which there are few sellers) for in such markets there is conflict and yet scope for co-operation between sellers. Each firm cannot *simultaneously* maximise its profit and each realises this. Morgenstern and von Neumann[7] saw this difficulty quite clearly and their theory of games, which is considered in the appendix to this chapter, brings it out well. Nevertheless, a number of valuable models of oligopolistic behaviour exist. Each allows for common reactions which arise between firms, and more recent models even allow for interfirm learning.

In imperfectly competitive markets, competition does not only occur through variations of price. Advertising can be important and variations in the composition, design, etc., of the product may be significant as it is, for example, with cars. But the theory of competition via the characteristics of products is not well developed. However, the ideas of Lancaster, mentioned earlier,[8] may eventually lead to a breakthrough in this case. The models which will now be considered for monopoly, monopolistic competition and oligopoly concentrate on variations of price with some allowance for advertising, but competition via product differentiation is not specifically discussed.

II. Monopoly

Monopoly can be regarded as the polar opposite of perfect competition. It is necessary for its existence that there be just one supplier of the product. But this is not sufficient for an effective monopoly. For a monopoly to be effective, there must be barriers to the entry of new suppliers and there must not be any other goods which are perfect substitutes for the supplier's product. It has already been observed that if a product can be produced at a constant per-unit cost and entry is extremely easy, no effective monopoly exists. For all relevant purposes, the market is perfectly competitive. Entry conditions are extremely important for competition and a later chapter will be devoted to them.[9]

In order to explore a pure case without complications, economists have traditionally begun with the assumption that entry is impossible in a monopoly market. Furthermore, other prices and sales are assumed to be virtually independent of the monopolist's. However, both of these assumptions are stronger than necessary for the two main conclusions which are drawn, namely

(i) a monopolist may be able to maintain the price of his product above long-run average cost and earn above-normal profit; and

(ii) he will not supply an output which equates marginal cost to the price of the product.

In consequence, resources are likely to be misallocated. The monopolist will usually produce less than optimal of his product. Everyone, including the monopolist, can be made better off by an increase of his output *if* a suitable method of compensation can be devised. It is on these grounds that the traditional criticism of monopoly by economists arises. This may also be reinforced by the belief that monopolies lead to an unfair distribution of income. Let us examine this type of market.

A. A MONOPOLY MODEL

Assume that the monopolist does not influence the price of the inputs which he purchases so that his cost curves have the same properties as those for the perfectly competitive firm and are derived by the same method as that which was outlined for the perfectly competitive firm.[10] The demand curve for the monopolist's product is the same as that for the industry and this *normally* slopes downward. As a rule, the demand conditions faced by a monopolist are distinctively different from those faced by a perfectly competitive firm and the contrast is well brought out by Figs. 9.1 and 9.2.

Because an industry demand curve normally slopes downward, a monopolist's marginal revenue curve usually lies below his average revenue curve, whereas these latter curves coincide for a perfectly competitive firm. In any case in which a demand curve is not horizontal, the average and marginal revenue curves differ and it is easy to show that the marginal revenue curve must lie below the demand curve (average revenue curve) if the demand curve is negatively sloped. It is the divergence between average and marginal revenue which causes the monopolist's actions to differ from those of the perfectly competitive firm, even though both firms are motivated to maximise profit.

The relationship between the slope of the demand curve (which also equals the average revenue curve) and the marginal revenue curve is easily seen from the following mathematics: letting X indicate the quantity of the firm's product and p its price, the demand for the product, other things being constant, might be represented by

$$p = f(X). \tag{9.1}$$

The firm's total revenue, R, can then be expressed as

$$R = pX = f(X)X \tag{9.2}$$

and, consequently, by the product rule of differentiation, its marginal revenue is

$$\frac{dR}{dX} = \frac{df}{dX}X + f(X). \tag{9.3}$$

It follows, since df/dX is the slope of the demand curve, that the marginal revenue curve and the demand curve (equals the average revenue curve because $pX/X = p$) *only* coincide if $df/dX = 0$, that is, if the demand curve is horizontal. If the demand curve is downward-sloping, df/dX is less than zero and, consequently, a monopolist's marginal revenue curve lies below his average revenue curve.

This can be illustrated easily for the case in which the industry demand curve is

Imperfect Competition

linear and downward-sloping. The demand for a monopolist's product can then be expressed as

$$p = f(X) = a - bX \qquad (9.4)$$

and his total revenue is

$$R = aX - bX^2. \qquad (9.5)$$

Therefore, his marginal revenue is

$$\frac{dR}{dX} = a - 2bX \qquad (9.6)$$

and declines twice as fast as his average revenue. The relationship between his demand curve (which is the same as his average revenue curve in this case) and his marginal revenue curve is shown in Fig. 9.3. Note that the marginal revenue curve (MR) divides any horizontal line from the p axis to the demand curve (D) in half.

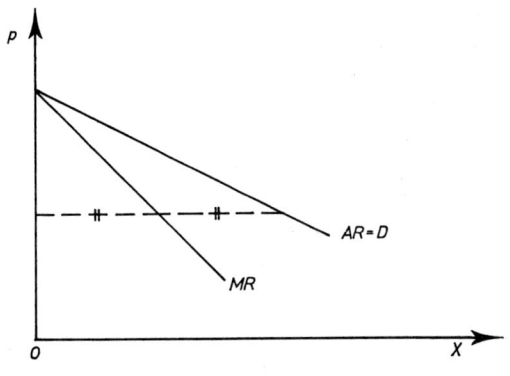

Fig. 9.3

Given the relationship between a monopolist's marginal revenue and average revenue, we can now proceed to analyse the monopolist's determination of price and supply in both the short and the long run. The standard analysis will be followed. In the short run only some factors are variable and entry of new competitors is supposed to be impossible in both the short run *and* the long run. It is assumed that the monopolist aims to maximise profit. Profit maximisation is the important driving force of the process.

The Short Run

In the short run, the monopolist's scale of plant is fixed but he is free to alter his employment of variable factors. Given his particular scale of plant, represent his total cost by $C(X)$. $C(X)$, if only one plant is operated, is found by the method which was outlined in Chapter 7. The cost function is constructed on the assumption that cost is minimised for each output.

The monopolist acts to maximise his profit which can be represented by

$$\pi = pX - C(X) \qquad (9.7)$$
$$= f(X)X - C(X) \qquad (9.8)$$
$$= R(X) - C(X). \qquad (9.9)$$

The problem is to find the value of X, the quantity of supplies, which maximise this expression. Once this is found, the price level and the monopolist's maximum profit can be determined. Assuming appropriate differentiability conditions, a local maximum of profit can only occur for a quantity of supplies which ensures that

$$\frac{d\pi}{dX} = \frac{dR}{dX} - \frac{dC}{dX} = 0. \tag{9.10}$$

A local maximum of profit can only arise for an output which ensures that marginal revenue equals marginal cost. This necessary condition for maximum profit is the same as that for the perfectly competitive firm. However, for the monopolist marginal revenue does not equal price as was shown by the argument surrounding Equation (9.3).

But the condition of Equation (9.10) is also satisfied for minimum and inflection levels of profit. However, a local maximum can be confirmed if at the output for which Equation (9.10) is satisfied, profit is decreasing for increases of X. A local maximum exists if

$$\frac{d^2\pi}{dX^2} = \frac{d^2R}{dX^2} - \frac{d^2C}{dX^2} < 0 \tag{9.11}$$

that is if the slope of the MC curve (d^2C/dX^2) exceeds that of the MR curve (d^2R/dX^2) at the output for which $MC = MR$.

Strictly, these conditions only isolate *a local* maximum. But multiple local maxima can be ruled out under usual conditions. (See the discussion of Chapter 2.) However, it is still possible for a boundary maximum to occur. It may be most profitable for the monopolist not to produce at all. In the short run this is so if short-run average variable cost exceeds average revenue for all possible levels of output.[11] Let us illustrate some different optimal levels of supply and price.

Figures 9.4 and 9.5 illustrate for a monopoly a local profit maximum which is also a global maximum. The curves are labelled by natural notation. Figure 9.4 indicates total revenue and cost as a function of output, and the difference represents profit. As shown, the maximum of profit occurs for a supply of $\bar{X}$. Note that the total revenue curve is not a straight line as for the perfectly competitive firm but is a *strictly* concave function. Figure 9.5 illustrates a similar situation to that of Fig. 9.4 by means of per-

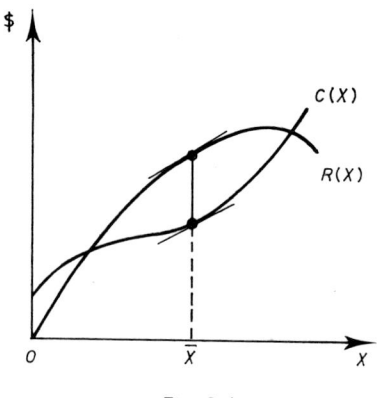

Fig. 9.4

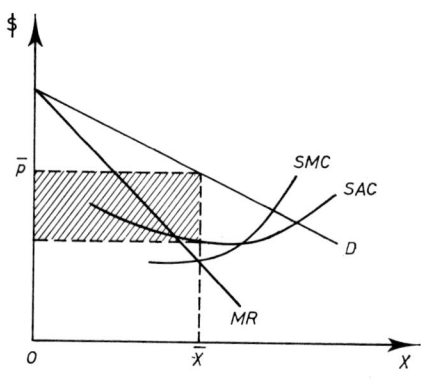

Fig. 9.5

Imperfect Competition

unit curves. There the profit maximising output is $\bar{X}$ and the price $\bar{p}$ and above-normal profit is shown by the hatched area.

In the case illustrated above, eventually increasing marginal cost occurs. But even if marginal cost is decreasing, a monopolist may have an equilibrium level of output. As Sraffa[12] and Joan Robinson[13] have pointed out, this contrasts with the position under perfect competition. If a perfectly competitive firm's marginal costs decline continually, it will be encouraged to produce an infinite output and perfect competition must break down. In the case of a monopolist, however, the size of the market puts a limit upon his profitable expansion, provided that the slope of his marginal cost curve exceeds that of his marginal revenue curve. In Fig. 9.6 a case is shown in which the monopolist's marginal cost declines. His profit maximising output is $\bar{X}$, his price $\bar{p}$ and his above-normal profit is shown by the hatched area.

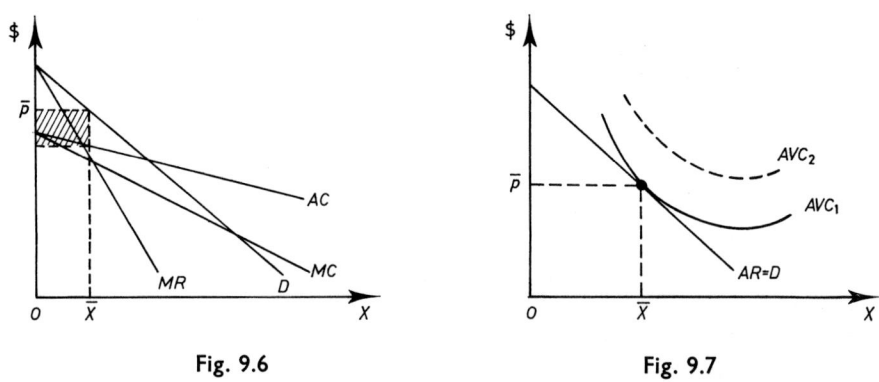

Fig. 9.6   Fig. 9.7

Figure 9.7 is drawn to emphasise that a monopolist may be unable to make a profit in the short run. This is also possible in the long run. If the monopolist's average variable-cost function is AVC_1, his profit is maximised by producing $\bar{X}$ or nothing. He loses his fixed cost in either case. If his average variable-cost function exceeds his average revenue function for all levels of output, it will be most profitable for the monopolist to produce nothing,[14] for example, if his average variable curve is AVC_2.

Variations of the monopolist's market behaviour have so far been limited to variations of price (and of quantity supplied). But it may also be of some interest to allow advertising expenditure to vary. If advertising effort is variable, the monopolist needs to determine this in conjunction with the price and output of his product so as to maximise his overall profit. Assume that the shift in the demand function as a result of advertising can be related to advertising expenditure, A. Then it is usually possible to express profit as

$$\pi = R(A,X) - C(X) - A, \qquad (9.12)$$

where R represents total revenue and $C(X)$ is the total cost of production. If this function is to be maximised, advertising expenditure should be increased until the marginal revenue from advertising equals its marginal cost and at the same time output should be expanded until its addition to revenue equals its marginal cost. In other words, advertising expenditure and output should be determined at levels which ensure that the following equations are simultaneously satisfied:

$$\left.\begin{array}{l}\dfrac{\partial R}{\partial A}-1=0\\[2mm]\dfrac{\partial R}{\partial X}-\dfrac{dC}{dX}=0.\end{array}\right\} \quad (9.13)$$

The marginal cost of advertising expenditure is 1. To put it another way, the demand curve should be shifted up to an optimal height by advertising, and output should be adjusted to equate marginal cost and marginal revenue.

Advertising *usually* (but not always) leads to an increase in the price of the product. If the demand curve shifts up as a result of advertising and *if* the marginal cost of the monopolist is increasing (in the neighbourhood of the profit-maximisation points) increased advertising leads to a higher price. It is most profitable for the monopolist to increase the price of his product. However, if marginal cost is declining, then under certain conditions, it is optimal for the monopolist to reduce his price as he expands his market by advertising.

Which types of advertising are socially desirable is difficult to assess. Forms which increase the information of purchasers have generally been approved by economists, and those which convey a "status image" are scorned. Yet even this latter category may have its value. After all, some people are prepared to pay for an "image", and liberal economists accept that it is the preferences of consumers which should count. This is not to say that some forms of advertising are not a social waste. Some, as we shall see in the discussion of oligopoly, are self-defeating.

Advertising will not be discussed again for the long run. The previous discussion applies *mutatis mutandis,*

The Long Run

In the long run a monopolist is able to vary his scale of plant and (it is traditionally assumed) need not fear the possibility of entry of new firms. But it seems doubtful if any firm is really secure from entry in the long run and certainly there is always, as Schumpeter has observed, the possibility of close substitutes arising. This, therefore, is a weak link in the traditional theory of monopoly which will be considered in detail in Chapter 19. If entry is possible, a monopolist may engage in limit pricing. He may charge a price low enough to forestall entrants and below the price predicted by traditional theory. But let us examine the extreme position.

If entry is impossible and if the monopolist finds it profitable to produce at all, his profit is maximised by charging a price and producing an output which equates his long-run marginal cost and marginal revenue from supplies at a level where the slope of the long-run marginal-cost curve exceeds that of the marginal revenue curve. The mathematical argument is akin to that for the short run. The only change is that long-run functions now replace short-run ones in the profit function of Equation (9.7).

Figure 9.8 illustrates the long-run profit maximising strategy of a monopolist who is able to make an above-normal profit. His profit is maximised by producing an output X_0 and selling it at a price p_0. His above-normal profit is shown by the hatched area. In this case, the monopolist does not operate his plant at minimum average cost nor does he adopt the plant which gives minimum average cost. His operations are on the lower output side of the minima. But for other cost curves they may be above or even, in some cases, at the minimum. (This latter situation arises if the minimum of the *LRAC* curve occurs for a point on the *MR* curve.)

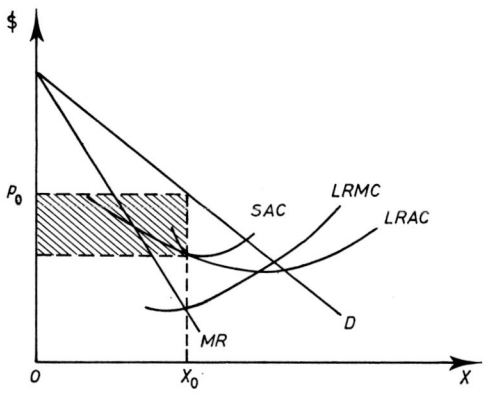

Fig. 9.8

It is sometimes wrongly believed that a monopolist must necessarily make an above-normal profit. A monopolist may, indeed, sometimes make a loss by producing, or make no more than normal profit. The former situation arises if the monopolist's long-run average-cost curve exceeds his average revenue (demand curve) for all positive levels of output.[15] The monopolist's optimal policy is not to produce. The latter circumstance eventuates if the monopolist's *LRAC* curve is just tangential to his demand curve at one point. By producing the output which corresponds to this point the monopolist just makes a normal profit and this is his maximum possible profit. The traditional hostility of economists to monopoly is not based so much on its possible income distribution effects[16] but more on the argument that monopoly usually leads to a less than Pareto optimal allocation of resources. If monopoly prevails, it usually is possible to make some people better off without making anyone else worse off. Let us give this some consideration.

B. PURE MONOPOLY VERSUS PERFECT COMPETITION AS A FORM OF ECONOMIC ORGANISATION

Under certain circumstances, a monopolised market is economically less efficient than a perfectly competitive market, *but* under others monopoly may be more efficient than any *feasible* perfectly competitive alternative. Efficiency is interpreted here in the sense of Pareto. The view that monopoly may be more efficient than any feasible perfectly competitive alternative even under static conditions is not often expressed. This may be due to some confusion. Even though a monopoly is less than Paretian optimal, it may be Paretian *preferable* to perfect competition or to production of a commodity by several firms. The discussion below should help to clarify this.

But before embarking on the comparison, it needs to be pointed out that perfect competition and monopoly are not always alternatives *under the same technological conditions*. First, internally decreasing marginal cost is incompatible with perfect competition, but not with monopoly. A monopoly in such an industry might be compared with perfect competition on the assumption that technology under perfect

H

competition is *limited* (in terms of known technology) to that which ensures increasing marginal costs and sufficient numbers of producers. Alternatively, an increasing marginal tax might be imposed on the production of each firm to raise the numbers of firms. But this is no longer perfect competition. The *feasible* "perfectly competitive" alternatives, as we shall see, may be inferior to the monopoly situation.

Second, economies or diseconomies may stem from operating several plants. As a result of multiplant economies, the long-run marginal-cost curve of a monopolist can diverge from the long-run supply curve of a perfectly competitive industry in which each firm's span of control does not exceed one plant or very few plants. Multiplant economies may arise from a reduction in administration costs as the number of plants rises.

While multiplant firms have not been discussed, it is necessary to touch on them now for it is easiest to compare a multiplant monopoly with a perfectly competitive alternative. Ruling out economies or diseconomies due to multiple plants, and assuming eventually rising marginal costs, a multiplant firm which wishes to maximise its profit will produce its overall output at minimum cost, if it allocates its output between plants (assuming a large number) to equalise the increasing long-run marginal cost from each. The overall long-run marginal cost curve of such a firm if it happened to be a monopolist would then be identical to the long-run supply curve for a perfectly competitive alternative.

The traditional comparison between monopoly and perfect competition can be made by supposing that multiplant economies or diseconomies are absent and that eventually increasing marginal cost arises at a level of plant output which ensures the profitable existence of a large number of plants in the industry. To make the traditional comparison, assume for simplicity that the long-run supply curve of the industry, under perfect competition, is a horizontal straight line equal in height to the minimum long-run average cost of each firm. It is indicated in Fig. 9.9 by *LRS*. Under a multiplant monopoly, and given the above conditions, the monopolist's overall marginal-cost curve coincides with this supply curve.

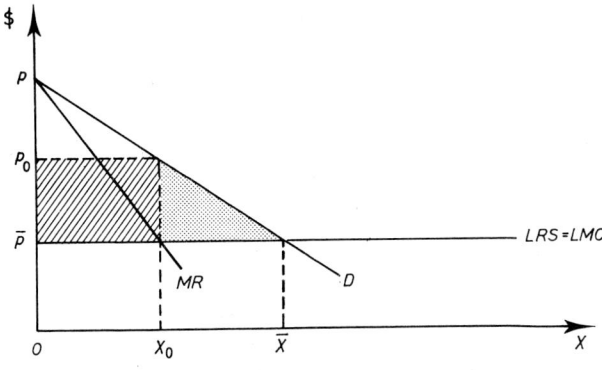

Fig. 9.9

Consider the long run. If the industry is organised on a perfectly competitive basis, $\bar{X}$ of the product is produced and sold at a price of $\bar{p}$. However, if the industry is monopolised, output is cut to X_0 (in this particular case by half) and prices rise to p_0.

The monopolist is able to earn an above-normal profit, as indicated by the hatched area, whereas under perfect competition profit was only normal. In the monopoly situation, overall marginal cost and price differ, whereas they coincide in the perfectly competitive situation. This difference, as will be seen, is very important from an allocation point of view. Incidentally, if plants are of equal size, a monopolist would reduce output by closing down one half of the plants in this instance.

If the long-run supply curve of the industry is increasing, the argument is basically the same as that above. The overall long-run marginal-cost curve of the monopolist coincides with the long-run supply curve of the industry. A monopoly take-over of such a perfectly competitive industry leads to the closure of "marginal" plants, to a reduction in output and increase of price, and a divergence between marginal cost and price. The monopolist will also make above-normal profit if the perfectly competitive industry was viable.

But it is not so much monopoly profits which have been a cause for complaints against monopoly; rather it is the deadweight loss which results from a divergence of price and marginal cost. Let us look first at the cruder argument. Any point on the demand curve indicates the value to consumers of an extra unit of production and, in the absence of externalities, the supply curve (the overall marginal-cost curve) denotes the cost to the community of an extra unit of output. If price exceeds marginal cost, the value to consumers of extra output exceeds its cost and thus there seems to be a social case for expanding output. On the other hand, if marginal cost exceeds price there is a case for contracting output. The optimal output is that for which marginal cost equals price. This is ensured under perfect competition but, under monopoly, price exceeds marginal cost and so output is lower than is socially desirable. This argument can be slightly refined by making use of the notions of producers' and consumers' surplus. The gain of profit by the monopolist as a result of his monopolisation (compared to profit under perfect competition) is less than the loss of consumers' surplus. In Fig. 9.9 the gain of profit by the monopolist is the hatched area but the loss in consumers' surplus is equal to the hatched area plus the dotted triangle. Hence, the loss to consumers exceeds the gain to the monopolist. Consumers would be prepared to pay a bribe to the monopolist of greater than his above-normal profit, in return for his producing the perfectly competitive output, $\bar{X}$. The net loss of welfare due to monopoly (with several serious reservations) might be measured by the dotted triangle. This is the deadweight loss due to monopoly.

A rather more general argument which takes account of interdependence of supply is as follows. Consider two goods, 1 and 2, which are interrelated in their supply and represent their prices by p_1 and p_2 respectively. Consumers, being price-takers, will equate their marginal rates of indifferent substitution to the price ratio p_1/p_2 of these goods. Thus p_1/p_2 indicates a rate at which consumers are *prepared* to exchange these goods. Represent the marginal cost of the two goods by MC_1 and MC_2. In the absence of externalities MC_1/MC_2 is the rate at which the two products can be *technically* transformed one into the other. It is the rate of product transformation and indicates the quantity of product 2 which *must* be forgone to obtain an additional unit of product 1. Thus if $MC_1 = 2$ and $MC_2 = 4$, one extra unit of product 2 can only be produced by forgoing two units of product 1. If the relative rate at which consumers are prepared to exchange the goods differs from the technological rate at which the goods can be transformed, it is possible to effect a Pareto improvement for the rate of indifferent substitution and the rate of product transformation diverges. It will be shown in Chapter 13 that under usual increasing cost conditions these two latter rates must be equal for a Pareto optimum. Since the rate of indifferent substitution equals p_1/p_2, for a Pareto optimum we require that

$$\frac{p_1}{p_2} = \frac{MC_1}{MC_2}. \tag{9.14}$$

If perfect competition prevails in the market for both products, the price and the marginal cost of each will be equated by firms maximising their profit. Consequently Equation (9.14) holds and a Pareto optimum occurs. But if a monopoly arises in one of the markets and perfect competition continues in the other, the position is changed. If the monopoly occurs in market 1, $p_1 > MC_1$ and, with perfect competition in the other, $p_2 = MC_2$. Consequently, Equation (9.14) does not hold, and the situation is not Pareto optimal. Too few resources are used in industry 1 and too many in industry 2.

What would happen if both industries happened to be monopolised? By a sheer fluke it might turn out that the price of the product of each monopolist exceeded its marginal cost in the same ratio. Thus Equation (9.14) would be satisfied. Given the employed resources (and assuming that these are only transferable between the industries) a Pareto optimal *allocation* exists. But even then a lower than optimal quantity of resources may be employed overall.[17] Activity may be at a lower than socially desirable level.

The argument against monopoly seems to be a strong one. But it needs to be tempered considerably, first by considering the results of empirical work and then by taking into account several important factors which the traditional comparison neglects.

Harberger's calculations for the U.S. economy suggest that, under static allocative conditions, the welfare loss which is due to the existence of monopoly or imperfect competition is small. Basing himself on data from the 1920s, Harberger claims[18] from his empirical evidence that the gain in consumers' surplus to be expected from elimination of imperfect competition in American manufacturing amounts to not more than *one-tenth of one per cent* of national income, a very small fraction indeed. Although one may disagree with some of the hypotheses upon which Harberger bases his estimate (he assumes that average costs are constant, that the elasticity of demand for each product is unity, and he defines monopoly profit to exist if the general level of profits in an industry is above the average in the economy), his result is striking.

But the traditional argument against monopoly ignores certain important possibilities. Under decreasing internal marginal cost, perfect competition is not possible and monopoly or oligopoly may be preferable to any *feasible* perfectly competitive alternative. A perfectly competitive alternative might be created by banning any technique which, relative to the market, gives rise to substantial decreasing marginal costs for any firm or by taxing increased production at a rate which rises sufficiently with the firm's volume of output. In both cases the alternative is a contrived rather than a natural possibility. In the contrived situation, the long-run supply curve of the perfectly competitive industry is in excess of the overall possible minimum long-run marginal-cost curve. Consequently, in the perfectly competitive alternative it is possible for an output to be lower and price to be higher than under monopoly. The monopoly

Imperfect Competition

alternative may be socially superior in the sense that all can be made better off than in the perfectly competitive alternative. Nevertheless, this does not imply that monopoly is Paretian optimal. The monopolist's behaviour is likely to be less than Paretian optimal but may be Paretian superior to any feasible perfectly competitive alternative. This is illustrated in Fig. 9.10. Under a monopoly, $LRMC$ is shown to decrease and the monopolist's profit-maximising output is X_0 which he sells for p_0. But under monopoly the socially optimal output is X_1 since this equates price and marginal cost. Note, however that this output is not sustainable under perfect competition and that unless means of compensation are devised for the monopolist, he makes a loss by selling X_1 at p_1 since his average costs exceed p_1. (It may be possible to compensate the monopolist by a subsidy or he may be able to engage in price discrimination, which is discussed below.) If the only feasible perfectly competitive long-run supply curve for the industry is LRS', price $\bar{p}$ is higher, and output $\vec{X}$ is lower under perfect competition than under monopoly.

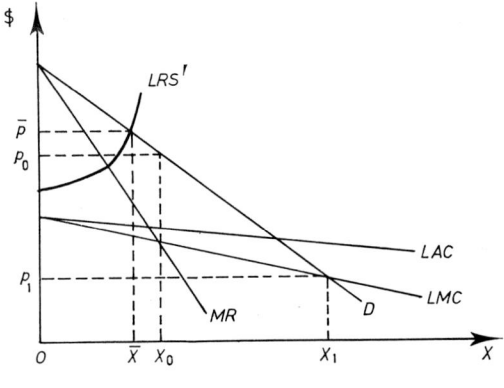

Fig. 9.10

The previous argument rests upon technological economies from a single plant. But economies may also arise due to the operation of a number of plants by the one firm. These multiplant economies (or diseconomies) cause the overall long-run marginal-cost curve of a monopolist to diverge from the long-run supply curve of the perfectly competitive alternative, if the perfectly competitive firm is limited to one plant. Under such circumstances, it is theoretically possible for price to be higher and output to be lower under the perfectly competitive alternative. The monopoly form of organisation can be Paretian superior to the feasible perfectly competitive alternative. But, once again, the monopolist's behaviour is not ideal; it is possible, by varying his profit maximising behaviour, to increase social welfare even more. This possibility is illustrated in Fig. 9.11. The long-run supply curve of the feasible perfectly competitive alternative is shown by LRS' and the overall $LRMC$ of the monopolist is shown to diverge from LRS', due to multiplant economies. The monopolist's output is X_0 and his price p_0 whereas under perfect competition output, $\bar{X}$, is lower and price, $\bar{p}$, is higher. Nevertheless, the monopolist's output is not socially optimal. An expansion of his output to X_1, for which marginal cost equals average revenue, is necessary for Paretian optimality. But this optimum cannot be achieved under perfect competition. Note that multiplant economies *may* mean that price is lower and output greater under monopoly, but do not ensure that this is so. $LRMC$ must be sufficiently less than LRS' if this result is to arise. If the empirical results of Bain's study[19] are an indication of the general situation, multiplant economies seem to be

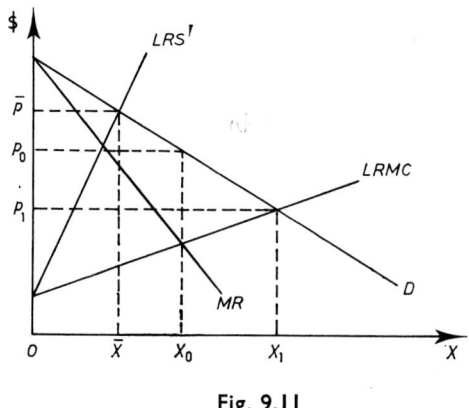

Fig. 9.11

comparatively small in magnitude so that the case shown in Fig. 9.11 might be un likely to arise in practice. On the other hand, plant economies are quite important in some industries, for example, chemicals.

The above arguments concentrate on static aspects of allocative efficiency and do not take technological change into account. Schumpeter [20] and others have suggested that technological change might be more rapid under monopoly than under perfect competition. The reward for invention and innovation may be higher for a monopolist than for a perfectly competitive firm, and he has a greater surplus which may mean a larger investment in research and development and innovation. (It is sometimes argued that in countries in which savings are low, monopoly is advantageous since it results in a greater surplus and more saving and investment.) In effect, Schumpeter is arguing that if we compare the alternatives of monopoly and perfect competition, after a stretch of time the overall long-run marginal-cost curve of the monopolist is likely to be below the long-run supply curve which would prevail if perfect competition had existed in the industry for the same stretch of time. The difference arises because technological change is supposedly faster under monopoly. After allowing for differences in technical change, price *may* be lower and output higher for a monopoly than for perfect competition over the same number of periods. Let us take an example: imagine that in an initial period there is a given LRS curve equal to the overall $LRMC$ of the industry. Consider the possible long-run supply curve for the industry after perfect competition has existed for T periods from the initial period. The curve is indicated by LRS_T in Fig. 9.12. If monopoly had existed for the same interval, the overall long-run marginal-cost curve might be like $LRMC_T$ in Fig. 9.12. Consequently, if monopoly rather than perfect competition exists for T periods, the price of the product is lower and its output higher. In period T, the output-price combination, given perfect competition over the whole time interval $0 \leqslant t \leqslant T$, is $(\bar{X}, \bar{p})$ and given monopoly over the whole interval (X_0, p_0). At any point of time the monopolist does not produce a socially optimal output (one for which price equals $LRMC$), but this non-optimal behaviour may be necessary for his superior performance when taken

Imperfect Competition

over a number of periods.[21] Schumpeter correctly stresses this point.[22] However, greater technical progress under monopoly alone is not sufficient to ensure that, after

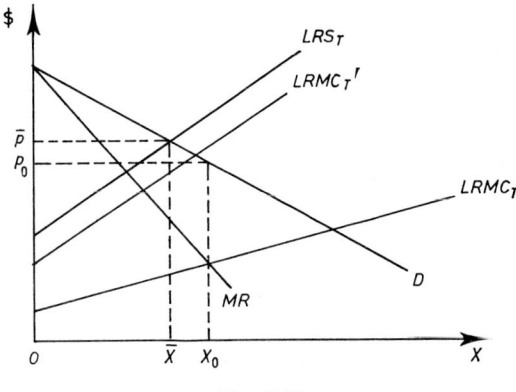

Fig. 9.12

an interval of time, monopoly results in a lower price and greater output for the product. If after T periods the monopolist's long-run marginal-cost curve is $LRMC_T'$, even though this is below LRS_T, the monopolist's price is higher and output lower than for the perfectly competitive alternative after T periods. Finally, of course, there is no guarantee that technical progress will be greater under monopoly, it might be slower, even though Schumpeter argues the reverse.[23] We shall return to this argument in a later chapter,[24] when workable competition is discussed.

C. PRICE DISCRIMINATION

In the discussion of Fig. 9.10 it was noted that a monopolist might be able to produce, at the point where his long-run marginal cost equals price, without making a loss if he is able to engage in price discrimination. Indeed, if the income effects due to the discrimination are small, the discriminating monopolist may find that his most profitable output occurs at the level where the demand curve equals marginal cost. This is so if each consumer can be charged the maximum amount which he is prepared to pay for each additional unit of product. Consumers are then left with no surplus. Let us examine some aspects of price discrimination.

Price discrimination is only possible if exchange between purchasers is subject to barriers. Otherwise, arbitrage will take place—units of the goods purchased at a lower price will be resold by purchasers in markets in which the monopolist is attempting to obtain a higher price. Thus the discrimination will not be effective. If the monopolist charges a lower price in one region and a higher one in another, and if transport and other barriers are absent, traders will find it profitable to purchase in the first region and resell in the second, until the price in both markets is equal. Barriers, however, may arise due to transport costs, because of the intrinsic non-transferable nature of the product or service (for example, medical attention) or because of the existence of artificial barriers, such as tariffs, import embargoes or legal controls, on transferability of goods.

In order for discrimination to be profitable between markets, the marginal revenue curve of the product must differ in the markets. The total revenue from all the separate markets for the product is maximised when the total output is allocated between the markets, so as to equate the marginal revenue from sales in each market. This implies that price should be highest in the market for which demand is most inelastic and lowest in the market in which demand is most elastic, if it is profitable to supply both of these markets. (It may not be profitable to supply one because demand is so low relative to the other.) The optimal allocation of a particular output is illustrated in Fig. 9.13 for two markets, 1 and 2, and the curves are indicated by standard natural notation. A total output of $X = \bar{X}_1 + \bar{X}_2$ is allocated so as to maximise revenue if

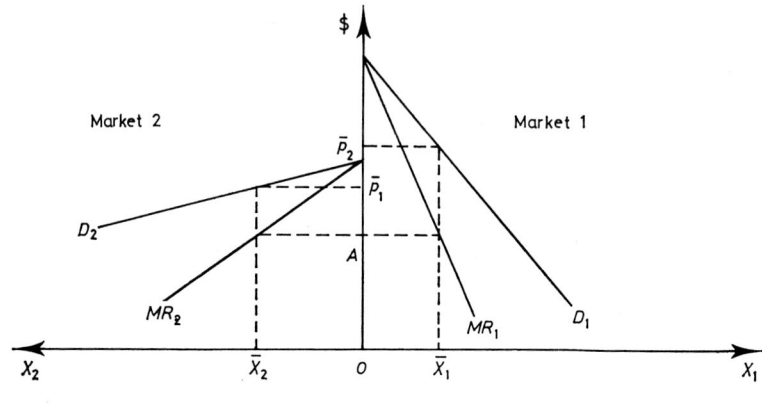

Fig. 9.13

$\bar{X}_1$ is allocated to market 1 and $\bar{X}_2$ to market 2. In that case the marginal revenue from sales in both markets is equalised. The additional revenue, which would be obtained by allocating a greater proportion of output to market 1, would be less than the loss of revenue from market 2. As indicated, price is higher in the market for which demand is more inelastic if supplies are allocated so as to maximise revenue.

Production variations have not been considered. If output can be varied, profit is maximised by allocating output so as to equalise the marginal revenue from the various markets, and producing an output for which marginal cost equals the common marginal revenue. To find this output by means of a diagram, we can add MR_1 and MR_2 horizontally to give a new curve and draw in the overall marginal-cost curve. The point of intersection of the two curves gives the optimal level of output.

Price discrimination between markets is fairly common. In many countries the home market is protected and demand is more inelastic than abroad. A home producer, therefore, is likely to charge a higher price in the domestic market than abroad. Price discrimination in the supply of public utilities is common. The price of electricity to firms may be lower than that to households, since more elasticity of substitution of other power sources exist for firms.

D. REGULATION OF MONOPOLY

Many countries place legal barriers in the way of the formation of monopolies. This is true in the United Kingdom, the United States and Australia for example, although monopolies themselves are not necessarily illegal. In Australia and the United Kingdom most public utility monopolies (electricity, telephones, railways) are government-

Imperfect Competition

owned and a fewer number are operated by the government in the United States. But those which are not owned by the government are normally regulated by it (for example, telephones in the United States) and very often this takes the form of fixing maximum prices for the product of the monopolist. An attempt may be made to fix the price so as to give the monopolist an average return on capital. In Australia such price-fixing is rare, but the Tariff Board indirectly has an influence over local prices. In certain instances, it may decide to fix a tariff to maintain a home price which just gives an Australian monopolist a normal return on capital. Let us analyse the situation by assuming that a government fixes a maximum price for the monopolist's product.

If a maximum price is set for a product, the monopolist's demand curve is like $P_{max}bD$ in Fig. 9.14 and his marginal revenue curve is discontinuous and consists of the two segments $P_{max}b$ and cMR. If the monopolist's marginal cost curve passes through the gap bc, then the monopolist maximises his profit by producing the output X_1 and selling it at P_{max}. In the absence of control, the monopolist's demand curve is aD, and his output X_0 and his price is p_0. If P_{max} is set equal to the value for which marginal cost equals demand, then this results in a socially optimal level of output by the monopolist, if he finds it profitable to produce at all. He will only find it profitable to produce if average cost is not decreasing at the output for which P_{max} equals marginal cost. (If average cost is decreasing, marginal cost is below it and thus if P_{max} equals marginal cost, average revenue is less than average cost and a loss is made.)

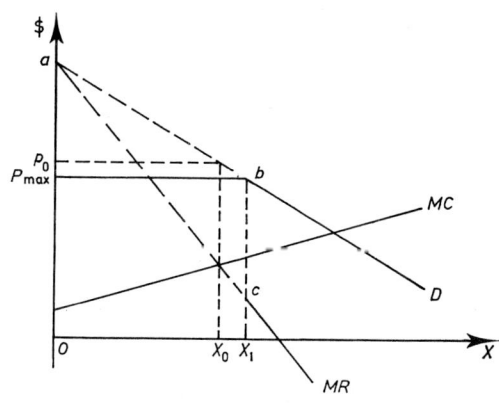

Fig. 9.14

Another way of influencing a monopolist's behaviour is to subsidise his output at an increasing marginal rate while at the same time imposing a lump sum tax on the monopolist (if this seems to be justified on income distribution grounds). By a judicious application of these measures, the monopolist may be enticed to produce the socially optimal output and yet be left in receipt of only a normal profit.

But the difficulty with all these measures is that they presume considerable knowledge on the part of the regulating authority. The authority must know the demand function and marginal costs within the critical range. This may be difficult to discover if accounts of the monopolist must be relied upon and the apparent marginal cost may include costs due to organisational slack, for example inflated expense accounts for employed personnel. But even allowing for estimation errors, measures of this type are likely to be of social value for public utilities and other important commodities which are monopolised. One problem faced in such regulations is that a monopolist may engineer shortages in an attempt to have the government authority increase the maximum allowable price. We shall see that this can also be a problem under competitive socialism.[25]

III. Monopolistic Competition

Monopolistic competition can be regarded as both a variant of monopoly and of perfect competition. In a monopolistic market, individual sellers have some influence on the terms of trade but not a considerable influence, product differentiation exists and long-run entry is easy. So many sellers exist in the area of competitive supply that the behaviour of any individual supplier is independent of that of any other individual. Since the products of the industry are slightly differentiated, Chamberlin[26] does not refer to an industry, but to a group. A group of suppliers is in the same industry if the cross-elasticity between their products is high.

The most noteworthy feature of this type of market is that it leads to excess capacity and the operation of plants which are smaller than those required to minimise long-run average cost. Some small retail establishments, nurseries, and moulders of plastics might roughly be monopolistic suppliers.

Following Chamberlin,[27] let us consider the position of a representative firm. This approach is justifiable if the demand and cost curves of all firms are identical. Two types of demand curves are relevant to the representative firm: demand curves which are drawn on the basis that the prices of all other firms are constant, and a demand curve constructed on the assumption that the price of each firm's product is the same. In Fig. 9.15, assuming a fixed number of firms in the industry, D is the representative firm's demand curve *if* all firms charge the same price. A demand curve such as d_0 or d_1 in Fig. 9.15 indicates the demand for the representative firm's product if the prices of all other firms are constant. The curve d_0 is drawn on the assumption that other firms charge p_0 for their product and d_1 on the assumption that other firms charge p_1. The higher the price charged by others, the higher the demand curve of the representative firm. If, in fact, other firms are charging p_1, the representative firm, since it believes the action of others to be independent of its own, will act on the basis of d_1 and produce an output which equates the marginal revenue corresponding to

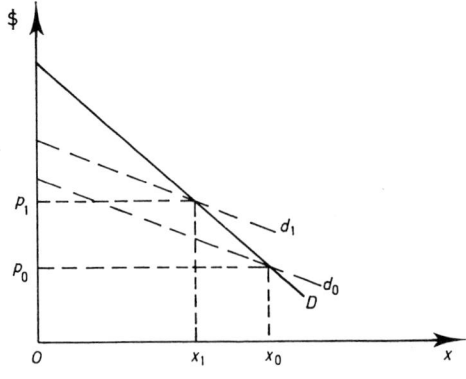

Fig. 9.15

Imperfect Competition

d_1 with its marginal cost. If p_0 is the price of others, then it acts similarly on the basis of d_0. But every firm does this. Thus *ex post facto* their predictions about the prices of others being unchanged may not be justified. There is equilibrium only if their combined production results in the price anticipated by everyone. The optimal (output, price) combination of each firm must be simultaneously on D and a d curve. In Fig. 9.16, the output x_0 and price p_0 result in overall equilibrium for the group if no entry is possible. Each firm has no reason to deviate from an output of x_0. If, however, each

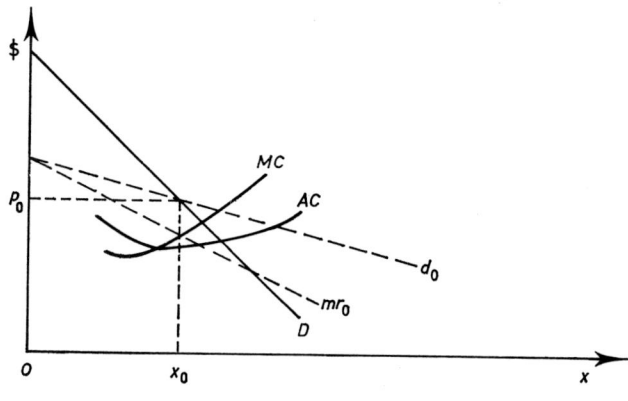

Fig. 9.16

had anticipated that the price of the products of other firms would be in excess of p_0, the industry would not be in equilibrium.

Imagine that MC is the long-run marginal-cost curve of the firm and AC its long-run average-cost curve then, in the absence of entry, the firm (shown in Fig. 9.16) is able to make above-normal profit. But this above-normal profit will induce entry of new firms into the industry in the long run. In consequence, the curve D will become steeper, since total output is now shared amongst more firms and the d curves may become flatter. Furthermore, the equilibrium price for the group will be lower and so, therefore, is the relevant d-curve for the representative firm. Indeed, the relevant d curve will continue to move down until it is just tangential to the long-run average-cost curve of the representative firm, for while it is above this cost curve above-normal profits are earned and entry is thus encouraged.

The long-term equilibrium of a representative firm is illustrated in Fig. 9.17. Its D-curve, D', is somewhat steeper than previously and its relevant d-curve, d', is lower than d_0 since the sustainable price for the product falls below p_0 as entry proceeds. In the long-term equilibrium, the sustainable price, p', is just equal to long-run average cost and d' is just tangential to long-run average cost. The firm makes only a normal profit and produces an output of x'. In doing so, it operates its plant below the capacity which ensures minimum cost and adopts a plant which is smaller than that which enables cost to be minimised. The firm is, however, maximising profit since it equates marginal revenue and its increasing long-run marginal cost.

Monopolistic competition does not result in maximum economic efficiency since for each firm marginal cost does not equal price. Marginal cost is less than price. Hence, the argument in respect of monopoly applies *mutatis mutandis*. Assuming that

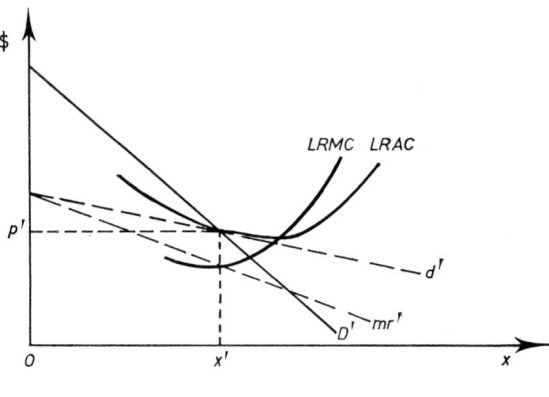

Fig. 9.17

per-unit cost curves are U-shaped, monopoly and monopolistic competition can be compared. Output is likely to be lower if the group is monopolised and prices higher than if monopolistic competition exists. If each firm (plant) produces a slightly different product the number of varieties of the same product is likely to be lower under monopoly. The argument is similar to that given in the comparison of monopoly and perfect competition, it being assumed that no multiplant economies or diseconomies are present and decreasing cost is of limited significance.

But under some conditions variety is greater under monopoly. For example, this may occur if multiplant economies are important. Furthermore, if plant economies are significant, monopolistic competition may not be a viable alternative to monopoly, or if monopolistic competition is artificially maintained by banning or taxing certain techniques, or by suitable taxes on the volume of output, it may be a socially inferior alternative. In view of the argument of the previous section, this seems to be fairly clear.

It is impossible to compare perfect competition and monopolistic competition meaningfully, for product homogeneity is essential to perfect competition and product differentiation to monopolistic competition. The closest one might come to some sort of a comparison would be to consider a situation in which supply is limited by legislation to a standard product and to compare this with monopolistic competition. Even assuming that a standard product of optimal specification could be designated, the resultant social and economic outcome could well be inferior to monopolistic competition. Though the price of the standard product would be lower than the same product under monopolistic competition, the majority of consumers might prefer to pay a higher price in order to have greater variety. At the moment, we have no satisfactory analysis of the comparison. We cannot, however, conclude that perfect competition is superior to monopolistic competition nor that monopoly is inferior. Comparisons of market forms are possible, but these must proceed on a realistic basis and take account of the technological characteristics of production and product differentiation of each situation, as well as performance as far as technical progress is concerned. The crude ranking of perfect competition as the best market form, followed by monopolistic competition and then monopoly, in the absence of any further qualification, is hardly a considered one. This is an important point which comes out

Imperfect Competition

of the discussion of economists such as John Maurice Clark[28] of the concept of "workable competition". To place oligopoly in this ranking somewhere between monopolistic competition and monopoly is equally unsatisfactory and crude.

IV. Duopoly and Oligopoly

As technical progress takes place, economies of scale seem to occur which frequently give rise to oligopolistic markets, markets in which there are few sellers. Chemicals, automobiles, aluminium and many other manufactured goods are produced by a few sellers. An oligopolistic market is characterised by a few sellers, all of whom are interdependent and able to exert considerable influence on the terms of exchange. A change in the terms of exchange offered by one seller is likely to be matched by others or more than matched so that each seller must take this into account in determining his market behaviour. Thus an oligopolistic market differs from the previous three types.

A duopolistic market is a special case of an oligopolistic one and consists of two sellers. Economic theorists have traditionally treated duopolistic and oligopolistic markets in a similar fashion and arguments given for two sellers have been assumed to apply to a few. However, von Neumann and Morgenstern [29] have suggested that, in markets involving more than two sellers, coalition formation amongst the sellers can be important and that this may call for modifications of the theory. Nevertheless, since the necessary modifications are insufficiently clear at this time, the traditional approach to oligopoly is outlined in this chapter. In the appendix to this chapter, the theory of games is sketched and applied to oligopolistic markets.

Various models of duopolistic and oligopolistic market behaviour have been suggested. By differentiating between oligopolistic market situations (for example, in terms of the degree of collusion between sellers and whether or not the collusion of sellers is formally organised), it is sometimes possible to select the model which is appropriate to the situation under investigation. No one model typifies the whole range of oligopolistic behaviour.

Several models are discussed below. The Cournot model is unique, since it assumes the complete absence of collusion, either tacit or overt. The cartel model is at the other extreme. It assumes the existence of a formal organisation among the oligopolists to direct a policy of maximising their joint profit. Let us consider the Cournot model, the cartel solution, the price leadership model and the kinked demand curve phenomenon in turn.

A. COURNOT'S SOLUTION

Cournot's model[30] which was presented in 1838 highlights the interdependence of sellers in an oligopolistic market. For simplicity, imagine that there are two sellers of a product which is freely available to the sellers and in sufficient supply to meet all potential demands. Cournot quoted mineral waters from natural springs as an example which might satisfy these conditions. Furthermore, suppose the product is homogeneous and represents the overall market demand for it by the linear expression

$$p = a - bX \qquad (9.15)$$

where p is the product's price and X represents the aggregate supply of the product. Representing the supply of duopolist 1 by x_1 and of duopolist 2 by x_2,

$$X = x_1 + x_2. \qquad (9.16)$$

Cournot assumed that in any period of time each duopolist acts on the assumption that his rival's output of the previous period is unchanged. Each duopolist attempts to maximise his own profit on the basis that the output of his rival is the same as in the previous period. Each acts as though their behaviour is independent.

In this model, the profit (also revenue) of firm 1 is

$$R_1 = [a - b(x_1 + x_2)]x_1. \tag{9.17}$$

Hence, given x_2, the output of firm 2, the profit of firm 1 is only at maximum if

$$\frac{\partial R_1}{\partial x_1} = a - 2bx_1 - bx_2 = 0. \tag{9.18}$$

Rearranging this equation, the profit of firm 1 is only at a maximum if its output of the product satisfies

$$x_2 = \frac{a}{b} - 2x_1. \tag{9.19}$$

This equation specifies the reaction curve of firm 1. The equation indicates the output which firm 1 finds to be most profitable to produce for each output of firm 2.

Similarly, a reaction line can be obtained for firm 2. It indicates the optimal output of firm 2 for the different possible levels of output of firm 1. The total profit of firm 2 is

$$R_2 = [a - b(x_1 + x_2)]x_2, \tag{9.20}$$

and this is only at a maximum if

$$\frac{\partial R_2}{\partial x_2} = a - bx_1 - 2bx_2 = 0. \tag{9.21}$$

Rearranging the equation, the reaction function of firm 2 is

$$x_2 = \frac{a}{2b} - \frac{1}{2}x_1. \tag{9.22}$$

The reaction functions indicated in Equations (9.19) and (9.22) can be easily graphed. They are illustrated by a case which is shown in Fig. 9.18. The use of these reaction curves is readily seen. Suppose that in the initial period, output combination J is produced. In the next period, firm 1 will produce an output corresponding to a point A on its reaction curve, since it assumes the output of firm 2 to be unchanged.

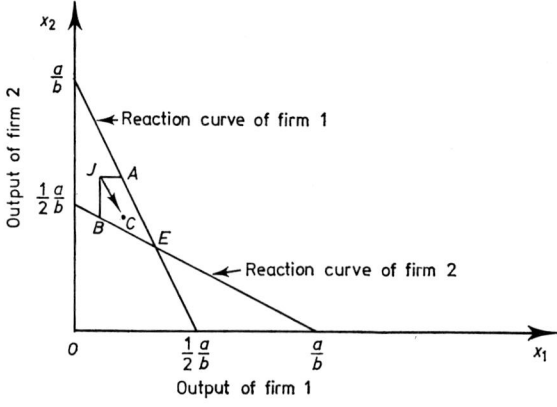

Fig. 9.18

Similarly, firm 2 produces an output corresponding to B. The result is that the actual overall combination of output is at C. This process of adjustment is repeated and point E is approached. Point E is an equilibrium point. Once it is reached each oligopolist does not vary his output any further.

By solving Equations (9.19) and (9.22) it can be shown that in equilibrium each duopolist produces an output of $\frac{1}{3}\frac{a}{b}$, so that total output is $\frac{2}{3}\frac{a}{b}$. This total output is greater than the monopoly output which is $\frac{1}{2}\frac{a}{b}$. It is, however, less than the perfectly competitive output which is equal to $\frac{a}{b}$ if the product falls in price to its average cost of production under perfect competition. The product becomes a free commodity under perfect competition.

But is Cournot's assumption reasonable? Surely duopolists would learn about their interdependence and take it into account because, except in equilibrium, the prior hypothesis of each duopolist always proves to be wrong. Indeed, they may collude formally and supply a joint profit maximising quantity to the market, sharing the market equally. In that case, their joint supply to the market will be the same as that of a monopolist.

B. A CENTRALISED CARTEL

If firms set up a formal organisation for direction of the economic activity of their industry, this can be called a cartel. The cartel may aim to maximise the joint profit of its members and, if it succeeds in doing so, its behaviour will not differ materially from that of a monopolist. In some countries, for example Australia, some of the agricultural boards act in a cartel-like fashion (for example, in the sugar industry). In turn, there are often international cartel arrangements for primary produce which allocate product quotas by countries. Few cartels succeed, however, in maximising the joint profit of their members.

The formal conditions for profit maximisation in an industry are obtained fairly easily. If the marginal costs of all firms are increasing, any output for the industry as a whole should be allocated between firms so as to equalise their marginal cost, otherwise the cost of the industry's output is not at a minimum. The industry's marginal-cost curve which is obtained on this basis should be equated to the marginal revenue for the industry, in order to obtain the profit maximising output for the industry as a whole. If, however, marginal costs are declining in the industry (indeed, even if long-run average costs are declining) the total output should be allocated to one firm only, if joint profit is to be maximised. Remaining firms might be compensated for not producing.

But distribution of joint profit may be a source of conflict and may very well result in a departure from joint profit maximisation. If each firm's share of profit aggregate is based upon its actual output, then each participant will require a quota and each is likely to clamour for a higher quota. However, if the request of all for a higher quota of output is granted, the cartel will be completely ineffective in raising the incomes of its participants. Depending upon bargaining skills, the share of some participants in total output may be biased away from the joint profit maximising allocation of output.

Usually a cartel is under the twin threats of internal dissolution and an external threat from new entrants. The more successfully it raises prices, the greater both these threats are likely to be. Any firm already in the cartel can greatly increase its sales by slightly undercutting the cartel price. Thus there is an incentive for each member to break away unless effective retaliation is possible and fairly certain to occur. Thus individual interest pulls in the opposite direction to joint interest and the cartel may collapse. For this reason cartel-like arrangements in agriculture are very often enforced by the State.

Entry is another problem. The profit maximising conditions given above ignored the possibility of entry. If price variations can reduce entry, a cartel may keep its price somewhat lower than otherwise. If entry proceeds nevertheless, two possibilities exist. The entrants may join the cartel, or remain aloof. In either case the profit of the industry declines, but most dramatically in the latter case. If entrants remain aloof from the cartel, they are likely to bring about the dissolution of the cartel by undercutting its price.

C. PRICE LEADERSHIP

Co-operation in an oligopolistic market may take a different form. One firm may be a recognised price leader and all other firms may respond in a known way to its variation of price or other terms of exchange. The price leader may be a low-cost producer and may be able to dominate the market because of this. However, this is not the only possible basis for leadership.

Consider the determination of price and output in such an industry if the product is homogeneous. In Fig. 9.19, the demand curve for the industry is shown by D. The supply of producers other than the price leader is shown by S'. These producers are price-takers. Hence, the demand curve for the price-leader's output is the difference between S' and D. The price-leader's demand curve is shown by d and his marginal-cost curve by MC. Thus it is most profitable for the price-leader to set a price of p_1 since mr is his marginal revenue curve. For a price of p_1 and a supply of X_1, the price leader's marginal revenue equals his marginal cost and his profit is at a maximum. At the price of p_1, followers in the industry will supply an output of $X_2 - X_1$.

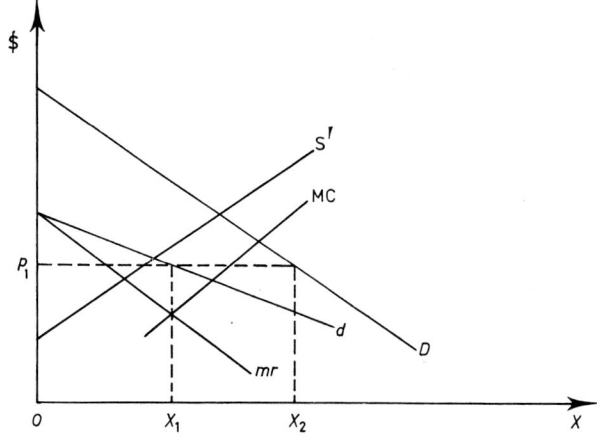

Fig. 9.19

D. THE KINKED DEMAND CURVE PHENOMENON

Hall and Hitch, and Sweezy[31] have suggested that an oligopolist in an unorganised industry may typically face a kinked demand curve. Once a pattern of price is established in an industry, an oligopolist who raises his price above the accepted level will not be followed by others. On the other hand, if he lowers his price below the established level, others will retaliate by lowering their prices too. In consequence, the individual oligopolist's demand curve is kinked like d in Fig. 9.20 and his marginal revenue curve is discontinuous like mr. The price p_1 is assumed to be the accepted price level for this oligopolist's product. In the case shown, the oligopolist's optimal output is x_1.

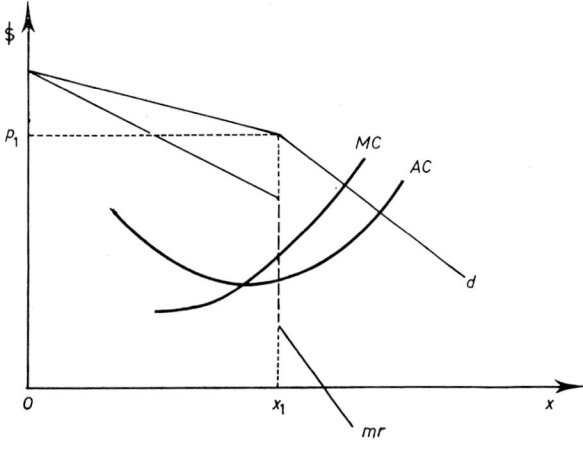

Fig. 9.20

Clearly, the oligopolist's costs can move up and down considerably and yet, if p_1 remains the accepted price, it is not profitable for him to depart from this price or to produce an output different to x_1. Only if his marginal-cost curve passes through the upper or lower segment of his marginal revenue curve, is it most profitable for the oligopolist to deviate from the accepted price. Furthermore, the demand for the oligopolist's product may expand or contract considerably and yet it is not profitable for him to deviate from the accepted price. This is illustrated in Fig. 9.21. The oligopolist's demand curve is shown to shift up from d_0 to d_1 but with marginal cost and the accepted price unchanged, it is most profitable to charge the accepted price and expand output. In the case illustrated, the optimal level of output expands from x_1 to x_2. Sweezy believed that this kinked demand curve phenomenon is helpful in explaining price rigidity under oligopolistic conditions.

However, Stigler[32] has contended that price rigidity is not as characteristic of oligopoly as is sometimes supposed. If the accepted price is subject to frequent change, prices may not be rigid.

How is the accepted price determined? What causes it to vary? Traditional theory has little to say about these questions. However, it is commonly believed that accepted prices are likely to be revised upward if costs rise generally in the industry or if demand expands generally. Customary formulas may be used for variations or one firm may be a recognised price leader under such circumstances and the analysis of the previous

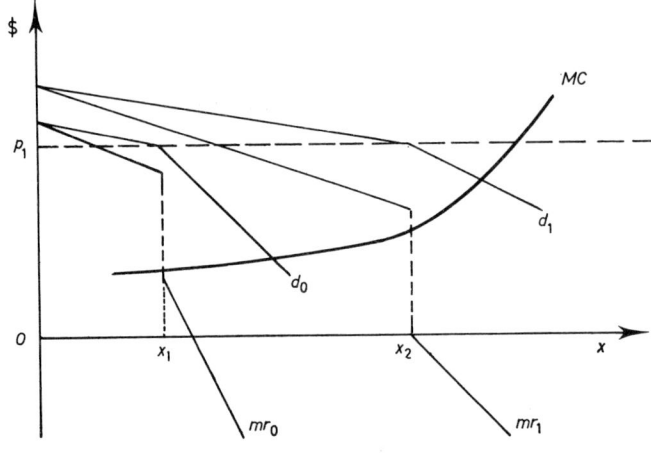

Fig. 9.21

section might be relevant. Once, however, the new price levels are attained, the kink is likely to be relevant again.

Cyert and DeGroot[33] have recently given an explanation of the kink using some crude learning theory. One firm is imagined to be aggressive and to be anxious to find the maximum matching price. Up to the maximum matching price, other firms will match the price increases of the active firm. As the active firm tests various prices, it learns more about the maximum matching price of others and after a point will not be tempted to experiment further. Thus its behaviour can be predicted. But the theory takes the maximum matching price as datum and is thus less than adequate.

None of the above theories alone cover the whole spectrum of observed oligopolistic behaviour, nor do they do so in combination. Yet each one highlights important aspects of oligopolistic behaviour and all emphasise important interdependencies between firms. They give helpful pointers for the examination of specific oligopolistic markets. Models from the theory of games add further insights and these are briefly discussed in the appendix to this chapter.

Finally, let me emphasise that, from an efficiency point of view, oligopoly is not necessarily inferior to perfect competition. The arguments given in the comparison of monopoly and perfect competition apply *mutatis mutandis*. It is evident that many of the traditional alternatives for market competition are unrealistic or unworkable and that the virtues of perfect competition have been much inflated. From a policy point of view the ideas of John Maurice Clark[34] on workable competition seem more relevant than the traditional hackneyed comparisons.

NOTES AND REFERENCES

[1] As mentioned earlier, the term *impure* might be used for markets in which participants influence the terms of trade but do not have perfect knowledge.

[2] They are in a position to influence prices, although some oligopolistic firms may, in fact, be followers of others in their determination of prices (see discussion later in this chapter).

[3] A. BERLE and G. MEANS, *The Modern Corporation and Private Property*, The Macmillan Company, New York, 1932.

[4] W. BAUMOL, *Business Behavior, Value and Growth*, The Macmillan Company, New York, 1959.

[5] Ibid.
[6] EDITH PENROSE, *The Theory of the Growth of the Firm*, Basil Blackwell, Oxford, 1959.
[7] J. VON NEUMANN and O. MORGENSTERN, *The Theory of Games and Economic Behavior*, Science Edition, John Wiley, New York.
[8] See the last section of Chapter 6.
[9] See Chapter 19.
[10] See Chapter 10.
[11] It is assumed that price discrimination is impossible.
[12] P. SRAFFA, "The Laws of Return under Competitive Conditions", *Economic Journal*, 1926, **36**, pp. 535-50, reprinted by the American Economic Association in *Readings in Price Theory*, Allen and Unwin, London, 1953, Reading 9.
[13] JOAN ROBINSON, *The Economics of Imperfect Competition*, Macmillan, London, 1st ed. 1933; 2nd ed. 1969, p. 4.
[14] This assumes that price discrimination is impossible.
[15] It is once again assumed that price discrimination is impossible.
[16] This is not to say that income distribution effects are unimportant. The hostility of the public at large often is based on this ground and on opposition to the concentration of power in few hands. See, for instance, ESTES KEFAUVER, *In a Few Hands: Monopoly Power in America*, Penguin, London, 1966.
[17] This is likely to occur if any factor is not in perfectly inelastic supply.
[18] A. C. HARBERGER, "Monopoly and Resource Allocation", *Proceedings of the American Economic Association*, May 1954, pp. 77-87. For a criticism of this article, see G. J. STIGLER, "The Statistics of Monopoly and Merger", *Journal of Political Economy*, 1956, **44**, pp. 33-40.
[19] J. BAIN, *Industrial Organization*, 2nd ed., John Wiley, New York, 1968, Ch. 6.
[20] J. SCHUMPETER, *Capitalism, Socialism and Democracy*, Allen and Unwin, 4th ed., 1954, Ch. 7.
[21] There is, of course, a time stream problem to take into account here. Furthermore, increased research and development expenditure is at the expense of other alternatives (for example, greater expenditure on social services) and it cannot be assumed that increases are necessarily desirable. However, one may wish to encourage temporary monopolies by patents in order to speed up technical progress. This aspect is discussed in Chapter 20.
[22] SCHUMPETER, op. cit.
[23] Monopoly may be even less restrictive than suggested above. A monopoly may internalise effects which would otherwise be external if many firms exist, and react to these effects in its economic calculation. A monopolist may also be better informed about market opportunities than purely competitive firms and so social losses due to errors may be less. Finally, a monopolist may not be under pressure to maximise profit and under the Baumol hypothesis (see reference 4 and referenced material) may not restrict output as much as is otherwise suggested.
[24] Chapter 14.
[25] See Chapter 22.
[26] E. CHAMBERLIN, *The Theory of Monopolistic Competition*, 6th ed., Harvard University Press, Cambridge, 1950.
[27] Ibid.
[28] J. M. CLARK, "Towards a Concept of Workable Competition", *American Economic Review*, No. 2, 1940, **30**, pp. 241-56. See also Chapter 14 of this book.
[29] J. VON NEUMANN and O. MORGENSTERN, op. cit.
[30] A. COURNOT, *Researches into the Mathematical Principles of the Theory of Wealth*. Published in French, 1838. Translation by N. BACON, The Macmillan Company, New York, 1897.
[31] R. HALL and C. HITCH, "Price Theory and Business Behaviour", *Oxford Economic Papers*, 1939, pp. 12-45. P. SWEEZY, "Demand under Conditions of Oligopoly", *Journal of Political Economy*, 1939, **47**, pp. 404-9.

[32] G. J. STIGLER, "The Kinky Oligopoly Demand Curve and Rigid Prices", *Journal of Political Economy*, 1947, **55**, pp. 432-49.
[33] R. M. CYERT and M. DEGROOT, "Interfirm Learning and the Kinked Demand Curve", *Journal of Economic Theory*, September 1971. Also by the same authors, "Bayesian Analysis and Duopoly Theory", *Journal of Political Economy*, 1970, **78**, pp. 1168-84.
[34] J. M. CLARK, op. cit.

FURTHER READING

CHAMBERLIN, E. H., *The Theory of Monopolistic Competition*, Harvard University Press, Cambridge, 6th ed., 1950, Chs 4 and 5.

COHEN, K., and R. CYERT, *Theory of the Firm*, Prentice-Hall, Englewood Cliffs, 1965, Ch. 12.

HENDERSON, J., and R. QUANDT, *Microeconomic Theory*, McGraw-Hill, New York, 1958, Ch. 6.

KAHN, R. F., "Some Notes on Ideal Output", *Economic Journal*, 1935, **45**, pp. 1-35.

KEFAUVER, E., *In a Few Hands*, Penguin, London, 1966.

KUENNE, R. (Ed.), *Monopolistic Competition Theory*, John Wiley, New York, 1967, Chs 5 and 7.

MACHLUP, F., *The Economics of Sellers' Competition*, Johns Hopkins Press, Baltimore, 1964.

ROBINSON, JOAN, *The Economics of Imperfect Competition*, 2nd ed., Macmillan, London, 1969, Books II and IV.

SCHUMPETER, J., *Capitalism, Socialism and Democracy*, 4th ed., Allen and Unwin, London, 1954.

STIGLER, G., "The Kinky Oligopoly Demand Curve and Rigid Prices", *Journal of Political Economy*, 1947, **55**, pp. 432-39.

Appendix to Chapter 9

Game Theory and Oligopolistic Behaviour

A. INTRODUCTION

Economic and social situations which involve conflict have much in common with parlour games. John von Neumann and Oskar Morgenstern exploited this relationship in their *Theory of Games and Economic Behavior* (1944)[1] to produce an analysis and a way of looking at the economic world which is one of, if not the most, significant of this century.

A game consists of a number of *players*, individual decision makers, each of whom has a number of alternative *strategies*. But no player controls all of the strategies on which the final *outcome* of the game depends. Each player finds that some of the strategies are controlled by other players with goals which differ from his and thus there is conflict. "The individual must consider how to achieve as much as is possible, taking into account that there are others whose goals differ from his own and whose actions have an effect on all. The decision maker in a game faces a cross-purposes optimisation problem."[2] Depending upon the outcome of the game, each player receives a *payoff* and there are *rules* which specify how the game is to be played.

A game can be formally represented in two different ways. It can be presented in an *extensive* or a *normal* form. The extensive form indicates all the possible ways in which the game can move step-by-step and is, therefore, quite cumbersome. On the other hand, the normal form does not consider step-by-step choices but rather portrays the game as one grand choice; an initial choice of which strategy to employ. A strategy prescribes how an individual player will act in particular circumstances and with the passage of the game. Once an individual makes his chosen strategy known, the game could be played according to his wishes by a representative. The combined strategies of all the players determine the outcome of the game and thus the payoffs to individual players. The number of possible strategies for a game may be fantastically large, but the normal form makes it easier to perceive formal similarities in the structure of games and to suggest likely outcomes for them. The concept of game theory can be readily illustrated by two-person zero-sum games.

B. TWO-PERSON ZERO-SUM GAMES

Any two-person game in which the preferences of the players for outcomes are diametrically opposed can be represented by a zero-sum game. A zero-sum game is one in which the loss to one player equals the gain to the other, so that the net overall gain adds up to zero. A game in which a money sum may merely change hands depending upon the outcome is a zero-sum game. A gain of $100 for one player is a loss of $100 for the other. Games of this nature are strictly competitive. The players cannot gain by co-operation.

Given that each of the players is entirely rational, how ought any player act? To decide on this, it is helpful to characterise the game by its normal form.

To represent the game suppose that player 1 has a finite set of alternative (pure) strategies. Letting a_i represent ith strategy of player 1, his set of alternative strategies is

$$S_1 = \{a_1, a_2, \ldots, a_m\}.$$

Letting β_j represent jth strategy of player 2, his set of alternative strategies might be indicated by

$$S_2 = \{\beta_1, \beta_2, \ldots, \beta_n\}.$$

The outcome of the game and the payoff to each player depends upon which strategy is adopted from S_1 and which is adopted from S_2. The relationship between the strategies and the payoffs can be set out in matrix (tabular) form. Listing strategies of player 2 across the top margin of the matrix and strategies of player 1 down the left hand margin, payoffs of player 1 are indicated in the body of the matrix. Because the game is zero-sum, it is only necessary to list the payoff for one player since it is easily remembered that the other player's payoff is equal to the listed values with a negative sign attached. In the matrix immediately below, P_{ij} represents the payoff to player 1. Since the game is zero-sum, the payoff to player 2 is $-P_{ij}$.

Pure Strategies of Player 2

	β_1	β_2	β_j	β_n
a_1	P_{11}	P_{12}	P_{1j}	P_{1n}
a_2	P_{21}	P_{22}	P_{2j}	P_{2n}
a_i	P_{i1}	P_{i2}	P_{ij}	P_{in}
a_m	P_{m1}	P_{m2}	P_{mj}	P_{mn}

Pure Strategies of Player 1

Take a specific example. Imagine that there are only two firms distributing petroleum products. These are the two players. Suppose further that during a particular period of time the goal of each is to maximise his market share. The game is zero-sum since the share lost by one firm is gained by the other. For simplicity, suppose that each firm has two alternative strategies. Each might not advertise at all or alternatively spend half a million dollars on advertising during the period. This information with the corresponding payoffs is shown in the matrix below. The figures in the body of the table indicate the percentage share of the market which goes to firm 1. If both firms advertise, each obtains a 50 per cent share of the market. If firm 1 fails to

Strategies of Firm 2

Strategies of Firm 1		β_1 = No Ads	β_2 = $\$\tfrac{1}{2}$m on Ads
	a_1 = No Ads	40	20
	a_2 = $\$\tfrac{1}{2}$m on Ads	60	50

advertise and firm 2 promotes his own product, firm 1 gains only 20 per cent of the market and "loses" 80 per cent of it to firm 2. In a situation like this, which strategies are likely to be adopted? It is argued below that both firms are likely to adopt their advertising strategies. But in order to predict this we suppose that each player is

Game Theory and Oligopolies

aware of the preference patterns of the opponent, the alternatives available to each player and the payoffs. In other words, he is considered to be at least implicitly aware of the normal form of the game.

Von Neumann and Morgenstern suggest that player 1 will adopt the strategy which maximises his minimum possible gain and that player 2 will select the strategy which minimises his own maximum possible loss. Under the circumstances, *neither player is being conservative* but is maximising his payoff, given that he has a rational opponent who is trying to minimise this. If, however, a player's opponent has some weakness, for example, if he does not know of particular strategies, then a player may take advantage of this. But the basic solution *is not* a conservative one and this will be given extra emphasis below.[3]

Consider the above example, which involved petroleum distributors. The previous matrix is restated below in a shorter form. Since player 2 is considering his own gain,

	β_1	β_2	Row minimum
a_1	40	20	20
a_2	60	50	**50**
Column maximum	60	**50**	

he is determined to keep the share of player 1 to a minimum. The likely payoffs for player 1 are shown on the right of the matrix. The best of these is **50**. Thus a_2 ensures the greatest gain for player 1 in the circumstances. On the other hand, player 1 is determined to maximise the loss of player 2. The maximum losses of player 2 for his alternative strategies are shown at the foot of the matrix. By adopting β_2, player 2 cannot lose more than 50 per cent of the market. This strategy minimises his maximum possible loss. The maximum gain and minimum loss figures are the same, namely 50 per cent. Thus (a_2, β_2) is the likely strategy pair of the game. This pair forms a stable solution. Player 1 finds it optimal to choose a_2 if β_2 is the known choice of player 2. Player 2 finds it optimal to choose β_2 if a_2 is the known choice of player 1. But not all zero-sum games have a stable equilibrium solution in terms of pure strategies.

Consider the game with the following normal form:

	β_1	β_2	Row minimum
a_1	3	1	1
a_2	2	4	2
Column maximum	3	4	

On the basis of the previous argument, the strategy a_2 might seem to be optimal for player 1 and β_1 for player 2. But (a_2, β_1) does not represent a stable solution. If player 1 reasons that player 2 will adopt β_1, it is optimal for player 1 to employ strategy a_1 rather than a_2. Similarly, if player 2 believes that player 1 will adopt a_2, it is optimal for player 2 to adopt β_2 in preference to β_1. The situation is not a stable one and is unlike the previous one. No determinate solution exists for pure strategies.

This difficulty was met by von Neumann and Morgenstern in an ingenious fashion.[4] Suppose that the players are permitted to select their strategies by using a random device. For example, player 2 might have a six-faced die with β_1 on two faces and β_2

on four faces. Using this device, the probability that β_1 is chosen is 1/3 and that β_2 is chosen 2/3. Similarly, player 1 could select his strategies by random means. Assuming that each player aims to maximise his *expected* utility (expected gain if utility varies linearly with the gain) von Neumann[5] was able to show that every two-person zero-sum game has a stable equilibrium solution for either mixed (that is randomly selected) or pure strategies. A pure strategy is one which is *not* selected by chance.

In the example, considered last, the appropriate mixed strategy is not difficult to determine. Figure A9.1 is informative in this respect. This figure indicates the expected payoff to player 1 if strategy a_2 is selected with a probability of p and a_1 with a probability of $1-p$. In Fig. A9.1, p_0 yields the maximum expected gain for player 1. Thus a_2 should be selected with a probability of p_0, and a_1 with a probability of $1-p_0$ by player 1 if he is rational.[6] In that case, minimum *expected* gain of player 1 rises above 2 but there is also some *probability* that his actual gain will fall below 2 to 1. The optimal mixed strategy for player 2 can be found in a similar fashion.

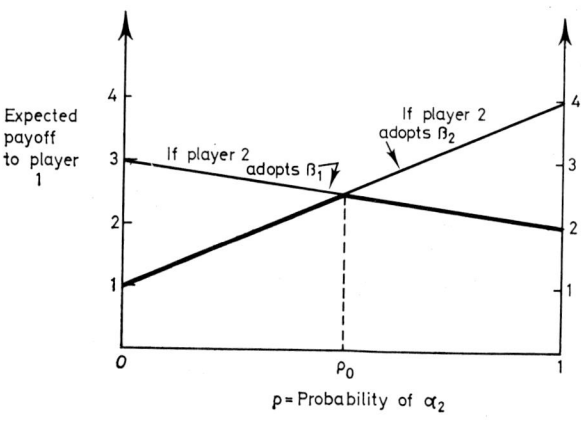

Fig. A9.1

Ingenious though this solution is, it does rely on the adequacy of *expected* utility maximisation as a predictor of behaviour.[7] Furthermore, few economic and social situations fit into the pattern of a zero-sum game, for there is generally conflict as well as some scope for co-operation in behaviour.[8] If profit rather than market shares are important, the duopoly model considered above is no longer a zero-sum one, for there is scope for co-operation.

C. CO-OPERATIVE GAMES

If the two petroleum distributors considered in the above example aim to maximise their profit, the normal form of their game is not the same as that previously outlined. It might be like that indicated in the following matrix:

$$\begin{array}{c c} & \begin{array}{cc} \beta_1 & \beta_2 \end{array} \\ \begin{array}{c} a_1 \\ a_2 \end{array} & \begin{bmatrix} (2,4) & (0,5) \\ (5,0) & (1,1) \end{bmatrix} \end{array}$$

The first strategy of each player corresponds to no advertising and the second to advertising. The pairs in the body of the table indicate the profit which is earned by the two firms. The first figure in the brackets is the profit of firm 1 in millions of dollars and the second figure is profit for firm 2. The game is not zero-sum. What is the likely outcome of this game? In the absence of communication, co-operation or trust, (a_2,β_2) seems likely to be the chosen set of strategies. No matter which strategy player 2 adopts, player 1 gains most by adopting strategy a_2. Irrespective of which strategy player 1 selects, player 2 maximises his gain by adopting β_2. It is always in the self-interest of player 1 to use strategy a_2 and always in the self-interest of player 2 to adopt β_2. But each player is led by his own self-interest to collective action which is inferior from the point of view of both. By acting selfishly each firm advertises and makes a profit of \$1m. By co-operation both could earn more by not advertising. Firm 1 could earn \$2m and firm 2 could earn \$4m. Thus if trust is present and communication is possible, both may agree to (a_1, β_1).

In this example, unrestrained self-interest leads to an outcome which is mutually disadvantageous. The situation is of the prisoner-dilemma type.[9] (This situation was originally illustrated by a problem in which two prisoners were given a chance to confess or not to confess to a crime. It was in their joint interest not to confess. But their own self-interest led both to confess.) Problems of a similar type frequently arise. For example, if no penalties are imposed, it is in the selfish interest of every individual to litter, to destroy native flora and fauna or other natural wonders. It is in his "self-interest" to do so irrespective of the action of others. In consequence, a situation may be reached which is inferior from everybody's point of view.

Von Neumann and Morgenstern considered the solution of games which give scope for co-operation. However, they point out that coalition formation and co-operation depend upon complex historical, sociological and psychological factors and are wary about claiming too much for their abstract theory. They suggest that whenever co-operation takes place

(i) the players will agree to strategies which are Pareto optimal from *their* point of view, and

(ii) assuming that transfers can be made between players, no player will accept less than he can ensure himself without co-operation.

In the case of duopolists, they would agree to maximise their joint profit and share this in such a way that no duopolist gets less than he could ensure himself of without co-operating. Thus the price, output and profit of the duopolists can be determined (in fact, the cartel solutions apply) but their actual shares in profit are indeterminate to some extent.

Attempts have been made to determine the shares precisely (for example, by Nash[10]) by taking account of the threat which one player can pose to the other. In *n*-person games another condition is sometimes added to the ones of von Neumann and Morgenstern, namely that no potential coalition should accept less than it can ensure itself of in the absence of co-operation. This is designed to locate more precisely the shares of players in the joint payoff.

However, co-operation does not always take place even when players can gain by it. Disagreement about their share in the gain may forestall co-operation of the players. Trust, too, is important. No player is likely to co-operate who believes that he will be "double-crossed". Game theory, by creating a new conception of social choice, indicates that matters like these are of fundamental social importance. It is in this, rather than in specific solutions, that its present value lies.

NOTES AND REFERENCES

[1] J. VON NEUMANN and O. MORGENSTERN, *Theory of Games and Economic Behavior*, 1st ed., Princeton University Press, Princeton, 1944; Science Edition, John Wiley, New York, 1964.

[2] M. SHUBIK (Ed.), *Games Theory and Related Approaches to Social Behavior*, John Wiley, New York, 1964, p. 9.

[3] Yet the minimax criterion which is sometimes used in decision theory is conservative if one is not opposed by a rational, well-informed opponent. See, for example, C. TISDELL, *The Theory of Price Uncertainty, Production and Profit*, Princeton University Press, Princeton, 1968, Ch. 2.

[4] VON NEUMANN and MORGENSTERN, op. cit., Ch. II, Sec. 17.

[5] J. VON NEUMANN, "Zur Theorie Gesellschaftsspiele", *Math. Annalen*, 1928, **100**, pp. 295-320.

[6] Maximises expected utility, is fully informed of possibilities and is faced by a rational opponent.

[7] For further discussion of this aspect, see H. MARKOWITZ, *Portfolio Selection*, John Wiley, New York, 1959, pp. 229-34.

[8] As a rule, too, we find that individuals are much less well-informed about possibilities than has been generally assumed in game theory. Deficiencies of knowledge lead to weaknesses in opponents which can easily be exploited.

[9] For further details, see R. D. LUCE and H. RAIFFA, *Games and Decisions*, John Wiley, New York, 1957, Ch. 5.

[10] J. F. NASH, "Two-Person Cooperative Games", *Econometrica*, 1953, **21**, pp. 128-40.

FURTHER READING

BAUMOL, W. J., *Economic Theory and Operations Analysis*, 2nd ed., Prentice-Hall, Englewood Cliffs, 1956, Ch. 23.

FELLNER, W., *Competition among the Few*, Knopf, New York, 1949.

HURWICZ, L., "The Theory of Economic Behavior", *American Economic Review*, 1945, **35**, pp. 909-25.

*LUCE, R. D. and H. RAIFFA, *Games and Decisions*, John Wiley, New York, 1957.

SHUBIK, M., *Game Theory and Related Approaches to Social Behavior*, John Wiley, New York, 1964, Part I.

---

*More advanced.

CHAPTER 10

The Pricing and Employment of Factors

Introduction

Whereas the previous two chapters concentrated on the markets for products, this one focuses on the markets for factors of production. The latter markets are important. The *prices* which factors fetch as well as their ownership by an individual determines his income. Yet factor prices are not only important from the angle of distribution of income, but also from the point of view of economic efficiency. The incorrect pricing (valuation) of factors leads to economic inefficiency, for under such circumstances it is possible to produce the same output by using a smaller quantity of inputs, or to produce a greater output using the same quantity of inputs, or to improve the allocation of factors between products so that all individuals are made better off.

All markets are subject to general supply and demand relationships yet factor markets have some special features which warrant mention. First, it is obvious that one factor, labour, is a very personal one. Second, the demand for factors is usually a *derived* demand. While the demand for entertainers, waiters, etc. is not a derived demand, the demand for factory hands is derived from the demand for the product of the factory. Derived demand will be assumed to be the general case. Consequently, the employment and price of factors depend not only upon conditions in the factor markets but also upon conditions in the related product markets. Thus if a firm has a monopoly in the sale of a product, this affects the demand for factors. Also, if there is monopsony in the purchase of a factor (a single buyer of a factor), the demand for the factor is altered. Imperfections, in either factor or product markets, influence the pricing and employment of factors.

Aspects of the theory of the employment of factors were mentioned earlier. In Chapters 1 and 3 economic efficiency and the allocation of factors were briefly considered, and in Chapter 7 the employment of factors by perfectly competitive firms was examined. But the overall market for a factor has not been dealt with, nor have market imperfections been adequately taken into account. Using the marginal productivity theory, we shall now examine the pricing and employment of factors in perfectly competitive markets and then in imperfectly competitive markets. Limitations of the theory are noted and some of its implications for the distribution of income are considered.

I. The Pricing and Employment of Factors under Perfect Competition

If perfect competition exists in both product and factor markets, no firm can influence the price of its product nor the price of any factor which it purchases. Also, no supplier of a factor is able to alter its price. Let us explore the demand and supply curves for a factor under these conditions.

If one factor alone is variable, call it L, the demand and supply curves of L for a firm and in aggregate are like those shown respectively in Figs. 10.1 and 10.2. Consider Fig. 10.1 which represents the supply and demand situation for a firm. The curve indicating the supply of the factor to the firm is a horizontal line equal to $\bar{w}$, the going wage rate. If an individual firm is willing to pay the going price of the factor, it can hire as much of L as it wishes. Consequently, $\bar{w}$ is the firm's average per-unit cost of the factor (sometimes abbreviated to average factor cost, AFC) and also the firm's marginal cost of the factor (sometimes called marginal factor cost, MFC). The firm's MFC is its cost of an additional unit of the factor, and is the first derivative of wl (total cost of L to the firm) with respect to l. The price of the factor is represented by w and l indicates the quantity of its employment by the firm.

The curve showing the demand of the firm for the factor is not horizontal. A firm's demand for an additional unit of a factor depends upon the extra revenue from the output produced by the extra unit of the factor. Clearly, it is profitable (unprofitable) to employ an extra unit of a factor if its addition to revenue exceeds (is less than) its cost. The firm's demand for a factor depends upon the marginal revenue product of the factor, MRP—the extra revenue from the output produced by an additional unit of the factor. As long as the MRP of a factor exceeds the cost of an extra unit of the factor, MFC, it is profitable for the firm to increase the employment of the factor. At any given price of the factor, the firm finds it profitable to employ the factor up to the point at which the price of the factor equals its marginal revenue product.[1] Thus the marginal revenue product curve of the factor is the firm's demand curve for the factor.

Now
$$MRP = MR \times MPP, \qquad (10.1)$$

that is the marginal revenue product of the factor is equal to the marginal physical product (MPP) of the factor times marginal revenue (MR), the additional revenue from the extra production. The demand for the factor depends upon its productivity and the demand for its product. Under perfect competition, an individual firm has no influence on the price of its product and so the price and marginal revenue of its product coincide. Hence, if perfect competition prevails, a firm's

$$MRP = p \times MPP \qquad (10.2)$$
$$= VMP, \qquad (10.3)$$

that is the marginal revenue product of the factor equals the price of the product times the marginal physical product of the factor. The expression on the LHS of Equation (10.2) is called the value of the marginal product, VMP. Under perfect competition, since p is constant, the slope of the firm's demand curve depends solely on the slope of the marginal physical product curve of the factor. If the marginal physical product of a factor falls as the factor is increasingly used, the firm's demand curve for the factor, d in Fig. 10.1, also falls as the firm's employment of the factor increases.

Unless the marginal revenue product of each factor employed by a firm equals its marginal factor cost, the firm is not maximising its profit. Ruling out an end-point

Pricing and Employment of Factors

profit maximum, the variable factor must be employed in a quantity which ensures that

$$MRP = MFC \qquad (10.4)$$

if the firm is to maximise profit. Under perfect competition, $MR = p$ and $MFC = w$ so that Equation (10.4) reduces to

$$VMP = w. \qquad (10.5)$$

Under perfect competition, profit maximisation requires that a factor be employed in a quantity which ensures that the value of its marginal product equals the price per unit of the factor. In Fig. 10.1, this condition is satisfied if the firm employs l_0 of the factor.

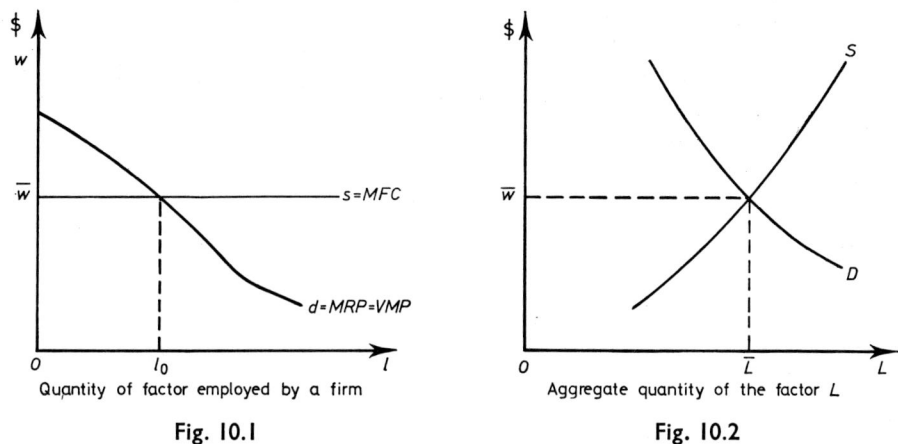

Fig. 10.1   Fig. 10.2

But the condition mentioned in Equation (10.4) is not sufficient to ensure a maximum of profit. Second-order conditions, at least, should be examined as a step towards distinguishing between minima, maxima and inflection points of profit. If, under perfect competition, the marginal physical product of the factor is declining for an employment which satisfies Equation (10.4) or (10.5), MRP is declining and a relative maximum of profit occurs. In Fig. 10.1, the firm clearly maximises its profit by employing l_0 of L. For the employment of l_0, $\bar{w} = MRP$ and MRP is declining. Note that if MRP increases over a sufficiently large range, perfect competition may break down because firms find it profitable to expand until they become very large. Consequently, their size may increase to such an extent that they are able to influence prices.[2]

In Fig. 10.2, aggregate supply and demand curves are shown for factor L. The equilibrium price of the factor is $\bar{w}$ and its equilibrium employment is $\bar{L}$. The aggregate demand curve D depicts the value of the marginal product of L, assuming that L is allocated between firms so as to equalise the value of their marginal product, and that allowance is made for any change in the price of products as a result of increased output due to an increase in the aggregate employment of L. Because the demand curves of individual firms for a factor are based on constant product prices, the aggregate curve for a factor can rarely be obtained by adding individual demand curves such as d together. The only exception arises if the market demand curves for the products of the factor are all perfectly elastic.

An example may help to clarify the notion of the aggregate demand curve for a factor. Imagine that factor L produces only one product, X, and let

$$p = f(X) \tag{10.6}$$

represent the demand function for that product. Let

$$X = G(L) \tag{10.7}$$

represent the production function for the industry as a whole, supposing that the aggregate quantity of L is allocated between firms so as to maximise the output of X for any employment of L. The optimal allocation requires that the marginal physical product of L be the same for all firms and (as was pointed out in Chapter 3) this condition is automatically satisfied under perfect competition.[3] The aggregate demand curve for L is given by

$$D(L) = f(X) \times G'(L) \tag{10.8}$$
$$= f(G(L)) \times G'(L) \tag{10.9}$$

where $G'(L)$ is the marginal product of L. As L varies, both the price of the product, $f(X)$, and the marginal product of L are likely to vary. Since usually $f(X)$ is likely to decrease as L increases, the aggregate demand curve D is steeper than the curve which would be obtained by adding demand curves, such as d, together.

Usually it is believed that the aggregate supply curve of a factor can be obtained by adding together the supply curves of individuals. Although this may normally be the case, snob and bandwagon effects could influence the supply of some factors. In that case, simple addition of individual curves would not give the aggregate curve. It is possibly also worthwhile noting that the supply curves of some factors may be backward-bending. Increased real wage rates may lead to increased supply of labour up to a point, but increased wages beyond that point may reduce the supply of labour as labourers prefer to take more leisure.

Consider now the effect upon equilibrium factor prices and employment of changes in some of the parameters of the market model. It is clear that if the demand curve for the end-product shifts upward so too does the demand curve for the factor. If the supply curve of the factor is positively sloped, the price of the factor and its employment rises. Second, an increase in the marginal physical productivity of the factor could lead to increased employment of the factor and could raise its rate of reward but need not do so. The more elastic the demand for the end-product, the more likely the favourable effect for the factor.[4] However, if the demand for the end-product is perfectly inelastic, the employment of the factor falls and its price per unit falls as a result of a general rise in its marginal physical productivity.[5] The employment and rewards to a factor can be influenced, amongst other means, by altering the demand for its end-products or by varying the productivity of the factor. Of course, variations of the supply curve of a factor also influence rewards and employment in an industry. If the demand curve is negatively sloping, a shift upward in the supply curve (for example, due to barriers to entry, such as long registration periods and unreasonable qualifications) raises the price of the factor. On various occasions, trade unions have attempted to influence both the supply and demand sides of labour markets to obtain better conditions for their members.

Consider economic efficiency and the use of the single variable factor. If perfect competition exists, economic efficiency occurs inasmuch as it is impossible to increase

Pricing and Employment of Factors

the output of any product without decreasing that of another. Furthermore, the factor is so allocated to the various products that it is impossible to make any consumer better off without making another worse off. (Externalities are assumed to be absent.)

While this is discussed in a later chapter,[6] a rough sketch of some of the important relationships is worthwhile at this stage. Imagine that two products, 1 and 2, can be produced. (There is no problem in taking a greater number.) Under perfect competition, the prices of these two products, p_1 and p_2, are the same for all consumers and all firms. Consequently, the marginal rate of substitution of these products is the same for all consumers and it is impossible to make one better off without making another worse off, given the available stock of goods. The stock (output) of goods is also at a maximum, given the quantity of the factor which is employed. Furthermore, the composition of products is optimal, for the relative value of an extra unit of one product at the expense of any other just equals its comparative cost. This is easily seen. The price of the factor, w, is the same for each firm. Since firms are maximising profit,

$$\frac{w}{p_1} = MPP_{1j} \qquad (j = 1, \ldots, n) \tag{10.10}$$

and

$$\frac{w}{p_2} = MPP_{2j} \qquad (j = 1, \ldots, n) \tag{10.11}$$

where there are $(j = 1, \ldots, n)$ firms. Hence, the marginal physical product of L in producing product 1 is the same everywhere and the marginal physical product of L in producing product 2 is the same for each firm. Now Equations (10.10) and (10.11) can be rearranged to give

$$p_1 = \frac{w}{MPP_{1j}} \qquad (j = 1, \ldots, n) \tag{10.12}$$

and

$$p_2 = \frac{w}{MPP_{2j}} \qquad (j = 1, \ldots, n) \tag{10.13}$$

$\frac{w}{MPP_{1j}}$ is the marginal cost to firm j of producing product 1 and $\frac{w}{MPP_{2j}}$ is its marginal cost of producing product 2.[7] Hence,

$$\frac{p_1}{p_2} = \frac{MC_{1j}}{MC_{2j}} \tag{10.14}$$

where MC represents marginal costs. The comparative value placed by consumers on an additional unit of product 1, p_1/p_2, just equals its comparative cost, MC_{1j}/MC_{2j}.

It is not, however, reasonable to suppose that just one factor is variable. Fortunately, the addition of other variable factors does not change the argument. Let alphabetical subscripts indicate alternative factors. Then let w_A represent the price of factor A, w_L that of L, and MPP with the appropriate subscript indicate the marginal physical product of any corresponding factor. Taking any product (product 1 will do) each firm will equate

$$p_1 = \frac{w_A}{MPP_{1A}} = \ldots = \frac{w_L}{MPP_{1L}} = \ldots \tag{10.15}$$

in order to maximise profit. But $\frac{w_A}{MPP_{1A}}$ or any other of these factor ratios indicate the marginal cost to the firm of an extra unit of product 1. Thus the firm's marginal cost, MC_{1j} is given by any of the terms to the right of p_1 in Equation (10.15). Thus, since prices are the same for all, the previous argument applies *mutatis mutandis*. At the margin, the comparative value of products under perfect competition is equated to their comparative cost.

But we must not conclude that perfect competition is necessarily the most efficient means of economic organisation. Decreasing costs may rule out perfect competition and there are all the problems to consider which were mentioned in the previous chapter.

II. The Pricing and Employment of Factors under Imperfect Competition

Although the general rule that firms find it most profitable to employ factors until their marginal revenue product equals their marginal factor cost still holds, firms have some influence over prices in imperfect markets. In consequence, the behaviour of firms does not lead to a Pareto optimum. Consider first a situation in which a firm has a monopoly in its product market but perfect competition prevails in its factor market, and then consider a monopsonistic case.

A. A MONOPOLY IN THE PRODUCT MARKET BUT PERFECT COMPETITION IN THE FACTOR MARKET

If monopoly exists in the product market and perfect competition in the factor market, the monopolist does not maximise his profit unless he employs factors in quantities which equate the price of the factors to their marginal revenue product. Because a monopolist is able to influence the price of his product, his marginal revenue product and the value of the marginal product diverge;

$$MRP \neq VMP \quad (10.16)$$

under monopoly. Since marginal revenue is below average revenue under monopoly, a monopolist's marginal revenue product curve is below his value of the marginal product curve. Given that one factor, L, is variable for the monopolist, and indicating his employment of it by L_1, the curves marked respectively VMP and MRP in Fig. 10.3 indicate possible values of marginal product and marginal revenue product curves for the monopolist.

If $p = f(X)$ represents the demand curve for the monopolist's product, X, and if $X = G(L)$ is his production function,

$$VMP = f(X) \times G'(L) \quad (10.17)$$
$$= f(G(L)) \times G'(L) \quad (10.18)$$

and $$MRP = \left[f(X) + \frac{df}{dX} X \right] G'(L). \quad (10.19)$$

These equations indicate that if df/dX is negative, if the demand curve for the product is negatively sloped, MRP is less than VMP. (This is true for $X > 0$ and $G'(L) > 0$.)

Given that perfect competition exists in the factor market, the monopolist can obtain an "unlimited" supply of L by paying the going price per unit for the factor. If that price is $\bar{w}$, his supply curve for the factor is the curve marked s in Fig. 10.3. In the case shown, since his marginal factor cost is $\bar{w}$, his most profitable employment of the factor is L_1^*. But the socially desirable employment of L by the monopolist

Pricing and Employment of Factors

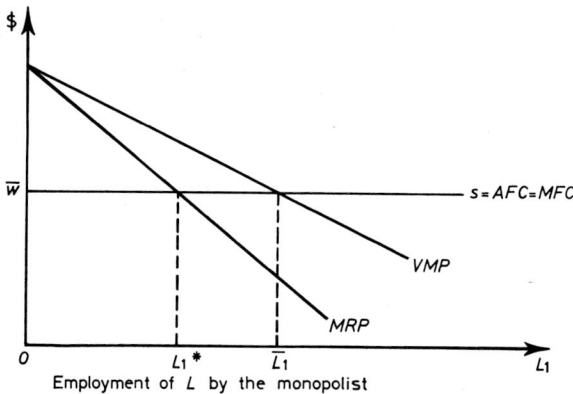

Fig. 10.3

is $\bar{L}_1$ if perfect competition exists elsewhere in the economy. If $\bar{L}_1$ of the factor is employed, its value at the margin in producing the monopolist's product is just equal to its value in producing products at the margin elsewhere. If perfect competition could be viable in the monopolised market and if technological conditions are no different to those under monopoly, perfect competition results in the employment of $\bar{L}_1$, the ideal level of employment, since each firm acts to equate the going price of the factor with the value of its marginal product.

The factor is not optimally allocated amongst products if monopoly occurs in one of the markets and perfect competition exists in others. In the monopolised market, $MC_1 \neq p_1$ but equals MR which diverges from p_1. If there is one other product market, call it market 2, in which perfect competition exists, there $MC_2 = p_2$. Consequently, as a result of monopoly in one of the markets $p_1/p_2 \neq MC_1/MC_2$; the factor is not allocated so as to equalise relative values and costs at the margin.

B. MONOPSONY AND THE PRICING AND EMPLOYMENT OF FACTORS

Sometimes a single buyer is able to affect the price of a factor by varying his purchases of it. If there is just one purchaser of the factor, a monopsony exists and it is likely that the single purchaser will be able to influence the price of the factor. If this influence is present, the profit maximising firm needs to take it into account in determining its employment of the factor.

Take a firm which has a monopsony in the purchase of a single factor, L, and which sells its product on a perfectly competitive market. Imagine further that L is the only variable factor. If the firm wishes to maximise its profit, it should employ L to equate its marginal factor cost with the value of its marginal product. The case is illustrated in Fig. 10.4 where L indicates the employment of L by the monopsonist. The supply curve is shown as sloping upward and is indicated by S. The monopsonist can obtain greater supplies of L only by paying increased prices for it. The supply curve is also equal to the average cost of the factor. Hence, the monopsonist's marginal factor cost curve is above the supply curve of the factor, for an average value can only rise if the marginal value exceeds it. The value of the marginal product is indicated by VMP in Fig. 10.4 and the firm finds it most profitable to employ $\hat{L}$ of the factor. This is a lower amount than would be employed if the demand for the factor happened to be perfectly competitive and technological conditions unchanged. Under those conditions, $\bar{L}$ of the factor would be employed. This is "socially" optimal. At the monopsonist's employment of $\hat{L}$, resource holders are willing to supply more of L at a price which does not exceed the value of its marginal product. Potentially, of consumers, resource owners and buyers can be made better off by the increased use the factor. The price paid for the resource, $\hat{w}$, is lower than under perfect competition, that is than price $\bar{w}$. The suppliers of the factor are "squeezed" by the monopsonist.

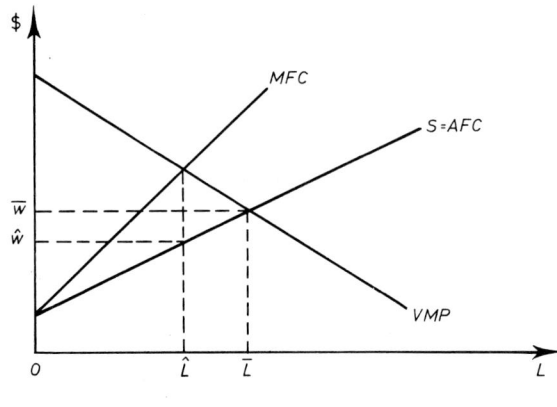

Fig. 10.4

Monopsony in the factor market coupled with perfect competition in the product market might be thought to be unusual. Yet for various types of primary produce, there is often only one processor in the immediate area of supply.[8] If the cost of transport of the raw produce is high, the processor has a virtual monopsony in his immediate region of supply. The finally processed commodity, because transport charges for it are less important, might be sold on a market which is very nearly perfectly competitive.

It is, of course, possible to have monopoly in the product market combined with monopsony in the factor market. If suppliers of the variable factor do not co-operate and if consumers do not countervail, the employment and pricing outcome for the factor can be illustrated by Fig. 10.5. The monopolist-monopsonist employs L^0 of the factor, a lower quantity than in any of the other market situations if technological and demand conditions are the same. He also pays a lower price for it, w_0, than in any of the alternative market situations *assuming* that technology and the demand for the final product are the same.

A firm need not have a complete monopsony to be able to influence the price of a factor and to create a distortion in the use of factors. To illustrate this and take account of interdependence, simply assume that a factor can be used in two markets, for example, to produce two different products, 1 and 2, and that there is no hindrance to the movement of the factor between the markets. Imagine that the market for product 1 is monopolised and the market for the other is perfectly competitive. Furthermore, suppose that the one variable factor L is in inelastic supply overall. Let the overall supply of L be L_A. The quantity of L which is not absorbed by one market is absorbed by the other. The situation can be depicted by Fig. 10.6. The perfectly competitive

Pricing and Employment of Factors

market is shown on the left and the imperfectly competitive one is indicated on the right. The supply curve of the factor to market 1 is shown by S_1. None of the factor is supplied to market 1 if a price less than w_m is offered there. Market 2 absorbs all supplies. At higher prices, S_1 rises until at a price of w_t market 1 employs the total supply of the factor. S_1 is equal to the difference between L_A and VMP_2.

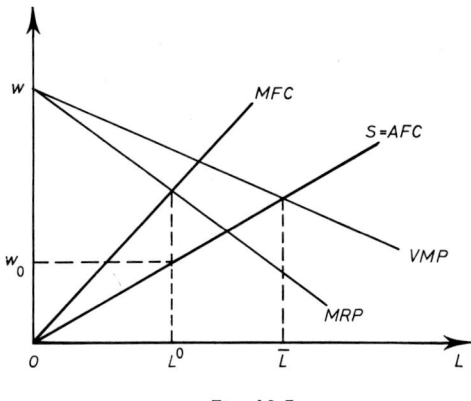

Fig. 10.5

If both markets are perfectly competitive (assuming that technological conditions and product demand are the same as those supposed in Fig. 10.6) $\bar{L}_1$ of L_A is allocated to market 1 and $\bar{L}_2$ to market 2. The price of the factor is $\bar{w}$. But with the type of imperfection mentioned, employment in market 1 drops to L_1^0, whereas that in market 2 increases to L_2^0. The price of the factor falls to w_0. The factor L is misallocated. Insufficient quantity of L is used in market 1, for the value of its marginal product there is much higher than in market 2.

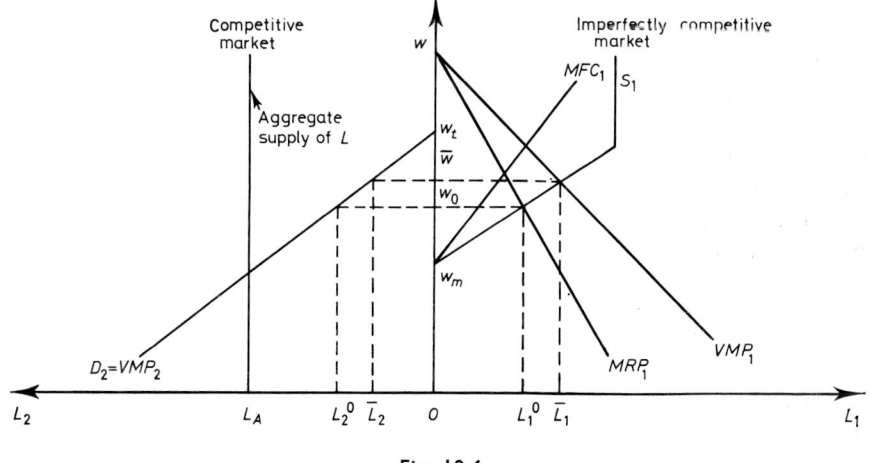

Fig. 10.6

Similarly, divergences from a social optimum can be shown to exist if the monopolist has an influence only on the price of his product and not on factor prices. Or, again, if in market 1 the firm influences the price of L but sells its product on a competitive market, the allocation of the factor diverges from a Paretian optimum. Figure 10.6 easily illustrates that the value of the marginal product of L in market 1 in all these cases exceeds that in market 2. In the absence of externalities, divergences in the private value of the marginal products are less than Pareto optimal.[9]

The aggregate supply of the factor is assumed to be perfectly inelastic in the model just discussed. But the model can be simply modified to allow for variations in aggregate supply of the factor. (The aggregate supply curve above L_A may slope down to the right and S_1 must be modified in Fig. 10.6.) Even if the supply of the factor is variable, the employed quantity of the factor is not optimally allocated between markets if imperfect competition occurs in only one market. The distortions are similar to those which have already been noted. Furthermore, given variability of supply, if imperfection arises in one market, the overall employment of the factor is lower than if perfect competition exists, provided that technological conditions and final demand relations are the same in both cases. The aggregate employment of the factor is less than optimal, since in one of the markets the price paid to the factor is less than the value of its marginal product. Some units of the factor are unable to find employment even though their owners wish to dispose of the units at a price which does not exceed the value of their marginal product.

The models which are considered above do not allow for imperfection in the supply of a factor. Trade unions in certain industries are able to exert an influence on wage rates. As previously noted this might be achieved by creating shifts of the supply and demand functions which are favourable to the trade union members. But trade unions may have an impact in other ways. Wages in excess of equilibrium levels may be negotiated by cohesive unions. If trade unions face organised employers or large employers, the outcome of bargaining or control of labour supply is to some extent indeterminate. The theory of games, however, does highlight some of the important interrelationships.[10]

In this chapter, the discussion has been limited principally to one variable factor. If more than one factor is variable, factor substitution is possible and the simple diagrammatic exposition which has been given needs to be modified. Nevertheless, the types of distortions in the allocation of factors which arise from imperfect competition remain the same.

Most importantly, the comparison made here between the economic efficiency and perfect competition must be qualified in accordance with the points made in the previous chapter. Perfect competition may not be viable under the same conditions as imperfect competition and technological progress may vary with different market forms.

III. Limitations of the Marginal Productivity Theory

Writers delineate the marginal productivity theory of income distribution and employment differently. Some restrict the coverage of the term to perfect competition only. However, I shall take it that the theory assumes that factors are employed up to the point where each firm finds that its marginal factor cost equals its marginal revenue product irrespective of whether competition is perfect or imperfect.

For the theory to be exactly applicable, firms must be profit maximisers. Organisational slack must be absent and goals which stress revenue etc., must be unimportant.

The marginal revenue product curve of a firm for the factor considered needs to

Pricing and Employment of Factors

be continuous and differentiable. This is only likely to be so if the demand curve for the firm's product and its production function possess these properties. If the factor is lumpy (available only in discrete quantities), the firm's production function is not continuous and the theory cannot be applied exactly. But it yields an approximation, and these discontinuities may become irrelevant in aggregate.

It has also been objected, by Stigler[11] amongst others, that if several factors co-operate in production, it is often impossible to disentangle the marginal revenue product of each. Indeed, there may be no individual marginal product, for example, if factors are required in fixed proportions for production. Again, in the provision of public goods (in which the price mechanism is deficient) the theory is no guide to optimal allocation of factors.[12]

Naturally, if the theory is restricted just to perfect competition, it fails to take account of imperfect competition which is a serious shortcoming. But even allowing no such restriction, a shortcoming of the theory is that it fails to explore bargaining aspects of wage settlements.

Furthermore, it is debatable whether the theory gives a satisfactory explanation of the division of national income between factors. Kaldor,[13] building on Keynes' theory, suggests that it does not and presents an alternative theory in which the share of profits in income depends on the ratio of investment to output in the economy. Kaldor's theory is able to explain the relative constancy of the wage share in national income but so, too, is a version of the marginal productivity theory.

IV. Marginal Productivity and Income Distribution

Marginal productivities influence factor rewards and, therefore, the share of each factor in national income. It is reasonable to inquire whether the marginal productivity theory is able to explain the overall shares of factors in the national income.

In its original version, the marginal productivity theory of income distribution states that, in the long run and under perfect competition, inputs receive a real rate of return or price per unit, equal to their marginal physical product. This original theory can explain the distribution of the total product without assuming that a production function for the economy is linearly homogeneous.[14] Note that perfect competition must be assumed to exist and a long-run view must be taken.

To prove the above proposition, assume that each firm produces one product X and that two factors A and B are employed. The profit of any firm in the economy is given by

$$\pi = px - w_A l_A - w_B l_B \qquad (10.20)$$

where p, w_A, w_B are the prices of the product and the factors, x is the output of the product, and l_A and l_B the quantities of the factors employed by the firm. In the long run, each firm earns zero profit even though it earns enough to pay the going interest rate on capital.[15] Thus in the long run, $\pi = 0$. Under perfect competition profit maximisation ensures that each factor is paid the value of its marginal product. Hence,

$$w_A = p\frac{\partial x}{\partial l_A} = pMPP_A \qquad (10.21)$$

and

$$w_B = p\frac{\partial x}{\partial l_B} = pMPP_B. \qquad (10.22)$$

Substituting in Equation (10.20) and remembering that $\pi = 0$,

$$\pi = px - p\frac{\partial x}{\partial l_A}l_A - p\frac{\partial x}{\partial l_B}l_B = 0. \tag{10.23}$$

Dividing Equation (10.23) by p,

$$x - \frac{\partial x}{\partial l_A}l_A - \frac{\partial x}{\partial l_B}l_B = 0 \tag{10.24}$$

or, rearranging,

$$x = MPP_A l_A + MPP_B l_B. \tag{10.25}$$

Hence, the distribution of total output is ensured by paying each factor its marginal physical product, or the value of its marginal product. Since profit is zero for all firms, the distribution of total output is accounted for. The argument extends without difficulty to a greater number of products.

But how relevant is the theory? Clearly, perfect competition is not universal and most economic systems are in disequilibrium. Uncertainty is a factor which is ever present, and windfall profits and losses are a matter of common occurrence. Imperfect competition needs to be allowed for and macroeconomic supply and demand influences such as those suggested by Kaldor[16] might be important.

Nevertheless, Cobb and Douglas[17] have come out in support of the marginal productivity theory on the basis of their empirical evidence. They estimated production functions for various economies and used these to predict the share of wages and profit in national output on the basis of the marginal productivity theory. Their predictions were then compared with actual shares. They found that the predicted and actual shares were remarkably close to one another.

For different countries, Cobb and Douglas fitted the production function

$$Y = AN^\alpha K^\beta \tag{10.26}$$

to their data. Y is an index representing real national output, N is an index indicating the employment of labour, K is an index measuring the use of capital and A, α and β are parameters to be estimated from the data. Both cross-sectional and time-series data were used to estimate these parameters for several countries.

Cobb and Douglas reached the conclusion that, allowing for rounding errors and minor divergencies, $\alpha + \beta = 1$ in the economies investigated. In other words, the production function exhibits constant returns to scale, or is linearly homogeneous. It is easily shown that if labour is paid its marginal physical product and capital its marginal physical product that, given this production function, the total product is just distributed. Further, the proportion α goes to labour and $1-\alpha$ to capital. Labour's overall income is

$$\frac{\partial Y}{\partial N}N = N[\alpha A N^{\alpha-1} K^{1-\alpha}] = \alpha A N^\alpha K^{1-\alpha}$$

$$= \alpha Y \tag{10.27}$$

and capital's is

$$\frac{\partial Y}{\partial K}K = K[(1-\alpha)A N^\alpha K^{-\alpha}] = (1-\alpha)A N^\alpha K^{1-\alpha}$$

$$= (1-\alpha)Y. \tag{10.28}$$

Thus the shares of labour and capital are α and $(1-\alpha)$ respectively and total output is accounted for.

Time-series data for the United States for the period 1899-1922 gave Douglas the following production function:

$$Y = 1.35 N^{0.63} K^{0.30} \qquad (10.29)$$

The exponents of N and K do not quite add to one. After taking account of random errors, Douglas concluded that the exponent of N was in the neighbourhood of 0.66 and K in the vicinity of 0.33. Given this production function, the marginal productivity theory predicts that wages should be two-thirds of the national output and profit the other third.

On examining actual shares, it was found that wages were remarkably steady at two-thirds of output. Hence, the actual distribution income is in accordance with that which would be expected from the marginal productivity theory. Douglas' investigations for Australia and South Africa gave similar results.

Solow[18] and others have challenged Douglas' production function. Douglas takes no account of technical progress and does not allow for increased human capital as a result of greater education of "labourers". Theories such as Kaldor's and modifications of it can also explain the relative constancy of labour's share in national output. The argument about the applicability of the marginal productivity theory remains unsettled.

From a social point of view, the personal distribution of income is important. The distribution not only depends on factor prices but on the possession of factors. If there are prejudices in a society, some may be debarred from educational opportunities and have their future incomes reduced because of their lack of education. Some may be fortunate to inherit factors and others may be unfortunate to be born into this world with deficiencies. To what extent should individuals gain or be penalised by such chances? Even though we may never arrive at a satisfactory answer, this question is not to be avoided.

NOTES AND REFERENCES

[1] Differentiality of the firm's profit function is assumed and an end-point solution has been supposed not to occur.
[2] This is the same point as was made by Sraffa and Joan Robinson. It was mentioned in Chapter 9.
[3] Provided that externalities are absent.
[4] If demand for the end-product is perfectly elastic and if the supply curve of the factor is positively sloped, the rate of payment to the factor rises.
[5] The supply curve of the factor is assumed to be normally sloped. Its slope is positive.
[6] See Chapters 13 and 14.
[7] To give an example that w/MPP_{1j} is the marginal cost to firm j of producing an extra unit of product 1: imagine that one unit of factor L produces two units of product 1 at the margin and costs firm j \$1 to purchase. Its marginal cost of producing an extra unit of product 1 is $1/2 = 50$ cents.
[8] This might be true of produce like coffee, cocoa, rubber, some vegetable oils and dairy products.
[9] This is explored in Chapter 13.
[10] See A. M. CARTTER, *The Theory of Wages and Employment*, Irwin, Homewood, 1959.
[11] G. STIGLER, "Production and Distribution in the Short Run", *Journal of Political Economy*, 1939, **47**, pp. 305-27. Reprinted in A.E.A., *Readings in the Theory of Income Distribution*, The Blakiston Company, Philadelphia, 1949, pp. 119-49. Pages 139 and 149 are particularly relevant.
[12] The theory of public goods is discussed in Chapter 21.

[13] N. KALDOR, "Alternative Theories of Distribution", *Review of Economic Studies*, 1955-56, **23**, pp. 83-100.

[14] By Euler's theorem, if a function
$$x = f(l_A, l_B)$$
is homogeneous of degree k,
$$\frac{\partial f}{\partial l_A} l_A + \frac{\partial f}{\partial l_B} l_B = kf(l_A, l_B).$$

Interpreting the function as a production function, where x represents quantity of output and l_A and l_B quantities of the factors, if $k = 1$, the production function is linearly homogeneous (or exhibits constant returns to scale) and it follows that if factors are paid their marginal physical product, the total product is just exhausted. On the other hand, if $k > 1$, payment at a rate equal to marginal physical product more than exhausts total product but, if $k < 1$, such payment does not exhaust it. Thus, it might appear that the marginal productivity can explain the distribution of the total product only if $k = 1$. Yet, as is argued later, this is not so.

[15] In the long run, the firm's normal profit is equal to the rate of interest on its capital. It is not necessary to suppose that the rate of interest falls to zero for the argument below to apply. Capital is treated as a factor in the firm's production function.

[16] KALDOR, op. cit.

[17] For a summary of their view, see P. DOUGLAS, "Are There Laws of Production?", *American Economic Review*, 1948, **37**, pp. 1-41.

[18] R. SOLOW, "A Skeptical Note on the Constancy of Relative Shares", *American Economic Review*, 1958, **48**, pp. 618-31.

FURTHER READING

CARTTER, A. M., *The Theory of Wages and Employment*, Irwin, Homewood, 1959, Chs 5-6.

DOUGLAS, P. H., "Are There Laws of Production?", *American Economic Review*, 1948, **37**, pp. 1-41.

HALEY, B. F., "Value and Distribution", in H. ELLIS (Ed.), *A Survey of Contemporary Economics*, I, Irwin, Homewood, 1949.

KALDOR, N., "Alternative Theories of Distribution", *Review of Economic Studies*, 1955-56, pp. 83-100.

LESTER, R. A., "Shortcomings of Marginal Analysis for Wage-Employment Problems", *American Economic Review*, 1946, **34**, pp. 62-83.

ROBINSON, JOAN, *The Economics of Imperfect Competition*, Macmillan, London, 2nd ed., 1969, Chs 18, 24-26.

SOLOW, R., "A Skeptical Note on the Constancy of Relative Shares", *American Economic Review*, 1958, **48**, pp. 618-31.

CHAPTER 11

General Equilibrium

I. Introductory Ideas

The demand for any commodity depends not just on its own price but on the price of other commodities. The supply of any commodity depends too on its own price and other prices. Consequently, important interconnections exist between markets. Some of these interdependencies have already been noted. For example, the Hicksian formulation of demand theory (outlined in Chapter 6) emphasises that an individual's demand for any product is a function of the *relative* prices of products and his real income. Our discussion of the production of the perfectly competitive firm stressed the significance of relative factor and product prices for its production and employment decisions. The theory did not exclude the possibility that the demand for (and the supply of) any commodity is dependent on the price of all commodities, although for simplicity a partial view was often taken.

While all markets possibly interact, links outside a particular area can be negligible and, hence, concentration on a limited number of markets may be justifiable. In the analysis so far, either isolated markets have been considered as in Chapter 3 or, at most, two or three interrelated markets isolated from the rest of the economy have been examined as in the last chapter. This approach is described as *partial* analysis. A theory which embraces the overall interrelationships of markets or the overall economic system is a *general* one. Such theories frequently aim to determine whether or not the economic system has an equilibrium and, if it does, to examine the properties of the equilibrium. Such theories are described as *general equilibrium* theories, although the term is sometimes loosely applied to models which embrace the general interrelationships of the economy irrespective of whether equilibrium is an important component of the model.

Some problems can be successfully treated by partial models and others are only amenable to analysis in a general framework. The influence of a general rise in prices, of an increase in the general level of money wages, of the devaluation of a currency or an increase in the supply of money are matters which can hardly be analysed in a partial framework. But the consequences of a rise in the demand for a single commodity (such as pins) can be adequately considered in a partial theory. To use a general model in the latter case would involve "hair-splitting" and would be cumbersome and unworthy of our ability to abstract.

But general equilibrium models vary in their complexity. Some, such as that of Walras, involve equations for *each* consumer and *each* producer in a society and others as well. Even for a country with a moderately-sized population, millions of equations need to be simultaneously solved. To make the number of equations and variables manageable, many general equilibrium models are cast in terms of aggregates or are, in other words, macroeconomic models. Some markets or commodities are lumped together and treated as one while at the same time portraying an *overall* view of the economy. For example, Keynes[1] treats consumer goods as one complex and capital goods as another; Leontief,[2] in his input-output analysis, aggregates the supply of products, for example, the steel sector might be treated as one entity and steel as one product, although many different types of steel exist. Aggregative procedures simplify models by eliminating minor links so that the main links in the economy as a whole are emphasised. Other methods, too, are used to reduce complexity. The economic relationships may be assumed to take a particular mathematical form, for example, production functions might be supposed to be linearly homogeneous or, as for input-output models, factors might be assumed to be required in fixed proportions to output. If many problems are to be solved or approximately solved with the feasible means at our disposal, abstraction from micro-details is essential. It is, however, an art to determine whether the exact abstraction used is appropriate.

The earliest markets considered in this book were isolated markets (Chapters 4 and 5). The supply and demand for a commodity were expressed as functions of its price only. This is a very partial approach. The models were of the form

$$D = D(p) \qquad (11.1)$$
$$S = S(p) \qquad (11.2)$$

where p represents the price of the commodity and D and S the quantity demanded and supplied of it respectively. The market was surmised to be in equilibrium if

$$D(p) = S(p). \qquad (11.3)$$

Thus the equilibrium quantity of the commodity is dependent only on its price.

A slightly more general system allows for interdependence in two markets. If subscripts 1 and 2 indicate different commodities, the following demand and supply relationships might occur:

$$D_1 = D_1(p_1, p_2). \qquad (11.4)$$
$$S_1 = S_1(p_1, p_2). \qquad (11.5)$$
$$D_2 = D_2(p_1, p_2). \qquad (11.6)$$
$$S_2 = S_2(p_1, p_2). \qquad (11.7)$$

The quantity demanded of any single commodity and its supply depend on its own price and the price of the related commodity. The two markets might be supposed to be in equilibrium if the following equations are simultaneously satisfied:

$$D_1(p_1, p_2) = S_1(p_1, p_2) \qquad (11.8)$$
$$D_2(p_1, p_2) = S_2(p_1, p_2). \qquad (11.9)$$

Consequently the equilibrium quantity of any one commodity depends upon its own price and the price of the related commodity. A shift upward in the demand function in one market has repercussions on both markets. To give an example, an increase in consumers' preferences for margarine will not only have a repercussion on the equilibrium price and output of margarine, but also upon the equilibrium price and output of butter. Maybe other markets will be affected, too, for example, those for shortenings

General Equilibrium

of various types and for vegetable oils. Our system of equations would need to be extended to embrace these. By extending it suitably, we might at last include all markets in the economy with their interconnections and equilibrium conditions. Below we shall consider models which do include all markets.

Before examining these general equilibrium models, it is well to recall some difficulties which we foresaw for equilibrium in isolated markets, for these difficulties do not disappear in general equilibrium models. The first possibility is that the system has no equilibrium at all. The set of equations describing the system might be underdetermined or overdetermined—the number of independent equations might be less than or in excess of the number of variables to be determined. Information could be insufficient to determine an equilibrium or the information could be inconsistent. Even if the number of independent equations and unknowns are equal, the equation system describing the economy might not have a solution which has economic meaning. A solution in terms of real numbers for prices and quantities might not exist. A case of this type is illustrated in Fig. 11.1 for a single market. Again, the system has an economically meaningless solution if it implies equilibrium for negative prices and quantities of commodities. A solution of this type is indicated by $(\bar{p}, \bar{X})$ for the single market example of Fig. 11.2 where, for any positive price, supply exceeds demand. Given the restrictions $X \geqslant 0$ and $p \geqslant 0$, a "quasi-equilibrium" might in fact be

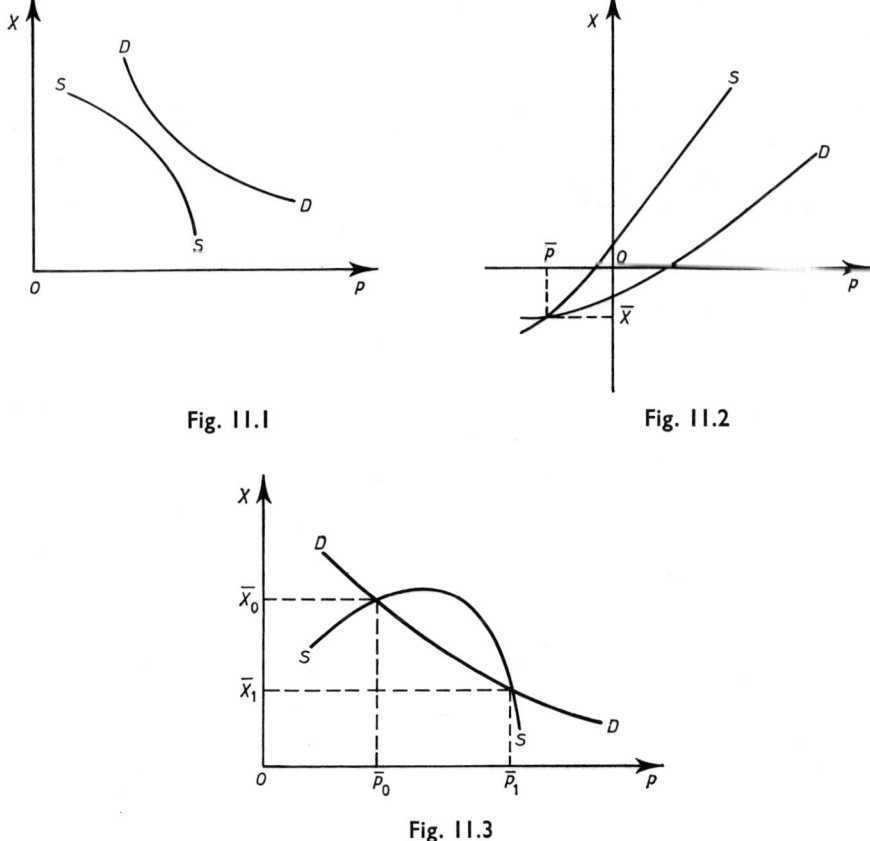

Fig. 11.1   Fig. 11.2

Fig. 11.3

established for ($p = 0$, $X = 0$). To give Fig. 11.2 a crude macro-interpretation, assume that p is the money wage-rate and X the overall employment of labour. Imagine that initially the supply and demand curves are such that the equilibrium employment of labour is in the positive quadrant of Fig. 11.2 but that the curves subsequently take up the position depicted. Consequently wages begin to fall and a movement is set up which, in the absence of exogenous restraints, drives the economy to complete unemployment of labour. Furthermore, the quasi-equilibrium position of unemployment may be stable. (The case shown is stable for Walrasian and Marshallian reaction assumptions.) Again the solution of a general equilibrium system need not be unique; the system might possess multiple equilibria. Equilibrium may correspond to high and low levels of activity as in the single market example of Fig. 11.3 in which equilibria arise for a price of $\bar{p}_0$ and $\bar{p}_1$. Or again, as in some general equilibrium models of an economy, the equilibrium might be unique only for prices and the quantity of money.[3]

Other dimensions of importance are the stability or otherwise of equilibria and the speed and direction of approach to an equilibrium. As was emphasised in Chapter 4, for practical purposes it is vital to more than determine whether stability exists because the path of approach to an equilibrium can be of crucial importance. Taking a macro-example, it is not enough just to know that an economy has an equilibrium at full employment if it does indeed have one. This equilibrium might be stable or unstable and not unique. But, even if it can be shown that an economy has a unique and globally stable equilibrium at full employment, this is little comfort if the economy has deviated from its full-employment equilibrium and its return, although certain, is expected to be slow or to occur only after unemployment has considerably worsened. Economic policy which is based just on comparative statics and which fails to take paths to equilibrium into account can have inhuman consequences.

Arrow, McKenzie, Debreu and others[4] have shown that general equilibrium can be achieved with perfect competition throughout the economy. At least, they have extended the set of conditions under which it is proved that perfect competition results in a general equilibrium. But even their systems fail to encompass many general relationships of our existing economies, for example, the occurrence of monopolies in particular sectors and the provision of public services. Even though the conditions under which general equilibrium can be shown to occur have been widened, significant decreasing costs and other factors must lead us to question the relevance of their models. Furthermore, as we have already indicated, perfect competition *throughout* the economy can and most likely is incompatible with economic efficiency, given that decreasing cost is significant in some areas of activity.

Contemporary general equilibrium models can only be regarded as a first step towards the building of more realistic ones. Nevertheless, even these models have allowed us to tackle significant issues. For example, what role do money balances play in helping to restore equilibrium in an economy? Neoclassical economists allotted an important role to these, whereas Keynes believed that increases of the money supply would fail to restore full-employment equilibrium in an already depressed economy. In order to give some examples of general equilibrium systems and to bring out the significance of money, let us consider a barter economy and then introduce money.

General Equilibrium

II. A Barter Economy

Imagine an economy in which perfect competition is universal but commodities are merely bartered one for another. We could, as Walras[5] originally did, specify demand and supply relationships for all the commodities of this economy in detail, even specifying those for individual consumers and firms. But rather than do this, let us adopt simplified Walrasian models due to Samuelson and Hicks.[6] We shall deal with market aggregate demand and supply (or excess demand) relationships only, although it will be realised from the earlier discussion that individual decisions lie behind these.

Assume that the economy involves $i = 1, \ldots, n$ commodities of which $i = 1, \ldots, k$ might be factors of production and $i = k+1, \ldots, n$ might be products. No money prices exist in the economy, only ratios in which commodities exchange. Select one good arbitrarily as a *numéraire* commodity and list the rates (ratios) at which one unit of the *numéraire* commodity exchanges for other commodities. The exchange ratios can be designated by $\{p_1, p_2, \ldots, p_k, p_{k+1}, \ldots, p_{n-1}, 1\}$ if commodity n has been chosen as the *numéraire*. Indicating the quantity supplied of the ith commodity by X_i^s and the quantity demanded by X_i^d, the market demand and supply functions for each of the commodities of the economy can be written as follows.

There are n demand equations, one for each commodity, and the demand for any commodity depends upon its rate of exchange with every other commodity.

Demand functions $X_i^d = X_i^d(p_1, \ldots, p_{n-1}), \quad (i = 1, \ldots n).$ (11.10)

Similarly, there are n supply equations and the supply of any commodity depends upon the rate at which it can be bartered for every other commodity.

Supply functions $X_i^s = X_i^s(p_1, \ldots, p_{n-1}), \quad (i = 1, \ldots n).$ (11.11)

The economy is only in general equilibrium if all the commodity markets are simultaneously in equilibrium. The exchange ratios and quantities of commodities must be such that the amount which buyers are willing to purchase and the amount which sellers are willing to dispose of are just equal in all markets. The exchange ratios must satisfy the following n equations simultaneously:

Equilibrium conditions $X_i^d(p_1, \ldots, p_{n-1}) = X_i^s(p_1, \ldots, p_{n-1}), (i = 1, \ldots, n)$ (11.12)

If this set of equations has a solution in $(p_1, \ldots, p_{n-1})$, the equilibrium quantities can be determined by substituting the solution values into Equations (11.10) or (11.11). I shall return to the question of whether or not a solution exists presently. But note that the relationships indicate that a change in a demand or supply function for any one product (or a variation in any exchange rate) *might* set off a wave of reactions which alters equilibrium in all markets.

Before considering the existence of a solution, let us divide the above system into product and factor markets. The system restated is

Factor markets $\begin{cases} X_i^d = X_i^d(p_1, \ldots, p_{n-1}), \ (i = 1, \ldots, k). & (11.13) \\ X_i^s = X_i^s(p_1, \ldots, p_{n-1}), \ (i = 1, \ldots, k). & (11.14) \end{cases}$

Product markets $\begin{cases} X_i^d = X_i^d(p_1, \ldots, p_{n-1}), \ (i = k+1, \ldots, n). & (11.15) \\ X_i^s = X_i^s(p_1, \ldots, p_{n-1}), \ (i = k+1, \ldots, n). & (11.16) \end{cases}$

General equilibrium requires

$$X_i^d = X_i^s, \ (i = 1, \ldots, n). \qquad (11.17)$$

One might, of course, wish to group the markets in various ways. Markets for different types of labour might be grouped together, for example, and those for capital goods might be "bunched" together. One might even wish to go further and aggregate the items which appear in categories of this type, as macro-theories do, in order to achieve simplicity. But we shall not follow that path here.

Returning now to the question of whether the set of equations in (11.12) have a solution, there are n equations and $n-1$ unknowns, the exchange ratios, so at first sight the system seems to be overdetermined. But it can be shown that one of these equations is linearly dependent on the others and can be eliminated, thus making the number of equations and unknowns equal.

In this barter system it must be true that

$$\sum_{i=1}^{n} p_i X_i^s \equiv \sum_{i=1}^{n} p_i X_i^d. \tag{11.18}$$

This we might equally well call *Walras'* or *Say's Law*. The value of goods disposed of by sellers when expressed in terms of the *numéraire* equals the value of goods received by buyers. Rewriting Equation (11.18),

$$\sum_{i=1}^{n-1} p_i X_i^s + X_n^s \equiv \sum_{i=1}^{n-1} p_i X_i^d + X_n^d, \tag{11.19}$$

whence it follows that if

$$X_i^s = X_i^d \text{ for } i = 1, \ldots, n-1, \tag{11.20}$$

$$\sum_{i=1}^{n-1} p_i X_i^s = \sum_{i=1}^{n-1} p_i X_i^d \tag{11.21}$$

and
$$X_n^s = X_n^d. \tag{11.22}$$

If all markets except one are in equilibrium, the remaining one is automatically in equilibrium. Thus *any* $n-1$ equations of Equation (11.12) can be selected to determine the $n-1$ unknowns, the price ratios. Once solutions for the price ratios are determined, the equilibrium quantities of demand and supply can be determined in the straightforward manner mentioned earlier.

However, it has been observed by mathematical economists, such as Lancaster,[7] that an equal number of equations and unknowns is neither necessary nor sufficient for a solution to a set of equations; and that non-negativity restraints of an economic system should be explicitly taken into account. These restraints have been allowed for in the Arrow-Debreu-McKenzie model.[8] Arrow, Debreu and McKenzie have used topological methods to prove the existence of general equilibrium for their representation of the competitive economy. The exposition is beyond an elementary book of this kind.[9]

An even simpler general equilibrium system for a barter economy has been presented by Hicks. Since it is frequently used in theory, it might be of interest to give a brief outline of it. It relies upon *excess demand* functions. The excess demand, X_i^E for the ith commodity, is the difference between the quantity demanded and the quantity supplied of the commodity as a function of prices or exchange rates.

The concept is easily illustrated for an isolated market. Let X represent the quantity of the good under consideration and p indicate its price. Figure 11.4 shows supply

General Equilibrium

and demand curves of normal slope and Fig. 11.5 illustrates their corresponding excess demand function for the good. This excess demand function shifts if either the demand or supply functions shift. Note, too, that if Walras' reaction law holds, then an equilibrium is stable if the excess demand function has a negative slope and unstable if it has a positive slope. With this background, the Hicksian system for a barter economy can be outlined.

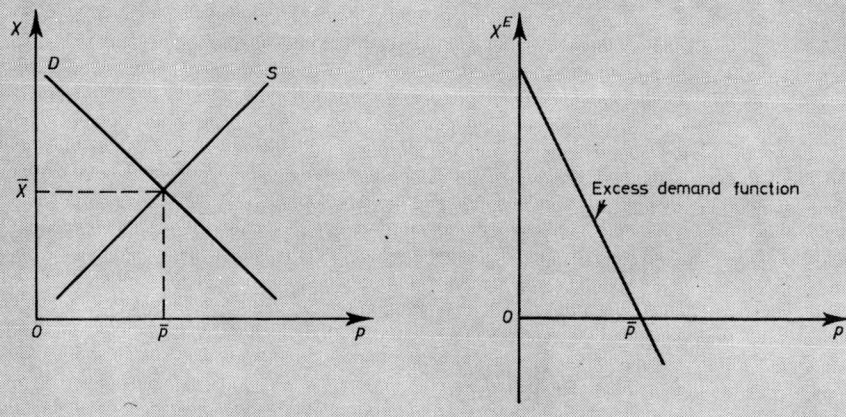

Fig. 11.4   Fig. 11.5

The excess demand for the ith commodity is $X_i^E = X_i^d - X_i^s$. Excess demand for any commodity depends upon all the exchange ratios and general equilibrium requires that there be no excess demand in any market. General equilibrium in the Hicksian system requires

$$X_i^E(p_1, \ldots, p_{n-1}) = 0, \ (i = 1, \ldots, n). \tag{11.23}$$

Once again, there are $n-1$ unknowns, the exchange ratios, and n equations. However, using Walras' Law (Equation 11.18) it can be shown that one equation is unnecessary. Subtracting the left hand side of Equation (11.18) from the right hand side,

$$\sum_{i=1}^{n} p_i X_i^E \equiv 0. \tag{11.24}$$

Rearranging and remembering that product n is the *numéraire* commodity and therefore has an exchange ratio of 1,

$$X_n^E \equiv -\sum_{i=1}^{n-1} p_i X_i^E. \tag{11.25}$$

Consequently, if $n-1$ markets are in equilibrium so is the nth. If $X_i^E = 0$ for $i = 1, \ldots, n-1$, then from Equation (11.25), $X_n^E = 0$. One market equation can be dropped and the choice of which one to eliminate is arbitrary. The number of equations and unknowns becomes equal and the likelihood that the system has a solution increases.

Stability of the general equilibrium of this system has been studied by Lange and Samuelson.[10] Using the correspondence principle (outlined in Chapter 5), Samuelson has proved *a fundamental proposition of general equilibrium theory*.

Assume that one of the equations has been eliminated on the basis of Walras' Law so that Hick's system is

$$X_i^E(p_1, \ldots, p_{n-1}) = 0, \quad (i = 1, \ldots, n-1). \tag{11.26}$$

Furthermore, suppose that the change of exchange ratios can be described by Walras' reaction hypothesis so that

$$\frac{dp_i}{dt} = f_i(X_i^E), \; f_i(0) = 0, \; f_i' > 0, \quad (i = 1, \ldots, n-1) \tag{11.27}$$

This is a set of $n-1$ differential equations in the exchange ratios $\{p_1, \ldots, p_{n-1}\}$ since excess demand in any market depends on all exchange ratios. A stationary solution is reached if $\frac{dp_i}{dt} = 0$ for $i = 1, \ldots, n-1$. Putting $\frac{dp_i}{dt} = 0$ for $i = 1, \ldots, n-1$, it is observed that Equation (11.27) reduces to Equation (11.26) which implies that Equation (11.26) (or (11.23)) is its corresponding static model. Using the correspondence principle, Samuelson has shown along similar lines to that outlined for the isolated market in Chapter 5, that $\frac{dp_i}{dt}$ ($i = 1, \ldots, n-1$) approaches zero only if in the *static* system, Equation (11.26), an increase in the excess demand (an increase of demand or decrease of supply) of any commodity, other things being equal, leads to an increase in its exchange ratio. Hence, the general equilibrium system is stable *only* if in a comparative static framework an increase in the excess demand for any commodity, other relationships being unchanged, leads to an increase in the exchange ratio of the commodity. This, however, is assuming that Hicks' general equilibrium system and Walras' Law of motion are relevant. *Conversely*, if the general equilibrium system, Equation (11.27), is stable, an increase in the demand for any commodity or a decrease in its supply, all other relationships being unvaried, results in an increase in the exchange ratio of the commodity. This is so *after all repercussions* throughout the entire market system have been taken into account.

So far no money has entered the system. The existence of a pure barter economy has been assumed. However, an economy without money of some form is almost unimaginable and certainly deviates far from our own economies. Let us, therefore, consider general equilibrium systems in which money is present.

III. Money and General Equilibrium

Economists have differed widely in their assessment of the influence of money on general equilibrium and the manner in which it influences the economic system. Classical economists regarded money as a veil and of no significance for real relationships in the economy, at least in the long run. In the classical economic system, general *equilibrium* exchange ratios of goods (the real part of the economic system) are completely unaffected by variations in the quantity of money. According to classical theory, the barter models discussed in the last section are sufficient to determine equilibrium exchange ratios for commodities (excluding money) and absolute price levels can be determined independently by reference to a quantity of money equation.

Take the first general equilibrium system outlined above in Equations (11.10), (11.11) and (11.12). The variables, $\{p_1, \ldots, p_n\}$ may be interpreted as exchange ratios or as relative prices. This system is solved by the means indicated, one real equation being eliminated by Say's Law. Let $\bar{X}_i^s$ represent the equilibrium quantity for the ith commodity and $\bar{p}_i$ represent its equilibrium exchange ratio in terms of the *numéraire*, n.

Absolute price levels are obtained by multiplying exchange ratios by a common factor, λ, which is equal to the money price of the *numéraire*. Classical economists determine λ from either Fisher's equation of exchange (quantity theory of money equation) or the Cambridge version of the quantity theory of money.

Fisher's equation of exchange is

$$MV = PT \tag{11.28}$$

where M represents the supply of money, V the velocity of its circulation which is assumed to be constant and known, and PT the value of transactions. In terms of the above model, Equation (11.28) can be written as

$$MV = \sum_{i=1}^{n} \lambda p_i X_i^s. \tag{11.29}$$

The equilibrium values of X_i^s and p_i having been determined from the real set of equations and M and V being known, λ is known.

$$\lambda = MV / (\sum_{i=1}^{n-1} \bar{p}_i \bar{X}_i + \bar{X}_n). \tag{11.30}$$

In equilibrium, money prices rise in the same proportion as the quantity of money. It follows that an increase in the quantity of money does not affect relative prices, nor real quantities (in general equilibrium).

Alternatively, the system might be completed by using the Cambridge equation rather than Fisher's. The Cambridge equation is $M = bY$ where b is a constant and Y is national income. M represents the supply of money and bY the demand for money which is assumed to be proportional to income. Expressing the Cambridge equation in the above terminology,[11] it becomes

$$M = b\lambda \sum_{i=1}^{k} p_i X_i. \tag{11.31}$$

With M given, b known and p_i, X_i ($i = 1, \ldots, k$) determined from the real system, the multiplicative factor, λ, can be resolved from Equation (11.31). Money prices are then determined by multiplying the equilibrium exchange ratios by λ.

This supply and demand equation for money implies in conjunction with the remainder of the system that an increase in the quantity of money increases all equilibrium prices in the same proportion. Since an increase in the quantity of money raises absolute prices in the same proportion, the relative prices of commodities are unaltered and so, too, are the equilibrium quantities of commodities. Taking the system as a whole, the equilibrium quantities of commodities other than money (the real part of the system) are homogeneous of degree zero in absolute prices *and* the quantity of money. Note that, taking all markets together, the real system is not homogeneous of degree zero for absolute prices alone. Imagine that the system is initially in equilibrium and let all prices increase in a fixed proportion without the quantity of money increasing. The system then is clearly put into disequilibrium for using either Equation (11.29) or (11.31) and assuming no change in the velocity of circulation, the "money market" moves from equilibrium to disequilibrium. Real cash balances become short. In an attempt to increase cash balances, sellers may increase their supplies and buyers may reduce their demands, so lowering absolute prices. This continues until absolute prices are such that Equation (11.29) or (11.31) is satisfied, and the original equilibrium level of absolute prices is restored. (This is one possible mechanism of readjustment. Actually the dynamic factors involved may prevent a return to exactly the old equilibrium. In disequilibrium, the distribution of wealth might be changed thus altering some of the demand and the supply equations. Nevertheless, the comparative static system above is homogeneous of degree zero in absolute prices and the quantity of money.)

Both Lange and Patinkin[12] have pointed out deficiencies in the classical method of introducing money into the general equilibrium system. They object to the assumption of Say's Law which in a monetary system does not necessarily hold and, indeed, observation indicates that it is not satisfied. Second, they feel that interpretation of the quantity theory exchange equation as the demand and supply of money leads to certain inconsistencies. Third, Patinkin holds that the demand and supply equations for commodities should specifically include real money balances as a variable. Classical theory does not explicitly include money in utility functions. But clearly money itself does possess utility—it facilitates transactions and is, because of its liquidity, valuable for meeting uncertainty. The utility of money is a function of an individual's real balance of it, that is his nominal balance deflated by the general price level.

In the non-barter economy, Say's Law is

$$\lambda \sum_{i=1}^{n} p_i X_i^s = \lambda \sum_{i=1}^{n} p_i X_i^d \qquad (11.32)$$

and asserts that the total value of commodities supplied (other than money) equals the total value of commodities (other than money) exchanged in return. Every demand for a commodity (other than money) is matched by an equal supply in dollar terms of some other "real" commodity. But this equality does not necessarily hold.

In a monetary economy the value of goods (excluding money) supplied may be less than, greater than, or equal to the spending on real goods during any given period of time, differences being accounted for by changes in money balances. Nevertheless, Walras' Law applies here. The value of the supplies of all commodities *including* money is equal to the value of all demands including the demand for money. Adding money as commodity $n+1$ and letting p_i represent the absolute price of commodities (remembering that the price of a unit of money is 1), Walras' Law asserts that

$$X_{n+1}^s + \sum_{i=1}^{n} p_i D_i^s \equiv \sum_{i=1}^{n} p_i X_s^d + X_{n+1}^d. \qquad (11.33)$$

In general equilibrium models (such as that of Patinkin) Walras' Law, Equation (11.33), enables unknowns and equations to be equated so that there is no need to resort to Say's Law which in a monetary economy is not likely to hold.

Some aspects of Patinkin's general equilibrium system are worth noting.[13] His supply and demand functions for commodities other than money may be expressed as

$$X_i^d = X_i^d\left(\frac{p_1}{P}, \ldots, \frac{p_n}{P}, \frac{\bar{M}}{P}\right), \quad (i = 1, \ldots, n), \qquad (11.34)$$

$$X_i^s = X_i^s\left(\frac{p_1}{P}, \ldots, \frac{p_n}{P}, \frac{\bar{M}}{P}\right), \quad (i = 1, \ldots, n). \qquad (11.35)$$

P is the average level of the prices of commodities and $\bar{M}$ represents the supply of money. The demand and supply of any real commodity depends upon all relative prices *and* upon the level of real money balances. In order to complete Patinkin's system, the demand and supply equation for money must be added to the above. This is his system if credit markets are absent.

Note that real money balances are explicitly stated to affect the supply and demand of a commodity. If the supply of money is constant, a rise in P affects the demand and supply for all "real" commodities and the demand for money. Other things being equal, a rise in the supply of money influences the demand and supplies of all real commodities. Yet, as in the classical system, equilibrium quantities of supply and demand of real commodities are unvaried in Patinkin's system (in the absence of credit markets) if prices *and* the quantity of money rise in the same proportion. Within the comparative static framework, Patinkin's system implies that, if a system is in equilibrium and the quantity of money is increased, disequilibrium results if all other things remain unchanged. Equilibrium can only be restored if all prices increase in the same proportion as the quantity of money. The result is similar to the earlier classical one but is achieved without assuming Say's Law and within a model which seems to be more realistic.

Observe that, if the real balance effect is important for the demand and supply of commodities, this calls for a modification of the partial theories which were discussed earlier in this book. Take consumption, for example. A rise in the price of a product, all other prices being constant, not only has a substitution and income effect but also has a real balance effect. If only one or a limited range of commodities rise in price by a small fraction, the real balance effect might be minimal, but this need not be so for general price increases. Yet even in the general context the significance of the real balance effect has been disputed. Keynes[14] doubted its importance, whereas Pigou[15] believed it to be significant. Keynes foresaw little chance of a depressed economy being returned to full employment through the operation of the real balance effect. This is an important issue in macroeconomics.

IV. Conclusion

Economic models can just as easily founder on excesses of realism as on lack of realism; and an admirable abstraction for one purpose can be entirely inappropriate for another. Thus, partial and general equilibrium analyses both have their uses.

In partial analysis some interdependencies between markets are deliberately left out in order to simplify. This is not a failing. Provided that significant relationships for the problem under investigation are not neglected, partial analysis can be the optimal approach to problem solving.

But, as pointed out earlier, some problems can only be tackled by general analysis. The ideal allocation of resources for a society can only be resolved ultimately in a general framework which allows for interdependencies in an economy. However, occasionally a partial analysis can give valuable insights and, if the assumption of groups of non-competing factors is satisfied, can resolve particular allocation issues. In Chapter 13 the ideal allocation of resources in a general framework will be considered.

Yet general equilibrium models are abstractions. Once again this in itself is an asset because actual economies are so complex in their details that any model which included all the details would be beyond manipulation and of limited value. Simplification of general models has been achieved both by aggregation and by assuming that particular mathematical relationships are satisfied in the economy generally. Input-output analysis, which is outlined in the next chapter, adopts both means for simplification.

NOTES AND REFERENCES

[1] J. M. KEYNES, *The General Theory of Employment, Interest and Money*, Macmillan, London, 1936.

[2] W. LEONTIEF, *The Structure of the American Economy 1919-1939*, Oxford University Press, Oxford, 1941; 2nd ed., 1951.

[3] If the level of money prices and the quantity of money are increased in the same proportion, the equilibrium quantities which are traded may remain unchanged.

[4] K. J. ARROW and G. DEBREU, "Existence of an Equilibrium for a Competitive Economy", *Econometrica*, 1954, **22**, pp. 265-90. G. DEBREU, *Theory of Value*, John Wiley, New York, 1959. L. W. MCKENZIE, "On the Existence of General Equilibrium for a Competitive Market", *Econometrica*, 1959, **27**, pp. 54-71. For an excellent coverage of these and related contributions, see J. QUIRK and R. SAPOSNIK, *Introduction to General Equilibrium Theory and Welfare Economics*, McGraw-Hill, New York, 1968, Ch. 3.

[5] L. WALRAS, *Elements d'économie politique pure* (1874). Translated by W. JAFFE, *Elements of Pure Economics*, Irwin, Homewood, 1954.

[6] J. R. HICKS, *Value and Capital*, Clarendon Press, Oxford, 1939; 2nd ed., 1946. P. SAMUELSON, *Foundations of Economic Analysis*, Harvard University Press, Cambridge, 1947.

[7] K. LANCASTER, *Mathematical Economics*, The Macmillan Company, New York, 1968, Ch. 9.

[8] See the references given in Reference 4.

[9] For a comparatively easy exposition see QUIRK and SAPOSNIK, op. cit., Ch. 3.

[10] O. LANGE, *Price Flexibility and Employment*, Blakiston, Bloomington, 1944, Appendix. SAMUELSON, op. cit.

[11] The term bY rather than the traditional kY is used here to avoid confusion with the kth factor.

[12] O. LANGE, "Say's Law: A Restatement and Criticism", in O. LANGE et al. (Eds), *Studies in Mathematical Economics and Econometrics*, Chicago University Press, Chicago, 1942. D. PATINKIN, "A Reconsideration of the General Equilibrium Theory of Money", *Review of Economic Studies*, 1950-51, **18**, pp. 42-61.

[13] PATINKIN, op. cit. See also D. PATINKIN, *Money, Interest and Prices*, 1st ed., 1956; 2nd ed., Harper and Row, Evanston, 1965.

[14] KEYNES, op. cit.

[15] A. C. PIGOU, "Economic Progress in a Stable Environment", *Economica*, 1947, **14**, pp. 180-8.

FURTHER READING

BALDERSTON, J., "Models of General Equilibrium", in O. MORGENSTERN, (Ed.), *Economic Activity Analysis*, John Wiley, New York, 1954, pp. 3-38.

BAUMOL, W. J., *Economic Theory and Operations Analysis*, 2nd ed., Prentice-Hall, Englewood Cliffs, 1965, Ch. 15 and Secs 1-3 of Ch. 20.

HANSEN, B., *Lectures in Economic Theory*, Studentlitteratur, Lund, 3rd ed., 1969, Part I, Lectures 3-8.

HENDERSON, J., and R. QUANDT, *Microeconomic Theory*, McGraw-Hill, New York, 1958, Ch. 5.

HICKS, J. R., *Value and Capital*, 2nd ed., Clarendon Press, Oxford, 1946, Chs 4, 5, and 8.

MANSFIELD, E., *Microeconomics*, W. W. Norton, New York, 1970, Ch. 14.

*QUIRK, J. and R. SAPOSNIK, *Introduction to General Equilibrium Theory and Welfare Economics*, McGraw-Hill, New York, 1968, Ch. 3.

*SAMUELSON, P. A., *Foundations of Economic Analysis*, Harvard University Press, Cambridge, 1947, Ch. 9.

---

* More advanced.

CHAPTER 12

Input-Output Analysis

I. Introduction

Wassily Leontief, while being profoundly impressed by the general equilibrium theories of Walras and Pareto,[1] was aware that the theories were too complex, too general in their mathematical relationships for the parameters describing the system to be found empirically for any existing economy. Even manipulation of neo-classical general equilibrium theories is difficult and the theories may, because of their detail, obscure the main interconnections between industries. To remedy these defects and yet emphasise interindustry connections, Leontief suggested[2] and championed input-output analysis, a general system which portrays all interconnections between industries by linear relationships. Leontief's simplification is to depict all relationships and interconnections in the economy by linear relationships and bring general theories of the economy, which still have details on individual industries, into the realm of the measurable. His method enables the structure of any *particular* economy to be analysed.

In terms of its detail of the economy, Leontief's approach stands midway between general theories, such as that of Walras,[3] and very aggregative macro-theories, such as that of Keynes.[4] Walras' system even describes the behaviour of individuals, whereas Keynes' macro-theory abstracts from individual industries. Leontief, in his approach, deals with industries or sectors of the economy, but neglects individual economic decision-makers.

The aim of interindustry analysis is to employ national accounting data (on an industry-by-industry basis) which for each industry indicates its deliveries to other industries and its inputs from others. The values of these transactions are then used to calculate coefficients indicating the dependence of one industry on another for inputs. Given these coefficients, the effect of increasing the output of an industry upon the output of all others can be predicted. Or again, if targets have been set for the net bill of goods (output after allowing for production used up in the process), one can calculate if these targets can be achieved and the variation of the economy's production which is needed in order to meet the targets. Clearly, these relationships are important for planning and predicting changes in an economy. Under certain conditions, the impact upon the cost of each product of a price rise of one product or of a primary input can be also calculated. In a period when a government is trying to restrain price increases of "key" products in order to check inflation, details of this nature can be of considerable help in selecting key products.

Although interindustry economics has applications to all economies, it would seem to be most applicable to centrally planned and directed economies. In the Soviet

Union, pioneers of input-output analysis, such as Kantorovich,[5] have repeatedly urged its increased application. As yet it seems only to have been used on a limited experimental basis. Perhaps its heroic simplifications constitute serious shortcomings after all.

Input-output analysis assumes that each unit of output of a commodity requires inputs in unvarying amounts and fixed proportions. Not only are constant returns to scale imagined to be the case but inputs are supposed to be required in fixed proportions. However, Samuelson has shown[6] that the latter assumption can be relaxed under circumstances which are mentioned below.

A variety of input-output models now exist. Models may be static or dynamic, and closed or open. In the dynamic models some of the outputs of the previous period become inputs in the next. A model is closed if all of its variables are endogenously determined. The demands of labourers, the government and others might be given from the model itself. Normally, however, input-output models are open. Some of the demand variables are given from outside the model. The government itself may set targets (exogenously given) for the final net bill of goods of the economy, that is, provide a list of the quantities of commodities which it wishes the economy to produce after allowance has been made for any output used up in production. Only closed static input-output models will be considered in this book. These models examine only interconnections between industries in the same period and while the demand for intermediate goods (commodities required in the production of others) is endogenously determined, final demands (those of the households, governments and for exports) are exogenously provided.

Generally, interindustry analysis presents its information in tabular form, since this is a very convenient way of showing interindustry connections. Inputs, both interindustry inputs and primary inputs, such as labour, land, and so on, are listed down the columns and the output of an industry (dissected into its allocation industry by industry) is presented across the rows. This is illustrated below. A simple model which involves only two industries (sectors) and one primary input is outlined first. Limitations of the general approach are then discussed and a more general formulation, in terms of matrix algebra, is given.

II. A Simple Input-Output Model

Consider an economy with only two sectors ("industries")—agriculture and manufacturing. Agriculture requires inputs from a manufacturing industry, such as tractors, fertilisers, etc., as well as inputs from agriculture itself, such as fodder crops for animals, seeds for new crops and so on. Agriculture depends upon inputs from both sectors. Manufacturing industry also requires inputs from both sectors. The requirements of both industries can be shown in a tabular form which brings out their interdependence. Since a diversity of products are involved, rather than show the physical amount of goods passing interindustry, let us state the value of goods flowing between industries. Observations of a previous year might indicate transactions of the value indicated in Table 12.1. This is a transactions matrix. This one indicates that, say, for 1970, the economy observed produced $10m of agricultural products and $20m of manufacturing products, it being assumed that labour is the only primary input. The values of the economy's gross outlays (which equal, by national accounting identity, the value

Input-Output Analysis

Table 12.1. A Transactions Matrix

		User of the output	
		Agriculture	Manufacturing
Producer of the output	Agriculture Manufacturing	$1m $2m	$3m $4m
Primary input	Labour	$7m	$13m
	TOTAL	$10m	$20m

of its gross output) were $10m and $20m for agriculture and manufacturing respectively. Each dollar's worth of agricultural output required 10c of agricultural produce, 20c of manufactures and 70c of labour. Manufacturing output required 15c of agricultural goods, 20c of manufactures and 65c of labour per dollar of output. Taking dollars as the unit of measurement, input-output coefficients based upon the data of Table 12.1 are shown in Table 12.2, a technology matrix. The entries in the body show the fraction, by value, of inputs listed on the left hand side which are required to produce a dollar's worth of the output of the product, listed at the top of the matrix. Leontief assumes that these technology coefficients are constant. Inputs are required in the same proportions indicated no matter what is the level of output. Given these coefficients, it is possible to describe the production possibilities of the economy.

Table 12.2. A Technology Matrix

		User of the output	
		Agriculture	Manufacturing
Producer of the output	Agriculture Manufacturing Labour	0.1 0.2 0.7	0.15 0.2 0.65
	TOTAL	1.0	1.0

For example, if A represents the total output of agriculture in dollars, M the total output of manufacturing in dollars and if the availability of primary inputs is not a problem, the net surplus available from a gross agricultural output of A is

$$C_1 = A - 0.1A - 0.15M. \quad (12.1)$$

$$\begin{bmatrix} \text{Net surplus of} \\ \text{agricultural} \\ \text{output} \end{bmatrix} = \begin{bmatrix} \text{Gross value of} \\ \text{agricultural output} \end{bmatrix} - \begin{bmatrix} \text{Use of} \\ \text{agricultural output} \\ \text{in agriculture} \end{bmatrix} - \begin{bmatrix} \text{Use of} \\ \text{agricultural output} \\ \text{in manufacturing} \end{bmatrix}$$

The item C_1 is termed the *final demand* for agricultural output. It may be set as a target figure by the government. This net surplus is available after the productive process to meet the demands of householders, of the government and of export. Similarly, the net surplus available from a manufacturing output of M is

$$C_2 = M - 0.2A - 0.2M. \quad (12.2)$$

$$\begin{bmatrix} \text{Net surplus of} \\ \text{manufacturing} \\ \text{output} \end{bmatrix} = \begin{bmatrix} \text{Gross value of} \\ \text{manufacturing output} \end{bmatrix} - \begin{bmatrix} \text{Use of} \\ \text{manufacturing output} \\ \text{in agriculture} \end{bmatrix} - \begin{bmatrix} \text{Use of} \\ \text{manufacturing output} \\ \text{in manufacturing} \end{bmatrix}$$

With targets for C_1 and C_2 set, it is clear that we can solve these two equations to determine the output of agriculture and manufacturing which is necessary to meet the targets. In doing so, account is taken of all technological interdependencies.

Let us abstract the problem slightly. Coefficients such as those in Table 12.2 can be represented by the elements a_{ij} as in Table 12.3. For example, a_{11} corresponds to 0.1. Rewriting Equations (12.1) and (12.2) using these coefficients, the net surplus of agricultural output becomes

$$C_1 = A - a_{11}A - a_{12}M, \tag{12.3}$$

Table 12.3. A Technology Matrix

		User of the output	
		Agriculture	Manufacturing
Producer of the output	Agriculture	a_{11}	a_{12}
	Manufacturing	a_{21}	a_{22}
	Labour	a_{31}	a_{32}

and the net surplus of manufactured goods,

$$C_2 = M - a_{21}A - a_{22}M. \tag{12.4}$$

If the surpluses C_1 and C_2 are *given* by the government, it ought to be possible to solve these equations to find the output of agriculture and manufacturing which is necessary. There are only two unknowns, A and M, and there are two equations.

Rearranging Equation (12.3),

$$A = \frac{a_{12}}{1-a_{11}}M + \frac{1}{1-a_{11}}C_1. \tag{12.5}$$

This can be inserted in Equation (12.4) to give a solution for M which we can represent as $\bar{M}$. $\bar{M}$ in turn can be substituted in Equation (12.5) to give the necessary level of agricultural output, $\bar{A}$. In turn, the labour requirement can be calculated. It is $a_{31}\bar{A} + a_{32}\bar{M}$.

Let us graph variants of functions, Equations (12.3) and (12.4), and indicate solutions for A and M. Equation (12.5) is a linear function of M and is indicated in Fig. 12.1 by the line marked "D for agricultural output". Equation (12.4) can also

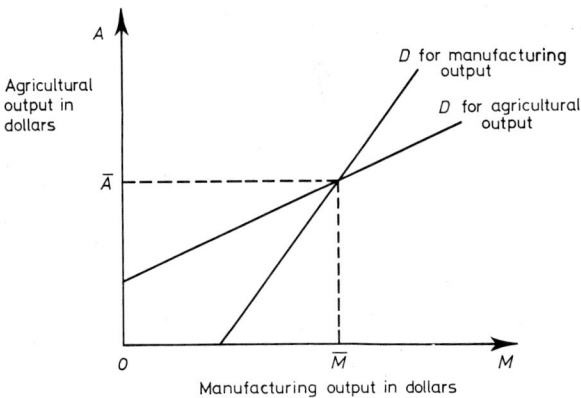

Fig. 12.1

be re-expressed as a linear function of manufacturing output and is shown by the line marked "D for manufacturing output". The solution to the two depicted functions occurs for a manufacturing output of $\bar{M}$ dollars and an agricultural output of $\bar{A}$ dollars. The targets C_1 and C_2 are attained if these outputs are produced.

Is it possible that the linear equations describing the economy and its targets are without a solution in the positive quadrant? Yes. This can occur, as Hawkins and Simon point out,[7] if the cost of producing one of the commodities is in excess of its value. We shall, however, suppose that for the commodities under discussion a solution occurs for non-negative values of their quantities of output.

So far limitations due to the availability of primary inputs have not been considered. If primary inputs are in limited supply, the final demand targets C_1 and C_2 and their associated requirements for A and M might not be attainable. If, for example, labour is the only primary factor and limited in supply to L, the solution $(\bar{A}, \bar{M})$ above is feasible only if

$$a_{31}\bar{A} + a_{32}\bar{M} \leqslant L. \tag{12.6}$$

The solution must fall in the space on or below the line

$$A = \frac{L}{a_{31}} - \frac{a_{32}}{a_{31}}M,$$

if it is to be feasible. The case indicated in Fig. 12.2 is feasible. If the industry solution fails to meet the input availability restriction, then targets need to be reduced or it

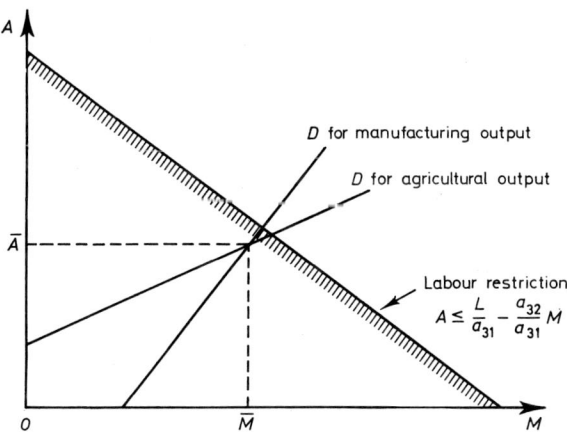

Fig. 12.2

may be possible to vary some of the technological relations, for example, as a result of new inventions or adopting new innovations or eliminating some organisational slack, or even to increase supplies of the primary factor with some effort, for example, to increase labour by immigration.

The target method of solution is very primitive. It is more of a "satisficing" approach than an optimising one. An economy which for the case shown in Fig. 12.2 produces the output $(\bar{A}, \bar{M})$, although able to meet the targets, is failing to produce the maximum net output from its *available* quantity of labour. If labour is involuntarily unemployed, then the economy is needlessly forgoing net output. Given that some value is attached to the net output of at least one of the goods under consideration, the economy ought to produce an output which enables it to reach its net bill of goods frontier.

The economy's net bill of goods frontier can be derived from the information normally required to apply the target approach. The frontier is, in fact, linear, corresponds to the full employment of labour (assuming one primary input only) and the comparative cost of one product in terms of another is equal to its relative labour content. Along the frontier the rate of substitution of one product for another is constant. A frontier of this type is indicated in Fig. 12.3. The gross output $(\bar{A}, \bar{M})$ of Fig. 12.2 corresponds to a point, such as E, and is within the frontier. Consequently, the net surplus of at least one of the products can be increased without decreasing that of another. Only points along the frontier can maximise net output from the available labour. Once the frontier of the set of possible combinations (hatched in the Fig. 12.3) is reached, the net output of one product can only be increased at the expense of the other. An "either or" and not "both" type of choice problem arises.

With the aid of a preference or objective function and having defined the feasible set of net bills of goods, one can hope to select the optimal combination of net output. The preference function may be given by an authority responsible for the planning of the economy. It need not be specified in detail to be useful for problem solving. Away from the true optimum, the preference ordering can be quite coarse, but should be finer in the neighbourhood of the optimum. In Fig. 12.3, three indifference curves from a possible preference function are shown and combinations on higher indifference curves are assumed to be preferred. The optimum attainable net bill of goods for the economy (given the particular preference function) is that corresponding to point H. Associated with this net output is a consistent level of gross output of the products which involves the full employment of labour.

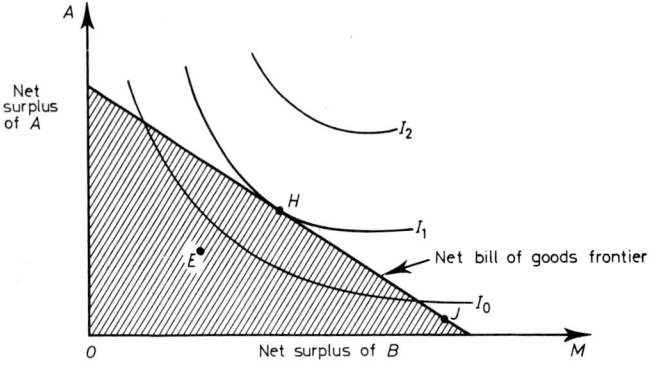

Fig. 12.3

The two-sector model, dealt with above, is nothing short of a caricature of the economy. A greater number of industries and primary inputs must be taken into account if the model is to have practical value. Unfortunately, however, the number of column entries in the technology table (matrix) excluding primary inputs is n^2, where n is the number of industries, so that the number of entries rises rapidly and the number of computations required to solve the system increases at an even faster rate as n increases. A forty-industry table, for example, involves 1,600 interindustry technology coefficients and such a table is still very coarse. Nevertheless, in the United States, a technology table has been constructed for 450 industries. But no input-output system has yet been solved for such a large number of industries. While matrix algebra and computers make the computation easier, the solution of realistic input-output tables is still a formidable task and the difficulties and costs of data collection should not be underestimated.

III. Limitations of the Approach

Despite the admirable aims behind input-output analysis and despite some of its merits mentioned earlier, it does have a number of shortcomings some of which might be serious in practice. The analysis assumes not only (a) that constant returns to scale occur throughout the economy, but (b) that each product requires the input of factors in fixed proportions.

No economic system satisfies these assumptions precisely and it is debatable whether any system roughly meets them. Certainly decreasing costs are known to be important in some industries (such as chemicals) and increasing costs are important in others (agriculture, for example). However, on the same principle as is used in differential calculus, a linear approximation may be adequate if the contemplated changes are small. Again, factor substitution does take place. However, Professor Samuelson has indicated[8] that the factor substitution assumption can be relaxed if constant returns to scale exist, if no joint production takes place, and if labour (or any single primary input) is the only scarce input. Even if factor substitution is possible under such circumstances, it will not occur because one combination of inputs is most profitable—expansion paths are straight lines through the origin. Nevertheless, Samuelson's conditions are still very restrictive.

There are also other more minor matters. The division of an economy into a set of industries is to some extent arbitrary. Because of the broad classifications required in order to make input-output tables manageable, products which are not close substitutes may be grouped into the same industry; and technical coefficients may vary widely between different products included in the same industry. Take the steel industry. Some types of steel are not substitutes at all. Furthermore, the ingredients of different types differ—some require the addition of manganese, others of nickel, etc. Expansion of the steel industry will involve very different requirements depending upon the expansion of the array of different types of steel.

Of course, and this is not peculiar to input-output analysis, it is not easy to collect reliable data on such a vast scale. There is the additional factor that all the data relate to the past so that the estimated coefficients are frequently those of a past year. How stable are these coefficients? If technical progress is rapid and the coefficients change quickly, input-output analysis based on historical technology coefficients will be a poor planning device. More attention is given to input-output analysis as a planning device when socialism is discussed later.[9]

Incidentally, one side-point must be mentioned: input-output tables have some value in indicating the areas in which partial analysis might be justified. Tables, such as those of Leontief[10] for the U.S. economy, indicate on the supply side that there are breaks or almost breaks in the chain of interdependence at some points.

The purpose of the remainder of this chapter is to show how input-output analysis can be extended to cope with a greater number of sectors by using matrix algebra. A method of solution using matrices is outlined and various matrices, such as Leontief's and the inverted Leontief matrix, are interpreted.

IV. Matrices: Extensions and Solutions

The analysis given above can be extended readily to n industries. Table 12.4 below is a transactions matrix set up in abstract form. The entries X_{ij} in its body indicate the value of output supplied by the ith industry (listed at the left) to the jth industry (listed at the top). Thus X_{12} is the value of output supplied by industry 1 to industry 2. The entries C_i in the column marked "final demand" are the net surpluses which the government wishes to have after all interindustry requirements of the ith product are taken care of. The total gross output of any product is listed in the last column. Clearly, the surplus of any product plus its deliveries to all industries equals its gross output. In symbols,

$$X_i = \sum_{j=1}^{n} X_{ij} + C_i, \quad (i = 1, \ldots, n). \tag{12.7}$$

In the last row, the value of the primary input used in each industry is shown by L_j. All the entries in the body of the transactions matrix are total values.

Table 12.4. Transactions Matrix

User of the output Producer of the output	Industry 1 2 .... n	Final demand	Total output
Industry			
1	$X_{11}\ X_{12}\ \ldots\ X_{1n}$	C_1	X_1
2	$X_{21}\ X_{22}\ \ldots\ X_{2n}$	C_2	X_2
.	.	.	.
.	.	.	.
.	.	.	.
n	$X_{n1}\ X_{n2}\ \ldots\ X_{nn}$	C_n	X_n
Primary input	$L_1\ \ L_2\ \ldots\ L_n$		

The technology matrix is calculated from the transactions matrix in a straightforward fashion. The proportion of commodity i involved in the production of a dollar's worth of commodity j is

$$a_{ij} = X_{ij}/X_j. \tag{12.8}$$

Thus the proportion in value terms of commodity 1 required per dollar's output of commodity 2 is

$$a_{12} = X_{12}/X_2.$$

The interindustry technology matrix can then be represented by the matrix presented in Table 12.5.

Input-Output Analysis

Table 12.5. Technology Matrix

$$\begin{array}{c|cccc}
\text{Industry} & 1 & 2 & \cdots & n \\
\hline
1 & a_{11} & a_{12} & \cdots & a_{1n} \\
2 & a_{21} & a_{22} & \cdots & a_{2n} \\
\vdots & \vdots & \vdots & & \vdots \\
n & a_{n1} & a_{n2} & \cdots & a_{nn}
\end{array}$$

Given these coefficients, the set of equations in Equation (12.7) can be rewritten since, from Equation (12.8),

$$X_{ij} = a_{ij}X_j. \tag{12.9}$$

Rewriting Equation (12.7)

$$X_i = \sum_{j=1}^{n} a_{ij}X_j + C_i, \quad (i = 1, \ldots, n). \tag{12.10}$$

In rather longer notation,

$$X_i = C_i + a_{i1}X_1 + A_{i2}X_2 + \ldots + a_{in}X_n, \quad (i = 1, \ldots, n) \tag{12.11}$$

so that, for example, the value of the output of commodity 1 is given by

$$X_1 = C_1 + a_{11}X_1 + a_{12}X_2 + \ldots + a_{1n}X_n. \tag{12.12}$$

The problem normally posed is to solve the set of equations given in (12.11) which indicates all technological interdependencies between industries. Given the values of C_i, the final demands required by the government, the problem is to determine the necessary industry outputs. Once these are discovered a check can then be made to find if the bill of goods is feasible given the availability of the primary factor.

Equations (12.11) can be rearranged by putting only C_i on the left hand side. Equation (12.12), for instance, becomes

$$C_1 = (1-a_{11})X_1 + a_{12}X_2 + \ldots + a_{1n}X_n.$$

The whole array of the rearranged equations has the following pattern:

$$C_1 = (1-a_{11})X_1 - a_{12}X_2 - \ldots - a_{1n}X_n$$
$$C_2 = -a_{21}X_1 + (1-a_{22})X_2 - \ldots - a_{2n}X_n$$
$$\vdots$$
$$C_n = -a_{n1}X_1 - a_{n2}X_2 - \ldots + (1-a_{nn})X_n.$$

Consequently, these equations can be written in matrix form as

$$C = (I-A)X \tag{12.13}$$

where C is a column vector of n elements, the final demands, X is a column vector of n elements, the gross outputs of each industry, and $(I-A)$ is an $n \times n$ matrix. A is the technology matrix, Table 12.5, and I is a conformable identity matrix. Now, the problem can be systematically solved by means of matrix inversion.

The matrix $(I-A)$ is known as the Leontief matrix and its inverse $(I-A)^{-1}$ is the inverted Leontief matrix. The solution of Equation (12.13) is then[11]

$$X = (I-A)^{-1}C. \tag{12.14}$$

Multiplying the vector of final demands by the inverted Leontief matrix we obtain the gross output of each industry necessary to meet interindustry demands and the final net bill of goods. The matrix is inverted by a series of simple steps which are outlined in most mathematical texts which deal with matrices.[12] We shall return to the solution of Equation (12.14) in a moment, but before doing so let us interpret the inverted Leontief matrix, $(I-A)^{-1}$.

An inverted Leontief matrix indicates the required change in the gross output of industries listed in the rows for a unit increase in the final demand on any industry listed at the top of the matrix. Let us imagine a two-sector case, sectors 1 and 2, and suppose that the inverted Leontief matrix is as in Table 12.6. This table indicates

Table 12.6. Inverted Leontief Matrix

Industry	1	2
1	1.15	0.25
2	0.3	2.4

that, if final demand on industry 1 is increased by one unit, it is necessary to raise the output of industry 1 in gross by 1.15 units and that of industry 2 by 0.3 units. Taking into account that industry 1 uses some of its own output and requires inputs from industry 2, the expansion indicated for both industries is necessary if one unit of net output of product 1 is to remain.

Ruling out any particular mathematical difficulties,[13] such as non-singularity of $(I-A)$, let us suppose that the solution to Equation (12.14) is X^0. This gross-output vector meets final demands and all interindustry requirements. Nevertheless, it is not attainable if the primary input is in short supply. Let V represent the vector of the input coefficients of the primary factor for all industries and L represent the upper limit of its supply. Then the solution is only feasible if

$$VX^0 \leq L. \tag{12.15}$$

As we shall see later[14] or as may have been observed, input-output analysis is a simple form of linear programming. Theorems from linear programming can, therefore, be applied to input-output problems. Furthermore, linear programming techniques enable extensions to be made in interindustry analysis, for example, alternative techniques can be allowed for. Possibly linear and non-linear programming will eventually make it possible to build more realistic yet general theories of the interdependence of the economy.

NOTES AND REFERENCES

[1] L. WALRAS, *Elements d'économie politique pure* (1874). Translated by W. JAFFE as *Elements of Pure Economics*, Irwin, Homewood, 1954. V. PARETO, *Cours d'économie politique*, 2 volumes, F. Rouge, Lausanne, 1896-97.

[2] W. LEONTIEF, *The Structure of the American Economy 1919-1939*, Oxford University Press, Oxford, 1941; 2nd ed., 1951.

[3] WALRAS, op. cit.

[4] J. M. KEYNES, *The General Theory of Employment, Interest and Money*, Macmillan, London, 1936.

[5] L. V. KANTOROVICH, *The Best Use of Economic Resources*, translated from the Russian by P. F. KNIGHTSFIELD, Pergamon Press, Oxford, 1965.

[6] P. A. Samuelson, "Abstract of a Theorem Concerning Substitutability in Open Leontief Models", in T. C. Koopmans (Ed.), *Activity Analysis of Production and Allocation*, John Wiley, New York, 1951, Ch. VII.
[7] D. Hawkins and H. Simon, "Some Conditions of Macroeconomic Stability", *Econometrica*, 1949, **17**, pp. 245-8.
[8] Samuelson, op. cit.
[9] Chapter 22.
[10] Leontief, op. cit.
[11] See, for example, R. G. D. Allen, *Mathematical Economics*, Macmillan, London, 1959, Chs. 14 and 15. A. C. Chiang, *Fundamental Methods of Mathematical Economics*, McGraw-Hill, 1967, Ch. 5.
[12] See, for example, Allen, op. cit. and Chiang, op. cit.
[13] See Chiang, op. cit., Section 5.5 ("Cramer's Rule").
[14] Chapter 15.

FURTHER READING

Baumol, W., *Economic Theory and Operations Analysis*, 2nd ed., Prentice-Hall, Englewood Cliffs, 1965, Ch. 20.

Cameron, B., *Input-Output Analysis and Resource Allocation*, Cambridge University Press, Cambridge, 1968.

Dorfman, R., "The Nature and Significance of Input-Output Analysis", *Review of Economics and Statistics*, 1954, **36**, pp. 121-43.

Dorfman, R., P. Samuelson, and R. Solow, *Linear Programming and Economic Analysis*, McGraw-Hill, New York, 1958, Ch. 9.

Eckstein, O., "The Input-Output System—Its Nature and Use", in O. Morgenstern (Ed.) *Economic Activity Analysis*, John Wiley, New York, 1954.

Hansen, B., *Lectures in Economic Theory*, 3rd ed., Studentlitteratur, Lund, 1969, Part I, Lecture 15.

Leontief, W., "Input-Output Economics", *Scientific American*, October 1951; and "The Structure of the U.S. Economy", *Scientific American*, April 1965. An abridged version of these articles appears as Section 32 in H. Kohler, *Readings in Price Theory*, Holt, Rinehart and Winston, New York, 1968.

CHAPTER 13

Welfare Economics

I. Introduction

Welfare economics, which is inseparable from the whole study of economics, is concerned with the social desirability of feasible economic alternatives. The problem mostly under consideration is that of selecting the economic possibility which is best from society's point of view. In order to choose, one needs a value (preference) ordering of the economic possibilities and knowledge of which economic states are actually possible. Both a knowledge of the economic world as it really is and a satisfactory value ordering are essential. It is, of course, difficult enough to select an acceptable value ordering, but many of the policy prescriptions of welfare economics go astray because the positive part of the model (the part concerned with what is, rather than with what is desirable) is ill-founded in practice. Some of the long established doctrines about the social desirability of perfect competition founder because the technological and knowledge conditions, which are supposed to be typically present in the economy, are in fact far from satisfied. The importance of the study of welfare economics remains however.

It is not coincidental that this chapter on welfare economics follows two chapters on general equilibrium systems. Being concerned with social choice, welfare economics must in its value ordering scan society as a whole. This is true even if it is decided that the preferences of some individuals will have no impact on the social ordering. In principle, the views of these individuals have been considered and it has been decided to disregard them. Second, the economic alternatives for society are basically determined by its availability of resources, the distribution of these resources or inputs to the production of alternative commodities and the allocation of the commodities between consumers. If inputs are being used efficiently, it is impossible to increase the output of any product without decreasing that of at least one other or without increasing the employment of inputs. For any given employment of inputs (including their full employment) in an efficient economy, the output of one product can only be increased by decreasing that of others, that is by shifting resources into one industry from other industries. Hence, no product's output can be considered in isolation—it must be related in principle to a general context. Optimal resource allocation, in the final analysis, needs to be set in a general (equilibrium) framework. Yet we should not conclude that no welfare questions can be settled in a partial framework. As far as technical efficiency is concerned, relevant social conclusions can be made on an industry basis, for example, if the marginal physical product of a factor is not the same for all firms in an increasing cost industry, it is possible to increase the output of the industry without employing more factors or reducing the output of any other industry by re-allocating the factor concerned. There is a rather dismal section of economists who insist that no welfare questions can be settled except upon a holistic basis, and since no adequate general theory of the economy exists, no welfare questions can be decided. Their negative approach has been widely accepted but is, in my opinion, unduly gloomy.

Social choice requires not only knowledge of the economic possibilities but also a social welfare function. Theoretically, an infinite number of different welfare functions are possible, each depending upon its own set of value judgements. Social welfare functions, for example, may differ in the method by which they amalgamate individual preferences to obtain social preferences. In some functions the preferences of each individual are entered and in others only those of a limited section of the population counts. It is even conceivable that a society could be ruled by a code or custom which respected the social preferences of no individual. Again, if a society is agreed about the method of amalgamating individual preferences and the properties which it wishes the social preference function to possess, there may be no function which meets these stipulations. Professor Arrow[1] has outlined a set of stipulations which preclude the existence of a social welfare function. These stipulations are the very ones which many regard as the fundamental basis of democratic decision-making.

Neo-classical welfare economics begins from the presumption that every individual in the society should count. The preference of each should be able to change the economic system. With practically no exceptions, each individual is taken to be the best judge of his own welfare. The welfare of each individual is assumed to depend upon his *own* consumption of goods and services.

We observe immediately that no real allowance is made for non-materialistic or non-economic wants, such as individual liberty and freedom, love, the sense of belonging, and so on. Any method which provides the same bundle of goods for the same effort is or is in danger of being regarded as being of equal social value, no matter what its non-economic advantages or disadvantages are.[2]

Furthermore, the individual's preference is determined by his *own* consumption. He is not sympathetic to the plight or fortunes of others around him. One presumes that any redistribution of income in this system only comes about in order to avoid violence from the "have-nots". Alternatively, redistribution of income may be treated in an exogenous fashion. Benevolent philosopher-kings redistribute income to maximise their paternalistic welfare function.

Take the classical utilitarian tradition in which A. C. Pigou was the last great member. Social welfare, the tradition postulated, is at a maximum when the grand total of utility in a society is maximised. The grand total of utility is equal to the sum of individual utilities. The utility enjoyed by any individual depends upon his own consumption of commodities alone and increases with his consumption of these goods.[3] Hence, if the grand total of utility is to be at a maximum it must be impossible, given the employed resources, to increase the output of any product without decreasing that of another. Furthermore, it must not be possible *by exchange* of the product to make any individual better off without making another worse off nor to be able to do this by varying the composition of production. These requirements or necessary conditions also appear in Pareto's theory[4] which involves a much weaker welfare ordering.

The distinctive feature of the utilitarian tradition is that it makes interpersonal comparisons of utility. Utility depends significantly on the income of the individual and utility can be measured and compared between individuals. Hence, not only should the conditions mentioned above be satisfied but income should be distributed so as to maximise utility.

The implications of the theory for the distribution of income vary widely, depending upon the nature of the utility functions of the individuals. Let $U_i(y_i)$ represent the utility of individual i from an income of y_i and imagine total income (or output) for society to be given at some level Y. The utilitarian distribution problem is one of maximising

$$W = \sum_{i=1}^{n} U_i(y_i) \tag{13.1}$$

subject to

$$\sum_{i=1}^{n} y_i = Y \tag{13.2}$$

where there are n individuals in the society. Utilitarians assumed as a rule that utility increases with income ($dU_i/dy_i > 0$) and that it does so at a decreasing rate ($d^2U_i/dy_i^2 < 0$). While an extra dollar gives extra utility, it gives an individual less additional utility the richer he is.

But how does utility differ between individuals? Is it the same function of income or does it vary in some systematic way depending upon the individual's social group? Depending upon the answers, a utilitarian's desirable distribution of income is entirely different.

If it is accepted that individuals are roughly equal in their capacity for happiness, then $U_1(y_1) = U_2(y_2) = \ldots = U_n(y_n)$. The Fabian socialists and other socialists accepted this. It follows logically that if $U_i' > 0$ and $U_i'' < 0$, income must be *equally* distributed if W, social welfare as defined by the sum of utilities, is to be at a maximum.[5] Figure 13.1 illustrates this proposition for a society of two individuals. The marginal utility curves of both are the same. If a sum $Y = \bar{y}_1 + \bar{y}_2$ is to be distributed, utility is at a maximum only if it is equally divided, that is if $\bar{y} = 0.5Y$ is allocated to individual 1 and $\bar{y}_2 = 0.5Y$ is allocated to individual 2. Adding any number of units to $\bar{y}_1$ and subtracting the same number from $\bar{y}_2$, we can see from the figure that the addition to the utility of individual 1 is less than the loss to 2. A vice versa variation also reduces total utility.

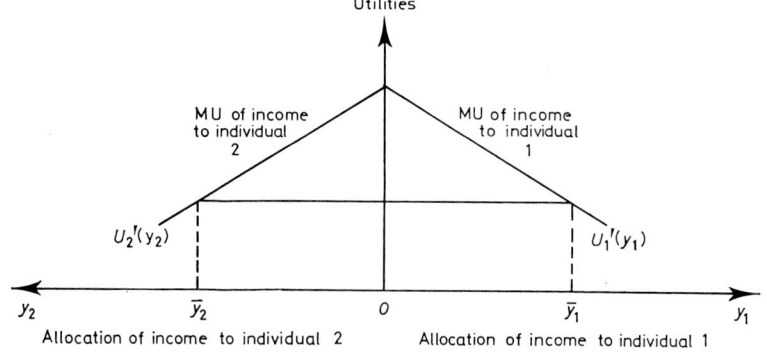

Fig. 13.1

Welfare Economics

But not all utilitarians believed that men are equally able to derive utility from income. The famous Oxford economist, F. Y. Edgeworth, author of *Mathematical Psychics* (1881)[6], held an extreme view. Wesley Mitchell's description of the view which Edgeworth put forward in *Mathematical Psychics* is rather humorous:

> He assumed without argument that men differ in their capacity as pleasure machines. Broadly speaking he contended that the members of the upper class were better pleasure machines than those of the lower classes; they were more sensitive individuals, they were susceptible of more education. He went on to argue that men, generally speaking are better pleasure machines than women, a contention that he supported by reciting two lines from Alfred Tennyson's "Locksley Hall":
>
> > Woman is the lesser man, and all thy
> > passions matched with mine
> > Are as moonlight unto sunlight
> > and as water unto wine.
>
> On the basis of assuming that the aristocracy are better pleasure machines than the common run of mankind and that men are better pleasure machines than women, he argued with perfect logic that to maximise happiness larger incomes should go to the aristocracy, than to the common folk and to men rather than women.[7]

The logic of Edgeworth's position can be illustrated by Fig. 13.2. Let individual 1 be a man or an aristocrat and individual 2 be a woman or a commoner. As shown, $U_1'(y_1) > U_2'(y_2)$ for $y_1 = y_2$. $U_1'(y_1)$ only equals $U_2'(y_2)$ if $y_1 > y_2$. Income inequality is necessary if utility is to be at a maximum. The fixed income, $Y = \bar{y}_1 + \bar{y}_2$ if there are only two individuals, must be allocated so that individual 1 gets the greater share. Otherwise, the marginal utility of income is not the same for both individuals and utility overall is not at a maximum.

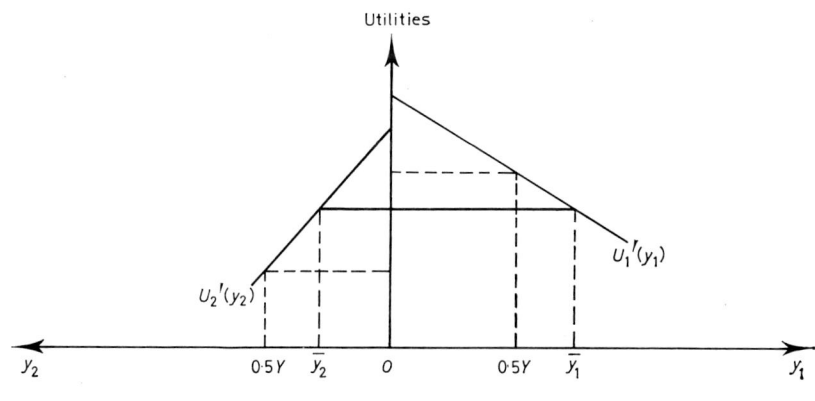

Fig. 13.2

Economists such as Pareto, Hicks and Robbins[8] attacked the utility doctrine. Measurement of utility and interpersonal comparisons of utility were held to be impossible and the conclusions of the utilitarians were therefore questionable. The weaker criterion of Pareto which neglects income distribution will be considered presently.

But in many ways the new welfare economics (of Pareto and Hicks) has undermined the study of welfare economics. Practically, no economic change can be made without affecting income distribution and there is a good case for making one's views about income distribution explicit. Even if utility is not measurable and interpersonal comparisons are without scientific basis, nevertheless some social preference function which takes account of incomes is needed. Our judgements about the desirable distribution of income should be made explicit and their consequences followed up. At least, the utilitarians did make their views explicit.

The welfare criterion suggested by Pareto[9] avoids the concept of measurable utility and sidesteps interpersonal comparisons and the question of the optimal distribution of income. Pareto posits that no matter what the distribution of income, welfare is not at a maximum if it is possible to make one or more individuals better off without making any others worse off. Hence, it is a necessary condition for maximum social welfare that it should be impossible by an economic re-organisation to place any individual in a preferred position without putting another in a less preferred situation. In theory, Pareto's approach is neutral about the desirable distribution of income. With equality or inequality in income, his criterion is equally applicable. But in practice, it is charged that his view tends to maintain the *status quo* distribution of income. By diverting attention from the optimal distribution of income to the question of economic efficiency in production and exchange, Pareto's approach leads to the neglect of the former problem.

Although Pareto's criterion seems relatively unobjectionable at first sight, it is not without its limitations. For example, is the individual always the best judge of his own self-interest? Are the relevant preference orderings those of the individual himself, "individualistic" preference orderings implying individual sovereignty, or should the orderings be adjusted in a paternalistic fashion to reflect the "true" interest of the individual which may not be known to him? My own ethics favour the individualistic approach. However, there is a real problem.[10] All of our existing societies recognise that an individual is not always able to judge his own self-interest and I would accept this. For this reason, (and others, such as externalities), societies place restrictions on drugs. For similar reasons, too, they may subsidise low-cost housing, operas, etc. The dangers of the paternalistic approach are, however, apparent to us all; for example, witness the lively debate about book and film censorship.

There is a further problem, too. Our preferences, to a considerable extent, are products of our education and environment. If these have objectionable features, should we really respect the preferences which emerge?[11] In the final analysis, Pareto's criterion shows itself to be inadequate, especially inadequate the further one moves from the demand for common goods, such as bread, potatoes, rice, grapefruit and so on, to consider brand products and general matters, like the demand for education, a social framework and hierarchy, etc. But then Pareto never intended his criterion as a complete prescription for social action.

Another possible objection to Pareto's criterion is that it disregards changes in the relative income of individuals. Social welfare is increased, provided that each in his own individual world is made better off. But is this a reasonable view? If, for example, the rich gain relatively much more than the poor by a social change this may increase social conflict and tension. Consequently, it can be reasonably doubted if social welfare is increased.

The conditions which production and exchange must satisfy if a Paretian optimum

Welfare Economics

is to be reached, depend crucially upon the type of production and consumption relationships which are assumed. Thus, for example, the allocation of resources, and the form of economic organisation which achieves a Paretian optimum if increasing costs are the case, differ entirely from those which are appropriate if decreasing costs are the case. This requires more than ordinary emphasis since the traditional argument that perfect competition ensures a Paretian optimum rests on the supposition that firms experience decreasing returns to scale for comparatively low levels of output. Amongst other things, too, externalities are assumed to be absent.

Conditions for a Paretian optimum in exchange and production are stated below. First, a simple exchange model is considered, followed by a look at a slightly more general scheme of an economy which takes account of production as well as exchange. But it is stressed that the conditions obtained are greatly influenced by the choice of the particular functional relationships. Given certain functional relationships, it is traditionally indicated that perfect competition leads to a Paretian optimum. In theory the same Paretian optimum could be obtained by central direction. But are the functional relationships an adequate representation of present economies? Hardly. The seriousness of the deviations and their implications are discussed in Chapter 14. Nevertheless before we can discuss this, we must be aware of the traditional position.

II. A Simple Exchange Model

Consider the following social problem: given an available stock of products, how should these be allocated between the individuals in society if a Paretian optimum is to be achieved? To decide this we need to know the preference functions of each individual for the products. Traditionally it is assumed that each individual's preference function depends only on his consumption of the products and possesses the properties of the Hicksian preference-ordering, outlined earlier in the chapter on consumption theory; for example, the ordering is transitive and continuous and the indifference curves are convex and differentiable. Assuming an interior solution, a Paretian optimum in exchange is not reached unless products are allocated in a way which ensures that the rate of indifferent substitution of the products is equal for all consumers. This can be proven generally but it is convenient to illustrate the proposition by a particular case.

Imagine that two products only, 1 and 2, are available and that the set of individuals in the society consists of two, A and B. Let x_1 and x_2 represent quantities of product 1 and product 2 and these quantities with superscript A or B added represent the allocation to A and B respectively. Given the traditional assumptions, the preference ordering of A and B can be represented by the functions

$$U^A = U^A(x_1^A, x_2^A), \tag{13.3}$$

$$U^B = U^B(x_1^B, x_2^B). \tag{13.4}$$

Note that each individual is completely insensitive to the lot of the other as would not be the case if, for example, $U^A = U^A(x_1^A, x_2^A, x_1^B, x_2^B)$ and

$$\frac{\partial U^A}{\partial x_1^B} \neq 0 \text{ and } \frac{\partial U^A}{\partial x_2^B} \neq 0.$$

Given the preference functions of Equations (13.3) and (13.4), their corresponding indifference curves can be drawn in an Edgeworth-Bowley box, whose dimensions are equal to the available quantity of the products 1 and 2. This box enables the optimal allocation of the products to be found. Such a box is shown in Fig. 13.3. The length of its base equals the total available quantity of product 1 and its height is equal to the total stock of product 2. Reading the allocation to A away from the point marked O_A and that to B from the point marked O_B, points in the box represent feasible allocations of the total product. Thus the point marked ζ corresponds to an allocation of $(\bar{x}_1^A, \bar{x}_2^A)$ to individual A and a distribution of $(\bar{x}_1^B, \bar{x}_2^B)$ to individual B. Two of A's indifference curves are shown in the diagram. One is indicated by $I_0^A I_0^A$ and another by $I_1^A I_1^A$. Similarly, two of B's indifference curves are illustrated and these, of course, are convex from O_B but concave when viewed from O_A. Given the usual non-satiety assumptions, individual A is made better off by movements in a NE direction and B by changes in a SW direction.

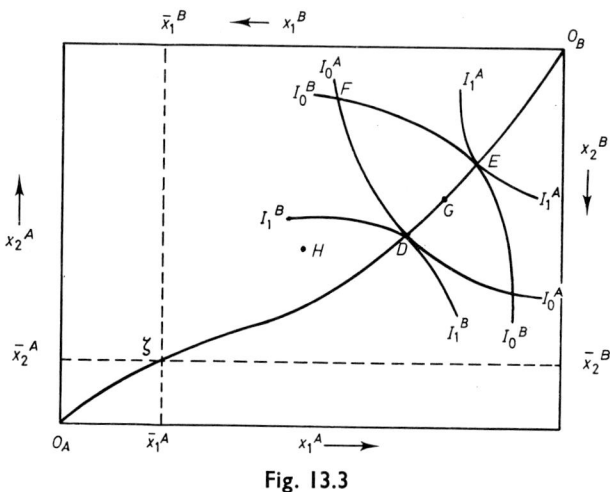

Fig. 13.3

From Fig. 13.3 it is evident that an allocation such as that corresponding to point F cannot be Paretian optimal, for a movement to a point such as D or E results in an improvement for one individual and is no worse for the other. Or, alternatively, an allocation anywhere between D and E on the line DE is better than the allocation F for both individuals.

An allocation such as D corresponds to a Paretian optimum. Any movement away from this point results in a reduction in utility for at least one individual. E also corresponds to a Paretian optimum. Any movement away from this allocation makes at least one individual worse off. For example, a movement from E to D makes individual A worse off although B is made better off.

Points E and D correspond to points of tangency of the indifference curves of the two individuals. At each point, individual A's (marginal) rate of indifferent substitution of product 1 for product 2 equals individual B's (marginal) rate of indifferent substitution of the two products. The rates at which the individuals would be prepared to trade the two products are equal. But there is an infinite number of points of tangency of the indifference curves, for each individual has an infinity of indifference curves. Taking all points of tangency, a curve such as $O_A DEO_B$ in Fig. 13.3 may be traced out. Edgeworth called this curve the contract curve for the very good reason

Welfare Economics

that if the two individuals happened to have an initial allocation corresponding to a point off the curve they might be expected to trade (if the trade is possible) their way to an allocation on the curve.[12] Starting from point F, it is clear that both parties can make *mutually* beneficial trades. For example, individual B could barter some of product 1 for product 2, so that the parties ended up at point G. At point G or at any point on the contract curve, no further trading takes place since parties cannot mutually gain.

All combinations along the contract curve and only combinations on the contract curve are Paretian optimal. Under the above conditions, a Paretian optimum does not occur unless the stock of available products is allocated in a manner which equalises the (marginal) rate of indifferent substitution of the products. Taking any point in Fig. 13.3 where this condition is not satisfied, two indifference curves (one for each individual) intersect at the point and enclose a set of allocations which are feasible and preferred by *both* individuals to the original allocation. Hence, the original allocations cannot be Paretian optimal. On the other hand, if an allocation is selected which corresponds to the point of tangency of two indifference curves, the indifference curves enclose no points which are preferred by both individuals. The allocation corresponding to the tangency point is Paretian optimal.

It is, however, to be emphasised that Pareto's criterion defines *only* the conditions for efficient exchange. Given an initial allocation of the products, it prescribes the *necessary* conditions for the maximisation of overall satisfaction. But it in no way specifies the optimal initial allocation of the products, the optimal distribution of income in this context. It remains silent on whether combination D is socially better than E or even whether combination E is preferable to H, because these combinations involve an improvement in real income for one individual (one individual is placed on a higher indifference curve) and a reduction in real income for the other. It does point out that E is socially preferable to F and that there are some allocations which are preferable to H. However, it cannot determine a social ordering of economic reforms which make some better off and others worse off. Pareto's condition is solely concerned in this context with *efficiency in exchange*.

In order to determine the optimal distribution of the product, given that the initial endowment of each individual is variable, a stronger method of ordering is required which must include judgements about the desirable distribution of income. But given the optimal distribution of income and if there is a positive association between individual preference and social preference, the final allocation of goods must end up on the contract curve if a social optimum is to be attained.

Samuelson has formalised the problem by means of a utility possibility frontier. In a similar way to a production possibility frontier, the utility possibility frontier indicates the maximum *attainable* utility of any one individual given the level of utility of the other. For our two-person case, a possible utility frontier is shown in Fig. 13.4. The points on the frontier correspond to combinations along the contract curve in Fig. 13.3. For example ξ may correspond to point D in Fig. 13.3 and then (U_0^A, U_1^B) is an index of the utility associated with the indifference curves I_0^A and I_1^B. Each point on the utility frontier has a corresponding point on the contract curve and vice versa. If non-consumption of some of the stock is allowed, the utility possibility set is similar to the hatched area in Fig. 13.4.

If *some* social welfare ordering of these indices (U_A, U_B) of real income is selected

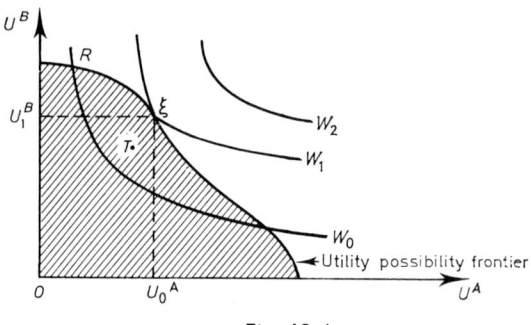

Fig. 13.4

and if the ordering is transitive and complete, the optimal attainable real income allocation and distribution of products can be found. If W_0, W_1, W_2 in Fig. 13.4 represent contours of this social welfare function and if a higher level of social welfare is reached as both individuals are made better off, ξ is the optimal attainable real income distribution. Thus the allocation corresponding to point D in Fig. 13.3, which corresponds to ξ by assumption, is selected as optimal. Both the optimal distribution and allocation of the stock are settled.

The social preference function was taken as datum. However, there is absolutely no reason to suppose that individuals will agree on a common social welfare function. There may be some agreement but consensus is not likely. But given any social welfare function which positively associates individual and social preference, the optimum occurs on the utility possibility frontier and requires Paretian optimality. Since the social welfare function (in Samuelson's formulation) can be anyone's (Professor Samuelson's, Friedman's or Mao Tse Tung's) the formulation is of limited help. Again, given agreement on a simple and, at first sight, reasonable set of axioms for social choice as Arrow[13] has shown, there may be no social ordering which satisfies these.

If social and individual preferences are positively associated, it is apparent from Fig. 13.4 that Paretian optimality is necessary but not sufficient for a social optimum. For example, the point R corresponds to a Paretian optimum but it is inferior to the Paretian optimum indicated by ξ. It is even inferior to a number of allocations which are not Paretian optimal, namely those in the feasible area above the contour W_0. For example, it is inferior to the allocation corresponding to T.

An important conclusion can be drawn. Suppose that the distribution of income corresponding to point R has been established. R is attainable given the distribution of goods in the society and its system of exchange. However, even though R is Paretian optimal, ξ is also Paretian optimal and socially preferred to R. Ought not social action be directed towards moving the economic system to the ideal, ξ? In principle, yes. But there may be significant social barriers which are certain to prevent this movement in the near future. Yet given the strength of vested interests, it might be possible to push the economic system to a point such as T. Rational social action for the near future is to push the system to T and forgo Paretian optimality. Because institutional barriers to redistribution are strong, short-term policy can with perfect social justification temper the efficiency goal to improve income distribution. For example, looking at the politically feasible, it may be socially optimal in the circumstance to tamper

Welfare Economics

with the pricing system and forgo some economic efficiency for an improvement in the distribution of income. This is not to deny, however, that one should try to remove the institutional barrier and move to ξ as soon as possible. But in the interim a rational society should not suffer by remaining at the Paretian optimal point, R, which is socially inferior to T. In practice, politics complicates the matter in a far from trivial way. From the political point of view, one must ask whether the movement from R to T will hasten or retard the eventual possible movement to ξ and weigh these matters up. From the practical standpoint, welfare economics cannot ignore political constraints, and it must inevitably take account of game-like behaviour. Nevertheless, the main point remains valid. Given political constraints, it is socially legitimate and can possibly be ideal in the circumstances to forgo some economic efficiency (even by altering the pricing system) for a preferable distribution of income. The outcome is not absolutely ideal but, if the absolute ideal is unattainable at the time, the objection is of no immediate import. Untold suffering can be caused by policy which awaits the absolute ideal before engaging in social reform.

Figure 13.4 enabled us to select an ideal distribution of the products, given the social preference function shown. In principle, the social ideal could be attained by directing the quantities implied by D (Fig. 13.3) to the two individuals. The individuals would, of course, then have no reason to exchange any of their goods. Our model assumes no production. But let us imagine a type of production which is compatible with this model. Imagine that the two products are gifts of nature or God and are allocated over space (land)—they might be coconuts, bananas, berries, manna, etc. However, the productivity of this land cannot be augmented by human effort nor can the composition of its output. Thus depending upon the way in which this resource is distributed to individuals so, too, shall individuals share in the product. Society could distribute the resource in a manner to achieve D in Fig. 13.3. No fundamental problem seems to be involved. (This would not be the case if the factor was human ability. Society is not completely free to determine the distribution of this factor.)

Yet the social optimum can also be achieved without prescribing original endowments to the individuals as indicated by D. If exchange is allowed, and if suitable exchange ratios for the goods exist, individuals can be given an original endowment which diverges from D and yet by trading can finish at D. The final outcome depends not only on each individual's initial endowment of the factor but also on the nature of the exchange ratios.

Consider Fig. 13.5 which is an Edgeworth-Bowley box with the same interpretation as Fig. 13.3. Now KDL is a line such that with movements in the allocation from D towards K both parties are made worse off and with shifts from D towards L both parties are also made worse off. Every increment of movement away from D worsens the lot of both parties. Suppose that an authority determines that goods can be exchanged between individuals if they maintain the swapping rates dictated by KDL. Clearly, any initial endowment which results in an original allocation on the line KDL, leads by exchange to point D. There will be other trading curves like KDL which, given the initial allocation, lead by exchange to the point D. It is vital and it is assumed that the trading curve through D is equal to the slope of both the indifference curves at that point. In final equilibrium, the rate of exchange equals the common rate of indifferent substitution of the goods if this assumption is granted. There is no unique optimal trading path to D and the trading path need not be linear.

The exchange rates considered above were assumed to be determined by an authority. What happens if individuals are free to determine their own exchange rates? If numbers are small (for example two), the exchange rates are indeterminate within a range. Certain possibilities can be ruled out but nevertheless a range of uncertainty is liable to remain. For example, take the two-person case shown in Fig. 13.3, and

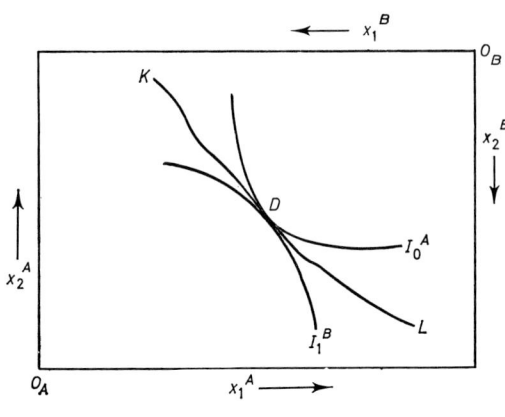

Fig. 13.5

imagine an original endowment of F. If we can expect the individuals to exhaust all their opportunities for mutual gain (we cannot, in practice, always expect this)[14] the final allocation is certain to fall somewhere between D and E on the contract curve. Given the approach of Edgeworth, and that of von Neumann and Morgenstern to the theory of co-operative games, the area of indeterminancy in this bilateral case is the curve DGE.[15]

As the number of individuals who hold stocks is increased, it has been shown that the area of indeterminancy shrinks.[16] Once a sufficiently large number of persons are involved, there must be a sufficient number holding the products, the area of indeterminancy reduces to a single point. Each individual can exchange his products at a given exchange ratio. This exchange ratio is an outcome of each individual seeking his own self-interest and being kept in check by the competition of others who also seek their own self-interest. The individual has no influence over the exchange ratio; it is set by all in competition. But the final exchange ratio is certainly affected by the way in which the original endowment of the resources are distributed. In determining the original distribution of the endowment, one must have regard to the resultant exchange ratios which are established and whether in the light of these the economy will be led to an ideal allocation of the products. Exchange and the distribution of income cannot be divorced in the final analysis.

One thing, however, is clear. Perfect competition does lead to a Paretian optimum (but not necessarily to a maximum of social welfare function). If perfect competition exists, the exchange ratios of the products must be the same for all. (This is the so-called Parity Theorem.) Given his initial allocation, each individual striving after his own gain equates this exchange rate to his (marginal) rate of indifferent substitution of the products. Since the exchange rate is the same for all, the (marginal) rate of indifferent substitution must be equalised for all. But if this is so, the individuals

Welfare Economics

must be on their contract curve and a Paretian optimum occurs. Perfect competition leads to a Paretian optimum. However, if the initial distribution of income is socially unsatisfactory and cannot be altered easily, perfect competition may be socially less desirable than other forms of economic organisation and exchange. For example, if a group only has its labour to sell and has depressed incomes, it might be argued that it is socially preferable (preferable according to some welfare functions) for this group to collude rather than engage in perfect competition. (Consider the earlier discussion of Fig. 13.4.)

The simple exchange model discussed above has structural limitations. For example, the preference system is assumed to meet Hicksian specifications. If preferences do not meet these specifications, a Paretian optimum need not require the fulfilment of marginal equivalences. Corner solutions or boundary solutions may be optimal. Take a particular case.[17] Imagine that, in our two-product two-person example, indifference curves are straight lines. Furthermore, suppose that the rate of indifferent substitution of the products is not the same for both individuals, so that their indifference curves have different slopes. A Paretian optimum only occurs if one individual consumes all of one product, and, at the optimum, the rates of indifferent substitution of the products by the two individuals differ. In the case illustrated in Fig. 13.6, individual B has a comparative preference for product 2. Therefore, the contract curve follows

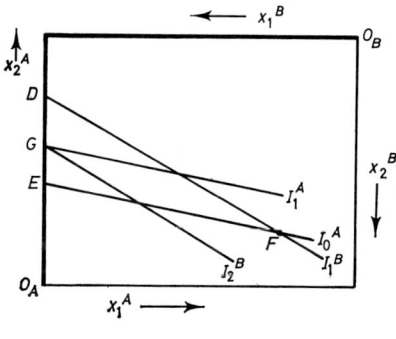

Fig. 13.6

the $x_2{}^A$ and $x_1{}^B$ axes. Given an initial distribution of F, both individuals can be made better off by exchange which leads to a point such as G. In fact, any point between D and E is preferable to F. At the Paretian optimum, G, the rate at which individual B is prepared to forgo product 1 *exceeds* the rate at which individual A is prepared to exchange the product. However, once point G is reached, individual B has exhausted his stock of product 1, so further trade is impossible. An attainable Paretian optimum has been reached. Nor is it difficult to enumerate other circumstances in which marginal equivalence is unnecessary, and indeed contrary to the fulfilment of a Paretian optimum. Nevertheless, in *some* of these circumstances (as in the linear case discussed above) it can be shown that perfect competition leads to a Paretian optimum.[18]

However, if externalities occur, perfect competition need not result in a Paretian optimum even though the conditions are sufficient otherwise to ensure an optimum. In the above model, an externality arises if any individual's satisfaction depends not only on his consumption of the products but also on that of others. Problems raised by externalities are discussed in the next chapter.

The above model did not allow for any variation of production and some provision ought to be made for the fact that production is variable. As a result the conditions for a Paretian optimum are extended. But basic welfare choices, for example, the multiplicity of Paretian optima and the necessity of a decision about the desirable distribution of income are well brought out by the original model. In the light of the extended model, it is not necessary to modify the main conclusions of this section.

III. A More General Model: Exchange and Variable Production

Variability of production can be simply allowed for if the following assumptions are made:

(i) production is possible by the use of two inputs. Each input is homogeneous, perfectly divisible, and its aggregate supply is inelastic. Let the two factors be N and L, land and labour, for example;

(ii) the economy produces two products, 1 and 2. Represent their quantities by x_1 and x_2 respectively. Where subscripts represent the quantity of the factor allocated to the production of the particular product, the production function of product 1 is

$$x_1 = f_1(L_1, N_1) \qquad (13.5)$$

and that of product 2 is

$$x_2 = f_2(L_2, N_2). \qquad (13.6)$$

These are aggregate production functions—it is assumed if several firms operate in the industry that factors are efficiently allocated between firms so that it is impossible to increase the output of the product by re-allocating the factors employed. Each of these production functions is supposed to be *strictly* concave and to be at least twice differentiable. In other words, decreasing returns are supposed to be the rule and isoquants are imagined to be *strictly* convex. Note that externalities are ruled out, for example, x_1 does not depend upon x_2 nor upon L_2 nor N_2.

(iii) as before, two individuals, A and B, are taken to be the only consumers. Each has an ordinal preference function. That for individual A is represented by

$$U_A = U_A(x_1^A, x_2^A) \qquad (13.7)$$

and that for B by

$$U_B = U_B(x_1^B, x_2^B) \qquad (13.8)$$

Superscripts indicate the consumption by the individual of the relevant product. The preference ordering is assumed to satisfy the usual Hicksian conventions, for example, the preference functions are *strictly* concave.

The task now is to determine simultaneously the Paretian optimal allocation of factors, the Paretian optimal composition of production and its Paretian optimal exchange between consumers. As in the previous model, we shall find that the Paretian optimal allocation is not unique. As the distribution of income varies so, too, do the allocations which correspond to a Paretian optimum. Economically efficient allocations vary with the distribution of income. Let us now examine efficiency in production.

Welfare Economics

A Paretian optimum is only achieved if, given the employed resources in the economy, it is impossible to increase the output of any product without reducing that of another. If this condition is not satisfied, it is unambiguously possible to increase overall output without greater effort. Consequently, if all goods are in demand, it is possible to make at least one person better off without making any other worse off. Hence, if this condition is not satisfied, a Paretian optimum has not been achieved.

Let us try to discover the allocation of factors between the products which ensures efficiency in production. For this purpose an Edgeworth-Bowley box is shown in Fig. 13.7. Its dimensions reflect the total employed quantities of the L and N, labour and land. From the origin O_1 allocations of the factors to product 1 are measured off and from O_2 the allocations to product 2 are indicated. Isoquants (contours) of production function Equation (13.7), that for product 1, radiate from the axes L_1 and N_1 and those of production function Equation (13.8), that for product 2, fan out from the axes L_2 and N_2. Superscripts to Q in Fig. 13.7 identify the product corresponding to the isoquants, and subscripts reflect the level of output. Higher values of the subscripts indicate greater levels of output.

It is apparent from Fig. 13.7 that the allocation of the factors shown by point K is an inefficient allocation. To allocate $\hat{L}_1$ of L and $\hat{N}_1$ of N to product 1 and the remaining quantities of these factors to product 2, that is ($\hat{L}_2$, $\hat{N}_2$), is inefficient. By reallocating the factors, the output of at least one of the products can be increased without reducing that of the other. For example, the allocation corresponding to point Z results in an increased output of product 2 and no change in the output of product 1. Indeed, any allocation on the line ZMN leads to a greater output than allocation K as does any allocation in the set enclosed by the two isoquants $Q_0^1 Q_0^1$ and $Q_0^2 Q_0^2$. But the points on ZMN are along the efficiency locus and thus have a special status. The efficiency locus is comprised of all allocations of the factors such that it is impossible to increase the output of one product without decreasing that of another. (Of course, the employed quantity of the factors is assumed to be given.) Once the efficiency locus is reached, it is impossible to increase production merely by improving the allocation of resources.

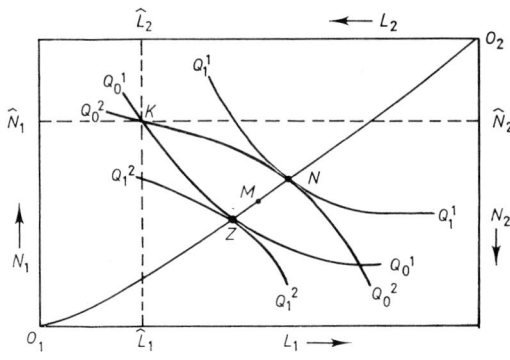

Fig. 13.7

The efficiency locus in Fig. 13.7 is indicated by O_1ZNO_2. Any movement away from this locus inevitably involves a reduction in the output of at least one product. But, most importantly, unless the allocation of factors is on the locus, it is possible to increase the output of at least one product without reducing that of any other. Note, too, that points along the efficiency locus, for example, M and N, correspond to tangencies of the isoquants. In fact, in this model these tangency-points together form the efficiency locus. *Efficiency requires that the (marginal) rate of technical substitution of the factors in the production of each product be equal.* However, I hasten to point out that this is on the assumption that interior optima alone arise and that the isoquants are convex and differentiable. If not, another set of conditions might prescribe the efficiency locus.[19]

Given the available quantities of the factors, a production possibility frontier for the products can be constructed. The production possibility frontier indicates for the economy as a whole the maximum output of any product for any given level of output of the other products. Clearly, points on the frontier correspond to allocations of factors along the efficiency locus. The method of moving from the efficiency locus and Edgeworth factor box to the production possibility frontier was outlined in Chapter 7 (Section III) so there is no need to repeat this here. A product possibility frontier is shown in Fig. 13.8 by the curve EHJ. The frontier is concave and hence indicates that as more of any product is produced an increasing amount of the other has to be forgone to produce an extra unit of the first mentioned product.

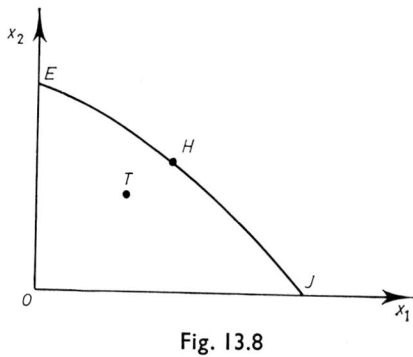

Fig. 13.8

All output-combinations on and in the figure $OEHJ$ are attainable but only those on the frontier EHJ can be Pareto optimal. If the economy is not on this frontier, its output of one product (or more) can be increased without reducing its output of other products and without increasing its use of resources. For example, if the system is at point T, the economy can move to H and increase its output of both products. T might correspond to point K and H might correspond to M in Fig. 13.7.

Now, no matter what output is produced, it must be distributed to consumers in a manner which makes it impossible to increase the satisfaction of one without decreasing that of another, otherwise a Paretian optimum (in exchange) has not been attained. This is equally necessary whether output is at a frontier point, such as H, or even at an interior point, such as T, in Fig. 13.8. Granted our assumptions about the preference curves of consumers, we know from the last section that, if there is to be a Paretian optimum from exchange, the marginal rate of indifferent substitution of the products must be the same for all individuals.

To illustrate this, select any attainable combination in Fig. 13.8. Take a point V,

Welfare Economics

for example, on the frontier. An Edgeworth-Bowley box, as drawn in Fig. 13.9, can be constructed for this combination, one origin of the box situated at O, the other at V. Possible allocations to individual A can be measured off from origin O and those to B from origin V, and the preferences of the individuals for the quantities can be indicated in the usual manner by a series of indifference curves. The indifference curves of individual A have a SW orientation and those of B have a NW orientation. Only allocations of output V along the contract curve ORV in Fig. 13.9 can be Paretian optimal. No matter what is the level of output to be distributed, the (marginal) rate

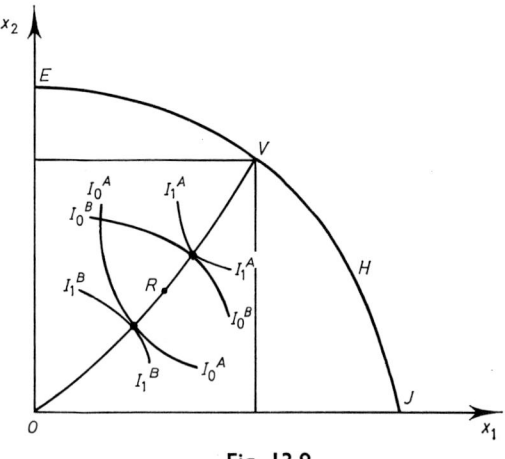

Fig. 13.9

of indifferent substitution of the products must be the same for all consumers, otherwise there is not a Paretian optimum in exchange.

Necessary conditions for a Paretian optimum in *production* and in *exchange* have been explored. But for a Paretian optimum a third condition must be satisfied. There must be an optimal conformance between production and the preferences of consumers. Pareto optimality requires that the rate of technical product substitution (also called the rate of product transformation) equals the rate of indifferent substitution of the product by consumers. That this is a requirement, can be seen from Fig. 13.10.

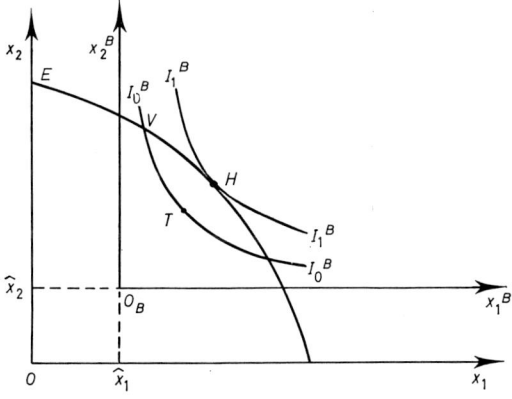

Fig. 13.10

Imagine that individual A's consumption is fixed at any level $(\hat{x}_1, \hat{x}_2)$ and that the remainder of production is allocated to B. The possible allocation to B can be measured off from the origin shown as O_B and B's preferences can be represented in relation to this origin. Two of B's indifference curves are shown in Fig. 13.10. At point H, individual B reaches his highest attainable indifference curve and here the rate of product transformation equals his rate of indifferent substitution. A combination such as V or T is inferior to that at H. As a result of a movement from an inferior position, such as V or T to H, individual B is made better off and A's position remains unchanged. A Paretian improvement takes place. The above argument can equally as well be applied to individual A. Or, since for optimal exchange the rate of indifferent substitution must be equal for all individuals, it follows from the above argument that if the rate of indifferent substitution for any one must equal the rate of product transformation, the rate of indifferent substitution of all must equal the rate of product transformation. Otherwise, given the nature of this model, a Paretian optimum has not been achieved.

Collecting our results together, if a Paretian optimum is to be achieved, given this model, the following conditions must be simultaneously satisfied:

(i) the rate of technical substitution of the factors must be the same for all products; and
(ii) the rate of indifferent substitution of the products must be the same for all consumers and, in turn, be equal to the rate of product transformation.

The convexity and other assumptions are such that if these conditions are satisfied, a Paretian optimum is ensured.

In other models, which could conceivably be more realistic approximations to present economic systems, the satisfaction of the above conditions does not ensure a Paretian optimum. If increasing returns to scale occur in one industry, the above condition (ii) may result in minimum rather than maximum economic efficiency. There are also complications raised by externalities in production and consumption which need to be specifically allowed for. This will be done in the next chapter.

In this model, as in the last, a Paretian optimum is not unique but varies with the distribution of income. Each point on the utility possibility frontier corresponds to a point on the product transformation frontier for the economy. This follows directly from our discussion of Fig. 13.10. The utility possibility frontier for the two-person case might be similar to the one which is set down in Fig. 13.11. If the appropriate social welfare function is indicated by social indifference curves such as those marked by W_0 and W_1, the optimal utility combination is that at point ξ. This point might correspond to production possibility V in Fig. 13.9 and imply the final distribution of products represented by R in that figure. The combination V implies that factors are combined in a way which places the economy on its efficiency locus, for example, the factor combination Z in Fig. 13.7 might correspond to V in Fig. 13.9. Note that all the combinations along the utility possibility frontier in Fig. 13.11 are Paretian optimal and one is powerless to choose between these until a social welfare function has been selected.

The social welfare functions must be able to differentiate between the social desirability of alternative attainable distributions of income or utility. Once an appropriate social welfare function is selected, the optimal production of goods and their optimal

Welfare Economics

distribution can be completely determined. However, it remains true, as was amply demonstrated in the simple exchange case, that a solution which is less than Paretian

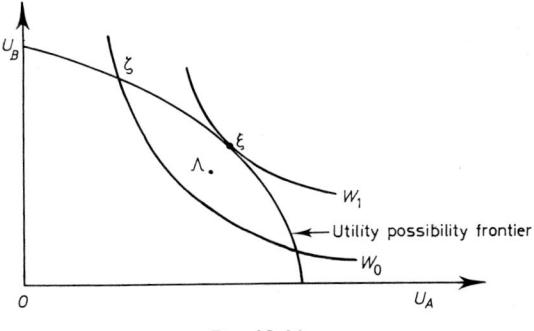

Fig. 13.11

optimal can be superior to a Paretian optimal solution. For example, in Fig. 13.11, the combination Λ which is not Paretian optimal is socially superior to ζ which is Paretian optimal.

Conceivably the social optimum in Fig. 13.11 corresponding to ξ could be achieved by fiat. A central authority might order factor allocations and product distributions in accordance with this optimum. Alternatively, ownership of factors of production might be so varied that if suitable exchange conditions are created the outcome corresponding to ξ is reached. However, some factors cannot be redistributed, for example, inborn qualities or acquired human capabilities at any point of time. Furthermore, the supply of some factors is dependent on suitable incentives: human effort, for example. In all economic systems restrictions of this type may be final bars to attaining a socially ideal state. If the Paretian assumption of inelasticity in the supply of factors is relaxed, it becomes even clearer that production and income distribution questions cannot be completely separated. It might be thought that a system of lump-sum taxes and subsidies would suffice to redistribute income and avoid these difficulties. Being lump-sum, the taxes or subsidies are not varied with one's income. But on consideration, it is readily seen that such a system is impossible. If one is to redistribute income there must be some relation between income and the taxes and subsidies. Even if lump-sum subsidies are paid to low-income groups and lump-sum taxes are only paid by high-income groups, at the borders of these groups the rate of taxation changes dramatically and must influence effort. Furthermore, a person may be in a low-income group not because his original personal endowment is inferior, but because he has a high desire for leisure; he is lazy, if you like to put it that way. To detect this would not only involve an intolerable intrusion on individual freedoms but would be, in practice, next to impossible. In my opinion there are, in the final analysis, insuperable barriers to redistribution of the output or the ownership of factors in every way that we wish. This is not to deny, however, that very significant changes can be made in the distribution of income.

IV. The Optimality of Perfect Competition

In the simple exchange case, it was indicated that perfect competition results in Paretian optimum if externalities are absent. It remains to extend this result to the simple production and exchange case of the last section. The task is to prove that the conditions for a Paretian optimum, namely the following, are automatically satisfied under perfect competition. The Paretian optimal conditions are that, as was pointed out above:

(i) the rate of technical substitution of the factors must be the same for all products; and
(ii) the rate of indifferent substitution of the products must be the same for all consumers and, in turn, be equal to the rate of product transformation.

Consider each of those conditions in the above order.

If perfect competition prevails (and if each firm finds it profitable to produce some of both products 1 and 2) a firm employs factors in producing each product until the value of their marginal product equals their per-unit cost. Otherwise, as was indicated in Chapter 7, the perfectly competitive firm is not maximising its profit.

Letting p_1 and p_2 represent the prices of products 1 and 2 respectively, w_L and w_N the prices per unit of the two factors and letting MPP_{L1} indicate the marginal physical product of factor L allocated to product 1 and giving a similar type of interpretation to the terms MPP_{N1}, MPP_{L2} and MPP_{N2}, each perfectly competitive firm, if it is maximising profit, must employ and allocate factors so that the following conditions hold for it:

$$\begin{cases} p_1 \, MPP_{L1} = w_L & (13.9) \\ p_1 \, MPP_{N1} = w_N & (13.10) \\ p_2 \, MPP_{L2} = w_L & (13.11) \\ p_2 \, MPP_{N2} = w_N. & (13.12) \end{cases}$$

From the discussion surrounding Equation (7.42), it is known that the rate of technical substitution of the factors in producing product 1, RTS_1, is

$$RTS_1 = \frac{MPP_{L1}}{MPP_{N1}} \tag{13.13}$$

and in producing product 2,

$$RTS_2 = \frac{MPP_{L2}}{MPP_{N2}}. \tag{13.14}$$

Dividing Equation (13.9) by (13.10) and Equation (13.11) by (13.12), it can be seen that

$$\frac{w_L}{w_N} = \frac{MPP_{L1}}{MPP_{N1}} = \frac{MPP_{L2}}{MPP_{N2}}. \tag{13.15}$$

Consequently, each firm in maximising its profit equates the rate of technical substitution of the factors in producing each product. Since, by the parity rule, w_L and w_N are the same for all firms under perfect competition, the rates of technical substitution of all are equalised and, taking the economy as a whole, the rate of technical substitution of the factors is equal for both products. Hence, it is confirmed that, in the absence of externalities, perfect competition results in the satisfaction of condition (i).

Turn now to the second condition. It was demonstrated in the discussion surrounding Equation (7.49) that if a perfectly competitive firm has a given quantity of factors and can produce more than one product profitably, it cannot maximise its profit unless it equates its rate of product transformation to the price ratios of the products.

Welfare Economics

Let the allocation of factors between firms be such as to satisfy conditions of Equations (13.9) to (13.12) for all. *Given* these allocations, then profit maximisation implies for *each* firm that its rate of product transformation

$$RPT = \frac{p_1}{p_2} \qquad (13.16)$$

or the equivalent

$$\frac{MC_1}{MC_2} = \frac{p_1}{p_2}. \qquad (13.17)$$

Since p_1 and p_2 are the same for all firms if perfect competition exists, their rates of product transformation are equalised by their profit maximising behaviour.

On the consumption side, it follows from Hicks' theory that any consumer is not maximising his utility unless his rates of indifferent substitution of the available goods equals their price ratios. (See the discussion of Equation (6.13)). For *each* consumer, the rate of indifferent substitution of the products,

$$RIS = \frac{p_1}{p_2}. \qquad (13.18)$$

Since prices are the same for all consumers under perfect competition, their rates of indifferent substitution are rendered equal. Consequently, there is Paretian efficiency in exchange. In our two-person example,

$$RIS_A = RIS_B = \frac{p_1}{p_2}. \qquad (13.19)$$

But since p_1 and p_2 are the same for all and the condition of Equation (13.16) holds, there must also be a Paretian optimal conformance between production and consumption. In our example

$$RPT = \frac{p_1}{p_2} = RIS_A = RIS_B. \qquad (13.20)$$

Hence, condition (ii) is automatically satisfied. As a result of perfect competition, the rate of indifferent substitution of the products is the same for all consumers and, in turn, is equal to the rate of product transformation. Merely by each seeking his own self-interest in a competitive environment, a Paretian optimum results.

Thus under the conditions outlined, that is given the absence of externalities and assuming certain convexity assumptions, perfect competition ensures a Paretian optimum. In the example given, interior solutions were supposed to be the only relevant ones and thus marginal equivalences were necessary for a Paretian optimum. However, if for example, the indifference curves tilt sufficiently or are not convex, corner (boundary) solutions can correspond to the Paretian optimum and certain marginal inequalities must hold for the optimum to be attained. Yet, provided that suitable convexity assumptions are retained, it can be shown by topology and the theory of sets that perfect competition leads to a Paretian optimum.[20] On the other hand, if increasing returns are significant in some parts of the economy, the mathematical convexity requirements are violated and perfect competition cannot exist and cannot be used to propel the economy to a Paretian optimum. The presence of externalities and other factors also leads us to the firm conclusion that, *in practice*, perfect competition does not result in a Paretian optimum, even if conditions for its possible existence are satisfied. It is necessary for governments to interfere to some extent with even a perfectly competitive market system in order to improve economic efficiency. This point will be elaborated in the next chapter.

But to show that, under the above economic conditions, perfect competition does lead to Paretian optimality does not *ipso facto* rule out the possibility that other forms of competition might do this, too. Yet, taking an overall view of the economy and supposing the above static production and consumption relationships, it can be shown that it is extremely likely, almost certain, that imperfect competition results in economic activity which is less than Paretian optimal.

For simplicity imagine that only one factor, L (labour), is used in the production of two goods, and suppose that there is perfect competition in the factor market and in the purchase of the final goods but that firms have a monopolistic arrangement (for example, some cartel arrangement) so that they do not compete perfectly in the sales of the products. If each firm is maximising its profit, it must be the case for *each* firm that

$$RPT = \frac{w_L/MPP_{L1}}{w_L/MPP_{L2}} = \frac{MC_1}{MC_2} = \frac{MR_1}{MR_2} \qquad (13.21)$$

if we suppose that all firms produce both products. In addition, if the group is to maximise profit, MR_1 and MR_2 must be equal for all so that RPT is the same for all.

Assume that the *exceptional* case arises where

$$\frac{MR_1}{MR_2} = \frac{p_1}{p_2}, \qquad (13.22)$$

the relative marginal revenues from the products equal their relative prices. This occurs, for example, if $MR_1 = kp_1$ and $MR_2 = kp_2$, that is if price exceeds the marginal cost or marginal revenue by the same fraction for each product. Hence, even though competition is imperfect

$$RPT = \frac{p_1}{p_2} = RIS_A = RIS_B \qquad (13.23)$$

and the above Paretian condition (ii) is satisfied. Indeed, if the supply of L is completely *inelastic* (the position is the same when there are a number of factors, all in inelastic supply), a complete Paretian optimum is achieved. The employment of L remains unchanged but, as a result of imperfect competition, the real wage is lower and real profit higher than under perfect competition. Under the above circumstance, the sole effect of change from perfect to imperfect competition is a change in the distribution of income, and an alteration of a type which many would regard with disfavour. Economic efficiency is maintained.

However, this is not the outcome if labour is not in inelastic supply. As the result of a fall in the real wage caused by the advent of monopolistic competition, the supply and employment of labour fall and the output of the economy is reduced. Output falls below its Paretian optimal level because labourers are paid less than the value of their marginal product by firms and reduce their supply of labour. Nevertheless, labourers are willing to supply extra labour for the value of its marginal product and could (assuming suitable social arrangements) be made better off without making anyone else worse off. Since the likelihood is great that some factors are not in inelastic supply, in the static setting of increasing costs the case against imperfect competition is strong on

Welfare Economics

efficiency grounds. Add to this the fact that there are no forces under imperfect competition which ensure that Equation (13.22) is the case, and the static case against imperfect competition becomes stronger. Unless perfect competition exists, the ratios of the marginal revenue terms of Equation (13.22) are equal to price ratios by a sheer fluke so that it is also likely that the composition of production is less than Paretian optimal. But if imperfect competition seems likely to lead to deviations from Paretian optimality, it will also be abundantly clear from the next chapter that, once a more realistic view of the economy is taken, perfect competition on its own does not ensure a Paretian optimum either.

NOTES AND REFERENCES

[1] K. J. ARROW, *Social Choice and Individual Values*, John Wiley, New York, 1951. There has been a number of criticisms of Arrow's axioms. See R. LUCE and H. RAIFFA, *Games and Decisions*, John Wiley, New York, 1957, Ch. 14 and J. ROTHENBERG, *The Measurement of Social Welfare*, Prentice-Hall, Englewood Cliffs, 1961.

[2] Neo-classical and present-day economists are deeply aware of non-economic factors and their importance. Pigou, in particular, gave considerable emphasis to the importance of externalities. But I believe that economists, on the whole, have not incorporated sociological factors in their models. Economic factors tend to be considered in isolation. No doubt this problem worried Pareto who turned to the study of sociology later in life.

[3] Once again, this is a caricature. Marshall and Pigou, for example, did give considerable emphasis to externalities.

[4] V. Pareto, *Cours d'économie politique*, 2 volumes, F. Rouge, Lausanne, 1896-1897. *Manuel d'économie politique*, 2nd ed., Giard, Paris, 1927.

[5] A given output or aggregate income has been assumed in this model. In reality, attempts to redistribute income may lead to a lessening of effort. Total output may be reduced. Eventually losses of output may annul advantages from improved distribution of income. Problems of this type are discussed later in this chapter.

[6] F. Y. EDGEWORTH, *Mathematical Psychics*, Kegan Paul, London, 1881.

[7] W. MITCHELL, *Types of Economic Theory*, Augustus M. Kelley, New York, 1967, Vol. I, p. 230. Reproduced with the kind permission of Augustus M. Kelly.

[8] PARETO, op. cit. J. HICKS, "Foundations of Welfare Economics", *Economic Journal*, 1939, **49**, pp. 696-712. L. ROBBINS, *An Essay on the Nature and Significance of Economic Science*, Macmillan, London, 1932.

[9] PARETO, op. cit.

[10] Note that Pareto's criterion can be applied on either an individualistic or paternalistic basis. But the policy implications of preferences on these different bases can be vastly divergent. The matter is of fundamental political significance.

[11] For the stimulating and excellent review of these problems, see JOAN ROBINSON, *Economic Philosophy*, Doubleday, New York, 1964, Ch. 1.

[12] See EDGEWORTH, op. cit. If only two individuals are involved in trading (a bilateral exchange situation) negotiation problems, that is jockeying to ensure just how the gains will be shared along *ED*, may prevent a movement to the contract curve.

[13] See Reference 1.

[14] Negotiation difficulties may stand in the way of a movement to the contract curve or a Paretian optimum. For a review of some of the difficulties, see C. TISDELL, "Some Bounds upon the Pareto Optimality of Group Behaviour", *Kyklos*, 1966, pp. 101-18.

[15] For further details, see M. SHUBIK, *Strategy and Market Structure*, John Wiley, New York, 1959.

[16] The theory which is involved is based on game-theoretical concepts. See M. SHUBIK, "Edgeworth Market Games", in R. D. LUCE and A. W. TUCKER (Eds), *Contributions to the Theory of Games*, Princeton University Press, Princeton, 1958, Vol. IV, pp. 267-78. H. SCARF and G. DEBREU, "A Limit Theorem on the Core of an Economy", *International Economic*

Review, 1963, **4**, pp. 235-47. P. NEWMAN, *The Theory of Exchange*, Prentice-Hall, Englewood Cliffs, 1965.
[17] For further examples, see J. QUIRK and R. SAPOSNIK, *Introduction to General Equilibrium Theory and Welfare Economics*, McGraw-Hill, New York, 1968, Ch. 4.
[18] See QUIRK and SAPOSNIK, op. cit., Secs 4-5. Important extensions appear in K. J. ARROW and G. DEBREU, "Existence of an Equilibrium for a Competitive Economy", *Econometrica*, 1954, **22**, pp. 265-90; D. GALE, "The Law of Supply and Demand", *Mathematica Scandinavia*, 1955, **3**, pp. 155-69 and G. DEBREU, *Theory of Value*, John Wiley, New York, 1959.
[19] See QUIRK and SAPOSNIK, op. cit.
[20] See the references listed in Reference 18.

FURTHER READING

BATOR, F. M., "The Simple Analytics of Welfare Maximisation", *American Economic Review*, 1957, **47**, pp. 22-59.

BOULDING, K. E., "Welfare Economics", in B. HALEY (Ed.), *A Survey of Contemporary Economics*, Vol. I, Irwin, Homewood, 1949.

HANSEN, B., *Lectures in Economic Theory*, 3rd ed., Studentlitteratur, Lund, 1969, Part 2, Lectures 9 and 13.

HENDERSON, J., and R. QUANDT, *Microeconomic Theory*, McGraw-Hill, New York, 1958, Ch. 14.

MANSFIELD, E., *Microeconomics*, Norton, New York, 1970, Chapter 15.

MISHAN, E., "A Survey of Welfare Economics, 1939-1959", *Economic Journal*, 1960, **70**, pp. 197-256.

*QUIRK, J., and R. SAPOSNIK, *Introduction to General Equilibrium Theory and Welfare Economics*, McGraw-Hill, New York, 1968, Ch. 4.

*SAMUELSON, P., *The Foundations of Economic Analysis*, Harvard University Press, Cambridge, 1947, Ch. 8.

---

* Advanced.

CHAPTER 14

More on Markets, Efficiency and Growth

I. Market Failure

Certain conditions were indicated in the last chapter which ensure that perfect competition results in Paretian optimality. Despite the relative generality of the economic conditions under which perfect competition leads to Paretian optimality, non-transient production and consumption relationships arise in practice which imply that perfect competition does not always result in a Paretian optimum. Hence, even under conditions of perfect competition, markets can fail to organise economic activity in a Paretian optimal fashion.

A number of possible causes of market failure exist. For example, if consumers are unable to pursue their true self-interest because of lack of knowledge or weakness, they will choose a consumption pattern which is not truly optimal for them. The question then arises of whether interference with consumers' sovereignty is justifiable. Externalities, too, can cause deviations from Paretian optimality, even if markets are perfectly competitive, and are extremely important in the case of pure public goods. Furthermore, increasing returns and uncertainty are other possible sources of market failure. Each of these aspects is discussed below.

In the light of these aspects, the impact of various market arrangements on economic growth is analysed. It becomes clear that under certain conditions perfect competition cannot exist or is less desirable than other alternatives. Consequently, the concepts of "workable competition" and "countervailing power" are introduced and the question examined of whether forces of countervailing economic power could contribute to economic efficiency. Finally, the question of the second-best is raised. If one (or some of) the conditions for Paretian optimality cannot be fulfilled in the economy, is it desirable to fulfil the other conditions? For example, if imperfect competition exists in one section of the economy, thus creating a deviation from the Paretian conditions in that sector, and cannot be eliminated, is it desirable to promote perfect competition in the remainder of the economy and so fulfil certain Paretian conditions there? Obviously, the answer is important for policy purposes.

A. CONSUMERS' SOVEREIGNTY AND MARKET FAILURE

Whether or not an individual is able to judge his own self-interest is a matter of considerable importance. If an individual knows and is able to pursue his own self-interest, without damage to others, then there is a strong presumption that he should be left free to make his own choices. This would also be so if he happened to be a better judge of his own self-interest than any other (identifiable) individual. Now, classical liberal economists such as John Stuart Mill[1] and many economists since, have accepted the proposition that, with a few exceptions (for example, lunatics and children), each individual is the best judge of his own self-interest.

Applying this to markets, their stand can be reasonably stated as follows: on the whole, an individual is the best judge of his own self-interest and so a consumer, subject to the restrictions of the market, can be expected to choose his truly optimal consumption-bundle, or at least one which can be expected to be truly better on average than one selected for him by another individual. In essence, if markets are perfectly competitive and externalities are absent, a true Paretian optimum results for the economy.

But is an individual always the best judge of his own self-interest and bound to act in accordance to it? The answer is *no*. A consumer might be less well able to judge his own self-interest in some matters than an expert in these matters. For example, a consumer may well have less knowledge about the technical characteristics, health effects, etc. associated with the consumption of some products than specialists in certain fields, such as engineering and medicine. Ignorance is a problem for consumers, especially in this age in which products have become highly complex. Yet even if a consumer is not ignorant, he still may fail to act in his own self-interest. He may perceive his interests well and yet because of personal weaknesses he may be unable to pursue these steadfastly. Weaknesses lead him to prefer short-term gains over his long-term goals. The individual might be well aware of this and indeed welcome a restraining influence by others on his behaviour. If society as a whole is considered, these two failures might be much rarer than economists like Mill supposed. To point to their existence, however, is not to argue that government interference with consumers' sovereignty is called for.

Nevertheless, all governments do restrict consumers' sovereignty (but not just on the above two grounds).[2] Often, for example, gambling, alcohol and tobacco are taxed at high rates, whereas products like housing, opera and milk are subsidised. Some items are completely banned or are restricted in their use, for example, "hard" drugs, and "obscene" material.

A pictorial representation of a divergence between true and apparent preferences of individuals is given in Fig. 14.1. Housing and gambling are assumed to be the only two variable consumption goods available to the society. The solid indifference curves represent the *true* preferences of individuals for housing and gambling. The dashed set of indifference curves is the revealed preference set of indifference curves in a free market allowing short-term weaknesses, impetuosities, etc. to take their toll. Given the product transformation curve *ABD*, equilibrium in the absence of governmental intervention is attained at combination *C*. But this is not the true Paretian optimum.[3] The true Paretian optimum is at *B*. The government, by taxing gambling and subsidising housing, or doing just one of these things to a suitable extent, can shift the economy to point *B*, the true Paretian optimum. This is so unless this interference leads to some reduction in effort because short-term satisfaction (real income) is reduced. But even then the economy might only be slightly below *B* so that real preferences are better satisfied than in situation *C*. Whether or not individuals should rely on governments to correct their personal weaknesses is a moot point. However, if the divergence between apparent and real preferences is a result of faulty information rather than personal weakness, then a social case would seem to exist for provision of improved information by the government.

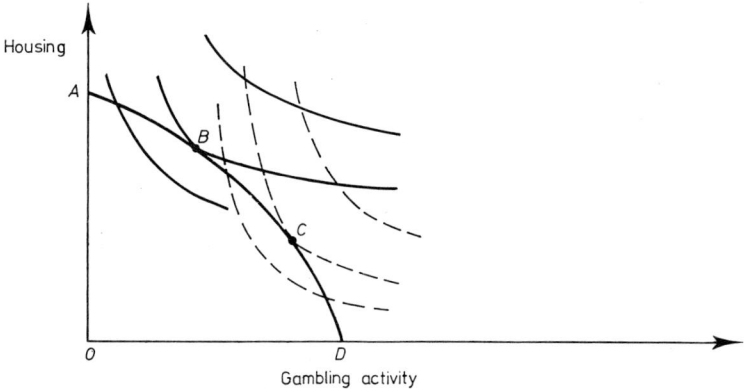

Fig. 14.1

But interference with consumers' sovereignty may be based on other grounds. An individual's consumption activity may damage others. Drunkards and drug addicts may become a risk to others (for example, by increasing the probability of car accidents). Or, more directly, they may have a very adverse impact on their dependants, neglecting them materially or causing injury to them. A society which has regard to the welfare of *all* individuals surely feels compelled to interfere in these cases to control consumption of the products concerned.

There do, therefore, seem to be some grounds for interference with consumers' sovereignty. But for those of us who believe that, on matters which do not directly affect others, the individual should have the right to choose even to be wrong, freedom in this matter will not be forgone lightly. Freedom of individual choice is regarded by many as a desirable thing in itself.

B. EXTERNALITIES

As mentioned earlier, externalities can be a source of market inefficiency. If externalities exist, perfectly competitive markets are unlikely to yield a Paretian optimum. Externalities occur if there are direct interactions between the activities of economic agents—interdependencies which are external to the price system and consequently escape being priced, that is being valued by the market.

Externalities may be favourable or unfavourable to others. The classical example of an unfavourable externality is that of a company which emits smoke and other pollutants into the atmosphere free of cost. The marginal cost to the company of this method of disposal is zero or low, but the real cost to the community can be great. As a consequence of the pollution, health suffers, buildings of others decay at a faster rate and the cleaning costs of others rise. Economists, such as Pigou,[4] advised that governments should tax activities of this kind so that private cost and social cost are brought more into line. But not all externalities are unfavourable to others. An orchardist might contribute to the output of a nearby apiary by planting trees, a householder might add to the satisfaction of his neighbours by maintaining a pleasant garden, or an individual, by adding to knowledge, might make the discoveries of others easier. In free markets, no reward is paid to an economic agent for his favourable external effects. Consequently, resources under perfect competition might not be allocated in a Paretian optimal way. This can be illustrated by two simple examples.

Consider first an example in which one-way external dependence occurs between the production of firms. Let the output of firm 1 depend upon *its* use of a single factor alone so that its production function can be expressed as

$$x_1 = f_1(l_1) \qquad (14.1)$$

where x_1 represents its output of product X and l_1 its use of factor L. Take a second firm and suppose that its output of product X depends not just on its employment of factor L but also upon the use of the factor by firm 1 so that the production function of firm 2 can be expressed as

$$x_2 = f_2(l_1, l_2) \qquad (14.2)$$

where x_2 indicates the output of product X by firm 2 and l_2 its employment of factor L. The productive activity of firm 1 has an external effect on the output of firm 2. Interdependence of this type might arise in a river valley. If farmers in the headwaters apply greater quantities of fertilisers, those in the lower reaches might make some gain in their output as a result of deposition of superior alluvium during floods. Other examples can be invented to fit the case. For illustrative purposes, let us limit our attention to two firms while fully realising that, in a perfectly competitive market, it would be really necessary to have a large number of firms.

Suppose that perfect competition occurs and that the overall supply of L is inelastic. As was noted in Chapter 3 and subsequently, profit maximisation under perfect competition ensures that the private marginal physical product of the factor is equalised for all firms. In turn this implies, if diminishing marginal productivity is the rule *and* externalities are absent, that the total product is maximised for the employed quantity of L. But if externalities are present, profit maximisation under conditions of perfect competition does not ensure a maximum of output.

Take the above example. In order to maximise its profit, each firm employs the factor up to the point where the factor's price per unit, w, equals the value of its private marginal product, that is to the point where w equals the price of the product, p, times the marginal physical product which the firm *itself* obtains from the factor. If each firm is maximising its profit, the following equations are satisfied for firm 1 and firm 2 respectively:

$$w = p\frac{df_1}{dl_1}, \qquad (14.3)$$

$$w = p\frac{\partial f_2}{\partial l_2}. \qquad (14.4)$$

Hence,

$$PMP_1 = \frac{w}{p} \qquad (14.5)$$

and

$$PMP_2 = \frac{w}{p} \qquad (14.6)$$

and, consequently, perfect competition renders the *private* marginal physical products

Markets, Efficiency and Growth

(*PMP*s) of the factor equal. If no marginal externalities are present, that is if $\frac{\partial f_2}{\partial l_1} = 0$, and if marginal physical product is declining, overall output of X is maximised for the employed quantity of L. But if a marginal externality arises, the allocation of the factor between the firms, which arises from profit maximisation, does not maximise the output of the employed L. For example, if employment of L by firm 1 has a favourable marginal impact on the output of firm 2, that is if $\frac{\partial f_2}{\partial l_1} > 0$, the relative use of the factor by firm 1 (assuming that it maximises profit) is less than necessary to ensure maximum output from the employed resources.

If overall output is to be maximised for the employed L, the social marginal products from each firm's use of L must be equal. Social marginal product includes not only additions made to the output of the firm concerned by its extra employment of the factor but also any repercussions on output elsewhere. Thus, in this example, the social marginal product of L for firms 1 and 2 respectively, is

$$SMP_1 = \frac{df_1}{dl_1} + \frac{\partial f_2}{\partial l_1} \tag{14.7}$$

and

$$SMP_2 = \frac{\partial f_2}{\partial l_2}. \tag{14.8}$$

Because of the external effect, the social marginal product of firm 1 from employing L exceeds its private marginal product. However, the necessary conditions for profit maximisation, Equations (14.3) and (14.4), imply equality only of private marginal products, that is

$$\frac{df_1}{dl_1} = \frac{\partial f_2}{\partial l_2} \tag{14.9}$$

and *not* equality of social marginal products, that is *not*

$$\frac{df_1}{dl_1} + \frac{\partial f_2}{\partial l_1} = \frac{\partial f_2}{\partial l_2}. \tag{14.10}$$

Hence, output is not maximised under perfect competition for the employed L.

This is illustrated in Fig. 14.2. Employment of L by firm 1 is shown to the right of the origin and that of firm 2 to the left. The vertical axis gives a measure in terms of units of X and the social and private marginal products of the curves are indicated by obvious nomenclature. If the real wage rate is $\frac{w}{p} = OA$, profit maximisation leads firm 1 to use l_1 of the factor and firm 2 to employ l_2. However, output from the employment $L = l_1 + l_2$ is not maximised. Only by re-allocating L so that its social marginal product is the same for all firms can a maximum be attained. In the illustration, this maximum occurs if firm 1 increases its employment of the factor to $\hat{l}_1$ and firm 2 reduces its employment to $\hat{l}_2$. The net *increase* in output as a result is the difference between the hatched area and the dotted area.

The externality which is shown in Fig. 14.2 is Paretian relevant. However, externalities which are not Paretian relevant can easily arise. In the above case, if SMP_1 happened to exceed PMP_1 for employments of $l_1 < \hat{l}_1$ and to equal it for larger employments of l_1, although an externality would arise, it would not exist at the margin and the allocation of $L = l_1 + l_2$ in a perfectly competitive market would maximise output from L. Externalities are not necessarily inconsistent with the attainment of Paretian optimality under perfect competition.[5]

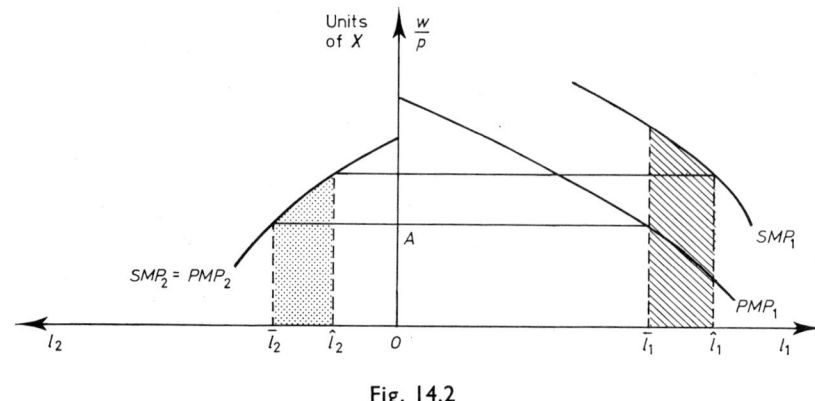

Fig. 14.2

More complicated patterns of externality can occur than that in the above example. Externalities may, for example, be mutual and they can arise in consumption as well as in production. Nevertheless, the main point continues to hold. If externalities exist, the self-seeking of economic agents in a perfectly competitive market does not ensure a Paretian optimum. As a result of externalities, the social marginal cost of a product can diverge from its private marginal cost or its private marginal value may differ from its social marginal value, and so the invisible hand of Adam Smith fails to ensure the economy of a Paretian optimum.

An extreme type of externality occurs in the consumption of goods which have been called *pure public goods*. *Pure* public goods have the property that any individual's consumption of the goods does not subtract from their possible consumption by others. Thus they differ markedly from *private* consumption goods. Any individual's enjoyment of a private consumption excludes its enjoyment by others. For example, bread is a private consumption item since, given the total stock of bread, the increase in one person's consumption of bread is at the expense of the possible consumption of others. Examples of pure public goods are difficult to find. The services of lighthouse is one case. Its use by one ship in no way detracts from its use by another. Radio and television constitute another. If an extra individual tunes in to a radio or television channel, this does not prevent others with different sets from doing so. Malaria eradication would also fit the pattern. But many goods which are not pure public goods nevertheless have characteristics akin to these. For example, my consumption of a product might only partially exclude others from its consumption. If I purchase tickets close to the opera stage, I exclude others from that place but I do not exclude them from watching at a greater distance. Private defence or security forces, too, might provide some "spin-off" protection for others, but not the same degree of protection as for their owners. However, if an externality exists, if the supply of a commodity provides marginal benefits to others which cannot be made conditional on a price payment, government interference is called for because the community, if left

C. DECREASING COSTS

To have a number of producers in a decreasing cost industry, that is one in which the long-run average costs of firms are falling, is less than Pareto optimal. Indeed, cost conditions in the industry are such that perfect competition cannot be sustained and either oligopoly or monopoly is likely to result.[6]

But there is a social problem. If the product is homogeneous, it is socially optimal to have just one producer in the industry. However, unless perfect price discrimination is possible, the producer will not supply a Paretian optimal quantity of the product. The Paretian optimal quantity of output does not maximise the profit of the producer and, worse, it involves a loss. A loss is made since, if average cost is declining, marginal cost is below it and thus, if price is equated to marginal cost, average revenue is less than average cost. The Paretian optimal behaviour (externalities absent) of equating price and marginal cost results in a loss. This is illustrated in Fig. 14.3.

In Fig. 14.3, the demand curve, D, for a single producer of a product X is shown and his declining average cost is indicated by AC. The corresponding marginal revenue and marginal cost curves are marked by MR and MC respectively. The Paretian optimal output is $\bar{x}$ but this results in the loss represented by the hatched area. However, if the firm is a profit-maximiser, it produces an output $\hat{x}$ which is less than the Paretian optimal output.

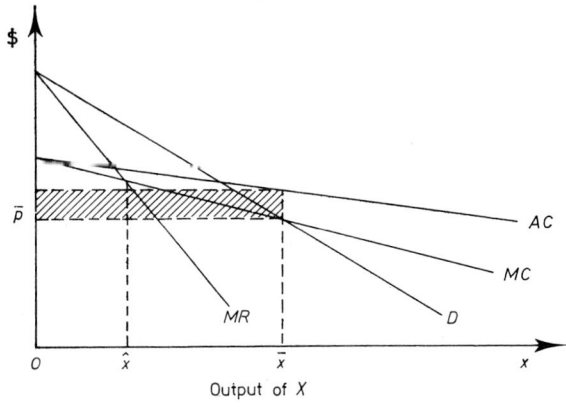

Fig. 14.3

What policy should a government adopt in these circumstances? Clearly, it cannot control the monopoly merely by setting a ceiling price of $\bar{p}$, for then production would be completely unprofitable. However, by paying a suitable progressive subsidy, the government could induce the firm to produce $\bar{x}$. But this assumes that the Hotelling-Lerner output[7] (the one for which marginal cost equals demand) as well as characteristics of cost and demand are known to the government. Furthermore, the subsidy would have to be provided out of taxes and these might be a cause of inefficiency elsewhere. If the government nationalises the industry, it still must determine an optimal output and pricing policy. This is considered in Chapter 21. At this stage sufficient has been said to indicate that decreasing costs are barriers to achieving Paretian optimality in a (free) market system.

D. ERRORS AND UNCERTAINTIES

Our world is one of less-than-perfect knowledge, even if it is not one of complete ignorance. At any point of time, economic agents are rarely aware of åll the prices of commodities everywhere which interest or involve them. Even in the absence of transport costs, the parity price theorem is violated because economic agents are not fully informed. Because of ignorance, the same commodity often fetches different prices at the same point of time. Consequently, some marginal conditions for a Paretian optimum are violated. Or again, divergency in expectations about future prices can lead to a violation of the Paretian conditions. For example, if production must be planned and if there is a lag before it is realised, divergencies in price expectations by firms lead to a Paretian loss. Indeed, deficiencies of knowledge can cause *every* condition for a Paretian optimum to be violated. Spatial as well as temporal ignorance about market prices can be a cause of market failure.

Take a simple example. Consider two firms which produce a single product X and use a single variable factor L, and suppose that each has no influence on prices. Let the respective production functions of firms 1 and 2 be

$$x_1 = f_1(l_1) \tag{14.11}$$
$$x_2 = f_2(l_2). \tag{14.12}$$

Then, given their employed L, their production is not at a maximum unless

$$f_1'(l_1) = f_2'(l_2), \tag{14.13}$$

that is, unless the marginal physical product of L is the same for both. Suppose that the price per unit of L is known to both and is w, but that each must estimate p, the price of the product. Let the estimate of firm 1 be $\hat{p}_1$ and that of firm 2 be $\hat{p}_2$ and suppose that each firm acts to maximise its anticipated profit on this basis. Consequently, firms 1 and 2 respectively employ quantities of L which ensure that

$$w = \hat{p}_1 f_1'(l_1) \tag{14.14}$$

and

$$w = \hat{p}_2 f_1'(l_2). \tag{14.15}$$

Hence,

$$f_1'(l_1) = w/\hat{p}_1 \tag{14.16}$$

and

$$f_2'(l_2) = w/\hat{p}_2. \tag{14.17}$$

Therefore only if $\hat{p}_1 = \hat{p}_2$, is the condition of Equation (14.13) satisfied, and is output at a maximum for the employed L. Since it is most likely that expectations will diverge to some extent, due to lack of knowledge, it is likely that $\hat{p}_1 \neq \hat{p}_2$ and thus a necessary condition for Paretian optimality, Equation (14.13), is probably violated.[8]

If the production functions of the two firms are the same, the divergency in their estimate of p causes their employment of L to differ. In Fig. 14.4, the firm which anticipates the lower product price might, for example, employ only $\bar{l}_1$ of labour and the other $\bar{l}_2$. Their total output is equal to 2 OA. But if each holds less divergent expectations, the output from the employed L is higher. If each has a common expectation about p which leads to each employing $\frac{1}{2}(l_1+l_2)$ of L, total output *from the same quantity of* L expands to $2\,OB$. (The point D in the figure corresponds to $\frac{1}{2}(l_1+l_2)$. Governmental interference to reduce the range of price expectations could lead to a Paretian improvement. Divergent expectations do *not* cancel out in their effect. On other occasions, too, *if* the government has superior market knowledge, there might be a case for interference. For example, if firms grossly overestimate the likely future demand for a product and begin investing in specific equipment, a social loss can eventuate unless their optimism is checked. A case can also be made out for the government's subsidisation of some market knowledge since externalities generally stem from its provision.

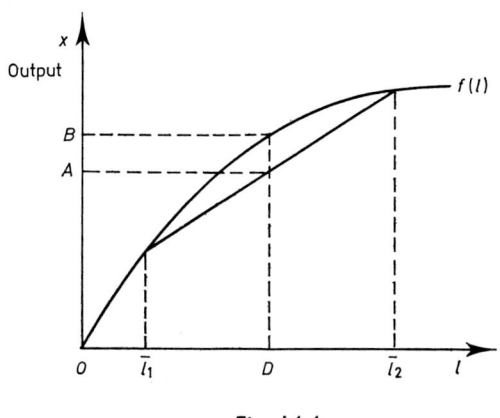

Fig. 14.4

II. Schumpeterian Ideas and Dynamics

Our investigations of Paretian optimality have not been extended to optimisation over time. In the previous chapter, optimisation within a single period was implicitly assumed. Although time creates certain complications (some of which will be mentioned presently) by regarding the commodities of different periods as different goods, one can extend the static model in a comparatively easy way. While perfect competition might in principle (ruling out externalities and decreasing costs) result in a multiperiod Paretian optimum, in practice it seems to be impossible to satisfy the knowledge requirements for its operation. In a multiperiod setting, Paretian optimality is achieved only if it is impossible to make anyone better off (who is either alive now or is to be born in the future) without making another worse off. Even disregarding the fact that individuals change their apparent lifetime preferences as they go through life, it seems almost impossible to predict the preferences of generations yet unborn and to know their number. Yet, if by some miracle, firms could predict all future prices then, under certain circumstances, perfect competition does ensure multiperiod Paretian optimality.[9] But externalities, decreasing costs, and deficiencies of knowledge must be absent.

In reality these factors are important, so it hardly seems conceivable that Paretian optimality can be achieved by the operation of perfectly competitive markets. In practice, too, some forms of imperfect competition might, as Schumpeter[10] suggested, be economically superior in the long run to perfect competition. Schumpeter's view was mentioned earlier but our discussion of market failure enables us to put it in new perspective.

In the decreasing average cost case, there are clear arguments against attempting to promote a perfectly competitive structure in the industry, so let us put this case to one side. Schumpeter is concerned with something rather different. He contends that, while perfect competition might result in Paretian optimality (at any point of time), it can be nevertheless inferior in the long run to imperfect competition which leads to Paretian optimality at no point of time.[11] Invention and innovation might proceed at a faster rate under imperfect competition and so in the long run make for greater productivity of employed resources than would be the case under perfect competition. However, the problem which Schumpeter poses does not, if correctly considered, result from a conflict between static and dynamic efficiency but from the fact that externalities and uncertainties are important under pure competition. Monopolies enable some externalities to be internalised and uncertainties to be reduced. If a monopoly exists in a field, inventions and successful innovations are not quickly copied by rivals. Rivals are absent. If there is no patent system and if rivals are present, they are at liberty to adopt inventions without payments to inventors. Even if a patent system is in operation some aspects of new knowledge can be of value to rivals and yet not be subject to the protection of the patent.[12] Monopolies by reducing externalities of invention and innovation and rendering a larger share of the gains to the firm (inventor) may stimulate research and development expenditures and innovations.

Again, monopolies may reduce uncertainties. A monopolist, if he has several plants supplying the same market, is hardly likely to operate these on the basis of divergent demand expectations and will, as a rule, find it more profitable to know more about demand than a series of individual perfectly competitive firms. Furthermore, if the firm is large, it may be diversified and research and innovation for it may constitute a smaller risk, so that it is likely to act more in accord with expected returns than would a large number of small firms. Economies of scale in the production of knowledge could also give a monopolist an advantage.

But Schumpeter's case in favour of monopoly and oligopoly does not only rest on these arguments. The very survival even of monopoly and oligopolistic firms can be threatened by the advent of new products or substitutes for theirs. A superior synthetic fibre replaces an earlier one, plastics replace glass in some uses and the very survival of the firm can be at stake. Thus in order to survive, firms, even in industries where there are few, cannot safely abandon their quest for new products and for new qualities in old ones. Even though oligopolists might not actively compete by means of price, nevertheless they may be in very active competition in attempting to improve the quality of their products. On the whole, if too little effort is directed to research activity under atomistic competition, for example, because favourable externalities occur, then this deficiency might be corrected to some extent under imperfect competition. This is not to deny that there might be an even better way of dealing with the problem.

Professor Samuelson states the position clearly.

> In admitting the superiority of monopoly to atomistic competition in certain respects, we do not imply that it is the best possible organisation of an industry. There necessarily exists a still better third alternative, which may or may not be less Utopian than the restoration and maintenance of atomistic competition.[13]

The social desirability of alternative types of competition in a market cannot be

Markets, Efficiency and Growth

sensibly settled on an *a priori* basis. Technological characteristics and any other peculiarities of the market must be specifically taken into account. Because of the realisation that perfect competition is not always attainable nor ideal, some economists have suggested "workable competition" as a new benchmark concept. While concepts of "workable competition" differ, the motivation behind the discussion is the same, namely to provide simple and realistic guidelines for bodies which are charged with regulating competition in the public interest.

III. Workable Competition and Countervailing Power

A concept of workable competition was first advanced by John Maurice Clark in 1940.[14] Clark's ideas about competition are very similar to those of Schumpeter.[15] Clark pointed out that imperfect markets are not insulated against competition in the long run and long-term competitive forces might be so great that the behaviour of firms approaches an economic efficiency ideal. The fear of entry might keep prices down, substitutes might keep demand curves relatively flat and entry forestalling behaviour might spur the adoption of new techniques. Although numbers are not great in any industry, competition can nevertheless be a major factor influencing its operation.

Other writers, such as Stigler,[16] have tried to define workable competition or effective competition by market structure. A market is workably competitive if it reasonably approximates the structure of a purely competitive market; for example, numbers are not small and entry is not difficult. Naturally, this leaves some scope for interpretation. The closer an industry approaches a perfectly competitive structure the better, by apparent implication, are the economic consequences for the community. But our previous discussions, for example, of the decreasing average-cost case, indicates that this is not so. A sweeping structural approach is not an adequate policy guide.

In assessing the social acceptability of the state of competition in any market one must at least answer the following questions:

(i) Can any other forms of competition exist freely in the market?

(ii) How do the alternatives compare from an efficiency point of view? Here one needs to keep in mind all those circumstances in which perfect competition is not the most efficient market form.

(iii) If a socially more desirable alternative exists, is it politically attainable and, if so, how does the social cost (that is, of policing and enforcing rules) compare with gains in direct economic efficiency?

In addition, one might also want to take into account the impact of changes on the distribution of income and non-economic factors. For example, a market which encourages individual independence and reduces the power of a few might be welcomed, for a society might value these attributes. A society might be prepared to forgo some output for the preservation of desired characteristics of this kind.

Economic performance cannot be judged by market structure alone and lack of competition need not result in inferior economic performance, although it might do so. The structural approach to workable or effective competition seems inadequate from a policy point of view. Depending upon different technological and market conditions, varying market structures are the most efficient (although there might be non-market structures which are even better than these again) and the appropriate market organisation may change with historical developments. A most realistic view has been expressed by Markham. He says:

> A possible alternative approach to the concept of workable competition may be one that shifts the emphasis from a set of specific structural characteristics to an appraisal of a particular industry's overall performance against the background of possible remedial action. Definitions of workable competition shaped along these lines might accept as a first approximation some such principle as the following: An industry may be judged to be workably competitive when, after the structural characteristics of its market and the dynamic forces that shaped them have been thoroughly examined, there is no clearly indicated change that can be effected through public policy measures that would result in greater social gains than social losses.[17]

But is it not somewhat misleading to call this workable competition since the satisfaction of the condition can require the absence of competition? Possibly a market which satisfies Markham's criterion should be described as "workably efficient" or "workably acceptable", rather than "workably competitive".

Atomistic competition is not always possible and it can be inefficient. In some industries because of decreasing average cost, there is a natural tendency towards concentration of market power. Economic power in many industries is concentrated and, in practice, it is hard to find any market which is regulated by the purely independent behaviour of a large number of economic agents because, even in industries where a large number of firms exist, there are generally associations for the advancement of the joint interests of members. Does the concentration of economic power in an industry result in economic inefficiency and exploitation of individuals? Not only are the points mentioned above relevant to answering this question but so also are matters raised by Galbraith.[18] It is his thesis that concentration and use of power in any part of the economy leads to the affected groups forming countervailing coalitions: "Those who are subject to the aggressions of economic power—to monopoly or to a strong buyer of their labour or of their products—have both a positive and a negative incentive to organise resistance."[19] One economic coalition leads to a counter-coalition and so on. Galbraith suggests that as a result of this countervailing tendency the exploitative power of unilateral control in markets is mitigated and that economic efficiency might be greater than otherwise.

There can be little doubt that the phenomenon which Galbraith mentions is important in current society, but its effects are less clear. It is not certain to lead to greater distributive justice, but may do so. The main problem is that not all groups are equally well able to countervail. Some, such as consumers, are not cohesive as a group and others, such as pensioners, have little threat power. As a result of the formation of large coalitions in society (for example, business associations, trade unions) negotiation in economic transaction becomes more important and the cost of transactions themselves is likely to increase. Furthermore, the conditions of exchange become more indeterminate.[20] Clearly any formal development of Galbraith's approach must be linked with results in Game Theory but as yet there has been little formal development of the approach in this respect.

While countervailing power can increase economic efficiency, it is not certain to do so. For example, if price is raised above marginal cost in one sector, other sectors (by countervailing and also raising their price above marginal cost) *might* improve rather than reduce economic efficiency. A case of this nature was discussed at the end of the last chapter. Countervailing power may help to promote a second-best optimum. Given that cartels, oligopolies and so on exist in one sector of the economy, for example, amongst manufacturing firms, there may be a case for encouraging associations of economic agents elsewhere, for example, in agriculture and amongst labourers. The real problem, however, is that the outcome is not certain to increase efficiency and improve distributive justice. There also seems a real possibility of cost push inflation being hard to control in a society of powerful associations.

IV. The Theory of the Second-Best

As has already been observed,[21] certain systematic deviations of price from marginal cost need not be inconsistent with the achievement of a Paretian optimum. A. C. Pigou seems to have been the first to mention this idea and it was further developed by Kahn in an article of 1935.[22] Not long after this Samuelson reiterated the main point and mentioned a closely connected but different one.[23] If for some reason it is impossible to achieve some of the Paretian conditions for an optimum, it is usually necessary to diverge from the rest. He said:

> A given divergence in a subset of the optimum conditions necessitates alterations in the remaining ones. Thus, in a world where almost all industries are producing at marginal social cost less than price (either because of monopoly or external economies) it would not be desirable for the rest to produce up to the point where marginal cost equals price. Neither would it be quite correct to seek the same percentage or absolute divergence from optimum conditions in each case; although in this particular example, if the elasticity of the supplies of the factors of production were zero, the proportionality of prices to marginal cost would be as good as the exact equality.[24]

If monopoly or imperfect competition is present in one sector, for example, in the manufacturing sector and cannot be eliminated, it might be (some economists would say it is) undesirable to promote perfect competition in places where this can be done, for example, in agriculture; or to adopt the "price equals marginal cost" rule for output in public enterprise. Desirable is interpreted as Paretian optimal, *given* any constraints which prevent the attainment of a position which is Paretian preferable. The Paretian optimum which can be achieved in the absence of constraints can be described as a *first-best* optimum and the Paretian optimum subject to the constraints can be called a *second-best* optimum. Because restrictions do exist in most countries (for example, it is virtually impossible to eliminate imperfect competition in secondary industry) the conditions for a second-best optimum are important for policy purposes.

Although a number of writers had discussed second-best solutions in particular contexts, Lipsey and Lancaster were the first to treat the solutions generally.[25] On the basis of their general considerations, they contend that if it is impossible to satisfy one or more of the conditions for a first Paretian optimum then a second-best optimum can *only* be achieved by departing from *all* the other first-best Paretian conditions. Furthermore, if a restriction occurs which prevents the attainment of one or more first-best conditions, increasing the number of first-best conditions which are satisfied in the economy may but need not increase welfare. No *a priori* judgement is possible. The exact nature of the interdependence must be explicitly taken into account.

The theory of Lipsey and Lancaster has a rather negative policy inference. Their theory condemns "piecemeal welfare economics", the putting into effect of first-best

Paretian conditions on a partial basis. They say: "To apply to only a small part of an economy welfare rules which would lead to a Paretian optimum if they were applied everywhere, may move the economy away from, not toward a second-best optimum position." If imperfect competition cannot be eradicated in one sector of an economy, a policy of promoting perfect competition in others or of producing an output which equates marginal cost and price can decrease welfare.

To illustrate their point, Lipsey and Lancaster[26] take an economy which consists of three industries. Designate these industries by A, B and C. Industry A is imperfectly competitive, C is perfectly competitive and B is operated by the government. The problem which they pose is this: Given the competitive situation in industries A and C, what should the level of production be in B?

If monopoly existed in A and perfect competition in the other two industries, the quantity of output of the monopolised product would be less than optimal and production of the non-monopolised goods as a group would be greater than optimal. If industry B behaves in a perfectly competitive fashion, it tends to produce more of its product relative to the monopolised product than a second-best Paretian optimum requires. On the other hand, if industry B acts in a monopolistic way, its output is reduced relative to the monopolist but, assuming that factors are in inelastic supply, the excess output of industry C increases. A second-best policy is required. Rather than produce an output which equates price and marginal cost, it is socially preferable to produce an output which ensures that price is in excess of marginal cost in industry B but by a smaller fractional difference than in industry A, the monopolised industry. At least this is so under the conditions outlined by Lipsey and Lancaster.[27]

However, using the Kahn-Samuelson argument, if *both* industries, B and C, can be controlled, the optimal output in both industries is that which ensures that price exceeds marginal cost by the same proportion as in the monopolised industry. If price exceeds marginal cost by the same proportion in all industries and if factors are in *inelastic* supply, a Paretian optimum is achieved. Nevertheless this optimum may be attained at the expense of the real income of labour. Even though a Paretian optimum can be achieved if monopoly is general and "equi-proportional", real wages are likely to be lower than under perfect competition. Thus welfare judgements in this area require us to evaluate the social desirability of differences in the distribution of income.

Problems raised by the second-best are difficult to represent graphically. Yet some graphical representation is possible. Consider a simple and rather artificial example. Assume that two firms (two regions can be substituted if this is more appealing) are both able to produce two goods, products 1 and 2. Imagine that each firm possesses a fixed quantity of resources and that they have identical product transformation possibilities. Represent the output of product 1 by x_1 and of product 2 by x_2 and let the curve passing through DAB in Fig. 14.5 indicate each firm's product transformation function. Suppose that one of the firms (regions) produces an inflexible combination of products, for example, the combination at B, but that the other remains completely flexible. Given the restraint imposed by the inflexible firm, the production possibility frontier of the economy *divided by two* is indicated by the curve which passes through $KBCE$. The economy's frontier in the absence of restraint is, *after dividing by two*, DAB. The constrained attainable frontier $KBCE$ is the locus of the mid-point of a chord which has one end-point fixed at B and the other free to move along DAB.

Markets, Efficiency and Growth

Modifying the social welfare function to take account of the fact that the quantities of goods available to society are twice those shown in Fig. 14.5, some contours of a modified social welfare function are shown by the curves marked W_0, W_1 and W_2. In the case illustrated, if there are no restraints on product transformation, the social optimum corresponds to point A. Each firm produces a combination equivalent to A. At this first-best position, rates of product transformation are equal for both firms and, in turn, equal to the rate of indifferent social substitution of the products. But if the production of one firm is restricted to B, the second-best optimum corresponds to point C.

If the output of the economy, divided by two, is at point C and if one firm is producing at B, the other must be producing at point D. Hence, for a second-best optimum, since the slope of the individual transformation functions differ at B and D, the rates of product transformation of the firms must diverge. Furthermore, equalising the rates by ensuring that both firms produce at B reduces social welfare. Putting some of the first-best conditions into effect reduces welfare.

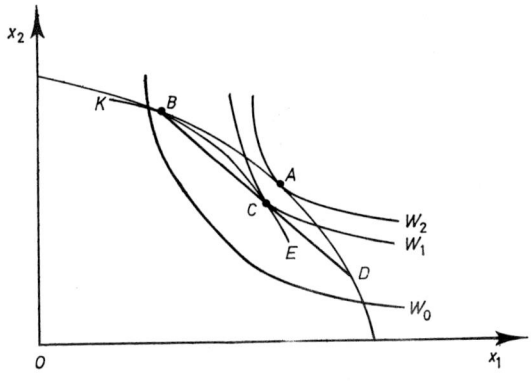

Fig. 14.5

Lipsey and Lancaster claim general application for their propositions about the second-best. But it is not hard to show that their propositions are not universally valid. Consider a simple example. Imagine that only a single product is being produced and requires one variable factor, say labour, for its production. Suppose that the overall supply of labour is inelastic. Then, a first-best optimum requires that labour be allocated so that its marginal physical product is equal everywhere.

Now imagine that, in this one-product world, a region which has a high marginal productivity restricts the inflow of labour so as to maintain its marginal physical product above that elsewhere in the world. Given this limitation what should be done to maximise output? It follows, in a straightforward fashion, that output is maximised if the marginal physical productivity of labour is equalised inside the restricted region and also equalised outside of it. Of course, the real wage rate will be lower outside the restricted region than inside, and lower than in the absence of the migration constraint. In the absence of externalities and given the necessary convexity conditions, perfect competition in both areas maximises output subject to the constraint. The promotion of competition in any sub-region adds to output; putting into effect more of the first-best marginal conditions adds to output, even though constraints prevent the attainment of a first-best level of output.

Other exceptions to the general theory of second-best have been noted by Ferguson, for example.[28] These can arise if one group or sector is not closely linked with the remainder of the economy. Nevertheless, Lipsey and Lancaster's main point remains. Promotion of competition in one area or the fulfilment of first-best conditions in one sector may reduce welfare if deviations from perfect competition occur in other related areas. In cases like this one cannot rely on partial theories for policy guidance.

NOTES AND REFERENCES

[1] John Stuart Mill, (1806-1873), *Collected Works*, University of Toronto Press, Toronto, 1963.

[2] For example, some of the items mentioned below may be taxed because of their revenue yield to the government and others may be subsidised so as to raise the incomes of favoured groups of individuals. No high ideals may be involved.

[3] That is, it is not a Paretian optimum based on "true" preferences.

[4] A. C. PIGOU, *The Economics of Welfare*, 4th ed., Macmillan, London, 1932.

[5] For other examples of Paretian irrelevant externalities, see J. E. MEADE, "External Economies and Diseconomies in a Competitive Situation", *Economic Journal*, 1952, **62**, pp. 54-67. J. BUCHANAN and W. STUBBLEBINE, "Externality", *Economica*, N.S., 1962, **29**, pp. 371-84. C. TISDELL, "On the Theory of Externalities", *Economic Record*, March 1970, pp. 14-25.

[6] Cf. P. SRAFFA, "The Laws of Returns under Competitive Conditions", *Economic Journal*, 1926, **36**, pp. 535-50. Reprinted in A.E.A., *Readings in Price Theory*, George Allen and Unwin, 1953.

[7] H. HOTELLING, "The General Welfare in Relation to Problems of Taxation and of Railway and Utility Rates", *Econometrica*, 1938, **6**, pp. 242-69.

[8] For further discussion of social loss due to divergent expectations and errors of prediction, see C. TISDELL, *The Theory of Price Uncertainty, Production and Profit*, Princeton University Press, Princeton, 1968, Chs 8 and 9.

[9] See G. DEBREU, *Theory of Value*, John Wiley, New York, 1959. But the conditions are very restrictive. In this respect consider the comments of T. KOOPMANS, *Three Essays on the State of Economic Science*, McGraw-Hill, New York, 1957, Sec. 2-6. See also R. DORFMAN, P. A. SAMUELSON and R. SOLOW, *Linear Programming and Economic Analysis*, McGraw-Hill, New York, Chs 11 and 12.

[10] J. SCHUMPETER, *Capitalism, Socialism and Democracy*, 2nd ed., Harper and Brothers, New York, 1942, Chs 7 and 8.

[11] Ibid., p. 83 and pp. 103-6.

[12] For a discussion of the patent system see Chapter 20.

[13] P. A. SAMUELSON, *Foundations of Economic Analysis*, Harvard University Press, Cambridge, 1947, p. 253. Reproduced with the kind permission of Harvard University Press.

[14] J. M. CLARK, "Toward a Concept of Workable Competition", *American Economic Review*, 1940, **30**, No. 2. pp. 241-56.

[15] SCHUMPETER, op. cit.

[16] G. STIGLER, "Extent and Basis of Monopoly", *American Economic Review*, 1942, **32**, Papers and Proceedings, pp. 2-3.

[17] J. W. MARKHAM, "An Alternative Approach to the Concept of Workable Competition", *American Economic Review*, 1950, **40**, p. 361. Reproduced with the kind permission of the American Economic Association and J. W. Markham.

[18] J. K. GALBRAITH, (i) "Countervailing Power", *The American Economic Review*, 1954, **44**, No. 2, pp. 1-6. (ii) *American Capitalism: The Concept of Countervailing Power*, Houghton Mifflin, Boston, 1952.

[19] Ibid., (i), p. 2.

[20] This problem was considered by Edgeworth as early as 1881. See F. Y. EDGEWORTH, *Mathematical Psychics*, Kegan Paul, London, 1881.
[21] See the end of Chapter 13.
[22] A. C. PIGOU, *The Economics of Welfare*, 4th ed., Macmillan, London, 1932. R. F. KAHN, "Some Notes on Ideal Output", *Economic Journal*, 1935, **45**, pp. 1-35.
[23] P. SAMUELSON. op. cit.
[24] Ibid., pp. 252-3. Reproduced with the kind permission of Harvard University Press.
[25] R. G. LIPSEY and K. LANCASTER, "The General Theory of Second Best", *Review of Economic Studies*, 1956-1957, **24**, pp. 11-32.
[26] Ibid.
[27] Ibid.
[28] C. E. FERGUSON, *The Macroeconomic Theory of Workable Competition*, Duke University, Durham, 1964. See. p. 17, Footnote 45. However, it ought to be noted that Ferguson believes that second-best problems are the rule rather than the exception.

FURTHER READING

BATOR, F. M., "The Anatomy of Market Failure", *The Quarterly Journal of Economics*, 1958, pp. 351-79.
CLARK, J. M., "Towards a Concept of Workable Competition", *American Economic Review*, 1940, **30**, No. 2, pp. 241-56.
FERGUSON, C. E., *A Macroeconomic Theory of Workable Competition*, Duke University Press, Durham, 1964.
HANSEN, B., *Lectures in Economic Theory*, 3rd ed., Studentlitteratur, Lund, 1968, Part II, Lectures 12 and 14.
KAHN, R. F., "Some Notes on Ideal Output", *The Economic Journal*, 1935, **45**, pp. 1-35.
*LIPSEY, R. and K. LANCASTER, "The General Theory of Second Best", *The Review of Economic Studies*, 1956-1957, **24**, pp. 11-32.
MARKHAM, J. W., "An Alternative Approach to the Concept of Workable Competition", *American Economic Review*, 1950, **40**, pp. 349-61.
NATH, S., *A Reappraisal of Welfare Economics*, Routledge and Kegan Paul, London, 1969.
ROTHENBERG, J., *The Measurement of Social Welfare*, Prentice-Hall, Englewood Cliffs, 1961.

*More advanced.

CHAPTER 15

Linear Programming, Activity Analysis and Economic Choice

I. Background

Linear programming is a recent mathematical technique which along with related activity analysis enables problems to be solved and analysed, which could not be handled by previous methods. Since comparatively little information is needed to apply linear programming methods and since the approach is more general than input-output analysis, some economists believe that it may provide a practical way for devising overall plans for centrally controlled economies.[1] But even if this later view is somewhat Utopian, it is true that linear programming can often be used by smaller units, such as firms, in their decision-making and that it, and related linear activity analysis, might give pointers for overall economic planning.

The application of linear programming techniques has been made comparatively easy due to the discovery by G. Dantzig[2] of the simplex method of solving linear programmes and the rapid development of computer technology which has made such methods economically possible. Linear programming involves the maximisation (minimisation) of a *linear* objective function of a number of variables subject to a number of constraints on these variables in the form of *linear* inequalities. Linearity is central to the problem. Non-linear programming has developed, too, but its progress has been slower and much more information is needed to apply it. Consequently, this chapter will concentrate on linear programming and on simple linear activity models.

Why should economists be interested in linear programming techniques which are essentially mathematical techniques? First, some are convinced that the economic world or parts of it exhibit linear relationships or, at least, can be reasonably approximated by linear relationships. To some extent this might be wishful thinking, since little data is required to determine the parameters of a linear equation or inequality. However, if the hypothesis is correct, linear models and linear programming have obvious economic applications. If the objective of a firm or the state (or any other economic agent) is a linear function of the economic variables which it controls, in a linear world one can determine the optimal values of its controlled variables by solving an appropriate linear programme. Directives might then be issued to ensure that the optimal programme is carried out. Alternatively, a suitable set of prices combined with profit maximisation can also be used to achieve the same result. The suitable price values to set (shadow prices) are yielded by the solution of a linear programming problem. The same result can be achieved by fiat or by profit maximisation

Programming and Activity Analysis

on the basis of efficiency prices which reflect the values of the central controllers. The latter method permits some decentralisation of decision-making.[3]

Input-output models assume that factors are combined in fixed proportions and rule out the possibility of factor substitution. However, linear programming and general linear activity analysis are able to allow for the possibility of factor substitution. But the constant return to scale assumption is retained. Nevertheless, the approach is more general than that of input-output analysis; it includes input-output analysis as a special case.

An economist too might be expected to advise in certain circumstances whether a linear model is appropriate for decision-making. In economic models technological and market conditions may determine whether a linear model is relevant. For example, a profit function, if this is the objective function of a firm, is linear under perfect or pure competition but not under conditions of monopoly.

In addition, linear programming and linear activity analysis can deal with problems of choosing between a limited number of techniques, a problem which is neglected in traditional analysis. Some economists are convinced that the number of available alternative techniques is limited. If this is so, important economic problems are involved, some of which have implications for underdeveloped countries.

Let us look at a traditional linear programming problem and then at some activity analysis which concentrates on the optimal choice of techniques. The strict application of our results will depend upon the absence of significant non-linearities.

II. Convex Sets and Linear Programming Solutions

Properties of convex sets which were discussed earlier[4] have important applications in linear programming and provide connecting threads throughout the whole theory of allocation. In particular, the properties of linear functions which are maximised subject to convex sets are important. In linear programming the (objective) function which is to be maximised or minimised is always linear and is normally to be maximised or minimised subject to a convex set which forms a convex polygon. This will be explained presently.

But, at this stage, let us recall some properties of point sets. A set S is convex if all points on a line segment connecting any two points of S also belong to S. The sets shown in Figs 15.1 and 15.2 are convex, whereas that of Fig. 15.3 is not convex. Extreme points are of fundamental significance in linear programming. An extreme

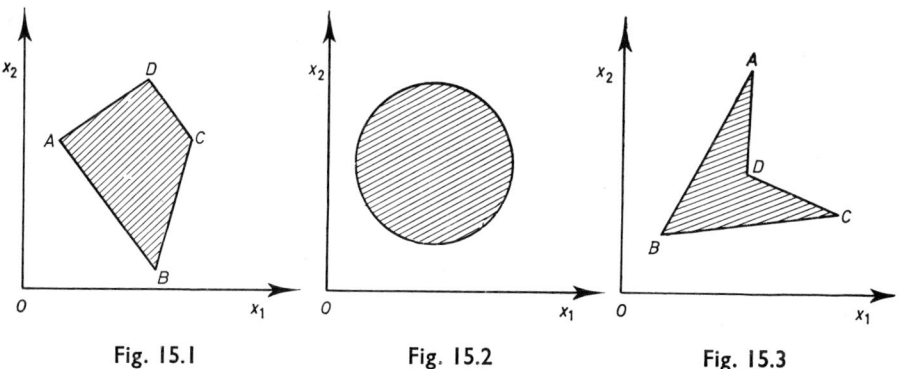

Fig. 15.1   Fig. 15.2   Fig. 15.3

point of a set is a point which cannot be expressed as a linear combination of two different points in the set.[5] In Fig. 15.1, the points A, B, C, and D are the only extreme points of the set. All points on the boundary (circumference) of the set in Fig. 15.2 are extreme points. In Fig. 15.3, the points A, B and C are extreme points but point D is not, since it can be expressed as a linear combination of other points in the set. The set of all the extreme points of a set is called the *extremal* of the set.

An important theorem can now be stated. *The maximum and minimum value of a linear function subject to a compact*[6] *set S occur for extreme points of S*. By considering *only* extreme points of the set S we are sure to find both the maximum and the minimum value of the linear function. Thus the theorem gives an efficient method of searching for an optimum value of a constrained linear function.

To illustrate, imagine that the linear function depends on two variables, x_1 and x_2, so that it can be written as

$$\pi = a_1 x_1 + a_2 x_2 \tag{15.1}$$

where a_1 and a_2 are parameters. This might be a profit function and x_1 and x_2 might indicate the level of sales of two different products. This function, π, is to be maximised subject to a set S which indicates limitations on x_1 and x_2. These, for example, might be production limitations. It follows from the above theorem that

(i) if set S is as in Fig. 15.1, the maximum of π occurs for the (x_1, x_2) combination at point A, B, C or D;

(ii) if S is as in Fig. 15.2, the maximum occurs for one of the points on the circumference of S; and

(iii) if the set of Fig. 15.3 arises, a maximum eventuates at either point A, B or C.

To make the economic illustration more specific, imagine that a linear profit function is to be maximised subject to a set of production possibilities which are represented by the convex polygon in Fig. 15.4. The shaded set there represents the firm's production possibilities, given that x_1 and x_2 indicate the quantities of products 1 and 2 which it produces. The production set is unlike the traditional set in so far as the production possibility frontier is not smooth. It has a number of corner-points and is composed of linear segments. Because of its corner-points, differential calculus methods cannot be applied.

The general theorem stated above informs us that if the profit function is of the type in Equation (15.1), its maximum occurs at one of the extreme points (or corner-points) of the production possibility set. In the parlance of linear programming, the attainable sets of production combinations are called *feasible solutions*. The corner-points of the convex polygon in Fig. 15.4 are called *basic feasible solutions*. One of these values maximises the linear profit function.

In Fig. 15.4, all points on and in the convex polygon $OABCD$ constitute feasible solutions. But *only* the points O, A, B, C and D correspond to *basic* feasible solutions. These are the extreme points of the attainable production set. From the above basic theorem, by substituting the (x_1, x_2) values corresponding to these points into profit function Equation (15.1) in turn and selecting the highest π value discovered and its associated output levels, one has found a production activity which maximises profit. The simplex method takes advantage of this simple theorem.

To complete the diagrammatic exposition of the problem, the linear profit function should really be projected on to the (x_1, x_2) plane. This can be done by a series of

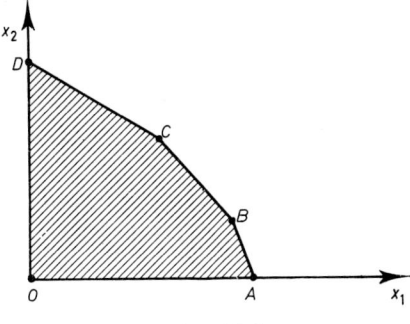

Fig. 15.4

isoprofit lines: each isoprofit line designates all (x_1, x_2) combinations which yield a particular level of profit. The isoprofit line corresponding to a particular level of profit, π_0, can be found by rearranging

$$\pi_0 = a_1 x_1 + a_2 x_2 \tag{15.2}$$

to give

$$x_2 = \pi_0/a_2 - (a_1/a_2) x_1. \tag{15.3}$$

Given the parameters a_1 and a_2 and assuming these to be positive, some isoprofit lines from a possible set are shown in Fig. 15.5. These parallel lines are indicated by $\pi_0, \pi_1, \pi_2, \pi_3$ and higher ones correspond to higher levels of profit. In this instance, profit is maximised by producing the output combination at C, an extreme point of the production possibility set.

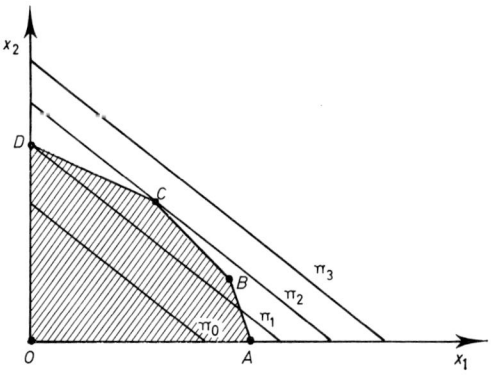

Fig. 15.5

However, it is difficult to overstress the point that the basic theorem requires the objective function to be linear. Otherwise as was illustrated in the appendix to Chapter 7, the objective function does not necessarily reach a maximum and a minimum value in the extremal of the constraining set of possibilities.

As yet the correspondence between linear programming and the above convex set problem has not been demonstrated. This will now be done by taking a particular example. Usually there are three sets of important ingredients in a linear programming model—a linear objective function, a set of structural inequalities and a set of non-negativity conditions. All three are present in the following example but it is not impossible to have cases in which non-negativity is not a requirement.

Assume that a firm is able to produce two products, 1 and 2. One of the resources which it requires for their production, labour, is available in unlimited supply at the going price. Each unit of output of the products requires a constant fraction of labour. Let λ_1 represent the fraction of labour input needed for a unit output of product 1 and let λ_2 represent the corresponding requirement for product 2. Indicate the price of product 1 by p_1, that of product 2 by p_2, of labour by w and let x_1 and x_2 represent the quantities of products 1 and 2. Then, the firm's unconstrained profit function, its *objective function*, can be written as

$$\pi = p_1 x_1 + p_2 x_2 - w\lambda_1 x_1 - w\lambda_2 x_2 - K, \qquad (15.4)$$

(Profit = total revenue − labour costs − fixed cost)

where K represents fixed costs. Letting $a_1 = p_1 - \lambda_1 w$, the profit per unit of product 1 if fixed cost is ignored, and letting $a_2 = p_2 - \lambda_2 w$, Equation (15.4) can be abbreviated to

$$\pi = a_1 x_1 + a_2 x_2 - K \qquad (15.5)$$

The firm's unconstrained objective function is linear. Suppose that other resources, too, are needed for the production of products 1 and 2 but that the available quantities of these are limited. The firm's problem then is to maximise its linear objective function, Equation (15.5), subject to limited availability of other resources.

Imagine that, in addition to labour, three resources are called for in order to produce the products. Indicate the quantities of these three resources by r_1, r_2, and r_3. Suppose that all are available up to a particular level, need not be employed to capacity, and that their cost is fixed. Examples of such resources might be floor space, containers on hand where the products need to be packed, or processing capabilities built into plant. Further, suppose that each unit of the products requires these inputs in fixed quantities. One unit of product 1 requires θ_{11} units of r_1, θ_{21} units of r_2 and θ_{31} units of r_3. Each unit of product 2 needs θ_{12} units of r_1, θ_{22} units of r_2 and θ_{32} units of r_3. Hence, the demands on any resource can be expressed as a linear function of quantities of the products. For example, the demand for r_1 is

$$r_1 = \theta_{11} x_1 + \theta_{12} x_2 \qquad (15.6)$$

and the demand for the other resources can be shown in a similar way. If the demand for any resource is to be satisfied, it must not exceed the upper limit of the available quantity of the resource. Let C_1, C_2, C_3 represent the maximum available quantities of r_1, r_2, and r_3 respectively. Then, clearly, Equation (15.5) is to be maximised subject to the following restrictions:

$$\theta_{11} x_1 + \theta_{12} x_2 \leq C_1 \qquad (15.7)$$
$$\theta_{21} x_1 + \theta_{22} x_2 \leq C_2 \qquad (15.8)$$
$$\theta_{31} x_1 + \theta_{32} x_2 \leq C_3. \qquad (15.9)$$

This set of inequalities formalises the fact that the use of the factors cannot exceed the quantities available. This set of inequalities specifies the *structural* or capacity restraints of the problem.

In addition, the possibility of negative outputs should be ruled out. This can be done by imposing the following conditions:

Programming and Activity Analysis

$$x_1 \geq 0. \tag{15.10}$$
$$x_2 \geq 0. \tag{15.11}$$

These *non-negativity conditions* complete this linear programming problem. The problem is to maximise the linear profit function of Equation (15.5) subject to the structural inequalities (15.7) to (15.9), and subject to the non-negativity conditions, (15.10) and (15.11).

The inequalities in this linear programming problem give rise to a convex polygon of production possibilities for (x_1, x_2). Each inequality forms a half plane and their intersection, which indicates output combinations which satisfy all of the inequalities, is a compact convex set. To illustrate this, take the structural inequality

$$\theta_{11}x_1 + \theta_{12}x_2 \leq C_1. \tag{15.12}$$

This inequality restricts the feasible (x_1, x_2) combinations to all points on and below the line.

$$x_2 = C_1/\theta_{12} - (\theta_{11}/\theta_{12})x_1. \tag{15.13}$$

This line is a boundary line of the closed half-plane corresponding to Equation (15.12). The closed half-plane of Equation (15.12) is indicated in Fig. 15.6 by the cross-hatched area. Similarly, half-planes can be derived for the other inequalities. For example, the restriction $x_2 \geq 0$ limits the possible output combinations to those on and above the horizontal axis.

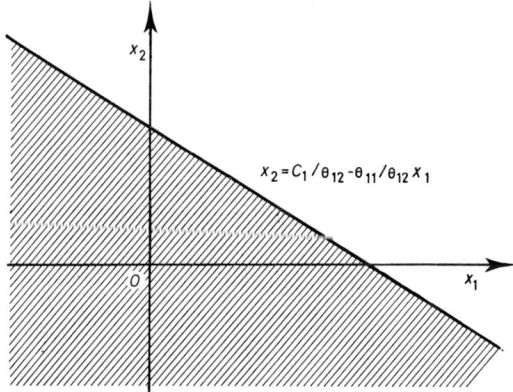

Fig. 15.6

The intersection (product) of a finite set of closed half-planes forms a polygonal convex set, that is a convex polygon. The structural and non-negativity requirements in the above linear programming problem form a series of half-planes and the intersections (products) of these are the only output combinations which meet all the limitations on (x_1, x_2). The boundary lines of the five half-planes formed by the inequalities might, for example, be like those shown in Fig. 15.7. The boundary lines which result from structural or capacity restrictions have been marked by their corresponding expression number. The non-negativity constraints restrict the feasible (x_1, x_2) to the positive quadrant in Fig. 15.7 and the capacity restrictions limit these possibilities even further. In Fig. 15.7 only those combinations of (x_1, x_2) in the polygon $OABCD$ satisfy all the inequalities. Every point of this compact set, and only points of this set formed by the convex polygon $OABCD$ satisfy all the limitations on (x_1, x_2).

The area $OABCD$ in Fig. 15.7 is the firm's production possibility set. In linear programming terminology, values in this set are *feasible solutions* to the linear programming problem. In this instance, as in most, the linear programming problem reduces to one of finding the maximum (or depending on the problem, the minimum) of a linear function subject to a compact polygonal set. From the general theorem on extreme values of a linear function subject to a convex set, it is true that a linear function defined over a convex polygon takes on its maximum value at a corner-point of the polygon. In this linear programming example, net profit, subject to the production restraints, reaches a maximum for an output combination at either O, A, B, C or D. In the terminology of linear programming, the corner-points O, A, B, C and D are *basic* feasible solutions. It is easy to solve the problem once these points are located. The (x_1, x_2) values which correspond to each of the corner-points can be substituted into the net profit function, Equation (15.5). This gives five net profit values, the largest of which is the maximum net profit value.

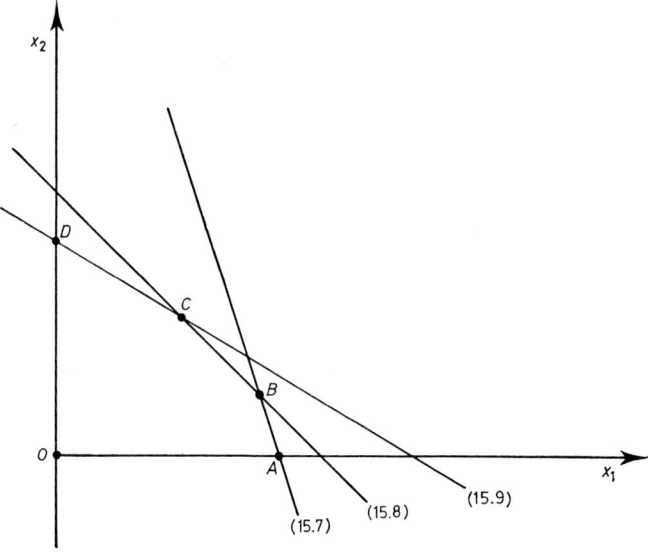

Fig. 15.7

Having determined the (x_1, x_2) values which yield maximum profit, the optimal employment of the factors can be determined in a straightforward fashion. For example, in Fig. 15.8, some iso-net profit functions have been indicated. In this case, the profit maximising combination is that at C, $(\hat{x}_1, \hat{x}_2)$. It follows that the optimal employment of labour is $\lambda_1 \hat{x}_1 + \lambda_2 \hat{x}_2$ and that the optimal utilisation of the other resources is

$$r_1 = \theta_{11}\hat{x}_1 + \theta_{12}\hat{x}_2, \qquad (15.14)$$

$$r_2 = \theta_{21}\hat{x}_1 + \theta_{22}\hat{x}_2, \qquad (15.15)$$

$$r_3 = \theta_{31}\hat{x}_1 + \theta_{31}\hat{x}_2. \qquad (15.16)$$

Programming and Activity Analysis

Note (by comparing Figs 15.8 and 15.7) that only two of the resources are used to capacity. In linear programming problems in general, the number of processes used to capacity equals or exceeds the number of activities which are engaged in.

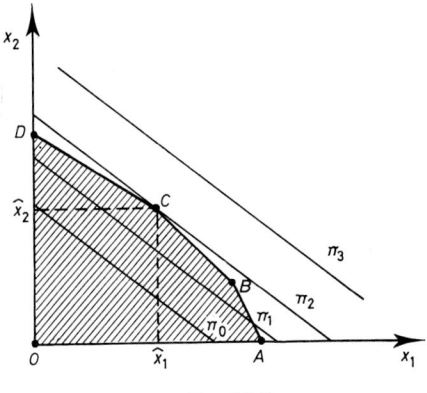

Fig. 15.8

While it is inappropriate to outline computational methods of solving linear programming models in an economic text, the basic approach of the *simplex method* might be indicated. The fundamental steps are:

(i) find any basic feasible solution, that is any corner-point. In Fig. 15.8, this might be O;

(ii) compute the value of the objective function at the adjacent corners. In our example, compute profit at points A and D;

(iii) if any adjacent corner-point yields a higher (lower) value of the objective function and if the objective function is to be maximised (minimised) move to the adjacent point which yields the highest (lowest) value. Test the values of the objective function at the adjacent points and continue moving to points which cause the value of the objective function to improve, until no adjacent points yield a better value for the objective function. Once a corner-point of this nature is achieved, it optimises the value of the objective function. In the example of Fig. 15.8, having computed profit at A and D one moves to D. At D comparison of the adjacent corner-points indicates that C gives greater profit. Moving to C, a comparison of the adjacent corner-points, D and B, indicates lower profit than for the product combination at C. Hence, combination C maximises profit.

The application of the simplex method to the example of Fig. 15.8 required an evaluation of all extreme points of the feasible set. But in many instances, it economises on the number of extreme points which must be evaluated. For example, let us suppose that instead of having two facets between C and A, the feasible set had a number of facets so that a number of extreme points in addition to B lie between C and A. If everything else about the feasible set is unaltered, it is clear that starting from O only five extreme points still have to be evaluated to locate the optimum at C though the number of extreme points is now in excess of five. Some computational economies are achieved. However, this should not lead one to suspect that in actual complicated problems (many cannot be represented graphically) it is a simple matter to locate corner-points. Computational procedures involving pivoting exist,[7] but in complicated problems one must rely on electronic or mechanical computers to speed up the calculation.

Every linear programme has a *dual* programme. The original programme is called the *primal* and it is also the dual of its dual. If the original linear programme involves the maximisation of an objective function, its dual is a linear programming problem which requires the minimisation of an objective function. Standard rules exist for converting a linear programme to its dual.[8] One might wish to make such a conversion because it is sometimes easier to solve the dual programme than the primal one and having solved the dual, one can infer the solutions of the primal programme.

Also the dual programme frequently has a more valuable economic meaning. In the profit minimisation example above, the dual involves the determination of so-called *shadow prices*. These are not real but imputed or accounting prices which indicate the marginal contribution to profit (marginal revenue product) of a resource as far as the firm is concerned. Only resources which are used to capacity have a positive shadow price; all other resources which are not used to capacity have a zero shadow price. If somehow a resource which is used to capacity could be just expanded a little, the shadow price would indicate its addition to total revenue. An expansion in the supply of a resource which is not scarce, one which is not used to capacity, would make a zero addition to revenue, hence it has a zero shadow price.

Note that if resources happen to be charged for at their shadow prices, profit is zero. One can see then how a firm or productive unit which satisfied the above linear relations might be controlled. The controller might determine the prices of the products to give the composition of production which he desires and compute on this basis the shadow prices for the resources available to the firm. If the firm's inputs and products are valued at these shadow prices by the controller, the firm will be carrying out the controller's plan efficiently only if it makes zero profit. A loss will indicate a deviation from plan. Even though no market system exists, prices in the form of constant per-unit valuations can sometimes be used to control production in an efficient fashion. This device might be useful in planning if a company has a number of plants and wishes to control production in these, while at the same time leaving some decentralisation of decision-making. The method leaves units free to react to the centrally administered accounting prices. It has also been suggested that this procedure may be useful for administering a centrally planned economy. The values which the controlling group places on various products are determined and in the light of these, the values of various inputs are imputed. At these prices (values) firms are instructed to maximise profit. But, of course, the computational task for the whole economy is tremendous and the problem of information-gathering enormous. In all these cases our enthusiasm must be tempered by realism. If constant returns *to scale* do not prevail, if non-constant returns are important, a linear programming model is inapplicable and yields misleading answers.[9]

III. Choice of Techniques for Production

Linear programming and associated linear activity analysis[10] can give us new insights into production. Production has been already discussed in an earlier chapter

Programming and Activity Analysis

using neo-classical methods. However, these assume that the choice of optimal techniques has already been made and that sufficient range and variety of techniques exist, so that isoquants are smooth, continuous and differentiable. In practice this last assumption might not be satisfied. The number of alternative techniques might be very limited. In circumstances like this, activity analysis can be used to determine which technique or combination of techniques is optimal. In this respect it differs from the neo-classical approach which assumes that the problem of optimal choice of techniques is solved, presumably by engineers. But the optimal choice of techniques is not just, or even primarily, an engineering problem. Activity analysis indicates that the optimal choice of techniques is to a considerable extent an economic problem because it is influenced by the relative scarcity (endowment) of factors, and the choice greatly affects the employment of factors like labour.

It is assumed (as a rule) in activity analysis that a finite set of alternative productive processes are available.[11] By supposition, any process requires inputs in fixed proportions to produce any unit of its output and constant returns are assumed to hold. Thus strong linearity conditions underlie the analysis. Furthermore, if a number of processes are in use, it is imagined that there is no interaction between the processes. If the input to any one process is held constant, the output from this process remains constant even if the outputs and inputs of other processes are altered. At least in simple models, externalities are ruled out.

Let us take a very simple case first, in order to illustrate the approach. Assume that one product is being produced and that there is the choice of producing it by two different techniques. Imagine, too, that one variable factor is used, L, labour, and represent the quantity of the output by x and the quantity of L employed by l. The production relationship using process 1 might be indicated by

$$x = a_1 l \quad (l \geqslant 0) \tag{15.17}$$

and that using process 2 by

$$x - a_2 l \quad (l \geqslant 0) \tag{15.18}$$

where a_1 and a_2 are constants which indicate the marginal productivity of L using the alternative techniques. Constant returns prevail for each process and L is required in a fixed proportion to output. The production relationships for the two processes are shown in Fig. 15.9.

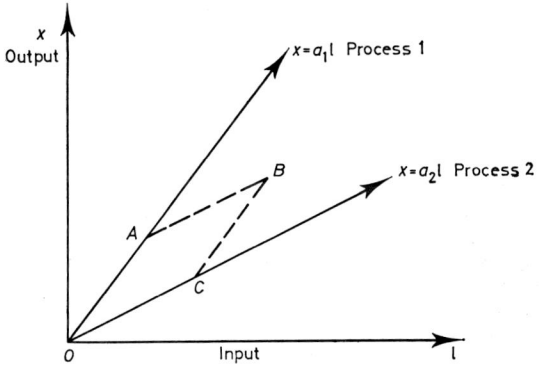

Fig. 15.9

The production relationship for each process is represented by a ray or a half-line. If we allow that all of the employed factor need not be used, the production possibility set is the set enclosed by the top ray and the horizontal non-negative axis, and includes points on these half-lines. It is clearly a convex set. This particular type of convex set is called a convex *cone*. In this example, only process 1 is efficient since it always results in greater output for any employment of L than the other process or possible combinations of the two processes. The ray for process 1 forms the efficiency frontier of the production possibility set.

Note that the output corresponding to B in Fig. 15.9 might be produced in two ways. One is by using process 1 and keeping some of the hired L idle. Another is to fully employ the hired L but use a combination of processes 1 and 2 to achieve the desired output. If an output corresponding to point A is produced by process 1 and an output corresponding to point C is produced by process 2, the resultant is the input-output combination represented by B. Given B, the corresponding points A and C are found by completing the parallelogram $OABC$ by drawing the side AB parallel to the ray $x = a_2 l$ and AC parallel to the ray $x = a_1 l$. (B corresponds to the addition of the vectors A and C.)

In the above example, the optimal choice of techniques is a trivial problem. Process 1 alone is optimal (that is it maximises output for any employment of resources) and this is so whether the availability of L is restricted or not. But the matter becomes less trivial if the number of variable factors of production is increased. Let there be two variable factors, L and K, and two alternative processes, 1 and 2, producing one product, x. Representing the corresponding quantities by L, K, and x, the efficient production relationship using process 1 might be

$$x = a_1 L + b_1 K \quad (L \geqslant 0, K \geqslant 0) \tag{15.19}$$

and using process 2,

$$x = a_2 L + b_2 K \quad (L \geqslant 0, K \geqslant 0). \tag{15.20}$$

Each process involves constant returns to scale and requires inputs in fixed proportions. The proportions in which the factors are combined can be represented by the slope of a ray in two-dimensional space. The slope of the ray passing through OA in Fig. 15.10 might indicate the factor proportions appropriate to process 1 and the

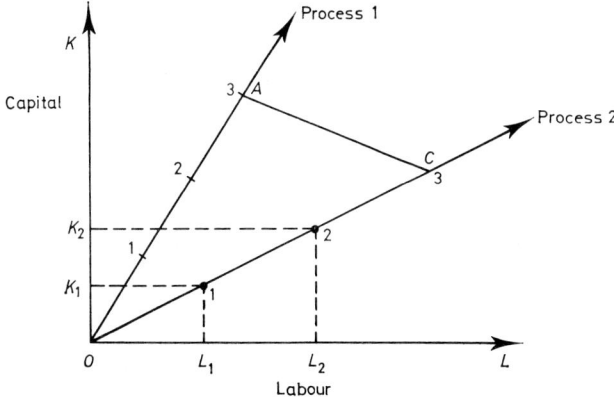

Fig. 15.10

Programming and Activity Analysis

slope of the ray passing through OC might represent these for process 2. If K represents capital and L represents labour, process 1 is capital-intensive whereas process 2 is labour-intensive.

Given any process, the units of output which result from the employment of any quantity of inputs along its ray can be indicated by units marked off along the ray. The units marked off along the rays in Fig. 15.10 indicate the quantities of output of product X for the various processes. For example, using process 2, one unit of output results from the employment of L_1 of labour and K_1 of capital; doubling these to reach (L_2, K_2), while using the same process, results in two units of output. After the unit measure of output is defined, each unit of output is indicated at an equal distance along a ray since constant returns to *scale* prevail. But depending upon the relative productivity of processes, the unit of *distance* can be different for alternative processes, that is, variable from process ray to process ray.

In activity analysis, it is imagined that processes can be combined in any proportion to produce output without a loss or gain of output due to the very fact of joint processes being used. By producing a suitable proportion of output by process 1 and the remaining proportion by process 2, factors can be substituted anywhere along the interval AC in Fig. 15.10 and output remains unchanged at 3 units. AC is a linear isoquant. Similarly, by joining other points of equal output on the rays by straight lines, other isoquants can be obtained. Unlike input-output analysis, the more-general activity analysis permits factor substitution.

Any point on an isoquant between the process rays implies that output is produced by means of more than one process. The contribution of each process can easily be found by graphical means by completing the relevant parallelogram. In Fig. 15.11, AC is assumed to be an isoquant and, as in the last case, two processes are imagined to be available. Suppose that one wants to find the level of operation of the processes which correspond to point B. The parallelogram $BCDE$ is then completed by drawing through B a line BE parallel to the ray for process 2 to cut the other ray in point E. From the point E, the remaining side of the parallelogram ED is drawn parallel to BC. Then by employing level E of factors in process 1 and $C-D$ in process 2 (where the points are vectors) the combined result, since $B-E = C-D$, is the employment

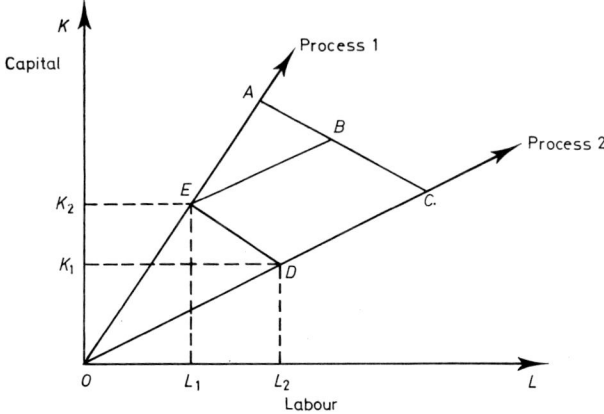

Fig. 15.11

316   Microeconomics

of the combination of factors at B and the output represented along the isoquant AC.[12] The output due to process 1 is the distance OE measured in output units for process 1 and production due to process 2 is CD measured in output units for process 2. Of the total output OE/OA is contributed by process 1 and the remainder is due to process 2. The remainder can be found by subtracting the first ratio from unity, or it is also equal to CD/OC. In this instance, production at point B involves the simultaneous use of the capital-intensive and the labour-intensive process. It might be surprising that these very different processes working side by side can be efficient.

So far only two alternative processes have been considered. But activity analysis can take account of any number of finite processes. In Fig. 15.12, the rays corresponding to three alternative processes are indicated. However, in this instance process 3 is inefficient and will not be used if maximisation of output is the goal. Points A, B and C correspond to equal outputs along the process rays. Each combination of factors along ABC results in the same output if the processes adjacent to the combination are used in suitable proportions. Combinations of inputs in the interior of the interval AB correspond to the use of processes 1 and 3, and those in the interior of BC to the use of processes 2 and 3. However, combinations of inputs along the interval AC can produce the same output, and involve only the use of processes 1 and 2 in varying proportions. Since combinations within this interval involve the use of less of both factors for the same output, the use of process 3 is inefficient. The relevant isoquant is AC and is convex.[13] But process 3 need not be inefficient (be dominated by the others). In Fig. 15.13, the rays of three processes are indicated and an isoquant for a particular output is shown by $EABCD$. Factor combinations in the interval BC involve the use of processes 2 and 3 and those in the interval AB imply the adoption of processes 1 and 3. Combination A involves the use of process 1 alone; B, the adoption of process 3 alone; and C uses only technique 2. The isoquant has been "filled out" by adding the horizontal segment CD and the vertical AE. These are the so-called "disposal" segments and indicate that, with the processes available, extra supply of the relevant factor (the other constant) adds nothing to output. Note that the isoquant is convex and is generally similar in shape to the Hicksian one. The difference is that it is composed of linear segments and has corner-points, which means that it is not differentiable everywhere. By the way, in this case, it is never efficient to use processes 1 and 2 together. If these processes are used together exclusively, the input requirements for the same output are along the segment AC. Actually, if we allow the processes to be used in any proportions, the whole set of alternative input employments

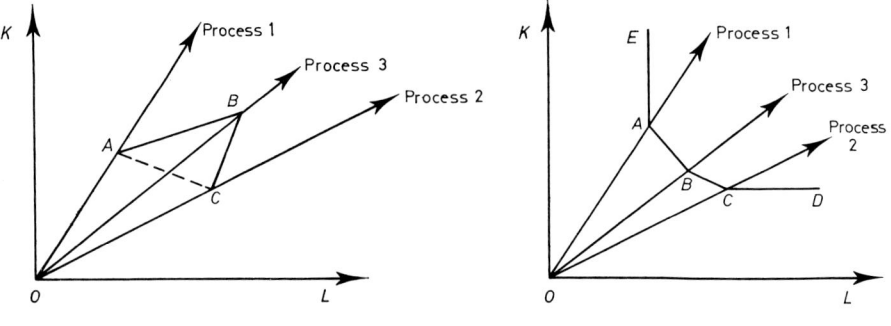

Fig. 15.12   Fig. 15.13

which give the same output is the triangular set formed by triangle ABC. ABC indicates the efficient points of the set. Any number of processes can be taken into account by this method so that convex isoquants consisting of linear segments can be constructed. Such isoquants allow some factor substitutability.

As an application of the above analysis, consider a country which produces one product by means of two factors, capital and labour, and imagine these factors are in limited supply. The upper limit to capital is K^* and to labour L^*. Its problem might be to maximise its production given limitations on the availability of factors and the available processes. For simplicity, assume that two alternative processes are available. Let the capital to labour requirement of process 1 be r_1 and the capital to labour requirement of process 2 be r_2; and assume that process 2 is the least capital-intensive so that $r_1 > r_2$. Then, if none of the processes are inefficient, maximum output requires

(i) the exclusive use of the capital-intensive technique, if $K^*/L^* \geqslant r_1$;

(ii) the use of both the capital-intensive and the labour-intensive technique, if $r_2 < K^*/L^* < r_1$; and

(iii) the exclusive use of the labour-intensive technique, if $K^*/L^* \leqslant r_2$.

Propositions (ii) and (iii) are illustrated in Figs 15.14 and 15.15. In the figures, the set of available factor combinations are those contained by the rectangles OK^*BL^*. In the first instance, the availability ratio K^*/L^* is intermediate (as indicated by the slope of the line OB) to the K/L, capital to labour ratios for the processes, indicated by the slopes of their rays. The point B is situated on an isoquant marked AC and output is maximised by producing the proportion OE/OA of total output by process 1 and the remainder by process 2. Both factors are fully employed and capital and labour-intensive processes are employed side by side. In Fig. 15.15, the unhappy circumstance is illustrated in which $K^*/L^* < r_2$, that is, labour to capital availability exceeds that which is required for the most labour-intensive process. Output is maximised by employing the labour-intensive process alone. This leads to the input combination (L_0, K^*) in Fig. 15.15 which enables the economy to reach the isoquant AC. Unfortunately, the economy in maximising its output (operating efficiently) is left with $L^* - L_0$ of labour unemployed. Because capital is short in relation to labour, the goal of efficiency conflicts with a full employment goal.

Eckaus[14] and others have studied the factors underlying unemployment in underdeveloped countries which typically have low capital to labour ratios. In many

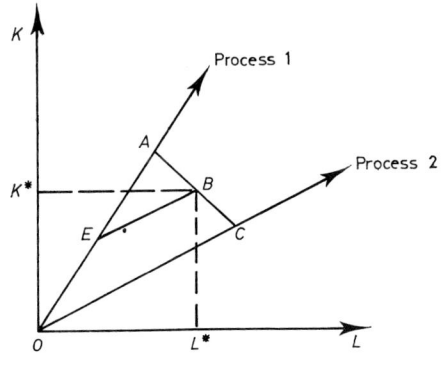

Fig. 15.14

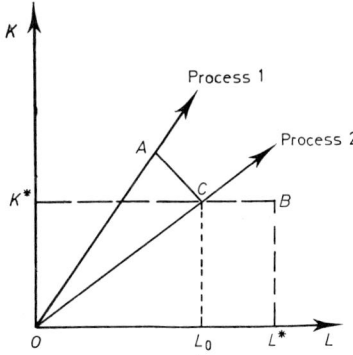

Fig. 15.15

instances, choice of productive methods by underdeveloped countries is limited. They can either adopt a capital-intensive method of developed countries or use a traditional labour-intensive method, and this discreteness of choice may be the basis for some of their unemployment problems. Eckaus says:

> It is fairly common for observers to report finding modern, capital-intensive equipment and techniques used in underdeveloped areas where relative factor prices would suggest the use of labour-intensive techniques. I should now like to suggest that the use of 'modern' techniques is not necessarily irrational emulation but the result of real limitations in the technological choices available, and that this, in turn, is a major source of labour-employment problems in underdeveloped areas.[15]

If isoquants consist of linear segments, substantial changes in relative factor prices are needed in order to induce profit-maximising units to vary their relative use of factors and if a firm's isocost line happens to fall along a facet of its isoquant, the firm has considerable discretion about its profit-maximising factor mix; both capital-intensive and labour-intensive techniques might yield the same profit if employed in a range of proportions. Thus use of a technique is not closely related to relative factor prices. However, the worst social situation arises if labour is in relative oversupply as in Fig. 15.15. Firms cannot be induced to employ all the available labour at any positive price. Furthermore, there is a natural floor to the wage rate in excess of zero (no one can exist on a zero wage, and work itself involves extra inputs for the individual concerned) and there is likely to be a union-negotiated or customary floor in excess of this again. Thus with labour in relative oversupply, unemployment is a structural problem. In Fig. 15.16, an isoquant for an economy has been marked in by $Q_1 Q_1$ and the available quantities of the available factors are L^* and K^*.

$C_1 C_1$ indicates an isocost line and is drawn on the assumption that the wage rate is at its lower limit. Consequently, K^* of capital and L_0 of labour is employed and $L^* - L_0$ is unemployed. Even if $C_1 C_1$ happened to be less steep, indicating that labour is relatively cheaper, labour unemployment is unchanged. However, the unemployment situation is worsened if trade unions are able to negotiate a wage rate which means that the isocost lines become steeper and resource use shifts to a corner-point such as A. This is the crude version of Eckaus' reasoning.

Nevertheless, the crude model raises the very real possibility that an underdeveloped country might not aim for unqualified maximisation of output from its available resources. Rather it might aim to *maximise its output subject to the full employment of*

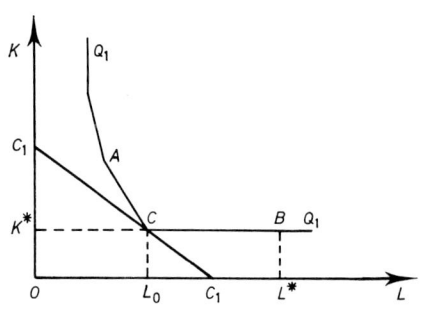

Fig. 15.16

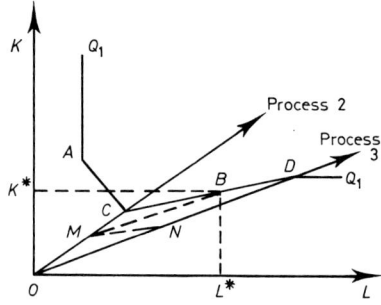

Fig. 15.17

Programming and Activity Analysis

labour and be prepared to use comparatively inefficient techniques to do so. Activity analysis can help with the solution of this problem, provided that the basic linearity assumptions are approximated.

Imagine that, as in Fig. 15.15, K^*/L^* is less than the capital-labour ratio required for process 2, an efficient process. But suppose that in addition to the two processes indicated there, a third process is available, which requires a capital-labour input of not more than K^*/L^*. However, this third process is inefficient in comparison to process 2; it requires greater input of capital and labour for the same output. Hence, the isoquant corresponding to this situation is like Q_1Q_1 in Fig. 15.17 and has a positively sloping segment CD. Given that the available factor combination is $B = (L^*, K^*)$ labour is fully employed and output is maximised *subject* to this full employment of labour if combination M of the factors is allocated to process 2 and the quantity $D-N(=B-M)$ is devoted to process 3. Output is lower than the attainable, but full employment of labour is efficiently preserved by simultaneously operating the most labour-intensive technique and one which is moderately labour-intensive. Observe, however, that at non-negative factor prices, profit maximisation could at most move the economy to the highest attainable point on the ray for process 2.

IV. Extensions and Limitations of Linear Analysis

The activity model which has just been discussed can be equally applied to a firm as to a country, provided that the basic mathematical assumptions are satisfied. If product and factor prices are constant, the same basic mathematical model can also be adopted to show profitability and to determine which techniques maximise profit, and how much output should be produced by the alternative techniques.[16] Diagrammatically, in a case such as that of Fig. 15.13, the process rays are drawn in and linked by isoprofit lines which are composed of linear segments like the isoquants considered earlier.[17] Given factor limitations, it is clear how the profit-maximising employments can be determined. The problem is to reach the highest attainable isoprofit line and the previous arguments can be followed through *mutatis mutandis*, on the assumption that the lines previously representing isoquants represent the isoprofit lines for the firm. Note, however, that besides constant returns to scale, prices must be constant. This is only likely to be completely satisfied if pure (or perfect) competition exists. Normally, in linear programming and activity models, the price assumptions are only strictly compatible with pure (or perfect) competition. Use of constant prices in other cases needs special justification.

Although linear activity analysis is based on *constant returns to scale*, it does not rule out diminishing "marginal" productivity. In the analysis of the last section, if one factor is held constant and the other is increased, marginal product may decrease in a step-like fashion, even though the marginal product function does not diminish continuously. A position like that indicated in Figs 15.18 and 15.19 can arise. In Fig. 15.18, the rays for three efficient processes (the only ones available) are shown, and we imagine a set of isoquants, one of which is shown as Q_1Q_1. Suppose that factor L is fixed at L^* but that capital, K, can be varied. Factor combinations along and to the left of the half-line going through L^*A are possible. The addition to the product as a result of increasing K is illustrated in Fig. 15.19. At $K \leqslant K_1$, process 3 alone is used. If $K < K_1$, each unit addition of K allows a constant quantity of labour to be taken into employment and a constant addition to be made to output. Hence, the segment DE in Fig. 15.19. In the interval, $K_1 < K < K_2$, processes 2 and 3 are both used in varying proportions, and FG of the marginal product curve corresponds to this in Fig. 15.19, and so on. The discontinuities of the marginal product function correspond to capital availabilities which are just in excess of those which render the use of one process optimal. Because activity analysis can make some allowance for variations of marginal productivity, this makes it more general than otherwise.

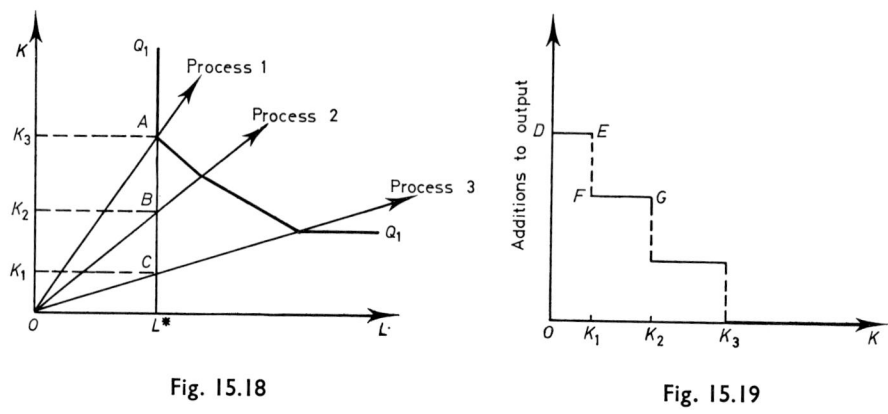

Fig. 15.18   Fig. 15.19

Certainly, activity analysis enables input-output analysis to be extended. Input-output relations are indicated by a single ray and no factor substitutability is possible. But the general variant, like its special case, assumes constant returns to scale. For some planning problems, especially those of underdeveloped countries, activity analysis can be a helpful planning device, at least, to give a rough approximation. However, one despairs at its prospects for planning any economy fully, especially complex advanced types, such as that of the U.S.S.R. It is difficult to obtain data on alternative techniques and even though computational problems are great, they are probably the lesser problems.

NOTES AND REFERENCES

[1] See, for example, L. KANTOROVICH, "Mathematical Economics", *Problems of Economics*, September 1965, pp. 12-15 and, in the same issue, "Pro and Con—Compare Conclusions", pp. 16-22.

[2] See G. DANTZIG, "Maximization of a Linear Function of Variables Subject to Linear Inequalities", in T. C. KOOPMANS (Ed.), *Activity Analysis of Production and Allocation*, Wiley, New York, 1951, Ch. 21. See also Ch. 2 of the same book.

[3] See T. C. KOOPMANS, "Efficient Allocation of Resources", *Econometrica*, 1951, **19**, pp. 445-65.

[4] See Chapter 2 and the appendices to Chapters 6 and 7.

[5] It is assumed that the multiples of the two different points must add to unity, and that each multiple is positive.

[6] A compact set is both bounded and closed. For further explanation see Chapter 2.

[7] For an outline of the method, see W. J. BAUMOL, *Economic Theory and Operations Analysis*, 2nd ed., Prentice-Hall Englewood Cliffs, 1965, Ch. 5.

[8] These are outlined by Baumol. For instance, ibid., Ch. 6.

[9] This is considered in Chapter 22.

Programming and Activity Analysis

[10] For a general outline of linear activity analysis, see T. C. KOOPMANS, *Three Essays on the State of the Economic Science*, McGraw-Hill, New York, 1957, Essay I, Sec. 3. Linear activity analysis refers to models which involve linear economic relationships alone.

[11] See Reference 10.

[12] An alternative construction is to draw a line through B parallel to OA to cut OC in, say, a point J. By vector addition, $E + J = B$. If quantity J of factors is used in process 2 and quantity E in process 1, the quantity B of factors is employed.

[13] By suitably mixing the techniques, one can produce the same output by any combination of factors in $\triangle ABC$. But AC is the efficiency frontier of this set.

[14] R. S. ECKAUS, "The Factor-Proportions Problem in Underdeveloped Areas", *American Economic Review*, 1955, **45**, No. 4, pp. 539-65.

[15] Ibid., p. 544. Reproduced by the kind permission of the American Economic Association and the author. Note in particular that it may be optimal to use capital-intensive and labour-intensive processes side by side to produce the same product in an underdeveloped country.

[16] For a full outline of this, see BAUMOL, op. cit., Ch. 12.

[17] As before, each ray indicates the proportions in which factors must be combined for each process.

FURTHER READING

BAUMOL, W. J., *Economic Theory and Operations Analysis*, 2nd ed., Prentice-Hall, Englewood Cliffs, 1965, Chs 5, 6 and 12.

BAUMOL, W. J., "Activity Analysis in One Lesson", *American Economic Review*, 1958, **58**, pp. 837-73.

BOULDING, K. E. and W. SPIVEY, *Linear Programming and the Theory of the Firm*, The Macmillan Company, New York, 1960, Chs 1-4.

DORFMAN, R., "Mathematical or 'Linear' Programming: A Non-mathematical Exposition", *American Economic Review*, 1953, pp. 797-825.

DORFMAN, R., P. A. SAMUELSON and R. M. SOLOW, *Linear Programming and Economic Analysis*, McGraw-Hill, New York, 1958, Chs 2 and 6.

ECKAUS, R. S., "The Factor-Proportions Problem in Underdeveloped Areas", *American Economic Review*, 1955, **45**, No. 4, pp. 539-65.

CHAPTER 16

Resource Allocation over Time

I. Introduction

So far the allocation of resources over time has not been discussed.[1] This is, of course, a limitation of the earlier analysis but it is not as serious as it might seem at first sight. It turns out that the within-period conditions, which we have explored, must continue to hold in plans which extend over several periods. Furthermore, the interperiod conditions for an optimum are, at least if certainty exists, analogous to intraperiod conditions. This is not to deny that economic choice which extends over several periods brings basic issues like uncertainty and learning to the fore and requires account to be taken of new factors like borrowing and lending, the discount rate and time preference.

The chapter first introduces basic ideas about the bond rate, discount rate and present or discounted value. A theory of the consumer's multiperiod consumption is then sketched and followed by a discussion of a perfectly competitive firm's multiperiod production. Towards the end of the chapter there is some discussion of uncertainty and learning.

Neither borrowing nor lending were considered earlier, but obviously both consumers and firms can borrow and lend resources over time, and this must be taken into account in multiperiod analysis. In practice, borrowing and lending takes place almost continually and involves a variety of credit instruments and risks. However, if our theory is to be of value only the essential ingredients must be abstracted from the situation. Consequently, a number of simplifying assumptions are made in the multiperiod analysis which is discussed below. First, time is treated as a discrete variable and *exchanges* of all types are limited to single points (for example, market days) spaced equidistant in time (for example, occurring every week). Thus consumers and firms can enter into borrowing and lending contracts only on each "market day". Furthermore, it is assumed that they can do so by the use of only one credit instrument, bonds. If any individual wishes to lend, he buys bonds and if any wishes to borrow, he sells bonds. The market for bonds is supposed to be perfectly competitive and the capital sum lent at one market date is assumed to be repaid at the next, plus interest. However, this does not prevent a debtor from taking out another loan at the later date and so remaining in debt, nor similarly does it prevent a creditor from continuing to lend. It also assumes that bonds are issued in exchange for specified quantities of current purchasing power expressed in terms of the money of account.

The borrowing charge can also be stated in the money of account or expressed as a proportion of the amount borrowed. Let i_t represent the proportion of interest

Allocation over Time

payable on a loan entered into in t and repayable at $t+1$. Thus $i_t = 0.08$ indicates an interest rate of 8 per cent on sums borrowed in t and repayable in $t+1$. While the rate of interest is liable to vary over time, for simplicity it will be assumed to be a constant per period rate of i.

At a per-period interest rate of i, y dollars of purchasing power when lent in period i should yield in $t+1$,

$$A = y(1+i), \tag{16.1}$$

the present value of the investment plus the accrued interest. Hence, the present value of A dollars available in $t+1$ is

$$y = \frac{A}{1+i}. \tag{16.2}$$

Clearly, if $i > 0$ the value of A dollars now is greater than A dollars one period later. If an individual is given A dollars now, not only does he have the opportunity of using this A dollars one period later but also (if it is lent) an additional iA dollars, the interest earned. For example, the present worth of $100 in one period's time, if the interest rate is $0 \cdot 05$, is $\$\frac{100}{1 \cdot 05}$. If $\$\frac{100}{1 \cdot 05}$ are invested now at the going interest rate of 5 per cent, it yields $100 after one period.

Similarly, the present value of A dollars t periods from now, if the interest rate is i per period, is

$$y = \frac{A}{(1+i)^t} \tag{16.3}$$

which is smaller the more distant is the sum of $\$A$, that is, A is more heavily discounted the further away it is in time. The sum of $\$y$, the amount which if invested now yields $\$A$ at the end of t periods, is called either the *present value* of $\$A$ or its *discounted value*. The discount rate, the rate by which a future sum must be discounted to give its present value, is

$$\beta_t = \frac{1}{(1+i)^t} = (1+i)^{-t}. \tag{16.4}$$

Consequently, the present value of a *stream* of purchasing power over a number of periods of time, where 0 represents the initial period and T the final one, is

$$V = A(0) + \frac{A(1)}{(1+i)} + \frac{A(2)}{(1+i)^2} + \ldots + \frac{A(T)}{(1+i)^T} \tag{16.5}$$

$$= \sum_{t=0}^{T} \frac{A(t)}{(1+i)^t} \tag{16.6}$$

where $A(t)$ represent the sum available in period t. The sum available in any period can either be negative or positive. A negative figure indicates indebtedness.

Any economic agent prefers an income stream which has the greatest current value because it dominates or can be made to dominate those with lower current values. By borrowing and lending using the first income stream, an individual can assure himself of just as much income at *every* date as in the latter case, and *additional* income. Firms which have alternative possible income or profit streams, if profit is their objective, are likely to prefer those with greatest present value. This will be discussed shortly. But first let us consider the position for the consumer.

II. Multiperiod Consumption

The pattern in which a consumer earns income over his lifetime or over several periods rarely matches his desired expenditure period by period. In some periods, his expenditure is likely to exceed income and the difference is made up by borrowing or drawing on past savings and at other times the individual may wish to save. A fairly typical lifetime pattern is for a consumer's expenditure to exceed his income while he is receiving his training and begins on the task of rearing a family—purchasing a car, home etc. During this period his borrowings increase not only because of the special demands placed on him, but also because his income is usually below its maximum. After middle age, indebtedness is decreased until positive savings exist by retirement—the individual is lending by the time of his retirement. During retirement, these savings are gradually depleted, that is, in our model his loans are gradually reduced. Of course, not everyone's pattern is of this nature and even within this pattern of expenditure there are many variations. In our economic model, the consumer can reconcile his desired expenditure or consumption stream with his actual income stream by borrowing and lending. But what motivates the consumer in making these decisions? How do his decisions mesh together? Consider Hicks' theory.[2]

One way to approach this problem is to assume that the individual has a preference function over his lifetime consumption of goods. The individual is presumed to estimate his life expectancy. Let this estimate be one of T periods from the initial marketing date. His Hicksian-type preference function for consumption of commodities over the T periods might be expressed as

$$U = U(x_{10}, \ldots, x_{q0}; x_{11}, \ldots, x_{q1}; x_{1T}, \ldots, x_{qT}) \tag{16.7}$$

where x_{rt} is the quantity of the rth commodity purchased by the consumer on the tth marketing date and consumed by him during the tth period.

There are clearly some limitations to this approach. First, the risk of a variable length of life is ignored. Second, new and unknown products may appear and lifetime preferences may change. It is clear, too, that because of uncertainties and the costs of decision-making, no individual works out his more remote consumption plans in any detail. However, let us put these matters to one side for a moment.

In the multiperiod case, as in the single period case, the individual is not free to satisfy his consumption preferences without restraint. He is limited in his lifetime consumption possibilities by his "earned" income, interest rates, and prices of the commodities at different points of time. Let $(M_0, M_1, \ldots, M_T)$ represent the individual's earned income at the various marketing dates. Then if an individual has zero initial assets and at his terminal date plans to have no assets nor debts, his present discounted expenditure over his lifetime must equal his present discounted income. This can be shown to be so even allowing for borrowing and lending opportunities. Consequently, the consumer's objective is to maximise (16.7) subject to

$$\sum_{t=0}^{T} \frac{M_t}{(1+i)^t} - \sum_{t=0}^{T} \sum_{r=1}^{q} \frac{p_{rt}}{(1+i)^t} x_{rt} = 0; \tag{16.8}$$

$$\boxed{\text{present discounted income}} - \boxed{\text{present discounted expenditure}} = 0,$$

where p_{rt} is the price of the rth commodity in period t. The term $p_{rt}/(1+i)^t$ is the discounted price of product r in period t. Note that it is assumed that future prices of the products and future earned incomes as well as the interest rate are known. These hardly seem reasonable assumptions if a long time interval is involved. In most instances, all of these variables are subject to uncertainty.

The necessary condition for a maximum of Equation (16.7) subject to Equation (16.8) is that the marginal rate of indifferent substitution between every pair of commodities be equal to the ratio of their *discounted* prices. In this formula the same commodities at different time-points are regarded as different commodities. The conditions are exactly the same as for the single-period case, except that discounted prices replace actual prices and each commodity is identified not only by its type but also by the time at which it is available. The necessary condition implies that *within each period* the relative (actual) prices of goods must equal the consumer's marginal rate of indifferent substitution of goods within the period. This condition is the same as the one which was obtained earlier in the single-period analysis. The necessary condition, however, has further implications. For example, it indicates that the consumption of any product should be allocated between any two periods in a way which equates the consumer's marginal rate of indifferent substitution of the product (as between the two periods) to the ratio of the discounted prices of the product for the two periods. The above rule only specifies the first-order or necessary conditions for a maximum of the preference function. However, second-order conditions are automatically satisfied if the preference function is strictly concave as is often assumed. Nevertheless, technical (mathematical) problems similar to those of single-period demand analysis remain in the Hicksian formulation of multiperiod analysis.[3] Non-negativity constraints are ignored in both formulations.

The effect of parameter changes in the multiperiod model are analysed in similar manner to those of single-period analysis. Interest rates being constant, the income and substitution effects of variations of the discounted prices of goods can be separated out and used to make predictions about the demand for the goods.

One problem of the theory, if we accept it at its face value, is that it involves a very large number of variables indeed. This makes it rather unwieldy. One way to simplify it is to split consumption decisions into two parts. The individual's prime decision might be imagined to be one of allocating his expenditure optimally by marketing dates. His subsidiary decision then is to allocate his predetermined expenditure (budget) of each marketing date optimally. But this formulation glosses over the interdependence which exists between these two decisions. Nevertheless an individual's time preference for expenditure can be isolated for special consideration, by assuming that the individual's expenditure *in* each period is allocated amongst commodities to maximise his utility from expenditure in each period concerned. Under these circumstances and supposing given prices, the individual has a preference function for expenditure through time. Where C_t represents his expenditure of period t, his time preference function for consumption expenditures might be expressed as

$$U = \psi(C_0, C_1, \ldots, C_T) \qquad (16.9)$$

His objective is to maximise this function subject to his lifetime budget restraint, Equation (16.8). An optimum requires that the individual's rate of time preference for consumption in one period rather than another be equal to the rate at which income can be transferred (either backwards or forwards) through the bond market between the first and the latter period.

A simple example should clarify the situation. Assume that only two periods are involved, so that period 1 is the terminal period. An individual's time preference for consumption expenditures can be indicated by

$$U = \psi(C_0, C_1). \tag{16.10}$$

Imagine that the present value of the individual's earned income is y^0. Then his lifetime restraint, if discounted expenditure must equal discounted income over the whole span, is

$$C_0 + \frac{C_1}{1+i} = y^0 \tag{16.11}$$

where i is the interest rate. Constraint Equation (16.11) can be rearranged to give

$$C_1 = (1+i)(y^0 - C_0). \tag{16.12}$$

Both the preference function Equation (16.10) and the restraint Equation (16.12) can be easily represented in a two-dimensional diagram with axes which indicate expenditure in the initial and later period. As in Fig. 16.1, the preference function can be represented by a series of indifference curves. The curves marked I_0I_0, I_1I_1 and I_2I_2 are three from the possible set. The constraint is indicated by the straight line LM which has a slope of $-(1+i)$. The point $M = y_0$ is the present discounted value of all lifetime earned income, and $L = (1+i)y^0$ is the amount which would be available in the second period by refraining from consumption in the initial one and lending the savings. The line LM indicates the possibilities for varying the time pattern of consumption using the bond market. In the case shown in Fig. 16.1, the rate of interest is assumed to be zero and so LM is at 45° to the axes. A ray, dashed from O, indicates expenditure patterns which involve no time preference. However, the individual shown has a positive time preference, for his optimum expenditure pattern over an interval of time is represented by point C. He prefers to consume the greater proportion of his income in the initial period. If the time-pattern of his income is as indicated by A, that is, if his income is equal in both periods, in the initial period the individual borrows BC and in the subsequent period repays this amount which equals AB. Many factors can cause time-preference to be other than neutral. Neo-classical theory does not analyse one of the more important ones, namely, the uncertainty

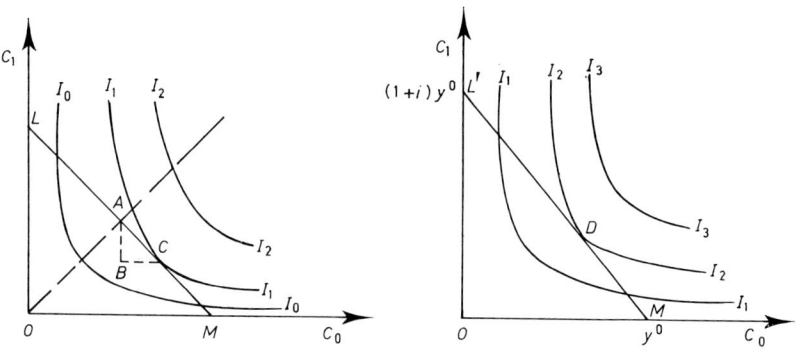

Fig. 16.1   Fig. 16.2

Allocation over Time

factor. Note that at point C the slope of the indifference curve, the marginal rate of indifferent substitution of expenditures in time, just equals the rate at which these can be substituted in the market. This rate is equal to the slope of LM.

Fig. 16.2 illustrates a case in which the rate of interest is positive. The expenditure transformation line $L'M$ has a slope of $-(1+i)$ and is steeper than LM of Fig. 16.1 because of the positive interest rate. The optimum allocation of expenditure corresponds to point D.

Diagrams of this type can be used to isolate the substitution and income effects of interest rate changes. In this two-period model, the *substitution* effect of a rise in the interest rate works towards reducing expenditure in the first period and increasing it in the second.

The limitations of the Hicksian single-period demand analysis are magnified in multiperiod analysis. Uncertainty and costs of decision-making are left out of explicit account and this point will be taken up later in this chapter. Nevertheless, the theory does provide a consistent framework for analysing multiperiod consumption and this in itself is no mean achievement. It provides a consistent reference point. Also, the theory enables the significance of factors like time preference and the interest rate to be appreciated. Neither element enters single-period demand theory. Yet the general defects of the Hicksian single-period theory remain. For example, the impact on demand of social influences is ignored.

III. Multiperiod Production

Just as a consumer can borrow and lend over an interval of time, so can a firm. Any temporary excess of a firm's costs over receipts can be covered by borrowing and the firm may also lend. Clearly, other intertemporal relationships are also likely to arise, for example, output in later periods is likely to depend upon output, and the application of factors, in earlier periods. A multiperiod theory of production must take account of these possibilities.

In the single-period analysis of production it was taken for granted that the firm maximised profit, that is, the excess of its revenue in the period over its cost. But in the multiperiod case the firm has a stream of profits and/or losses and its alternative streams, which depend on its alternative production strategies or plans, may have very different time profiles. The question then is which alternative will it choose. Hicks supposes that the firm will choose that production plan which maximises the capitalised or present value of the firm.[4] The capitalised or present value of the firm equals the discounted value of the firm's stream of profits.

There is a very good reason for supposing this to be the equivalent of profit maximisation in the single-period case. The plan with the highest present value enables the firm (or its owners) to have (if they so desire) more purchasing power at every date than with any other plan or to have the same purchasing power at every date with the exception of having more at one date. In a perfect bond market, the plan with the highest present value can be made to dominate all others in regard to purchasing power through time. Both in the case of a company in which management and ownership is separated and in owner-operated companies, Hicks sees maximisation of capitalised value as the motivating force behind the firm's production plans.[5]

Whether or not profit maximisation is the typical aim of a firm is a moot point.

In recent years, profit maximisation (maximisation of capitalised value) has been claimed by some economists not to be the main aim of many firms. Sales may be expanded at the expense of profit or capitalised value, for example. These alternatives are discussed in the next chapter. For the time being, let us accept Hicks' hypothesis.

The firm is assumed to have a finite planning horizon. Its plan extends from the initial marketing date, 0, to the horizon at the final marketing date, T. Its problem is to find the production plan which maximises its capitalised value,

$$K = \sum_{t=0}^{T} \frac{\pi(t)}{(1+i)^t} \tag{16.13}$$

where $\pi(t)$ represents its profit of period t. Letting p_{rt} represent the price of commodity r in period t and x_{rt} its quantity, and supposing that commodities numbered $1, \ldots, m$ are products and those numbered $m+1, \ldots, q$ are factors, the capitalised value of the profit of period t is

$$K_t = \frac{\pi(t)}{(1+i)^t} = \frac{1}{(1+i)^t} \left[\sum_{r=1}^{m} p_{rt}x_{rt} - \sum_{r=m+1}^{q} p_{rt}x_{rt} \right] \tag{16.14}$$

that is, equal to the discounted value of revenue in period t less the discounted value of cost. Hence, the present value of the whole stream of profits is

$$K = \sum_{t=0}^{T} \left[\sum_{r=1}^{m} p_{rt}x_{rt} - \sum_{r=m+1}^{q} p_{rt}x_{rt} \right] \frac{1}{(1+i)^t}. \tag{16.15}$$

The firm's aim is to maximise Equation (16.15) subject to the technical possibility of transforming commodities as indicated by its production function. Where x_{rt} indicates the quantity of the rth commodity exchanged by the firm at period t (if x_{rt} is a factor, the firm purchases it at that date, t, and if it is a product, the firm sells it at that date) the firm's production function might be expressed as

$$f(x_{10}, \ldots, x_{q0}; x_{11}, \ldots, x_{q1}; \ldots; x_{1T}, \ldots, x_{qT}) = 0. \tag{16.16}$$

Since no stocks are assumed to be held, the firm's available output of each marketing date is completely sold if perfect competition exists. Perfect or, at least, pure competition is assumed throughout the discussion of this chapter but the theory can be modified to allow for imperfect competition.

The necessary conditions for a maximum of the firm's capitalised value, Equation (16.15), subject to its production possibilities, Equation (16.16), are as follows:

(i) the marginal rate of substitution between outputs of any two dates must equal the ratio of their discounted prices;

(ii) the marginal rate of substitution between inputs of any two dates must equal the ratio of their discounted prices;

(iii) the marginal rate of transformation of any input into any output must equal the ratio of their discounted prices.

These rules can be summarised by saying that *the marginal rate of technical transformation of any commodity into any other must equal the ratio of their discounted prices*. This rule is equivalent in form to the one for a consumer's multiperiod optimum. Note, too, that the rules are identical to those for the single-period case, except that price terms are discounted and commodities are distinguished by type and time.

Allocation over Time

Again, it might be pointed out that the analysis ignores *some* non-negativity constraints, for example, the impossibility of negative output, and these might make it impossible to fulfil the above "necessary" conditions. Also, it is necessary to check the second-order conditions to decide whether a relative maximum of capitalised value is achieved by the production plan which satisfies the above necessary conditions. If the firm's production function is supposed to be strictly concave, as is traditionally assumed, then any plan which satisfies the necessary conditions automatically yields the global maximum of the firm's capitalised value.

But it is not correct to conclude that the traditional economic theory of production introduces no non-negativity conditions. It is explicitly stated, for example, by Hicks,[6] that a firm will not produce after any date for which the present value of its profit from that date to its horizon is negative. The firm makes a discounted loss by producing in these circumstances.

To illustrate the multiperiod theory of production, take two simple cases. In both instances, it is imagined that only two planning periods are involved, the initial period and the subsequent period.

In the first model, suppose that the firm's supply of factors through time is fixed and that it produces one product, x. Let x_0 represent its quantity of output of product x in the initial period and x_1 represent its output in the subsequent period. The firm's maximum output of x in period 1 is imagined to be dependent on its output in period 0. For example, if the firm is engaged in mining, this sort of dependence seems a clear possibility; if it is also engaged in agriculture, land use and output at an early stage influence production possibilities at a later stage and so on. The production function of the firm can be written as

$$f(x_0, x_1) = 0. \tag{16.17}$$

For simplicity, suppose that this function can be rewritten in the explicit form

$$x_1 = g(x_0). \tag{16.18}$$

Equation (16.18) specifies the product transformation curve for the firm which, assuming a diminishing rate of product transformation between the output of period one and period zero, that is $g''(x_0) < 0$, is indicated by the curve ABC in Fig. 16.3. Equation (16.18) indicates the production constraint faced by the firm.

Next, the firm's objective must be specified. Let p represent the actual price of x and its subscript indicate the date to which this refers. Then the capitalised value or discounted profit stream of the firm is

$$K = p_0 x_0 + \frac{p_1}{1+i} x_1 \tag{16.19}$$

where i is the rate of interest. Equation (16.19) must be maximised subject to Equation (16.19). Carrying out this simple mathematical operation, the necessary condition for a maximum is found to be

$$g'(x_0) = -p_0/p_1' \tag{16.20}$$

where $p_1' = p_1/(1+i)$, that is, the discounted price of x in period 1. The rate of product transformation must equal the ratio of the initial price of x divided by its discounted subsequent price. This is illustrated in Fig. 16.3. Equation (16.19) can be used to obtain a number of isocapitalised earnings or isodiscounted profit lines. Rearranging Equation (16.19),

$$x_1 = K/p_1' - (p_0/p_1')x_0. \tag{16.21}$$

where $p_1' = p_1/(1+i)$. For any specified value of K and given prices and the interest rate, Equation (16.21) yields a straight line with a negative slope equal to the ratio of the discounted prices of commodity x. This line is an isodiscounted profit function which indicates time patterns of production which yield equal discounted profit.

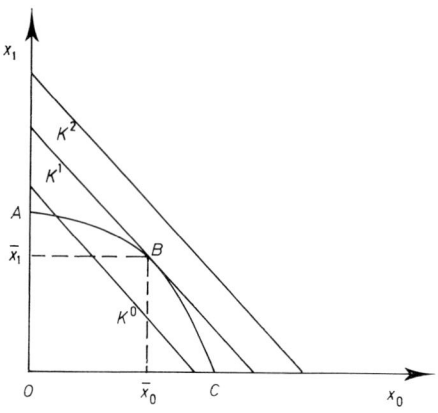

Fig. 16.3

As K varies, other parameters being constant, it generates a series of parallel isodiscounted profit lines. For given parameters, three such possible lines are indicated by K^0, K^1 and K^2 in Fig. 16.3. The highest attainable one is reached for production plan B which involves producing an output of $\bar{x}_0$ in the initial period and $\bar{x}_1$ in the subsequent one. At point B, the slope of K^1 is equal to the slope of the product transformation curve ABC, which implies that the appropriate discounted price ratios and rates of product transformation are equal.

One can, of course, easily trace through the consequences of variations of price and interest rates in this model. A rise in the interest rate, other things being constant, encourages current production at the expense of future production. A rise of the present price of the product *relative* to the future price, other things being constant, also encourages present production at the expense of future output. However, if present and future prices discounted increase in the same proportion, other things being equal, the optimal production plan is unchanged.[7]

Consider a second illustration. Imagine that the firm produces only one product x and that its output depends solely upon one input l but with a lag of one period. Thus the output of x in period 1, x_1, depends upon the firm's purchases of factor l in the initial period. Represent the quantity of these purchases by l_0. The firm's production function can then be written as

$$x_1 = g(l_0). \tag{16.22}$$

If w_0 represents the price per unit which is paid for l in the initial period, the discounted profit of the firm is

$$K = \frac{p_1}{1+i}x_1 - w_0 l_0. \tag{16.23}$$

Allocation over Time

The multiperiod theory of production predicts that discounted profit, Equation (16.23), is maximised subject to the production function, Equation (16.22). The necessary condition for a maximum is that l be hired in the initial period up to a level which ensures that

$$w_0 = \frac{p_1}{1+i} \frac{dg}{dl_0}, \qquad (16.24)$$

the price of the factor = the discounted price of its product × its marginal product.

In the initial period, l should be hired in a quantity which ensures that its price per unit is equal to the discounted value of its marginal product. Second-order conditions are automatically satisfied if diminishing marginal productivity is the case, that is, if $g'' < 0$.

The optimal production plan can easily be indicated by diagrammatic means. Indeed, Figs. 7.6, 7.7 and 7.8 are all easily modified to show the optimal plan by placing l_0 on the horizontal axis and in the case of Figs. 7.7 and 7.8, x_1 on the vertical axis. The discounted price of the product replaces the actual price of the earlier version. The straightforward modifications can be safely left to the reader.

These two illustrations have possibly led the reader to infer that a wide range of dynamic production relationships are possible and that various lags can arise. Of this there is no doubt. In principle, the Hicksian formulation which involves multiperiod inputs and multiperiod outputs covers all interdependencies. Yet many interesting applications are possible by considering special cases of interdependence. Some possible interdependencies are as follows:

(i) point-input, point-output dependence. The output of a period depends on the input of a particular period;

(ii) interval-input, point-output dependence. The output of a particular period depends upon the inputs of several periods;

(iii) point-input, interval output dependence. The output of several periods depends on the input of a single period;

(iv) interval-input, interval-output dependence. Output over several periods depends upon inputs over several periods.

This list is by no means exhaustive but problems involving all of these types arise.

The point-input, point-output case is particularly interesting. In some cases, it is possible to vary the point of output and sale as in the maturing of spirits. The problem for the firm is then one of determining an optimal length of time for maturing in order to maximise the present value of the return. It turns out that the optimal length of time for maturing is the one which equates the marginal rate of return from maturing with the rate of interest.[8]

As in the case of consumption theory, the Hicksian theory of multiperiod production[9] provides a consistent framework which is useful as a starting point for introducing "complicating" factors such as uncertainty about prices, interest rates etc. It seems a serious limitation of the theory that it does not take adequate account of uncertainty and does not consider the costs of decision-making. Both of these matters are taken up below. Many economists, too, would challenge the basic hypothesis that firms aim to maximise their capitalised value, the present value of their stream of profits. It is possible that firms are, as Baumol[10] suggests, prepared to

IV. Uncertainty, Futures Markets, Expectations

Until recently, comparatively little attention has been given by economists to the impact of uncertainty on economic planning and much remains to be done. This is not to say that the importance of lack of information has been unrecognised by economists.

In *Value and Capital*, Hicks[11] does make a limited allowance for uncertainty in his multiperiod theory. Considering uncertainty about prices, he says:

> If we are to allow for uncertainty of expectations in these problems of the determination of plans, we must not take the most probable price as the representative price, but the most probable price ± an allowance for uncertainty of the expectation, that is to say, an allowance for risk.[12]

An adjustment should be made to the most probable price of a commodity in any period to allow for uncertainty or risk associated with the estimate of the price.

However, since no guide is given by Hicks on the procedure for calculating these allowances, the theory is somewhat incomplete. Yet one thing is clear as far as Hicks' theory is concerned. An economic agent acts upon the basis of a specific vector of discounted adjusted prices. The probability distribution of the price of a commodity in any period t is represented by a *single* (adjusted) price value.

Let X be the vector of commodity quantities for the planning interval. In our previous models, $X = [x_{10}, \ldots, x_{q0}; \ldots; x_{1T}, \ldots, x_{qT}]$. Let R be the corresponding vector of the most probable discounted prices of the commodities. These prices must be adjusted to allow for uncertainty. Let the adjusted discounted price vector be represented by R'. The multiperiod optima are then found by using this vector.

For example, consider multiperiod production. Allowing for price uncertainty, the problem for the firm is to maximise

$$K = R'X \tag{16.24}$$

subject to its production function

$$f(X) = 0. \tag{16.25}$$

If $f(X)$ is strictly concave, the solution occurs for a unique value of vector X. Represent this solution by $\bar{X}$. It specifies unique input and output values for each period.

In the initial period, it specifies, for example, $[\bar{x}_{10}, \bar{x}_{20}, \ldots, \bar{x}_{q0}]$ as being optimal. Hicks would accept this as the optimal plan for the initial period. Yet, he would not hold the firm to $[\bar{x}_{11}, \bar{x}_{21}, \ldots, \bar{x}_{q1}]$ in the subsequent period but would contend that learning might occur and the firm will adjust to its new price estimates. Thus, in period 1, another vector of discounted adjusted prices is used to redetermine the production plan of the period and so on. Production beyond the initial period is *implicitly* treated by Hicks as a function of learning.

But learning possibilities may render initial period plans which are obtained by the Hicksian method less than optimal. Present production sets limits to future flexibility of production and the actual *range* or *spread* of future possibilities has consequences for the optimality of present production. This is certainly obscured by the Hicksian analysis, that is, it is not evident how optimal initial period plans are affected by the range of learning possibilities in later periods. This has been investigated in recent years by Henri Theil and others.[13]

It might be noted, too, that the theory paid little regard to the role of money Money was regarded as a neutral factor useful as a standard of account but of very little other significance. In lending and borrowing, only transfers of real purchasing power or securities were considered. In practice, an excess of expenses over receipts can be covered not only by selling bonds but by drawing an accumulated cash balances or borrowing money. But if bonds pay interest and idle money balances do not, why should individuals wish to hold money balances which pay no interest? Because the liquidity of money makes it convenient for meeting irregular and uncertain excesses of expenses over receipts, and it can be used to diversify portfolio investment and reduce risk. As Keynes contended[14] and as Tobin has elaborated,[15] uncertainty has a considerable impact on the desire of individual economic agents to hold money balances. Thus uncertainty is seen to be important in another regard.

It might be thought that an emphasis on uncertainty is unwarranted because futures markets exist and their coverage could be extended. If futures markets happened to work perfectly, then future prices could be calculated relatively easily by economic agents from a knowledge of futures prices contracted. But, in practice, futures markets are less than perfect—speculators have much less than perfect foresight, and thus a probability of error remains. Of course, too, any producer who sells futures does not really eliminate his risk. He merely replaces one risk, possibly a more acceptable risk to him, by another. If the future spot price rises substantially above the futures price at which a producer has contracted for delivery of produce, then considerable profit is forgone by him as a result of the contract. If the reverse happens, then he is protected from a loss.

Other elements which are ignored in the Hicksian multiperiod theory of decision-making are the costs associated with the decision process itself. These are the costs of searching for information, organising it and carrying out the actual operations of finding an optimum. It is not always optimal to improve our knowledge, even if it is possible to do so, for the additional costs can outweigh the additional benefits. Thus, even if the prices of a period could be predicted with certainty, the gains from improving the accuracy of predictions to this level might not justify the extra cost. Similarly, it does not always pay to differentiate too finely between the characteristics of production and consumption plans. The cost of specifying the alternatives finely outweighs the gain. Typically, plans might be classified into bunches, the members of each bunch being regarded as similar or equally satisfactory, since it is not worthwhile to differentiate between them on the basis of profitability, for example. Consequently, pure chance determines which plan is selected from the optimal bunch. The procedure is not irrational. We shall return to the cost of decision-making and uncertainty towards the end of the next chapter which examines the profit-maximisation hypothesis generally.

NOTES AND REFERENCES

[1] This is not quite true. It was touched on in Section II of Chapter 14.

[2] The basic theory outlined in this section and Section III is that of Hicks. See J. R. HICKS, *Value and Capital*, 2nd ed., Clarendon Press, Oxford, 1946, Chs. 15-18.

[3] Ibid. Other factors, such as social influences on demand and the problem of changing tastes, are not allowed for, nor is allowance made for the cost of decision-making.

[4] HICKS, op. cit., Ch. 15.
[5] Ibid. pp. 243, 244, and also p. 196.
[6] Ibid. p. 201.
[7] Increasing p_0 and p_1' in the same proportion does not change the left hand side (16.20) and so its solution is unaltered.
[8] Details of this model can be found in J. HENDERSON and R. QUANDT, *Microeconomic Theory*, McGraw-Hill, New York, 1958, pp. 253-5.
[9] HICKS, op. cit.
[10] W. J. BAUMOL, *Business Behavior, Value and Growth*, The Macmillan Company, New York, 1959, Chs. 6-8.
[11] HICKS, op. cit.
[12] Ibid., pp. 125-6.
[13] H. THEIL, *Economic Forecasts and Policy*, 2nd revised ed., North-Holland Publishing Company, Amsterdam, 1961.
[14] J. M. KEYNES, *The General Theory of Employment, Interest and Money*, Macmillan, London, 1936.
[15] J. TOBIN, "Liquidity Preference as Behaviour towards Risk", *Review of Economic Studies*, 1958, **25**, pp. 65-86.

FURTHER READING

ALCHIAN, A. A., and W. R. ALLEN, *Exchange and Production Theory in Use*, Wadsworth Publishing, Belmont, 1969, Ch. 9.

*COHEN, K. J. and R. M. CYERT, *Theory of the Firm*, Prentice-Hall, Englewood Cliffs, 1965, Ch. 5.

HENDERSON, J. M., and R. E. QUANDT, *Microeconomic Theory*, McGraw-Hill, New York, 1958, Ch. 8.

HICKS, J. R., *Value and Capital*, 2nd ed., Clarendon Press, Oxford, 1946, Parts III and IV.

*LUTZ, F. and V., *The Theory of Investment of the Firm*, Princeton University Press, Princeton, 1951.

---

*More advanced.

CHAPTER 17

Objectives of the Firm: Profit Maximisation Reconsidered

Our analysis has been based upon the assumption that firms maximise their profit or capitalised value. But some economists claim that this assumption is unrealistic. In their opinion firms do not typically desire to maximise profit but have different objectives. Moreover, there is an even more radical view than this. A few economists claim that firms do not pursue any conscious objective consistently.[1]

Alternative views about the firm's behaviour can be conveniently introduced by first supposing that the firm operates under conditions of certainty and then considering the situation if uncertainty exists. Even if one accepts the profit-maximisation objective as a rough guide to the firm's behaviour, the hypothesis must be modified in some way or other if uncertainty is important. One must distinguish between the desire of a firm to maximise profit and its ability to do so. Although a firm may desire to maximise profit, it may be unable to do so because of its lack of knowledge. In the latter circumstances, the predictive value of the profit-maximisation hypothesis is much reduced.

Yet the adequacy of a hypothesis can be rarely judged in isolation from its purpose. Traditional economic theory is concerned with the broad factors which determine the production and prices of goods, so that the degree of its abstraction is not completely unwarranted. Traditional theory is not concerned with the organisation and administration of firms—more detail is required in a theory which is concerned with these matters. But if business administration has important consequences for output and price formation then the orientation of economic theory needs to change. Economists like Galbraith,[2] Cyert and March[3] believe that this change in orientation is necessary because firms have become large administrative units and many production decisions are made outside the market.

Thus there is a diversity of opinion about which hypothesis is appropriate for describing a firm's behaviour. Some of the alternatives will now be considered by first examining the firm's behaviour under certainty and then its decisions under uncertainty. In the light of this discussion, a few observations on the cost plus controversy are also made.

I. The Behaviour of the Firm under Conditions of Certainty

Traditionally firms are assumed to maximise their profit or capitalised value if conditions of certainty prevail.[4] One may be asked to accept the hypothesis on the grounds that it can be checked against observation, or it may be supported by argument. Both Alchian[5] and Penrose[6] have supported the hypothesis by further theory. Let us consider Alchian's view now.

Alchian argues[7] that profit maximisation is necessary for the survival of the firm. If perfect competition prevails, then in the long run above-normal profit is zero. In these circumstances, if the firm is unable to earn a normal return and needs to borrow because of losses, it will be unable to meet all of its commitments, that is to meet its running expenses, interest and capital repayments from revenue, and will normally go out of existence. Furthermore, if the view of J. M. Clark[8] on the workably competitive nature of imperfect competition in the long run is accepted, the argument also extends to imperfect competition.

While profit as a rule is necessary for survival of the firm, is profit maximisation a necessity? Even under perfect competition some entrepreneurs may be prepared to accept less than normal profit in order to run their own firm rather than, say, lend their capital at the going rate of interest. This is so, even though the latter course is financially more attractive to the capitalist. If an individual has his own capital, then he has leeway in his own firm to accept less than a normal return. Also, if he provides some of his own managerial skill and/or labour, he may be prepared to supply these to his own firm in a quantity which implies that his marginal revenue product is less than the marginal return which he could receive elsewhere for these factors. He may be prepared to forgo income for the sake of his own firm.

The social Darwinistic view that profit maximisation is necessary for survival of the firm is too strong, but it does highlight the fact that some attention to profit is necessary for survival. A lessening of competition possibly widens the scope for pursuing objectives other than profit maximisation. Monopolists can pursue a variety of alternative objectives. As Hicks once observed,[9] the greatest reward of a monopolist might not be the possibility of making above-normal profit, but of being able to lead a quiet life in which he worries little about (maximising) profit. If we accept the view that profit maximisation is not a necessity for the survival of the firm, we open the door to a consideration of other objectives. The views of Scitovsky, Berle and Means, Williamson, Baumol, Cyert, Marris, Simon and others can be considered.[10]

Scitovsky[11] supposes that the firm is operated by a single entrepreneur producing one product. He imagines that the entrepreneur has a preference function which depends both on the profit of the firm and its physical output. This might be represented by

$$U = U(\pi, x) \qquad (17.1)$$

where U is an ordering function, π represents the profit of the firm and x the output of its product. The indifference curves for (π, x) combinations can be shown in a two-dimensional diagram. Three possible sets are indicated in Figs. 17.1, 17.2 and 17.3. In Fig. 17.1, the indifference curves are positively sloped as a function of x—increased output requires compensation by increased profit, whereas in Fig. 17.3 they are negatively sloped—increased output is to some extent rewarding to the entrepreneur. In Fig. 17.2, profit is the sole consideration of the entrepreneur and his indifference curves are horizontal.

Indifference curves of the type shown in Fig. 17.1 by I^1, I^2, I^3, might arise if the entrepreneur has a strong preference for leisure, provides effort for the firm and if his required effort rises with output. Also there might be, depending upon the society,

Objectives of the Firm

strong social pressures against maximising profit. The situation shown in Fig. 17.3 might arise because the entrepreneur enjoys putting effort into production or because he obtains more prestige from an extra volume of sales than from extra profit.

Although he allows for all of the above possibilities, Scitovsky believes that the entrepreneur typically derives satisfaction from his work.

> The person who derives satisfaction from his work—other than that yielded by the income he receives from it—will to a large extent be governed by ambition, a spirit of emulation and rivalry, pride in his work and similar considerations, when he plans his activity. We believe that the entrepreneur usually belongs to the latter category.[12]

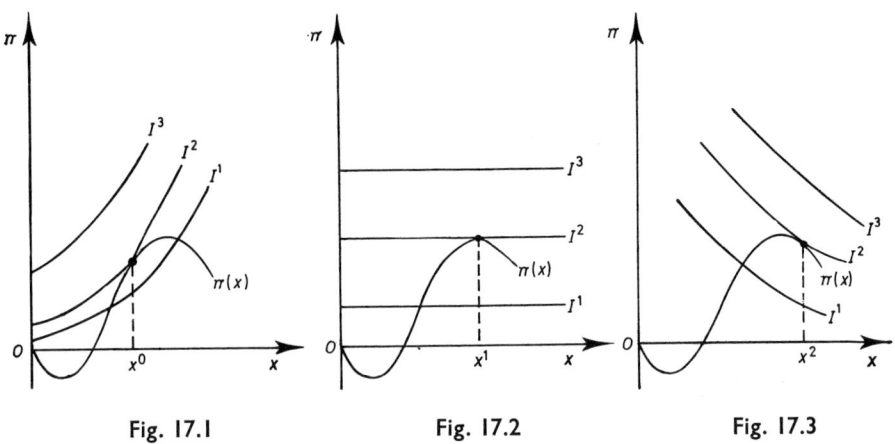

Fig. 17.1   Fig. 17.2   Fig. 17.3

The profit function (assuming the absence of organisational slack) is shown in the diagrams by $\pi(x)$. Optimal output is lower in Fig. 17.1 than the profit-maximising output in Fig. 17.2. Output is lower or greater than the profit-maximising output depending upon whether there is an aversion or a preference for production. Deviations from a pure preference for profit have also other consequences.

If the profit-maximisation hypothesis holds, a lump-sum tax or an increase in fixed cost, other things being unchanged, do not alter the output of a non-marginal firm. In Fig. 17.2, the effect can be considered by a vertical downward displacement of $\pi(x)$. But this relationship does not hold if the entrepreneur's utility function depends upon his output as well as his income or profit. If the entrepreneur has an aversion to extra output (as illustrated in Fig. 17.1) output may *expand* as a result of a lump-sum tax. In contrast, if there is a positive preference for greater output (as illustrated in Fig. 17.3) output may be reduced by a lump-sum tax. Hence, taxation policies have entirely different consequences depending upon the nature of the preference function of entrepreneurs.

Scitovsky is concerned with owner-operated firms (for example, his model might be applicable to farms and small businesses) but today the owners of many firms are remote from the managers. The growth of large companies with many shareholders often means that shareholders have little direct influence on the policies which are pursued by professional non-owner managers of companies. Does this separation of ownership and management alter the effective objectives of the firm?

Views about this differ. Berle and Means (1932) were amongst the first to state that the division of ownership and management changes the objective of the firm.[13] Because of the division entailed by the corporate form, a company is unlikely to be operated in the interest of shareholders but in accord with the interest of managers. They summarise their view as follows:

> If we are to assume that the desire for *personal* profit is the prime force motivating control, we must conclude that other interests of control are different from and often radically opposed to those of ownership; that the owners most emphatically will not be served by a profit-seeking controlling group.[14]

They quote[15] examples in which managers have lined their own pockets at the expense of others but do not develop a specific theory. Recently, however, specific theories have been developed by economists such as Williamson, Baumol and Marris.

Williamson[16] indicates the objectives of management by a utility or preference function. Several possibilities are canvassed but basically it is assumed that management has a preference for managerial slack but is prepared to forgo some slack for the sake of greater funds for discretionary investment spending. Managerial slack may take the form of a greater number of inferiors than the number necessary for reporting to top management (a staff larger than is most profitable) or perquisites of various kinds, for example, liberal entertainment and travel allowances which are greater than those required to retain managers. Funds for discretionary investment are seen as depending on the reported profit of the firm less its tax and less the minimum profit necessary for paying dividends and meeting essential investments. Although profit still has significance, it does not have an overriding significance. Williamson puts his model into an operational form and explores its implications. An interesting feature is that a tax change or a demand variation can have an impact on managerial slack and give rise to results not predicted by the profit-maximisation approach. For example, an increase in the tax rate leads to increased output and an increase in managerial slack since salary and other expenses are tax-deductible.

Baumol's model[17] is somewhat simpler. Baumol asserts that "the typical oligopolist's objectives can usefully be characterised, approximately, as sales maximisation subject to a minimum profit constraint."[18] He has *value* of sales or total revenue in mind, not quantity of sales. In the business world, so he contends, the value of a firm's sales is regarded as a significant indicator of success and status. Furthermore, the *salaries of managers tend to increase with the sales of their firm* and therefore managers have a personal interest in the expansion of the firm's value of sales. This often results in the expansion of the firm's output beyond the level which maximises profit. Yet management is restrained in its expansion of sales by the need to pay shareholders a satisfactory return on their investment.

Unless a firm pays its investors the going rate of return, it may be unable to obtain funds for growth and investment. The capital market provides a restraint. Baumol says that

> In order for all incorporated firms to be able to obtain funds from the sale of their securities, there must, over the long run, be some sort of rough parity among the earnings of the securities of listed firms (whether or not they are oligopolists) after some appropriate corrections for risk premiums.[19]

Provided that a firm pays (and will continue to pay) the going return, its supply of external funds is perfectly elastic. A firm need not pay the going return in dividends but

Objectives of the Firm

may reinvest its profit or a proportion of it in the firm so that shareholders gain by appreciation of the market value of their shares.

Baumol's hypothesis can be easily illustrated for a firm which produces one product. Indicate quantity of its product by x. The total revenue of the firm is then shown by the curve, $R(x)$, in Fig. 17.4, and its profit by the curve marked $\pi(x)$. $R(x)$ reaches its maximum for an output of $\hat{x}$. At that output marginal revenue equals zero. If marginal cost is positive when it cuts marginal revenue from below, profit is at a maximum for a lower output than $\hat{x}$. In the case shown, profit is at a maximum for an output of $\bar{x}$. If a profit of π_0 is necessary to ensure investors the going rate of return, Baumol suggests that the firm produces an output of x_0 which in this instance is greater than the output necessary for profit-maximisation and less than the output necessary for revenue-maximisation. If the required profit is greater than π_0, say π_1, output is even lower. As the profit constraint varies, actual output may vary in the range $\bar{x} \leqslant x \leqslant \hat{x}$. If Baumol's hypothesis is correct, the output of the firm is likely to be in excess of $\bar{x}$, the profit-maximising output. One implication of this is that output under imperfect competition is likely to be less restricted than suggested by the traditional profit-maximising theory.[20] Furthermore, an increase in fixed cost or the imposition of a lump-sum tax causes the firm to reduce its output (because $\pi(x)$ has a downward vertical displacement), a result not in accord with traditional theory.

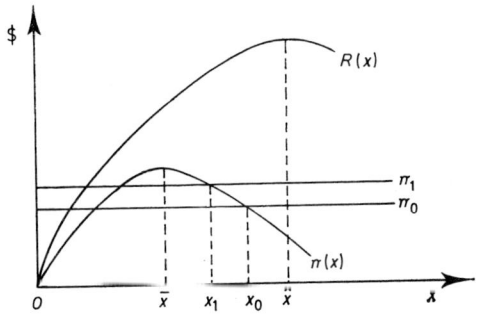

Fig. 17.4

Edith Penrose,[21] unlike Williamson and Baumol, believes that despite the separation of ownership and management in most corporations, the traditional profit-maximising hypothesis is still applicable. Managers still try to maximise the corporation's profit because they wish to maximise its growth rate, and retained earnings are the most important source of funds for the firm's growth. According to Edith Penrose, managers desire the company's growth because this enables them to realise their personal ambitions. The salary, power and prestige of the company's executives increase with its growth. A basic difference between the positions of Baumol and Penrose is that the latter puts greater emphasis on internal funds as a source for growth and survival.

However, some aspects of Penrose's hypothesis are puzzling. Maximisation of capitalised value may conflict with the objective of largely self-financing a company in its early stages.[22] The strategy which maximises capitalised value may be one which involves considerable early deficits. Will this be preferred to a strategy which has a lower capitalised value but which makes internal funds available at an earlier stage?

Edith Penrose gives us little indication. But if the latter strategy, a short-run profit goal, is supported by her view then, after all, her theory is in conflict with the traditional view that firms maximise their capitalised value.

Other hypotheses which pay particular attention to the modern corporation have been developed or are being developed. For example, Marris[23] suggests the managers aim at maximum growth of their company subject to ensuring some probability of survival of the company as an identity under their control. Since the probability of a take-over of the company depends in part on its retentions from profit, this aim can be used to predict retention-ratios.

A rather unusual view is that of Simon, Cyert, Cohen and March.[24] They believe that *non-maximising behaviour* is the rule. A firm may aspire to *satisfactory* levels for its profit, market-share, inventories, etc. without thought of maximising any objective function at all. Various models have been developed on this basis. In one of their models, Cyert and Cohen[25] assume that the firm reacts to satisfactory *changes* in its profit by increasing its organisational slack, and to unsatisfactory changes in its profit by reducing organisational slack. Given that the firm takes some time to react to profit changes and that there is randomness in the firm's demand function, the firm's actual output is a random variable within limits. Cyert and Cohen have simulated some of the possible output paths by using computers.[26] Yet little or no analytical advance has been made by this approach. Another factor which has been stressed by Simon, Cyert *et al.*[27] is the significance of the costs of decision-making—the costs of searching for a satisfactory strategy. These costs are considered in the next section which examines decision-making under uncertainty.

II. The Behaviour of the Firm under Conditions of Uncertainty

Even if a firm wishes to maximise profit, it may be unable to do so because of its lack of knowledge about prices and future technological changes etc. Consequently, the profit-maximisation hypothesis cannot be used to predict its precise behaviour. Nevertheless, if bounds can be put on the possible values of relevant variables, the aim of maximum profit limits the strategies which could possibly maximise profit. This last point can be simply illustrated by a single-period model.

Imagine that a purely competitive firm must contract for its factors in advance and that at that time it is uncertain only about the price which it will receive for its product. Its profit can be expressed as

$$\pi = px - C(x) \qquad (17.2)$$

where p is the actual price which prevails for its product and C represents its cost. At the time factors are hired to produce x, p is of uncertain magnitude. But imagine that the firm believes that p will fall in the range $p_0 \leqslant p \leqslant p_m$. Let x_0 be the output which maximises profit if p_0 is the case and x_m be the output which maximises profit if p_m is the case, and assume that if p_0 occurs, average variable cost can be covered. Then output in the ranges $x < x_0$ and $x > x_m$ is not consistent with profit maximisation. Only quantities of output in the range $x_0 \leqslant x \leqslant x_m$ could possibly maximise profit but the actual quantity which maximises profit is indeterminate at the time a decision must be reached, even if this quantity must fall within the limits.

In order to predict the firm's output precisely, some additional criterion is needed. A firm may react to uncertainty in a variety of ways depending upon its willingness

Objectives of the Firm

to take risks, and a large number of criteria have been suggested for decision-making under uncertainty. It is not possible to discuss all of the alternatives here.[28] Yet a few of the more commonly suggested ones might be mentioned.

One possibility is that the firm will aim to maximise its expected profit, that is the average profit it could expect to earn if the chance situation which it believes that it faces could be repeated a large number of times. "Expected value" is used in the mathematical sense, that is, it is the summation of the possible values of the relevant variable weighted by their probability of occurrence. Thus the expected value of a product's price, if $j = 1, \ldots, k$, different price values are possible and p_j is the probability of the jth price, is

$$E[p] = \sum_{j=1}^{k} p_j \, p_j \tag{17.3}$$

In the single-period model introduced above, a firm's expected profit is at a maximum if

$$E[\pi] = E[p]x - C(x) \tag{17.4}$$

is maximised. The necessary condition for a maximum of this expression is that

$$E[p] = \frac{dC}{dx}. \tag{17.5}$$

Planned output should be at a level which equates the expected price of the product to the marginal cost of production. But the rule has limitations.

The expected profit maximisation rule does not take any account of the dispersion of profit possibilities. For example, the rule ranks the following alternatives as equally desirable:

Alternative I: 0.5 probability of $0 and
0.5 probability of $100;

Alternative II: 0.5 probability of −$100 and
0.5 probability of $200.

Both alternatives give an expected gain of $50 but the second one involves more risk. Certainly not everyone is indifferent about these alternatives.

A desire to maximise expected money gain can be regarded as a *special* case of a desire to maximise the expected utility from money gain. Imagine that the utility of money gain to the firm (or an individual) can be expressed by a function (in terms of a von Neumann and Morgenstern utility index).[29] If the firm's utility function depends linearly on money gain, it desires to maximise expected profit but in the case of diminishing marginal utility this is not so. Fig. 17.5 shows a case in which the firm's utility function $U(\pi)$ is linearly dependent on its profit and Fig. 17.6 a case in which the marginal utility of additional profit is declining.

It is easy to see that the different functions give rise to different decisions. For example, imagine two alternatives:

Alternative I: π^* with certainty;

Alternative II: π^0 with a probability of 0.5 and
π' with a probability of 0.5.

π^0 is as far below π^* as π' is above π^* so that $E[\pi]$ is *the same* for both alternatives. But differences in the utility function lead to unlike rankings of the alternatives. In the first instance (Fig. 17.5) both alternatives give an expected utility of $E[U]$. The firm is indifferent between them. In the second instance (Fig. 17.6) the first alternative gives an expected utility of $E_1[U]$ and the second yields $E_2[U]$. Thus the first alternative, the one with less dispersion, is preferred. Indeed, the firm would be prepared to pay a sum (an *insurance premium*) to avoid the risky alternative. It would be prepared to pay up to $\pi^* - A$ to ensure itself of π^*. If increasing marginal utility had been the case, the firm would have preferred the alternative which offered a greater range of payoff.

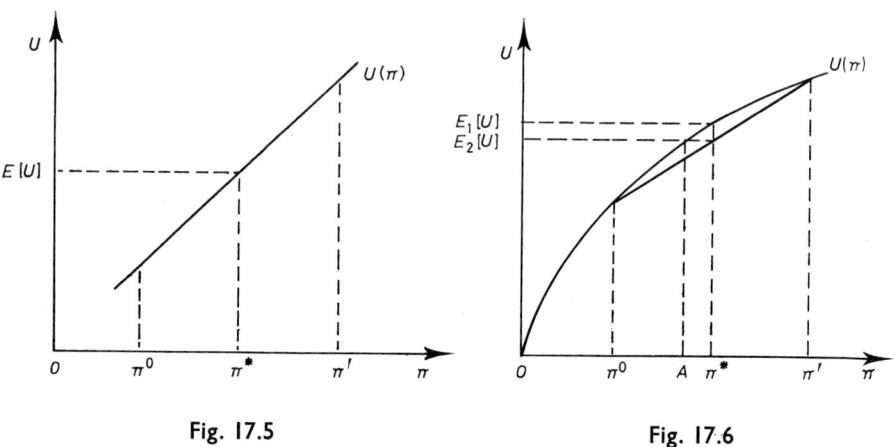

Fig. 17.5   Fig. 17.6

Diminishing marginal utility results in the firm being more conservative. If it maximises expected utility, its optimal output is below that which maximises expected profit. Just the opposite occurs if increasing marginal utility is the case.

Several other criteria are also possible. In particular, it might be noted that criteria which have been discussed so far rely on some type of a probability distribution. Sometimes, uncertainty may be so great that no probability distribution can be constructed. Various criteria attempt to predict behaviour in these cases.[30] For example, the maximin approach assumes that the economic agent will base its decision on the worst eventuality. In the above single-period production example, the firm would act on the assumption that the lowest possible price p_1 is going to occur and would produce an output which ensures that this price equals marginal cost.

It is doubtful if any single criterion does justice to the diversity of behaviour which arises under conditions of uncertainty. Much of the discussion of the decision-making of economic agents under uncertainty is also limited by the implicit assumption that knowledge is stationary. Implicitly, the decision rules mentioned above assume that the probability distribution of prices is *given*. But in reality learning takes place with time and probability distributions or information can be increased by effort.

While neglect of these factors might be excusable in single-period models, it is an important oversight in multiperiod models. As A. G. Hart and H. Theil[31] stress, passive learning (that is changes of probability with time) can make it desirable to build biases into earlier decisions in multiperiod decision-making. This was mentioned also in the last chapter. Future learning *prospects* can make an important difference to the optimal decision today.

Objectives of the Firm

But a great deal of learning is not passive but is of an active type. Knowledge can be increased with effort. To decide how much effort to expend in this task is also a significant optimisation problem. If maximisation of expected gain is the aim, then the knowledge about a relevant variable should be increased until the marginal expected cost of doing so equals the additional expected gain. Since the marginal cost of extra knowledge is likely to be positive, one *normally* will stop short of perfect knowledge about the variable, even if perfect knowledge should be attainable.

Because the knowledge which an economic agent may discover is likely to be a random function of search and since the passive knowledge which comes to hand with time may exhibit some randomness, the future output of a firm, if predicted from an initial period, is, within limits, a random variable. The future levels of output of a firm cannot be predicted with certainty. That search behaviour can lead to random results is evident from sequential sampling.

The likelihood of this randomness has been noted by Baumol and Quandt[32] who speak of optimally imperfect decisions due to the cost of information gathering and of more precise calculation. They point out that "one can easily formulate the appropriate marginal condition for what one may call *an optimally imperfect decision*, which requires that the marginal cost of additional information-gathering or more refined calculation be equal to its marginal (expected) gross yield". Given the costs of collection and processing of information, it can be shown that approximate procedures and rules of thumb may be optimal under the circumstances.

Simon suggests that individuals do not always optimise but are often prepared to accept a satisfactory outcome below the optimum.[33] Firms, for example, may only aspire to a satisfactory level of profit. Why? Is it because the costs of search and calculation really make it unprofitable to have higher aspirations? This is certainly a possibility, although it is not the view which Simon canvasses since he rejects maximisation-descriptions of behaviour. According to Simon, the individual or firm sets itself on aspiration level. If the firm can reach its aspiration level it is satisfied and does not wish to maximise. If it does not reach its aspiration level, the firm begins searching for a superior strategy and, if a sufficiently better one is not discovered after a time, may reduce its aspiration level. This certainly seems a reasonable *description* of much behaviour.

Yet this type of behaviour does not necessitate the rejection of maximisation or optimisation approaches to behaviour. Behaviour of this nature can be generated by models in which firms (or individuals) aim to *maximise* expected gain taking account of all costs including costs of calculation and information-gathering. If firms are uncertain of relevant variables and can learn more about them at a cost, models not unlike those with sequential sampling may be relevant and firms may revise their expected variables (aspiration levels) as they gain experience. Whether optimisation models of this nature are the best predictors of a firm's behaviour is as yet unknown. Models of the type which I have in mind have analytical advantages but, of course, these alone do not justify their application.

The increasing inclusion of decision costs in models to describe choice by economic agents is a radical departure from orthodox theory, and brings out new relationships, such as the likelihood of randomness in choice. But the inclusion of decision costs does complicate matters and one must always consider whether this is justified in models which abstract to give a broad sweep of the economy.[34]

III. The Marginalist and Cost-Plus Controversy

The discussion of the last section has some relevance to the cost-plus controversy. The observation that businessmen add a fairly constant percentage to their average cost to obtain the price which they charge[35] sparked off a debate about the relevance of marginalism and profit maximisation to business behaviour. One conclusion which can be drawn from the debate is that profit maximisation is not necessarily inconsistent with cost-plus behaviour. Furthermore, maximisation of expected profit is not inconsistent with this behaviour if the costs of decision-making and uncertainties are taken into account. Let us consider this in more detail.

Observation indicates that businessmen in many markets act in the following way:

> Sellers normally determine their prices by adding a fairly fixed percentage to a per-unit cost base (such as average cost of production at standard volume). Prices which are determined by this "mark-up" method tend to be stable despite variations of demand and some changes of cost.[36]

Two contentions can be distinguished, namely that price tends to be relatively constant despite variations in the demand for the firm's product, and that the margin is a constant percentage of the cost base. Consider the first aspect now.

If the firm is a price-setter and if its available supplies (from output plus inventory) can be varied without much lag and further if the demand for its product varies in a fashion which is difficult to predict, the firm may maximise its expected profit by setting a fairly constant price. In attempting to predict short-term fluctuations of demand, it will make errors and the losses due to these errors may outweigh the gains to be had from the occasionally correct prediction and adjustment.[37] This could be a significant explanation.

But there are additional elements to consider. If the firm is a price-setter, there are costs involved in actually changing prices, for example, price schedules must be reprinted, price tags altered, inventory revaluation must take place, advertisements of prices must be changed. Although these costs might be minor, they add to the picture that it can be *unprofitable* to change prices frequently *and* by small amounts. There is another factor, too, which operates in favour of price inflexibility. Consumers resent frequent variations of prices and the demand for a product with frequent price variation about the same average might be lower than when this variation is absent. Consumers establish certain habits in spending their income, that is in determining their "budget", and these habits are often based in the first place upon some optimising procedure. If prices change frequently, habits need to be revised. This is distressing to some and involves the effort and costs of recalculation. A product which requires these calculations often may become less preferred (on entirely rational grounds).

The price of a firm's product might also tend to be relatively constant for another reason. As Sweezy and Hall and Hitch point out,[38] this constancy is implied in oligopolistic markets in which the demand curves of the firms are kinked. The kink arises when a firm's price increases are not matched by competitors but its price-cutting touches off a retaliatory price-cutting by others. As illustrated in Fig. 9.21 and the attending discussion, the demand for the product of an individual oligopolist may vary greatly without a price alteration being profitable for the firm.

But constancy of price does not necessarily imply a constant margin of price over average variable cost. This, for example, is apparent from Fig. 9.21 in which per-unit costs are increasing with output. However, if average variable costs happen

Objectives of the Firm

to be constant then marginal cost is also constant and equal to average variable cost. In this case, and given a kinked demand curve, a constant mark-up on average direct costs maximises profit, no matter what is the level of demand. Evidence has been presented by J. Dean and J. Bain[39] to indicate that average direct costs are constant over a wide range in many manufacturing industries. If this is so, and a kinked demand situation exists, cost-plus behaviour also maximises profit for variations in demand over a wide range.

Cost-plus behaviour is not necessarily inconsistent with profit maximisation or expected profit maximisation. More generally it is not inconsistent with optimisation of some objective function. Furthermore, some of the above points indicate that infrequent changes of prices can be consistent with expected profit maximisation or optimisation generally. I suggest that small or marginal and frequent changes are not as a rule optimal and are not characteristic of economic life. This view is different from the traditional one but is implied by the logic of *optimally* imperfect decision-making.

NOTES AND REFERENCES

[1] See, for example, R. M. CYERT and J. G. MARCH, *A Behavioral Theory of the Firm*, Prentice-Hall, Englewood Cliffs, 1963.
[2] J. K. GALBRAITH, *The New Industrial State*, Houghton Mifflin, Boston, 1967.
[3] CYERT and MARCH, op. cit.
[4] See J. R. HICKS, *Value and Capital*, 2nd ed., Clarendon Press, Oxford, 1946, p. 196.
[5] A. A. ALCHIAN, "Uncertainty, Evolution and Economic Theory", *Journal of Political Economy*, 1950, **58**, pp. 211-21.
[6] EDITH PENROSE, *The Theory of the Growth of the Firm*, Basil Blackwell, Oxford, 1959.
[7] ALCHIAN, op. cit.
[8] J. M. CLARK, "Toward a Concept of Workable Competition", *American Economic Review*, 1940, **30**, No. 2, pp. 241-56.
[9] J. R. HICKS, "Annual Survey of Economic Theory: The Theory of Monopoly", *Econometrica*, 1935, **3**, pp. 1-20.
[10] References to these views are given in the succeeding footnotes.
[11] T. SCITOVSKY, "A Note on Profit Maximisation and its Implications", *Review of Economic Studies*, 1943, **2**, pp. 57-60. Reprinted in A.E.A., *Readings in Price Theory*, George Allen and Unwin, London, 1953.
[12] Ibid., p. 358 in A.E.A., *Readings in Price Theory*.
[13] A. A. BERLE and G. C. MEANS, *The Modern Corporation and Private Property*, The Macmillan Company, New York, 1932.
[14] Ibid., pp. 345-6. Reproduced by the kind permission of The Macmillan Company.
[15] Ibid.
[16] O. E. WILLIAMSON, *The Economics of Discretionary Behavior: Managerial Objectives in a Theory of the Firm*, Prentice-Hall, Englewood Cliffs, 1964.
[17] W. J. BAUMOL, *Business Behavior, Value and Growth*, The Macmillan Company, New York, 1959.
[18] Ibid., p. 49.
[19] Ibid., p. 50. Reproduced with the kind permission of Professor William Baumol.
[20] In turn this has important welfare implications. For example, the output of imperfectly competitive firms might be closer to Paretian optimal than has been previously supposed.
[21] PENROSE, op. cit.
[22] If uncertainty happened to be absent and the capital market is perfect, no conflict would exist. But in reality both of these conditions are violated.
[23] R. MARRIS, *The Economic Theory of "Managerial" Capitalism*, Macmillan, London, 1964.
[24] H. A. SIMON, "A Behavioral Model of Rational Choice", *Quarterly Journal of Economics*, 1955, **79**, pp. 98-118. CYERT and MARCH, op. cit. K. COHEN and R. CYERT, *Theory of the Firm*, Prentice-Hall, Englewood Cliffs, 1965, Chs. 17 and 18.

[25] Cohen and Cyert, op. cit., pp. 363-73.
[26] Ibid.
[27] See Reference 24.
[28] For a discussion of a number of the alternatives, see C. Tisdell, *Theory of Price Uncertainty, Production, and Profit*, Princeton University Press, Princeton, 1968, Ch. 2.
[29] J. von Neumann and O. Morgenstern, *Theory of Games and Economic Behavior*, Science Edition, John Wiley, New York 1964. See also Section VII of Chapter 6 of this book (*Microeconomics*) and the discussion of Fig. 2.21.
[30] For an outline of several of these, see Tisdell, op. cit., Ch. 2.
[31] A. G. Hart, "Risk, Uncertainty, and the Unprofitability of Compounding Probabilities", pp. 110-18 in O. Lange, F. McIntyre and F. Yntema (Eds), *Studies in Mathematical Economics and Econometrics*, The University of Chicago Press, Chicago, 1942. H. Theil, *Economic Forecasts and Policy*, 2nd revised ed., North-Holland Publishing Company, Amsterdam, 1961.
[32] W. Baumol and R. Quandt, "Rules of Thumb and Optimally Imperfect Decisions", *American Economic Review*, 1964, **54**, pp. 23-46.
[33] H. A. Simon, "A Behavioral Model of Rational Choice", *Quarterly Journal of Economics*, 1955, **79**, pp. 98-118.
[34] This is not to deny that these elements can be important. They are most important in managerial economics.
[35] R. L. Hall and C. J. Hitch, "Price Theory and Business Behaviour", *Oxford Economic Papers*, 1939, **2**, pp. 12-45.
[36] Compare the findings of Hall and Hitch, op. cit. Their article is reprinted in T. W. Wilson and P. W. S. Andrews (Eds), *Oxford Studies in the Price Mechanism*, Clarendon Press, Oxford, 1951, pp. 107-38. See especially p. 125.
[37] The model, which is outlined by C. Tisdell, "Economic Policy, Forecasting and Flexibility", *Weltwirtschaftliches Archiv*, 1971, pp. 34-54, can be applied to this matter. Treat price, p, as the controlled variable and quantity of sales (output) as the uncontrolled variable.
[38] P. Sweezy, "Demand under Conditions of Oligopoly", *Journal of Political Economy*, 1939, **47**, pp. 568-73.
[39] J. Dean, *Managerial Economics*, Prentice-Hall, New York, 1951, Ch. 5. J. Bain, *Industrial Organization*, 2nd ed., John Wiley, New York, 1968, Ch. 6.

FURTHER READING

Alchian, A. A., "Uncertainty, Evolution and Economic Theory", *Journal of Political Economy*, 1950, **58**, pp. 211-21.
Baumol, W. J., *Business Behavior, Value and Growth*, 1st ed., The Macmillan Company, New York, 1959, Chs. 6 and 7, 2nd ed., Harcourt, Brace and World, New York, 1967, Chs. 6-8.
Baumol, W. J., *Economic Theory and Operations Analysis*, 2nd ed., Prentice-Hall, Englewood Cliffs, 1965, Ch. 13.
*Cohen, K. J. and R. M. Cyert, *Theory of the Firm*, Prentice-Hall, Englewood Cliffs, 1965, Chs. 15-17.
Hall, R. L., and C. J. Hitch, "Price Theory and Business Behaviour", *Oxford Economic Papers*, No. 2, 1939, pp. 12-45.
Lanzillotti, R. F., "Pricing Objectives in Large Companies", *American Economic Review*, 1958, No. 5, **48**, pp. 921-40.
Machlup, F., "Marginal Analysis and Empirical Research", *American Economic Review*, 1946, **36**, Part I, pp. 519-54.
Simon, H., "Theories of Decision-making in Economics", *American Economic Review*, 1959, **54**, pp. 253-83.
Tisdell, C., *Theory of Price Uncertainty, Production and Profit*, Princeton University Press, Princeton, 1968.

* Advanced.

CHAPTER 18

Measurement and Estimation in Microeconomics

I. Econometrics: Some General Matters

The measurement and estimation of microeconomic relationships is a necessary part of scientific endeavour. The field of study and research connected with the measurement of economic relationships on the basis of observed data is called *econometrics*. Generally, econometric analysis involves a combination of mathematical and statistical techniques. This type of analysis can be used to estimate the values of parameters in models, to check theories against observation and to make predictions. Its value is difficult to overestimate. It is a check against irrelevant theories, and by placing bounds on the parameters of particular economic models it renders these more useful for policy purposes.

The following procedures have something to recommend them as steps in obtaining economic knowledge:

(i) first, postulate a theory, model or hypothesis on the basis of assumption and observation;
(ii) secondly, derive some consequences of the theory;
(iii) thirdly, take further observations to see if they accord with the predictions of the theory;
(iv) fourthly, if observations accord with the predictions of theory they lend support to the theory, otherwise the theory is refuted (as a complete description of reality) and *might* be rejected or modified. However, as will be argued in a moment, we might continue to use a theory even if its predictions do not accord exactly with observations.

A theory arises in an attempt to explain and/or regularise certain observed phenomena, and a successful theory has the major practical result that it enables the consequences of particular events to be predicted in advance. Should we expect the predictions of a theory to accord exactly with observation? Such a test seems to be too stringent. In assessing the value of a theory, it seems preferable to weigh the costs of applying the theory (both the estimation and calculation costs) against its accuracy and the expected returns from increased accuracy. On the basis of this criterion, the optimal theory is the one where complications proceed only to the point at which the additional expected benefits equal the expected additional cost. An imperfect theory, one which does not predict extremely well, may be optimal on this basis.

To take an example, suppose that it is asserted that the demand for a product X is

$$x = 100 - 0.001p \qquad (18.1)$$

where x is the quantity demanded and p is the price of the product. Suppose that a number of (p, x) values are observed in the market. Three possibilities exist: all observations might agree with the values predicted by the demand hypothesis (Equation (18.1)); some might not coincide and others coincide; and no observations might agree with predictions. Should the hypothesis be rejected if either of the last two possibilities arise? Not necessarily. Even if there is no exact correspondence, the theory might be optimal for *some* applied purposes. The extra cost of deriving a more accurate theory might offset the extra benefit.

This pragmatic approach may cause some economists to wince but after all it is a method of judging a theory, if not the only possible one. If one takes the pragmatic view, the value of a theory or a hypothesis can change with circumstances. Theories which at earlier times are less than optimal can become optimal at later times because more information becomes available or the costs of calculation and information-gathering fall, due to the growth of computer technology, for example, or because the theory is being applied to problems in which the cost of errors has increased and the returns from increased accuracy have risen. Variations of applicability due to these factors must be distinguished from historical (real) changes in the relationships of variables, for example, from an increase in the elasticity of a demand function with the passage of time. Historical changes, too, may necessitate the revision or adoption of a new theory with the passage of time.

In econometrics one does not normally demand an exact correspondence between observations and the predictions of a theory. The error which one is prepared to tolerate depends upon the purpose of the model, the cost of errors and the possibilities for improvement of the model.

Econometrics can help in the specification of theories, their testing and verification, and in making predictions. For example, suppose that one requires a demand function for a product. One hypothesis might be that it is a linear function of the price of the product. The demand function is of the form

$$x = a + bp \qquad (18.2)$$

where x represents the quantity demanded of the product, p is its price and a and b are parameters. Given time series or cross-sectional observations of x and p, one might wish to estimate a and b by econometric means. These estimates might be stated as point values (for example, the most likely values of the parameters) or as interval estimates. Or again, one might wish to check the hypothesis that the demand function is linear. On the basis of observations, how probable is it that the demand function is linear? This is amenable to statistical analysis.

But it is not always possible to estimate parameters and check theories by econometric means. There are special difficulties in economics which arise because it is usually impossible to carry out controlled experiments. The relevant variables of an economic model cannot be manipulated as a rule by an observer and he is forced to rely on whatever observations are thrown up in the process of people going about their ordinary economic life. An economist can rarely manipulate the variables of his model independently. Consequently, it can be difficult, sometimes even impossible, to estimate the parameters of an economic model.

First, there may be insufficient variety in the data to make a reliable estimate

Measurement and Estimation

possible. For example, if the parameters of a single linear equation need to be estimated and only one value of the independent variable has been recorded, an estimate of the linear function is impossible. If only a few values are available, an estimate from the data is likely to be unreliable. The data admit too many degrees of freedom.

Again, even when data are plentiful, they might not be varied enough if equations depend on several variables, and the problem of *multicollinearity* might arise. Two variables might be so closely related that it is impossible to disentangle their independent contributions by examining one's observations. The observations are highly correlated.

For example, imagine that one wishes to estimate the parameters of

$$x = a - bp + \beta y \tag{18.3}$$

from data where x is the quantity demanded of a commodity, p is its price and y represents income per head. In all observations in which p has increased, y might have risen also in a systematic way so that, for example, all (p, y, x) observations cluster on or around a straight line. For example, taking an extreme case, the observations might cluster on a straight line, such as BC in Fig. 18.1. Although the actual plane indicated by Equation (18.3) must pass through BC, an infinite number of planes pass through BC and there is no way to decide which is the relevant one. However, if p could be held constant and y varied independently, it would be possible to fix the relevant plane and determine all the parameters of Equation (18.3). Unfortunately, this course is rarely available to the econometrician.

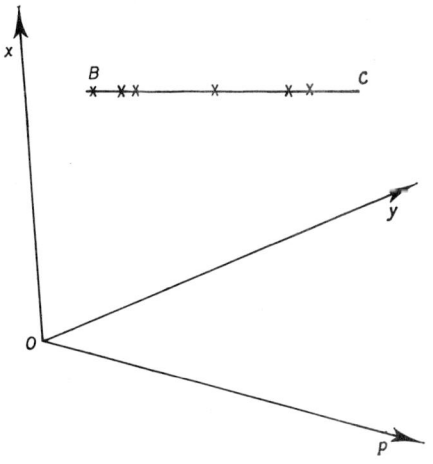

Fig. 18.1

In the given example of multicollinearity, observations were assumed to be on or in the approximate neighbourhood of the true demand curve even though they were not sufficiently varied to estimate the parameters of that curve. But it can happen that the observations do not identify a demand curve at all. If variables are determined by simultaneous equations, the observations may not describe the functional relationships of the model or describe particular relationships which are not the ones that the econometrician is searching for. This raises the problem of *identification*.

The problem of identification arises because economic relationships are often described by a set of simultaneous equations (for example, market behaviour is described by supply and demand equations). The problem of identification will be discussed when the empirical derivation of demand and supply curves is considered.

Other problems may also arise in econometric work. Predictions based on econometric estimates might be wrong because the economic theory which has been fitted to the data is inappropriate, the estimation procedure itself may be inadequate or there may be errors of observation. But to see possible difficulties in applying econometric methods is not to depreciate their great and growing value. Let us consider their value for measuring some microeconomic relationships.

II. Empirical Determination of Demand (and Supply) Functions

Imagine that one is faced with the problem of estimating from observations the market demand function for a particular product. No progress can be made with this matter until a decision is reached about which variables are or might be relevant determinants of demand. Is advertising expenditure important, or the price of the product, or the price of related products and income per head? Our preconceptions about these factors influence the results.

Suppose that the demand for the product depends only on its price. How might one discover the actual demand curve? There are at least four possibilities:

(i) one might attempt to estimate the demand function by interviewing a sample of consumers. The interviewer asks of each respondent how much of the product the respondent would be willing to purchase at alternative prices. The difficulties of this approach are apparent. Respondents might be untruthful, especially if they hope to keep the price down by exaggerating the reduction of demand which would be occasioned by price increases, or consumers might not really be able to predict their own behaviour very well. There are also the usual difficulties associated with sampling and non-response;

(ii) it might be possible to estimate the demand curve in various markets by cross-sectional means. Suppose that the demand for the product can be divided by geographical regions. Regional markets are to some extent separate. If the price of a product is different in the regional markets and *if* consumers are much the same in all regions, an average *per capita* consumption function might be calculated for the whole community. For example, the price of petrol varies in different states and regions of Australia. By fitting a curve to the observations on price of petrol and consumption per head for petrol in the different regions one *might* approximate the overall *per capita* demand curve for petrol as a function of its price. Of course, the results might be spurious. For example, if income per head, or sparseness of population also influence demand and if these tend to be correlated with the higher prices, a multicollinearity or an identification problem exists. If systematic relations of this kind occur, the cross-sectional data are inadequate for the purpose of yielding an overall demand curve;

(iii) if the price of the product is controlled by a monopolist or some association or government board, experimentation might be possible in a partially isolated geographical sector of the market. Price might be varied in the experimental

Measurement and Estimation

region, consumers response noted, and inferences drawn about demand in the whole market. A problem, however, is whether the experimental region is representative of the market as a whole. Furthermore, not only the price level but the frequency of its change is significant. There is possibly a time-lag in altering consumption patterns, and consumers may be averse to a product which has frequent price variations. Thus it might be hazardous to infer overall demand from price variations in a regional market.

Because of his particular market power, a monopolist might be able to vary price in a regional market. However, if pure competition exists, variations of price in regional markets might not occur. If this is the case, there is a fourth possible way of estimating market demand;

(iv) time series data from the whole market might be used to estimate the market demand curve. Observations of the past prices and past quantities of the product sold may be recorded and a demand curve might be fitted to these observations.

But simply to fit a curve to these observations and call it a demand curve is misleading. Indeed, the curve might, in fact, turn out to be a supply curve, or neither a demand nor a supply curve. The problem is that price and quantity values are determined simultaneously by supply and demand relationships and hence there are problems of identification.

Let us consider some problems of identification by first taking market models in which random elements are absent and then models in which randomness is significant.

Suppose that, in a particular market, the market situation is correctly described by the following theory: in any period, the demand for the product is a monotonically decreasing function of the price of the product during that period and supply is a monotonically increasing function of the price of the product during that period. Furthermore, in every period, price and output are adjusted so that demand and supply are in equilibrium. The theory can be summarised as follows:

$$D_t = D_t(p_t), \qquad D_t' < 0; \qquad (18.4)$$
$$S_t = S_t(p_t), \qquad S_t' > 0; \qquad (18.5)$$
and
$$D_t = S_t, \qquad (18.6)$$

where D_t represents the quantity demanded of the product, S_t is the quantity supplied, p is the price of the good and t identifies the period. If this theory holds, the observed price and quantity of the product for any period is the equilibrium price and quantity for that period.

The demand and supply curves are liable to shift from period to period. If they do not vary at all or vary in such a way that the same price and quantity is recorded for each period, then it is impossible to identify either a supply or a demand function on the basis of this single observed point.

If the demand curve alone shifts over the period, then the observed (output, price) combinations identify a supply function. This is indicated in Fig. 18.2. In this diagram, observations of (output, price) combinations for five periods are circled. During these periods, the supply curve S, which is unknown to the observer, remains unchanged. The demand curve D_t shifts and five possible demand curves are shown, the curve belonging to a period, which is, of course, unknown to the observer, is indicated by the appropriate subscript to D. Clearly, the observations trace out the supply curve.

On the other hand, if the demand curve is stationary and the supply curve is subject to fluctuation, observed (quantity, price) combinations identify a demand curve. This is indicated in Fig. 18.3 where the supply curves of five periods are shown and the associated observations are circled. Observations fall along the demand curve marked by D.

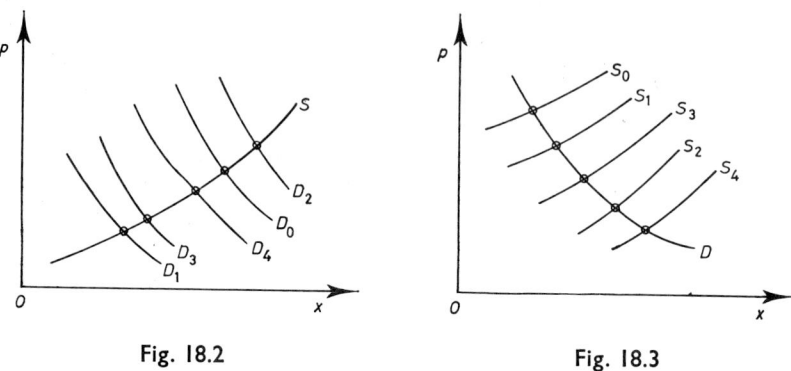

Fig. 18.2   Fig. 18.3

Observations in other instances (for example, if both the demand and supply curves are subject to variation) might fail to identify either a demand or a supply curve. In Fig. 18.4, observations are circled for three periods and the shifting supply and demand curves for the three periods are indicated by the appropriate subscripts to S and D. The three observations fall along a line KK' but KK' is neither a demand nor a supply curve. It is sometimes described as a *mongrel curve*.

Yet even if both the demand and the supply curve are subject to variation, the observations may approximately identify a demand or a supply curve. If the supply curve varies considerably and the demand curve hardly at all, observations approximately identify a demand curve and, if the reverse is the case, a supply curve. In the illustration of Fig. 18.5, a demand curve is approximately identified by the observations which are indicated by dots, and limits to the fluctuation of the demand curve are shown by D_0 and D_m and for the supply curve by S_0 and S_m. In this instance, the

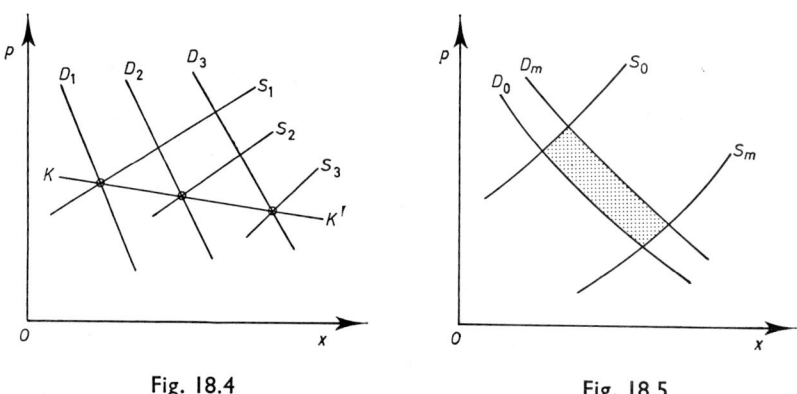

Fig. 18.4   Fig. 18.5

supply curve is subject to considerable variation whereas the demand curve does not vary much.

As a rule, neither a demand nor a supply curve can be *exactly* identified from time-series data. Both demand and supply curves are liable to some variation through time. Sometimes the possible variations of supply and demand are described by a random variable. For example, agricultural supplies might exhibit random variation because weather is unpredictable. In this case, if demand is stationary and non-random, if price adjusts to clear the supplies of each period and if there is sufficient random variation of supply, observations of output and price identify the demand curve. If both demand and supply exhibit random variation, it might be impossible to identify either a demand or supply function. However, if the random variation of supply is sufficiently great in relation to that of demand, a demand curve can be approximately identified.

Generally, observations do not fall along a single function but are scattered, as in the example of Fig. 18.5. The problem then is to fit a curve to this scatter. The procedure which one adopts is naturally influenced by the underlying theory of the process. Do the observations represent random deviations from a "true" demand curve? They might. They would not, however, if the first equilibrium market model applied.

Nevertheless, the problem of which type of function to fit to the scatter of observations (a linear function, a quadratic etc.) and of the method by which to fit it still remains. Is a least-squares method appropriate or should the parameters of the equation be estimated by a maximum likelihood method or some other method? These all involve important statistical questions and theories which cannot be delved into here.[1] Yet, it might be noted that to fit a linear "demand" curve to the observations of Fig. 18.5 by the least-squares method would give rise to a misleading estimate. The estimated demand curve would be steeper than any of the actual ones. The approximate least-squares estimate is shown by the line LL' in Fig. 18.6. Actual demand curves lie between D_0 and D_m. LL' coincides with no demand curve and gives a biased impression of the responsiveness of demand to price changes.

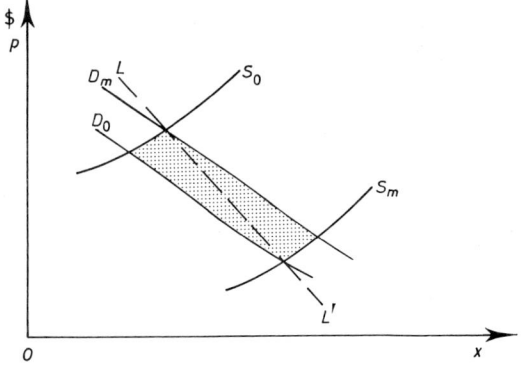

Fig. 18.6

The estimate of the demand function is likely to be unreliable if the adopted theory of demand or markets is inadequate. For example, the theory might exclude important determinants of demand; perhaps the demand for a product might depend not only on its own price but on the price of other products. Or again, the demand for a commodity might depend not solely upon its price but also upon the length of time for which its price remains at any particular level. Furthermore, a cobweb relationship could be present in the market. A cobweb relationship does not prevent the demand curve from being identified but it can make identification of the supply curve difficult.[2] But if the reaction of producers is known, for example if their supplies of a period are based on the assumption that the price of the last period will prevail, it is frequently possible to identify *both* the demand and the supply function because output depends on the price of the last period and, assuming the simple cobweb outlined earlier, the price of any period adjusts to demand to clear available supplies. Hence the influence of price on supply can be separated from its influence on demand in this case.[3]

The techniques which are suggested above for the estimation of demand curves can also be applied to the estimation of supply curves if pure competition is present. The difficulties encountered remain much the same and the scope for creativity, since each product seems to have its peculiarities, remains great. Alternatively, one might try to estimate the supply function in a more primitive way. A sample of the production functions or cost functions of firms might be taken and one might try to infer supply responses from these, using standard theory. Let us consider the estimation of production and cost functions.

III. Empirical Determination of Production and Cost Functions

In principle, a number of methods exist for estimating production and cost functions. Production functions might be obtained first and, if factor prices are known, cost functions could be based on these; or cost functions might be estimated directly from data. Production functions might be inferred from known physical principles, experimentation using pilot studies, cross-sectional data or time-series data. All these methods have been employed and all have their limitations.

It might seem surprising that an economist should be interested in deriving a production function from data. Surely, this is the role of the natural scientist and engineer. To some extent this is so. But the production function is basic to economic analysis and an economist needs to be aware of possible shortcomings in the actual functions which are put forward. Furthermore, a choice of technique problems underlies the production function and, as was observed in Chapter 15, relative scarcity of factors can affect the optimal choice of technique.

While inference from established principles may suffice to establish a production function, sometimes situations are too complex and involve too many interacting factors to make this feasible. There is also the danger that the principles are not correct or some vital elements have been excluded from consideration.

Direct pilot experiment is another alternative. For instance, imagine that one wishes to know the influence of varying quantities of nitrogenous fertiliser and superphosphate on the output of a particular type of corn. One might try to calculate this from an experimental plot of corn in which the application of nitrogenous fertiliser and superphosphate are varied by blocks in the plot. The levels of output are then compared with the variations of fertiliser application and a production function is fitted to the output-input combinations which are observed.

But, of course, errors can creep into the data. Increasing fertiliser application may, in fact, occur on soils in the plot which are progressively more deficient in the chemicals which are being added. To overcome this to some extent, the application of fertiliser by blocks might be randomised. Again, the growing season for which the test is conducted might be unusual. It might have been less rainy than usual. This would affect the utilisation of the fertiliser by the corn. The production function for corn on the plot is likely to be influenced by weather and other factors. Because of these elements, the output from a particular quantity of fertiliser cannot be exactly predicted. Observations over a number of years are likely to lead to a number of different output recordings for the same rate of application. There is no guarantee, either, that the production function which is obtained in one region is applicable to others; for example, soils might differ.

Once the production data has been obtained, one must decide upon the form of function to fit to the data. On this matter Heady and Dillon observe:

> Numerous algebraic equation forms can be used in deriving production functions. No single form can be used to characterise production under all environmental conditions ... Guides on appropriate algebraic forms may come from previous investigations and the theory of the sciences involved. Selection of any specific type of equation to express production phenomena automatically imposes certain restraints or assumptions in respect to the relationships involved and optimum resource quantities which will be specified.[4]

For example, if one fits a linear function to the data, the production function can exhibit only constant returns to scale and constant marginal products are the rule. Thus if decreasing returns are important, this form would be an inappropriate one to fit to the observations. Possibly a log linear, quadratic or square root function should be fitted since all can show decreasing returns. The actual choice depends in part on the computation costs involved in fitting the various alternatives.

Heady[5] and others have, in fact, estimated a production function for the response of corn output to nitrogen (contained in ammonium nitrate) and P_2O_5 contained in superphosphate from experiments conducted in Western Iowa in 1952 using a randomised block design. They fitted various functions to their data. Two of these were the log linear and the square root function. These can be written generally for this problem as

$$x = aP^{b_1}N^{b_2} \tag{18.7}$$

and

$$x = a - b_1 P - b_2 N + b_3 P^{0.5} + b_4 N^{0.5} + b_5 P^{0.5} N^{0.5} \tag{18.8}$$

where x is the output of corn in bushels per acre, N and P are the pounds per acre of nitrogen and P_2O_5 respectively and the remaining elements are parameters. The actual estimated functions are

$$x = 0.442 P^{0.4090} N^{0.2877} \tag{18.9}$$

and

$$x = -5.68 - 0.316N - 0.417P + 6.3512N^{0.5} + 8.5155P^{0.5} + 0.3410N^{0.5}P^{0.5}. \tag{18.10}$$

Of course, the large numbers of entries after the decimal points indicate spurious accuracy.

They[6] concluded that the data were characterised best by the square root function. Then they considered various expansion paths and cost functions for the firm on the basis of this production function.[7] (The reader may wish, as an exercise, to compute the marginal products of the factors in the above production functions.)

Other methods for estimating production functions are also employed. The cross-sectional method is often used. The input-output combination of firms operating at different levels of output can be observed and *if* firms have the same production function, this function might be inferred from the data, or if the observations are for output and cost and if factor prices as well as production functions are the same for all firms, a total cost function might be estimated for all firms in the industry. For example, Marc Nerlove[8] has estimated returns to scale in electricity generation by taking a cross-section of plants operating at different scales in the United States. He concludes that there is evidence of a marked degree of increasing returns to scale at the firm level; but the degree of returns varies inversely with output. One problem of the cross-sectional approach is that production functions and cost functions may vary systematically with the sample; for example, firms with a larger output might have lower per-unit *cost functions* and be more efficient at most levels of output than firms with low levels of output. If so, cross-sectional observations give rise to a "mongrel" cost function and the computed function is applicable to no firm.

Time-series data can also be utilised to estimate production and cost functions. For example, Joel Dean[9] undertook early influential studies of the cost curves of two manufacturing firms from different industries, using time-series data. One involved study of the costs of a hosiery mill and the other of a leather-belt factory. He found that the cost functions in both instances were linear and the marginal cost was constant thus lending support to the view that marginal cost might typically be constant in manufacturing industry.

Consider Dean's leather-belt enquiry.[10] This study is based upon a factory's cost records for the monthly accounting periods of the years 1935-39. The cost of belting is assumed to depend upon X, its output in thousands of square feet of single-ply equivalent belting and weight W, in pounds per square foot of belting. W is added to allow the density of the product to affect its costs. Using regression methods, Dean estimated the cost function of the factory to be

$$C = -60.178 + 0.77X + 70.181W \tag{18.11}$$

where C represents total cost in dollars. The equation indicates that the marginal cost of an extra 1000 square feet of belting of fixed weight is 77 cents and thus is constant. Dean's cost function is linear. He tested for possible non-linearity of the total cost relationship by fitting functions of higher degree in X but found no statistically significant departure from linearity.

Naturally, it cannot be concluded from Dean's results that the total cost curves of all firms in manufacturing industry are linear and hence their marginal costs are constant. Decreasing and increasing marginal costs might occur also in manufacturing. It is possible, too, that Dean's result is biased because his observations were taken during a depressed period of trade and it is likely that his factory was working below capacity. In Fig. 18.7, a true cost curve is indicated by C. If observations are clustered as shown in the diagram by the crosses, a linear curve indicated by C might give a good fit to these. Nevertheless it does not characterise the total cost curve over a wide range and gives a misleading view. As capacity is reached, total cost increases at an increasing rate.

Measurement and Estimation

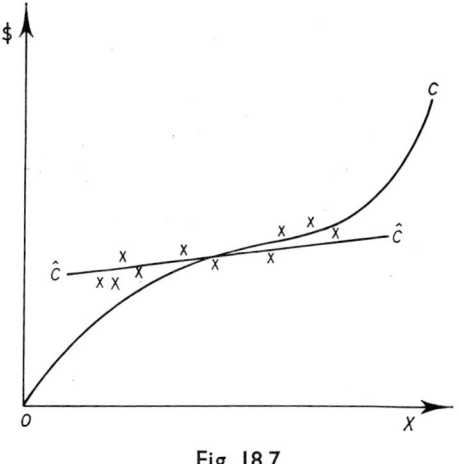

Fig. 18.7

There are also other difficulties in estimating cost curves from accounting data. If absolute prices of the factors change during the period of data collection, a correction must be made for this. If relative factor prices change or if technological progress takes place, observations may correspond to different cost curves. Again, it cannot always be presumed that management is efficient. Management may alter its attitudes to efficiency or organisational slack over time. Hence, the observed costs may not minimise the cost of producing the output considered.

Although there are difficulties in estimating microeconomic relationships from observed data, the scope for estimation is great. With the growth of computer technology, the cost of estimation is falling. Therefore one expects that econometric methods will be increasingly applied to microeconomic problem-solving.

NOTES AND REFERENCES

[1] For further discussion of this matter, see W. J. BAUMOL, *Economic Theory and Operations Analysis*, 2nd ed., Prentice-Hall, Englewood Cliffs, 1965, Ch. 10 and Appendix.

[2] This is so if the cobweb relationship outlined in Chapter 5 applies.

[3] For general information about identifying supply and demand functions if cobweb patterns arise, see L. R. KLEIN, *An Introduction to Econometrics*, Prentice-Hall, Englewood Cliffs, 1962, Ch. 2.

[4] E. HEADY and J. DILLON, *Agricultural Production Functions*, Iowa State University Press, Ames, 1961, p. 73. Reprinted by permission from *Agricultural Production Functions*, by Earl O. Heady and John Dillon, © 1961 by the Iowa State University Press, Ames, Iowa, U.S.A.

[5] Ibid, pp. 475-525.

[6] Ibid.

[7] Ibid.

[8] MARC NERLOVE, "Returns to Scale in Electricity Supply", pp. 167-98 in C. CHRIST (Ed.), *Measurement in Economics*, Stanford University Press, Stanford, 1963.

[9] J. DEAN, (i) *Managerial Economics*, Prentice-Hall, New York, 1951, Ch. 5; (ii) *The Relation of Cost to Output for a Leather Belt Shop*, N.B.E.R., 1941.

[10] J. DEAN, op. cit., (ii).

FURTHER READING

BAUMOL, W. J., *Economic Theory and Operations Analysis*, 2nd ed., Prentice-Hall, Englewood Cliffs, 1965, Ch. 10.

BRENNAN, M., *Preface to Econometrics*, 2nd ed., South-Western Publishing Company, Cincinnati, 1965, Chs. 23, 25.

DEAN, J., *Managerial Economics*, Prentice-Hall, New York, 1951, Ch. 5.

FISHER, F. M., Z. GRILICHES and C. KAYSEN, "The Costs of Automobile Model Changes since 1949", *Journal of Political Economy*, 1962, **70**, pp. 433-51. Reprinted in D. KAMERSCHEN, *Readings in Microeconomics*, John Wiley, New York, 1969.

HEADY, E., and J. DILLON, *Agricultural Production Functions*, Iowa State University Press, Ames, 1961.

KLEIN, L. R., *An Introduction to Econometrics*, Prentice-Hall, Englewood Cliffs, 1962, Chs. 2 and 3.

WALTERS, A. A., *An Introduction to Econometrics*, W. W. Norton, New York, 1968, Part III.

WORKING, E. J., "What do Statistical 'Demand Curves' Show?" *Quarterly Journal of Economics*, 1927, **41**, pp. 212-35. Reprinted in A.E.A., *Readings in Price Theory*, George Allen and Unwin, London, 1953.

CHAPTER 19

Returns to Scale and Barriers to Entry

The optimal degree of market concentration in an industry depends amongst other things upon the returns to scale enjoyed by firms in the industry. Indeed, if increasing returns stem from increased concentration of production, something might even be said in favour of a monopoly.[1] But there is not complete agreement amongst economists about the significance and frequency of increasing returns in manufacturing industry. Some of the empirical evidence and alternative views about this subject are briefly examined in this chapter.

Economies of scale not only have implications for concentration in an industry, they also create barriers to the entry of new firms and this, in turn, influences the market behaviour of established firms. Barriers to entry may also arise from product differentiation, capital requirements and absolute cost advantages. Because of these barriers, above-normal or above-average returns may persist in an industry. Thus maximum economic efficiency might be thwarted. Traditionally, barriers to entry have been seen by economists as impediments to the attainment of a social optimum[2] but, as pointed out below, there are circumstances in which some barriers seem to be in the general interest. But this is not to deny that there are other cases in which the traditional view requires no qualification.

I. Returns to Scale

A firm's long-run costs per unit of output may fall for a number of reasons as the firm expands its production. Physical and other economies may arise from operating larger plants at any location, or economies may result from the management and operation of multiple plants. Overheads resulting from basic indivisibilities (for example, of presses of various types) can be spread over a greater volume. The indivisibility factor contributes substantially to economies of scale but it is not the only element at work.

For example, economies may result from increasing the size of plant at a particular location because labour, management and machinery can be more specialised for their tasks with a greater volume of output. In other words, the division of labour, management and machinery can proceed further and this may cause the cost per unit of output to fall with volume. Furthermore, other technical relationships might be important. The surface area of containers which are needed to hold or convey substances usually increases proportionately less than the volume of the substances. For example, if the ratio of height to diameter is kept constant, the surface area of a cylinder must be increased by only 0.5 per cent if the volume of its content is to be raised by 1 per cent. In this instance, if the same thickness of the walls of the cylinder suffices, the cost per unit of volume declines with volume. This would apply, too, when increase in the thickness of the walls is only slight.

By increasing the number of plants which it operates, a firm might reap further economies. Its average cost of production might fall if it operates several optimal scale plants or a number of plants which have a combined output in excess of one plant operating at minimum optimal scale. Because of the increased volume of output, management may become more specialised, technological aids to management (such as computers) might become more profitable and the costs of information (such as market information) can be spread more widely. Furthermore, if plants are at different locations, the cost of distributing the firm's product might fall. With larger volume, the firm may also be able to purchase its inputs at a discount.

The nature of plant and multiplant economies in some industries in the United States have been studied by J. Bain.[3] Bain suggests that typically in manufacturing industry, as the output of a single plant increases, long-run average cost falls, then is constant *over a wide range* and finally increases or in some cases remains constant. In Bain's opinion, the typical long-run average cost curve associated with expansion of a plant is like that shown in Fig. 19.1 by LAC. In some instances, long-run average cost does not rise but remains constant after a certain volume and the branch marked LAC' in Fig. 19.1 is applicable.

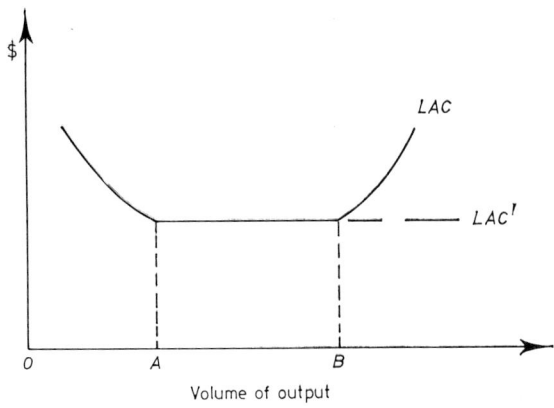

Fig. 19.1

In estimating the importance of plant scale economies in various United States' industries,[4] Bain took into account two factors: the percentage rise in cost per unit of output if a plant happened to be below minimal optimal scale, and the proportion of the market which can be supplied by a minimal optimal scale plant.

Bain estimated the percentage rise in cost per unit of output if a plant happened to be of half minimum optimal scale, for example, of a scale optimal for an output of $\frac{1}{2}OA$ in Fig. 19.1. Bain found that average costs of production were raised by more than 5 per cent in the production of cars, typewriters, farm machinery, tractors, rayon and steel at half minimum optimal output. Volume plant economies were regarded as significant in these industries. Economies of this type were found to be unimportant in the manufacture of cigarettes, liquor, soap, shoes, flour and canned goods.

Scale and Entry

The importance of scale economies was also assessed in relation to the size of the market. This Bain measured by the proportion of output produced by a minimal optimal scale plant in relation to the volume of sales of the product in the relevant geographical market. The proportion was high for automobiles and typewriters (over 20 per cent) and for fountain pens, tractors, copper and gypsum (10-20 per cent). In markets smaller than those of the United States, such as the Australian and those of some of its Asian neighbours, these ratios would be much higher. The proportion for cigarettes, soap, rayon fibre, farm machinery and steel was 5-6 per cent.

On the basis of both Bain's measures, production of automobiles and typewriters gave rise to important plant scale economies, and production of cement, farm machinery, tractors, rayon and steel exhibited moderately important plant scale economies. Cigarettes, liquor, petroleum products, soap, rubber tyres, shoes, flour, meat packing and canned goods had no important scale economies. While products which give rise to most important plant scale economies in the United States will continue to be very significant in a smaller market, scale economies of other products may also be significant. Again, one must be careful in applying these results because the importance of scale economies in an industry can change with time as technological progress takes place.

Bain doubts if any substantial economies stem from the operation of a number of plants. He maintains that

> We find a substantial fraction of industries in which [multiplant] economies are not present, and in which the one-plant firm is as efficient as the multiplant one ... Where economies of the multiplant firm are encountered, they are ordinarily quite slight in magnitude. In these cases, the unit costs of production and distribution with several plants (whatever number appear to be required for greatest efficiency) are typically only one or two per cent below those of a firm with one plant of minimum optimal scale.[5]

Bain's results indicate that plant scale economies are significant in some industries. Studies of other manufacturing industries and the practices of engineers suggest that decreasing average costs are important in a wide range of manufacturing activities.

For example, in several industries engineers use the "rule of 0.6" to calculate the capital expenditure requirements for the expansion of plants. If a is the cost of a plant of "standard capacity", the capital cost of a plant of N times that capacity is estimated to be

$$K = aN^{0.6} \qquad (19.1)$$

Increased capacity of 1 per cent requires only an increase of 0.6 per cent in capital expenditure. In a special supplement dealing with petrochemicals, *The Economist*, 1970, October 3, p. xvi, said,

> By the so called "rule of 0.6" it has become virtually accepted in the petrochemical industry, that a big plant double the size of a small one will nevertheless only cost 50 per cent more and will only use (by the "rule of 0.2") 15 per cent more labour.

By the "0.2 rule", if λ is the labour cost associated with a plant of "standard" capacity, if V represents labour costs, and N is the capacity of a proposed plant in relation to the capacity of a standard plant, then

$$V = \lambda N^{0.2} \qquad (19.2)$$

In the petrochemical industry, at least, substantial economies in per-unit capital and labour costs stem from an expansion of scale.

The engineering rule of thumb has been noted by a number of economists and several, including F. Moore,[6] have fitted a generalised version of the 0.6 function to output and capital expense observations in several industries. The generalised version of the capital expense equation, (19.1), is

$$K = aN^b \qquad (19.3)$$

which can be expressed as

$$\log K = \log a + b \log N. \qquad (19.4)$$

The coefficients of the equations are a and b.

If b is less than unity, capital costs per unit of output fall as capacity expands, remain constant if $b = 1$, and rise if $b > 1$. Chilton[7] estimated b for 36 products in chemical and metal industries. His average estimate of b was 0.68 and the median value was 0.66. In only three cases did the value of b exceed unity. A similar study by Professor Leontief[8] gave an average of 0.8 for b. Research along these lines was conducted by Moore[9] into alumina production, aluminium rolling, cement and oxygen production. His estimated values of b were less than unity and, although the difference was substantial for oxygen production, the deviations were not significant on a sampling basis. Nevertheless, all estimates suggested economies of size. But, as Moore points out, "these economies should not be interpreted as being identical with economies of scale since variable costs must also be considered in the latter case; however, there are some indications that labour, power, and utilities cost also decrease with scale while the costs of materials embodied in the final product remain constant."[10] Thus there is evidence that substantial economies of scale occur in important segments of manufacturing industry.

The entry of a new firm to an industry may be blocked by economies of scale. If economies of scale are important in an industry, established firms may earn above-normal profit without attracting new entrants. The situation can be illustrated by a simple model. Imagine that production in the industry requires a unique scale of plant which produces an output $\bar{x}$ at a per unit cost of $\$z$.

Using a postulate of Sylos and Modigliani,[11] it can be shown that the greater is $\bar{x}$, the scale of plant required for entry, the greater is the sustainable excess of the product's price over its per-unit cost of production. In other words, the greater is $\bar{x}$, the greater is the excess profit which established firms can maintain without encouraging entry. This is hypothesised on the assumption that demand is not perfectly elastic and that other things are unchanged. Furthermore, the steeper is the demand curve the greater is the sustainable excess of price over average cost; and the less responsive is demand to price variations. The postulate of Sylos and Modigliani is that existing firms react to entrants by keeping their output unchanged and reducing their price to clear this output.

Because of scale barriers, the maximum sustainable price for the product of the industry indicated in Fig. 19.2 is p_m if the industry demand curve is D_0. This price is well in excess of z, the minimum cost of production per unit of output. If the industry is producing an output of $X_c - \bar{x}$, a firm is tempted to enter the industry. If a firm enters, it adds $\bar{x}$ to total output and so industry output expands to X_c and price falls to z, the average cost of production. This is, of course, assuming that the

Scale and Entry

Sylos and Modigliani postulate holds. If the output of the industry is less than $X_c - \bar{x}$, a firm finds that it is more profitable to enter this industry than to seek a normal return elsewhere. But if the combined output of established firms exceeds $X_c - \bar{x}$ and even though established firms earn above-normal profit, new firms find it unprofitable to enter the industry. New firms must enter at a large scale of output and their production would depress prices below average cost if the combined output of established firms happened to be in excess of $X_c - \bar{x}$.

It is easily appreciated from Fig. 19.2 that if the industry demand curve is downward-sloping, the maximum sustainable price is greater, the greater is $\bar{x}$, the scale which is necessary for production. For example, $X_c - \bar{x}$ is nearer O, the greater is $\bar{x}$ and thus p_m is higher if D_0 is the relevant demand curve. Furthermore, for any given value of $\bar{x}$, the maximum sustainable price is greater the steeper is the demand curve. For example, the maximum sustainable price for the demand curve D_1 is greater than for D_0.

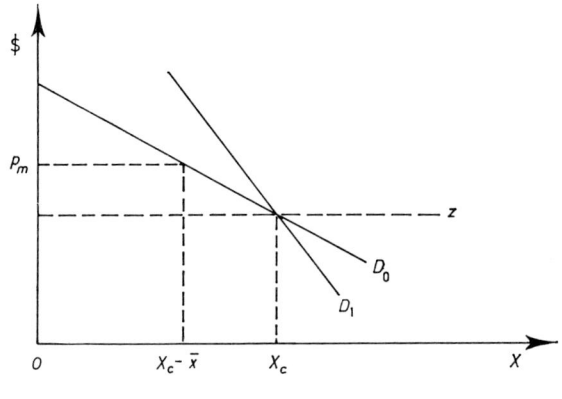

Fig. 19.2

Of course, it is rare for the level of production to be as unique and lumpy as in the above example and Modigliani has extended the model to permit firms to vary their output. Nevertheless, the propositions which are mentioned above (if z is interpreted as minimum average cost) are basically unchanged. However, an additional proposition is advanced. The steeper is the long-run average cost function of firms in an industry, the higher is the maximum sustainable price in the industry.[12]

While the Sylos and Modigliani postulate is a special one, nevertheless the model makes it clear that established firms can reap and continue to reap above-normal profits because indivisibilities and economies of scale create barriers to entry. If established firms also deliberately build plants with excess capacity in areas where scale economies are significant, entry barriers can be formidable. But, unfortunately, potential entrants have to contend with other barriers as well.

II. Entry and Entry Barriers

In addition to barriers created by economies of scale, barriers to entry may stem from product differentiation advantages of established firms, or established firms may have easier access to capital or have advantages which give them lower absolute costs. Bases of absolute cost advantages may be superior techniques which are protected by patents or kept secret from rivals, or an established firm might have advantages in the employment of factors (for example, in a metal industry, it might have a long-term, advantageous lease of a higher-grade ore than is generally available), or an established firm might be able to obtain capital at a lower interest rate. If the capital requirements for entry to an industry are large and if potential entrants have less ready access to capital, this can be a significant deterrent to newcomers. The product differentiation barrier is also important in some industries. Product designs may be protected by patents or established firms might have built-up "loyalty" to their products, for example by advertising. Habits in the use of branded products also establish themselves after a period of time and there may also be problems in obtaining retail outlets for the output of an entrant in some industries.

On the basis of his study,[13] Bain ranked various industries in terms of the importance of scale economies, product differentiation, absolute cost differences and capital requirements as barriers to entry. A sample of his results are indicated in Table 19.1.

Table 19.1

Barriers to Entry in Various United States Industries

Industry	Scale Economies	Product Differentiation	Absolute Costs	Capital Requirements
A. *Very High Barriers*				
Automobiles	1	1	3	1
Cigarettes	3	1	3	1
Liquor	3	1	3	2
Tractors	1	1	3	1
Typewriters	1	1	3	n.a.
B. *Substantial Barriers*				
Farm machinery				
Petroleum Refining	2	2	3	1
Soap	2	2	3	2
Steel	2	3	1	1
C. *Low Barriers*	Rayon, Tyres and tubes, Shoes, Meat packing, Cement			

In this table, 1 indicates a very high barrier, 2 a substantial barrier and 3 a low barrier. Note the consistent importance of product differentiation and capital requirements as barriers in the group with very high barriers. Indeed, in cigarettes and liquor, scale economies and absolute costs are unimportant but the other barriers are very great. In Australia, and many other countries, one would expect a broadly similar pattern, although the barriers might be substantial in some industries which are assessed as having low barriers in the United States.

The barriers mentioned above are either an outcome of technology or result from behaviour in the industry. In addition, governments sometimes maintain entry bars by law. Competition with state postal services may be prohibited and competition with other state industries is not infrequently restricted. In addition, a government agency sometimes restricts entry into certain industries by imposing higher qualifica-

Scale and Entry

tions and standards than may be demanded, and by other means. The practice of medicine is, for example, restricted in this way. At the other pole, in Australia at least, entry into sugar-cane growing and some other agricultural industries is limited by a government board. One of the most unusual methods of limitation is in the taxi business in some parts of Australia. Taxi registrations are limited and new registrations are allocated by ballot (a lottery) to potential entrants. This method leaves the lucky ones free to enjoy part of the above-normal profit from the restrictive policy. This would not be the case if registrations happened to be offered for sale by public auction.

Adam Smith was firmly of the opinion that restrictions on entry reduce the level of attainable national income and welfare.[14] Restrictions prevent the equalisation of returns to factors everywhere and may cause a divergence in the value of the marginal product of factors. Consequently, a Paretian optimum is not achieved.

However, is it not conceivable that barriers to entry are sometimes in the general interest? Without wishing in the slightest to extol all barriers to entry, let me point out that there are some circumstances in which entry barriers might be in the general interest. The Paretian condition is an equilibrium one and, in practice, disequilibrium seems to be the general rule. Therefore, social decisions require a consideration of the time-paths of production. Some industries are subject to waves of entry and exit and develop a cobweb pattern. Above-normal profit brings excessive entry which, in turn, is followed by excessive exit with the cycle repeating itself and the industries tending tardily, if at all, to equilibrium. These are generally industries in which comparatively small amounts of capital are required, and are lures to the inexperienced. Some barriers, possibly government-enforced, may stabilise the industry and cause a speedier convergence towards equilibrium even if equilibrium is not reached. In the absence of this interference, deviations from the equilibrium are liable to be even greater. Impediments or obstructions can make for a speedier and more certain convergence to an equilibrium since they permit learning to take place more effectively.

There is another circumstance, too, in which restrictions of entry might be in the public interest. An inventor might be given an exclusive property right in his invention by a patent. Consequently, he might earn a monopoly profit by excluding potential competitors. Although entry is restricted, the rate of technical progress might be speeded up and an economic position reached which is superior to that attainable in the absence of patents. This argument was mentioned earlier and will be discussed in more detail in the next chapter.

Lastly, it might be noted that the threat of entry is sometimes more effective than actual entry in keeping the price of a product down. For example, consider an industry in which there is one established firm and one potential entrant. Imagine that there is a price, M, for the product which, if it is charged by the established firm, just forestalls entry. The potential entrant enters only if the price of the product is raised above M. Furthermore, suppose that the established firm is the price leader after entry so that the price of the entrant's product is a function of the established firm's price and so, too, is its share of the market.

To determine the optimal price for its product the established firm must compare its profit in the absence of entry and its profit should entry take place. An entry-preventing policy might be most profitable. But it is not necessarily most profitable to charge an entry-forestalling price. The situation is somewhat complex but can be sorted out with the aid of Fig. 19.3.

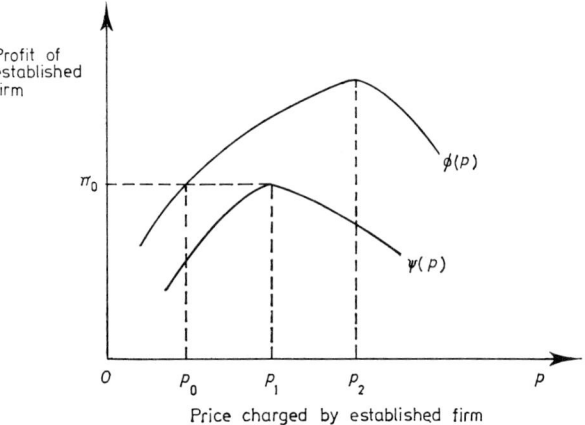

Fig. 19.3

In Fig. 19.3, let $\phi(p)$ represent the profit function of the established firm in the absence of entry and $\psi(p)$ be its profit function if entry occurs. Let $\phi(p)$ reach its maximum for p_2 and $\psi(p)$ attain its greatest value for p_1. Suppose also that $\psi(p_1) = \phi(p)$ for $p = p_0$; that is, at a price of p_0, profit in the absence of entry equals the established firm's maximum profit, given entry. The profit-maximising policy of the established firm is then as follows:

(i) if the entry-forestalling price exceeds the profit-maximising monopoly price, that is if $M \geqslant p_2$, the established firm acts as a monopolist and charges a price of p_2;

(ii) if $p_0 \leqslant M \leqslant p_2$, the established firm charges the entry-forestalling price, M;

(iii) if $M < p_0$, the established firm charges p_1 and precipitates entry.

In all these instances, supply is assumed to be adjusted to meet demand at the price being charged. In particular, note that, if $p_0 \leqslant M < p_1$, the established firm charges M for its product which is lower than p_1, so the threat of entry causes the established firm to charge a lower price than would be charged if entry occurs. Hence, the threat of entry can be a more powerful force than actual entry for keeping price down and output up.

This model is somewhat special. For example, allowance should be made for uncertainties associated with entry. But the basic point remains.

Established firms may well be able to raise M with the passage of time by advertising and other strategies. But no strategy is likely to proceed beyond the level at which its additional cost exceeds its expected benefit to the established firm. Nevertheless, considerable social-economic waste can occur even at these levels of exclusion activity. For example, the advertising which is undertaken for exclusion purposes may be misleading. An examination of these strategies would be interesting but would take me beyond the scope of this book.

NOTES AND REFERENCES

[1] See, for example, C. TISDELL, "Efficiency and Decreasing Cost Industries", *Australian Economic Papers*, 1970, pp. 256-72.
[2] Adam Smith put a well-argued case for absence of impediments on entry as early as 1776. See ADAM SMITH, *The Wealth of Nations*, Everyman's edition, J. Dent, London, 1910; Book I, Ch. 10 in particular.
[3] The results are reported in J. BAIN, *Industrial Organization*, 2nd ed., John Wiley, New York, 1968, Ch. 6.
[4] Ibid.
[5] Ibid., p. 195. Reproduced by kind permission of John Wiley & Sons, Inc.
[6] F. T. MOORE, "Economies of Scale: Some Statistical Evidence", *Quarterly Journal of Economics*, 1959, **73**, pp. 232-45.
[7] Reported by MOORE, op. cit.
[8] Ibid.
[9] MOORE, op. cit.
[10] Ibid, p. 235.
[11] The postulate which is stated at the end of the paragraph, appears in P. SYLOS LABINI, *Oligopolio e progresso tecnico*, Giuffrè, Milan, 1957, and F. MODIGLIANI, "New Developments on the Oligopoly Front", *Journal of Political Economy*, 1958, **66**, pp. 215-32.
[12] See MODIGLIANI, op. cit.
[13] J. BAIN, *Barriers to New Competition*, Harvard University Press, Cambridge, 1956. See also Bain's *Industrial Organization*, which is cited above.
[14] SMITH, op. cit.

FURTHER READING

BAIN, J. S., *Price Theory*, 1952, Science Edition, John Wiley, New York, 1966, pp. 197-225.
BAIN, J. S., *Barriers to New Competition*, Harvard University Press, Cambridge, 1956.
BAIN, J. S., *Industrial Organization*, 2nd ed., John Wiley, New York, 1960, Chs. 6-8.
MODIGLIANI, F., "New Developments on the Oligopoly Front", *Journal of Political Economy*, 1958, **66**, pp. 215-32. Reprinted in D. KAMERSCHEN, *Readings in Microeconomics*, John Wiley, New York, 1969.
MOORE, F. T., "Economies of Scale: Some Statistical Evidence", *Quarterly Journal of Economics*, 1959, **73**, pp. 232-45.
TISDELL, C., "Efficiency and Decreasing Cost Industries", *Australian Economic Papers*, 1970, pp. 256-72.
The Economist, Supplement, 3 October 1970.

CHAPTER 20

Markets and Knowledge, Research and Innovation

I. Market Shortcomings and Knowledge

Markets influence both the transmission of existing knowledge and the production of new knowledge. However, if left to themselves, markets do not ensure that these activities are conducted in an optimal manner and to an optimal extent. Normally, some governmental interference with the market mechanism is required to advance knowledge and transmit it.

Knowledge creation and transmission is a major source of growth in more developed countries. Edward Denison, for example, has estimated that 20 per cent of the increase in the real national income of the United States over the period 1929-1957 could be attributed to the advance of knowledge and 27 per cent to improvements of education which increased the quality of labour.[1] Thus, in this period, improvements in quality, rather than variations in quantity, contributed 47 per cent of the observed increase in real national output. This is a considerable amount by any standard.

This chapter concentrates more on the production of new knowledge than on the economics of education.[2] But it might be noted that governments are not prepared to leave education to be determined in free markets for a number of reasons. Education gives rise to some favourable externalities. For example, educated individuals might be (this is not certain) more harmonious in a community and socially more aware and constructive. On this ground a government might subsidise education. Yet one feels that the main basis for subsidisation of education is the desire to provide equality of opportunity. There is a general feeling that children should not be the victims of their parents' low incomes and that their education ought to be subsidised to provide some modicum of equality of opportunity. Furthermore, the state is likely to make basic education compulsory. This might be done on two grounds: to protect children and parents who are ignorant of the value of education (see Chapter 14); or to protect children against parents who are not prepared to make sufficient sacrifices for them. But let us turn to new knowledge and research and development.

Externalities are a major problem for inventors and the discoverers of new knowledge. In the absence of special protection by a patent or similar device, the use of an inventor's discovery by others cannot be made dependent upon a price payment. Exclusion subject to a price payment is impossible. Others may use the inventor's invention without paying him for this. Furthermore, the faster is the rate of diffusion and adoption of the idea, the less is his lead in commercial exploitation of the idea and the lower his personal gain. Indeed, if there is practically no lag in the adoption of the idea by rivals, an inventor (inventing firm) might not even be able to recoup the development cost of the invention. For example, if perfect competition exists and the invention reduces the minimum long-run average costs of production, and all firms (including entrants to the industry) adjust to the invention just as quickly as the inventor, the inventor obtains no extra profit by the invention. If all firms happened to be making a normal profit prior to the invention, they also earn only a normal profit afterwards because competition forces prices down to the minimum average costs of production. In such a circumstance, a firm is unable to earn any profit from research and development and even in cases where the inventor obtains a small lead in the adoption of the invention, his returns from research and development may be low. In circumstances like this, the social return from his research and development activity greatly exceeds his private return.

The real problem is that, because of exclusion difficulties, inventors (or their capitalist backers) obtain a private marginal expected gain from research and development expenditure which is less than the expected social marginal gain. Consequently, if economic agents aim to maximise profit, fewer resources are likely to be allocated to research and development activity than is socially optimal. How then can the private marginal return from research and development expenditure be brought more into line with the social marginal return?

There are a number of alternative means which can be employed separately or in conjunction. For example, cash prizes may be given for new inventions or bonuses which vary with the economic application of the invention may be paid. However, the problem in each case is how to determine the appropriate level of reward.

Alternatively, or as well, research and development expenditure can be subsidised. The problem again is to determine the appropriate subsidy. In some cases (for example, in basic research) the required subsidy may be 100 per cent since the commodity produced is virtually a pure public good. In cases like this, in order to avoid or reduce the risk of corruption, the research might be undertaken by a government agency or closely supervised by the government.

Still another device is the issue of a patent. A patent grants a temporary monopoly to an inventor and gives rise to a dilemma. For maximum static efficiency, knowledge (in the absence of any externality) should be available to all at its marginal transmission cost which may be zero or very low. But by giving the inventor a property right in his invention, a patent enables a patentee to charge others a price for the use of his invention in excess of the marginal transmission cost of his idea. Thus, although patents may raise the return to invention and increase research and inventions, they also lead to less than optimal adoption of inventions. Arguments for and against the patent system will be considered presently along with the Schumpeterian dilemma which the system poses.

A government may also wish to adopt some of the above measures for reasons other than the externalities involved in research and development. For example, the returns from research and innovation may be comparatively uncertain.[3] Consequently, if firms underestimate their returns or are risk-averters on an average, insufficient resources to maximise overall output will flow to research and innovation activities. The risks of returns from investment projects which yield uncertain returns is lower for the community than for an individual investor who invests in one or a few of these projects. If the returns from different risky ventures are not correlated, then by the law of large numbers their actual returns in aggregate tend to the mean return.

II. Patents, Subsidies and Other Measures

Let us consider some of the measures for dealing with market shortcomings in research and innovation in slightly more detail, concentrating on the patent system in particular.

One way to combat the research problems mentioned before is for the government to conduct in-government research through its own or closely affiliated institutions, such as some universities. In cases like these, the new knowledge may be made available at its marginal cost of transmission, or even at a lower cost if externalities are expected to flow from its application. Thus static efficiency can be combined with the growth of new knowledge. Nevertheless, some economists are of the opinion that in-government research alone does not lead to optimal growth in the composition of knowledge. Government institutions may not concentrate sufficiently on development of ideas to the application stage and may lose contact with economic considerations. This will be discussed below. Yet there is some role for in-government research, particularly on the basic research side where externalities are almost complete and thus 100 per cent subsidisation or support is called for. Also not only because of externalities but because of the public safety factor, the government needs to undertake research. For example, in testing the effectiveness and safety of drugs, it can be argued that since the consumer is relatively ignorant there is a case for this activity. A private organisation is unlikely to supply the information since it can easily be communicated from one recipient to another (there is an immense externality) and, furthermore, how reliable is the private organisation likely to be?

Yet there is a limit to the effectiveness of in-government research. It is claimed that there must be some balance between in-firm and in-government research because government research institutes are liable to pay insufficient regard to development and expected returns, and a communication gap is liable to develop between the government research institutes and industry—institutes may fail to do research that is of relevance to industrial firms or, because of their relative lack of research facilities and funds, firms may fail to perceive and develop the ideas originated in the institutes to the stage of commercial application.[4] Thus a case exists for the continuance of a certain amount of in-firm research. This, of course, still gives rise to externalities and may have high associated risks.

As in Australia and Canada, for example,[5] private industrial research and development might be subsidised to allow for these elements. However, there is still the problem of determining the appropriate subsidies to be paid. Taxation concessions are also a variant of the subsidisation approach. Yet, unless a negative income tax policy operates or loss offset is available, firms will be treated differently by taxation concessions rather than grants. Those with net incomes below the taxable level gain no benefit from the taxation concessions.

The patent system has been commonly used to support research and to make *knowledge* of research results available to the community as a whole. A patent confers upon a patentee the exclusive property right of his invention during the term of the patent and thus makes it possible for an inventor to charge a price for the use of his invention by others, and restrict its use. The duration of a patent varies from country to country but generally the period is in the range of 14-20 years. Extensions beyond this period may also be granted. In some countries, a patent may be revoked for non-use of the invention or the patentee may be ordered to license others to use the discovery.[6] But indications are that these powers are rarely used.

A patent grants to the patentee a legal monopoly of his invention which may (if it involves a significant advance) enable him to monopolise or control the production of a particular product and earn monopoly profits. Sometimes the exclusion principle of the system is abused. For example, a patentee may threaten patent litigation against potential entrants to an industry even if they do not intend to violate any of his patent rights. Nevertheless, this might dissuade entrants since patent litigation can be long, costly and uncertain. Furthermore, members of an industry sometimes administer their patents in a common pool. Naturally, this creates a tremendous barrier to entry and can lead to a permanent cartel.

In assessing the patent system, one must weigh the restrictions which the system imposes on output against the amount of technical advance which it makes possible. But even if one finds that the system is a net advantage, one needs to go further and enquire whether preferable means exist.

Professor Machlup[7] has gathered together a number of views which have been put in favour of the patent system. Some no longer have many avid supporters. They can be conveniently classified as

 (i) the natural law thesis,
 (ii) the reward by monopoly thesis,
 (iii) the exchange-for-secrets thesis, and
 (iv) the monopoly-profit-incentive thesis.

(i) According to the *natural law thesis*, man has a right to property and a right to remuneration for its use by others. It is claimed that an individual's invention is his property and so he ought to be remunerated for its use by others. This rather moralistic view does not have universal appeal. Also an inventor generally has a debt to earlier inventors and discoverers. In many cases he builds on the ideas of others, so just where does his contribution begin?

(ii) The *reward by monopoly thesis* presumes that a patent is a *just* reward for the inventor's services in making his new idea or product available to society. But this begs the whole question of justice since discovery is to a large extent a lottery. Ought a person who discovers a new idea by chance or little effort (as sometimes happens) be entitled to a large reward?

(iii) The *exchange-for-secrets thesis* assumes a contract between the inventor and society. The patentee on his part makes the knowledge of his invention available to society and society in return grants him temporary protection by means of the patent. Thus the stock of communal knowledge is assumed to increase. The availability of this knowledge can be of benefit to other inventors.

But not everyone agrees that the patent system raises the stock of communal knowledge. Some claim that inventions which can be kept secret are unlikely to be patented, particularly if there is any chance that patented material will give promising leads to competitors. Yet a firm cannot be certain of keeping an invention secret and a patent is a safeguard against leaks of information or subsequent discovery of the idea by rivals. Hence, on balance, one would expect the patent system to increase the stock of communal knowledge even if a few ideas are not patented.

(iv) According to the *monopoly-profit-incentive thesis*, patents encourage research and development expenditure by raising the expected return from this activity and likewise promote innovation. The number of inventions is increased and industrial progress is speeded up. As Machlup puts it,

> The monopoly-profit-incentive thesis assumes that industrial progress is desirable, that inventions and their industrial exploitation are necessary for such progress, but that inventions and/or their exploitation will not be obtained in sufficient measure if inventors and capitalists can hope only for such profits as the competitive exploitation of all technical knowledge will permit. To make it worthwhile for inventors and their capitalist backers to make their effort and risk their money, society should intervene to increase their profit expectations ....[8] [by granting *temporary* monopolies in the form of patent rights for inventions].

But this hypothesis is not accepted by everyone. Some believe that patents do not raise the expected return from research and development significantly, for the bulk of inventors and their capitalist backers already have a high degree of protection via secrecy and entry barriers, such as arise from product differentiation, so they do not gain by additional protection. Others, while prepared to concede that patents and other means of support for research and development might raise expected returns, are sceptical about the possibility of increasing the number of inventions by increased research and development expenditure. Taussig,[9] for example, believes that the number of inventions depends basically on inventive talent and society's inventive talent is strictly limited both in the short and in the long run. The number of inventors is limited and, beyond a point, their inventiveness does not benefit substantially by improved facilities.

In evaluation of the desirability or otherwise of the patent system, three factors need to be considered: namely, its influence on the quantity and quality of inventions, its effect on the speed of innovation and its impact on the rate of imitation or diffusion of new techniques. The benefits from speedier invention and innovation, if these occur, must be weighed against restrictions of production which are likely to follow a successful patented invention. The output-expanding impact of faster technical progress can be annulled by the counteracting restrictive impact of monopoly on output.

This can be illustrated by means of Fig. 20.1. Assuming perfect competition, imagine that in the absence of a patent system a product, X, has a per-unit cost of p_0. The aggregate output of the industry is then shown in Fig. 20.1 by X_0 and the product sells for p_0. Under these conditions, let us postulate an absence of technical progress so that with the passage of time price and supplies remain unchanged. However, if a patent system operates, this might stimulate a firm to invent a technique which lowers the per-unit cost of producing the product to OA. Consequently, the patentee is able to undercut firms which use the old technique, drive them from the industry and establish a monopoly. Having established the monopoly, the patentee may revert to the previous output, X_0, and price, p_0, for the product. The consumer of the product makes no gain, though there is an advance in so far as fewer resources are now required for the old effect. Only if the patented technique causes per-unit cost of output to fall by more than $p_0 - A$, does the patentee-monopolist charge a lower price and produce a greater output than that in the absence of the patent system; only then does his monopoly-restriction of output fail to annul the output-expanding effect due to technical progress. Conceivably, even though technical progress takes place, price can be higher for the product under a patent system. For example, if the patentee's technique reduces per-unit cost below p_0 but not below OA, he might still decide to drive competitors from the field. Having done so, he might raise price above p_0. At this price, other things being unchanged, it would be profitable for new firms to start production with the old unpatented technique. But they may fail to enter the industry. The patentee might threaten to ruin them by reducing the price if they enter and this is in his power, or he might threaten patent litigation against entrants even though no infringement might be intended. Thus the patent system may raise entry barriers and even lead to higher prices in the midst of technical progress. But this effect is by no means certain and the actual influence of the patent system may vary from industry to industry. Even the overall impact of the patent system is far from clear. As Machlup says,

> No economist, on the basis of present knowledge could possibly state with certainty that the patent system, as it now operates, confers a net benefit or a net loss upon society.[10]

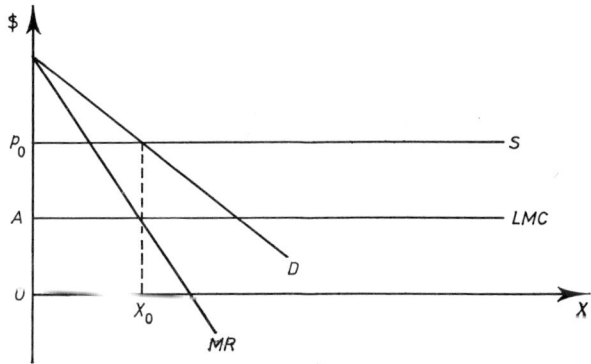

Fig. 20.1

But even if the patent system as it now stands confers a net benefit on society, improvements in the present patent system might still be possible. Furthermore, measures, other than patent protection, for the encouragement of technical progress might be better again. We must remind ourselves that the patent system encourages static inefficiency and ask ourselves if there are alternatives which avoid this and yet ensure technical progress. Possibly the present patent system could be improved by varying the length of the patent period depending upon the nature of the discovery, and, in cases where considerable static economic inefficiency or hardship to consumers arise from monopoly (for example, in the case of an important new drug), by not granting a patent to the discoverer, but a bonus or reward which is related to the benefit of the advance.

III. Some Empirical Findings about Research and Innovation

As was noted in earlier chapters,[11] Schumpeter[12] advanced the hypothesis that innovation would be faster and research and development possibly greater under imperfect competition than under perfect competition. All in all, Schumpeter believed that technical progress might be faster under imperfect competition (monopoly and oligopoly) than under perfect competition. This hypothesis has proved difficult to test but recently considerable research has been done which relates research and development effort to firm size and industry concentration.

Studies in the United States by D. Hamberg, F. Scherer, E. Mansfield, J. Schmookler and J. Worley[13] related observed research and development expenditures of firms to their size. Their studies indicate a tendency in any industry for research and development expenditure to increase with a firm's size first at an increasing rate and then at a decreasing rate. For a sufficiently large size, the expenditure might even fall. Markham suggests that the central finding of recent empirical studies is

> ... up to a certain size [of the firm], innovational effort increases more than proportionately to size; at that size which varies from industry to industry, the fitted curve has an inflection point and among the largest few firms innovational effort generally does not increase and may decline with size.[14]

Consequently, in any industry research and development expenditure as a function of the size of a firm tends to be like a logistic curve. For example, it might be like the curve shown in Fig. 20.2.

The curve which is shown has an inflection point at A. However, contrary to Markham's apparent assertion above, the proportion of funds committed to research and development as a fraction of the firm's size is *not* at a maximum at the size corresponding to this inflection point. Rather it is at a maximum at size B, the point at which the rays which pass through points of the research and development function have maximum slope. In Fig. 20.2, the ray OC is the one which has maximum slope. The

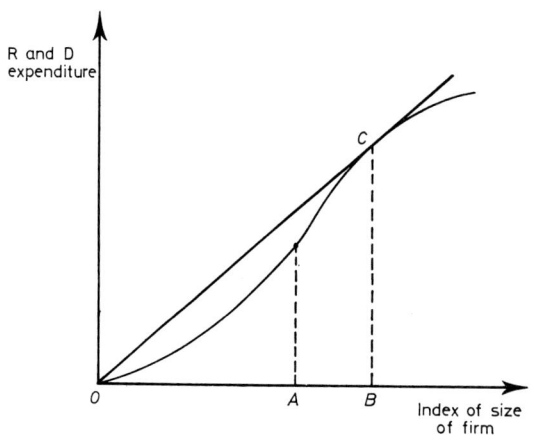

Fig. 20.2

size at which maximum research and development expenditure per unit of size occurs varies from industry to industry, and it seems probable that, beyond a point, bigness results in a decline in *proportionate* research and development expenditure.

The above finding is not inconsistent with the further observation that the greatest proportion of research and development expenditure is concentrated amongst a few large firms and in the oligopolistic core of the economy, for example, in chemicals, electrical equipment and automobiles. Firms in these categories are relatively large.

Does research and development effort increase with market imperfection? Hamberg[15] has found some positive correlation between concentration ratios and research and development expenditure from observations of seventeen industries in the United States, but the relationship is weak. Thus judgement must be suspended on this issue. At this stage, too, evidence on the variation of the productivity of research and development effort with its size (at the level of the economic unit) is inconclusive but, as Jewkes[16] has pointed out, many important inventions have come from smaller laboratories.

Empirical studies of innovation and diffusion have also been undertaken. For example, lags in innovation of one to twenty years have been observed. Griliches and Mansfield[17] have done some interesting work on the diffusion of new techniques which indicates that the percentage of firms adopting a profitable technique is likely to conform to a logistic curve and proceed at a faster rate the more profitable is the new technique and the smaller is the investment which it requires. The adoption curve is like that shown in Fig. 20.3.

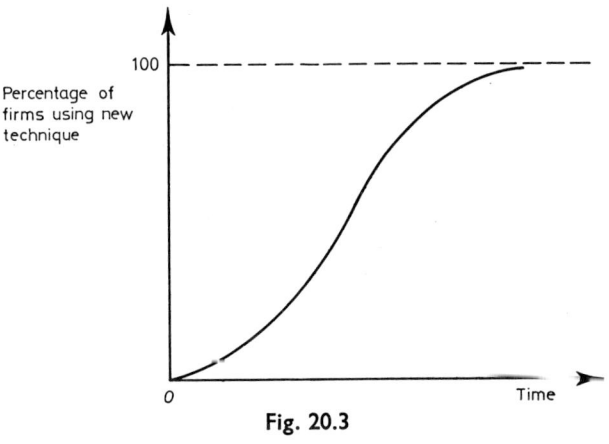

Fig. 20.3

At the moment the economics of knowledge is a subject of considerable interest for economic research and significant advances in this field may be expected in the future. This chapter provides only a brief survey of some aspects of the economics of knowledge. Consequently, the reader may wish to add to the survey by drawing upon the sources mentioned in its footnotes.

NOTES AND REFERENCES

[1] DENISON, E., (i) *The Sources of Economic Growth in the United States and the Alternatives before Us*, Committee for Economic Development, New York, 1962; (ii) *Why Growth Rates Differ*, Brookings Institution, Washington, 1967.

[2] For information on the economics of education, see, for example, M. BLAUG, *Economics of Education*, Penguin, Harmondsworth, 1968. P. H. KARMEL, *Some Economic Aspects of Education*, Cheshire, Melbourne, 1962. J. VAIZEY, *Education in the Modern World*, Weidenfeld and Nicolson, London, 1967.

[3] See K. J. ARROW, "Economic Welfare and the Allocation of Resources for Invention", in NATIONAL BUREAU OF ECONOMIC RESEARCH, *The Rate and Direction of Inventive Activity*, Princeton University Press, Princeton, 1962, pp. 609-26.

⁴ This matter is a problem for economic policy-makers in both socialist and capitalist countries. See C. TISDELL, "Commonwealth Industrial Research and Development Grants: An Economic Evaluation" to appear in *Economic Analysis and Policy*, 1971, **2**, No. 2, Queensland University Press, Brisbane, and J. WILCZYNSKI, "Technological Progress in Centrally Planned Economies", a paper read to Section 24, 43rd Congress, Australian and New Zealand Association for the Advancement of Science, May 1971.

⁵ In Australia, grants are controlled by *Industrial Research and Development Grants Act 1967*, No. 51 of 1967.

⁶ Patents are regulated in Australia by the *Patents Act* 1952-1969. Part XII of the Principal Act provides that the High Court, upon petition, may order the compulsory licence of patented inventions after three years if this is in the public interest, and revoke a patent for non-use after two years from the date of sealing of a patent.

⁷ F. MACHLUP, "An Economic Review of the Patent System", A UNITED STATES SENATE STUDY, *Committee on Patents, Trademarks, and Copyrights*, U.S. Govt. Printing Office, Washington, 1958.

⁸ Ibid., p. 21.

⁹ F. TAUSSIG, *Inventors and Money-Makers*, Macmillan, New York, 1915.

¹⁰ MACHLUP, op. cit., p. 79.

¹¹ Chapters 9 and 14.

¹² J. SCHUMPETER, *Capitalism, Socialism and Democracy*, George Allen and Unwin, 4th ed., 1954, Chs. 7 and 8.

¹³ D. HAMBERG, "Size of Firm, Oligopoly, and Research: The Evidence", *Canadian Journal of Economics and Political Science*, 1964, **30**, pp. 62-75. E. MANSFIELD, "Size of Firm, Market Structure, and Innovation", *Journal of Political Economy*, 1963, **71**, pp. 556-76. F. SCHERER, "Size of Firm, Oligopoly, and Research: Comment", *Canadian Journal of Economics and Political Science*, 1965, **31**, pp. 256-66. J. SCHMOOKLER, "Bigness, Fewness and Research", *Journal of Political Economy*, 1959, **67**, pp. 628-35. J. S. WORLEY, "Industrial Research and the New Competition", *Journal of Political Economy*, 1958, **68**, pp. 183-6.

¹⁴ J. MARKHAM, "Market Structure, Business Conduct, and Innovation", *American Economic Review*, 1965, **55**, No. 2, pp. 323-32; quotation in text comes from p. 329.

¹⁵ HAMBERG, op. cit.

¹⁶ J. JEWKES, D. SAWERS and R. STILLERMAN, *The Sources of Invention*, 2nd ed., Macmillan, London, 1969. See also F. M. SCHERER, "Firm Size, Market Structure, Opportunity, and the Output of Patented Inventions", *American Economic Review*, 1965, **55**, pp. 1097-125. Scherer concludes from his study that inventive output increases with firm sales, but at less than a proportional rate.

¹⁷ Z. GRILICHES, "Hybrid Corn: An Exploration in the Economics of Technological Change", *Econometrica*, 1957, **25**, pp. 501-22. E. MANSFIELD, *Industrial Research and Technological Innovation*, W. W. Norton, New York, 1968.

FURTHER READING

ARROW, K. J., "Economic Welfare and the Allocation of Resources for Invention", in NATIONAL BUREAU OF ECONOMIC RESEARCH, *The Rate and Direction of Inventive Activity*, Princeton University Press, Princeton, 1962, pp. 609-26.

BLAUG, M., *Economics of Education*, Penguin, London, 1968.

MACHLUP, F., "An Economic Review of the Patent System", *A United States Senate Study, Committee on Patents, Trademarks, and Copyrights*, **15**, 85th Congress, 2nd session, U.S. Govt. Printing Office, Washington, 1958.

MANSFIELD, E., *Microeconomics*, W. W. Norton, New York, 1970, Ch. 16.

MARKHAM, J., "Market Structure, Business Conduct, and Innovation", *American Economic Review*, 1965, **55**, pp. 323-32.

NELSON, R. R., "The Simple Economics of Basic Scientific Research", *Journal of Political Economy*, 1959, **67**, pp. 297-306.

SCHUMPETER, J. A., *Capitalism, Socialism and Democracy*, 4th ed., George Allen and Unwin, London, 1954, Chs. 7 and 8.

CHAPTER 21

The Government and Resource Allocation

I. Public Expenditure and Investment: General Points

The public sector today has a significant direct effect on resource allocation, so much so that any examination of resource allocation is grossly deficient if it neglects the role of the public sector. In countries such as the United States, United Kingdom, Canada and Australia, expenditure by the public sector on goods and services amounts to between 20 per cent and 25 per cent of total expenditure. The public sector is also responsible for something like 25 per cent to 30 per cent of all investment (capital formation). In addition to this direct impact on resource allocation, the public sector (which includes local governments, state and federal governments, and instrumentalities) has indirect influences by its transfer payments (social service benefits), taxation and subsidies, legislation to control restrictive practices, and so on, but it is the direct impact which will be considered in this chapter.

The composition of public expenditure varies from country to country. The largest expenditure item is usually for defence. Expenditures upon education, public health, transport and communication, public utilities, justice and public order are all likely to be important. Some differences in emphasis occur. For example, public utilities are more often operated by the public sector in Australia and the United Kingdom than in the U.S.A., although their operation by private enterprise in the United States is regulated by the government.

Why is there so much public investment and expenditure in "free enterprise" economies? Why is there a need for public expenditure? The basic reason seems to be that markets, while they can be useful organising mechanisms in some spheres, fail to provide a socially optimal quantity of goods and services in other spheres. Some of the reasons for market failure and deficiencies were outlined in Chapter 14.

Public expenditure might be justified on one or more of the following grounds:

(i) it is necessary to ensure an optimal supply of collective goods (sometimes also called pure public or social goods) or goods which give rise to extremely favourable externalities;

(ii) the expenditure is necessary to reduce ignorance or deal with merit wants;

(iii) full or satisfactory levels of employment will not be maintained in the absence of government expenditure;

(iv) government production might lead to greater efficiency and/or a more satisfactory distribution of income (for example, in the case of natural monopolies);

(v) expenditure on some commodities (for example, education) might promote greater equality of opportunity.

This list is not exhaustive but possibly covers the main economic grounds for expenditure by the government. Before considering these grounds in more detail, a closely related question might be noted. How much production should be carried out by the government itself? Clearly, the government itself produces many of the goods which it requires. But, in fact, practically all of the services which are provided by the government could be produced by the private sector on behalf of the government. At the moment governments, such as those of Australia, frequently let contracts for their construction activities, country mail deliveries etc., and in principle this system could be extended (in some countries it has been already done in the past) to cover the provision of the police force, defence (the army), tax collection, etc. But why are most countries reluctant to proceed thus far? In part, it is because of the risks associated with private execution of these activities. The loyalty of physically powerful and well organised bodies to the government is more readily retained if these bodies are under the direct control and supervision of the government. Factors such as loyalty, ease of supervision and efficiency have a bearing on decisions about just how much of its goods and services should actually be produced by the government. The desirable amount of government expenditure and the desirable extent of its direct involvement in productive activity can be treated as separate issues. The latter matter is important and to a considerable extent involves non-economic considerations, but I shall concentrate on the first problem.

Public expenditure influences the level of aggregate demand in the economy and so the level of employment or, in certain circumstances, the rate of inflation. Under the influence of Keynesian theories, some economists have come to regard variations of government expenditure as primarily a stabiliser of employment in the economy. But this is a dangerous view. Government expenditure is not merely an instrument for stabilisation but also a means of providing goods and services whose production is required for Paretian optimality but which either will not be supplied by free markets at all or will be supplied in less than optimal quantities. Furthermore, it ought to be realised that there is still an allocation problem if unemployment exists, for government expenditures of the same amount generally can be directed to a number of alternative activities. A choice of expenditures might in this case be made both on the basis of employment-creating effects of projects and their contribution to the output of goods and services.

Pigou[1] and others have also maintained that individuals are too shortsighted and that this causes them to prefer increased consumption at the expense of investment thus reducing the benefits for future generations. One way to offset this tendency is to increase public investment at the expense of private consumption. But this is not the only way to deal with this matter, assuming that it requires action. Interference on these grounds is contentious since it involves an imposition on existing generations of consumption and savings patterns which are not preferred by them.

In many circumstances, the average costs of production fall with volume and duplication of productive facilities is wasteful of resources. There may be a natural tendency towards monopoly in these instances. But there is a dilemma. Maximum economic efficiency is not achieved if more than one productive unit operates. However, if a monopoly is achieved, the profit maximisation goal leads to a less than ideal level of output. Even worse, it may be impossible to produce the ideal level of output without making a loss. In situations like this, a government may decide to produce the commodity in question (for example, it might be a public utility like electricity or gas) or, at least, to regulate the industry. Policy matters raised by the state's operation of industry where exclusion is possible are discussed in the next section.

For some goods exclusion is impossible or uneconomical. These are called public or collective goods. Pure public goods, unlike private goods, have the quality that consumption of them by any one or number of individuals does not subtract from possible consumption by others. The classic example is that of a lighthouse. Its use by one passing ship does not prevent its use by another. While pure public goods might be rare, many goods have significant externalities and are quasi-public goods. Unless such goods are provided by or subsidised by the state, they are unlikely to be available in Paretian optimal quantities. This is also discussed in the next section.

Thus production and pricing in state enterprises is discussed below, first on the assumption that exclusion is possible (economical) and then on the assumption that exclusion is impossible. The last section of this chapter deals with cost-benefit analysis and thus introduces dynamic considerations into the resource-allocation problems of the public sector.

But before becoming involved in the government's resource-allocation problems, let me make a few general points. In some instances, state operation of enterprises and provision of resources can be an alternative or a supplement to their provision by a free market. In comparing the two alternatives, it needs to be borne in mind that neither the state nor the market is likely to make perfect decisions—both are liable to shortcomings. There is little point in contrasting a real market with a perfect government or a real government with a perfect market.

This is not to deny that real net benefits may flow from operation of certain enterprises by the state, but to point out that the state is not a perfect instrument. It is subject to all the problems of administration and the shortcomings of bureaucrats etc. In the context of an economy which wishes to make maximal use of markets, the role of the state would seem to be

(i) to produce or subsidise the production of goods which cannot be supplied in Paretian optimal quantities by the market mechanism,

(ii) to correct specific defects in the operation of markets, for example, to control restrictive practices, and

(iii) to improve the working of markets by improving mobility and information.

These grounds give the government a wide scope for interference, much wider than might be imagined at first sight.

II. The Public Supply and Pricing of Products

Just how large should be the quantity of output by state enterprises? What prices should they charge for their product? Should they be expected to make a profit? If they make a loss, how should the loss be covered?

As a first approach, one might set up the requirement that public enterprises ought to be operated in a manner which achieves Paretian optimality. But this goal is difficult to achieve or even approach. Not only is the non-public sector far from perfectly competitive and thus second-best problems arise,[2] but public production often gives rise to externalities which are difficult to evaluate. Furthermore, the public production of goods in which internal decreasing average costs are the rule, requires a monopoly for maximum economic efficiency and may, when operated at the most efficient level of output, involve a loss.

It is convenient to divide the discussion of optimal supply into two parts by first considering the production of goods for which exclusion is possible (that is goods from which public enterprises can exclude consumers by price charges, and for which externalities are absent) and then goods in which exclusion is impossible or only partially successful (the case of public or collective goods).

A. PUBLIC SUPPLY AND PRICING OF PRODUCTS, GIVEN THE POSSIBILITY OF EXCLUSION

In the case of a number of government enterprises, it is possible to make the availability of their product to a consumer dependent on a price payment. For example, this is true of public utilities such as electricity, postal services, roads, railways and many others. If it is desired to achieve Paretian optimality, if externalities are absent, and if the output of each firm in the private sector of the economy is such that marginal cost equals price, production by public enterprise ought to be such as to equate the marginal cost of output and the price (value) of the product. The principle of equating price and marginal cost is called the Hotelling-Lerner rule in honour of two economists who suggested it.[3] But if prices in the private sector are somewhat in excess of marginal cost, the application of the Hotelling-Lerner rule can lead to a relative overexpansion in the output of public enterprise.[4] A second-best problem arises. It might be best in these circumstances for public enterprises to restrict their output to some extent so that their price, too, is in excess of marginal cost, for example, by the same percentage as in the rest of the economy. But as was pointed out in Chapter 14, we cannot be categorical about the extent of the correction which is required.

However, let us proceed on the assumption that the Hotelling-Lerner rule is appropriate. Even if it is not appropriate and some correction needs to be made because of second-best problems, it may still turn out that the optimal operation of some state enterprises involves a loss. The special case then serves to illustrate problems which arise also in these cases.

Consider production and pricing in state enterprises which experience decreasing average total costs of production as their output expands. Industries of this type, such as those providing roads, bridges, transport, public utilities, etc., are frequently state monopolies. In cases like this, duplication of productive units wastes resources, for example, to have two sources of electricity supply in competition means costly duplication of transmission lines and failure to take full advantage of economies of scale in power generation. (Consider Nerlove's finding which is mentioned in Chapter 19.) Operation by a private monopoly also leads to a deviation from the Hotelling-Lerner rule if the monopolist maximises his profit and is unable to engage in perfect price discrimination. A private monopolist equates marginal cost to marginal revenue and, since marginal revenue is less than price, produces a lower than Paretian optimal output.

Government and Resource Allocation

However, if a state enterprise adopts the Hotelling-Lerner rule in this case and is unable to engage in price discrimination, it faces a loss. If average total cost is decreasing, marginal cost is *less* than average total cost. Hence, if output is such as to equate marginal cost and price (equals average revenue), average cost exceeds average revenue. The enterprise makes a loss. Note that if marginal cost is less than average cost, the marginal cost curve may be constant, decreasing or even increasing. These three possibilities are shown in Figs 21.1, 21.2 and 21.3 respectively. In these figures, average total cost is marked by *ATC* and marginal cost by *MC*. The demand curve for the enterprise's product is marked by *D* and the corresponding marginal revenue by *MR*. The Hotelling-Lerner ideal output is $\bar{x}$ and results in losses indicated by the dotted rectangles if the output is sold at $\bar{p}$ per unit. Under private monopoly the output is $\hat{x}$ which is lower than $\bar{x}$ and price is higher. The Hotelling-Lerner output gives a Paretian optimum if the overall value of the product to consumers (the amount which they would be willing to pay if all consumers' surplus could be eliminated by perfect price discrimination) exceeds the total cost of producing the Hotelling-Lerner level of output. Otherwise, the product should not be produced at all.[5] A boundary Paretian optimum occurs. But if production is necessary for a Paretian optimum, then at first sight it appears that the Hotelling-Lerner level of output yields a Paretian optimum.

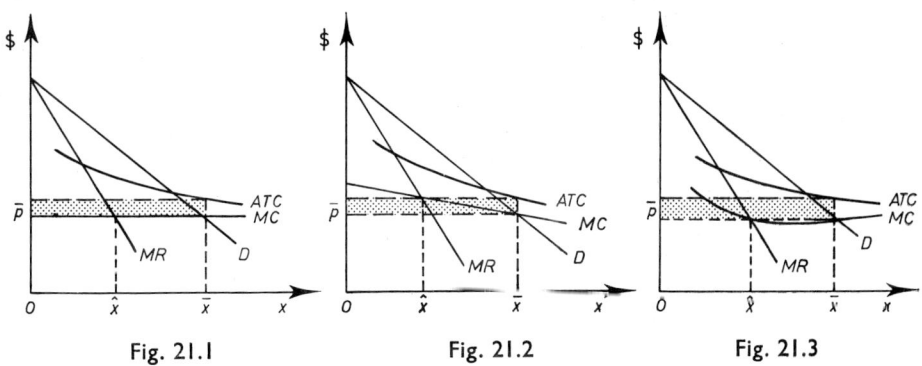

Fig. 21.1   Fig. 21.2   Fig. 21.3

But it may be necessary to revise the view that the Hotelling-Lerner level of output leads to a Paretian optimum. If decreasing costs occur, the rule leads to a loss which has to be covered in some way. For example, it might be met by increased taxation. But increased taxation is liable to affect the supply of effort and also economic efficiency. Once the overall impact is taken into account, some divergence from the Hotelling-Lerner rule may recommend itself. Clearly, the manner of meeting the deficit must be taken into account in our assessment.

The following matters need to be weighed up if the deficit of a state enterprise is to be met by increased taxation:

   (i) the taxation might unfavourably redistribute income;
   (ii) the beneficiaries from the supply of the product might not pay or might only partially pay for their benefits;
   (iii) if the taxation is marginal, which is very likely, production elsewhere in the economy may be adversely affected and the conditions for a Paretian optimum violated;

(iv) a public enterprise might become inefficient if it knows that its losses will be covered. The idea might build up amongst management that costs do not matter much.

Each of these elements need to be taken into account. But it should be noted that none necessarily dictate against the use of the Hotelling-Lerner rule. For example, the increased taxation might lead to a more favourable distribution of income. If one holds to the principle that he who benefits ought to pay (and on distributional grounds one might not), then there might be some preference for local taxation to meet the losses of enterprises with principally a local impact. But if all regions have a similar cluster of public enterprises so that each region obtains similar benefits, there may be little ground for differentiating between local and national taxation as desirable means for meeting the deficits of these enterprises.

Nevertheless, it is useful to consider whether there are any suitable alternatives to taxation as a means for meeting the deficits. If price discrimination is possible, the potential loss can be reduced or even eliminated by a multipart tariff system without in many instances deviating from the Hotelling-Lerner level of output.

Multipart pricing is frequently used in charging for electricity, telephone calls, even water. Very often a flat charge, a "rental" charge is made for continued access to the service and then the marginal charge to the consumer falls with the volume of the commodity which is purchased by him. Frequently, the fall in per-unit charges is not continuous but discrete so as to keep administration and computation costs down. For instance, Fig. 21.4 indicates that if for the commodity X (shown there), a per-unit charge of p_1 is made for X_1 units and of $\bar{p}$ for the remainder, the enterprise suffers no loss and produces the Hotelling-Lerner level of output. Total revenue is $p_1 X_1 + \bar{p}(\bar{X} - X_1)$ and costs are $B\bar{X}$. The latter rectangle is less than the stepped figure in diagram 21.4 which indicates total revenue. If the demand curves of consumers are the same, and if there are n consumers, each consumer might be charged p_1 on the first X_1/n units purchased and $\bar{p}$ for the remaining unit which he buys.

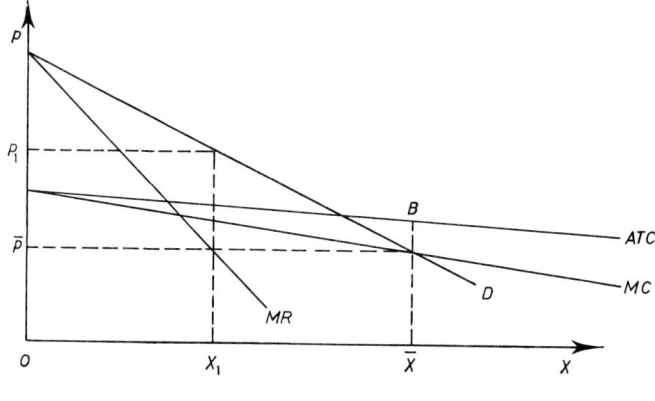

Fig. 21.4

As a result of multipart pricing he-who-benefits-pays, the enterprise may be able to operate at a profit, and Paretian optimality may be achieved. Therefore it might be thought that multipart pricing is the optimal solution.

Government and Resource Allocation

However, price discrimination is not always possible. It requires the absence of arbitrage possibilities. If a commodity can be easily resold on purchase, for example, if units which are purchased at lower marginal cost can be resold by the initial buyer at a higher price and with no (or little) transfer cost, price discrimination is liable to break down. Furthermore, the effect of price discrimination on the distribution of income must be taken into account. Again, discrimination may require costly metering devices, reading of meters and computation and this must be weighed against any possible gain.

Frequently, cases in which average cost is decreasing and short-run marginal cost is zero or near zero are singled out for particular attention. Possibly, these are fairly common for public facilities, for example, museums, parks, bridges. But they are merely special cases of the decreasing average cost situation discussed above. The price at the margin of using any facility which has zero marginal cost should be zero, unless demand exceeds the capacity of the facility. If a capacity restriction is not effective, the facility should be free at the margin. For example, if the marginal cost of crossing a bridge is zero, crossings (at the margin) should be free, unless demand exceeds the capacity of the bridge. If demand exceeds capacity, Paretian optimality requires that price equates supply and demand.

The situation is illustrated in Fig. 21.5. The supply curve of crossings for a bridge per unit of time is shown by the curve $O\hat{X}S$. Up to $\hat{X}$ crossings, marginal cost is zero and then capacity is reached. If demand does not exceed $\hat{X}$ when the crossings are free, for example, as is the case when the demand curve is D_0, the *marginal* crossings should be free. In practice, this may require all crossings to be free if discrimination is not possible or the cost of collecting tolls is too high. If crossings are free, average total cost (equals total fixed costs) is uncovered. On the other hand, if demand exceeds capacity when the facility is free as, for example, occurs when the demand curve is D_1, it is necessary to charge a price or toll if Paretian optimality is to be achieved. If the demand curve is D_1, the appropriate marginal charge per crossing is p_1.

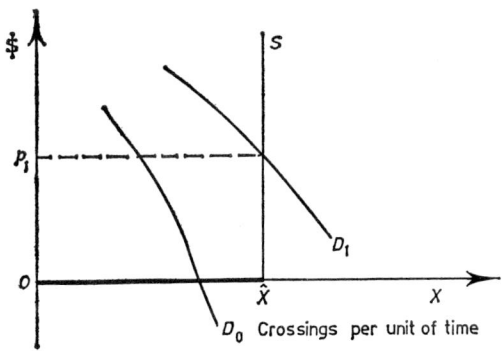

Fig. 21.5

The finite capacity assumption which is employed in Fig. 21.5 involves an abstraction. In practice, as the number of crossings per unit of time increases, the probability of delay increases so that a rather more complicated model is needed to deal with this sophistication. Also, even if demand exceeds capacity, it might not be optimal to charge a toll if the excess is small because the cost of collection might exceed the revenue. But, on the whole, these matters might be regarded as minor. The position is much more complicated if goods are of a type which does not permit exclusion. Many goods which are produced by public enterprise are of this type so let us consider the optimal supply of these.

B. PUBLIC SUPPLY OF GOODS IN THE ABSENCE OF EXCLUSION

Pure public or collective goods form a special class. A pure public good (commodity) has the property that any individual's consumption of it leads to no reduction in its possible consumption by others, and the exclusion of others from the enjoyment of the good (commodity) is impossible or uneconomical. The classic example is that of a lighthouse, cited on p. 379. In general it is impossible or uneconomical to make its use dependent on a price payment. Another example is that of flood mitigation in a river valley. The residents of a river valley may all gain from a flood-mitigation reservoir in the headwaters of their river. Gain from flood control by one resident does not preclude gain nor reduce the possible gain by another, and benefits to an individual cannot be made dependent on a price payment.

While *pure* public goods are rare, many goods produced by the state have partial characteristics of pure public goods. Exclusion may be impossible or only partial and the supply of the commodity and its consumption by one individual may still leave some "spin-off" consumption for others. For example, private protection and security measures may primarily benefit the person providing these for his personal use but there may be *some* "spin-off" to others in that crime may become less profitable and less prevalent. The spin-off is an external effect. To some extent, the problems raised by pure public goods arise in these cases. These problems do not arise with private consumption goods. In the case of a private consumption commodity, one individual's consumption of the commodity is at the expense of that of another and exclusion is possible. Bread, for example, falls in this category.

While private consumption goods can be supplied by perfectly competitive markets in optimal quantities, this is not so for pure public goods. In the absence of government supply of pure public goods, they are liable not to be supplied at all (even if there is a social case for their supply) or not to be supplied in optimal quantities.

To illustrate this, consider a simple example. Imagine two individuals who are able to produce two types of goods, one a private consumption commodity and the other a pure public commodity. Assume, too, that the transformation function of the private commodity into the public commodity is linear and is the same for both individuals. Furthermore, for simplicity's sake, assume that the indifference map which indicates preferences for the possible combinations of the quantities of the private and the public goods is the same for both individuals. Fig. 21.6 illustrates the transformation possibilities available to one individual and his preferences. X_1 represents the quantity of the public commodity and X_2 the quantity of the private commodity; I_0, I_1 and I_2 indicate some of the selected individual's indifference curves and his product transformation frontier passes through DE. Thus, if each individual acts *independently* of the other, each produces the combination at E. Consequently, each individual has $\bar{X}_2$ of the private commodity available to him and $2\bar{X}_1$ of the public commodity: his own output plus that of the other individual. Hence, there is disequilibrium *ex post facto*. The optimal composition of production does not occur.

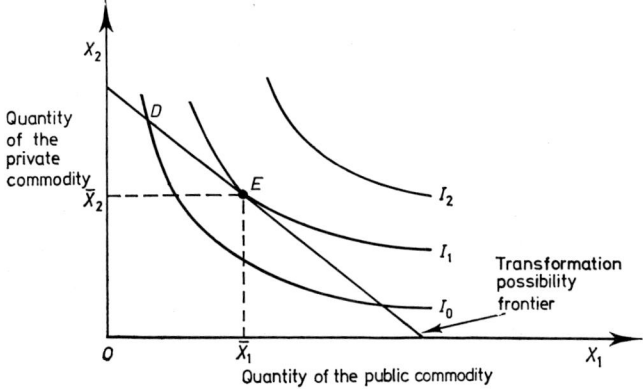

Fig. 21.6

The optimal composition of production can be found by using marginal evaluation curves. An individual's marginal evaluation curve shows the quantity of the private commodity which the individual is willing to forgo for additional units of the public commodity as the supply of the public commodity is increased by moving along the transformation frontier. Mathematically, its value for any level of output of the public commodity is equal to the slope of the individual's indifference curve for the corresponding output combination on the frontier. For example, the marginal evaluation for $\bar{X}_1$ in Fig. 21.6 is equal to the slope of I_1 at point E. In the usual case, one expects an individual's marginal evaluation curve to be decreasing. For example, it might be like the marginal evaluation curve shown in Fig. 21.7. In this diagram marginal costs of the public good in terms of the private good are represented by the curve MC. If each individual acts in *isolation*, he finds that it is optimal to produce $\bar{X}_1$ of the public commodity. Consequently, $2\bar{X}_1$ of the public commodity is produced and afterwards each individual finds that this production is greater than optimal. Thus one individual might discontinue production of the public commodity in the

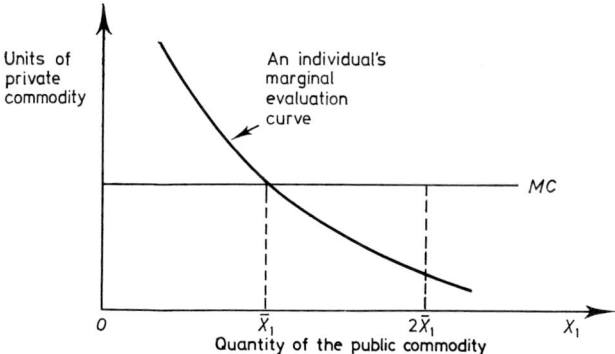

Fig. 21.7

hope that the other continues to produce $\bar{X}_1$ of it. If his hope is justified, the non-producer obtains a free ride and each, given the actions of the other, is optimising. *But the production of only $\bar{X}_1$ of the public commodity does not yield a social optimum.*

The optimal supply of the public commodity is the quantity which equates the *summed* marginal evaluations to the marginal cost of producing the public commodity. The *combined* marginal quantity of the private commodity which individuals are prepared to forgo for an additional unit of the public commodity should be equated to the marginal cost of the public commodity. Or, put differently, *the rates of indifferent substitution of the public for the private commodity summed for all individuals should be equal to the technical rate of substitution of these goods otherwise a Paretian optimum is not attained.* The summation is appropriate because of the extreme externality which arises from the availability of a pure public commodity.

In the example shown in Fig. 21.8, the optimal level of output of the public commodity is X_1^*. The curve AC is the marginal evaluation curve of individual 1, which is also equal to that for individual 2, and the sum of the marginal evaluation curves

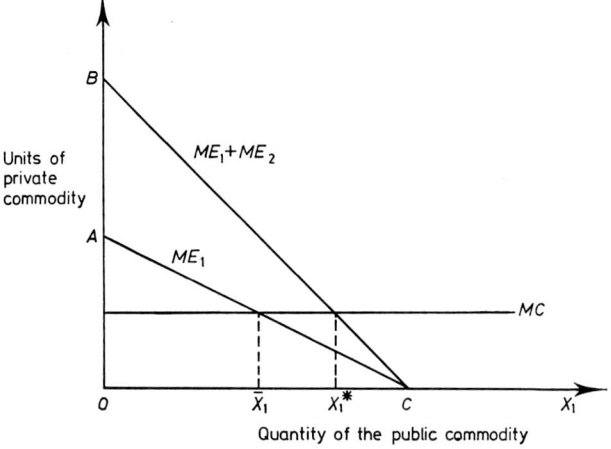

Fig. 21.8

is BC. BC equals the marginal cost of producing the public commodity if the quantity of output is X_1^*. Chances are that, unless each individual expects the other to produce the public commodity, some of the public commodity will be produced but not an optimal quantity. If each tries to free-ride, none of the public commodity might be produced.

However, in other circumstances and in the absence of governmental intervention it is *certain* that none of the public commodity will be produced even though its production is required for Paretian optimality. This, for example, is illustrated by the case which is shown in Figs 21.9 and 21.10. The same general position is assumed as before. Figure 21.9 indicates the preferences of one of the individuals for quantities of the private and public commodities and shows his transformation possibility frontier for the private and the public commodity. His optimal combination is at E, which implies that he produces none of the public commodity. The same is true for the second individual. The marginal evaluation curve of both might be like AC in Fig. 21.10. AC is below MC (marginal cost) throughout its whole length and maximum benefit occurs as far as the individual acting in isolation is concerned at $X_1 = 0$. Each individual, acting within his own sphere, finds that it is optimal to produce none of the public commodity. But the addition of their marginal evaluation curves reveals that an output of X_1^* is optimal. If X_1^* of the public commodity is produced, the summed marginal evaluations equal the marginal cost of producing the public commodity. Thus, even though no individual in isolation would find it worthwhile to produce or contribute to the production of the public commodity, its production is socially optimal in a community.

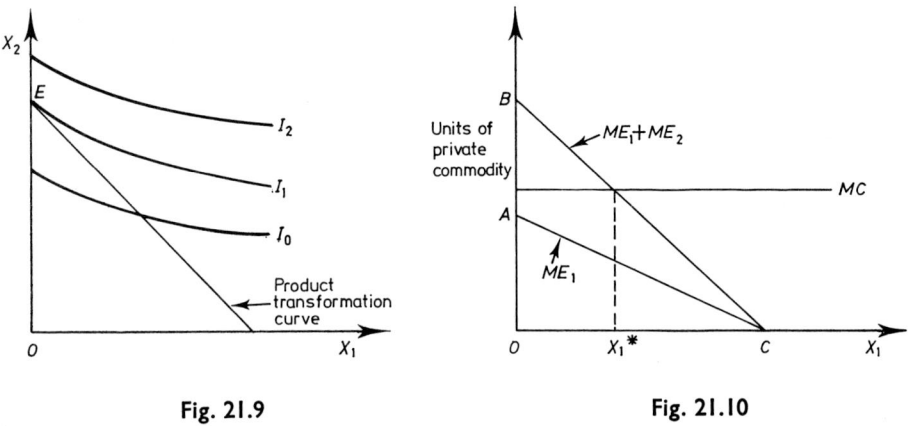

Fig. 21.9   Fig. 21.10

Each individual knows that his benefits from public goods are (practically) independent of his contribution and, hence, he cannot be relied upon to make a voluntary contribution. Where a social benefit accrues from provision of the public commodity, the government must step in and see that it is supplied and that individuals contribute to its supply. Compulsory contributions are required to avoid the free-rider problem. The supply of the public commodity and the actual contributions of individuals to its supply are then determined within the political arena and outside the free market. Nevertheless, the social principles which are enunciated above remain relevant.

The above models have been cast in real terms. Under certain conditions, they can be recast in money terms. The marginal evaluation curve of each individual then shows the value of private goods which the individual is prepared to forgo for additional units of the public commodity, or the maximum price which an individual would be prepared to pay for additional units of the public commodity. Individual demand curves for the public commodity, when added *vertically*, give the value of the summed marginal evaluation curves. In the case of private consumption goods, individual demand curves are added *horizontally* to obtain the aggregate demand curve. To obtain conformity, marginal cost is merely stated in money terms. The optimal supply of the public commodity is then the quantity which equates the summed marginal evaluation (expressed in money terms) of the public commodity to its marginal cost.

III. Cost-Benefit Analysis: Dynamic Factors

Cost-benefit analysis refers to techniques which can be sometimes used by governments to make systematic allocation decisions. Normally, the techniques take explicit account of time, a factor which was neglected in the static models discussed above. But, as we shall see, there is no universal method of treating the time-flows of benefits and costs.

Cost-benefit analysis can be regarded as a part of the general theory of capital budgeting. But its application to government rather than to private planning involves special difficulties. Cost and benefits are more complex in government undertakings. Let us, therefore, first consider some alternative approaches to capital budgeting or production planning over time and then the difficulties of evaluating cost and benefits for government undertakings.

A. ALTERNATIVE METHODS OF TREATING THE TIME-FLOW OF COSTS AND BENEFITS

A number of different criteria have been applied to the problem of choosing between projects with different cash flows. Four criteria deserve mention since they have sometimes been applied to public cost-benefit decisions. These are:

   (i) the pay-back or pay-out;
   (ii) the total return per dollar of outlay;
   (iii) the marginal efficiency or internal rate of return; and
   (iv) the discounted present value or discounted cash flow.

Consider each of these in turn.

The *pay-back or pay-out criterion* ranks projects according to the speed with which they repay the original investment. Projects which repay the original investment or outlay in the shortest period of time are preferred. Given a fixed amount of initial capital, projects are ranked in descending order of preference as their pay-back period becomes longer and projects are selected from the top of the list until the capital is exhausted.

But this is a crude rule of thumb. It ignores the flow of returns beyond the pay-back period and does not take account of the receipt pattern within the pay-back period. No account is taken of the possibility that some projects involve capital outlays in other than the initial period. Thus this criterion ignores much of the time pattern and, indeed, some of the net benefits from projects.

The total return per dollar of outlay criterion weighs up all costs and benefits but fails to make any allowance for the timing of these. Let R_j represent the sum of the net benefits (receipts or total benefits less cost) over the lifetime of the project and let K_j indicate the initial investment which is required in project j. Projects with the highest R_j/K_j values, those with the highest net return per dollar of initial investment, are preferred. Thus, if initial funds are limited, projects are ranked in descending order of preference, those with highest R_j/K_j values being preferred, and funds are allocated to those projects with the highest ratios until funds are exhausted.

This criterion takes no account of time. For example, it ranks the following projects or investments equally: imagine that both involve an initial investment of $1,000. At the end of one year, project 1 returns $100 net and the original $1,000 of capital and gives no other returns. Project 2 only involves a cash flow at the 100th year

Government and Resource Allocation

when it returns $100 net and the original $1,000. Clearly, it is unsatisfactory to rank these projects equally. A considerable return on capital is forgone in the latter case— the return which the individual might have earned by investing the capital elsewhere at the going rate of interest. The present discounted value criterion takes full account of the time-pattern and the alternatives forgone. But before examining this criterion, let us consider a closely related one, the marginal efficiency of investment criterion.

The marginal efficiency of an investment project is equal to that rate of interest which renders the discounted present value of the project's yields exactly equal to its initial investment cost. Or it is the rate of interest required to reduce the operating benefits plus realisation value of assets *less* operating costs and capital costs to zero. All costs and benefits are assumed to be stated in money terms. In the case of a firm, the benefits are equal to its revenues.

The *marginal efficiency or internal rate of return criterion* indicates that an investment should be undertaken as long as its marginal efficiency exceeds the rate of interest. Then there is a surplus or profit after the payment of interest (or after allowance for the interest forgone by not lending the capital sum involved). Provided that funds are in unlimited supply at the going interest rate, the projects selected by the marginal efficiency criterion and the discounted present value criterion as desirable investments do not differ. But if capital supplies are limited, and this is very common, their recommendations are not the same and the marginal efficiency criterion can be misleading.

Let us examine this last proposition. Taking any project, let $B(t)$ indicate the gross benefits from it in period t and $C(t)$ represent its costs in period t. If the life of the project or the planning interval extends over n periods beyond the initial period, and letting i represent the rate of interest, the present discounted value or capitalised value of the project is

$$V = \sum_{t=0}^{n} \frac{B(t) - C(t)}{(1+i)^t} \tag{21.1}$$

where $C(0)$ is the initial investment in the project, and all benefits, including salvage receipts or terminal values of the project, and all operating costs are included in the expression. Clearly V, the discounted present value of the project, is a decreasing function of i, the rate of interest. (If one is uncertain of the discounted present value concept, it might be worthwhile to refer to the beginning of Chapter 16).

The discounted present value of net benefits (V) from a project as a function of i might trace out a curve like that shown in Fig. 21.11. If the interest charge is 0.05, the present value of this project is $y and at an interest charge of 0.1, the present value is zero dollars. Thus the marginal efficiency of this project is 10 per cent. If the rate of interest is less than 10 per cent and capital is freely available at the going interest rate, the project is profitable and should be undertaken according to the marginal efficiency criterion.

But if capital is limited at the going interest rate, the procedure of selecting projects with the highest marginal efficiency of capital until all funds are allocated can be less than optimal. For example, assume that two independent projects A and B are available and let V_A and V_B represent their respective present values as a function of the rate of interest. For the example shown in Fig. 21.12, the curves of these present values as a function of i intersect. Imagine that both projects involve an identical

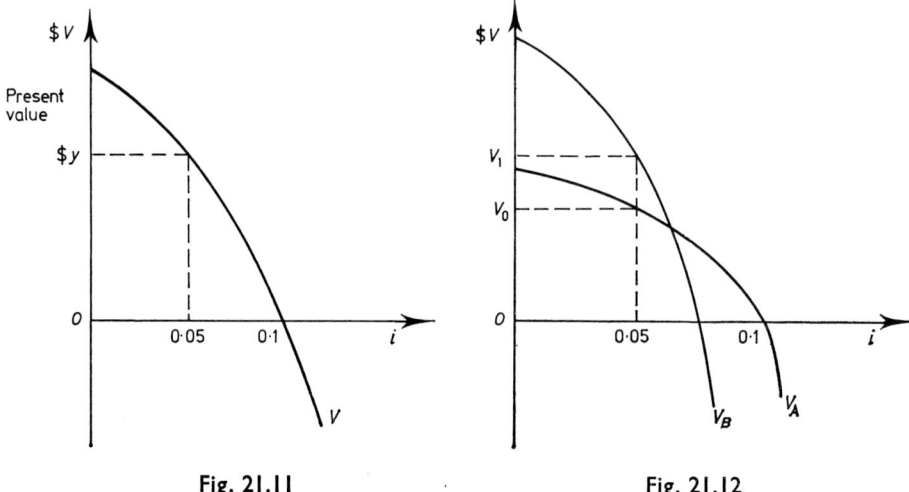

Fig. 21.11   Fig. 21.12

capital outlay and that there is just sufficient capital to proceed with one of the projects. Project A has a marginal efficiency of 10 per cent and project B a marginal efficiency of 7.5 per cent. Thus it might seem that project A is the optimal choice. But at low interest rates the present value of project B exceeds that of A. For example, if the interest rate is 5 per cent, the present value of project B is V_1 which exceeds V_0, the present value of project A. It seems reasonable that the project with the greatest present value should be preferred and not the one with the highest marginal efficiency of capital. If the capital market operates tolerably well, then the project with the greater present value can give the same net returns in time as the other and, on some occasions, more besides.[6] But, of course, this point of view is not applicable to all public investment since much of it has little or no market-realisable value at all. This is a matter which will be discussed later. But the interest rate (or adjusted interest rate) indicates the return on capital in the economy if used elsewhere and thus present values allow for the alternatives forgone.

The present value or discounted cash flow criterion indicates that funds ought to be allocated so as to maximise the overall present value of net returns from investment. The criterion implies (i) that only such projects should be considered which have a non-negative net present value and (ii) that, if funds are limited, projects with the highest discounted benefit to discounted cost ratios should be given preference. If there is no restriction on borrowing, all projects which have a positive present value should be undertaken. These are also projects for which

$$\frac{\text{discounted benefit}}{\text{discounted cost}} > 1. \qquad (21.2)$$

If funds are limited in the initial period and projects do not make additional demands on capital (that is if they are self-financing beyond the initial period) then allocation of the available funds to the projects with the highest discounted benefit-cost ratios should maximise the present value of the funds. This assumes that lumpiness in the size of investment projects is not a problem, for example, if the project with the highest benefit-cost ratio requires more than the available funds, one clearly must

Government and Resource Allocation

move down the ladder and look for the next-best combination which satisfies the availability of fund restriction.

There is another complication which can be very worrying in practice. Not all projects are self-financing beyond the initial period. Additional capital sometimes has to be found at a later date and new scarcities of funds might exist then. This must affect the evaluation procedure and the simple selection of projects by giving preferences to those with the highest benefit-cost ratios may be inadequate. The problem can be handled mathematically, but the above simple algorithm is inadequate.

It has been assumed implicitly that each project involves a unique cost and initial investment. While this might be approximately true for some undertakings, costs are variable in others and may have a variable influence on benefits. Yet even in these circumstances and taking account of calculation costs and difficulties, continuous variation possibilities might be profitably approximated by a number of discrete possibilities. Returns from each project might be calculated at a few discrete levels of investment and each level treated as a different project.

Nevertheless, there is nothing in principle which prevents a consideration of continuous variation. If discounted net returns are a function of initial investment and diminishing marginal returns are the case, the present value of initial funds which can be invested is only maximised if these are allocated so as to equalise the marginal discounted net benefits from all undertakings which have a discounted net benefit. But this is subject to the provision that no investment in a project should proceed so far as to make its marginal discounted net benefit less than zero.

Consider the following example. Imagine that only two alternative projects, 1 and 2, are available and that the discounted value of each is a continuous and differentiable function of the initial investment C_0. The present value of project 1 is

$$V_1 = V_1(C_{01}) \quad \text{where } V_1'' < 0 \tag{21.3}$$

and C_{01} is the initial outlay on project 1. Similarly, the present value of project 2 is

$$V_2 = V_2(C_{02}) \quad \text{where } V_2'' < 0. \tag{21.4}$$

Given that the total available funds are K in the initial period, the problem is to maximise

$$\Lambda = V_1 + V_2 \tag{21.5}$$

subject to

$$C_{01} + C_{02} \leqslant K. \tag{21.6}$$

This is satisfied if funds are allocated so that

$$C_{01}' = C_{02}' \geqslant 0 \tag{21.7}$$

and no more than the available funds are allocated to the projects.

Fig. 21.13 illustrates the optimal allocation of initial funds for the marginal discounted net benefits shown. If $K = \bar{C}_{01} + \bar{C}_{02}$, initial funds are optimally allocated if $\bar{C}_{01}$ is allocated to project 1 and the remainder to project 2. Marginal discounted returns are equal and positive. But if $K > \hat{C}_{01} + \hat{C}_{02}$, it is most profitable to allocate only $\hat{C}_{01}$ to project 1 and $\hat{C}_{02}$ to project 2 and to invest the remainder at the going rate of interest.

This is a particular example. In other cases the situation might be more complicated. For example, discontinuities might occur in the benefit and cost functions. A variety of benefit-cost relations may arise from time to time and require the use of diverse

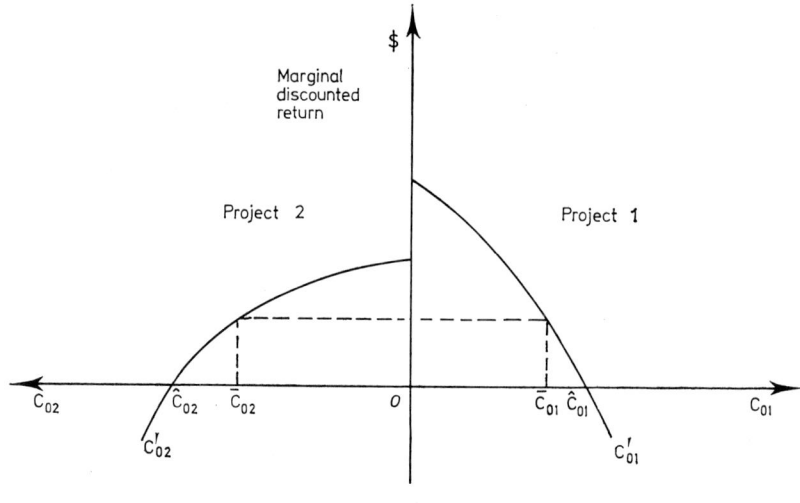

Fig. 21.13

mathematical methods for finding a maximum of present value of net returns. But irrespective of the mathematical technique which must be used to find an optimum, the present value criterion remains unchanged; that is, one should *adopt the strategy which, taking account of restrictions if any, maximises the present value of one's economic plans.*

B. DIFFICULTIES IN APPLYING COST-BENEFIT ANALYSIS TO PUBLIC INVESTMENT DECISIONS

All the criteria outlined in Section A involve evaluation of cost and benefits, all can be regarded as a part of cost-benefit analysis and all are capable of being applied and, at times, have been applied to public investment decisions. Yet the first three criteria have defects which only the present value criterion avoids. Thus, it is assumed that the present value criterion is likely to be most relevant to public investment decisions. Nevertheless, all criteria have the value that they call for a consideration of specific cost and benefits involved in projects and this at least gives a basis for rational choice.

This is not to suggest either that cost-benefit analysis can be applied to public expenditure decisions easily or that it avoids matters of judgement. Usually, the technique is much easier to apply in private enterprise since money receipts, and cost, and the resulting flow of net income or profit are of central concern. Benefits and costs are readily identified and only private returns matter to the firm. On the other hand, a government needs to take account of the overall benefits and costs of its undertakings to society and not all of these can be readily and objectively expressed in terms of money. Social benefits cannot be measured by the market value of the goods provided since some goods (collective goods) command no market price, although they do have value and there may be other market shortcomings and some benefits may be in terms of non-economic goods or a more favourable distribution of income.

Let us consider the problems of applying the technique to public investment and expenditure decisions systematically. Four main areas of concern might be distinguished:

(i) difficulties of defining and valuing benefits and costs;

(ii) problems of allowing for uncertainty and inadequacies of data;

(iii) the question of choosing the relevant discount rate; and

(iv) deciding on and allowing for the appropriate constraints on cost-benefit decisions.

Consider (i) *difficulties of defining and valuing benefits and costs*. Since the price mechanism does not function perfectly, it is often difficult to assign prices which adequately reflect social values of commodities. While market prices can sometimes be used to value the costs and benefits from projects, frequently these must be adjusted to allow for distortions in markets. First, prices outside the public sector are influenced by monopolistic practices and, furthermore, many prices are affected by governmental interference in the pricing system via subsidies, taxes, tariffs, etc. Therefore, existing prices may not correctly represent opportunity costs. Market prices may have to be adjusted if they are to be used in the valuation of public benefit and cost. Also, if non-marginal changes occur in prices as a result of government investment, some approximation needs to be made for the change in consumers' surpluses, for example, the value of the output might be assessed at a price per unit which is intermediate between the original price and the subsequent price of a product. Furthermore, if government services are provided free (for example, roads and schools in an irrigation development) a cost must be imputed to these. Again, if a subsidy is paid on produce, the output of which is to be increased by a public scheme, the extra output, in the absence of externalities, ought not be valued at the price paid to producers since this includes the subsidy and so exceeds marginal cost.

Secondly, in decreasing cost industries, extra profits do not adequately reflect the benefits of extra production. As was shown earlier,[7] if a price is charged which equates average revenue to the marginal cost of output, the activity may show a loss. This is so even though the value of output to consumers, as indicated by the maximum amount which they would be willing to pay for the product rather than go without it altogether, exceeds the total cost of its production. Once the commodity is produced, and an excess of this maximum over total cost might indicate that it ought to be produced, the Hotelling-Lerner output yields a Paretian optimum. (This is subject to qualifications mentioned earlier.) In these cases, it is necessary to obtain an approximation of the changes in consumers' surplus occasioned by the production. This may be comparatively easy if multipart pricing is possible.

Thirdly, some goods, collective or pure public goods, are not capable of being marketed, so that it is very difficult to impute a value to their production. For example, how does one value increased expenditure upon defence? But not all government expenditure falls in the pure or near pure public commodity category. Thus cost-benefit analysis can still be used for assessing the economic value of, for example, projects for power generation, roads, railroads, dams and water projects and even, despite increased difficulties, provision of educational and health facilities.

But even for public expenditures where the cost-benefit technique can be applied, externalities are liable to be important and difficult to evaluate. Nevertheless, if externalities differ significantly in value from project to project, account needs to be taken of these.

o

Fourthly, if involuntary unemployment exists the private cost of extra employment exceeds its social cost. Prest and Turvey suggest

> When there is an excess of supply at the current market price of any input that price overstates the social cost of using that input. Furthermore, when there is general unemployment, expenditure upon a project by creating a multiplier effect, will create additional real incomes in the rest of the economy. Hence, the use of market values to ascertain direct costs and benefits of a project overstates its social costs and underestimates its total benefits (by the amount of "induced benefits").[8]

But we must be cautious. If all projects have similar induced benefits, induced benefits will not be important for choosing between them.

In practice, in assessing net benefits, one must be careful to avoid double-counting. For example, one must not measure net direct benefits from a public project by combining the increased profits to enterprises with the increased value of properties which are affected. Increases in the value of properties reflect increases in their expected earnings.

In assessing social benefits and costs, there are often non-economic or intangible factors to take into account. For example, if individual self-reliance is valued, how does a project affect this and what allowance ought to be made for it? Factors of this kind can be important, but it seems best to calculate net costs and benefits of these separately and bring them in at the interpretation stage. The same might be said for the effect of projects on the distribution of income. Should not benefits be weighted depending upon their influence on the distribution of income? Might it not be reasonable to give a higher weight to benefits which accrue to those on lower incomes than to those which accrue to individuals on higher incomes. In the final analysis, benefits and costs need to be interpreted in the light of their influence upon the distribution of income. But once again it seems preferable that calculations should be *first* made without weights for the income distribution factor if only because the weights which different individuals find appropriate are often not the same.

Uncertainties of various kinds also make it difficult to value benefits. The future demand for products whose production is affected by a project may be uncertain and the life of some projects may be uncertain. Let us therefore consider (ii) *problems of allowing for uncertainty and inadequacies of data.*

In the public sector, as in the private field, data gathering and processing involve expenditure and any additional expected benefits from improvements on this score need to be balanced against additional costs. A public agency is likely to have imperfect data, and in any case it is rarely optimal to seek perfect data even if the goal is attainable. Only too often the goal is unattainable. Future benefit and costs cannot as a rule be perfectly predicted. There is a need to take account of uncertainty in some systematic way.

One crude method is to state costs and benefits for a few alternative predictions of the most important variables, for example, agricultural prices for products affected by an irrigation scheme. One might even attach probabilities to the alternatives but eventually leave the risk-takers or decision-makers of governments to make the final choice. At least, the main alternative possibilities can be simply communicated by this method.

Other methods of allowing for uncertainty also exist. For example,

Government and Resource Allocation

(a) some certainty equivalence method might be used,
(b) the planning horizon might be shortened to allow for uncertainty, or
(c) the discount rate might be biased upward to take account of increased uncertainty.

The first of these methods seems intellectually most satisfactory, but encounters problems in obtaining data and can involve high calculation costs. The other two have definite defects which make them dangerous and indeed inferior, in my opinion, to the simple approximate method mentioned above.

Consider (a) *certainty equivalence methods of allowing for uncertainty.* These involve preference ordering of the relevant characteristics belonging to the probability distribution of present discounted values of net benefits. The characteristics which the relevant decision-maker feels are important might vary. Some decision-makers might believe that the mode and the range of discounted net benefits are important, others prefer the mean and the variance of discounted net benefits, and there are still additional possibilities. (Under certain circumstances the relevant moments of the probability distribution can be inferred from a decision-maker's von Neumann-Morgenstern utility function, if it is known.[9])

To illustrate the method, imagine that the decision-maker's preference function U is

$$U = U(m, \sigma^2) \qquad (21.8)$$

where m is the mean of the *present value* of net benefits and σ^2 is the variance of present value of net benefits. Any project has a particular m and σ^2 value which can be used (if the decision-maker's preference function is known) to find the certain present sum which is equivalent to this uncertain prospect in the eyes of the decision-maker. This certainty equivalent sum, if estimated for each project, can be used to rank them by discounted cash flow methods outlined earlier.

In Fig. 21.14, for example, a set of indifference curves, I_0, I_1, I_2, I_3 is shown which indicates combinations of the mean and variance values of present discounted net benefits which the decision-maker finds to be a matter of indifference. In this case,

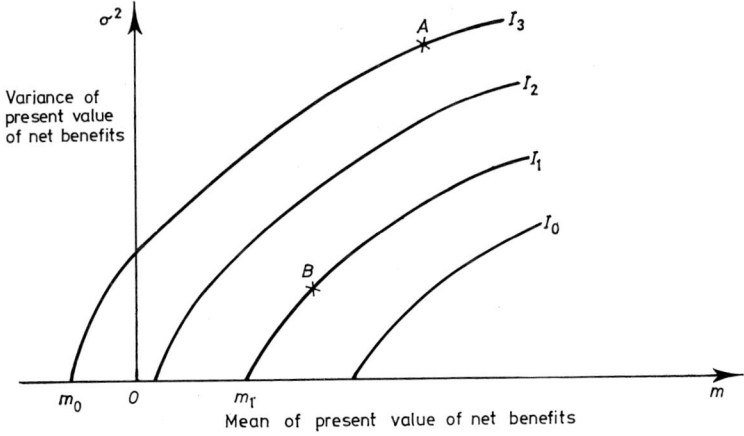

Fig. 21.14

the decision-maker is a risk-averter. He is unprepared to accept an increased variance if the mean present benefit is not increased.

Take two projects, A and B. Let point A, in Fig. 21.14, represent the (mean, variance) combination corresponding to project A and let B represent the corresponding combination for project B. Project A has a greater mean present value but a greater variance than B. The certainty equivalent value which corresponds to A is m_0 and to B, m_1. Since m_0 is negative, project A should not be undertaken. B shows a positive discounted present net benefit after allowing for risk and, if funds are available at the going rate of interest, ought to be adopted. The way in which the method can be used is fairly clear. A basic problem, however, is how to derive the relevant risk preference functions.[10] Possibilities of learning may also create complications for the analysis.[11]

Sometimes (b) *the planning horizon might be shortened to allow for uncertainty.* This can have a systematic basis. For example, the variance of present net benefits might increase with time and the mean of discounted benefits might decrease (due to the discounting) so that certainty equivalent net values of distant sums are likely to be zero or negative. But, sometimes, the shortening is quite arbitrary. An arbitrary shortening may exclude projects which give very high returns towards the end of their life and indeed involve less uncertainty than in the beginning.

Also (c) *the discount rate might be biased upward to take account of increased uncertainty*, that is, sometimes an allowance is made for uncertainty by adding a premium to the interest rate and using the resulting rate as a discount factor. Again, this method can lead to abuses if the premium is arbitrary and varied from project to project depending on the whim of individuals. The effect of adding the premium is to make the discount for uncertainty a regular compounding function of time. Although such an allowance goes some way towards typifying the general situation that uncertainty is likely to be greater the more distant are the costs and benefits, it is no more than approximation which might be quite misleading in some instances, for example, those in which uncertainty decreases after a time.

Nothing has been said about (iii) *the question of choosing the relevant discount rate for discounting net returns from public projects*, except that the interest rate might be adjusted in some instances to allow for uncertainty. But what is the market interest rate and just how applicable is it to public investment decisions?

Because of market imperfections, no single interest rate prevails in the capital market and so it is difficult to determine the risk-free interest rate. But a choice of an interest rate needs to be made somehow. In practice, the interest rate on long-term government bonds is often used for discounting public costs and benefits. But this interest rate might not correctly indicate the social opportunity cost of capital. The marginal *expected* (that is mean) return on capital in the private sector may exceed the government long-term bond rate because of the lower security of capital invested there. Thus if funds are allocated between the private and public sector using this criterion, the marginal productivity of capital in the public sector is likely to be lower than in the private. The return from employed capital is, therefore, not maximised. Hence, the appropriate rate for discounting public projects might be somewhat in excess of the long-term bond rate.

On the other hand, Pigou[12] and others contend that "social time preference attaches more weight to the future than private time preference and that it is the former which is relevant for determining the allocation of society's current resources between investment and consumption".[13] The appropriate interest rate for discounting net returns from public projects might be appropriately less than the market interest rate. But in the absence of government action to depress the market rate generally to the social rate, the use of a lower interest rate by the public sector involves a lower marginal return on capital in the public sector than that in the private and thus the returns from employed capital are not maximised. Furthermore, Pigou's argument is far from uncontentious. It involves value judgements about the desirable distribution of income between generations.

Thus it can be seen that there is room for disagreeing about the appropriate interest rate. Yet no one denies that a discount rate is necessary for a rational decision. Fortunately, the precise discount rate may be unimportant for if funds are limited so that only a few projects can be undertaken, the really optimal projects may remain optimal for slight changes in the discount factor. Thus where capital is really short and uncertainties important, determination of the appropriate interest rate to the last decimal point may be of no practical value at all.

Finally, there are problems of (iv) *deciding on and allowing for appropriate constraints on cost-benefit decisions* in allocating funds. The choice of projects by any governmental agency is likely to be constrained by the limited availability of capital. A government agency is unlikely to be able to obtain any amount of capital which it requires at the going rate of interest because of administrative constraints. As was noted earlier, this creates problems for capital budgeting especially if the availability of capital is liable to vary (uncertainly) over time. Political constraints upon the regional distribution of projects, for example, might also need to be taken into account. All these constraints add to the problems of maximising the present value of benefits because they must eventually be maximised *subject* to these constraints. The actual mathematical procedures for solution, difficulties of specification aside, can become very complex.

Resource allocation problems in the public sphere are a challenge and involve problems running the whole gamut of economising. To many of these problems, we have only tentative answers and to some no satisfying ones at all; for this whole area of economics is in a very experimental stage. The application of cost-benefit analysis to public expenditure does have its limitations and it is well to realise this. Above all its application requires ingenuity and often original thought. It provides no ready-made answers, but that does not make it of little value. The following conclusion to an Australian government publication on cost-benefit analysis seems to sum the position up:

> Yet when all is said, the [present value] technique, properly formulated and wisely used, does possess great advantages over less rigorous approaches, particularly because it does take into account the time-phasing of benefits and costs. With due appreciation of its limitations, it has already provided guidance on a number of large development projects, particularly overseas, but to some extent in Australia also. New projects of their very nature, involve the charting of new territory and an attempt to look into the future. For those reasons, those whose job it is to attempt to evaluate them are compelled to use often rudimentary data and to adopt heroic assumptions; benefit-cost analysis is proving to be a satisfactory way of organising this ostensibly unpromising material.[14]

Possibly one of the best ways to appreciate further the difficulties and prospects for cost-benefit analysis is to consider some of the specific studies which have been completed. Some references to these can be obtained from the reading list for this chapter.

NOTES AND REFERENCES

[1] A. C. PIGOU, *The Economics of Welfare*, 4th ed., Macmillan, London, 1932.
[2] See Chapter 14.
[3] H. HOTELLING, "The General Welfare in Relation to Problems of Taxation and of Railway and Utility Rates", *Econometrica*, 1938, 6, pp. 242-69. Reprinted in A.E.A., *Readings in Welfare Economics*, George Allen and Unwin, London, 1969. A. P. LERNER, *The Economics of Control*, Macmillan, New York, 1944.
[4] This was mentioned in Chapter 14. The problem is discussed by R. G. LIPSEY and K. LANCASTER, "The General Theory of Second-Best", *Review of Economic Studies*, 1956-1957, 24, pp. 11-32.
[5] This statement may need to be modified. For problems raised by the concept of consumers' surplus, see P. SAMUELSON, *Foundations of Economic Analysis*, Harvard University Press, Cambridge, 1947, pp. 206-10. For a discussion of the above criterion, see J. OORT, *Decreasing Costs as a Problem of Welfare Economics*, Drukkerij Holland, Amsterdam, 1958.
[6] This was discussed in Chapter 16.
[7] In Section II of this chapter.
[8] A. R. PREST and R. TURVEY, "Cost-Benefit Analysis: A Survey", in A.E.A. AND ROYAL ECONOMIC SOCIETY, *Surveys of Economic Theory*, Vol. III, Macmillan, London, 1966, pp. 155-207. The quoted passage appears on page 166. Reproduced by permission of St. Martin's Press Inc., The Macmillan Company of Canada and Macmillan, London and Basingstoke.
[9] See, for example, C. TISDELL, *The Theory of Price Uncertainty, Production and Profit*, Princeton University Press, Princeton, 1968, Ch. 2.
[10] Decision-makers within the same organisation may, for example, have conflicting attitudes towards risk-bearing.
[11] See A. G. HART, "Risk, Uncertainty, and the Unprofitability of Compounding Probabilities", in O. LANGE, F. MCINTYRE and F. YNTEMA (Eds), *Studies in Mathematical Economics*, The University of Chicago Press, Chicago, 1942, pp. 110-18.
[12] PIGOU, op. cit. pp. 24-30.
[13] PREST AND TURVEY, op. cit. p. 169.
[14] COMMONWEALTH OF AUSTRALIA, "Investment Analysis", *Supplement to the Treasury Information Bulletin*, July 1966, 7854/66-2 p. 28. Reprinted with the permission of the Australian Government Publishing Service, Canberra.

FURTHER READING

Reading for Section II

BUCHANAN, J., *The Demand and Supply of Public Goods*, Rand McNally, Chicago, 1968.
FLEMING, M., "Production and Price Policy in Public Enterprise", *Economica*, 1950, 17, pp. 1-22.
HEAD, J. G., "Public Goods and Public Policy", *Public Finance*, 1962, 17, pp. 197-221.
HOTELLING, H., "The General Welfare in Relation to Problems of Taxation and of Railway and Utility Rates", *Econometrica*, 1938, 6, pp. 242-69.
LANGE, O., *The Economics of Control*, Macmillan, New York, 1946.
LITTLE, I. M. D., *A Critique of Welfare Economics*, 2nd ed., Oxford University Press, London, 1957, Ch. 11.
SAMUELSON, P. "The Pure Theory of Public Expenditure", *Review of Economics and Statistics*, 1954, 36, pp. 387-9.

Reading for Section III

BAUMOL, W. J., *Economic Theory and Operations Analysis*, 2nd ed., Prentice-Hall, Englewood Cliffs, 1965, Ch. 19.

COMMONWEALTH OF AUSTRALIA, "Investment Analysis", *Supplement to the Treasury Information Bulletin*, July 1966, 7854/66-2, Australian Government Publishing Service, Canberra.

ECKSTEIN, O., "A Survey of the Theory of Public Expenditure", in J. M. BUCHANAN (Ed.), *Public Finances: Needs, Sources, and Utilization*, Princeton University Press, Princeton, 1961.

HINES, L. G. "The Hazards of Benefit-Cost Analysis as a Guide to Public Investment Policy", *Public Finance*, 1962, **17**, pp. 101-19.

McKEAN, R. N., *Efficiency in Government through Systems Analysis*, John Wiley, New York, 1963.

PREST, A. R., and R. TURVEY, "Cost-Benefit Analysis: A Survey", in A.E.A. and ROYAL ECONOMIC SOCIETY, *Surveys of Economic Theory*, Macmillan, London, 1966, Vol. III. pp. 155-207.

MATHEWS, R., *Public Investment in Australia*, Cheshire, Melbourne, 1967, Chs. 7 and 8.

MISHAN, E. J., *Cost-Benefit Analysis*, George Allen and Unwin, London, 1971.

CHAPTER 22

The Operation of Socialist Economies: Some Theories

I. Introduction

It seems logical that our discussion of the state operation of industry should be extended to the case of socialism, the case in which all industry is owned and operated by the state. But there are other reasons also for discussing this topic. The economies of many countries are organised on socialist lines and some thinkers see socialism as the best method for reducing or overcoming scarcity. Some of the earlier proponents of socialism even went so far as to claim that all economic problems would disappear with the advent of socialism. For example, Rosa Luxemburg claimed that "the victory of the working class constitutes the last act of political economy as a science".[1] Yet none of these predictions have proved to be correct so far. The basic economic problem of scarcity continues in socialist countries and they are concerned, like "capitalist" countries, with economic efficiency, economic growth, full employment and the distribution of income. The methods for dealing with these problems may differ but the problems remain.

Marx[2] never presented a blueprint for the operation of socialist economies. The task of exploring the merits of different methods of organising socialist economies has fallen to later economists. Two main rational means of organising socialist economies have been espoused. These are *central direction* on the basis of economic models of interdependence, and organisation via modified *market systems*. But since elements of central direction and of market mechanisms can be blended in many ways, there are, in practice, a large number of alternative procedures for operating socialist economies each with its merits and drawbacks.

Possibly Enrico Barone has the honour of being the first economist to demonstrate that, under ideal conditions in a socialist state, either central direction or perfectly competitive markets can be employed to achieve a Paretian optimum. His mathematical model of the economy is very abstract but his theory is a valuable starting point.

Barone demonstrated in 1908[3] that *given the technical requirements for perfect competition* and the absence of externalities, economic activity in a socialist state is not Paretian optimal, unless it coincides with economic activity which is implied by perfect competition. Paretian optimality in a socialist state requires the same levels of consumption production and economic activity as occur under perfect competition, provided that the distribution of income is the same.

For any distribution of income, there is an allocation of resources in the economy

Socialist Economies

which yields a Paretian optimum. If the technical requirements for perfect competition are satisfied and if externalities are absent, a Paretian optimal allocation of resources can be achieved, in theory, (i) by central orders to produce and combine resources in the optimal way or (ii) by the operation of perfectly competitive markets. Given the same distribution of income, the ideal levels of economic activity are the same in both instances. The Paretian optimal solution is independent of the persons who own the resources.

Drawing out the implications of general equilibrium models of the economy, Barone showed that a Paretian optimal ("rational") allocation of resources could be obtained in principle by fiat or central command. His view contrasted strongly with that of Ludwig von Mises who claimed that a rational allocation of resources in a socialist economy is a *logical* impossibility. The contention of von Mises has been summarised in the following way:

> There being no genuine markets for the means of production (capital and land) ... since they are collectively owned and used and never bought or sold, there can be no pricing them or their services. Hence, ... there can be no economising, because of the absence of a rational price system, but only groping in the dark. Every departure from the private ownership of the means of production is, in fact, a step away from rational economics. "Socialism is the abolition of rational economy".[4]

But von Mises is wrong. Under socialism, even shadow prices for land and capital can be estimated, in principle, by solving general equilibrium models of the economy. Barone pointed out that a central authority could, in principle, impute prices to both inputs and outputs and arrive at a fiat solution which does not differ from the perfectly competitive solution.[5]

But the very immense practical difficulties (practical impossibility) of a centralist ideal solution remained. Barone's model assumes that the central planning body of a socialist state has all the relevant knowledge about production conditions throughout the economy and about the preferences of individuals in the economy. The costs of obtaining this information are ignored and it is assumed to be available far enough in advance to be a basis of action. But even if, by some miracle, the central planning body had this required information, the task of solving the myriad of equations in a realistic general equilibrium model is extremely difficult. Certainly, in Barone's day, before the advent of advanced computer technology, such solutions were beyond practical possibility. However, the situation appeared to be that, although a Paretian optimum might theoretically be achieved under socialism, it was impossible to find the optimum in practice.

Endeavours were then made to show how a social optimum could *in practice* be approached or reached under socialism. Two lines of thought were developed. One relies upon the use of markets, the other upon the use of simplified general equilibrium models in conjunction with computers. Economists, such as Taylor, Lange and Lerner, pioneered market or competitive methods as a means for reaching or approaching a social optimum.[6] The second approach, an outgrowth of work by Leontief[7] and others in the field of input-output analysis, linear programming and activity analysis generally, has been championed in the U.S.S.R. by L. V. Kantorovich, V. V. Novozhilov, Nemchinov,[8] and others and has become a more practical means of planning as a result of improvements in computer technology.

There is no necessity for socialist economies to be operated in either of these ways. Non-systematic methods are often used and a mixture of central direction and market mechanisms may be employed. Neither ideal socialist nor ideal capitalist systems exist. Thus the models need to be interpreted warily. First, alternative centralist solutions to the allocation of resources in a socialist economy are examined. Next, theories of competitive or market socialism are outlined and evaluated.

II. Central Command and Centrally Directed Socialism

While central direction of the economy is not a necessary or unique concomitant of socialism, it is a common feature. Most socialist models, even Lange's, have a helmsman in the form of a central planning authority. But central direction can be exercised in a variety of ways and be more, or less, pervasive.

One extreme possibility is to operate the economy by commands which emanate from a central authority. Here I have in mind a system in which the physical quantities of resources are allocated and employed in response to specific commands about these quantities. Particular quantities of labour, for example, might be ordered to particular regions and particular productive units might be ordered to produce certain physical outputs. But this is not the only command possibility.

Economic agents of the state may be ordered to maximise profit on the basis of prices assigned to factors and goods by the central planning authority. These prices reflect the relative values of commodities in the opinion of the central planning authority and are called *shadow prices*. If the shadow prices are "correctly" calculated and economic agents carry out their orders, the composition of production is the same as that which is desired by the central planning authority. This may, but need not be, a mixture of production which is Paretian optimal from the point of view of consumers. The essential point, however, is that markets are by-passed as computers of relative values and, possibly, the relevant shadow prices are obtained from the solution of a set of general equations which typify the economy.

But a pure command system of either type can fail to be efficient. Commands must be translated into practice and human beings without *incentives* to do so may fail to carry out these plans or obstruct their fulfilment in all those subtle and less subtle ways which are known to us all. Thus, even though targets might be set, it is common under socialism to use material incentives to ensure that individuals are motivated to fulfil plans.

The method of maximising profits by command on the basis of shadow prices is no less effective (under a certain range of theoretical conditions) than direct allocation of all resources by fiat. It has the further advantage that the power of the state does not appear to be as pervasive as it really is and some independence of judgement is left to economic agents. There is also nothing to prevent the direct fiat method being applied to some commodities and the shadow-price and profit-maximising method being employed for the allocation of others.

Both of the above methods differ fundamentally from the competitive or market approach. This approach makes maximum use of markets as computational mechanisms for determining prices and responses to these. Profit maximisation by state enterprises is encouraged but in response to prices which are adjusted to reflect market values and take account of the wishes of consumers. The role of the central planning board is primarily one of making the market system work more efficiently, correcting market deficiencies and stepping-in in those areas in which market failure is inevitable. Though the system has a helmsman there is considerable decentralisation.

Command socialism may be operated in a number of different ways and with the help of various planning techniques.

Possibly the least sophisticated way is for a central planning authority to set physical targets for various outputs according to its feeling, and issue orders for this production, breaking the aggregate down to specific targets for individual productive units. But the targets might be quite incapable of fulfilment because of resource shortages either as a result of shortages of primary resources or of inadequate supplies of intermediate products, that is products required in the production of other goods. In the absence of any systematic review of interdependencies and physical possibilities of the economy, plans are either unlikely to be fulfilled or the goals of the planners may be attained in a less than optimal way. A slightly more sophisticated version of this method involves making a prior check with economic agents as to the feasibility of the targets set for them by the central planning authority. Individual economic agents report on the feasibility of targets set for them prior to the period of the operation of a plan and, in the light of this information, the central planning authority may adjust its plans. Thus by trial and error methods and review, the initial plan may be improved. But the method is cumbersome, individual productive units have an incentive to underestimate their productive potential and the system is not speedy enough to allow a number of checks on revised plans. However, the Soviet Union basically uses this method.

Yet systematic techniques of central planning have been suggested and the adoption of these is being studied by socialist countries such as the U.S.S.R. At this time in history, despite improvements in computers and information gathering, only simplified general interdependence or general equilibrium systems are within the bounds of practical application. Input-output analysis describes one of the simplest general interdependence systems. Slightly more complicated linear programming models and models of activity analysis of the economy are also available. Because these systems require comparatively little information and are not so difficult to solve because of their linearity assumptions, they have been given the most serious consideration by central planners.

Input-output analysis was outlined and discussed in Chapter 12. Input-output analysis simplifies interrelationships in the economy by dealing only with interdependencies of industries as a whole and by assuming linear relationships of a particular kind, namely that inputs are required in fixed proportions to the output of products. Given its particular assumptions, the analysis can take account of overall technological relationships between industries of an economy during a period of time.

If the final demand targets (the required net bill of goods or targets for end-products) are given, input-output analysis enables one, by means of matrix algebra, to determine the overall composition of production, including intermediate production, which is required to meet the targets and to check whether the targets are attainable given limitations which are imposed by the availability of primary inputs. This is, of course, assuming that the assumptions of input-output analysis apply to the economy. The general procedure was outlined in Chapter 12 so I shall not repeat it here.

Under socialism the targets for the end-products of the economy are set by the central planning authority. Having solved the appropriate input-output problem, the central planning authority can issue *orders* to industries to produce certain quantities and instruct each to make certain interindustry deliveries. The targets will all be consistent and attained if the basic structure of the input-output model is consistent with that of the economy.

But the simplification achieved by input-output analysis must be weighed against its shortcomings and one must consider whether it is really too crude an approximation. It is clear that every industry does not require inputs in a fixed proportion to output. Factor proportions may be varied and constant returns do not always prevail. There are also a number of practical difficulties. The gathering of information for and the solution of realistic input-output models is still costly. While the growth of computer technology has been reducing problems of attaining solutions, at the same time new products (new industries) have been arising so that realistic technology matrices are getting larger all the time, and realistic matrices must now be very large which still rules out their solution within the lag available before plans for the economy must be acted upon. More aggregative input-output models can, however, be solved in the requisite time but their value for planning is difficult to gauge. Another problem is that input-output coefficients are liable to differ amongst productive units in the same industry and thus results will differ depending upon the way in which any planned increase of output is distributed in the industry. The emergence of new industries may require guesses to be made about their input-output coefficients and technological progress is likely to call for continual revision of the Leontief technology matrix.

The system of input-output analysis has shortcomings but then so do its alternatives. Even though its recommendations are less than perfect, they might be superior to results achieved by *ad hoc* methods. A real problem, too, is that costs of decision-making must be taken into account. More realistic general interdependence systems involve greater problems in gathering data and for solutions. Does the extra sophistication justify the extra cost? Which approximation procedure is optimal? These are questions which need to be examined but which, I fear, can only be answered in a concrete situation.

Linear programming and general activity analysis, which are discussed in Chapter 15, can also be adopted to portray interconnections in the economy as a whole. In theory, these models can allow for factor-substitution and the choice of alternative techniques. While these approaches still retain linearity assumptions, they require more information and are more difficult to solve than input-output models.

Either direct orders for the production of particular quantities of products and the adoption of particular techniques may be based on the solution of these models *or* the central planning authority may use the models to determine its appropriate shadow prices for commodities. Productive units may be ordered to maximise profit on these shadow prices. In consequence, the bill of goods desired by the central planning authority may eventuate. Thus two alternative techniques of systematic realisation of control plans *seem* to exist. Considering the second method Kohler says,

> As Koopmans, for instance, has shown, such prices [i.e. appropriate shadow prices] would be rational in exactly the same sense as the prices of a perfectly competitive economy under identical circumstances of demand and technology. Once proper relative [shadow] prices for all outputs and primary factors have been established the execution of the plan might well follow monetary incentives

without direct central supervision. Firms making losses would indicate that they are misusing society's resources to produce something worth less [as evaluated by the central planning authority] than the opportunity of something else forgone (which is reflected in the cost of properly evaluated resources). By attempting to maximise profits, firms would in fact choose the correct technologies in producing whatever the *Central Planning Board is demanding of them*.[9]

Yet the "decentralised" method of shadow prices plus profit maximisation is not always capable of ensuring that the (feasible) targets of the central planning authority are fulfilled. It is not always an alternative to direct commands to resource holders, which specify the physical use of their resources. It is important to establish conditions under which the two methods are alternatives and others under which they are not, for the impression is too often given that the methods are always alternatives, that is that production goals which can be achieved by one method can also be attained by the other. Let us first consider circumstances in which direct command and the shadow price method are alternatives and then circumstances in which this is not so. Simple models, but ones not limited by linearity assumptions, will be used to illustrate the main points.

Consider the production possibility frontier for a productive unit (firm) of an economy assuming that the unit has a given quantity of factors. To what extent is it possible to manipulate the production of that unit by the shadow price method? If it is impossible for the central planning authority to vary the output of *individual* productive units in accordance with its desires by using shadow prices and profit maximisation, it is impossible for the authority to vary aggregate output in accord with its wishes. We shall see that the scope which the authority has for controlling production of any firm by the method of shadow prices depends upon whether the firm's production possibility *set* is *strictly* convex, convex but not *strictly* so, or non-convex in its efficiency frontier. Full control of efficient production is ensured in the first case, but not in the other cases. Indeed, in the last circumstance, it may be *impossible* to achieve an efficient production goal of the central authority by the shadow price and profit maximisation approach.

In Fig. 22.1, the production possibility set of a firm is indicated by the hatched figure and the set is strictly convex in its efficiency frontier. The firm is assumed to be in a position to produce two products, 1 and 2, the quantities per unit of time being indicated by x_1 and x_2 respectively. Any bundle of production which the central planning authority requires on the firm's efficiency frontier can be achieved with certainty by ordering directly that this bundle be produced *or* by setting suitable shadow prices and ordering or encouraging the firm to maximise profit. The applicability of the last method follows from some important properties of sets (and indeed the results of the appendices to Chapter 6 and 7 are very relevant to this discussion of control by shadow prices and enable the discussion to be extended). Since the production set of the firm is convex, every boundary point of it has at least one supporting hyperplane which implies in this context that an isoprofit line could support it there. (Here, a supporting hyperplane is a straight line with the property that it passes only through boundary points of the production possibility set.) But since the set is *strictly* convex in its efficiency frontier, the hyperplanes supporting the set at one point of the frontier are *different* from those supporting it at any other point on this frontier. This implies that the isoprofit lines corresponding to these supporting hyperplanes arise from different sets of relative prices for the products. If the central planning authority suitably selects shadow prices, its desired combination of production is reached when the firm reaches its highest attainable isoprofit line—a hyperplane which supports the production set at the desired output and *only* at the desired output. This is illustrated in Fig. 22.1. Assume that the central planning authority desires the firm to produce combination D. The production set is supported at D by the hyperplane MN. By setting p_1/p_2, the relative shadow prices of the products, equal to the absolute slope of MN, and ordering the firm to maximise profit, combination D, the combination *desired by the central planning authority* results and no other.[10] Possibly consumers do not desire to purchase the combination at D at the shadow prices which ensure its production. They may, for example, wish to purchase the combination at E which means a relative shortage of product 1 from their point of view. But if the authority decides that prices are to ration out D, the relative price of product 1 to consumers may be made higher than the relative shadow price for producers, for example, by imposing differential turnover taxes on the products as is done in the U.S.S.R. Yet as was pointed out in the appendix to Chapter 5, that depending upon the convex nature of indifference curves, consumers cannot *always* be manipulated by prices to purchase any combination of products which a central authority may desire. This is not to deny that there is great scope for control by this method but merely to caution that it is not universally effective.

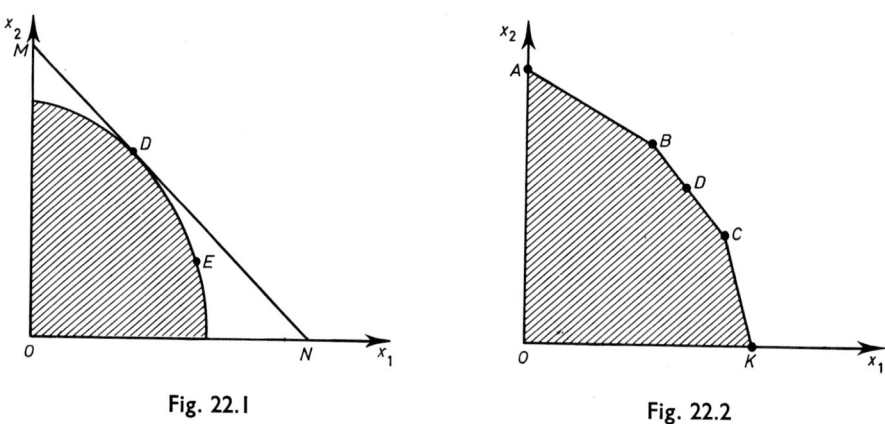

Fig. 22.1   Fig. 22.2

If the firm's production possibility set is convex in its efficiency frontier, but not *strictly* so, for example, as shown in Fig. 22.2, the central planning authority may be unable to attain its production goals by the shadow price approach. If corner-point combinations of output are desired, for example, at A, B, C or K in Fig. 22.2, there are supporting hyperplanes which support the production set only at each of these points and nowhere else. Hence, there are relative shadow prices, which in conjunction with profit maximisation, ensure output at whichever of these corner-points may be desired. But if the authority desires an output along a facet of the firm's production possibility set, for example at D, there is no set of relative shadow prices which, given profit maximisation, ensures D. The supporting hyperplane to the set at D passes along the facet BC. If relative shadow prices are set equal to the absolute slope of this hyperplane, profit is maximised for *any* combination along BC. Output D is not assured, but it is possible. The possibility of control of production in the absence of direct orders has deteriorated sharply.

The possibility of using *constant* shadow prices and profit maximisation to reach the authority's production goals becomes even more remote if the firm's production possibility set is to some extent strictly non-convex in its efficiency frontier. Some efficient levels of production cannot be reached by a combination of constant shadow prices and profit maximisation. Consider the example of Fig. 22.3. The firm's production set is strictly non-convex in its efficiency frontier. No combinations on this frontier, other than A or B, can be achieved by the shadow price approach. For example, imagine that the planning authority desires to achieve the combination at D. The production set has no supporting hyperplane at D. (The tangent to ADB at D passes through the interior of the production set and, therefore, is not a supporting hyperplane.) At any set of relative prices for the products, profit is higher at combination A or B than at D. Assuming positive shadow prices which are constant, the firm reaches its highest attainable isoprofit line (highest profit) at either A or B. The shadow price approach can only be used to steer the firm to efficiency point A or B. It cannot be steered by this method to point D.

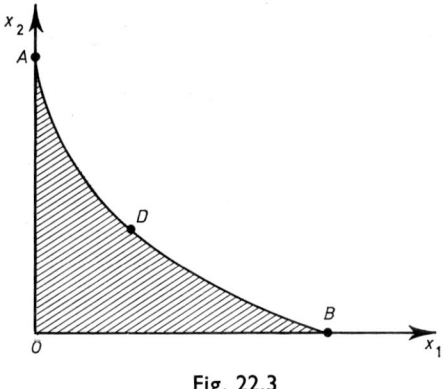

Fig. 22.3

Thus full control of the firm's efficient production by the shadow price method is possible if increasing marginal cost is the case, that is if the production of one commodity is at the increasing marginal expense of the other (the first case which was considered). But if constant marginal cost or decreasing marginal cost arises over some range of production possibility frontier, full control of a firm's efficient production by the shadow-price approach is impossible. Thus profit maximisation on the basis of constant shadow prices cannot always be a substitute for direct commands.

While this analysis takes account of the individual productive unit, some consideration needs to be given to the aggregate production of the economy. If there is no direct interaction in the production of firms so that total output is a simple sum of the output of all firms, and if the production set of each firm is *strictly* convex in its efficiency frontier, the efficiency frontier for the whole economy is *strictly* convex. The central planning authority can achieve any point which it may desire along the economy's frontier by establishing a suitable set of shadow prices (the same set for all firms) and ordering firms to maximise their profit on the basis of these. If the efficiency frontiers of the firms are differentiable, this method brings the rate of product transformation for all productive units into equality with the common set of shadow price ratios. Technical efficiency is achieved and the goals of the planners are satisfied.

But if any productive unit does not experience increasing marginal cost (if its production set is not *strictly* convex in its efficiency frontier) the central planners are not able to manipulate production precisely to *any* point on the economy's efficiency frontier by varying shadow prices and ordering firms to maximise profit on the basis of these. If it is impossible to control the output of any one firm by this method (and circumstances in which this is so are shown above) then aggregate output cannot be precisely controlled by this method. In these circumstances, shadow pricing by constant prices and profit maximisation by firms is not always a substitute for the allocation of resources by direct fiat.

Thus in areas of the economy where increasing marginal costs are the rule the shadow-price and profit-maximisation approach is an alternative to direct commands about resource allocation, but in areas where this is not so the method is not *always* an alternative. In theory, if sufficient information is available, a socialist economy might be operated efficiently to the goals of planners either by central commands which specify the use of all resources or, since all relevant production possibility sets are unlikely to be *strictly* convex in their efficiency frontiers, by shadow prices and profit maximisation in some areas, *supplemented* by central commands in others.

It ought to be noted once again that the shadow prices are set to reflect the desires of central planners whose wishes *may* differ from those of consumers. Direct sovereignty of consumers is absent, although prices may still be used to ration out the available production.

Shadow prices must be correctly determined if productive efficiency is to be attained. If increasing costs are the case and externalities are absent, the shadow prices must be the same for all firms and must reflect the value of opportunities forgone at the margin. This implies that all scarce resources including capital and land must be given a positive shadow price, otherwise these resources will not be allocated in a rational way. Firms, for example, may hoard capital (machines, spare parts etc.) as reputedly happened in the U.S.S.R. because no charge for capital or reward for its economic use was made. At the same time as this hoarding takes place, less fortunate firms with higher marginal physical productivities for capital may be unable to obtain capital. Thus the total output from the economy's capital is below its maximum.

Rarely does any socialist economy rely upon commands alone to ensure the fulfilment of its plans. Commands are usually supplemented by incentives for fulfilment or overfulfilment of plans. If material bonuses are paid to members of a productive unit, depending upon whether they fulfil or overfulfil physical output quotas, a number of side-effects can result. First, it is advantageous to the members of a productive unit to hide their productive potential to some extent and consequently obtain a quota which can be easily achieved and so obtain their bonus without difficulty. Secondly, production units may be reluctant to adopt new technology if this involves a temporary cut in production and so a loss of bonuses. More importantly, if their quotas are revised sufficiently upward in response to the new potential as a result of innovation, innovation is discouraged. Furthermore, if insufficient weight is given to the factors used in production when bonuses are determined, factors may be hoarded against shortages, the reserve being designed to ensure that the quota can be reached.

Socialist Economies

Fourthly, since it is impossible to check every product in detail, the setting of physical targets and the payment of bonuses based on these may lead to a deterioration in the quality of output. Volume rather than quality becomes the prime goal of productive units. Fifthly, the composition of production may differ from that which is really desired by the central planners. In reality, central planners cannot specify production to the last detail. Thus if quotas for nail production are set in tons this may result in the production of too many big nails, if productive units find it easier to fulfil or overfulfil their quotas in this way.

If bonuses are paid on profit calculated on shadow prices, none of the above problems disappear if target profit levels are set and bonuses are paid only if the target is achieved or more than achieved. It is assumed that the output of the firm is valued at the authority's shadow prices and enters the profit calculation irrespective of whether it is sold. After all, sales are matter for manipulation by the central authority.

In setting bonuses and targets, the central authority needs to take account of externalities and any differential rents which firms may enjoy. Thus command socialism of either kind, socialism which does not rely on markets for problem solving, involves considerable calculation and information-gathering costs.

III. Market or Competitive Socialism

Difficulties associated with command socialism can be reduced to some extent by using markets to perform calculations about economic variables. However, not all the limitations of command socialism, particularly of the shadow price type, are overcome by market socialism. For example, profit maximisation by firms in free markets does not result in a Paretian optimum if decreasing costs arise.

A number of slightly different methods of operating market or competitive socialism have been advanced. Two of the earliest models are due to Lange and Lerner.[11] In Lange's model[12] there is a Central Planning Board which sets prices but adjusts these according to the presence of excess demand in any market. The Board steers the economy by market signals. In Lerner's model,[13] markets operate freely. No board is used to interpret market signals. Consider Lange's model.

Lange imagines that the following conditions are satisfied in his socialist state:

(i) all resources other than labour are collectively owned;
(ii) labour is freely mobile;
(iii) subject to their income constraints, consumers are free to purchase any desired quantities of available consumer goods;
(iv) productive units (firms) exist but are collectively owned and are administered by socialist enterprise managers;
(v) on the basis of given input and output prices, enterprise managers are either instructed to maximise profit or are encouraged to do so by salary offers which are an increasing function of their firm's profit;
(vi) for each industry a board of socialist industrial managers is appointed. Its function is to control the number of firms in the industry to ensure that the marginal firm is just able to earn a normal profit;
(vii) a Central Planning Board which has a number of important functions in guiding the operation of the economy is established. Its functions are:

(a) *to determine the aggregate level of investment* or capital formation in the economy. The absolute level of this is not determined by any market mechanism. However, except for the allocation of funds for investment to public or social goods, the rate of interest is used to allocate the funds. Each firm is charged an interest rate on its borrowing which is a common rate for all firms and set so that funds which are not earmarked for social goods are allocated exactly. The Board obtains its funds for investment from its receipt of interest and from rents, profit and taxation revenue which accrues to the state;

(b) *to determine the supply of social or public goods*, such as defence, justice, public recreation, the supply of which cannot be rationally determined by a free market or which are not marketable at all;

(c) *to set the prices of all inputs and outputs* (that is of marketable commodities) *adjusting these prices to reduce any excess demands which exist in the markets* for commodities. The Board gropes towards the equilibrium prices in all markets by a trial and error process. As Lange puts it, "the right prices are simply found out by watching the quantities demanded and the quantities supplied and by raising the price of a commodity or service whenever there is an excess of demand over supply and lowering it whenever the reverse is the case, until, by trial and error, the price is found at which demand and supply are in balance".[14] The reactions of the Board to market disequilibrium are of the Walrasian type.

Subject to the centralised decisions about prices, some of which may be delegated to boards for particular industries, and the other two main spheres of central direction by the Central Planning Board, most decisions are decentralised. Each household is free to determine its purchases of commodities and the supply of its labour. Each enterprise manager decides on his employment of factors and the output of his enterprise, while industrial managers decide whether to expand or contract their industry by expanding or reducing the number of enterprises in the industry. Thus, with some guidance from the Central Planning Board, the system can be expected to operate like modified capitalism. In an economy in which externalities are absent, the system leads to Paretian optimality if demand and supply functions are stable enough and if increasing marginal costs are the rule.[15]

Consumers are sovereign in the system in so far as production adjusts to their changing demands. Their increased demand for a product causes an excess of demand if prices remain fixed at their old equilibrium levels. In response to this excess demand, the Central Planning Board increases the price of the product (and reduces the price of any product for which the demand has fallen). In response to the increased price of the product, firms in the industry expand their output since this is now profitable. Since the general profitability of the industry is likely to rise, industrial managers are likely to arrange for the entry of new firms and so increase supply further in response to the demands of consumers. This system contrasts strongly with the one in which consumers have freedom of choice but not sovereignty. In the latter system, prices are used to ration out available production to consumers but the composition of production is not necessarily responsive to the changing demands of consumers. An increase in the demand for a product leads to a rise in its price but not necessarily to an increase in its production.

The above statement that consumers are sovereign in the system needs to be qualified slightly. Just as in modified capitalism, Lange realised that it might be occasionally "necessary" to interfere with the freedom of choice by consumers, for example, to ban drugs and other products injurious to health or which have major external nuisance effects or to correct myopic choices. This question was discussed at some length in Chapter 14. In view of the matters raised, it was pointed out that there could be a case for imposing taxes and subsidies on various goods or even banning them altogether. The danger of this thin edge should also be apparent.

Just how efficient is Lange's system likely to be? Lange believes that his system is likely to be allocatively more efficient than freely competitive capitalism and even most forms of modified capitalism. In his view, the Central Planning Board is likely to have greater knowledge of the economy than the average entrepreneur would hope to have and could use this to achieve an equilibrium more quickly than would be the case under capitalism. Even if the knowledge of the Central Planning Board does not exceed that of the average entrepreneur under capitalism, its policies, as I have suggested in *Theory of Price Uncertainty, Production and Profit*,[16] might achieve an aggregate production and consumption level in excess of that under free competition. Essentially this is because in Lange's socialist system, the price expectations of firms in the same industry cannot differ, whereas under free competition they are likely to diverge. If increasing marginal cost is the case, divergent expectations lead to a loss of output. The results of overestimation and underestimation do not cancel out. A Central Planning Board, by causing prices to converge, causes aggregate production to rise and this gives the Board some leeway for making errors in predicting equilibrium prices and yet ensuring a greater output than under free competition. But note that this method of regulating prices is also possible under capitalism and, indeed, in some capitalist countries agricultural boards do set forward prices for agricultural produce. But though capitalism remains in this case, markets are not free in their operation.

However, not all economists accept Lange's view that equilibrium is likely to be approached more quickly under his system. For example, Hayek says that

> ... the Lange scheme, when tried *in reality*, would be slower, not faster, in chasing after an ever-changing equilibrium in a dynamic world. It would be impracticable to change *all* prices frequently, as would be needed, hence they would be changed only after long intervals. Even then such price changes could not take account of millions of details requiring price differentiation with respect to quality and other circumstances of time and place.[17]

But even in Lange's model, it would be possible to overcome this objection by letting prices freely find their own level in markets. Instead of prices being set by the Central Planning Board, firms may be permitted (as they are under free-market capitalism) to predict prices. Managers who predict best, make greater profits and reap greater rewards if their salary rises with the profit of the firm. Markets can be operated in exactly the same way as under free-market capitalism. The only difference is that the wealth of all productive enterprises is owned by the state. Indeed, Lerner advocated the free-market approach to socialism for all, except decreasing-cost industries.[18]

Not surprisingly, market socialism encounters many of the difficulties of free-market capitalism. For example, monopolies may occur in some industries and managers may engineer shortages of production in an attempt to induce the Central Planning Board to increase the price of their product so that they obtain bonuses on the basis of monopoly profits. Without a thorough investigation of the affairs of the monopolised industry, the Central Planning Board may be unable to tell the difference between a genuine and an "engineered" shortage. This is illustrated in Fig. 22.4 where per-unit cost curves of a monopolist are designated in the common way. The socially ideal output and consumption of the product is $\bar{x}$.[19] Profit maximisation results in this output if the Central Planning Board fixes the price of the product at $\bar{p}$. However, in its original trial, the Board might have set a price of p_0. At this price, the firm finds it profitable to produce x_0 only, even though x_1 is demanded. Thus a genuine shortage exists and price is then increased by the Board. But let us suppose that $\bar{p}$ is tried. The monopolist might deliberately "engineer" a shortage, that is not maximise profit at that price, in the hope that the Board will accept this as a genuine shortage and so raise the price. For example, the Board might raise the price to p_1. In this way, the firm earns monopoly profit and a Paretian optimum is not achieved.

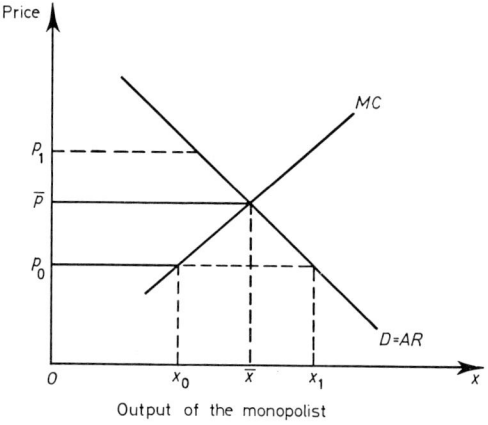

Fig. 22.4

As in a capitalist free-market economy, allowances must be made, as a rule, for external effects of consumption and production if Paretian optimality is to be achieved. This may entail the subsidisation of the production of firms with favourable external effects and the taxation of those with unfavourable effects.

Again, decreasing-cost industries also pose problems for market socialism since a single productive unit alone must carry on production of the commodity if economic efficiency is to be attained. Paretian optimality requires that output of the product be expanded until marginal cost equals the value to consumers of the last unit of the goods which is produced. But if all units of the product are priced at the level which equates marginal cost and demand, the firm makes a loss. (The argument was given in the last chapter.) Furthermore, the amount of the loss increases as the firm expands output towards the socially optimal level. Thus, if bonuses to management are positively related to profit, output may be restricted to a level below the social optimum. If bonuses are positively related to losses, this is unsatisfactory because managers have an incentive to inflate the costs of their productive unit by waste or inefficient use of resources. Thus the same types of problems occur as were discussed in the last chapter when dealing with the government operation of decreasing-cost industries and the same sorts of policy adjustments are available (for example, if possible, the firm might engage in price discrimination). If perfect price discrimination is possible, then a bonus which rises with profit will encourage the optimal level of output by the productive unit. However, price discrimination is not always possible.[20]

Under market socialism of either the Lange or Lerner type, markets fail to ensure a Paretian optimum in exactly the same circumstances as under market capitalism. If externalities are absent, then markets can be efficient controllers of resource allocation in increasing-cost industries. If various stability conditions are satisfied and if economic change is not too rapid, they can steer an economy towards a Paretian optimum at little cost of information-gathering and processing, though there would be some cost in Lange's scheme. But in practice, the situation is extremely complex. It cannot be shown on *a priori* grounds that market socialism is likely to be inferior from an economic efficiency point of view to command socialism or vice versa. The same is true of a comparison between (modified) capitalism and socialism.

Lange's system differs from the command shadow-price and profit maximisation approach in two important respects. In Lange's scheme the Central Planning Board searches for market equilibrium prices using markets as a guide, whereas in the other approach the appropriate shadow prices are found by solving a set of equations which represent interdependencies in the whole economy. Secondly, in Lange's model, consumers are sovereign. Yet both approaches are based on constant prices and both may fail to achieve social optima in similar circumstances, that is circumstances in which the production and preference sets do not form suitably convex point sets as is the case, for example, where decreasing costs arise.

Allowing for adjustments of investment, Lange's social ideal is a Paretian one based upon the preferences of all consumers expressed through the market, whereas the command approach gears the economic system to the preferences of the central planning authority. Nevertheless, the command method does not preclude the possibility, as a special case, that the authority desires to attain a Paretian optimum which takes account of the preferences of all consumers. Thus both approaches could give exactly the same economic or material result. Yet there is a vast political difference in the methods. In one, the response to consumer demands is more direct and certain. The other, at best, is benevolently despotic and the response is very indirect. Clearly, decision about the desirability of these alternative methods does not hinge on economic efficiency factors alone. This point will be taken up in the next section.

IV. Some Concluding Points

Theory seems to indicate that the static allocation of resources in socialist economies can be just as efficient (or inefficient) as in capitalist economies. The range of alternative methods for operating socialist economies is great and their operation can be made to approach the operation of capitalist economies very closely.

However, static allocative efficiency is just one factor which influences scarcity or the level of national output. Full employment and growth are also important and, from the individual's point of view, so is the distribution of income. Despite the problems of existing socialist economies (such as that of the U.S.S.R.) in maintaining economic efficiency, they have been very successful in maintaining high levels of employment. Certainly, they have not had the recent employment problems of countries like the United Kingdom and the United States.[21] This is not to deny, however, that some modified capitalist countries, like Australia, have been able to maintain high levels of employment.

Comparisons of income distribution between modified capitalist and socialist countries are difficult to make. No private income is earned in socialist countries by individuals from the ownership of property but it can be earned from the control of property, for example, by a manager. In the U.S.S.R., incomes from personal exertion vary widely. For example, the individual salaries of scientists, ministers, professors and managers are approximately twenty times as great as the salary of an unskilled worker.[22] This is a much greater difference than that which exists in a country like Australia. In addition members of the top echelon have various perquisites: for example, cars provided, a certain amount of free entertainment and so on.

Growth is another important consideration. In socialist countries such as the U.S.S.R., a high proportion of national output has been directed into investment, that is capital formation. At earlier times, this led to a high rate of growth in the U.S.S.R.'s national output but now the rate of growth has declined. According to Soviet official data, the growth of real national income during the 1950s was about 10 per cent p.a. but in the 1960s the rate dropped to a little over half this figure. (Western estimates indicate a fall from 7 per cent to 4 per cent.[23]) Many reasons are given for the decline. But important contributory factors would seem to be the increasing complexity of the economy, which makes central planning more difficult and increases the likelihood of inefficiency; and problems of technological progress, initiative and innovation in production.

Denison's studies[24] indicated that qualitative rather than quantitative factors may be the most important elements in growth. Sheer capital accumulation without technological progress, innovation and education may be relatively unproductive, especially once the scope for the most profitable forms of extensive investment have been exploited. Investment in education has been maintained at high levels in the U.S.S.R. The real problem might be in the area of technical change and innovation. Reports of the Central Committee of the Soviet Communist Party indicate that this is so.[25]

In maintaining technical progress, innovation and economic change, socialist economies may be at a disadvantage when compared with capitalist ones. Under socialism, the state is the sole source of all funds for investment and, therefore, of all risk capital. Thus the allocation of funds to novel projects may be stultified by conservative rules and many worthwhile projects may find no backing. In contrast, under capitalism, a potential innovator has a number of alternative sources of funds and may, depending upon the amount of his own funds and the size of his project, risk his own funds. While it is unlikely to be easy to raise funds in any society for risky ventures, the scope seems wider in capitalist economies. In practice, too, the actual rules of operation of a socialist economy may discourage innovation, for example, as mentioned earlier, if bonuses vary with physical output and if quotas are likely to be adjusted to eliminate potential gains in bonuses from an innovation.

However, the U.S.S.R. and other socialist countries are well aware of the technical progress and innovation problem and reforms have been instituted. For example, in the U.S.S.R., productive units are now to retain funds for discretionary investment, innovation and technical progress, so achieving some decentralisation and independence of decisions. Furthermore, the organisation of research institutes has been reviewed to permit greater decentralisation and to ensure that there is greater contact between these and production in particular industries. The latter contact is necessary if application of research is to be fostered and to ensure that the institutes are familiar with the problems and needs of the industries. In addition, lump-sum payments to individuals who suggest new ideas of economic value have been substantially increased.[26] Thus there is a problem, namely how to encourage individual initiative in a centralised framework.

Individuals alone are the ultimate source of ideas and the problem for any society is how to encourage the formation of ideas and take advantage of the beneficial ones. The problem with a centralised system is that it may hinder the formation of new ideas and the adoption of existing useful ones. But any society which represses the individual, be it capitalist or socialist, faces a fundamental problem which has been expressed by John Stuart Mill in the following way:

> A government cannot have too much of the kind of activity which does not impede, but aids and stimulates individual creation and development. The mischief begins when, instead of calling forth the activity and powers of individuals and bodies, it substitutes its own activity for theirs; when instead of informing, advising and upon occasion, denouncing, it makes them work in fetters, or bids them stand aside and does their work instead of them. The worth of the State in the long run is the worth of the individuals composing it, . . ., a State which dwarfs its men, in order that they may be more docile instruments in its hands even for beneficial purposes, will find that with small men no great thing can really be accomplished, and that the perfection of the machinery to which it sacrificed everything, will in the end avail nothing, for want of the vital power which, in order that the machine might work more smoothly, it has preferred to banish.[27]

An economic system, let me finally stress, cannot be reasonably judged just by its material achievements. Economic systems involve people in a web of social interrelationships and different patterns of social relationship have different psychological repercussions. Though two different systems of economic organisation achieve the same material ends, depending upon how individuals relate one to another in a system, systems are likely to have different psychological impacts. Means are important in themselves. They themselves are factors in human happiness. We must not only consider the influence of a method of economic organisation on scarcity but whether it promotes for individuals a sense of belonging or alienation, encourages individual responsibility, development and creativity and allows reasonable variety in their tasks, etc.. Sociological and psychological elements of this kind may be no less important than economic ones in reaching our decisions about desirable forms of economic organisation.

NOTES AND REFERENCES

[1] Quoted by J. WILCZYNSKI, *The Economics of Socialism*, George Allen and Unwin, London, 1970, p. 29.

[2] Karl Marx (1818-1883).

[3] E. BARONE, "The Ministry of Production in the Collectivist State", in F. A. VON HAYEK (Ed.), *Collectivist Economic Planning*, George Routledge and Sons, London, 1935, pp. 245-90.

[4] H. KOHLER, *Welfare and Planning*, John Wiley, New York, 1966, p. 68. Reproduced with the kind permission of John Wiley & Sons, Inc.

[5] BARONE, op. cit.
[6] F. M. TAYLOR, "The Guidance of Production in a Socialist State", in B. LIPPINCOT (Ed.), *On the Economic Theory of Socialism*, The University of Minnesota Press, Minneapolis, 1938, pp. 41-54. O. LANGE, "On the Economic Theory of Socialism", in B. LIPPINCOT, op. cit., pp. 55-142. Reprinted from *Review of Economic Studies*, 1936-1937. A. P. LERNER, *The Economics of Control*, Macmillan, New York, 1946.
[7] W. W. LEONTIEF, *Input-Output Economics*, Oxford University Press, New York, 1966 and earlier contributions. Kantorovich's contributions are contemporaneous, and the earliest ones may predate Leontief's.
[8] L. V. KANTOROVICH, *The Best Use of Economic Resources*, translated from the Russian by P. F. KNIGHTSFIELD, Pergamon Press, Oxford, 1965. V. NEMCHINOV, (i) *The Use of Mathematics in Economics*, Oliver & Boyd, Edinburgh, 1964; (ii) *Ekonomiko-matematicheskie metody i modeli*, Mysl, Moskva, 1965.
[9] KOHLER, op. cit., p. 121-22. Reproduced with the kind permission of John Wiley & Sons, Inc.
[10] This assumes that firms will, in fact, maximise their profit if ordered to do so or that non-distorting incentives are available which ensure that firms maximise profit. This condition may be difficult to satisfy.
[11] LERNER, op. cit.
[12] LANGE, op. cit.
[13] LERNER, op. cit.
[14] LANGE, in B. LIPPINCOT, op. cit., p. 89.
[15] K. J. ARROW and L. HURWICZ, "Decentralization and Computation in Resource Allocation", in R. PFOUTS (Ed.), *Essays in Economics and Econometrics*, University of North Carolina Press, Chapel Hill, 1960, pp. 34-104.
[16] C. TISDELL, *The Theory of Price Uncertainty, Production and Profit*, Princeton University Press, Princeton, 1968, Ch. 9. See also Chapter 14 of this book.
[17] KOHLER, op. cit., p. 79. Reproduced with the kind permission of John Wiley & Sons, Inc. See also F. VON HAYEK, "Socialist Calculation: The Competitive 'Solution'", *Economica*, 1940, 7, pp. 125-49.
[18] LERNER, op. cit.
[19] Externalities are assumed to be absent.
[20] Let me add that price discrimination in some cases might not be desirable on income distribution grounds.
[21] See, for example, H. KOHLER, *Economics: The Science of Scarcity*, The Dryden Press, Hinsdale, 1970, pp. 380-8.
[22] *The Monthly Labor Review*, April 1960, p. 362.
[23] A. BERGSON, "The Current Soviet Planning Reforms", in ALEX BALINKY et al. (Eds), *Planning and the Market in the USSR*, Rutgers University Press, New Brunswick, 1967.
[24] E. F. DENISON, (i) *The Sources of Economic Growth in the United States and the Alternatives Before Us*, Committee of Economic Development, New York, 1962; (ii) "Sources of Postwar Growth in Nine Western Countries", *American Economic Review*, 1967, 57, pp. 325-32.
[25] CENTRAL COMMITTEE OF THE COMMUNIST PARTY OF THE U.S.S.R., "The New Economic Model", in H. KOHLER, *Readings in Economics*, Holt, Rinehart and Winston, New York, 1968, Reading 53.
[26] Reported by J. WILCZYNSKI in "Technological Progress in Centrally Planned Economies" a paper read to Section 24, 43rd Congress, Australian and New Zealand Association for the Advancement of Science, May 1971.
[27] JOHN STUART MILL, "On Liberty", reprinted in the *The Six Great Humanistic Essays of John Stuart Mill*, Washington Square Press, 1963, p. 240.

FURTHER READING

BARONE, E., "The Ministry of Production in the Collectivist State", in F. A. VON HAYEK (Ed.), *Collectivist Economic Planning*, George Routledge and Sons, London, 1935, pp. 245-90. This article was published in Italian in 1908.

Hansen, B., *Lectures in Economic Theory*, 3rd ed., Studentlitteratur, Lund, 1968, Part II, Lectures 9 and 15.

Kantorovich, L. V., *The Best Use of Economic Resources*, translated from the Russian by P. F. Knightsfield, Pergamon Press, Oxford, 1965.

Kantorovich, L. V., "Mathematical Economics", pp. 12-15 and "Pro and Con—Compare Conclusions", pp. 16-22, *Problems of Economics*, September 1962.

Kohler, H., *Welfare and Planning*, John Wiley, New York, 1966.

*Koopmans, T. C., *Three Essays on the State of Economic Science*, McGraw-Hill, New York, 1957, Essay 1.

Koopmans, T. C. "Efficient Allocation of Resources", *Econometrica*, 1951, **19**, pp. 455-65.

Lange, O., "On the Economic Theory of Socialism", in B. Lippincot (Ed.), *On the Economic Theory of Socialism*, The University of Minnesota Press, Minneapolis, 1938, pp. 55-142. Reprinted from *Review of Economic Studies*, 1936-1937.

Lerner, A. P., *The Economics of Control*, Macmillan, New York, 1944.

Liberman, E. G., "Plans, Profits, Bonuses", *Problems of Economics*, July 1965, pp. 3-8.

Nemchinov, V., "Plan Target and Material Incentive", *Problems of Economics*, July 1965, pp. 9-13.

Wilczynski, J., *The Economics of Socialism*, George Allen and Unwin, London, 1970.

---

* More Advanced.

Index

activity analysis, 312-20
  limitations, 319-20
advertising, 199-200
  barriers to entry, 366
Alchian, A., 16, 336, 345
Allen, R. G. D., 39, 56, 62, 92, 125, 162, 263
Allen, W. R., 16
Archibald, G. C., 39
Arrow, K. J., 39, 126, 244, 246, 252, 265, 285, 286, 375, 416
Austrian School, 18, 39, 92

Bain, J., 219, 345, 346, 360, 361, 364, 367
bandwagon effect
  on demand, 118-19
  on supply of factors, 230
Barone, E., 400, 401, 415, 416
Baumol, W. J., 125, 126, 195, 218-19, 320, 321, 331, 334, 338, 339, 343, 345, 346, 357
Bentham, J., 14, 16
Bergson, A., 416
Berle, A., 134, 162, 195, 218, 337, 345
Blaug, M., 375
bond market, 322, 327
break-even output, 178
Buchanan, J., 302

capital budgeting, 388-92
capitalised value, 327
cartel, theory of, 215-16
Cartter, A. M., 239
central planning, production obstacle, 405-09
certainty equivalence, 395-6
Chamberlin, E., 210, 219
characteristics approach to demand, 123-4
Chiang, A. C., 39, 263
Clark, J. M., 213, 218, 219, 220, 297, 303, 336, 345
Cobb, C. W., 9, 16, 238
cobweb model, 76-8, 354
Cohen, K., 82, 340, 345, 346
command
  and attainment of a social optimum, 281
  and economic organisation, 11
Commonwealth of Australia, Cost-Benefit, 398
Communist Party of USSR, 416

compact set, 33, 320
comparative advantage, 51
comparative cost, 155, 232
competition,
  and resource allocation, 12, 264-86, 287-303
  and scarcity, 2
  classification of, 43-55, 221-5
  imperfect, 42, 194-218, 221-5, 284-5
  perfect, 42 (*see also* perfect competition)
  perfect and economic efficiency, 12
  pure, 42 (*see also* pure competition)
  workable, 12, 297-8
complementarity of inputs, 144
complements and indifference curves, 101
concave functions, 27-30, 35
concentration and economies of scale, 359
consumption, 22-5, 39, 92-126, 127-33
  and sets, 39, 127-33
  multiperiod, 324-7
  neoclassical marginal utility theory, 93-6
  revealed preference, 115-17
  socialist control, 133
contract curve, 271-2, 275
consumer's equilibrium, 103-05
consumers' sovereignty, 13-14, 408
  and market failure, 287-9
  and socialism, 410
consumer's surplus, 113-14
convex functions, 27-30, 35
convexity, 27
  and the average or expected value of a function, 29, 30
convex production sets and socialist control, 405-08, 413
convex sets
  and consumption, 101-02, 127-33
  and linear programming, 305-10
  and production, 163-73
  definition, 32-3
  differ from convex functions, 35
  optimality of perfect competition, 283
  strictly, 34
correspondence principle, 73-6, 247-8
cost, 155-60
  average, 157
  average fixed, 157
  average variable, 157

cost,—*continued*
  fixed, 156
  function, 150
  long-run, 158-60, 184
  marginal, 157-8
  short-run, 156-8
  variable, 156
cost-benefit analysis, 388-98
  and uncertainty, 394-6
  difficulties of applying to public investment, 392-8
  difficulties of valuation, 393-4
cost curve, empirical determination, 356-7
cost plus pricing and marginalism, 344-5
countervailing power, 298-9
Cournot, A., 18, 39, 213, 219
Cournot's model of duopoly, 213-15
cross-elasticity, 88-9, 210
custom, 10-11
Cyert, R. M., 82, 218, 220, 335, 340, 345, 346

Dantzig, G., 304, 320
Dean, J., 345, 346, 356, 357
Debreu, G., 93, 97, 125, 131, 133, 244, 246, 252, 285, 286, 302
decision-making, costs, 333, 340, 343
decreasing costs, 54
  and efficiency, 44
  and market failure, 61
  and monopoly, 204
  and planning, 407
  and socialism, 412
  and state enterprise, 380-4
DeGroot, M., 218-220
demand curve, 64-6, 111-12
  and price-consumption curve, 106-07
  best fit, 353
  empirical determination, 350-4
  for a factor, 230
  identification, 351-3
  social influences, 112, 117-20, 131
Denham, James Steuart, 13, 16
Denison, E., 368, 375, 414, 416
differential calculus and economics, 18-27
Dillon, J., 355, 357
discounted cash flow criterion, 390-2
Dorfman, R., 302
Douglas, P., 9, 16, 161, 162, 238, 239, 240
duopoly, 213-18
Dupuit, J., 113, 125
dynamics, 56, 57-8

Eckaus, R., 317, 321
econometrics and microeconomic measurement and estimation, 347-57
economic model building, 347

economics, positive and normative, 15
economies of scale, 359-63
  and monopoly, 205-06
  multiplant, 202, 361
  plant, 359-61
Edgeworth, F. Y., 15, 16, 267, 274, 285, 286, 303
Edgeworth-Bowley box, 269-70
education, 368
efficiency
  and decreasing costs, 44
  and employment of factors, 230-2, 317
  and income distribution, 272
  and markets, 41-55
  and prices, 11-14
  economic, 5-7
  of exchange, 271
  of imperfect competition, 194, 201-07, 212-13, 218
  of monopolistic competition, 212-13
  of monopoly compared to perfect competition, 201-07
  of perfect competition, 190-2
  of socialist systems, 413-14
  technical compared with economic, 6-7
efficiency locus, 153-4, 277
efficiency prices, 305
elasticity
  concept of, 83
  cross, 88-9
  of supply, 90-1
  own price, 83-8
employment, 4, 48, 49, 317 (*see also* unemployment)
Engel functions, 107-08
entry, barriers to, 195, 363-7
  and economies of scale, 362
  and patents, 371
  and pricing, 365-6
equilibrium, 56-61
  and dynamics of markets, 72
  and entry, 365
  and knowledge, 80-2
  general, 241-52
  of a barter economy, 245-8
  of a monetary economy, 248-51
  problems, 243-4
  stability, 56-9
  under pure competition, 68-9
excess capacity, and monopolistic competition, 210
excess demand functions, 246-7
exchange, 41-2
  and income distribution, 274
  and Paretian optimum, 269-76
expansion path, 149

Index

expected utility, 341-2
externalities, 14, 44, 54
 and invention, 368-9
 and market failure, 289-93
extrema (*see also* optimisation)
 and convexity and quasi-convexity, 27
 differential calculus and marginalism, 19-27
 global, 22
 local, 22
 mathematical theory, 18-19
extremal, 34
 and linear programming, 305-12
extreme points, 37
Euler's Theorem, 240

Fabian socialists, 266
factors, pricing and employment of, 227-37
 under imperfect competition, 232-6
 under perfect competition, 227-32
Ferguson, C. E., 302, 303
firm, definition of, 134
 behaviour under certainty, 335-40
 behaviour under uncertainty, 340-3
 profit maximisation under perfect competition, 145-53
free-rider problem, 387
futures markets, 333

Galbraith, J. K., 298, 302, 335, 345
Gale, D., 286
games, theory of, 221-6
 and Paretian optimality, 225
 co-operative, 224-6
 extensive form, 221
 prisoners' dilemma, 225
 normal form, 221
 two-person zero-sum, 221-4
general equilibrium, 241-52
 and socialism, 401
 Arrow-Debreu-McKenzie model, 246
 of a barter economy, 245-8
 of a monetary economy, 248-51
government and resource allocation, 377-99
Griliches, Z., 375, 376
growth, 7-9, 45

Hadley, G., 133
Hall, R., 217, 219, 344, 346
Hamberg, D., 374, 375, 376
Hancock, K., 55
Hansen, B., 56, 62
Harberger, A. C., 204, 219
Hart, A. G., 342, 346, 398
Haveman, R., 82
Hawkins, D., 263
von Hayek, L., 411, 416

Heady, E., 355, 357
Henderson, J. M., 62, 162, 334
Hicks, J. R., 27, 39, 56, 61, 92, 96, 97, 100, 101, 109, 115, 125, 126, 162, 246, 247, 252, 267, 285, 324, 327, 332, 333, 334, 336, 345
Hitch, C. J., 217, 219, 344, 346
Hotelling, H., 302, 398
Hotelling-Lerner rule, 293, 380, 381, 382
 and Paretian optimality, 381
Hurwicz, L., 416
Hyperplanes, 127-9
 bounding, 127-8
 separating, 127-8
 supporting, 127-8

identification, 349
 of demand curve, 351-3
imperfect competition (*see* competition)
imperfect decisions, 343
imperfect knowledge, 14, 41 (*see also* knowledge, uncertainty)
 and market failure, 294-5
 and profit maximisation, 340
 by consumers, 288
income distribution, 9-10, 15, 202
 and marginal productivity, 237-9
 and Paretian optimum, 276, 280
 and utility, 266
 and welfare, 267-8, 271-3
 difficulty of changing, 281
 influence on exchange, 274
income effect, 116-17
 and substitution effect, 108-12
indeterminancy
 of exchange, 274
 of supply, 184
indifference curves, 96-101
 social influences on, 131
inferior goods, 66, 89, 108, 110
inflation, 299
innovation, 368-75
 and diffusion, 375
 under socialism, 408, 414
input-output analysis, 253-63, 304, 305
 and central planning, 403-04
 inverted Leontief matrix, 261-2
 Leontief matrix, 261
 limitations, 259-60
 linear programming, 262
 matrices, 260-2
 net bill of goods, 254
 net bill of goods frontier, 258
 technology matrix, 255, 256, 260-1
 transactions matrix, 260
 types of models, 254

insurance, 342
interindustry analysis, 253-63 (*see* input-output)
internal rate of return, 389-90
international trade theory, 153
isocost, 147
isoprofit, 139
isoquant, 142
isorevenue, 162

Jevons, W. S., 18, 39, 92, 125
Jewkes, J., 375, 376

Kahn, R. F., 299, 303
Kaldor, N., 237, 238, 239, 240
Kantorovich, L. V., 254, 263, 320, 401, 416
Karlin, S., 39
Karmel, P. H., 375
Kefauver, E., 219
Kennedy, J. F., 13, 16
Keynes, J. M., 4, 16, 56, 61, 237, 242, 251, 253, 263, 333, 334
Klein, L. R., 357
Knight, F., 1, 15, 16, 156, 162
knowledge, and markets, 368-75
  and socialism, 411
Kohler, H., 15, 415, 416
Koopmans, T. J., 302, 320, 321
Kuenne, R., 56, 62
Kuhlman, J. M., 91
Kuhn, H. W., 39
Kuhn-Tucker conditions, 26

Lancaster, K., 62, 93, 123, 125, 133, 174, 195, 246, 252, 299, 300, 301, 302, 303, 398
Lange, O., 1, 15, 18, 39, 247, 250, 252, 401, 409, 411, 416
Lange's model of market socialism, 409-13
learning, 218, 332, 342-3
  and equilibrium, 365
Leftwich, R., 91
Leibenstein, H., 118, 126
Leibniz, G., 18
Leontief, W., 242, 252, 253, 259, 263, 362, 401, 416
Lerner, A., 398, 401, 409, 411, 413, 416
linear function, maximised subject to compact set, 163
linear objective function and linear programming, 304
linear programming, 304-12
  and central planning, 404
  basic feasible solutions, 306, 310
  dual, 312
  feasible solutions, 306, 310
  limitations, 319-20
  non-negativity conditions, 309
  primal, 312
  shadow prices, 312
  simplex method, 311
  structural or capacity restraints, 308
Lipsey, R. G., 39, 299, 300, 301, 302, 303, 398
long period, 156
Luce, R. D., 226, 285
Luxemburg, Rosa, 400

Machlup, F., 371, 372, 373, 375
McKenzie, L. W., 244, 246, 252
Mansfield, E., 374, 375
mapping of supply, 163
March, J. C., 335, 340, 345
marginal cost, 150
marginal efficiency of an investment, 389-90
marginal evaluation curve, defined, 385
marginalism and extrema, 19-27
marginal product, 5
marginal productivity, diminishing, 136
  and employment, 236-7
  and income distribution, 237-9
marginal rate of substitution, 50, 100
markets, classified, 42-4
  failure, 287-95
  mechanism, 11-14
Markham, J. W., 298, 302
Marschak, 39
Marris, R., 340, 345
Marshall, A., 18, 39, 72, 82, 91, 92, 113, 125, 126, 155, 156, 162, 176-7, 192
Marx, Karl, 400
maximin criterion, 342
Meade, J. E., 302
Means, G., 134, 162, 195, 218, 337, 345
Menger, C., 125
Mill, John Stuart, 14, 16, 288, 302, 415, 416
minimax criterion, 226
von Mises, L., 401
Mitchell, W. C., 16, 285
mixed strategies, 226
Modigliani, P., 362, 363, 367
money and general equilibrium, 248-51
monopolistic competition, 43, 44, 210-13
monopolist's objective, 336
monopoly, 14, 43, 195-213
  advantages, 219
  and efficiency, 191
  and employment, 232-3
  and income distribution, 219
  and Paretian optimum, 201-04
  and patents, 371-3
  and technical progress, 206-07
  deadweight loss, 203

Index 422

monopoly,—*continued*
  production set, 168-9, 173
  regulation, 208-10
  under socialism, 206-07
  vs perfect competition, 201-07
monopsony, 43, 233-6
Moore, F. T., 362, 367
Morgenstern, O., 39, 81, 82, 93, 120, 125, 126, 195, 213, 219, 221, 223, 226, 274, 346
multicollinearity, 349
multipart pricing, 382
multiperiod production, types of interdependence, 331
multiperiod resource allocation, 322-34
Musgrave, R., 115, 126

Nash, J. F., 225, 226
Nemchinov, V., 401, 416
Nerlove, M., 356, 357
von Neumann, J., 39, 81, 82, 93, 120, 125, 126, 195, 213, 219, 221, 223, 226, 274, 341, 346
Newman, P., 286
Newton, I., 18
normal good, 108, 110
Novozhilov, V. V., 401

oligopoly, 43, 213-18
  and game theory, 221-6
  kinked demand model, 217-18
  price leadership, 216
oligopsony, 43-4
Oort, J., 398
opportunity cost, 155
optimisation
  and rationality, 18
  constrained problems, 22-7
  significance for economics, 17-19
  solution principle, 35
  unconstrained, 22
optimum
  boundary and interior, 36
  global and local, 35
  and a linear function, 36-7
orderings, 97, 116
organisational mechanisms, 10-14
organisational slack, 150, 340
  and cost curves, 357
  and input-output analysis, 257
  and marginal productivity theory, 236

Paretian criterion, 4, 5, 15, 55, 268
  basis, 285
  limitations, 268-9

Paretian optimality, 280, 287-303
  and employment, 235-6
  and exchange, 269-76
  and imperfect competition, 284-5
  and income distribution, 276, 280
  and monopoly, 201-04
  and perfect competition, 44-55, 281-4
  and production and exchange, 276-85
  and socialism, 400-01, 410, 413
Pareto, V., 4, 9, 15, 16, 92, 96, 115, 125, 253, 263, 268, 285
Pareto's distribution, 9
parity theorem, 274
partial analysis
  and input-output analysis, 259
  compared to general, 241
  value, 251-2
patents
  economic effects, 370-3
  exchange-for-secrets, 371
  monopoly-profit-incentive, 372-3
  natural law thesis, 371
  reward by monopoly, 371
  Schumpeterian dilemma, 369
Patinkin, D., 250, 251, 252
pay-back or payout criterion, 388
Penrose, Edith, 195, 219, 336, 340, 345
perfect competition, 175-92
  and employment, 227-32
  and Paretian optimality, 281-4
  and scarcity, 44-55
  characteristics of, 64, 175
  efficiency of, 190-2
  vs monopoly, 201-07
Pigou, A. C., 14, 16, 251, 252, 265, 285, 289, 299, 302, 303, 378, 396, 398
point sets, 32, 33
pollution, 44
present value, 323, 327
present value criterion, 390-1
Prest, A. R., 394, 398
price-consumption curve, 105-07
price discrimination, 207-08
pricing, long-run, 182-90
  short-run, 176-82
product differentiation, 210, 212
production, 134-62, 163-73
  multiperiod, 327-32
production function, 135, 142-5
  CES, 162
  Cobb-Douglas, 161
  concave, 143
  empirical, 354-6
  homogeneous, 160, 239
  and production set, 164
  special types, 160-2

production possibility frontier, 50, 54
product transformation function, 154, 169
profit maximisation
　and resource allocation, 12
　and socialism, 402
　capitalised value, 327-8
　marginal productivity theory, 236
profit maximisation hypothesis, 134, 192, 195
　reconsidered, 335-46
public expenditure, bases of, 377
public goods, 14, 54, 292, 377, 384-7
　and employment, 237
　and resource allocation, 377-99
pure competition, 63-80
　characteristics, 63-4
　dynamics, 72-80

Quandt, R. E., 62, 126, 162, 334, 343, 346
quasi-concavity, 35-7
　and demand theory, 131-3
quasi-convexity, 27
Quirk, J., 174, 252, 286

Radner, R., 39
Raiffa, H., 226, 285
rationality, 18, 97
research and development, 219, 368-75
　and concentration, 374
　empirical results, 373-5
　means of support, 370-3
　and size of firm, 374
restrictive trade practices, 54
returns to outlay, 152
returns to scale, 152, 359-63 (*see also* economies of scale)
Ricardo, D., 8, 9, 16
risk (*see* uncertainty)
Robbins, L., 267, 285
Robinson, Joan, 192, 199, 219, 285
Rothenberg, J., 285
Rousseau, J-J., 3

sales maximisation hypothesis, 338-9
　welfare implications, 345
Samuelson, P. A., 39, 49, 55, 56, 57, 62, 69, 82, 83, 91, 92, 115, 125, 245, 247, 252, 263, 296, 299, 302, 303, 398
Saposnik, R., 133, 174, 252, 286
satisficing, 340, 343
　and input-output analysis, 257
Say's Law, 246, 250, 251
scarcity, 1-16
　basic problem, 1
　consequences, 1, 2
　economic alleviation, 3
　and economic organisation, 9-10
　solutions, universality, 3

Scarf, H., 285
Scherer, F., 374, 376
Schmookler, J., 374, 376
Schumpeter, J., 45, 55, 206, 207, 219, 295, 296, 303, 373-4, 376
Schumpeterian dilemma, 369
Scitovsky, T., 336, 337, 345
second best, theory of, 299-302
Seligman, B., 61
set, boundary point, 34
　bounded, 33
　closed, 34
　compact, 33, 320
　convex hull, 34
　convex polyhedral, 37
　extreme point, 34
　open, 34
sets and convex sets
　complement of, 32
　disjoint, 31
　empty, 31
　equality, 30
　intersection, 31
　and production, 163-73
　proper subsets, 30-1
　subset, 30
　union, 32
shadow prices, 311
　and efficiency, 408
　planning and socialism, 401, 402, 404, 405
short period, 156-8
Shubik, M., 226, 285
Simon, H., 17, 39, 340, 343, 345, 346, 398
simplex method, 311
Slutsky, E., 92, 96, 109, 111, 115, 125
Smith, Adam, 13, 16, 367
snob effect
　on demand, 118-20
　on supply of factors, 230
socialism, 400-17
　and Paretian optimality, 400
　and sets, 174
　command, 402-09
　competitive (or market), 210, 409-13
　vs capitalism, 413-15
social welfare and entry, 359, 365-6
social welfare functions, 265, 271-2, 280-1
sociological factors in economic models, 285
Solow, R., 239, 240, 302
specialisation, 49-54, 189
Sraffa, P., 16, 192, 219, 303
state, role of, 379
state enterprise
　and taxation, 381
　production and pricing, 380

statics, 56
  comparative, 56, 69-70
  and dynamics, 59-61
  and policy, 189
Stigler, G. J., 91, 217, 219, 220, 297, 302
Strotz, R. M., 126
Stubblebine, W., 302
subsidies, 80 (*see also* taxation)
substitution
  and indifference curves, 101
  and isoquants, 144
substitution effect, 116-17
supply, 134-62, 163-73
  by government, 379-88
  constant costs, 185
  decreasing costs, 187-9
  empirical, 354
  increasing costs, 186-7
  long run, 182-90
  mapping of, 163
  market, 66-7
  short run, 176-82
  under perfect competition, 137-41, 175-90
supply curve of perfectly competitive firm, 151
Swedish School, 56
Sweezy, P., 217, 219, 344, 346
Sylos, P., 362, 367
Sylos postulate, 362, 363

tariff and regulation of monopoly, 209
Taussig, F., 372, 376
taxation
  and market equilibrium, 79-80
  burden of, 114-15
Taylor, F. M., 401, 416
technical progress (*see also* innovation, growth, patents, research and development)
  and monopoly, 206
  under socialism, 414
technical substitution, rate of, 144
Theil, H., 333, 334, 342, 346
Thompson, R. G., 91
Thoreau, H. D., 11, 16
time-preference, 325-7
  social, 396-7
Tinbergen, J., 125
Tintner, G., 16
Tisdell, C. A., 126, 226, 285, 302, 346, 367, 375, 398, 416
Tobin, J., 333, 334

trade unions and employment and wages, 236, 318
Triffin, R., 91
Tucker, A. W., 35
Turvey, R., 394, 398

uncertainty
  and cost-benefit analysis, 394-6
  and market failure, 294-5
  and production, 332-3
  and socialism, 411
  demand under, 123
unemployment, frictional, 4
  involuntary, 4
Union of Soviet Socialist Republics, 401, 403, 408, 413, 414
utilitarianism, 265
utility
  and cost-benefit analysis, 394-6
  and Pareto's criterion, 268
  cardinal, 96
  index of von Neumann and Morgenstern, 120-3
  maximisation of expected utility, 224, 341-2
  maximisation and resource allocation, 12
  ordinal, 96
utility possibility frontier, 271

Vaizey, J., 375
value judgments, 9
Veblen, T., 120, 126
Veblen effect, 66, 112, 120
Viner, J., 184, 192

Walras, L., 72, 82, 92, 125, 241, 245, 252, 253, 263
Walrasian general equilibrium models, 245
Walras' Law, 246, 250
Wallace, R., 55
Walters, A., 162
Weierstrass's Theorem, 34
welfare economics, 15, 153, 155, 264-86, 287-303
  and general equilibrium, 264
  and social action, 272
  exchange and production, 276-86
  utilitarian, 265-7
Wilczynski, J., 376, 415, 416
Williamson, O. E., 338, 339, 345
workable competition, 297-8
Worley, J. S., 374, 376